David Irving is the son of a Royal Navy commander. Educated at Imperial College of Science & Technology and at University College London, he subsequently spent a year in Germany working in a steel mill and perfecting his fluency in the language. Among his thirty books the best-known include *Hitler's War; The Trail of the Fox: The Life of Field-Marshal Rommel; Accident, the Death of General Sikorski; The Rise and Fall of the Luftwaffe,* and *Göring: a Biography.* He has translated several works by other authors. He lives in Grosvenor Square, London, and is the father of five daughters.

In 1963 he published *The Destruction of Dresden.* This became a best-seller in many countries. In 1966 he issued a revised edition, *Apocalypse 1945,* as well as his important biography, *Goebbels. Mastermind of the Third Reich* and the second volume of *Churchill's War.*

David Irving

NUREMBERG

THE LAST BATTLE

'David Irving is in the first rank of Britain's historical chroniclers' — THE TIMES

F

FOCAL POINT

For Jessica

Parts of this book were first published by *Welt am Sonntag*, Hamburg, and as a paperback edition by Wilhelm Heyne Taschenbuchverlag, Munich. It has been revised and expanded on the basis of materials available since then.

This edition first published 1996 by
FOCAL POINT PUBLICATIONS
Duke Street, London W1M 5DJ

British Library Cataloguing-in-Publication Data
A catalogue record for this book is available
from the British Library

ISBN 1 872197 16 7

Printed and bound in Great Britain by
Butler & Tanner Ltd, Frome and London

NURREMBERG

THE LAST BATTLE

Contents

'There is more dynamite in this question than Krupp ever produced out of his plant!'

—JUSTICE ROBERT H. JACKSON at a secret meeting of the Nuremberg chief prosecutors, November 12, 1945

'The trials served both to illuminate and to falsify history. In the hand of the experienced historian, their documentation is a good guide; in the hand of a demagogue it is a dangerous knobkerry.'

—Naval judge advocate Captain OTTO KRANZBÜHLER, lecturing at the University of Göttingen in September 1949

Author's Introduction

THIS BOOK is an intimate look at the origins and conduct of the first post-war trial of major war criminals held at Nuremberg from 1945 to 1946. It has as its nucleus a series of articles which I wrote for the German weekly *Welt am Sonntag* in the late 1960s under the title *Nürnberg, die letzte Schlacht.* These articles were then published under one cover by Wilhelm Heyne Taschenbuchverlag in Munich under the same title, which has long been out of print.

Much research has been carried out since then. In the course of preparing my biographies of Hitler and some of his principal lieutenants (Göring, Milch, Hess, Rommel), I had already met many of the participants in this final drama of World War Two—those, that is, who had survived the hangman's noose—and I had had perforce to talk things over with several of their legal counsel too, in whose hands were still concentrated important historical records.

In the years since publishing that German newspaper series I collected additional significant materials on the trial, including the diaries of several of the German defendants, as well as of the Allied prosecuting counsel and judges; and after the British archives opened, I was enabled to adjust the balance of what had until then been investigated primarily from the American archival angle.

The richest quarry, and one to which I have returned several times in the intervening years, is the files of the American chief prosecutor, the late Justice Robert H. Jackson.

If this story needs a hero, then he is Jackson. As will be seen from the footnotes, I first used his private papers when they were held by Professor Philip Kurland of the University of Chicago Law School; a debt of thanks is owed to Professor Kurland for his patience and generosity in allowing me to delve into his files thirty years ago, and to review the contents of several filing cabinets of Jackson's private and legal papers which he was holding in his basement with the pious, but alas unfulfilled, intention of one day writing the definitive biography of the great jurist. The folder listed tantalisingly as 'diary kept by Jackson from April 27 to November 19, 1945' was at that time missing, but it turned up years later in box 95 of his confidential papers, which had by then been transferred to the Manuscript Division of the Library of

Congress in Washington, D.C., and William Eldred Jackson gave me the formal permission needed to make use of his late father's diaries.

Jackson's no less voluminous official papers, designated his Main Office files, now form part of Record Group 238 at the National Archives in Washington. The fact that my source notes indicate 'Chicago' as the location does not however imply that those papers are still held there now, over a quarter of a century later. As indicated above, most of them have been relocated in the Library of Congress and the National Archives, both in Washington.

Of scarcely less importance than Jackson's are the private papers of his *bête noire* at Nuremberg, Judge Francis Biddle, the senior American member of the Tribunal. The George Arents Research Library at the University of Syracuse, New York, allowed me to study his diaries, private letters, and trial notes, which often included caustic observations about the prosecutors and about the evidence heard before him.

After corresponding several years earlier with the former American commandant of Mondorf prisoner-of-war cage ('Ashcan') and Nuremberg prison, I was permitted by his son, Lieutenant-Colonel Burton C Andrus Jr., to make use of his late father's files of papers which were held at the family home in Colorado Springs, including his hand-written diaries dated from February 7 to November 18, 1946.

Similarly the son of the late Selkirk Panton, the journalist covering the trial for the *Daily Express*, gave me permission to use his father's papers in the National Library of Australia in Canberra. Among others to whom I express gratitude are Ben Swearingen, one of those indefatigable amateur historians to whom the professional is so indebted: he provided to me the ultimate clues on the suicide of Reichsmarschall Hermann Göring, about which he had already written a fine book. Dr Daniel P. Simon, director of the Berlin Document Center controlled by the U.S. Mission in Berlin, opened up for me the hitherto closed safe-file containing Göring's enigmatic last letters. John Taylor, of the Archives & Reference Branch of the Textual Reference Division at the U.S. National Archives, kindly provided me with magnetic tape copies of the original wire-recordings of selected passages of the trial, to enable me to verify the mimeographed and published transcripts against the words actually spoken.

As for the German records used, may I acknowledge here my thanks to Henrik Pastor of Berlin, for showing me Grand-Admiral Erich Raeder's prison diary and other important papers salvaged from Spandau. Wolf Rüdiger Hess provided excerpts from his father's prison diary, which I have already quoted in *Hess, the Missing Years* (Macmillan, London, 1987). The late Karl-Heinz Keitel allowed me to copy his personal notes on his prison conversations with his father. I was able to conduct lengthy interviews with Albert Speer, Erhard Milch, Karl Bodenschatz, and others about the trials, prison life, and interrogation methods.

Among the German lawyers whom I interviewed were Dr Alfred Seidl (defence counsel for Hans Frank and Rudolf Hess, and subsequently Bavarian minister of justice), a courageous fighter and a friend of many years' standing; Dr Dr Otto Nelte (counsel for Field-Marshal Keitel), Dr Friedrich Bergold (counsel for the absent Martin Bormann); Dr Rudolf Merkel (counsel for the Gestapo); Dr Robert Servatius (counsel for the Nazi Party's political organisation); and Professor Dr Hermann Jahrreiss (counsel for Alfred Jodl); I also spoke with Konrad Morgen about aspects of S.S. Obergruppenführer Ernst Kaltenbrunner's testimony.

In Britain I corresponded, as will be seen, with Lord Justice Harry Phillimore, as well as with the former Sir Hartley Shawcross, now Lord Shawcross. In the United States I had discussions with Ralph Albrecht, the international-law expert on Jackson's team, and with Ernst Engländer, the principal U.S. airforce interrogator. Somewhere in between these nationalities falls, or fell, the late Dr Robert M. W. Kempner, who after a brief debut as a legal officer in Göring's Prussian ministry of the interior, fled from Nazi Germany in 1933 and returned in 1945 in the uniform of a U.S. army colonel, designated as an assistant to an unwilling Robert Jackson; Dr Kempner, who after 1946 acted as chief American prosecutor in the 'subsequent proceedings,' answered my queries with as much patience as he could muster.

As with my earlier works, I have catalogued and placed much of these source materials on microfilms which are available to researchers.* For example the Oral History, in which Jackson had in 1952 dictated his often very frank personal reminiscences of the Nuremberg trials, is on my film DI–87 (Professor Kurland having allowed me to borrow and take back to England the relevant bound volume of the History for this purpose). The interrogations of Göring will be found on my film DI–34. My transcripts of the diaries of Field-Marshal Erhard Milch are on film DI–59. The early interrogation reports on Jodl and other top-level prisoners are on film DI–8. The secret reports from Jackson's papers on the chief prosecutors' meetings at Nuremberg are filmed on DI–70 and 71. (These minutes were written by the late Elsie L. Douglas, who acted as Jackson's private secretary during the trial, and also talked with me at length about her recollections). The original Schmundt File on Hitler's 1938 preparations to attack Czechoslovakia ('Fall Grün') is filmed on DI–78. The papers left by Dr Robert Ley after his suicide are filmed on DJ–79.

Miss Susanna Scott-Gall performed some of the leg work involved in utilising the more remote document collections. Karl-Heinz Höffkes of Essen made available to me the diaries and other papers of Julius Streicher from his collection. Professor Ian Maclaine, of the University

* From Microform Academic Publishers Ltd., Main Street, East Ardsley, Wakefield, West Yorkshire WF3 2AT, England (tel. +44 1924 825 700; fax 829 212).

of Wollongong in New South Wales, drew my attention to documents in the Public Record Office on the earlier British deliberations about how to dispose of the enemy leaders.

This list of acknowledgements is necessarily incomplete, and some of my helpers may feel slighted by their omission, but this is the place to record once more my thanks to my friend Dr Ralf-Georg Reuth, chief of the Berlin bureau of *Bild* Zeitung, and to Walter Frentz, who generously provided many of the unique colour photographs used in this book. Let me finally express my thanks to the two editors, who necessarily remain nameless but whose pens of various hues have ensured that this book is relatively free of error and not substantially more politically incorrect than it is.

DAVID IRVING
London, July 1996

1: In Which Stalin Says No to Murder

As the C–54 cargo plane of the U.S. Army droned eastwards across the Atlantic, a smell of coffee roused the sixteen passengers from an uncomfortable sleep; but Justice Robert H. Jackson had not slept since leaving Washington at mid-day, when the Supreme Court had adjourned for the summer recess after a hectic week of last-minute appeals.

Behind the round, gold-rimmed spectacles the broad forehead was creased by a worried frown; the usually humorous mouth was set in an expressionless line. It was June 18, 1945. Two weeks earlier, the president of the United States had entrusted him with the prosecution of the principal war criminals in Allied hands, and he and his hand-picked staff of lawyers, intelligence officers, and personal secretaries were flying to London on the first leg of the assignment.

To Jackson this was an unique opportunity to push out the frontiers of international jurisprudence, to encompass new areas hitherto beyond its pale. He was going to lay the foundations of a new kind of law, outlawing wars of aggression and making the very conspiracy to wage wars a crime against international law. He wanted to punish the entire organisations that had furnished to Adolf Hitler his temporary successes, such as the German General Staff and the S.S., and not just the individuals whose conventional criminality could be established under common law.

Behind him, in the United States, the controversy over his ambitions was just beginning. How would he persuade the British to agree, let alone the French, or the Russians? Each nation had its own agenda. He entertained few doubts about the magnitude of the task he had set himself.[1]

The heavy transport plane descended through the clouds, passed over Ireland, and then droned on further eastwards into England. The pilot had obtained permission for them to circle London once, so that they could see the areas damaged by German bombing.

As the plane rolled to a halt on the airfield at Bovingdon, eighteen hours after its take-off from Labrador, Jackson turned to his son, Ensign William Jackson, a navy lawyer attached to his staff for this historic mission.

'Bill,' he warned him, 'you're going to be defending me long after I am gone.' He took the cup of coffee offered to him. 'That's why I want you to be there,' he said. 'I want you to see what it was all like.'

PEOPLE JUST did not come any more American than Robert H. Jackson.

It was once unkindly said of Clement Attlee—by Winston Churchill, the master of the poisoned parliamentary barb—that he was a modest man, with much to be modest about. Jackson too was modest, but with much that he could be proud of too.

He was a plain man who had started his professional life as a country lawyer in the Pennsylvania town where he had been born on February 13, 1892. His great grandfather had settled the township of Spring Creek in Pennsylvania, and his grandfather and father had been born on the same farm as he. In 1913 he had hung out his shingle as a lawyer at Jamestown in upstate New York, where his father ran a livery stable; he never did take his law degree, and he tried his first case—defending four trade unionists—and won it, before he was even admitted to the Bar. He qualified as a lawyer by hands-on practice alone.

Despite his youth, Jackson developed a large trial practice and became a familiar figure in the New York appellate courts. His politics were left-wing liberal. Very early on, he had become a supporter of Franklin Roosevelt; a model New Deal lawyer, Jackson had led the anti-trust assaults on the big business combines in the United States. In Washington, his career seemed to climb as inexorably as the morning sun. In 1934 Henry R. Morgenthau Jr, the urbane and civilised secretary of the treasury, invited him to become general counsel of the bureau of internal revenue.

It was said of Jackson that he was a man of urgent idealism, and not without personal ambitions, but as a true Democrat he never wavered in his support for Roosevelt, whom he described in 1939 as 'the greatest natural resource we have.' By 1940, he was being openly tipped by newspapers as a possible future president himself.

For the time being he was content to be a major legal figure. In July 1941, Roosevelt appointed him to the Supreme Court. On that exalted bench Jackson was cherished and renowned for his forthright dissenting opinions: for example, he could opine at the height of World War Two that the Supreme Court was wrong to allow the military to set aside the Bill of Rights in evicting all people of Japanese ancestry from the West Coast after the Japanese attack on Pearl Harbor—it was 'racial discrimination' in his view; and as Roosevelt's attorney-general he had forbidden all wiretapping operations by J. Edgar Hoover's F.B.I. (They had carried on tapping, all the same.)

Topping just five feet eight-and-a-half inches, with brown hair and blue eyes, Jackson was like many American country folk a man of limited horizons—a criticism that could be levelled at most of the Nazi leadership too. He had rarely travelled outside the United States; his last passport, issued ten years before, had been lost years earlier, and he had needed to get a new one for this trip.[2]

If there was one man on whom the Germans could count to give them a fair trial it seemed to be this man—convinced that the United States had a solemn, almost God-granted duty to educate the world, to reward the good, and to punish the evil with an element of righteousness which his country could still afford in 1945, if not in more recent times. Equally, if there was one man on whom President Harry S. Truman could count to set the trials in motion and see them through to their completion it was Jackson.

EVEN BEFORE his appointment by Truman, Jackson had attacked the cynics who had expected war crimes tribunals to act merely as extended weapons of war. He had initially come out against any such trial. 'If we want to shoot Germans as a matter of policy,' he had said in one speech as the fighting in Europe sputtered to an end, 'let it be done as such, but don't hide the deed behind a court. If you are determined to execute a man in any case, there is no occasion for a trial; the world yields no respect to courts that are merely organised to convict.[3] It would bring the law into contempt, he argued, if mock tribunals were held with the verdict already decided. 'I ... expressed the opinion,' he recalled two weeks later in his diary, 'that if these persons were to be executed, it should be as the result of military or political decisions.'[4]

In this courageous view, that there must be due and proper process, Jackson stood virtually alone at first, for this was the early summer of 1945, and the world's newspapers were full of photographs and vivid eye-witness stories of the horrors revealed in the former Nazi-occupied countries and extermination camps; the air was loud with the cry for immediate, summary, and violent revenge on the perpetrators of these crimes. Tens of millions had been sacrificed to the Termagant of war. Stalin would claim to Churchill at Potsdam that the Soviet Union had suffered nearly five million losses in killed and missing. Of 5,700,000 Russians taken prisoner by the Wehrmacht, only some two millions had survived.

This why Jackson felt that it was not enough to single out isolated conventional atrocities and punish the handfuls of low-ranking guilty men or even their leaders. The criminal organisations themselves had to be indicted. The other cases could be dealt with by existing army court-martial procedure. 'These cases I regarded as the small change of crime,' he privately recorded. 'They were offenses that always occur when men are hot, frightened, and passionate.'[5]

No, Jackson was after the men who had sat at the top, the enemy leaders who had planned that kind of warfare, who had brutalised it, and who had above all made war itself an instrument of policy.

❖ ❖ ❖ ❖ ❖

By June 1945 Jackson already had the toughest fight for justice behind him.

Firstly, there was President Roosevelt. While he talked eloquently in public of pursuing the Nazi criminals to the ends of the earth, privately he too intended that they should be punished without trial. At a stag dinner held at the White House on June 7, 1944, he had regaled Polish prime minister Stanislas Mikolajczyk with stories of Stalin's plans to 'liquidate 50,000 German officers,' and he had laughed out loud as he recalled how his joint chiefs had listened with round eyes to these words. Talking, later that evening, about which of the victorious powers should acquire the great north German ports, Henry L. Stimson, the U.S. secretary of war, urged Roosevelt to caution. 'I felt,' Stimson recorded in his diary, in an oblique hint at the ethnic cleansing that would occur after those regions were turned over to the Poles, 'that repercussions would be sure to arise which would mar the page of our history if we, whether rightly or wrongly, seemed to be responsible for it.'[6] Still worried about the bloodbath in store for the defeated Germans, Stimson wrote two days later that occupying the southern sector of Germany would be more congenial as it 'keeps us away from Russia during occupational period. Let her do the dirty work but don't father it.'[7]

Such was the climate of hatred that even Cordell Hull, Roosevelt's secretary of state and a distinguished statesman, argued for nothing less than the summary liquidation of the Axis leaders as and when they fell into Allied hands. 'Hull surprised me,' admitted the British ambassador Lord Halifax in his secret diary after dining with him on March 16, 1943, 'by saying that he would like to shoot and physically kill all the Nazi leaders down to quite low levels!' In this belief Hull was on a par with the ambassador's barber in Washington, who perpetually told him: 'Kill every one. Leave one—they will breed again and you have to do the job again. It is like leaving one rabbit in a young plantation.'[8] In the autumn of 1944 Cordell Hull again graphically proposed: 'If I had my way, I would take Hitler and Mussolini and Tojo and their arch accomplices and bring them before a drumhead court-martial, and at sunrise on the following day there would occur an historic incident.'[9]

General Dwight D. Eisenhower, who has a well-manicured image in the history books as a military commander blessed with both chivalry and decency, was little better. He told Lord Halifax on July 10, 1944 that in his view the enemy leaders should be 'shot while trying to escape'—the common euphemism for murder used in Hollywood's cheaper films about the Nazis. Eisenhower's naval aide Harry Butcher heard his chief of staff, Lieutenant-General Walter Bedell Smith, an officer who nursed a phenomenal hatred for the Germans, urge that imprisonment was not enough for the enemy's General Staff, a body of some 3,500 officers. 'There was agreement,' noted the aide in his unpublished diary, 'that extermination could be left to nature if the Russians had a free hand.' Why just the Russians? inquired Eisenhower:

the victorious powers, he suggested, could temporarily assign zones in Germany to the smaller nations with scores to settle.[10]

He repeated these views to Henry Morgenthau when the latter visited the Portsmouth command post of the Supreme Headquarters, Allied Expeditionary Force (S.H.A.E.F.) on August 7—indeed, Morgenthau would, with some justification, point to Eisenhower as the father of his famous Plan.[11] According to Morgenthau's version, General Eisenhower opposed any soft line: 'The whole German population is a synthetic paranoid,' he told the treasury secretary. 'And there is no reason for treating a paranoid gently. The best cure is to let the Germans stew in their own juice.' 'General Eisenhower had stated,' Morgenthau told his officials five days later, '… that in his view we must take a tough line with Germany as we must see to it that Germany was never again in a position to unleash war upon the world.'[12] According to another witness, Eisenhower also said: 'The ringleaders and the S.S. troops should be given the death penalty without question, but punishment should not end there.'[13]

This discussion with the treasury secretary prompted the supreme commander to dilate on his own views about the basically 'paranoid' German character, which Eisenhower himself later summarised as follows: 'The German people must not be allowed to escape a personal sense of guilt for the terrible tragedy that had engulfed the world. Germany's war-making power should be eliminated. Certain groups should be specifically punished by Allied tribunals: leading Nazis, Gestapo members, S.S. members.' He added, 'The German General Staff should be utterly eliminated. All records destroyed and individuals scattered and rendered powerless to operate as body. In proper cases more specifically punished.'[14]

Morgenthau tackled the British prime minister Winston S. Churchill about this three days later, over lunch on August 10, 1944.[15] The prime minister indicated his 'general concurrence' with Eisenhower's viewpoint. Morgenthau then sketched the outlines of what later became his Plan—'In his opinion serious consideration should be given to the desirability and feasibility of reducing Germany to an agrarian economy wherein Germany would be a land of small farms, without large-scale industrial enterprises.' Morgenthau reported all this to his Washington staff a few days later, one of whom recorded: 'He said that in his conversation with Churchill the question of the program to be followed upon occupation of Germany had come up and that he had gathered from the Prime Minister's comments that he was in agreement with the view expressed by Morgenthau to the effect that during the early months Germany's economy ought to be let pretty much alone and permitted to seek its own level.' The Germans were to stew in their own juice, in other words.[16]

Morgenthau advised the president on August 19, on his return from Europe to Washington, that some people in Europe were planning a soft future for Germany. Roosevelt confidently assured him, 'Give me thirty minutes with Churchill and I can correct this.' He added, 'We have got to be tough with Germany and I mean the German people, not just the Nazis. You either have to castrate the German people or you have got to treat them in such a manner so they can't go on reproducing people who want to continue the way they have in the past.'[17] (The presidential interest in castration is worth bearing in mind.)

Worried about the rumours that he was hearing, on August 21 the secretary of war Henry L. Stimson, a Republican in a broadly Democrat administration, talked with Roosevelt's special adviser Harry L. Hopkins on the telephone. Hopkins however asked him to bear with Morgenthau over Germany. Stimson saw every reason to be concerned about treasury secretary's involvement with Germany, and at noon on the twenty-third he went to the president and put to him his own more measured views. Afterwards Stimson and his deputy John G. McCloy took lunch with Morgenthau at the war department, and listened in disbelief as the latter revealed triumphantly that the dismemberment of Germany had already been agreed upon between the Big Three eighteen months earlier at Teheran. This was news not only to Stimson. 'Although the discovery of this thing,' dictated Stimson shortly afterwards into his private diary, 'has been a most tremendous surprise to all of us, I am not sure that the three chiefs regard it as a fait accompli.'[18]

In the afternoon Stimson tried to collect his own thoughts about the future of Germany, drafting a document entitled 'Brief for Conference with the President on August 25,' in which he listed 'a number of urgent matters of American policy' including in particular their policy vis-à-vis the 'liquidation of Hitler and his gang.' Stimson's wording was very explicit. 'Present instructions seem inadequate beyond imprisonment. Our officers must have the protection of definite instructions if shooting [is] required. If shooting required it must be immediate; not post-war.' He also asked the question, 'How far do U.S. officers go towards preventing lynching in advance of Law and Order?'[19]

❖ ❖ ❖ ❖ ❖

Morgenthau got at Roosevelt first, lunching with him at the White House on August 23. Here he filled in more details of his Plan for punishing and emasculating post-war Germany—regardless of the effect which this 'running sore' would have on the rest of the European economy.

The treasury secretary visited Roosevelt early on August 25 to hand him his own memorandum on the German problem. Later that day he and Stimson both lunched with the president. Stimson again focused attention on the allocation of British and American zones of occupation in Germany. He now urged Roosevelt to dump on the British the occupation of northern Germany. 'By taking south-western Germany,' he recorded in his diary, 'we were … further away from the dirty work that the Russians might be doing with the Prussians in Eastern Germany'—another unsubtle reference to the mopping up or purification operations which the Russians would conduct in their own occupation zone. Worried that Allied troops would shortly be entering Germany without policy directives, Stimson suggested that Roosevelt appoint a cabinet committee. The president took the point, and after lunch all three men went together into cabinet.

At the very beginning of this cabinet meeting Roosevelt announced that he would appoint Secretaries Hull, Morgenthau, and Stimson as the members of that committee.[20] In the ensuing discussion, Stimson felt that he was able to put across his view that any penalties should be inflicted on individuals and 'not by destruction of the economic structure of Germany which might have serious results in the future.' 'The President,' he recorded discreetly, 'showed some interest in radical treatment of the Gestapo.'[21]

THERE HE left it for a while. For the last days of August Stimson remained on his farm, maintaining scrambler telephone contact with McCloy in Washington. 'In particular,' wrote Stimson in his diary,

> I was working up and pressing for the point I had initiated, namely that we should intern the entire Gestapo and perhaps the S.S. leaders and then vigorously investigate and try them as the main instruments of Hitler's system of terrorism in Europe. By so doing I thought we would begin at the right end, namely the Hitler machine, and punish the people who were directly responsible for that, carrying the line of investigation and punishment as far as possible. I found around me, particularly Morgenthau, a very bitter atmosphere of personal resentment against the entire German people without regard to individual guilt and I am very much afraid that it will result in our taking mass vengeance on the part of our people in the shape of clumsy economic action.[22]

Getting wind of this rising controversy, the British ambassador in Washington, Lord Halifax, sent a telegram to the Foreign Office on September 1 reporting that McCloy had told him of the Morgenthau committee, and its preoccupation with the question of the trial and punishment of Hitler, Himmler, and other leading Nazis 'as distinct from their mere arrest by Allied military forces.'[23]

The economic part of what was more properly called the Treasury Plan was drafted by Morgenthau's principal assistant Harry Dexter White (who was later accused of being a Soviet agent); White completed the first draft on September 1 and sent it over the next day to Morgenthau, who had retired to his country home in upstate New York for the Labour Day weekend, an American public holiday. When President Roosevelt and his wife motored over to take tea with Morgenthau beneath the trees of his estate, the treasury secretary showed him the draft.

Roosevelt's current thinking on Germany was still rather simplistic: no aircraft, uniforms, or marching.

Morgenthau said: 'That's very interesting, Mr President, but I don't think it goes nearly far enough.' He wanted to put eighteen or twenty million Germans out of work, and he wanted able-bodied Germans transported to Central Africa as slave labour on 'some big TVA project.' (The Tennessee Valley Authority hydroelectric project of Roosevelt's New Deal had generated employment for half the continent.)

How different was the staid, elderly Republican Stimson from the vengeful Democract Morgenthau. That Monday, September 4, the former flew back to Washington and conferred with General George C. Marshall, Roosevelt's chief of staff, about the treatment of Germany and ways of investigating and punishing the Gestapo. 'It was very interesting,' Stimson dictated afterwards in a note, 'to find that army officers have a better respect for the law in those matters than civilians who ... are anxious to go ahead and chop everybody's head off without trial or hearing.'

Invited to dine with Morgenthau that evening, Stimson found McCloy and Harry Dexter White already there. 'We were all aware of the feeling that a sharp issue is sure to arise over the question of the treatment of Germany. Morgenthau is, not unnaturally, very bitter, and as he is not thoroughly trained in history or even economics it became very apparent that he would plunge out for a treatment of Germany which I feel sure would be unwise.'[24]

The next day the cabinet committee on Germany met for the first time in Cordell Hull's office. Hull was reticent but it turned out that his ideas were no less extreme than Morgenthau's. Stimson found himself in a minority of one. 'This proposal,' he said of Morgenthau's Plan, 'will cause enormous evils. The Germans will be permanent paupers, and the hatreds and tensions that will develop will obscure the guilt of the Nazis and poison the springs of future peace.'

'My plan,' retorted Morgenthau, unabashed, 'will stop the Germans from ever trying to extend their domination by force again. Don't worry. The rest of Europe can survive without them.'

Stimson was unconvinced. 'This plan will breed war,' he said, 'not prevent it!'

TO GENERAL Marshall he wrote, 'It's very singular. I'm the man in charge of the Department which does the killing in this war, and yet I am the only one who seems to have any mercy for the other side.'

Stimson returned to his office and dictated this note for his diary:

> As soon as I got into the meeting it became very evident that Morgenthau had been rooting around behind the scenes and had greased the way for his own views by conference with the president

> and others.... I, to my tremendous surprise, found that Hull was as bitter as Morgenthau against the Germans and was ready to dump all the principles that he had been laboring for in regard to trade for the past twelve years. He and Morgenthau wished to wreck completely the immense Ruhr–Saar area of Germany into a second rate agricultural land.... I found myself a minority of one and I labored vigorously but entirely ineffectively against my colleagues. In all the four years that I have been here I have not had such a difficult and unpleasant meeting.[25]

It was decided that each of the three men would submit to the president a memorandum on the treatment of Germany. Stimson utterly rejected Hull's proposals, which closely tallied with Morgenthau's. 'I cannot treat as realistic the suggestion that such an area in the present economic condition of the world can be turned into a non-productive "ghost territory" when it has become the center of one of the most industrialized continents in the world, populated by peoples of energy, vigor, and progressiveness.'[26]

Lord Halifax sent a further telegram to London, briefing the foreign office at McCloy's request on what Morgenthau was up to. Two awesome questions were now being raised, on which the ambassador asked for formal instructions: 'Whom do we imprison or intern? On what scale? Is it by tens of thousands or hundreds of thousands?' And, more crucially, 'Whom do we shoot or hang? The feeling is that we should not have great state trials, but proceed quickly and with despatch. The English idea, once preferred but then withdrawn, was to give the army lists to liquidate on mere identification. What has happened to this idea? Besides individuals, what categories should be shot?'[27]

General Marshall was a wise, unhurried soldier–politician. On September 7, Stimson secured him as an ally. After reading the memorandum which Stimson had received from Morgenthau 'demanding,' as Stimson summarised it, 'that the leaders of the Nazi party be shot without trial and on the basis of the general world appreciation of their guilt,' Marshall gave it the reception that his political master had expected—'absolute rejection of the notion that we should not give these men a fair trial.'

Morgenthau nonetheless stuck to his guns and went to the very top, demanding of the president a re-hearing.

Learning of this, Stimson cast about for other allies. He dined with Justice Felix Frankfurter, one of the twelve members of the Supreme Court and one of Roosevelt's less extreme advisers. 'Although a Jew, like Morgenthau,' dictated Stimson afterwards, 'he approached this subject with perfect detachment and great helpfulness.' He went over the whole matter with the judge from the beginning, reading out Morgenthau's proposals on the future of the Ruhr and on the summary liquidation without trial of the Nazis, at both of which Frankfurter 'snorted with astonishment and disdain.' He fully backed Stimson's views and those of his army generals. The accused Germans, said Frankfurter, were to be given a fair hearing: 'They cannot be railroaded to their death without trial.'[28]

The fight nonetheless continued. By September 9 Morgenthau had his full Plan ready, 'a new diatribe' on the subject of how to deal with the Nazis. At a meeting that day with Roosevelt, Stimson waded into it. But the meeting was very unsatisfactory. Hull sat silent.[29] Morgenthau's record shows that Roosevelt said he wanted Germany partitioned into three parts. He flipped through the pages of Morgenthau's Plan, and kept prodding Morgenthau: 'Where is the ban on uniforms and marching?' Morgenthau reassured him it was all there.[30]

The president was planning to meet in a few days' time with the British war leadership at Quebec, in Canada, to decide on these and other matters. He now, as Stimson put it, 'pranced up to the meeting at Quebec,' leaving Hull and Stimson behind.[31] Morgenthau seized the opportunity to share the train journey north with the president as far as Hyde Park. Roosevelt's country home in upstate New York. He wanted to have the last word.

❖ ❖ ❖ ❖ ❖

What views did Churchill bring with him to Quebec?

His cabinet had displayed some differences of attitude on the punishment of enemy war criminals.[32] A number of German prisoners-of-war had been shot in Britain during the war, but the file on these episodes is closed to public scrutiny.[33] The treatment of the principal enemy leaders was clearly a different matter altogether. The archives show that as early as 1942 Churchill had decided that they should be executed without trial, and he repeatedly canvassed this proposal until long after the war was over, although there is no trace of it in his memoirs.

For example, when the British ambassador in Moscow conveyed a Foreign Office statement on the case of Rudolf Hess to Marshal Stalin on November 5, 1942, the Soviet leader put his concerns to Sir Archibald Clark Kerr outright: 'After the war it is customary to repatriate prisoners-of-war: do you intend to send Hess home?' and he added, 'If Goebbels landed in the U.K. tomorrow, would you send him back as a P.o.W. too?' He was perturbed about the plan to set up a United Nations commission to try these criminals. 'I would not like to see Hitler, Mussolini, and the rest of them escaping like the Kaiser to some neutral country.' (The German Kaiser had been given sanctuary by the Netherlands after World War One.)

It was then that His Majesty's ambassador reassured the dictator that Churchill proposed a 'political decision,' whereby the enemy leaders would be liquidated upon capture.

Both on this occasion and subsequently when Churchill tried to force this solution on him Stalin voiced wise objections. 'Whatever happens,' he lectured the ambassador in November 1942, 'there must be some kind of court decision. Otherwise people will say that Churchill, Roosevelt, and Stalin were wreaking vengeance on their political enemies!'

'I am sure,' persisted the ambassador laconically, 'that the political decision that Mr Churchill has in mind will be accompanied by all the necessary formalities.'[34]

This was not an isolated document, in which an ambassador had perhaps expressed an opinion without sufficient warrant from his superiors. From both the British and American archives it becomes clear that the British—from their autocratic prime minister Winston Churchill downwards—were set on executing against the Nazi leadership what can only be described as lynch justice without the palliative noun, or alternatively as judicial murder without the exculpatory adjective.

It was a matter on which Anthony Eden, the foreign secretary, equivocated. Cabinet papers show that in July 1943 he proposed that the United Nations warn all neutral countries that the harbouring of war criminals at any future time would be regarded as an unfriendly act.[35]

Responding to this, another cabinet minister, Duff Cooper, pointed out that the United Nations had yet to decide on the fate of Hitler and Mussolini if they should be taken prisoner. 'By what code and before what tribunal can the head of a conquered State be tried by his victorious opponents?' he perhaps naïvely asked. He predicted that such a trial would drag on interminably, bringing disrepute to the lawyers and sympathy to those in the dock. Hitler, he reminded his cabinet colleagues, had ultimately decided not to put the deposed Austrian chancellor Kurt Schuschnigg on trial for precisely this reason.

As for the alternative, 'punishment without trial,' Duff Cooper warned that this would shock the consciences of many people at the time and 'many more in retrospect.' Since Hitler and Mussolini would no doubt meet their deaths with dignity, the result would be that their 'memories would be enshrined for ever in the hearts of their people.' He argued that it would be infinitely preferable for the Axis leaders to creep into a despised and dishonoured exile than to have trials leading to a St Helena or, worse, to executions. Duff Cooper quoted historical parallels—showing that the exiles of James II, the Kaiser, and Charles X were fatal to their dynasty; while the harsher punishments meted out to Napoleon, Louis XVI, and Charles I built up legends on which restorations were later founded.[36]

In July 1943, after Mussolini's overthrow and arrest, the very real possibility arose that he and his fascist consorts, 'the head devil together with his partners in crime,' as Roosevelt had called them, might fall into Allied hands. 'We ought now to decide,' Churchill cabled to Roosevelt, 'in consultation with ... the U.S.S.R. what treatment should be meted out to them. One,' he continued, though still treading warily, 'may prefer prompt execution without trial except for identification purposes.' Others might however prefer that Mussolini and the others be kept in confinement until the end of the war in Europe and their fate then be decided along with the other war criminals. Not yet having discussed this delicate matter with the president, Churchill professed to be 'fairly indifferent on this matter,' provided that they sacrificed no solid military advantages for the sake of immediate vengeance.[37]

Roosevelt responded on this occasion that in his opinion a premature effort to seize the 'head devil' would prejudice the primary Allied objective which was, he reminded the prime minister, to get Italy out of the war. In due course they could set about capturing Mussolini and his assistants; only then could they determine the individual degrees of guilt for which 'the punishment should fit the crime.'[38]

Where did the Lord Chancellor, head of the British legal structure, stand on this? Parroting His Master's Voice, Viscount Simon agreed with Churchill: the enemy leaders should be put to the sword. When he saw Lord Halifax on September 9, 1943 Simon said that, if action were ever to be taken against Hitler or Mussolini, it could be done only on the basis of a United Nations declaration as a 'political act'—that is, outright execution without trial. 'Whether that would be wise or not,' remarked Lord Halifax dubiously in his diary, 'is another matter. One other thing is certain: that it would be very difficult to explain to the ordinary public why you shot the man who burnt Lidice, and did not shoot Hitler.'[39]

Part of the decision-making process was easy: following Churchill's lead, on October 8 the cabinet decided that any lesser war criminals whom the Allies captured should be turned over to be punished locally, in the country where they had committed their crimes. Churchill thoroughly approved this: it would shift the burden of 'administering retribution'—he did not use the word justice—from the hands of the Allies to those of the countries which had suffered.[40]

Eden, however, as foreign secretary listened to the cabinet debate with misgivings. He was just off to confer with the other Allied foreign ministers in Moscow. 'I am far from happy about all this War Criminals business,' he minuted the next day. 'When I come back I want to have a Departmental discussion about it all. Broadly I am most anxious not to get into the position of breathing fire and slaughter against War Criminals and promising condign punishment and a year or two hence have to find a pretext for doing nothing.'[41]

Nonetheless Churchill drafted a solemn declaration which he submitted to both Roosevelt and Stalin on October 12, 1943, undertaking to cart back all the minor enemy war criminals to the location of their atrocities where they should be put on trial. He published the text of this draft in his memoirs:

> Great Britain, the United States, and the Soviet Union have received from many quarters evidence of the atrocities, massacres, and cold-blooded mass-executions which are being perpetrated by the Hitlerite forces in the many countries which they have overrun and from which they are now being steadily expelled. The brutalities of the Nazi domination are no new thing, and all peoples or territories in their grip have suffered from the worst forms of government by terror. What is new is that many of these territories are now being redeemed by the advancing armies of the liberating powers, and that in their desperation the recoiling Hitlerites and Huns are redoubling their ruthless cruelties.

Accordingly, continued Churchill's draft, the three powers, speaking in the interest of the thirty-two United Nations, declared that at the time of any armistice with Germany, those Germans who had been responsible for the atrocities 'will be sent back to the countries in which their abominable deeds were done.' Thus Germans taking part in the wholesale shooting of Italian officers—a neat contemporary touch, that—or in the execution of French, Dutch, Belgian, or Norwegian hostages and so on 'will know that they will be brought back, regardless of expense'—a less neat turn of phrase—'to the scene of their crimes and judged on the spot by the peoples whom they have outraged.'

'The above declaration,' he was careful to end, 'is without prejudice to the case of the major criminals, whose offences have no particular geographical localisation.'[42]

Eden carried Churchill's draft to Moscow and, with minor amendments, it was adopted as the declaration issued there at the end of the foreign ministers' meeting on October 30. This Moscow Declaration became the basis of the post-war disposition of many of the German war criminals—though not of the Italian and Japanese. Churchill expressed relief at this, telling the cabinet, 'I am certain that the British at any rate would be incapable of carrying out mass executions for any length of time, especially as we have not suffered like the subjugated countries.'[43]

This left unresolved the awkward problem of how to deal with the major war criminals, particularly those 'whose offences however have no particular geographical localisation'—the major criminals like Hitler.

For these the prime minister reverted, in November 1943, to his own final solution. 'A list,' he suggested, 'shall be compiled by the United Nations of all major criminals other than those provided for by local jurisdiction.' This growing list, of fifty or at the most one hundred names, would include 'the Hitler and Mussolini gangs and the Japanese

War Lords.' From time to time at a conference of jurists the lists would be pruned, added to, and approved. 'Thereafter, the persons named on the approved list will, by solemn decree of the 32 United Nations, be declared world outlaws.'

The beauty of this proposal was that the 'outlaws' could be liquidated at will: 'No penalty will be inflicted on anyone who puts them to death in any circumstances.' 'As and when any of these persons falls into the hands of any of the troops or armed forces of the United Nations,' suggested Churchill, 'the nearest officer of the rank or equivalent rank of Major-General will forthwith convene a Court of Inquiry, not for the purpose of determining the guilt or innocence of the accused but merely to establish the fact of identification. Once identified, the said officer will have the outlaw or outlaws shot to death within six hours and without reference to higher authority.'[44]

2: **Lynch Law**

IT WAS perhaps infelicitous for the leader of a great democracy, the head of a nation fighting a war to re-establish the rule of law, to have put his name to such a document. It was drafted in November 1943, even as Churchill was issuing orders for the severest fire raids in history to be executed against the capital of Germany, with the specific aim of killing as many of its civilian inhabitants as possible. There is no historian writing on the Third Reich who has not shuddered with uncomprehending disgust upon finding broadly identical orders signed by Adolf Hitler for the summary execution or liquidation of commandos, commissars, and Allied 'terror fliers'—and precisely those were the documents which were to be used as prosecution exhibits in the Tribunal that forms the centrepiece of this narrative.

There was, it must be said, also a party-political sub-plot to Churchill's deliberations. He was replacing Lord Woolton with Jay Llewellin as minister of food, a move which was seen as 'a nasty blow for the Simonites'—the followers of Viscount Simon, the lord chancellor. According to his private secretary, Churchill had hoped thereby to get rid of Simon. 'But,' he told another minister, 'since it is now desired to send back as many war criminals as possible to the scenes of their crimes, there is no longer much of a job, as was at one time expected, for Simon as president of some great International War Criminal Tribunal, and so, for the moment, he sticks on.'[1]

Churchill's proposals to lynch the enemy leaders were put before the war cabinet on November 10, 1943. Surprisingly given the prevailing mood and their broad subservience to their prime minister, the proposals were not at once adopted. Instead the cabinet agreed that in the light of their sometimes heated discussion the lord chancellor should, together with the attorney-general and the minister of aircraft production Sir Stafford Cripps, redraft the prime minister's unfortunate wording.[2] The formula which these three, much wiser, men eventually proposed was adopted by Churchill without comment:

> It is now announced that a list of the inner ring of political leaders who must take responsibility for the barbarous way in which the war has been conducted will be drawn up (in due course) by the United Nations. (These individuals will be solemnly

declared World-Outlaws.) When any of these major criminals fall into the hands of any force of the United Nations, they will be kept in strict confinement until such time as the United Nations decide on their fate.[3]

Meeting for dinner at the Soviet embassy in Teheran later in November 1943, Churchill, Roosevelt, and Stalin touched upon the issue of how to deal with the major war criminals, again without reaching any definite conclusion.[4] The meeting did however produce one famous piece of gruesome banter.

It was November 29, and one of the Americans present, diplomat Charles Bohlen, took detailed notes. He recalled Stalin's peculiar attitude to the British prime minister: this was a mixture of jocularity and contempt, as Churchill still seemed to entertain misgivings about OVERLORD, the planned invasion of northern France in 1944.

'Stalin,' Bohlen recorded, 'lost no opportunity to get in a dig at Mr Churchill.' Soon the prime minister was on the defensive. 'In the discussion in regard to future treatment of Germans,' Bohlen noted, 'Marshal Stalin strongly implied on several occasions that Mr Churchill nursed a secret affection for Germany and desired to see a soft peace.' It was their duty to evolve 'really effective measures' to control Germany to prevent her resurgence in fifteen or twenty years' time. One of the conditions, said Stalin, that must be met was that 'at least 50,000 and perhaps 100,000 of the German Commanding Staff must be physically liquidated.'

Churchill, having been fiercely celebrating the eve of his seventieth birthday, with many toasts, was in poor condition to notice that Stalin was ragging him. He remarked pompously that it was not the British habit to slaughter prisoners-of-war, 'especially officers.'[5] There were glares at him from around the table. Charles Bohlen's written record has it: 'The Prime Minister took strong exception to what he termed the cold blooded execution of soldiers who had fought for their country. He said that war criminals must pay for their crimes, and individuals who had committed barbarous acts, and in accordance with the Moscow Declaration which he himself had written they must stand trial at the place where the crimes were committed. He objected vigorously, however, to executions for political purposes.' According to Churchill's own colourful account, published after the war, he had announced: 'I would rather be taken out into the garden here and now and be shot myself rather than sully my own and my country's honour by such infamy.'[6]

Those documents already quoted and those still to come provide sufficient reason for doubting whether he really nursed such powerful objections to liquidating the enemy out of hand.

Roosevelt could see that Stalin had been pulling Churchill's leg. 'The President,' continued Bohlen's note, 'jokingly said that he would put the figure of the German commanding staff which should be executed at 49,000 or more.'[7] He dined out on Churchill's humourless response for weeks afterwards.[8]

Was Stalin, the butcher of Katyn, joking, or was he not? Probably he was not serious, because when Churchill, with Roosevelt's backing, later ventilated a similar plan (in October 1944) it was Stalin alone who vetoed it.

WHEN GENERAL Eisenhower asked the British government in April 1944 for a statement to issue to the Germans about how they would be treated in defeat, Churchill wrote to the Foreign Office as follows:

> I have pointed out to the cabinet that the actual terms contemplated for Germany are not of a character to reassure them at all, if stated in detail. Both President Roosevelt and Marshal Stalin at Teheran wished to cut Germany into smaller pieces than I had in mind. Stalin spoke of very large executions of over 50,000 of the staffs and military experts. Whether he was joking or not could not be ascertained. The atmosphere was jovial, but also grim. He certainly said he would require 4,000,000 German males to work for an indefinite period to rebuild Russia. We have promised the Poles that they shall have compensation both in East Prussia and, if they like, up to the line of the Oder. There are a lot of other terms implying the German ruin and indefinite prevention of their rising again as an armed Power.[9]

Unlike Churchill, Stalin seemed inclined to take the judicial path, albeit using the trial procedures for which the Russians were already well known. On December 16, 1943 they opened a war crimes tribunal against three German officers taken prisoner in Stalingrad, accused of murdering Russian civilians by means of gassing-trucks. The trial ended after only three days with death sentences. The three officers were executed in a public square in Kharkov before forty thousand spectators.[10]

The Russians spliced together a gruesome documentary film about the Kharkov trials, and its message—the Soviet trial procedures—was not lost on Justice Robert H. Jackson when it was shown to him and his entire newly assembled staff on the evening of May 17, 1945. Limiting his own verdict on it, the judge diplomatically called it 'a very interesting exposition of the Russian method of proving a case by the defendants themselves'—that is, the tortured 'self-confessions' for which Soviet-style trials had long become renowned.[11] As the British attorney-general Sir David Maxwell Fyfe wrote, these trials were efficiently stage-managed examples of summary action, in which the defendants abjectly confessed to their crimes and were convicted and executed without further ado.[12]

The show trial in Kharkov was not without consequences in Berlin during that winter of 1943–4. Goebbels' senior colleagues Dr Hans Fritzsche, who would also be indicted at Nuremberg, would testify in June 1946 to having particularly clear recollections of the moment when he learned that the Russians had staged a trial after recapturing the city of Kharkov. It was then that he heard for the first time the allegations about people being killed with gas.

> I hurried in with this report to Dr Goebbels and asked him what was going on. He responded that he would look into the matter, talk it over with Himmler and Hitler. The next day he told me there would be an official denial. But the denial was in fact never issued, the explanation being that they wanted to clarify the whole thing in more detail in a German trial.

Dr Goebbels had however told him explicitly, he said, that 'The gas trucks that they mentioned in the Russian trial were a product of somebody's fevered imagination, without any basis whatever in fact.'[13]

In England the War Cabinet formally decided on March 13, 1944 that a select list of German, Italian, and Japanese criminals should be drawn up, including not less than fifty and certainly not more than one hundred names all told, of which the larger proportion would 'of course' be German. The intention was, the Foreign Office informed those drawing up the list, to keep 'these select few' quite distinct from the general run of those guilty of war crimes in the strict sense. The criterion for selection would be 'responsibility for bringing about the war.'[14] It is quite clear, though not explicitly stated, what was to happen to these fifty to one hundred who were to be selected and kept apart from the rest, because the lord chancellor continued throughout 1944 to assume that the Axis leaders would be summarily liquidated upon their apprehension. Before his prime minister departed to meet Roosevelt at Quebec in September 1944, Viscount Simon handed to him a memorandum setting out a suitable public formula as a basis for such summary liquidation of the enemy leaders.[15]

❖ ❖ ❖ ❖ ❖

The two Allied leaders met in Quebec from September 11, 1944 and thereafter in private at Hyde Park. Churchill seems to have indicated his intention of discussing the future of Germany straight away, because from Quebec, Roosevelt cabled on the twelfth to Henry Morgenthau, 'Please be in Quebec by Thursday September 14th noon.' No such invitation went to Stimson.[16] Morgenthau brought his Plan with him in a loose-leaf folder.

Left in Washington, Stimson was disgusted on hearing of his president's action. 'I cannot believe that he will follow Morgenthau's views,' he wrote on the thirteenth. 'If he does, it will certainly be a disaster.' He continued to seeth, dictating on the next day: 'It is an outrageous thing. Here the president appoints a Committee with Hull as its Chairman for the purpose of advising him in regard to these questions in order that it may be done with full deliberation and, when he goes off to Quebec, he takes the man who really represents the minority and is so biased by his Semitic grievances that he is really a very dangerous adviser to the President at this time.' Even Cordell Hull had found himself left behind.

In Roosevelt's defence it can be said that he was already a sick man. Much thinner in body and face, he had lost around thirty pounds in weight, his eyes were drawn, his haggard face had a sunless pallor, and he looked distinctly older and worn. There was electioneering abuse of him as 'a senile old man' and it had etched deeply into him; the truth was that his great brain had already deteriorated so far that at one banquet in August he had proposed a toast to the same Icelandic prime minister twice in twenty minutes. As he now leaned forward in his wheelchair to see the models which Churchill had brought over—of D-day invasion paraphernalia—beads of perspiration stood out on his forehead.[17]

Morgenthau's papers show that he brought the talk round to Germany immediately he arrived in Quebec, on the evening of September 13.

Roosevelt invited him to outline his Plan. Unexpectedly, Churchill's first reaction was hostile. When Morgenthau talked of physically dismantling the Ruhr industries, Churchill interrupted him. He was flatly opposed, he said—all that was necessary was to eliminate German arms production. He waspishly told Morgenthau that his proposal would be 'unnatural, un-Christian, and unnecessary.' 'I regard the Morgenthau Plan,' the prime minister said, 'with as much enthusiasm as I would handcuffing myself to a dead German.' He was truculent, even offensive, lisping at one point to Roosevelt , 'Is this what you asked me to come all the way over here to discuss?'[18]

Lord Cherwell (the former Professor F. A. Lindemann) glowered at him: Churchill had evidently not grasped the salient point that this one man, Roosevelt's treasury secretary, controlled America's purse-strings and hence the bankrupt Britain's financial destinies. Before leaving Quebec, they had to get Roosevelt's signature on the draft Lend–Lease Agreement for Phase II, the post-war years.

Privately conferring with Morgenthau the next morning (September 14) the Prof. apologised profusely for Winston's behaviour, and promised to dress up the Plan in a way more appetising to the Prime Minister.[19]

Churchill now got the message, writing later: 'We had much to ask from Mr Morgenthau.' When he discussed policy toward Germany with Roosevelt later that day he declared himself in favour of the Plan, as explained to him by Lord Cherwell (basically, that by smashing Germany's industries the British Empire could grab the defeated enemy's export markets.) Cherwell was instructed to draft a memorandum for signature and give it to Churchill.[20] Churchill was in no mood to display magnanimity. At one point their host, the Canadian prime minister William Mackenzie King, asked him how long the war was going to last. Churchill said he feared that it might drag on. 'Hitler and his crowd know that their lives are at stake,' he said, 'so they will fight to the bitter end.'

Lord Cherwell produced a one-page draft memorandum on the treatment of Germany. Out of earshot of Churchill, Morgenthau invited the Prof. and Harry Dexter White up to his room at eleven A.M. on September 15, read the Prof.'s draft—and expressed a profound dislike for it. It represented 'two steps backward,' he suggested. Since the last discussion, he said, Churchill had seemed to accept the Plan, and had himself spoken promisingly of turning Germany into an agricultural state as she had been in the last quarter of the nineteenth century. Morgenthau therefore urged them to scrap this milk-and-water draft and to return to the two leaders for fresh instructions.

They all met at noon on September 15. Anthony Eden, who had been peremptorily summoned to Quebec from London, noted in his diary that he 'felt somehow irritated by this German Jew's bitter hatred of his own land & also wasn't sure that [his] scheme was all that good from our point of view.' The foreign secretary became 'rather peevish' with Morgenthau and afterwards felt that he must have hurt his feelings.[21] Churchill however rejected the new draft made by the two men, Morgenthau and Cherwell, as 'not drastic enough.' In their presence he dictated the famous one-page memorandum on the destruction of the Ruhr and Saar industries which Roosevelt and he himself shortly initialed. It contained the words, 'This programme for eliminating the war-making industries in the Ruhr and in the Saar is looking forward to converting Germany into a country primarily agricultural and pastoral in its character.'[22] It went in fact far beyond the Morgenthau Plan in its punitive economic provisions.

HENRY STIMSON learned of Morgenthau's triumph at Quebec in a phone call from his deputy John J. McCloy that weekend. It hung like a cloud over him for days. 'I have yet to meet a man,' he dictated, 'who is not horrified with the "Carthaginian" attitude of the Treasury. It is Semitism gone wild for vengeance and, if it is ultimately carried out (I can't believe that it will be), it as sure as fate will lay the seeds for another war in the next generation. And yet these two men [Churchill and Roosevelt] in a brief conference at Quebec with nobody to advise them except "yes-men," with no cabinet officer with the president except Morgenthau, have taken this step and given directions for it to be carried out.'

Anthony Eden would later use similar language, terming Morgenthau's interference, in a hand-written minute poisonous with barely concealed antisemitism, 'a piece of gratuitous impertinence.' 'These ex-Germans,' he wrote, 'seem to wish to wash away their ancestry in a bath of hate. A.E., Nov 19.'[23]

The Morgenthau Plan included controversial provisions for the establishment of slave-labour battalions comprised of all the members of the 'S.S., the Gestapo and similar groups,' and it proposed to punish with death any person trying to leave Germany. As for the punishment of 'arch-criminals' the Morgenthau Plan seemed to convey more than just the spirit of Churchill's original 'outlaw' proposals.

> A list of the arch-criminals of this war whose obvious guilt has generally been recognized by the United Nations shall be drawn up as soon as possible and transmitted to the appropriate military authorities. The military authorities shall be instructed with respect to all persons who are on such list as follows: (a) They shall be apprehended as soon as possible and identified as soon as possible after apprehension, the identification to be approved by an officer of the general rank. (b) When such identification has been made the person identified shall be put to death forthwith by firing squads made up of soldiers of the United Nations.[24]

Morgenthau's friends in Washington acted rapidly upon learning that Roosevelt and Churchill had initialed the document. Only two days later, on September 17, the American joint chiefs of staff issued to Eisenhower a wide interim directive, instructing him to ensure that the Germans realised they would never again be allowed to threaten world peace. 'Your occupation and administration,' the document read, 'will be just but firm and distant. You will strongly discourage fraternization between Allied troops and the German officials and population.'[25] A political directive issued on October 14 by the American joint chiefs of staff stressed the elimination of the German officer corps: 'General Staff officers not taken into custody as prisoners are to be arrested and held, pending receipt of further instructions as to their disposal.'[26]

That sounded ominous. But it was no more than what Churchill had simultaneously persuaded President Roosevelt to approve at Hyde Park on September 17, a document which he intended to lay before Marshal Stalin for signature at the first opportunity. This hitherto unpublished document—typed by one of Churchill's private secretaries on a 10 Downing Street letterhead—reads in full:

'DRAFT OF A SUGGESTED TELEGRAM TO BE SENT BY
THE PRESIDENT AND THE PRIME MINISTER TO MARSHAL STALIN

'1. In the Moscow Conference of foreign ministers before Teheran, the

Prime Minister of Great Britain submitted a draft proposing the local punishment of war criminals in the countries, and if possible, at the scenes where their atrocities had been committed. With some small amendments this document was approved and has been published to the world with general acceptance and approval. This document however did not attempt to deal with the cases of the major war criminals "whose offences have no particular geographical localisation." This matter was touched on in conversation at Teheran without any definite conclusion being reached.

'It has now become important for us to reach agreement about the treatment of these major criminals. Would you [Stalin] consider whether a list could not be prepared of say 50 to 100 persons whose responsibilities for directing or impelling the whole process of crime and atrocity is [*sic*] established by the fact of their holding certain high offices.

'Such a list would not of course be exhaustive. New names could be added at any time. It is proposed that these persons should be declared, on the authority of the United Nations, to be world outlaws and that upon any of them falling into Allied hands the Allies will "decide how they are to be disposed of and the execution of this decision will be carried out immediately". Or, alternatively, "the nearest General officer will convene a court for the sole purpose of establishing their identity, and when this has been done will have them shot within six hours without reference to higher authority."

'2. It would seem that the method of trial, conviction and judicial sentence is quite inappropriate for notorious ringleaders such as Hitler, Himmler, Goering, Goebbels, and Ribbentrop.* Apart from the formidable difficulties of constituting the court, formulating the charge and assembling the evidence, the question of their fate is a political and not a judicial one. It could not rest with judges however eminent or learned to decide finally a matter like this which is of the widest and most vital public policy. The decision must be "the joint decision of the Governments of the Allies." This in fact was expressed in the Moscow Declaration.

'3. There would seem to be advantages in publishing a list of names. At the present time, Hitler and his leading associates know that their fate will be sealed when the German Army and people cease to resist. It therefore costs them nothing to go on giving orders to fight to the last man, die in the last ditch &c. As long as they can persuade the German

* On what grounds would the Nuremberg Tribunal have found it possible to indict Dr Goebbels? Dr Nelte, Keitel's attorney, described the Propaganda Minister as a very shrewd man, the ideological dynamo , who actually believed everything he wrote. 'Apart from the Jewish pogrom in [November] 1938 there was nothing Goebbels could have been accused of in this trial,' in Nelte's opinion.

people to do this, they continue to live on the fat of the land and have exalted employments. They represent themselves and the German people as sharing the same rights and fate.

'Once however their names are published and they are isolated, the mass of the German people will infer rightly that there is a difference between these major criminals and themselves. A divergence of interests between the notorious leaders and their dupes will become apparent. This may lead to undermining the authority of the doomed leaders and to setting their own people against them, and thus may help the break up of Germany.'[27]

CLUTCHING THESE horrendous documents in his briefcase, on September 19 Churchill boarded the Queen Mary for the return journey to England. Lord Cherwell, his *éminence grise*, remained for further talks in Washington. On the twentieth, McCloy warned Stimson that he had now heard from both Lord Halifax and Sir Alexander Cadogan, permanent secretary at the foreign office, that the president was 'very firm for shooting the Nazi leaders without trial.'[28]

Roosevelt was still under Morgenthau's influence. Both Stimson and Hull continued to lobby him against the Morgenthau Plan. Remarkably, almost overnight, he began to reconsider. It was of course an election year, and what finally helped change his mind was when the newspapers got wind of the Plan; details of it appeared on September 23 in the *Wall Street Journal*. There was a torrent of criticism directed at both the president and Morgenthau. The five biggest American engineering unions issued a declaration dismissing the Plan as economically unsound and warning that it 'contained the seeds of a new war.'

Pulling out all the stops, Morgenthau sent a copy of the full-length twenty-two-page final version of the Plan round to Lord Cherwell, who was still in Washington, asking him to show it to Churchill.[29] In London, Eden angrily rebuked Churchill for having initialed the agreement. On September 29 a Labour member of Parliament, Richard Stokes, challenged the foreign secretary to tell the truth about the Morgenthau Plan.[30]

Eden was however still completely caught up in Winston's web. On October 3 he circulated to the cabinet a copy of the telegram which the prime minister had drafted on September 17 at Hyde Park, New York, and was proposing to address together with Roosevelt to Marshal Stalin, recommending the lynching of the enemy leaders.[31] This telegram, quoted in full above, was a document of disturbing cynicism—even if one overlooks its literary licence, not least in the passage where Winston Churchill, of all people, describes the ascetic Adolf Hitler as living 'on the fat of the land.'

CONFIDENT OF gaining Stalin's support, Churchill now proposed to press the matter home. Regardless of Roosevelt's feelings in the matter, he sprang a surprise visit on Stalin in Moscow in October, securing his first meeting with the dictator in the Kremlin late on the ninth.

By now uncomfortably aware of Britain's slipping authority in the grand alliance, he intended to steal a march on the Americans with this visit. The series of meetings—code named TOLSTOY—was primarily to carve up post-war Europe, in precisely same way as the 'war criminal' Ribbentrop and Molotov had divided eastern Europe and the Baltic states between them under less auspicious circumstances in August 1939.

While things went swimmingly on the matter of the frontiers, on the issue of punishing the war criminals, as things turned out, Churchill did not get far with Stalin.

It had finally dawned on him that all their public talk of Unconditional Surrender and the Morgenthau Plan was just making the Germans fight even harder. He therefore suggested to Stalin that for a month or so they should shut up—not saying anything about their plans. He was all for setting hard surrender terms, but in the United States, he admitted, opinion was divided on just how hard. 'The problem was how to prevent Germany getting on her feet in the lifetime of our grandchildren,' he said.

Stalin disagreed with the whole concept. 'Hard measures,' he felt, 'would stir a desire for revenge.'

Molotov then asked outright for Churchill's view on the Morgenthau Plan.

Churchill admitted that Roosevelt and Morgenthau had been taken aback by its public reception. The prime minister repeated, according to the British record, that, as he had declared at Teheran, Britain would not agree to the mass execution of Germans, since he feared that 'one day' British public opinion would cry out. 'But it was necessary,' the British minutes record Churchill as saying, 'to kill as many as possible in the field.'

Stalin made no comment on that. A few moments later Churchill suggested that the population of Silesia and East Prussia should be 'moved' to other provinces in western Germany, explaining with disarming cynicism: 'If seven million had been killed in the war there would be plenty of room for them.'[32]

After a week dominated by Polish affairs—of which Churchill declared both British and Russia to be 'heartily sick'—the two leaders renewed their discussion on the future in a macabre humour.

British foreign secretary Anthony Eden had already secretly promised the Russians on October 16 that Britain would repatriate to the Soviet Union eleven thousand Russian prisoners-of-war 'without exception,' even if they did not wish to return. (The eleven thousand would be shot as soon as they arrived on Russian soil.) The next day Churchill regaled Stalin with an account of his bombing onslaught—boasting that three days earlier R.A.F. Bomber Command had put down ten thousand tons of bombs in twelve hours on one minor Ruhr town, Duisburg. 'The war,' boasted Churchill, 'is the most cruel since the Stone Age.' When Stalin allowed himself a witticism about cannibalism, Churchill chimed in, 'Talking of eating—Britain has managed to arrange for the despatch of 45,000 tons of corned beef to the Soviet Union.' With a guffaw he added, 'We are also sending eleven thousand Soviet ex-prisoners-of-war to eat the beef.'

The reader can almost hear the unkind laughter crackling from the pages in the archives—but they merit quoting here as an indication of the kind of reprehensible remarks which are exchanged at high-level conferences between men of war, and which hardly bear reading out by public prosecutors in the cold light of a war-crimes tribunal years later.

When Stalin asked point-blank what they were to do with Germany, Eden dutifully talked of dismemberment; and Churchill reverted to his old bugaboo, Prussia and her military caste as 'the root of the evil.' They should strip everything out of the Ruhr and the Saar, he said. 'This was the policy which Mr Morgenthau had laid before the President,' Churchill explained, adding, 'Mr Morgenthau's hatred of the Germans was indescribable.'

'A second Vansittart,' remarked Stalin approvingly, referring to the pathologically anti-German Lord Vansittart, a former adviser to the British foreign office.

Roosevelt, continued the prime minister, had liked what Morgenthau had said; so did he, and he quoted page after page from the Plan as they both pored over maps of Europe, Germany, and the Dardanelles Straits, pencils in hand.

It was a pity, Churchill murmured, that when God created the world he had not consulted the two of them. 'God's first mistake,' agreed Stalin.[33]

IT WAS not until his last day in Moscow that Churchill cautiously raised the Allied proposal to kill off the major enemy leaders upon capture, which he and Roosevelt had both initialed at Hyde Park earlier that month.

He ran into a solid wall of Stalinite yet again. The Marshal refused to endorse the proposed declaration, and Churchill quietly tucked it away.[34] He would sadly report to H. M. the King, as well as to Attlee and President Roosevelt on the failure of this part of his mission to 'Uncle Joe': 'U.J. took an unexpectedly ultra-respectable line. There must be no executions without trial otherwise the world would say we were afraid to try them. I pointed out the difficulties in International Law but he replied [that] if there were no trials there must be no death-sentences, only life-long confinements.'[35]

About this remarkably legalistic approach by the Soviet dictator, the record leaves no room for doubt.

❖ ❖ ❖ ❖ ❖

His own bloodlust aroused, Britain's lord chancellor did not readily abandon his case for judicial murder, and as Churchill departed for the Crimea conference at Yalta on January 26, 1945, Lord Simon again submitted to him a memorandum on the 'Punishment of Hitler and his Chief Associates'. 'I am still of opinion,' he wrote in this document, 'that the best course of the Allies would be to treat the punishment of Hitler, Mussolini and their principal colleagues and associates as a political matter and not to have recourse to judicial forms.' 'I have gathered,' he however continued, 'that Marshal Stalin did not agree but preferred the method of trial—no doubt on the Soviet model,' he added sardonically.[36]

In the United States, there had also been more discussion on what to do with the defeated enemy. Herbert Wechsler, the assistant attorney-general, had drawn up a secret memorandum at the end of 1944 commenting on the war department's latest proposal that the Nazi leaders be tried for 'conspiracy to achieve domination of other countries'—a crime of which nobody, he evidently felt, could ever accuse the United States leadership.[37]

The Supreme Headquarters, Allied Expeditionary Force (S.H.A.E.F.), which was General Eisenhower's headquarters, was consulted. Its views were formulated in a report by the Psychological Warfare Division and discussed in Washington on January 16, 1945. This document proposed to differentiate between the German people and the members of the government, high command and Nazi party. Something unappetising was evidently planned for the latter along the lines of the Morgenthau Plan, because the secretary of the navy, James V. Forrestal, at once objected. 'The American people,' he wrote, 'would not support mass murder of the Germans, their enslavement, or the industrial devastation of the country.' Henry Stimson vigorously agreed with him.[38]

Morgenthau continued to canvass vigorously for his Plan. He secured permission from the new secretary of state, Edward Stettinius, to address the senior department's senior officers on January 17, 1945; he told them of his dismay at the namby-pamby provisions of the joint chiefs of staff directive 1067 for the treatment of the Germans.[39] After further discussion between Francis Biddle, Stimson, Forrestal, and Stettinius, respectively the heads of the departments of justice, war, navy, and state, they initialed a plan six days later for submission to Roosevelt outlining their very different concept, which envisaged the full-scale trial of the major enemy war criminals before military tribunals. They reminded the president that putting these men to death without trial would violate 'the most fundamental principles of justice common to all the United Nations.' They suggested that Roosevelt carry this document to Yalta for discussion with the British and Russians.[40]

Arriving at Yalta without any of these men, and without even Morgenthau this time, President Roosevelt largely ignored their recommendations. Conferring with Marshal Stalin in private at the Livadia Palace on February 4, 1945, he confessed, according to the transcript once more made by interpreter Charles Bohlen, that he was more bloodthirsty now than a year earlier, and that 'he hoped Marshal Stalin would again propose a toast to the execution of 50,000 officers of the German Army.'[41]

Five days later, Churchill echoed similar thoughts at their plenary session, on February 9, 1945, raising the issue of war criminals, and again proposing a form of legalised lynching. According to the American Admiral William D. Leahy's diary the prime minister 'expressed an opinion that the "Great War Criminals" should be executed without formal individual trials.'[42] The transcript taken by James Byrnes shows, in rather more detail, that Churchill mentioned that the current proposal was to send the lesser criminals to 'the place where their crime was committed,' where they would be put on trial by the people living there. 'I want to call attention,' Churchill had then said however, according to Byrnes' note, 'to the grand criminals whose crimes have no particular geographic location.' He himself felt that the Big Three should draw up a list of these major criminals. 'Personally,' he added, still hankering after the plan that he had offered in October in Moscow, 'I was inclined to think they should be shot as soon as they were caught and their identity established.'

For a moment Stalin prevaricated, asking about Rudolf Hess, who was still in British hands. Churchill offered the laconic response that Hess would eventually 'catch up' with the others being returned to Germany. He pressed his earlier point: was it still Marshal Stalin's view that 'grand criminals' should be tried before being shot; in other words, did Stalin still believe the shooting should be 'a judicial rather than a political act'?

Stalin replied 'that that was so.'[43]

According to the American transcript, he then asked, evidently mindful of the international conventions on the treatment of prisoners-of-war: 'Would the prisoner-of-war come under the category of war criminal? So far,' he reminded Churchill, 'there has been general opinion that a prisoner-of-war could not be shot without trial.'

> THE PRIME MINISTER: A prisoner-of-war who has committed crimes against the laws of war can be shot.* Otherwise, they would only have to surrender. I gather, however, that the Marshal thought that before they could be put to death they ought to have a trial.
>
> THE PRESIDENT: I do not want it too judicial. I want to keep the

* Churchill's information was incomplete. Prisoners-of-war can be executed only after due court martial by officers of appropriate rank, after the protecting power has been notified, and after the lapse of a statutory period of time. It was a paradox that the British prime minister made the suggestion and that the Russian repudiated it, since Britain had signed the Geneva Convention on prisoners-of-war and the Soviet Union had not.

newspaper men and the newspaper photographers out until it is finished.[44]

The American's note on his president's words was overly discreet. The British transcript of Roosevelt's language at this point reads: 'He wanted to keep out newspapers and photographers until the criminals were dead.'[45]

❖ ❖ ❖ ❖ ❖

The position of Rudolf Hess was complicated by many factors. Ever since his dramatic arrival in Scotland on the night of May 11, 1941 as Hitler's deputy and titular head of the Nazi party, parachuting out of a Messerschmitt 110 fighter plane, wearing the uniform of a Luftwaffe lieutenant and demanding to see His Majesty the King, he had been held as Churchill's personal prisoner, first in the Tower of London and then in various secret service safe-houses.

Twice members of Churchill's Cabinet—Lords Simon and Beaverbrook—had been to see Hess. The verbatim transcripts of their talks in 1941 reveal Hess as a dedicated, upright ex-aviator of World War One who was haunted by nightmare visions of the all-out bombing war against civilians that seemed to be in prospect if the madness could not be halted immediately.[46] He had come on a peace mission, as he wrote in a letter addressed to the King, adding that Germany had no demands to make of Britain or her Empire. But, once he was being held in solitary confinement, the Hess story took a tragic twist. Recognising that his mission had failed he had developed all the raging symptoms of a latent paranoid schizophrenia.[47] Under the terms of the Geneva Convention he should have been repatriated along with hundreds of other disabled prisoners-of-war. On Churchill's instructions however the foreign office had fobbed off all the inquiries of the Swiss legation, as the protecting power, and Hess had been detained as a possibly useful pawn in the international power-game. He was held in a series of fortified mansions, where his rooms were bugged with hidden microphones that recorded every word.

He tried suicide twice—by plunging headlong from a second-floor balcony, and by thrusting a knife into his chest. Each time he failed. He had been left to vegetate, a matter of interest only for the doctors and psychiatrists who continued to infest his shrinking world. They tried everything, including truth drugs (in May 1944), to prise from him the secrets which he must have known.[48]

In 1942 the British government sent a secret report to Stalin admitting that eminent psychiatrists had diagnosed mental instability with signs of persecution mania. 'There is no doubt that Hess is mentally unbalanced,' this report said, 'though his condition varies considerably from time to time.'[49] The foreign office however warned Britain's ambassador in Moscow, when handing this document to

Stalin, to urge him to keep it secret. 'If Hess's mental instability becomes known to the German Government,' they explained, 'they might make out a good case under the Prisoners-of-war Convention for his repatriation.' Eden's telegram continued, 'We naturally do not intend to let Hess return to Germany and so possibly escape answering for his share in German war crimes.'[50]

Stalin remained deeply suspicious, and he at least once suggested putting the prisoner on trial immediately—an action which Eden had earnestly discouraged, explaining: 'Premature action might merely lead to reprisals against British prisoners-of-war in German hands.'

In July 1945 the research department of the foreign office would issue a brief on the Role of Hess in the Criminal Plan or Enterprise and his responsibility for specific war crimes. Quoting only sources like his published speeches the F.O. concluded that he was an unrepentant Nazi; even when he came to Britain on his peace mission, they said, Hess had proposed that Germany should be given 'a free hand in Europe,' which was proof of his aggressive intentions. It was however more difficult to pin specific crimes on to Hess because 'his sojourn of four years in this country has prevented him from adding his name to many overtly criminal acts.'[51]

That was the nub of the matter: He had personally issued a circular telegram to all the gauleiters in November 1938 halting the outrages of the Kristallnacht.[52] He had participated in none of the secret Hitler conferences in 1938 and 1939. As the British well knew, Hess had tried to stop the war and to end the bombing. He had left Germany before the attack on Russia in June 1941 and before the onset of what would in the 1970s become known as the Holocaust. There seemed little real reason to inscribe Hess's name on any list of war criminals. But as Eden had informed the cabinet on June 16, 1944, they felt bound to include his name 'both because of his former position and activities and because his omission would be likely to arouse unfavourable comment, particularly from the Soviet Government.'[53]

All of this seemed to have much to do with the moral cowardice of international diplomacy, and little to do with the inherent criminality or otherwise of the people being indicted.

❖ ❖ ❖ ❖ ❖

Upon his return to Washington from Yalta, Roosevelt instructed Judge Samuel I. Rosenman, a long-time friend and legal adviser who had been at Yalta with him, to travel to London and try to agree with the British a course of action on the war criminals. Rosenman visited the liberated areas of Europe first, and then flew on to England.

On April 5, 1945 the American judge heard Viscount Simon solemnly plead for the summary killing of Hitler *et al.*, with no kind of tribunal. The attorney-general (Sir David Maxwell Fyfe) was also recorded in the formal minutes as being 'personally in favour of the summary execution method.' While Rosenman may well have listened to these British proposals in dismay he diplomatically described them as 'novel, ingenious, and sound in principle.'[54] On the following day Simon however wrote to Rosenman informing him that Lord Halifax, the British ambassador in Washington, had now conveyed to them the strong feelings of the U.S. secretary of war that 'there ought to be a judicial proceeding before execution'—an unfortunate phrase even then, conveying as it did more than a whiff of foregone conclusions.[55]

The Americans were already represented at London discussions. Brigadier-General John M. Weir, head of the War Crimes Section of the U.S. judge advocate-general's department, raised one important question: precisely who was to be put to the sword in this mediæval way? The lord chancellor tossed off a few names—Hitler, Goebbels, Himmler, and Ribbentrop were the most obvious candidates for summary liquidation; he admitted that from what he knew the Russians were likely to favour an ordinary trial, 'although the president and Prime Minister had suggested summary execution as the best method.'[56] This was a reference to the memorandum drafted by Churchill at Hyde Park, New York state, the previous September.

ENLIGHTENED, IF not encouraged, by these talks with the British legal profession, Judge Rosenman drove down to Chequers to see the prime minister on April 8.

Churchill kept him up talking until three A.M.[57] 'I found him most interesting on the subjects of feeding the liberated peoples and the punishment of war criminals,' the prime minister wrote in a guarded letter to his wife afterwards.[58] Although he did not go into further detail in this letter, we know more of what he said from other sources. Referring yet again to his setback in Moscow in October 1944, Churchill told Judge Rosenman that he had already broached the subject with Marshal Stalin—he had suggested that they should not brook any delay by putting these men on trial, and that 'if these Nazi high officers were caught they should be taken out and shot.'

Marshal Stalin, so the prime minister related to Rosenman, had however solemnly replied that the Soviets never executed anybody without trial. Having as he put it stuck his neck out, Churchill immediately drew it in. 'Of course, of course,' he had lisped to Stalin, as though nothing had been further from his mind. 'We should give them a trial first.'[59]

Simon however clung tenaciously to his own (and Churchill's) radical ideas. Before Rosenman returned to Washington, the lord chancellor pressed into his hands a top-secret war cabinet paper in which he still recommended that the Allied generals be directed to take the law into their own hands.

IN THE United States fate would supervene before Rosenman returned to Washington. Morgenthau again visited Roosevelt as he was resting in his little wooden cottage at Warm Springs, in Georgia, on the evening of April 11, 1945 and badgered him to adopt the Plan. 'Mr President,' he said, 'I am doing a lot of things in regard to Germany, and I want you to know about it. We are having a lot of troubles.'

The president, looking grey and drawn, said nothing. Morgenthau then asked him if he wanted him to interest himself in the future treatment of Germany. Again the president did not answer directly. 'Look, Mr President,' persisted Morgenthau, 'I am going to fight hard, and this is what I am fighting for.'[60] He handed over the Plan. That was as far as he got with Roosevelt, because the very next afternoon the president suddenly slumped over and died. A new man with decidedly different views on international law, Harry S. Truman, took over at the White House.

❖ ❖ ❖ ❖ ❖

Upon arriving back in Washington, Rosenman showed Viscount Simon's cabinet paper to Judge Robert H. Jackson, of the Supreme Court, and to Henry L. Stimson, at the end of that month.[61] The document showed that the British legal experts still contemplated the idea of a proper trial of the enemy leaders with an wholly uncharacteristic *horreur*. As Rosenman told Jackson, the lord chancellor indicated that it was proposed to detach Hitler and his immediate associates from the trial of the main group, no doubt some other fate still being held in store for these higher Nazis despite Stalin's recriminations.[62] The British considered death sentences a certainty; the only question was whether to stage a mock trial first or not. 'It being conceded,' wrote Simon loftily in the cabinet paper, 'that these leaders must suffer death, the question arises whether they should be tried by some form of tribunal claiming to exercise judicial functions.' His Majesty's government, he added, duly recommended 'that execution without trial is the preferable course.'

This involved obvious departures from generally understood notions of law. Stimson, who was briefly staying on as secretary of war to the new president, was equally shocked. After reading this unsavoury British cabinet document, he dictated a note on April 25 to the effect that the Lord Chancellor supported lynching the enemy leaders and that the war cabinet in London had voted in favour. This was not what Stimson thought proper at all. He discussed it over the telephone with John McCloy: how should they now state the United States position on war crimes at San Francisco, where the Allied nations were meeting to lay the constitutional foundations of the United Nations? Stimson dictated into his diary: 'The British, as I think I have reported in this diary, have come out strongly against having a trial and wish to kill the people offhand—a most singular position.'[63]

He brooded for days on this, perplexed by Churchill's policy, and repeated that weekend: 'The British have to my utmost astonishment popped out for what they call "political action" which is merely a euphemistic name for lynch law, and they propose to execute these men without a trial. Sir John Simon [agrees with] the War Cabinet, who wish to execute them at once when they are captured.... Fortunately,' observed Stimson, 'the Russians and the French are on our side.'[64]

President Truman strongly supported Stimson's view that a trial was vital. He was a plain speaker, and he spoke plainly. The Nazis should be given a fair trial first—and then hanged.

3: Mr Morgenthau and the All-American Judge

IN LONDON the cabinet had given Viscount Simon full authority as lord chancellor to reach the necessary agreements with the Soviet Union, France, and the United States. A British War Crimes Executive was the outcome, which spent much time in committee, going over the details. The resulting proposal was for a military court consisting of high-ranking generals which would try the question of war guilt in two phases—first to establish that a general conspiracy had existed, aimed at conquering Europe and the whole world; and then to identify who had been a party to the conspiracy.

Several months had passed since the Crimea conference, however, and the war in Europe was about to end. The Russians, initially the most strident in the call for proper war crimes trials, were dragging their feet. American approaches to them through the state department brought no response. With not a little prompting from Samuel Rosenman, who regarded this as the legacy of the late president, President Truman decided late in April 1945 that the United States must take the lead.

This was how Justice Robert H. Jackson came in. Truman could think of no lawyer better fitted to stage the whole trial than Jackson, a judge on the Supreme Court. He wanted to see Jackson seize a dominant position for the United States—what would now be called the moral high ground. His initial belief was that Jackson should act as trial attorney not just for the American prosecution but for the entire United Nations.

At tea-time on April 26 the president asked Sam Rosenman to telephone the historic invitation to Jackson at the court. Jackson invited the other judge over to the courthouse, and Rosenman initiated him for the first time in what was being planned. If the Russians could be brought in to the trial, said Rosenman, they would no doubt be nominating Andrei Yanuar'yevich Vyshinsky, the prosecutor at the famous Soviet show-trials of the Thirties, to head their delegation, while the British team would probably be headed by the lord chancellor. Jackson knew Viscount Simon only vaguely, having met him once in 1924. 'Simon as a lawyer,' he dictated to his diary now, 'is entitled to the greatest respect, however inept he has been in some of his political ventures.' (Simon was anxious to expunge from the memory of History his record as a Liberal party spokesman for appeasement in the Thirties.)

Rosenman further assured the judge that the U.S. war department had been working for a long time intensively on the matter, and that it had amassed an 'extraordinary amount' of photographic and other evidence which made for an open-and-shut case against those who were to be accused of the conspiracy. Jackson suddenly remembered the speech that he had made only two weeks previously, in which he had seemed to be advocating the execution of the enemy leaders without trial; he very properly warned Rosenman that this might be quoted to embarrass the new president. Rosenman assured him it would not.[1]

He invited Jackson to read the January 1945 memorandum prepared by Roosevelt's department heads before Yalta. It was all very tempting—too tempting too ignore. For a brief moment Jackson did wonder whether directing the United Nations' prosecution of the major war criminals might take him away from the Supreme Court too long—long enough, in fact, to affect his career: but the court was about to hear the last arguments of the current term, and it would then be in recess until October 1945; the European thing would surely all be over before then. 'The trial of these war-guilt cases,' felt Jackson, 'must be prompt, and must be over with before the public turns to other things if they are to serve any real purpose.'[2]

'Immensely pleased at the offer, and challenged by the difficulty of the task,' as he entered in his diary, Jackson accepted.[3]

It was the mistake of a lifetime. The trial to be held eventually at Nuremberg would take a year longer than he had calculated, and it would bring ruination to his reputation and to his political and judicial aspirations.

❖ ❖ ❖ ❖ ❖

In his letter of acceptance to Harry Truman, dated April 29, 1945, Jackson foreshadowed some of the greyer areas of the forthcoming trial. He discouraged Truman from pressing for an American right to prosecute on behalf of all the United Nations. There might well be matters where considerations of domestic prestige for the Russians required that they present the evidence—and some of that evidence, Jackson righteously added, 'such as confessions, for example,' might have been obtained in such a manner that he as an American judge could hardly vouch for it.[4] Since Truman was in a hurry to announce the appointment on Wednesday, May 2, Rosenman sent his two best aides, Colonel Murray Bernays and Herbert Wechsler, the latter being assistant attorney-general and a fine international lawyer, to see Jackson on the last day of April. He found that these two lawyers had already drafted a suitable executive order for the president to sign.[5] Truman did so, signing Executive Order No. 9547 on May 2, 1945.[6]

The two lawyers also left with Jackson a document entitled 'Punishment of War Criminals', dated April 28, 1945—a draft instrument for each of the United Nations, whose foreign ministers were meeting at San Francisco, to sign creating the Tribunal and laying down its procedure. Jackson immediately found fault in its flowery and emotive language, reminding its authors of how much unwanted litigation might be hung onto a single thoughtless word of limitation, and warning of how the defence might cling to the document's superfluous adjectives and unnecessary phrases.[7]

Rosenman took the draft agreement with him to San Francisco on May 2. There, the new U.S. secretary of state Ed Stettinius showed it to Vyacheslav Molotov and Anthony Eden on May 3; now that Truman had stolen a march on them by announcing Jackson's appointment, the British were inclined to come into line on the issues of principle. 'The general attitude, of course, favours the trials,' Rosenman told Jackson, phoning him from San Francisco.[8] On May 7 Molotov, Eden, and Stettinius formally agreed that the war criminals should be put on trial. 'The British attitude has changed,' said the attorney-general Francis Biddle, discussing this with Jackson, 'and is entirely favourable to our point of view.'[9]

❖ ❖ ❖ ❖ ❖

This is the proper place to mention, before proceeding to consider the nature and enormity of Germany's crimes, the record of the victorious nations who now proposed to sit in judgement on her and on her soldiers, diplomats, industrialists, and political leaders.

One of the least palatable aspects of the coming trials was that there would be few crimes listed in the indictment of the German war criminals, as finally drawn up in October 1945, of which one or other of the four prosecuting powers was not itself guilty. In the cause of defeating Hitler, civilian populations had been—and were still being—burned and blasted, murdered, brutalised, intimidated, deported, and enslaved; aggressive wars had been launched, neutral countries had been occupied by pretext and deceit, and the unalterable paragraphs of the international conventions on the treatment of prisoners-of-war were still being flagrantly violated.

In this respect the Americans were still, as the war in Europe ended, relatively well placed, the world having yet to feel the searing flash of the first atomic bombs. True, in the fury of war American troops had committed a number of outrages in Sicily and on the Italian mainland, and even Lieutenant-General George S. Patton Jr, one of the war's most illustrious battlefield commanders, was found to have ordered and concealed the shooting of German prisoners. There had too been an unfortunate incident in Germany in the last weeks of the war when one hundred and thirty prisoners died of suffocation in a train of boxcars left standing at Frankfurt; but on that occasion General Eisenhower had ordered a personal apology telegraphed to the German High Command.[10] And there had been one less than heroic moment on April 29, 1945, for which nobody was ever called to account, when the army personnel at Dachau concentration camp surrendered, most of them ordinary German soldiers who had taken over from the fleeing S.S. guards. Of these 560 unarmed German prisoners, all but forty were put to death on the spot by the Allied liberators (or in a few cases by released inmates whom the Americans had temporarily armed); 358 of those killed, including a doctor carrying a Red Cross flag, were lined up against a wall by GIs of the 15th Regiment, 45th Infantry Division, and summarily put to death by one American army lieutenant, whose name is known, and his machine-gunner while former Hollywood film producer George Stevens and photographers of the U.S. Signals Corps recorded the scene in black and white and in colour.[11]

Many of the details of the pre-war crimes committed by the Bolsheviks were still not fully documented in 1945. They were not properly crimes of war, but in 1939 Britain had procured the universal censure of the Soviet Union for launching her unprovoked attack on Finland; and—most embarrassing of all—Stalin had not only sanctioned Hitler's aggression against Poland, but by a secret annexe to the Ribbentrop–Molotov Pact of August 1939 he had secured the eastern part of that much injured country for himself; the Red Army had invaded Poland on a pretext in mid-September, and had thereafter deported large numbers of the Polish inhabitants into the Soviet interior. The consequential horrors in the forest at Katyn need to be referred to, as does the subsequent Russian treatment of German captives taken on the eastern front, although here, technically speaking, the Geneva Convention did not hold sway since the Soviet Union had refused to become a party to it: each side had in consequence treated prisoners captured from the other with unbecoming barbarity. Of the quarter-million German soldiers taken prisoner at Stalingrad and forced into slavery, fewer than ten thousand would survive to return to Germany.

At Katyn and elsewhere in the spring of 1940, as is now known and commendably admitted by the Russian government, the Soviet secret police, the N.K.V.D., had liquidated fifteen thousand Polish officers and intellectuals captured during the Soviet invasion of Poland in September 1939 and recently removed from the prison camps at Kozielsk, Starobielsk, and Ostashkov. These men, their hands trussed in barbed wire and expertly shot with a single bullet in the back of the head, had been buried in mass graves.[12] The British government was well aware of the truth about this atrocity. Discussing the early reports on Katyn with Eden, Sir Alexander Cadogan had cynically disagreed with the inference that it was wrong to continue to consort with the murderers, although his private diary showed that he still had qualms. 'I pointed out,' he recorded, 'that years before Katyn the Soviet Government made a habit of butchering their own citizens by the 10,000s, and if we could fling ourselves into their arms in 1941, I don't know that Katyn makes our position more delicate. The blood of Russians cries as loud to heaven as that of Poles. But it's very nasty. How can Poles ever live amicably alongside Russians, and how can we discuss with Russians execution of German "war criminals," when we have condoned this?'[13]

The French too had committed crimes, but on a paltry scale—individual murders by General Charles de Gaulle's followers of his opponents, and routine, and by comparison relatively petty, atrocities against prisoners-of-war both during the 1940 campaign and in 1944. In May 1945 the—still undocumented—excesses of the *épuration*, the cleansing of liberated France of the tens of thousands of citizens alleged to have collaborated with the Nazis, had yet to start on a large scale. On a broader canvas, however, it is necessary also to take note of the joint planning by both Britain and France for the invasion of Norway and Finland in 1940, an 'aggression' which would fall well within the categories of crimes against peace as they were codified by the international lawyers who would meet in London in August 1945.

On Britain's 'war crimes' we are better informed since subsequent governments, and particularly that of John Major, have bared most of their predecessors' iniquities by opening the archives. Most of Britain's crimes were quite pointless, and provided for a needless sullying of the empire's otherwise immaculate escutcheon—of a record of unparalleled heroism by British troops fighting often against overwhelming odds. There were the questionable orders issued by Churchill in 1939 and 1940, as first lord of the admiralty, for unrestricted naval warfare, of which mention will be made later. These were orders of such criminality that the judges at Nuremberg, including the British members of the Tribunal, uniquely found them grave enough to mitigate the crimes committed by the Nazi admirals.* There were Churchill's 1940 orders for the invasion of Norway, which the British government successfully concealed from those same judges. There were crimes committed in the heat of action by subordinates but sanctioned by superiors—for instance, British officers were given the Victoria Cross, the highest medal for valour, after machine-gunning the fleeing survivors of the German fleet auxiliary *Altmark* in April 1940 and those of the sinking minesweeper *Ulm* in September 1942.

There were too Churchill's orders for the military occupation, on one pretext or another, of Iceland in 1940, of Persia in August 1941, only days after promulgating the Atlantic Charter, of Madagascar, or French North-West Africa, and of several other countries which were not belligerents. Churchill had planned the forcible seizure of the

* See pages 266–7.

Portuguese Azores in May 1943 but had been overruled by Attlee and Eden. Of questionable legality was the enforced return after the war by the British of tens of thousands of Russians captured with Hitler's troops, including not only the Cossacks but large numbers of White Russian pre-war émigrés whom the British sent back to the tender mercies of Stalin's secret police after the war, knowing what their likely fate would be.[14] At the end of May 1945 officers of the British Eighth Army had turned over to Tito three captured Serb guards regiments which had fought against him along with eleven thousand Slovenian auxiliaries. All were murdered in the forests of Gottschee. The same fate awaited the eighty thousand Croatian soldiers and thirty thousand Croatian civilians, most of them women and children, who had surrendered to the British around Maribor in the second half of May 1945; the British turned them over to Tito's partisan army.

As if the rain of fire, phosphorus—an illegal weapon—and slaughter by British bombers on cities like Hamburg, Dresden, and Pforzheim were not enough:[15] In one senseless, horrific incident on May 3, 1945 a single British fighter-bomber had attacked and sunk the German liner *Cap Arcona*, moored as a refugee ship in the Gulf of Lübeck. Emblazoned with the Red Cross, the ship was carrying thousands of civilian refugees and concentration-camp prisoners back from the east. It went down within minutes, with the loss of 7,300 lives. Throughout the summer of 1945 the bodies were washed ashore; they are buried in a single common grave on the beach at Neustadt, Holstein.[16]

That Churchill's scientists had also prepared for mustard-gas and anthrax warfare was arguably quite proper; he had ordered a quarter of a million four-pound anthrax bombs from the United States in February 1944.[17] By the summer of 1944 Britain had 26,000 tons of mustard-gas and six thousand tons of phosgene already filled into bombs or in bulk storage, 'enough,' as he was briefed, 'to cover Berlin, Hamburg, Cologne, Essen, Frankfurt, and Cassel put together.'[18] But enraged by Hitler's 'indiscriminate' use of the V–1 flying bombs, in a late-night Defence Committee session on July 6, 1944 Churchill had ordered his chiefs of staff, in an inebriated outburst, to prepare to 'drench' the six selected German cities with poison-gas attacks in violation of all treaties and conventions to the contrary (he dismissed these treaties as 'silly conventions of the mind,' and as a matter of changing morality, 'simply a question of fashion changing as she does between long and short skirts for women').[19] In a rare display of steadastness, his chiefs of staff finally overruled him.

In fact, Hitler had stockpiled thousands of tons of superior poison gases, the nerve gases Sarin and Tabun, but he had embargoed their use unless the Allies violated the convention first.[20]

It must not be forgotten either that Hitler's generals were often fighting an undeclared war against hidden armies of plain-clothes irregulars and *francs-tireurs* who considered themselves bound by none of the international treaties and conventions. Thus the Polish underground army had boasted to the Americans in 1943 that it was making successful use of both poison gas and typhus bacilli against the German occupation troops.[21]

NONE OF this can be read, of course, as justifying or even mitigating the Nazi excesses, particularly the horrors inflicted by the S.S. on the populations of eastern Europe. It is pointless to weigh, one against the other, such catalogues of horrors and atrocities. The deeper lesson is that war itself is a crime—and that the real crime of war is not genocide but the far broader bestiality which embraces genocide, and which we can label Innocenticide, the Slaughter of the Innocents. This slaughter was still not at an end, even as Robert Jackson was preparing to undertake his holy crusade against war, because there would soon follow the release by his own country of the atomic bombs above Hiroshima and Nagasaki. At the Potsdam conference of July 1945 Churchill and his successor Clement Attlee had both tacitly acceded to Harry S. Truman's decision to drop the bombs, documented tersely in Truman's files by the single-sentence signal to the Pentagon: 'Suggestions approved,' it said. 'Release when ready but not sooner than 2 August.'[22] British documents reveal that Churchill had been equally prepared to discharge such infernal weapons over Berlin if the European war had not ended first.

These were the nations who now proposed to pass judgement on the defeated enemy. Would it be ungenerous to suspect that this was perhaps one reason why some of the Allied leaders consulted had hoped to silence the enemy 'war criminals' by declaring them to be outlaws and killing them off quickly, without first giving them their day, or even hour, in court?

❖ ❖ ❖ ❖ ❖

Not long after President Truman appointed him, on May 4, 1945, Jackson was privately warned that the U.S. government had already agreed in principal to the immediate deportation of millions of Germans as forced labourers to the Soviet Union, as punishment for their membership of certain organisations. It was a few days before Field Marshal Wilhelm Keitel and General Alfred Jodl signed the documents of unconditional surrender in Europe. Jackson was telephoned at home by the war department's Colonel Murray Bernays: 'I understand our representative on the Reparations Commission, Edwin Pauley, is going to come and see you. I think I ought to come and show you something first.'

At ten o'clock next morning, Bernays arrived and slapped before the judge a document stamped TOP SECRET. It was a plan drawn up by the Reparations Commission, containing draft instructions for the Allied military government shortly to be set up in Germany. The draft contained dynamite, as Jackson immediately saw. It stated in part:

> It was agreed at Yalta that reparation in kind is to be exacted from Germany, partly through the 'use of German labor.'

It explained that punitive labour service was to be exacted from 'convicted war criminals and all individuals definitely determined by appropriate process to be members of the Gestapo, the Sicherheitsdienst (Security Service) of the S.S., leaders of the S.A. or collaborators, supporters of and participants in the Nazi party or administration.'

These organisations embraced millions of Germans. The deportation was apparently planned to last for a number of years, under what were called controlled and humane conditions.

Jackson was pole-axed by this document. It was totally inconsistent with the assumptions on which he had been working. 'It is plain,' he dictated to his diary, 'that the only country that can actually use slave labor in large numbers is Russia.'

What was the point of planning to sentence individual enemy war criminals to hard labour, if thousands if not millions of them were to be taken away for slave labour without conviction? From his point of view, to do so would be to abandon the moral position on which the Allies had fought the war.

He rapidly established that both the venerable and redoubtable Secretary of War Henry Stimson and his war department were also 'somewhat shocked' by the proposal. Then he learned that the pressure from within the U.S. government for the plan was 'said to have stemmed from Morgenthau,' the treasury secretary.[23] Morgenthau had switched his attentions to Truman the moment Roosevelt died. On May 9, he told the new president that General Brehon Somervell was holding up the implementation of J.C.S. directive 1067: But now was the time, while the American people were aroused over the Nazi atrocities, said Morgenthau. 'You will have to protect me on this,' Morgenthau dictated to the new president.[24]

This was just the first problem Jackson found. There were soon others. On May 7 they showed him a resolution, drafted by Congressman King, which the U.S. Congress was due to debate later that day, and which provided that the enemy war criminals 'shall be brought to trial or summarily punished.'

There was that unmistakable whiff of lynch justice again. Jackson however, anticipating coming under attack at some time in the future for having been 'too summary,' decided that while the wording went rather further than he would have, rather than being an embarrassment it was likely to be useful to have Congress going on the record as being gung-ho like this.[25]

ON MAY 10, 1945 Jackson received from Judge Rosenman and Colonel Bernays word on the outcome of the negotiations in San Francisco: the foreign ministers had agreed in principle that there should be an international military tribunal, and that there should be, as Jackson put it delicately, a 'trial rather than political disposition of the major war criminals'—the latter being the proposal to kill them out of hand without a trial.[26]

The foreign office still expressed mild disagreement with the proposed war crimes trials. While there was agreement that there should now take place talks in London on what laws to try the foreign leaders under, Sir William Malkin, their own expert on international law, predicted that unless these were very carefully framed there would occur a reaction in Germany ten years after any trials which would feed a future Nazi mythology. More importantly, anticipating controversies to come, Malkin felt that the planned London protocol should not try to arrive at a fundamentally new definition of what constituted a war crime, but merely declare it an 'existing doctrine'; that is, they should argue that such a law already existed. This would overcome the most serious problem which all the lawyers anticipated, that in years to come historians and others would claim that the Allies were guilty of convicting their vanquished prisoners on the basis of retroactive legislation—laws which did not exist at the time of the alleged offence.[27] This was no mere will-o'-the-wisp of an argument. It should be noted that on December 10, 1948 the United Nations ruled that the retrospective application of criminal laws was a violation of human rights.

A FURTHER problem was that Henry Morgenthau's henchmen were still trying to implement his unbecoming Plan. Any doubts that might have existed on this score were dispelled by two more clashes which Jackson had with them in Washington, as his unpublished private diary reveals.

The first was on May 12 over a luncheon served in the luxury hotel suite of Edwin Pauley. Morgenthau's representative at this hotel conference, Dr Isadore Lubin, produced the draft directive which was the subject of their meeting; probably it was one of the many offspring of joint chiefs of staff directive 1067. To Justice Jackson there seemed little to differentiate this directive from the treasury secretary's original Plan; it appeared to be 'a very tough document substantially reducing Germany to an agricultural state by stripping her of all industrial equipment.'

When Jackson reached the part of the document which pronounced that President Roosevelt, now dead, had already formally agreed to the victors' obtaining reparations through the 'use of German labor,' he dug his heels in and demanded to know precisely what F.D.R. had agreed to at Yalta. Ambassador Harriman, who had been at the Crimea conference, could not recall Roosevelt saying more than just that. The stenographic record of the conference was still top secret but Judge

Rosenman undertook to scrutinise it if he could.

Unhappy with the whole notion of slave labour, Jackson asked what figures were in mind: Lubin said that Russia wanted five million able-bodied Germans, France two million and England could also 'use' a small number.

In a daze when he heard these figures, Jackson again stoutly objected that he doubted whether the late president had agreed to any such thing. Rosenman explained that F.D.R. had 'thought the Germans deserved to be so punished,' as the judge noted in his diary, 'and emotionally was very bitter [and] had even seriously discussed sterilisation and more or less in fun had devised a machine to perform the operation on a mass-production basis.'

Only the rattle of the air conditioners in that hotel suite reminded Jackson that this was modern Washington, capital of the civilised world.

LUBIN SAID he resented the words 'slave labor' which both Rosenman and Jackson continued to bandy about. Justice Jackson however would not budge. He launched into a new counter-attack. The thought of transporting to Russia millions of Germans, who had been neither properly tried nor convicted, 'just because they are members of a vanquished race' shocked him, he said: he believed it would lead to the downfall of any western government that sanctioned it.

'Suppose,' Lubin drawled, 'the Russians promise to treat the Germans as well as we treat our chain gangs in Georgia?'

Harriman replied soberly that there was no comparison. He had seen conditions in Russia with his own eyes.

Jackson stuck to his guns. 'I told them,' he wrote in his diary, 'that I could not go ahead with pretended trials if this provision were agreed upon, that the trials would merely be farces.'[28]

He sent to Pauley a scathing attack on the draft instructions, marked TOP SECRET. Of the plan to condemn Germans to slave-labour service in Russia for the mere membership of certain organisations—the Gestapo, the S.S., the Sicherheitsdienst—as well as all senior officers of the S.A., 'or leading collaborators, supporters of and participants in the Nazi Party or administration,' the judge commented in this written riposte: 'That would make it farcical to conduct trials concerning the conspiratorial character of those organisations or the guilt of their membership.' Stating the seemingly obvious, he said that the trials must come before the punishment. And as for the punishment—deporting millions of Germans to Russia—he commented: 'I think the plan to impress great numbers of labourers into foreign service, which means herding them into concentration camps, will largely destroy the moral position of the United States in this war.'

Jackson's own position was plain. 'What the world needs,' he summarised, 'is not to turn one crowd out of concentration camps and put another crowd in, but to end the concentration camp idea.'[29]

4: If We Can't Lynch Them, Flog Them

As the war in Europe spluttered to its close Jackson began to gather about him in Washington and New York a number of friends and legal experts who would form his personal prosecution staff for the historic task. He wanted to use Bill Whitney, of the New York law firm Cravath, deGersdorf, Swaine, & Wood; Whitney had practised at the English Bar, had a country house in England, and was almost more English than the English. He phoned Sidney Alderman to ask if he would be free to go along as his associate counsel. Despite not liking the man personally, Jackson lunched too with Francis Biddle, the attorney-general, who promised every help, including the assistance of the Federal Bureau of Investigation, which came within his domain.[1] Biddle's assistant attorney-general, Francis M. Shea, also joined Jackson's team, as did the expert on international law Ralph A. Albrecht.[2]

The Office of Strategic Services, Roosevelt's wartime intelligence service, had always been interested in mounting such a trial, and its barnstorming director, Major-General William J. Donovan, himself a lawyer by training, had planted the first such thoughts in the late president's mind early on. 'Wild Bill' Donovan promised Jackson all the help the O.S.S. could give, but James B. Donovan, a lieutenant-commander in the U.S. naval reserve who was special counsel to the organisation, soon disabused Judge Jackson of any notion that it had mountains of incriminating material on enemy war criminals at its fingertips which would make a prosecution easy. 'In view of the size of the promises,' noted Jackson bitterly after talking to the younger Donovan on May 7, 1945, 'mighty little has been done toward their fulfilment.'

His visitor explained to him that the tasks of the O.S.S. had included counter-espionage, and both 'white' and 'black' propaganda, the latter being the spreading of rumours and generally 'bedevilling the enemy.' General Donovan had been eager to begin work on the war criminals, but he had been unable to get any specific target names from those who made the policy around here. In short, nothing had been done.

In his dealings with General Donovan, Jackson would run into a more fundamental problem, the basic hostility of the United States Army, including Donovan himself, to the notion of prosecuting enemy soldiers. He was more interested in settling accounts with the Gestapo and the S.S.—his opposite numbers—and with the Nazi politicos. James B. Donovan warned that over at the office of the judge advocate-general of the army, Jackson would find little sympathy for the idea of a trial. As for the navy department, he said, a certain Professor Robinson had been put in charge of the war crimes work there. Jackson knew Robinson, and had not been struck by his competence. Notwithstanding Stettinius' agreement in San Francisco, the state department, said James Donovan, was also in two minds, fearing the effects that any war crimes prosecution would have on opinion in neutral countries. This was all very discouraging. 'It is plain,' summarised Jackson, 'that our case will have to be built from the ground up, that despite the large talk there has been little done to really dig out evidence, which makes our task more difficult but nonetheless challenging.'[3]

A few days later, after weighing all the pros against the not inconsiderable cons, he telephoned to invite General Donovan to take a leading part on the trial staff as his special assistant, flattering the general that this offer was a mark of his gratitude to the O.S.S. for the 'foresight, energy and skill' which it had shown in organising the work done so far. Not only would it improve the political balance of the prosecution—Donovan was a Republican—but it would at least commit the entire O.S.S to helping prepare for the trial. Donovan, an ambitious and power-hungry man, leapt at the offer.[4] It would take six weeks, estimated the younger Donovan in a somewhat over-optimistic conference with Jackson on May 14, to put the American case into shape for the trial.[5] In a telephone call to Jackson on the following day Truman approved the O.S.S. chief's appointment.[6]

AT FIRST the collaboration went smoothly despite their differing views on prosecuting the officer corps. The two Donovans visited Jackson on May 15, 1945 and they all compared notes. Donovan senior, who was leaving for Europe two days later, lifted a little of the shroud of secrecy surrounding the structure of the O.S.S. He dropped intriguing hints about the links he had established to the Soviet N.K.V.D. and even to the German underground—he mentioned a witness now in Switzerland, one of the original organisers of the Gestapo, who would be available to Jackson as a witness (the first hint at the existence of Hans Bernd Gisevius, one of the more controversial members of the cast that now began to build.) Donovan told Judge Jackson he was proud to join the team—he wanted the judge to understand, he added fulsomely, that he, Jackson, was the captain and the general would be proud to play and serve wherever the judge put him to work.[7]

Rapidly staking out his own territory, Jackson persuaded General George C. Marshall to send a telegram to Europe instructing his commanders that there must be no more suicides by their prize prisoners—the Sudeten German leader Konrad Henlein had just swallowed poison—and that there were to be no more press interviews of suspected war criminals like Hermann Göring, since these might 'seriously prejudice [the] trial.'[8]

❖ ❖ ❖ ❖ ❖

After his first talks with the other lawyers, Jackson was especially sensitive to the danger that the Nazi defendants might turn the tables on their victors during the coming trial, pointing the finger at their prosecutors and accusing the victorious powers of having committed crimes that were equal to, if not worse than, those of which they were accused.

On May 14 army officers at the Pentagon showed Jackson for the first time leaflets which their bombers had dropped in millions over Japan with a picture of a Japanese family being consumed in flames; the Japanese text threatened more terror-bombing if they did not surrender. It was, noted Jackson, who was naïvely unaware of the millions of such leaflets dropped by the British and American air forces for five years over Germany, 'the boldest kind of violation of the Hague convention.' Jackson pointed out to these officers that in his opinion dropping such a leaflet would 'warrant the Japanese executing any American soldier' caught carrying out such a policy. (To his horror, the U.S. Army then sent a message to the Philippine theatre, quoting him as an authority; in his view this message increased the risk of such executions.)[9]

Later in May, Brigadier-General John M. Weir, of the judge-advocate general's office, revealed to him that they had evidence of an order issued by Hitler for the killing of Allied commandos and paratroopers.[10] The snag was, said Weir, that there were several well-documented cases where Americans had done exactly the same. An American officer in Italy had issued an order to 'take no prisoners,' and a U.S. Army sergeant had thereupon killed thirty-five German soldiers in his hands; the sergeant—but not General Patton, the officer involved—had been put on trial and, said Weir, 'narrowly escaped death,' and had recently even been restored to duty.[11]* Jackson, shocked by this revelation, recorded it in his diary and anticipated problems if the Germans should put up the defence known in Latin as *tu quoque*, roughly 'you did it too.'

There were other legal thickets to be negotiated. Colonel Murray Bernays pointed out to Jackson that some time previously chiefs of staff had issued an order forbidding trials of German prisoners. This order had been issued at a time when the Germans were threatening reprisals.

*There are several such instances cited in General George S. Patton's private diaries, e.g. January 4, 1945: 'The [American] 11th Armored is very green and took unnecessary losses to no effect. There were also some unfortunate incidents in the shooting of prisoners. I hope we can conceal this.' (Copy in the author's possession, from the estate of the late Ladislas Farago).

Machinery would now have to be set in motion to have the irksome ban lifted.

Anxious to get a start and make a public showing of activity, Jackson blithely suggested they take, say, fifty of the cases which the judge advocate-general's office had substantially ready for trial. Colonel John Harlan Amen, the former New York racket-busting lawyer who was now one of the army's top lawyers, replied in embarrassment that there were not fifty, nor twenty, nor even one case ready. In nearly every case on file, the identity of the actual perpetrator was unknown.[12] Jackson told Bernays the next day he was 'deeply distressed' by this complete absence of ready cases; he proposed that the army and navy get their twelve best cases ready for him to look at.[13]

General Donovan suggested that, even though the case files were nowhere near ready, they could rush through some of the lesser cases—the trials could take place at once, 'it would not be necessary to proceed immediately with executions.' Jackson agreed, stipulating however, 'No execution shall take place without the approval of the Assistant Secretary of War,' John J. McCloy.[14]

THERE WAS already a subtle Cold War element involved. Jackson was conscious of the need to prevent the trials taking an 'anti-German' shape which would drive the German population into the arms of the Russians. Regardless of Stalin's personal stand on precisely this issue, Soviet newspapers now began attacking the Allies for not having executed Reichsmarschall Hermann Göring, Germany's highest-ranking soldier, immediately upon capture; this kind of lawlessness made Jackson uncomfortable about any future participation of the Russians in a trial.

It seems that the Kremlin had suddenly been stricken with the same kind of misgiving as had beset Churchill since 1942—the Russians evidently fearing that if Germany were now to be charged with preparing an aggressive war against Russia, the defence would establish from German and captured Soviet documents that Moscow had been making much more extensive preparations to attack Germany than the world was yet aware of. Before General Donovan departed for Europe on May 17, Jackson therefore asked him to question Göring on the following topics: the Soviet preparations for war (or, failing that, the real reasons why Hitler had attacked Russia); information that might be of use to Jackson if and when Göring took the witness stand; and 'any positions he might be taking in defense.'

General Donovan warned Jackson in confidence that the Russians had had 'the code of the British Foreign Office' all the time; in consequence many communications which the British had thought secure were really known to the Russians, and this might also prove an embarrassment during the coming trials. Suddenly the whole thing did not seem such an open-and-shut case to Jackson after all. Practical problems also shortly arose. Eisenhower's headquarters cabled the Pentagon reporting that his Thirty-Sixth Corps had captured the former Hungarian regent Admiral Nicholas von Horthy. Was he to be turned over to the Russians, who now occupied his country? Jackson advised that he was a probable defendant, and certainly a vital witness, and should be held.[15]

Donovan left for London, arranging to keep in touch through the secure channels that the O.S.S. had established during the war for its other purposes.[16]

❖ ❖ ❖ ❖ ❖

At this time the secret row about 'slave labour' boiled over again in Washington.

On May 15, 1945 Jackson told President Truman that he refused to support any such provisions in the reparation instructions, except for Germans properly tried and convicted, and even then only under rigorously controlled conditions. 'I fully agree with you,' said Truman.[17]

Not to be outwitted so easily, Henry Morgenthau struck back. He called a second meeting between his henchmen and the judge at four o'clock on May 18, this time on home ground in his Treasury building. Justice Jackson found Morgenthau and many of his staff among the score or so officials crowded into the chamber. Morgenthau immediately pointed out the snag in Jackson's objections—supplying Russia only with those Germans duly tried and convicted would yield perhaps a couple of hundred thousand workers, whereas Stalin was thinking in terms of five million.

When John J. McCloy, a later military governor of Germany, suggested that the late president had surely been thinking of a proper trial as the only basis for the supply of forced labour, Morgenthau angrily rounded on him, protesting that this was the first time that he had heard such a limitation suggested. One of his aides, Joseph Dubois, chimed in that in view of the Yalta decision there did not appear to be any need for trials at all. Besides, a Gallup poll had shown a large percentage of Americans in favour of using the Germans for slave labour.

Jackson thumped the desk with his fist. 'Just watch the Gallup poll ratings change when the first slave-labour horror stories start coming out of Russia!'

Quietening, he prophesied, 'The problem of sending labour to Russia is that I don't think it would ever come back.' More pertinently he pointed out that the Geneva Convention provided no basis for holding prisoners-of-war as reparations once peace had been concluded.

Morgenthau's man Dubois protested at such legalisms. 'We already know that the S.S. and Gestapo are guilty—a trial would be farcical!'

'How do you know?' challenged the justice. 'This city is full of people who tell me there's no doubt about it. But when I ask for specific evidence I can't get a single item.'

SINCE PRESIDENT Truman had already signed the executive order giving Jackson his warrant for the task, Morgenthau had no option but to climb down. He did so with poor grace. 'I bet you won't have your trials through by Labour Day'—the first Monday in September—he mocked. Heading for the door, Jackson told him that Christmas 1945 was a better bet.

As the judge walked out into the Washington spring sunshine with Ralph Bard, a U.S. Navy officer who had been at Yalta, he heard still more details of the behind-the-scenes discussions there. The Russians, Bard told him, had seriously aired a proposal to deport to the Soviet Union millions of ordinary Germans—people who had not belonged to any of the organisations—sterilising the men, and breeding the women with Russians.[18]

Jackson counted on Morgenthau to pull one last dirty trick. Knowing how Washington worked, he was sure that his opposition memorandum would be leaked after this conference by the spin-doctors at the treasury, and he offered a wager to Elsie L. Douglas, his pretty secretary, that it would show up in the press within four days. In fact it was five days later, when Jackson was in Paris, that Drew Pearson's widely syndicated gossip column in the *Washington Post* published extracts from the document as part of a damning personal attack on Justice Jackson, claiming that he was canvassing a 'soft peace' for the Germans.

Jackson was not in the least surprised. 'The poor idiots think they are "planting" something to hurt me,' he wrote in his diary, conceding: 'It will embarrass now; but it will be a great strength in time to come if God really is in his heaven. Many are worried about the story. It may hurt our Russian relations.... Washington is full of cowards. Gallup-Poll patriots.'

The manœuvre was unsuccessful. Upon Jackson's return from Paris to Washington the chief justice of the United States, Harlan F. Stone, privately gripped his hand and congratulated him for holding out against a purely lawless and vindictive treatment of a defeated enemy. 'Some day,' Stone predicted, 'you will be very proud of that memorandum.'[19] Later however Stone would become vociferous in his criticism of the trials.

To the end of his days, Jackson refused to believe that the President Franklin D. Roosevelt whom he knew could have advocated the slave-labour proposal. (He kept an open mind on the castration.) 'I can't believe that a man who knew history as well as he did, and knew the American people, ever had believed that proposal was a wise thing,' he confidentially recorded. 'I think myself that it was Morgenthau's emotional reaction—I don't know about the motives of some of the men with him.'

On May 22, 1945, he set off for Europe to inspect what had to be done.

❖ ❖ ❖ ❖ ❖

Where were the war criminals at this time? For diplomatic reasons, the idea of putting Italy's wartime leaders on trial seemed to have been abandoned; Benito Mussolini and his principal ministers and aides had in consequence by this time been dead already for three weeks—lynched and machine-gunned in the back shortly after their capture by communist partisans.[20] It now appears possible that, pursuing his own long-held beliefs, Churchill had issued instructions to the directors of his Special Operations Executive (S.O.E.) for the murder of Mussolini and his henchmen as soon as they were captured. The S.O.E. and the O.S.S. had duly passed these instructions on to their contacts amongst the partisans, and the bloody events at Lake Garda in northern Italy at the end of April 1945 were the outcome.

As for the German leaders, Adolf Hitler, Dr Joseph Goebbels, Martin Bormann and a host of others, acting wholly without consideration for Jackson and the needs of international justice, had taken their own lives before they could be put on trial.

The remnants of Germany's Nazi government, including Grand-Admiral Karl Dönitz, whom Hitler had appointed Reich president, and Field-Marshal Wilhelm Keitel, chief of staff of the Oberkommando der Wehrmacht (the supreme high command), had withdrawn to an enclave in and around Flensburg, just below the Danish frontier, where they were penned in by British troops under Field-Marshal Bernard Law Montgomery, pending the receipt of further instructions from London. Among several career moves dictated by Hitler in his final will and testament, he had dismissed Heinrich Himmler as Reichsführer S.S., and replaced Ribbentrop as foreign minister by Count Schwerin von Krosigk.

Later—awaiting the gallows at Nuremberg—Keitel described these last days at Flensburg to his son. One day Himmler had come in for an hour-long talk with him and had asked Keitel to place himself at his disposal, as he was going to have to take over. The contents of Hitler's political testament however soon made clear that Himmler had been sacked as Reichsführer S.S., and that Dönitz had been appointed head of state. Dönitz had asked Keitel, 'What do you make of Himmler's being here?' Keitel had replied that he'd have to go, and agreed to tell Himmler as much—that he should put on some civvies and get out of there. Dismissed from all his offices on May 6, Himmler had hung around long enough to give Keitel a letter addressed to General Eisenhower, offering his services once the war was over. Keitel had read the letter and torn it up.[21]

It is not without significance that all three Allied governments initially accepted the Dönitz government's credentials and agreed to negotiate the surrender terms with the admiral's emissaries. At 2:41 A.M. on May 7 Colonel-General Alfred Jodl signed the overall surrender of the German armed forces at Eisenhower's headquarters in Rheims, France. But it was not due to come into force until May 9, to enable several hundred thousand soldiers, women, and children to escape the Soviet advance. On May 9 Field-Marshal Keitel signed once again the instrument of overall surrender, this time in the Soviet military headquarters at Berlin-Karlshorst. Keitel was arrested on May 13 and Jodl had to be put in temporary command of the German High Command, the O.K.W.

What was known at this time about the Nazi 'extermination camps'? The most horrific camps were in the zones occupied by the Soviet army and thus not immediately accessible to the Allies. At many camps liberated by the British or Americans, including Buchenwald, Bergen-Belsen and Dachau, they found and photographed for posterity disturbing scenes of death from starvation and pestilence—scenes which should not, in retrospect, have surprised the Allied commanders who had spent the last months bombing Germany's rail distribution networks and blasting the pharmaceutical factories in order to conjure up precisely these horsemen of the Apocalypse.[22]

FOR A FEW brief days, Dönitz tried to re-establish a German rule of law. On May 11 the Allied Control Commission, comprising a number of senior British and American officers, established contact with him in Flensburg.

Four days later, at the suggestion of Schwerin von Krosigk, the new foreign minister, Dönitz issued an ordinance appointing the Reich Court at Leipzig, as in 1921 after World War One, to pass judgement on and hand down punishments for the atrocities in German concentration camps. Dönitz had a copy of this ordinance sent to General Eisenhower, the Allied supreme commander, with the request that he enable the German courts to take appropriate action to punish the offenders. 'The German people,' wrote the grand-admiral to Eisenhower, 'unanimously and with a sense of outrage condemn the brutalities and atrocities described in Allied reports, as they are completely at variance with their basic principles and moral values. The real and authentic sense of justice of the German people demands that the crimes that have been committed be prosecuted immediately and with the utmost rigour.'[23]

There was no reply from the Allied commander. On May 17 Eisenhower sent his political adviser Robert Murphy and staff officer Major-General Lowell W. Rooks to meet Dönitz and to investigate the legality of his government. They reported that Dönitz had hinted at a combined Allied–German crusade against the Russians.

Such talk was quite unacceptable to Eisenhower. After waiting a few days to enable his Intelligence officers to grill Hitler's armaments minister Albert Speer and seize his voluminous files, he ordered the Dönitz government arrested. On May 23 Rooks and Murphy returned to Flensburg with truckloads of British troops. Dönitz was arrested together with every member of his interim government. Jodl was also arrested, and separated from his precious diaries.[24] Murphy later wrote: 'British military police made the arrests and, in the manner of soldiers from time immemorial, they simultaneously "liberated" some souvenirs for themselves. The German staff, including the helpful women secretaries and clerks, were ordered by the military police officers to hand over everything detachable, especially money and wristwatches.'[25]

On the same day Heinrich Himmler died shortly after his apprehension near Lüneburg, either summarily executed by the British troops or taking his own life more or less voluntarily. It was the end of Hitler's Reich. By virtue of the Berlin Declaration of June 5, 1945 the Allies arrogated to themselves all sovereign powers in Germany.

ONE BY ONE the future actors in the Nuremberg drama were taken into custody. Those whom the international media had long portrayed as major criminals were not treated with kid gloves. After first beating him savagely, the GIs transported Hans Frank, the hated Nazi governor of occupied Poland, to the municipal prison at Miesbach. They flung a tarpaulin over the prisoner to hide the worst weals left by the beating. Under cover of the tarpaulin, Frank tried unsuccessfully to open an artery in his left arm.[26]

They gave the gauleiter of Franconia and newspaper publisher Julius Streicher an even rougher ride after an American army officer, Major Henry Blitt, found him at a house in Waidbruck in the Tyrol on May 22. Challenged as to his identity, the former gauleiter admitted: 'Julius Streicher.' He was driven off to the prison at Salzburg. There he was handcuffed—the manacles were not removed for the next five days[27]

Still manacled and dressed only in a shirt and pants he was driven on May 23 to Freising in Bavaria, where he was thrown into a windowless cell without either a bed or chair. 'Two or three times a day,' he wrote a few days later, "I was made to stand against a wall with my handcuffed hands above my head while a Black or a military police officer beat me around the genitalia for up to one minute at a time with a leather whip. If I attempted to ward off the blows with my handcuffed hands they kicked me in the testicles. My private parts and testicles were badly swollen.'

Scarcely more pleasant was to have 'the white police officer' and the GIs order him to open his mouth two or three times a day so they could spit into it. If he kept his mouth shut, they forced it open with a wooden baton. They forced him to drink out of the urinal. When he once refused to, they beat him with the whip. 'Each time he visited my cell the white police officer ripped hairs out of my nipples and eye-brows.' Once when Streicher refused to eat the putrid leftovers that were dished out to him they threw him to the ground and forced him to lick the (Black) soldiers' feet.

On May 26 they finally told him to get ready for the drive to Wiesbaden. A couple of hours before that one of the GIs said to him with a smirk, 'Now you get "kill, kill"'—and he made the appropriate cut-throat motion across his neck. Then a Black soldier marched Streicher into the lavatories, tossed his clothing into the toilet and told him to get dressed—which was easier said than done, given his handcuffed condition. The manacles were removed only after he arrived at Wiesbaden. 'Since then,' wrote Streicher, 'I have been under medical care. The prison commandant at Wiesbaden (who says he is a Jew) has behaved with complete propriety.'[28]

❖ ❖ ❖ ❖ ❖

Judge Jackson was aware that the French, like the Russians, were only lukewarm about the idea of war crimes trials. Joseph Grew, the new under-secretary of state, had wired to Paris asking General de Gaulle's government to name negotiators promptly.

Flying with Colonel John H. Amen from Washington to Paris on May 22, Jackson found the French foreign minister Georges Bidault and ambassador Henri Bonnet sharing the same plane, travelling home from San Francisco. When the opportunity diplomatically arose, Jackson tackled Bidault on the subject; the judge confessed that 'all of the older international lawyers are against us,' holding as they did to the doctrine that 'all wars are legal.' The United States had however officially repudiated that position by adopting its Lend–Lease programme, argued Jackson. Bidault was not obviously impressed, except for the need for speed, whatever course of action they chose.[29]

Jackson and Amen were met on French soil by General Edward C. Betts, the American theatre judge-advocate, Colonel Bernard Bernstein, one of Morgenthau's men who had wangled his way onto Eisenhower's headquarters staff as chief of civil affairs, and the local O.S.S. chief.[30] It rapidly became plain to Jackson, and he remarked upon it in his diary, that Paris had suffered little or not at all under the Nazi occupation, and was suffering rather more under the American. They were housed at the Ritz Hotel, and drove over the next morning to the old Hotel Majestic which had once housed the headquarters of Field-Marshal Gerd von Rundstedt as Hitler's commander-in-chief, west.

Here Betts filled him in on the latest titbits, for example that the Polish ambassador in Brussels had told him that the Russians were filling seventeen new concentration camps in Poland with those who opposed the puppet government that they had set up in Warsaw. Betts had established at Wiesbaden a records centre, which also housed 'boxes of rings, jewels, teeth fillings etc., collected by the S.S. and left there with German banks.'

He said they had about six hundred war crimes cases on file, most of them little more than witness statements. About twenty cases had been tried by common law, and most of the defendants had been convicted and executed. Apart from two cases currently being tried, however, they had no others ready; and they were certainly were not prepared to mount a prosecution along the lines envisaged by Jackson—trying the conspiracy to make war as a crime in itself. The local American ambassador, Jefferson J. Caffery, told him that the local French trials were moving slowly, with that being staged against the widely respected Marshal Henri Philippe Pétain a 'special headache.'[31]

On May 25 General Eisenhower, who was resting briefly in Paris, invited Jackson over to the Hotel Raphaël. The general's position seemed to have shifted marginally since his talks with Morgenthau the previous summer. 'He said he is not for shooting anybody without trial,' recorded Jackson afterwards, 'and hopes trials will not take long.'

When Jackson outlined the plans he had for putting the entire Gestapo on trial as an organisation, Eisenhower responded with verve that he was all for it—he had seen so much that 'any bastard who belonged to that outfit' was guilty in his eyes at once. Betts interposed that he was planning to ask the war department for authority to keep these prisoners in common prisons rather than in prisoner-of-war cages; Eisenhower waved his hand and said to put them in jail on his responsibility—no need to bother Washington with that. 'Practical, decently profane, and a most impressive leader,' was how the judge summed up the Allied supreme commander.[32]

Afterwards Jackson lunched with French resistance leaders, who regaled him with small-fry stories of German plans to exterminate a whole camp, and of eleven villagers near Baden-Baden accused of lynching three American aviators who had parachuted into their hands; the local mayor had turned these miscreants over to the French occupation authorities. But Jackson was after bigger fish than these.

WITH ALL the round-eyed eagerness of the classic American tourist, the judge made his first foray into Germany the next morning, paying a brief visit to American army headquarters, code-named ROUND-UP, in Frankfurt-on-Main. The journey, flying at no great height in General Donovan's plane, took him over battlefields littered with wrecked war material, damaged buildings, and fields pocked with bomb craters.

Frankfurt, where the American army had taken over the well-appointed and already largely restored I.G. Farben administration buildings, was a mass of rubble—of burned and blasted railroad yards, tumbled trains, and roofless and windowless buildings. Whatever feelings Jackson may have had upon seeing destruction on such a scale, he kept them to himself both then and later. The masses of homeless Germans looked at him and the escorting American officers in dull wonderment, betraying neither hatred nor opposition.

As for the notion of war criminals, the subject that really interested Jackson, there was not much that the U.S. Army here could tell him; Eisenhower's chief of staff Walter Bedell Smith expressed bitterness against the Luftwaffe paratroop general Bernhard Ramcke, who had, he alleged, killed American prisoners at Brest, and against an S.S. officer who had shot perhaps as many as two hundred American prisoners in the Ardennes—evidently a reference to Jochen Peiper; Peiper was eventually acquitted of that charge, only to be killed thirty years later by terrorists who burned down his home in France. Otherwise, however, the general expressed a profound respect for Hitler's Wehrmacht, speaking particularly highly of General Johannes Blaskowitz, who as commander-in-chief, east, in 1939–40 had refused to carry out orders for mass executions in Poland, and had been replaced by an S.S. officer instead. (Blaskowitz was nonetheless held by the Americans in the jailhouse at Nuremberg, where he jumped to his death on the day the Generals' Trial began.)[33]

The irksome joint chiefs of staff directive 1067 was already causing major problems. Bedell Smith told Jackson that while the Americans troops were forbidden to 'fraternise' the Russians were cultivating the workers and peasants in their occupation zones to further the spread of communism. The Russians, said Bedell Smith, were refusing to co-operate in setting up the Allied Control Council as agreed. They were stripping eastern Europe bare, having rounded up and shot 'all leaders, intellectuals, lawyers, civil officials, scholars—any who might be a rallying point for opposition.' Mass shootings? Even lawyers? Jackson took note of all that Bedell Smith told him.[34]

A few days later, back in Washington, he would listen equally dispassionately to the American ambassador in Belgrade, Richard Patterson, reporting on the mass executions of intellectuals and businessmen beginning in that country on the orders of Marshal Tito, or rather of his Soviet puppet masters: 'Members of the Yugoslav government informed him that they had just executed the brother of a young woman employed in the American Embassy as a translator. He was not tried, no charges were placed against him, but they were of a family of bankers.'[35]

In an ideal world, it should all have provided much food for thought. But Germany in May 1945 was not the ideal world; Hitler's soldiers had committed crimes on a scale that beggared all comparisons in history, and Jackson's ambition now burned so fiercely within him that he would find no difficulty in putting on the blinkers that would be indispensable if he was to sit side by side with war criminals in prosecuting war crimes.

GENERAL DONOVAN had gone off by himself to Twelfth Army Group headquarters in Wiesbaden. He brought back to Jackson a number of minor case files that the judge-advocate general's branch there had already assembled—basically reports on the killing of American airmen and on the questioning of two doctors at hospitals where people had been put to death by morphine injections because they were a burden to society, or politically objectionable. 'These,' dictated Jackson, after reading the files in the plane on the way back to Paris, 'were buried naked, and without box, before they were cold.' The German nurses examined had seen nothing wrong in what they had done, he wrote: 'The state had ordered it.'[36]

Beneath their plane, as he flew back to Paris, his self-righteousness redoubled, to partake of dinner at the Ritz, there unrolled the devastated cities and villages of western Germany. They reminded him of Sodom and Gomorrah: they had perished for want of even one willing to stand up for simple decency.[37]

❖ ❖ ❖ ❖ ❖

In Paris things began to look up. Jackson dined with a bespectacled, square-jawed Allen Dulles who had headed the clandestine operations of the O.S.S. in neutral Switzerland; this secret service Lothario bragged (as General Donovan had earlier) that he had one witness on hand ready to testify who had been one of the original founders of the Gestapo. He also had a witness, noted Jackson, who 'for several years has furnished us telegrams and reports right out of the German foreign office.' Every month this man had sent such documents to Switzerland, and every three months he had come in person with more documents as a German foreign office courier and turned them over to Dulles.

Further, said Dulles, after much bargaining he had obtained the original diaries of Count Galeazzo Ciano, Mussolini's foreign minister, who had married the Duce's daughter Edda and had been shot by a German firing squad in 1944; sore at her papa for not having intervened to save him, Edda had smuggled five volumes of these pregnant diaries out of Italy strapped about her abdomen, and they were, said Dulles, loaded with succulent details against Joachim von Ribbentrop, Hitler's former foreign minister.[38] Finally, Dulles also claimed to have acquired a complete roster with photographs of the entire S.S. as of two years earlier.

'What a Godsend if it proves true,' wrote Jackson. 'I don't know why I should doubt his word, but I have followed so many rainbows to their ends to find there was no pot of Gold.'[39]

HE FLEW on to London. Driving into the empire's capital he found the effects of the bombing far less dramatic than he had expected, 'hardly noticeable in comparison with the total destruction visited upon the German cities.' He and his little advance party were billeted at Claridge's, the hotel where visiting kings and queens were housed, in a suite overlooking, he noted, the American embassy—several buildings in between having been removed by the German bombers.[40]

Over at Grosvenor Square, he heard from U.S. ambassador John G. Winant that Churchill had originally sent a minute to Anthony Eden directing that the lord chancellor, Viscount Simon, was to be Jackson's British counterpart in the prosecution. Simon was eager for this historic role; indeed he had long been lobbying for it. But Eden had scotched his ambitions, holding that the taint of Simon's pre-war policies still clung to him. He inclined toward the attorney-general Sir David Maxwell Fyfe instead.

Jackson did not mind one way or the other; he was however privately amused when later in the day Simon drew him aside and 'unctuously and at length' explained to him that his position made it impossible for him to serve, and that he had therefore arranged to have the attorney-general designated.[41]

At a conference with the British legal authorities assembled under Lord Wright, president of the U.N. War Crimes Commission, the decision was formally taken that the attorney-general should be Jackson's British counterpart at the trial. Churchill announced this in the House of Commons that same day.[42] Otherwise the British seemed to be as uninterested in the legal proceedings as ever. Dining with Eden, Jackson found that the British foreign secretary had only 'the vaguest remembrance' of what had been agreed at San Francisco about the trial of war criminals.[43]

On the following day, May 29, Sir David Maxwell Fyfe chaired a meeting in the panelled Room C at the House of Lords to report on the progress made with particular cases. It was not much: although all agreed on the need for a courtroom with all its splendid panoply of judges, robes—and wigs where possible—there was little or no agreement at all about the identity of the gentlemen to whose disadvantage the entire proceedings were to be staged.

Together, this panel of British and American officials crafted a first 'select list'—which is in British archives—containing inevitably the name of Göring, followed more hesitantly by those of '?Hess' and '?Von Papen.' General Donovan asked what was being done about the latter two; the British attorney-general assured him that he would find out. After more discussion they arrived at a new list running to fourteen names beginning with Göring, the labour front chief Robert Ley, and Nazi ideologist Alfred Rosenberg, and including the Hungarian regent Nicholas von Horthy, but omitting Hess and Papen.[44] When the list was written down again on May 31, there were no question marks, and it began confidently: 'Göring, Hess, Rosenberg.' It all seemed a very hit-or-miss affair.

Among Jackson's papers is a secret memorandum giving a clearer picture of this first session. On his side were Bill Donovan and Bill Whitney; on that of Sir David Maxwell Fyfe, the solicitor-general Sir Walter Monckton, the treasury solicitor Sir Thomas Barnes, Patrick

Dean for the foreign office, and Major-General Lord Bridgeman, the deputy adjutant-general. The British were clearly diffident about the whole thing, and content to follow the American lead. They had only minor points to offer, wishing to substitute a clause emphasising the Nazis' 'systematic policy with the aim of dominating Europe,' where the American text had spoken only of violations of German law.

When discussion turned to the list of names, it was Maxwell Fyfe who named Göring, Ley, Rosenberg, and Ribbentrop, to which he later added as an afterthought the name of Admiral Karl Dönitz, the German Navy's commander-in-chief and Hitler's successor as head of state; he stipulated that the British public would measure the trial's success or failure by what he called 'the disposition of Göring's case.' This was a more dainty way of stating what Lord Vansittart had once said—that the only question really left open was the site of the gallows and the length of the rope.

It was at General Donovan's suggestion that the names of Rudolf Hess and Franz von Papen were added. Jackson also had a few names jotted down, including Franz Xaver Schwarz, the Nazi party's treasurer; Wilhelm Frick, the minister of the interior; Hans Frank; Hjalmar Schacht, the former governor of the Reich Bank; and an enigmatic 'Woolf'—perhaps Karl Wolff, chief of staff of the now unavailable Heinrich Himmler. But these names were already too lowly for the Londoners' taste: they swiftly objected that the list must be restricted to the most senior officers and ministers, in order to obviate the defence of 'superior orders' that more subordinate officers were bound to employ.

As for the number and length of these major trials, Jackson wanted there to be only one, at which they could thrash out the whole history of the 'Nazi conspiracy'; it was a novel idea to the English, but they seemed willing to go along with him and his pet project. The British were thinking in terms of one swift trial of about ten German defendants—there was talk of it lasting two weeks. Jackson modestly indicated that he had something 'a little broader' in mind.

AS FOR the actual modes of punishment. Jackson suggested two basic principles—that all sentences would be reviewed by the Control Council in Berlin, which was now the supreme sovereign body in occupied Germany; and that death by hanging was the appropriate penalty for the principal offences. The British mentioned that their manual—presumably of military law—also 'permitted' shooting, but they seemed to agree that hanging appeared right for 'this type of crime.'

Some of their number thirsted after more mediæval penalties—Sir David Maxwell Fyfe revealing that they were considering corporal punishment (Jackson's hand-written note uses the word 'flogging'), since English law still permitted whipping for people convicted of burglary with violence or of living off immoral earnings.[45] Jackson and

Donovan demurred, suggesting that American public opinion would not stomach that.[46]

They still had no word from Moscow or Paris; the British and Americans agreed to prevail on their governments to invite the Russians and French to join in the prosecution of the criminals, but they also agreed to go it alone, as currently seemed quite possible.

Before leaving London, Jackson visited the Soviet ambassador together with Donovan and Winant, and expressed the hope that France and the Soviet Union would soon have appointed suitable prosecutors, so that the four powers could agree on procedures. The Russian informed him of the work being done by their own Extraordinary Commission on War Crimes (its Russian initials were the not unfamiliar Che-Ka), but otherwise maintained a Slav inscrutability.

Jackson told the Soviet ambassador bluntly that, whether or not the Russians came in, the People of the United States would be going ahead with war crimes trials.[47]

5: The Origin of 'Six Million'

HENRY MORGENTHAU had continued to hawk his Plan around Washington. Although momentarily thwarted by the death of President Roosevelt, as the war ended in May 1945 he would resume his campaign for the punishment by starvation of the entire German people. He telephoned Henry Stimson, who was lunching at home, and complained that the authorities in Germany were not carrying out his 'scorched earth' policy as harshly as he wanted, particularly as related to the destruction of all oil and gasoline and the plants for making them in Germany, and the joint chiefs of staff directive 1067 that ordained this.[1] The U.S. Army was protesting this senseless order, but Morgenthau wanted his will performed. Secretary of War Stimson dictated this comment the next day: 'I foresee hideous results from his influence in the near future.'[2]

In a memorandum addressed to Truman on May 16, Stimson outlined the probable consequences, of pestilence and famine in central Europe—and of 'political revolution and Communistic infiltration.' He added a warning against falling for the plans to punish every German by starvation: 'The eighty million Germans and Austrians in central Europe,' he wrote, 'today necessarily swing the balance of that continent.'[3]

THE AMERICAN Congress had also recently adopted its resolution calling for the summary punishment of the war criminals. Jackson proposed, with Truman's consent, to argue against this before the Congress Foreign Relations Committee. Instead, he found himself invited to a dinner party attended by several senators—a familiar ploy in Washington power-politics.

The senators made it plain that they too were out for German blood, although there were exceptions. Senator Alben W. Barkley of Kentucky had just returned from a guided tour of Heinrich Himmler's concentration camps, and his lurid description made Jackson's blood run cold. Thousands of prisoners, and not a few Allied officers, were still dying from the plagues sweeping through the squalid sites. But even Barkley made plain that he felt a trial was the proper course. Others loudly dissented. Senator William Fulbright of Arkansas, the most liberal and scholarly of those present that evening, suggested that there was no law under which the criminals could be tried. 'Therefore they must be executed forthwith as a political decision,' he insisted. 'A trial means delays—and it means giving the defendants a chance to tell their stories to the world.'

'What,' Justice Jackson patiently queried, 'are we afraid to hear them tell?'

Fulbright replied that they had all the authority they needed to kill the prisoners without trial. This, of course, did not address the question at all.[4]

The public shared this mood, and even Senator Barkley had to trim his sails. In a Memorial Day address he demanded early war criminal trials. 'I am not interested,' he added, 'in whether the courts are civil or military so long as they dispense with legalistic technicalities.' The popular press was whipping up a lynching fever. Writing in the New York *Post* and Chicago *Sun* in May 29, Edgar Mowrer, who had had his own dealings with Göring during the war, asked, 'We want to know the American line on war criminals—what we are waiting for to shoot Hermann Göring and turn German generals over to Allied judges. Is Ambassador Robert Murphy trying to save German industrialists, German generals and German clericals, as he saved his disreputable French friends?' Three days later a public opinion poll conducted by the Gallup organisation revealed that sixty-seven percent of the American public wanted Hermann Göring executed without trial, and that forty-five percent would like to see the Gestapo agents and Nazi stormtroopers liquidated the same way. 'Kill them … Hang them … Wipe them off the face of the earth,' were typical reactions. The war department informed Eisenhower: 'Dr Gallup's overall impression is that American people want *no* fooling around about punishing war criminals. The people want *no* delay in meting out of punishment.'[5]

To Justice Jackson, summary execution was as unthinkable as setting the prisoners free. 'To free them without a trial would mock the dead and make cynics of the living,' he would write eloquently to Truman early in June 1945. 'On the other hand we could execute or otherwise punish them without a hearing. But indiscriminate executions or punishments without definite findings of guilt, fairly arrived at, would violate pledges repeatedly given and would not sit easily on the American conscience or be remembered by our children with pride.'[6]

Pandering to domestic public opinion, Jackson insisted however that all the prospective defendants be denied the privileges due to their rank as prisoners-of-war and that they be treated with the rigours due to major criminals (in itself an infraction of international law). Jackson repeatedly stressed, as in a speech to newspaper correspondents at a luncheon in London on July 6: 'Our effort is to preserve at all stages the essence of fair play, even toward those whom we loathe.'

❖ ❖ ❖ ❖ ❖

This then was Justice Robert H. Jackson at the outset of the affair: the righteous American, the idealist endowed with clearly defined notions of justice and fair play. He was in as little doubt as Viscount Simon in London and the senators in Washington about the outcome for any defendants whom they chose to arraign. The identity, perhaps even the guilt, of the defendants was of less moment than the spectacle, the trial itself. The trial was the thing.

But given that there were to be executions, he wanted the blood to be shed with purpose—to sanctify the new framework of international law that he proposed to construct.

ON JUNE 6, 1945 Jackson delivered his first formal report to President Truman. He again requested that the State Department put pressure on London, Moscow, and Paris to appoint their representatives for a meeting in London to draw up the protocol which would become the 'legal' basis of the trial.[7] He jotted down a tentative list of those who would leave with him for England in ten days' time—Alderman, Shea, Donovan, Bernays, and public relations officer Gordon Dean, each bringing one or two female secretaries; Major Larry Coleman, Captain Morgan, Jackson's devoted secretary Elsie Douglas, and his lawyer son Bill would complete the party.

He proposed to leave behind Colonel Telford Taylor, a brilliant lawyer with a useful background in Intelligence and codebreaking, to supervise the collection of evidence in the United States. General Donovan was angry to find that Jackson seemed to be neglecting his protégé James Donovan and in a taste of things to come he phoned the judge threatening to pull out of the whole operation. Jackson invited the two prima-Donovans to lunch and smoothed their 'ruffled feathers' as best he could.[8]

❖ ❖ ❖ ❖ ❖

A few days before leaving for London Jackson visited F.B.I. officials in New York on June 11, 1945. Here he had, probably not at his own wish, his first meeting with several powerful Jewish organisations who had already made quite clear to him they wanted a hand in running the trial. In an office provided by the F.B.I. in the Federal Building, three leading lawyers, Judge Nathan Perlman, Dr Jacob Robinson, and Dr Alexander Kohanski, came to exert pressure on behalf of a coalition of representative American organisations.

They began by heaping picturesque praise on Jackson's first report to the president, which had now been published, describing it as 'like rain on the desert to the Jews.' While others had looked for precedents in the seventeenth or eighteenth centuries, they flattered him, Jackson had taken his 'from the twenty-second century.'

These lawyers, who greatly impressed him by their intelligence and erudition, had hopefully read into his report to the president the implication that he intended to treat the Nazi persecution of the Jews as a crime in its own right. Dr Robinson handed him a copy of the Treaty of Sèvres in which the Allies had laid down penalties on the Turks for their atrocities against the Armenians during World War One. This might serve as a useful precedent. Robinson also suggested that the tribunal prosecute Alfred Rosenberg in his capacity as chief Nazi philosopher: they were not seeking vengeance, swore Robinson, 'nor, of course, compensation for Jewish losses.'

HOW GREAT were those losses? inquired Jackson, seeking a figure to use at the coming trial. 'Six million,' responded Dr Robinson, and indicated that the figure included Jews in all Nazi-occupied lands 'from the Channel to Stalingrad.'

Jackson noted that day:

> I was particularly interested in knowing the source and reliability of his estimate as I know no authentic data on it.

Robinson said that he had arrived at his figure by extrapolation from the known statistics for the Jewish population in 1929 and those believed to be surviving now. In other words his figure was somewhere between a hopeful estimate and an educated guess. 'The differences are assumed to be killed or in hiding,' he said. Given the turmoils and tragedies of a war-torn Europe ravaged by bombs and plagues, it was not a data basis on which a statistician would properly have relied. Where were the shifting frontiers? Who, indeed, was a Jew? These were questions about which cartographers, ethnographers, religious fanatics, and politicians are still at each other's throats. Six million? By sad but extraordinary coincidence, the American Jewish community had raised a similar outcry about a 'holocaust' a quarter of a century earlier, after World War One. In a 1919 speech the governor of New York, Martin Glynn, had claimed that 'six million' Jews were being exterminated.[9]

The delegation expressed to Jackson their fears that the Allies would choose the less onerous course, of merely prosecuting the Nazis for lesser offences. These men wanted a decision based on the persecution of the Jews which, they averred, all the post-war trials so far conducted had side-stepped. They even asked for a separate court to try these charges, and failing that they asked for the right to have an *amicus curiæ* in Jackson's courtroom to 'represent the six million slaughtered.'

Foreseeing inevitable problems, Jackson demurred. All the other persecuted minorities would then feel entitled to the same rights. He gave the delegation no encouragement, but promised to think about it. Having obviously failed in that mission, they then asked him at least to appoint an officer on his staff specifically to handle their angle.[10]

❖ ❖ ❖ ❖ ❖

Ideas on how to conduct and promote the trial were crystallising in Jackson's mind, and he was keen to share them with others.

While in New York he visited Herbert Bayard Swope, who was angling for a position in directing a publicity campaign around the trial. Swope recommended that for European audiences to be impressed the coming trial must be surrounded by the proper pageantry. The British and French lawyers must wear their gowns and wigs. Even Jackson should assume a gown for this performance. The whole show, said Swope, must also be recorded from start to finish by moving pictures and in sound.[11] Later Swope phoned his hotel to recommend staging the trial at Munich, the seat of the Nazi party—possibly in their old headquarters which had a large hall, he seemed to remember. Swope also reminded Jackson that if the Nazis had killed 'six million Jews'—it was amazing how rapidly that figure had taken hold—it would mean that the Nazis had acquired 'at least' six billion dollars of Jewish property.[12]

In mid-June a committee of American psychiatrists and neurologists contacted Jackson, asking permission to examine the prisoners and to make sound recordings of the interviews. Their premise was almost racist in its implications: 'Aggressive leaders have been recurrently produced by the German people, who then follow them blindly. Detailed knowledge of the personalities of these leaders would add to our information concerning the character and habitual desires of the German people, and would be valuable as a guide to those concerned with the reorganisation and re-education of Germany.'

Rather unfairly, the writer proposed that these examinations should 'not be utilized to support pleas of insanity'—the results should remain secret until after the sentences had been executed. And, as for that, the doctors urgently recommended that 'the convicted be shot in the chest, not in the head,' as it would be desirable to have a detailed autopsy, especially of an undamaged brain.[13]

Jackson rather liked the idea. He had read the book *Is Germany Incurable?* by one of the committee, Dr Richard M. Brickner, and agreed with much that Brickner had written. 'There is more than a possibility,' he reflected, 'that after conviction, [a] finding of insanity, perversion, or other mental defect on the part of these leaders would do more to deflate their future influence in Germany than anything else could do.'[14]

He saw however a real danger that the defendants, who would of course be aware of these psychiatric examinations, would alert their attorneys, who would in turn demand to see the findings, resulting in the trial bogging down in endless litigation about to the fitness of the defendants to stand trial. On balance therefore he decided that there should be no examination until after the Tribunal had ruled on the question of guilt. As for the mode of execution, he reassured the committee of psychiatrists: 'The general attitude of the army is that those who are subjected to death sentence as criminals should be hanged rather than shot as the hanging seems to carry with it an implication of dishonor.'[15]

General Donovan had had much the same idea. Dr Douglas McG. Kelley, an army psychiatrist, would write a few weeks later that the general proposed he write up personality studies on each defendant; he asked for stenographers to facilitate this complex task.[16] Eventually Jackson would write to the New York committee giving its experts the go-ahead—authorising the secret examination of the defendants by qualified psychiatrists as soon as the Tribunal went into recess to consider its judgement; but again he ruled that the findings were not to be published until after any sentences had been carried out, and he was to have immediate access to them and the right to make such use of them before the Tribunal as he might 'deem desirable.'[17]

GENERAL DONOVAN had gone off alone to London. At a meeting of the British War Crimes Executive early in June 1945 he found general agreement that the first Nazi leaders to stand trial should include Göring, Hess, Ribbentrop, and Ley. Hess presented difficulties, as his medical and mental condition were well known to the British government by this time; the erstwhile deputy Führer was displaying all the symptoms of the latent paranoid schizophrenia which had become more acute during his solitary confinement in Britain.

In London on June 9, Donovan urged again that it would be a mistake to overlook Hess. 'He should be brought to trial as a major war criminal,' said the O.S.S. chief, 'and if he were to put forward the plea of unfitness he should be examined by a body of medical men and, if found unfit to plead, sent to Broadmoor.'[18] Broadmoor was Britain's windswept isolation prison for the criminally insane.

The list of proposed defendants was kaleidoscopic and by no means complete even now. After consulting with the foreign office, Patrick Dean ventured to suggest to Sir David Maxwell Fyfe on June 19 that they add the names of Keitel, Streicher, and S.S. Obergruppenführer Ernst Kaltenbrunner, Reinhard Heydrich's successor as chief of the Reichssicherheitshauptamt (R.S.H.A.), the Reich Main Security Office that came under Himmler's S.S.; he included Rosenberg, Frank, and Frick as well.[19] It all seemed rather haphazard.

Through secret service channels the Foreign Office cabled via Donovan to Jackson in Washington, agreeing to his proposal for a London conference of prosecutors to begin on June 25; Britain as host nation would issue the invitations to the United States, France, and the Soviet Union right away. The French had already nominated Professor Henri Donnedieu de Vabres, professor at the Paris Law Faculty, and an authority on international criminal law.[20]

BEFORE LEAVING for the London conference, Judge Jackson and General Donovan called to pay their respects on President Truman.

A leading freemason, like Roosevelt (and for that matter Jackson himself), Truman showed them the gavel presented to him as grand master of the Masons of Missouri, and then the Reichsmarschall's baton which a GI had stolen from Hermann Göring and mailed home; U.S. Customs had opened the parcel and confiscated the priceless bauble. Different cultures cherished different icons, it seemed. Göring's baton was about eighteen inches long, a cylinder about one-and-a-half inches thick, covered with symbols and encrusted with diamonds; it is now housed in the museum of the U.S. Military Academy at West Point.

They briefly discussed the case of Karl-Hermann Frank, who was in U.S. Army hands. This prisoner had been the deputy protector in Prague during the Nazi occupation, and the London war crimes representative of the newly reconstituted Czech government was demanding his extradition to face the music in Prague. In view of the major war crimes trial coming, the British had insisted however that Frank stay in American custody for the time being. Truman's initial attitude was that Frank was such a sonofabitch he would like to send him back as the Czechs would treat him more roughly than the Americans would; Jackson persuaded him to let wiser counsels prevail. Later that day the state department warned Jackson that Colonel Bohuslav Ečer, commanding officer of the Czech War Crimes Investigating Team in London, was emotionally unstable and quick to take offence; Dr Ečer had already interrogated Frank, and prestige was involved. But Jackson had now obtained a letter from Truman giving him carte-blanche to act as he saw fit, and instructing everybody to fall in with his requirements. He feared nobody.[21]

On June 18, 1945, as General Eisenhower was being given a hero's welcome by the city of Washington, Jackson and his little band of lawyers set out by plane in the opposite direction for Goose Bay, Labrador, and London, to direct the last battle of World War Two.

6: Architect of a New International Law

IN THE WEEKS which followed his optimistic arrival in London Robert H. Jackson found himself out of his depth. He campaigned valiantly, but he was up against brains scarcely less devious than any he was expecting to indict in Germany.

He spent the first day in London soothing the ruffled feelings of his staff. Most of them were leading American lawyers in their own right, who had led in cases time after time; they were no longer accustomed to acting in subordinate positions or to taking orders. One after another they came to Jackson with complaints about each other. Francis Shea, Biddle's deputy attorney-general, was the cause of most of their irritation, but Colonel Robert G. Storey, who would be chief of Jackson's evidence division, also annoyed Colonel Murray Bernays so much that the latter was returned home at his own request.[1]

The Soviet Union and France had now given their assent to Jackson's proposal to put the major war criminals on trial. In mid-June 1945 the four powers began their conferences on the appropriate procedures at Church House, Westminster, under the chairmanship of British attorney-general Sir David Maxwell Fyfe.[2] They made little or no progress; they bogged down in conferences, and then in conferences about conferences. Jackson soon had to send home Ruth, one of the secretaries he had brought over, as she became hysterical and could not cope with the unaccustomed tensions: and the trials had not even begun.[3]

He attended his first such four-power meeting on June 21. Their hosts, the British, apologised that the Russians were unlikely to arrive in time for the main session on the twenty-fifth; Andrei Vyshinsky had however promised to set out from Moscow on the twenty-third. At this first meeting the list of putative defendants was further amended. Some of the more charitable delegates now felt that including Rudolf Hess would 'overload the list.'[4] Jackson disliked this whole name-by-name approach that the British were following; it was not what he had envisaged: 'They proposed names such as Göring, Hess, Ribbentrop, Ley, Keitel, Streicher, Kaltenberg [*sic*], Rosenberg, Frank, and Frick,' he recorded after this meeting. 'From this they wanted to draw an indictment and build a case.'

The American position was more formalist, and perhaps less

practical; they preferred to gather the evidence first, and then consider the case. They agreed to appoint four sub-committees to review the position. Bearing Herbert Swope's advice in mind, Jackson cabled ahead to General Lucius Clay, the military governor of Germany's southern zone, to ask whether Munich would make a suitable site for the trial.[5]

With the arrival, one day late, of the Russian delegation the London conferences finally began at full strength on the twenty-sixth. The chief Russian prosecutor turned out to be Major-General Iona T. Nikitchenko, vice-president of the Soviet Supreme Court; rather tall, and with a pugnacious jaw-line, Nikitchenko appeared to Jackson somewhat inscrutable, hiding behind his glasses eyes that seemed to look straight past you. He was both a general and a judge, and undoubtedly a shrewd man. His adviser Professor A. N. Trainin seemed more versatile, though with great reserve and little trace of bonhomie about him. His eyes too failed to meet the Americans'. The Russian delegation did however make one very useful suggestion straight away, namely that they should aim at signing a short agreement or protocol, to which should be appended a 'Charter' setting out the rules and procedure of the resulting Tribunal.

The lawyers made only hideously slow progress. In the weeks and months that followed Jackson would never really grasp what made his Russian colleagues tick. They seemed to be poles apart, and after a while the Americans asked the Russians to prepare a memorandum on their position.[6] 'Their life and tradition and experience are so different,' he wrote home helplessly after a few days, 'that even after translation of language it is hard to understand each other.'[7]

It complicated matters further that the Soviet officials at these London talks showed little inclination, or had little licence, to compromise. The Russians insisted on several niggling changes to the draft protocol. The American ambassador Winant advised Jackson to put up a strong stand against the Russians. President Truman had offered the same advice earlier, saying that the Russians only respected people who stood up to them. It soon became clear, particularly from their meeting on June 29, that the Russians had not abandoned the idea of a swift trial and even swifter execution of all the war criminals.

Their argument had the benefit of simplicity. General Nikitchenko—who was to figure both as the Soviet chief prosecutor and negotiator at the London talks and as the Soviet judge at the Nuremberg trial—said with refreshing candour: 'We are dealing here with the chief war criminals who have already been convicted and whose conviction has already been announced by both the Moscow and the Yalta declarations and by the heads of the governments.' He objected, he said, to the 'fiction' that the Tribunal's judges were disinterested parties—they would have read the newspapers like the rest of the world, and the guilt of these criminals was perfectly clear. The judges should merely decide the just punishment of the criminals without time-wasting preliminaries; as for the prosecutors, their job would be, in Nikitchenko's view, merely to assist the judges. That was the Russian way of doing things.[8]

Jackson listened to these arguments with impatience. There were other complications too. Dr Ečer, the Czech war crimes official, came to see Jackson with his file on Karl-Hermann Frank; Frank was denying any responsibility for the infamous shooting of the male inhabitants of Lidice which had followed the assassination of Heydrich in 1942, but witnesses were now coming forward who had seen him there. While sympathetic toward the demands for Frank's extradition, Jackson expressed concern on several counts. If they agreed to hand Frank over, he said, thinking aloud, he was not to be mobbed or lynched, and he must be returned to the Americans in good condition for use in their own cases or for interrogation; and the Americans would want observers at any trial of Frank.[9] The Czechs expressed indignation at the imputation that their citizens might lynch Frank, and thus there were more ruffled feathers to be smoothed.[10] In the event, the Americans decided to hang on to this prisoner for a while.

The greatest problem that Jackson found was the conflict between the differing legal systems employed by the four powers. Weak though the American legal system was in many respects, his own guileless country-lawyer eyes detected that the European Continental systems smacked much of the kangaroo court, 'a Court organised to convict.' If the American system seemed over-tender to the defendant, the French and Russian procedures looked startlingly summary and loaded in favour of the prosecution. A compromise in this respect would have to be struck. Jackson frankly conceded, 'I have not seen fit to insist that these prisoners have the benefit of all the protections which our legal and Constitutional system throws around defendants.'

From the very outset he had nourished an unhealthy mistrust of the Russians. For all his bluster at the London conferences about going it alone, he preferred the Russians to have a prosecutor of their own at the trials since, the Russian record in this war hardly seemed less black than the German.

THIS WAS of course a conference of the victors; their purpose was to choose the defendants, and to draft the new laws they were to be accused of having broken, and the rules of the court which was retroactively to apply those laws.

The Germans were not represented at these sessions, so the trial would start with the dice already loaded against the defendants. But to Jackson it was of paramount importance to get an agreement—any agreement—between the four powers. Bit by bit he chiselled the concessions out of the others: he secured from the other prosecutors agreement to a concrete declaration that individuals who led their nations into aggressive wars should in future (and in the past, if they were Germans) be held accountable. When the final text was announced, the justice declared: 'The definitions under which we will try the Germans are general definitions. They impose liability upon war-making statesmen of all countries alike.' They were brave words, but they had not the slightest effect on the statesmen who would wage one hundred wars, large and small, in the half-century after he uttered them.

The 'all countries alike' referred only to the future. The final indictments resulting from these London conferences would narrowly state the crime to have been 'aggression or domination over other nations carried out by the European Axis in violation of international laws and treaties'—a definition that saved the Russians particularly from embarrassment (the Russian representative had insisted that the Tribunal limit the charge even more narrowly to 'aggressions started by the Nazis in this war'.) The Soviet conscience was troubled by its own actions against Poland and Finland in the first years of the war, while British consciences were no less exercised by the knowledge of Churchill's 1940 plans for the invasion of neutral Norway and Sweden.

❖ ❖ ❖ ❖ ❖

The British and U.S. armies had begun to concentrate the prisoners most likely to be required for trial as war criminals in a requisitioned four-star hotel, the Grand Hotel, at Bad Mondorf or Mondorf-les-Bains in the duchy of Luxembourg. The U.S. Army gave the camp the sarcastic code-name ASHCAN. (The British, determined to be different, called it DUSTBIN.)[11]

Eventually there would be seventy or more elite prisoners in this camp. They found that their camp commandant was a stiff-backed, crusty American cavalry colonel, Burton C. Andrus; he would move with them, and they were to remain on his charge until they left him for liberty, jail, or the gallows.

He was aware that there would be no laurels for him in this thankless task. After *Time* magazine later published an unflattering account of his career, he privately wrote to his family denying its more bizarre allegations and recalling that when he accepted the appointment he had been told that 'they' had not been able to find a brigadier-general available to take it. Several had evidently turned it down, realising that it was a job where it was 'impossible to win.'[12]

Andrus was an efficient, even calculating, professional army officer. He did everything by the book, and was swayed by neither blandishments, flattery, entreaties, nor threats. He wanted his prisoners to have no chance to evade their fate. There had already been several unfortunate suicides after Konrad Henlein's; Victor Bouhler, head of Hitler's private chancellery (and director of the 'T-4' euthanasia

Aktion) and a number of other Nazi party dignitaries had prematurely joined their Führer in his Valhalla without paying the necessary respects to their captors before departure. They had found one cyanide phial concealed in a tin of Reichsmarschall Hermann Göring's coffee. Andrus warned his staff to look out for more—which, he warned, had also been found 'concealed in the orifices of the body.' He enforced strict procedures to ensure that none of his prisoners was concealing any suicide instruments. On arrival each prisoner was held in isolation and strip-searched by the prison doctor; his shoes and clothing were searched for razor blades and scissors; all nail files, shoe laces, belts, neck-ties, watches, long pins with ribbons or insignia, and batons were taken from him. Some prisoners, Andrus admonished his men, had concealed weapons in the heels of their shoes or taped razor blades to the soles of their feet.[13]

Among the first prisoners to arrive at the Mondorf cage was Field-Marshal Keitel, together with Arthur Seyss-Inquart, who had been Hitler's Reich commissar in Holland. 'One by one the others arrived,' recalled Keitel later. 'Some of them had been taken into captivity in the most humiliating manner. Stripped naked, men on one side, women on the other, though with their backs to each other.'[14]

PROMINENT AMONG Mondorf's new guests was a somewhat crestfallen Albert Speer.

In the closing days of the war Speer, who had started as Hitler's chief architect and ended as his armaments minister, had worked out his own survival stratagems—four of them—and one by one he was seeing them fail.

In many respects he was like a capable, down-to-earth westernised businessman. From February 1942 he had brilliantly nurtured the German armaments miracle which the munitions minister Fritz Todt, killed in a plane crash, had set in train, and it is no surprise that the Allies had delayed the final swoop on the Flensburg enclave to enable their arms experts to pick his brains and to take his advice. He had remained in Hitler's thrall until the end. After his flying visit to the inferno that was Berlin to pay his final respects to the embattled Führer, he told his intimate friend Field-Marshal Erhard Milch of his 'good impression of the Führer, not so good of the "skulking" Göring.'[15] It is clear however that from March 1945 if not earlier Speer had begun back-tracking with an eye to his future welfare. He protested forcefully to Hitler about plans for a scorched-earth defence of Germany, and he sabotaged the destruction of bridges and factories.[16] Staying out at Milch's forest hunting-lodge in April, Speer dictated a broadcast script, calling on Germans to lay down their arms.[17]

But there was also an artistic element, an air of unreality about him. As the war ended he had told Milch that he was going to submerge—vanish from the face of the earth—and live in a canoe with the aviator

Werner Baumbach like Karl May's Red Indian heroes Old Shatterhand and Winnetou, to re-emerge two months later, by which time he expected the hue-and-cry to have died down; Speer then fully expected to be summoned to office by the desperate British and Americans as the only German capable of taking over and restoring order from the chaos of defeat.[18] This dream was shattered when he was rudely taken into British custody in Flensburg.

He had thereupon proceeded to the second stratagem: adopting the same tactics as Hans Frank, he turned over his entire files to the enemy 'intact' (or so he claimed: in fact he had hidden his incriminating Speer Office Chronicle.) This concession buttered no parsnips however, and he had now found himself thrown into the Grand Hotel at Mondorf with some very seedy characters indeed.

As the conditions of his imprisonment grew more acute, he proceeded to stratagem three. He began to bargain for a deal. He had every reason to huckster while there was still time because there is little doubt of Speer's criminality and he knew this might well soon be found out. He had been well aware from his friend S.S. Obergruppenführer Otto Ohlendorf of what was going on in the slave-labour camps.[19] He also claimed—though he recalled this only relatively late in his life—to have been told by his friend Karl Hanke, gauleiter and governor (Oberpräsident) of Lower Silesia, never to ask what was going on at a place called 'Auschwitz.' Be that as it may, Speer had certainly visited the underground missile and jet-engine assembly-plants tunnelled into a mountain at Nordhausen, and he had passed without comment or complaint the tens of thousands of slave labourers drawn from the adjacent concentration camp 'Dora.'[20] If Sauckel would be hanged for conscripting the labour, then the man who had exploited it most mindlessly could expect no mercy.

There is moreover evidence of Speer's direct complicity, as inspector-general of building for Berlin, in the fate of the fifty thousand Jews expelled from that city to the east between 1941 and 1943, evidence to be derived both from the unpublished diaries of Dr Joseph Goebbels and from his own wartime office chronicles—the genuine *Chronik*, that is, not the reworked and sanitised texts which Speer donated to a gullible German federal archives upon his release in 1966 from Berlin's Spandau prison. According to Speer's own figures there were over twenty-three thousand Jewish homes in Berlin in 1941; he decreed that these were to be vacated to house people affected by his grandiose slum-clearance programme. Working hand-in-glove with S.S. Obersturmbannführer Adolf Eichmann, of Heydrich's R.S.H.A., Speer's infamous Main Rehousing Office (Hauptabteilung Umsiedlung) had directed the eviction of these Jews, beginning on October 18, 1941; between that day and November 2, confirms Speer's diary, the first 4,500 Jews were 'evacuated,' releasing to him and Goebbels one thousand apartments. These were supposedly for bombed-out Berliners, but in fact the cream of them went to Speer's cronies.[21] On November 27, 1941 Speer reported to Goebbels that his third eviction *Aktion* was just beginning.[22] That day a thousand more Jews, already the seventh trainload, departed from Berlin, bound this time for Riga, capital of Latvia. All would die three mornings later, machine-gunned into two pits outside the city (against Hitler's specific orders to Himmler, as it turned out.)[23]

There was more. As the transcript of a speech by Himmler at Posen on October 6, 1943 showed, the Reichsführer had seemingly addressed a remark directly to 'party comrade Speer' during a passage describing in gruesome detail what he, Himmler, meant by the words Final Solution.

Speer would need all his wits about him to escape an Allied execution squad. Working to his advantage were the Americans' ignorance of these things and his own salesmanship, his smooth ability to deceive. So far he had managed to persuaded the Allies that they needed him. Even here at Mondorf the admiring Allied experts would march up to his cell door in column of four to talk with him. His first six interrogations were devoted solely to questions of arms and economics.

Then he pulled his trump card—stratagem four of his planned escape route. During the seventh interrogation session, at the end of May 1945, after asking his questioner O. Hoeffding to regard what he would now say as being 'off the record' and not to make any notes on it, he volunteered a sensational statement on anti-Hitler plotting which he claimed to have undertaken in February 1945. Here is what Hoeffding reported:

> In February 1945 Speer had intended to organise a 'second July 20.' As the builder of Hitler's Reichskanzlei and its underground Bunker he was closely acquainted with its structural details. Hitler's daily conferences on the situation were held in the Bunker, and Speer proposed to obtain some poison gas and have it pumped into the Bunker during one of these conferences. In this way he hoped to eliminate in one blow the whole faction which was in favor of continuing the war, including Hitler himself. Speer had asked Brandt (Hitler's physician?)[24] to procure the poison gas, and Speer was going to arrange for its introduction into the conference room through a ventilator shaft. He claims that there are other witnesses to his plans, whom he did not name.
>
> He changed his mind on his subsequent visit to the Ruhr, where he saw that not only the gauleiters but also many common miners still had a pathetic faith in the Führer and his ability to bring the war to a successful end. Their attitude convinced Speer that the only way of curing the German people from the delusions and the state of mind brought about by years of propaganda and isolation from the outside world was to make them 'drink the cup of

> bitterness' and be thoroughly disillusioned. Anything that afterwards might be presented to them as internal treason which ended the war by a 'stab in the back' would disturb their mental regeneration process. He therefore abandoned his plan.[25]

Hoeffding's report continued that Speer had repeatedly stressed that he did not care about his personal fate. He expected to be put on trial—perhaps for having been an efficient arms minister, which would be unfair, or for having been on intimate terms with Adolf Hitler, a charge which 'would not stand up to the judgement of history.' 'He "apologised" at the end,' reported Hoeffding, 'for not having been able to carry out his intention of delivering Himmler alive into the Allies' hands.'[26]

The stratagem worked. The unexpected happened: before the wondering eyes of his fellow-captives, Speer found himself extricated from the Mondorf camp. He took his leave of the others as he was driven off alone, as though for him the whole unpleasantness was over.[27] The Americans drove him in a limousine through Paris to Versailles, where he was housed in a luxury hotel and questioned at comfortable length by Eisenhower's experts about the Nazis' weapons developments. He found here several of his former closest colleagues including the loud-mouthed Karl-Otto Saur, the real dynamo of the munitions ministry.* Dr Hjalmar Schacht and Fritz Thyssen, released from Hitler's concentration camps—liberated from the Nazi frying pan, shortly to be tossed into the Allied fire—soon joined him. When Eisenhower's headquarters transferred to Frankfurt-on-Main, Speer and his colleagues were moved to nearby Kransberg castle, which he had himself converted for Göring's use as a headquarters in 1939. Gradually all the former senior members of his ministry joined him here, awaiting their captors' curiosity and pleasure. While all around them Germany starved, these men were free to come and go, and well fed too, on American army rations. Until one morning in September, when Speer was rudely awakened with the news that the radio had announced that both his and Schacht's names were to be found on the list of those who were to be put on trial for war crimes in Nuremberg. Schacht was taken there almost immediately, but Speer would not follow until the end of the month.

ALFRED JODL had also been brought to Mondorf. His reputation as a soldier was intact: American officers had presented arms as he had left his first prison camp at Flensburg. Indeed, they had invited him to write a strategic survey of Germany and the defence of western Europe, and this had attracted favourable comment in Washington.[28] He was unrepentant about the Führer however. Questioned at Mondorf about

* And founder of the present K. G. Saur Verlag in Munich.

whether Hitler, a suicide in his own capital, could rightly be regarded as a famous warlord, Jodl had stoutly defended him. 'Rome destroyed Carthage,' he pointed out, 'but Hannibal is still regarded as one of history's greatest warriors and always will be.'

This remark went through the prison camp at Mondorf like wildfire.[29]

The Americans forced the prisoners here and elsewhere to watch atrocity films into which they had spliced scenes of piles of corpses filmed after air raids on German cities and aircraft factories. Some of those interned spotted the deception—one former Messerschmitt worker said he had even recognised himself.

HERMANN GÖRING soon joined them at Mondorf.

The Reichsmarschall had surrendered to a Texas infantry division on May 7, 1945 in Austria. Three days later, accompanied by his expensive blue leather luggage, he was flown in a tiny plane to Augsburg to meet the press. It was this episode that had led Jackson to order an end to such press interviews.

At first Göring refused to believe that Hitler had appointed Dönitz, and not him, in his place—it must be a plot by Martin Bormann. He told the press of how he had opposed Hitler's plan to attack Russia, and of his dismay when the Americans produced their long-range fighter escort planes which enabled their bomber formations to range far across the Reich. For a week after press conference he was held at the Seventh Army's interrogation centre at the Villa Pagenstecher in Wiesbaden. One officer warned that he was far from mentally deranged: 'In fact he must be considered a very shrewd customer, a great actor and professional liar.' Shown news photographs of Dachau, he expressed the belief, that they must have been taken in the final chaotic days.[30]

Göring was flown to Luxembourg on May 20. He took small satisfaction from the fact that he was shortly joined here in the ASHCAN by his rival as Hitler's successor, Grand-Admiral Dönitz, too. The two men struck an uneasy truce. But the Reichsmarschall remarked combatively to the admiral's adjutant, 'You can be quite certain that if we're for the high jump, mine will be the first head into the noose!'

Andrus took an inventory of Göring's more valuable personal effects, all of which were to remain locked away out of the prisoner's reach from now on. The list included gold Luftwaffe badges, one encrusted with diamonds; a valuable collection of artefacts embellished with gold, silver, amethyst, emeralds, diamonds, rubies, and lapis lazuli; his famous medals including the Pour le Mérite, a World War One iron cross, and the Grosskreuz; several clocks and watches, including a Cartier and 'one large Swiss wristwatch,' and 'one fountain pen inscribed Hermann Göring.'[31] It is worth bearing in mind both of the latter items until the very end of this narrative. There were also leather cases full of personal items like toilet necessities and food. After Field-

Marshal Robert Ritter von Greim swallowed cyanide on May 24, the Americans stepped up security and evidently for the first time searched Göring's luggage. It was now that they triumphantly found and confiscated, concealed in a tin of American coffee, a screw-capped cartridge fashioned from a rifle bullet, containing hydrogen-cyanide in a glass ampoule.[32]

Göring had weighed in at 264 pounds; the American doctors found him extremely obese, flaccid, and generally in poor physical shape. He had suffered frequent heart attacks since 1941. They put him on a radical diet. Mugshots taken on June 22 and July 10 showed him wasting away, his cheekbones beginning to protrude. They found around 2,000 white pills in his possession, a weak morphine substitute, of which he took ten each morning and night. Andrus told S.H.A.E.F.: 'My surgeon reports that if we suddenly remove this [medication] he will become totally demented.' Eisenhower's headquarters replied that all they asked was that Göring remain coherent for a while. 'There are a number of things we wish to ask him before we finally lose interest in what happens to him.'[33] Interrogators on July 10 reported that he was very wary—he knew they were trying to convict him of something, 'But he is not quite sure what that is.'[34] Andrus reported a further reduction in the paracodeine dosage on July 23. He also reported that the Reichsmarschall was beginning to look very good on it.

The airforce's chief interrogator Major Ernst Engländer (known to Göring as 'Evans'—in real life a Wall Street financier) grilled the Reichsmarschall several times while hidden microphones taped every word. 'I found it easier,' Engländer would write, 'to deal with them by getting reasonably chummy and as a result Göring asked me to do a favor and see his wife for him.'[35] Engländer knew of the intense hatred that existed between Göring and his Luftwaffe commanders, and did what he could to fuel the flames of this hatred by conveying largely invented tittle-tattle between the generals and field-marshals about what they were saying about each other. Unaware of this, Göring gratefully gave 'Evans' a tattered snapshot of his wife Emma and daughter Edda to hand to his wife, and he inked on the back the words, 'Major Evans has my confidence.'[36]

Many of the prisoners had brought their old enmities with them to this prison camp, a baggage that could not be easily locked away. While Hitler's manpower boss Fritz Sauckel was one of Göring's intimates, there was no love lost between the Nazi labour leader Dr Robert Ley and the Reichsmarschall. 'Göring,' Ley told American interrogators, 'was never able to win the heart of the workers. He was considered a comical figure … the "pus-bag" not only of the party but of Germany as well.' He described the Reichsmarschall as a conceited, egotistical windbag, who by his measures had damaged the party.[37] Göring, noted his fellow-prisoner Julius Streicher with amusement, had had to kick his cocaine habit here: 'At Mondorf he actually wrote a letter to complain about the quality of the food. He still felt every inch the Reichsmarschall. He always was a glutton and always will be. Poor guy! He thinks that if he were to get out now the "people" would greet him with vestal virgins. As if!'[38] Göring told him he had never wanted this war, they couldn't pin the blame onto him as a soldier, every soldier had to do his duty. Streicher answered: 'The Jews will make sure enough that we hang.'[39]

Andrus ordered a further reduction in Göring's paracodeine allowance. Soon he was almost entirely weaned of the narcotics.[40] 'I don't know what they want to do with Göring,' the prison commandant wrote to Colonel Fritzsche—how confusing all these German-named Americans were—on August 4, 'but I think he should stay with me and my doctor. Göring states that his health is better now than it has been for years and is tremendously better than when we got him.' As the Americans reduced the dosages, Göring's health perked up. Andrus asked that the War Crimes Commission be notified of one thing: 'It is our purpose not only to keep Göring well but to eliminate any possible bar to trial or punishment.'[41]

On August 5, the United States Army forwarded to S.H.A.E.F. headquarters the list of prisoners to be turned over to the control of prosecuting counsel. As he had anticipated, Göring's name topped the list. On the following night, the drugs rehabilitation programme complete, Andrus halted Göring's paracodeine medication for good.

SHORTLY THE prisoners at Mondorf were joined by Joachim von Ribbentrop. He had been captured in Hamburg on June 14 after a long search. He would spend the remaining weeks here at the Grand Hotel writing his memoirs.[42] When he invited Göring to run his eye over eighty-five pages he had just written, the former aviator told him without undue politeness where he could file them. With the drug intake now halted completely, the Reichsmarschall had regained his old fight and *joie de vivre*.

Ribbentrop spoke a wooden but intelligible English, having spent some time in Canada in earlier years. A British officer interviewed the ex-foreign minister on August 4, assuring him that their conversation was in secret (in fact every word was picked up and recorded.) Despite these assurances, both now and later Ribbentrop refused to talk about the non-aggression pact he had signed in Moscow in August 1939 between Germany and Russia, invoking diplomatic secrecy.

The British officer changed to another, by implication more menacing, tack.

'You've seen, of course, what has happened in these concentration camps,' he began.

'I never knew,' confessed Ribbentrop, 'whether it is really true what has been published on the concentration camps.'

'It is true.'

'I only learned of all these things through the papers in Hamburg when I was not yet a prisoner. We all had not the slightest idea of it.'

'That astonishes us.'

'Would it possibly astonish you, I wonder,' questioned Ribbentrop, 'if you knew our system? If anyone had asked Himmler to visit a concentration camp, the result would have been that he would have ended up there but would never come back from there.'

'He was responsible for them?'

'Of course.'

'Who built them up?'

'He did.'

'But he alone couldn't have had the full responsibility: he must have had a staff under him. Did Bormann work on this?'

'Bormann is a man who worked a lot with Himmler. About concentration camps. You see, we knew there were concentration camps but we didn't know what was going on. Nobody knew. All these people in Mondorf—not one of them knew. Also the Jewish question.'

'You mean about the persecution?'

'We knew that there were concentration camps but we didn't know what was in them.'

'Do you think Hitler knew?'

After a long, painful pause, Ribbentrop replied: 'I have so often thought about that. It would absolutely ruin my picture of Hitler if I thought this. I know one thing, that after the Russians [in September 1944] had taken the concentration camp in Poland, Majdanek I think it was called, that was the first time I heard of these persecutions in concentration camps, misdeeds, atrocities. This was the first thing I heard when our representatives from abroad sent telegrams that Russian propaganda was making a tremendous row in neutral countries. I got these telegrams and placed them before the Führer. I said that if this were true in any respect it would be quite impossible to make foreign policy. So he took the matter in hand and said it was not my business to discuss this. That's the only thing I ever heard.'

The British officer asked if he had seen any pamphlets. Ribbentrop replied: 'I have seen one film in Mondorf. It was shown to us. It was a terrible film. There is no doubt about that. There was some propaganda. You see, we saw on a number of pictures where it was quite evident that it was done after bombardment.... If you ask me about Himmler,' he concluded, 'in the last years he was very touchy—*sehr böse*.' The adjective actually translates as wicked.[43]

THE FORMER gauleiter of Franconia, Julius Streicher, found that he was treated rather better here than he had been at Wiesbaden, although the other prisoners steered well clear of him, well aware of the hatred of their captors for this man. During the Third Reich many of these same Nazis had written letters of congratulation to Streicher or to his newspaper the *Stürmer*. Now they could not disown him fast enough.

He had been born the son of a village teacher near Augsburg on February 12, 1885, and had won three medals for gallantry in World War One. Joining Hitler in the 1923 putsch, he had shared imprisonment in Landsberg with him, and found himself forbidden afterwards to practise his profession as a senior-school teacher (*Berufsverbot*, the systematic destruction of a man's livelihood, is a cruel and unusual punishment used in Germany for political offences even now.)[44] From the 1920s on he had studied the teachings of the Old Testament and the Talmud, and he had concluded that so long as the Jews claimed to be the chosen people they would always find difficulties with their host nations.[45] Although he had turned away from Christianity, the distasteful references to Jesus Christ in the Talmud, many of which he had learned by heart, left their mark on him.[46] He had perceived the 'Jewish Bolsheviks' seizing power in Russia, murdering the Tsar and his family, and ruling by terror; he had seen the methods of, as he said, the Jewish 'Soviet' (*Räteregierung*), led by Kurt Eisner, in Bavaria; he had watched other Jews establish similar authoritarian regimes such as the one under Béla Kun in Hungary; and he had concluded that 'the Jews' were making it their objective to establish final supremacy over the gentile races by ramming multiculturalism and multiracism down their throats. He had campaigned, in response, for the destruction of the Jews, and that no doubt was why he now found himself here.[47]

He had however confined himself to this agitating, to creating a climate of hatred against the Jews: to words rather than deeds. Even his sworn enemy Benno Martin, the *Höherer S.S.- und Polizeiführer* in Nuremberg, had to confirm to interrogators that Streicher had opposed the Kristallnacht in November 1938, saying that the outrages would benefit only the Jews in the long run. Streicher had not however opposed the subsequent levelling of the main synagogue in Nuremberg, claiming that it was municipally necessary, its oriental architecture being out of keeping with the city's mediæval character; for him synagogues were not religious structures anyway, but—as the Talmud had taught him—hubs of moneymaking, wheeling-and-dealing, and intrigue.[48]

Streicher had founded two periodicals which enjoyed little success. After close study of the successful tabloids he started over, publishing from 1923 onward an unofficial, widely read, and often pornographic weekly tabloid, the *Stürmer*. The magazine was often the despair of both Hitler and Goebbels—it was literally beyond the Nazi party's control—but it was banned only once, from August 8 to 18, 1934, for publishing a libel on the Czech head of state. Because of the hard-core antisemitism that was the staple of the *Stürmer*, with liberal repetition of blood libels like the ritual slaughter of gentile children, Streicher became the public enemy No. 1 of the organised international Jewish community. One of his staff collected thousands of examples of the attacks on him published around the world, and he was about to publish them in an anthology ironically entitled 'Streicher, the Bloody Tsar of Franconia,' when Hitler's war intervened.[49]

His long-range ambition was to see the Jews emigrate from Germany. He believed that many of the foreign diplomats accredited to Germany silently applauded this, including the French ambassador André François-Poncet, who often saw him at the Nuremberg rallies; when the grand mufti of Jerusalem however made plain that there could no question of consigning the Jews to Palestine, Streicher, like Hitler, adopted the so-called Madagascar plan as the only viable final solution.[50]

He fell out of favour for quite different reasons. In 1939 he was forbidden to make public speeches (*Redeverbot*, another authoritarian German law that is still on the statute books), and in 1940 he was dismissed from all his party offices over allegations arising from the Aryanisation of property after the Night of Broken Glass.[51] He had withdrawn to the Pleikershof estate in his native Franconia, built a home above the cowshed there, and lived out the remaining war years with no contact whatever with the Nazi power structure. For years he had been Hitler's only intimate friend, on *du* terms with him; but the Führer's shortcomings, after the hearings that Streicher insisted on to clear his name, had dismayed him. Hitler had said that 'if anybody is found out to have lied he will be shot'; but nobody was dealt with in this manner, and Streicher could only conclude that when push came to shove Hitler lacked the necessary ruthlessness.

All that was in the distant past. Here at Mondorf, Streicher painted water-colours and wrote his political testament, for which purpose he read the Bible once more and sought out quotations.[52] Some of the prisoners noted in their diaries a sneaking admiration for Streicher's refusal to buckle under. 'I'm not worried about you,' Grand-Admiral Karl Dönitz whispered to Streicher as they left Mondorf to be trucked across southern Germany to Nuremberg prison, 'but I wonder how the others are going to come through!'[53]

The more fortunate prisoners, the witnesses, had been mustered and driven away from Mondorf first. Göring remained upstairs with heart trouble, and received the farewells of his former colleagues in bed. Walter Lüdde-Neurath, Dönitz's adjutant, found him in defiant mood. 'Whatever happens,' said the Luftwaffe commander, 'you can bank on me. There are one or two things I'm going to be saying at the coming trial.'[54]

7: Meeting with Two Traitors

On August 12, 1945 the seventy prisoners were transferred from Mondorf to Nuremberg, either as defendants or as witnesses. Albert Speer was no longer among them. The other prisoners had gathered that Speer, who had initially stood up manfully to his captors like the rest of them, now seemed to be trafficking with the Allies because they had whisked him away from Mondorf some weeks before.

The uglier formalities began—with a farce, framed in fictions. At four P.M. on the twelfth the Americans formally arrested Göring at 'Ansbach PW Processing and Discharge Camp (Nuremberg courthouse)' on the charge of being a war crimes suspect, and on the authority of Jackson's office; like Field-Marshal Keitel, arrested there on the same date by Second Lieutenant Martin M. Lewkowicz, Göring and the other military prisoners had first been discharged, on paper at least, from the Wehrmacht. The 'discharge' was a charade performed to enable the Allies to prosecute and hang their captives outside the protection afforded to them as prisoners-of-war by the Geneva Convention.[1] Milch, put through the same procedure a few weeks later, would impudently lecture the Americans: 'You were not the ones who appointed me, nor can you discharge me.' A field-marshal in Germany, as elsewhere, remains formally on active duty for life.

JACKSON'S OVERRIDING concern at this stage was whether the prosecution could obtain enough admissible evidence to support the charges which had been levelled so freely against the Nazis throughout the war.

The conferences in London had gone into tedious sub-committee stage. The lawyers had ruled out Munich as a trial location for want of a suitable intact building, and Jackson needed to line up another site ('Nuremberg probably'.) So he flew with his team to Germany on July 7, 1945, landing on a bomb-scarred airfield at Wiesbaden.[2] The hangars were fire-blackened skeletons. Disabled weapons, tanks, and jeeps, and the burned-out wrecks of crashed aircraft still littered the field. General Donovan's O.S.S. had requisitioned a comfortable house for the lawyers, and established its own headquarters in the Henkell sparkling-wine factory at Wiesbaden—a provident choice for the hard-drinking

Americans. (The head of the firm, Karl Henkell, had been killed in an air raid on February 10.)

For Jackson, this brief sojourn in Wiesbaden was one of the turning points in the preparation of his case. The army lawyer Colonel John H. Amen had just arrived from Paris with an armful of documents which soon had Jackson, starved until now of the kind of evidence he needed, salivating. Among them was the typescript copy of the first part of a document subsequently referred to portentously by historians as the Hossbach Protocol, recording a meeting held by Hitler on November 5, 1937 with Göring and his other commanders-in-chief and foreign minister Constantin von Neurath, describing his plans to expand into eastern Europe. From the judges' later deliberations during the trial, there is no doubt that they too regarded this as one of the key documents of the prosecution.

After viewing what the colonel had brought, Jackson wrote in his diary: 'He had obtained a copy of the minutes of a 1937 conference between Hitler and his top generals in which Hitler exposed the whole plan of aggressive war and of extermination of the Jews.'[3] While the document in fact makes no reference to the Jews it looked to him at first blush like proof of the Nazi conspiracy beyond his wildest dreams.[4] In English criminal law at least conspiracy is broadly defined as the incitement by one of another or others to effect an unlawful purpose, followed by the agreement of those others. Other legal authorities, including the French judges at Nuremberg, would however find the Hossbach document less impressive.* It did not show anybody 'conspiring,' as they pointed out: it showed Hitler setting out his intentions, and the others effectively clicking their heels in assent.

There were more documents than just this. '[Amen] also,' noted Jackson, 'had the documents by which the German police had been warned of forthcoming riots against the Jews and ordered not to interfere with them, and rather detailed instructions as to how the riots should be allowed to proceed.' This was a reference to telegrams issued to local Gestapo offices during the Kristallnacht in November 1938, which are now also in the archives.[5] Jackson had these papers delivered to the O.S.S. for reproduction.

This was not all. Shortly the academic-looking O.S.S. chief in Switzerland, Allen Dulles, came over to the house bringing with him four rather dishevelled 'Nazi refugees' who seemed likely to be of pivotal

* As one critic has pointed out, 'This document turned out to be a certified photocopy of a microfilm copy of a retyped "certified true copy," prepared by an American, of a retyped "certified true copy," prepared by a German, of unauthenticated hand-written notes by Hossbach, written from memory five days after a discussion led by Hitler on 5 November 1937.' *Spectator*, London, December 16–23, 1995, page 57. Despite its unprepossessing provenance, however, there is no doubt in this author's mind about the protocol's authenticity. Rear-Admiral Karl-Jesco von Puttkamer told him he saw it at the time; and it is referred to in Jodl's contemporary diary.

importance in building Jackson's case. The Americans—Jackson, Donovan, Amen, Dulles, and a couple of others—spent the afternoon in the library of the house questioning two of these Germans, while Elsie Douglas, Jackson's secretary, took down everything in detail.

First there was Fabian von Schlabrendorff, a lawyer who had been attached to the German Army as legal adviser (in post-war Germany he would rise to eminence as a judge.) Schlabrendorff said that he had seen with his own eyes the Nazi orders to kill American parachutists. In an embellishment which serious historians now find frankly improbable, Schlabrendorff also claimed to have planted a bomb, disguised as a square Cointreau bottle—in some versions he changed it to a (round) brandy bottle—in a briefcase in Hitler's plane in the spring of 1943; it had failed to detonate and 'at the risk of his life' he had returned to retrieve it from the plane. The gullible American prosecutors were thoroughly taken in—after all this man was a lawyer—and Schlabrendorff gushed with gratitude to Dulles for saving him when he fled for his life in January 1945.[6]

The second gentleman was no more likeable. This man was Hans Bernd Gisevius, an official of the Abwehr, the German secret service. Until a few weeks earlier, the Nazis had incarcerated his sister in Dachau concentration camp, largely in consequence of his treachery. But now that treachery paid off handsomely. In a letter to Jackson some months later Allen Dulles would summarise how useful Gisevius had been to the Allied cause from the time they had first met in Zürich, Switzerland, in January 1943. 'I personally have no doubt whatever,' wrote Dulles, 'that he is a confirmed anti-Nazi, who took extraordinary risks in order to help defeat the Nazis.' Here at Wiesbaden, Jackson learned that Gisevius had been active in anti-Nazi movements and 'was to have been "Minister of Purification" in the new government if Hitler had been disposed of.' A minister of purification sounded a singularly European kind of office, one concerned no doubt with correcting the political environment; but Jackson dictated to his diary that with one possible exception these two men were the only plotters against Hitler who had survived the purges that followed the assassination attempt in his headquarters on July 20, 1944. (Inevitably, in subsequent years a whole host of 'plot survivors' would discover themselves and come forward.)[7]

Working without remuneration as 'Agent 512' for the American secret service during the last two years of his country's ruinous war, Gisevius had been one of the most valuable German renegades. 'Gisevius,' noted Dulles in a memo, 'gave me frequent reports over a year and a half, from January 1943 to July 1944, with regard to the development of the anti-Nazi movement. Through him I was in touch with the circle of conspirators which included General [Ludwig] Beck, [Carl] Goerdeler, [Count Helmuth] von Moltke, General [Hans] Oster, [Adam] von Trott and others. Some days prior to July 20, 1944 I was forewarned by Gisevius of what was coming and given details of those who were in the plot to overthrow Hitler.'[8] Gisevius had returned to Berlin to reap the rewards of the July plot; after its failure he lay low for six months until Dulles smuggled papers in to him to enable him to escape to Switzerland in January 1945.

There are no doubt some who would balk at labelling Gisevius a traitor. But Dulles' written testimonial revealed the full extent of this German's activities for his country's enemies: 'In February 1943 Gisevius warned me that the secret cipher of the American Legation in Bern was being read by the Germans, proved this by bringing readings of deciphered telegrams, and thereby permitted me to warn the Legation and close what might have been a serious leak.' At a very early date moreover, Gisevius had provided Dulles with information on what later became the V–1 and V–2 missiles, and he helped to identify Peenemünde on the Baltic as the site of Hitler's missile research station.[9] In the consequent British air raid on Peenemünde eight hundred Germans and foreign workers were killed. It would be the spring of 1946 before O.S.S. 'Agent 512' Gisevius would testify before the war crimes tribunal. Somewhat remarkably he felt able to deny under cross-examination ever having acted on behalf of the secret service of any foreign power. Dulles was enthusiastic about these renegades. Jackson evidently less so, writing of them in a private letter in terms almost of reprobation.[10]

THE CASE was beginning to seem to Jackson 'so big, so sprawling, and so complex' that he wondered if it would ever prove possible to knock it into shape.[11] After supper they questioned the two other men Allen Dulles had brought—a lutheran minister jailed by the Nazis, and a German foreign ministry official who had been illicitly supplying secret documents to Dulles in Switzerland for years.

The latter gentleman, code-named 'George Wood' by Dulles, was most probably Fritz Kolbe, who had been a special adviser (*Sonderreferent*) to Ambassador Karl Ritter, Ribbentrop's liaison officer to the German High Command, the Oberkommando der Wehrmacht. This agent claimed to have been a member of the Schwarze Kapelle network—the catholic counterpart to the communist Rote Kapelle. Reporting to President Truman later, Donovan would state that Dulles had first established contact with 'Wood' in August 1943: 'Over a period of eighteen months [the] O.S.S. received over 1,600 true readings of secret and top secret German diplomatic correspondence between the [German] Foreign Office and German diplomatic missions in twenty countries.' The British secret service had rated this contact 'the prize intelligence source of the war.'[12] Wood's treachery had of course proven invaluable in enabling the British to break Germany's diplomatic codes.

Having taken all this in Jackson went to bed in his Wiesbaden billet, a building completely surrounded by ruins, a happier man. He heard the pop-pop of sporadic shooting during the night, but it disturbed him less than it did Elsie. Evidently some kind of purification had already begun.[13]

❖ ❖ ❖ ❖ ❖

Meeting him in Frankfurt the following day the American military governor General Lucius B. Clay advised that if the trials were to be held in Berlin they should at least be staged in the American sector of the city, as the Russians in their present truculent mood would hinder and not help. If, however, Jackson had a free choice, Clay advised him to plump for Nuremberg instead, as this was in the American occupation zone of Germany. Clay's veteran political adviser Robert Murphy also preferred Nuremberg.

Murphy told Jackson that the Americans had just released 450 tons of German foreign ministry documents to the British, since the O.S.S. did not have adequate microfilming capacity. Jackson was annoyed to hear this, since he felt he had a prior claim, as he would be needing the original documents as exhibits in court. Among the documents carried to England by a Colonel R. C. Thompson of the British C.I.O.S.* were some that contained political dynamite—the microfilmed papers of Carl von Loesch, of Ribbentrop's staff, which Thompson and Loesch had jointly retrieved on May 19 from a house at Schöneberg in the Soviet Zone, near Berlin. On these films were the entire surviving records of Hitler's dealings with Mussolini, Franco, Laval, and other foreign potentates (as well as, incidentally, the only surviving copy of the Ribbentrop–Molotov Pact of August 1939.)[14] A cable to the State department from Jefferson Caffery, the American ambassador in Paris, dated June 15, stated that the British had so far failed to return copies of these microfilms to the American authorities in Germany. Murphy had heard that the British ambassador Lord Halifax had been instructed by London to put pressure on Washington not to insist—it seemed that there were some embarrassing items in those Nazi files which the British were not keen to see aired in public now or at any time in the future. Among the items which the British seized and never returned to Germany were interpreter Paul Schmidt's transcripts of Hitler's meetings with leading members of the British aristocracy.[15]

As for co-operation with the Russians, Murphy was gloomy: he said he had asked them about Martin Bormann, one of the war criminals on Jackson's provisional list, and the Russians had just shrugged and professed ignorance about the fate of the former Reichsleiter. They had

* Combined Intelligence Objectives Sub-Committee of the foreign office.

† The author provided his copies of these microfilms to Soviet historian Lev Bezymenski on January 22, 1989; Bezymenski carried them to Moscow where they were solemnly produced to Mikhail Gorbachev's Politburo as proof that there had been such a pact with its aggressive secret additional protocol.

other fish to fry. Driving around Berlin, said Murphy, he had not seen one male labourer aged between eighteen and fifty: evidently they had already been deported as slave labour. He privately advised Jackson that the Soviet centralisation of power was just an alibi for doing nothing. When a Russian official really wanted to do something, he found ways of doing it; when he did not, he said he found it impossible to get authorisation from Moscow.[16]

WITH AN eye to ensuring that the Americans kept the upper hand the U.S. Army had provided Jackson with his own C–47 transport plane and crew.

This proved a good investment. He used it to ferry his team briefly across to Nuremberg that afternoon to make a flying inspection of the courthouse and jail. It was his first visit to the city. Over eighty-five percent of the buildings had been damaged by Allied bombing—the worst destruction Jackson had seen so far. There were few people in sight, and a sickly smell of death and decaying flesh hung over the ruins.

They picked their way through the rubble mountains to where the forbidding, stone-walled Palace of Justice was still standing; this was the building that the military governor General Clay proposed they use. It was windowless and largely roofless, its grey stone façade pock-marked by bullets and bomb fragments. Inside, its red-carpeted library was water-logged and ruined; in the courtroom on the third floor, a beer barrel had been set up on the judges' bench. But this courtroom could hold six hundred people, and Jackson heard that the jailhouse next door could accommodate 1,200 prisoners, so he gave Nuremberg the go-ahead and the army began the necessary rebuilding.[17]

He flew back to London. While the case that the army lawyers and O.S.S. officers were preparing was turning out to be stronger than he had dared to hope, over the next two weeks it was again the Russians who dragged their feet on the procedural preparations for the trial. 'Their whole background is so different,' sighed Jackson in a private letter. The Russians still wanted the trial to be in Berlin; but now that Jackson had seen Nuremberg he was not going to let go of that. Playing his trump card—the U.S. Army plane and crew placed at his permanent disposal—he invited the Russian, French, and British delegations to fly over from London to Nuremberg for a better look at the courthouse that weekend. The Russians, after consulting their central authorities in Moscow, cordially but firmly declined his invitation. 'So we are off for a weekend amid unbelievable destruction and desolation,' he wrote to his wife Irene.[18]

The entire Jackson circus flew to Nuremberg on Saturday July 21—without the Russians but this time taking along several British lawyers, including the attorney-general Sir David Maxwell Fyfe, Mr G. D. Roberts, KC, and Lord Bridgeman, as well as Professor Gros and Robert Falco, a judge at the Cour de Cassation, France's supreme court. Falco was Gallic and diminutive but a man of immense charm, shrewdness, and patience. Jackson's party on this junket included Alderman, Shea, Bernays, and Dean. It is clear from Maxwell Fyfe's memoirs that it was only now that he realised what the German civilian population had been through under Allied bombing, although he never once in the trial admitted the relevance of this ordeal. General Clay warned the visitors that there were still so many corpses buried beneath the rubble that he feared the city's water supply must be contaminated.[19]

After a slap-up lunch in the American officers' mess at Nuremberg's half-rebuilt Grand Hotel, Jackson toasted their British and French guests and declared emotionally that here in Nuremberg, where Hitler had once proclaimed democracy to be decadent, the democracies were in possession; and that here where the Nazis had said there should be no more law, the victors should re-establish the rule of law. Jackson was still a small-town lawyer at heart, but sophistries like these have always tripped lightly off the American tongue.

Everybody now agreed that this city's courthouse provided the right setting for the trial of the century. Shown over the Eberhard Faber castle—home of the pencil king—that afternoon, which the army had earmarked as their future billet, Jackson had no difficulty in rejecting it, with its vast dining rooms and cavernous bedrooms.[20] It would be turned over to the press corps instead, since journalists were people beset with fewer sensitivities than lawyers. At the badly damaged opera house, Jackson and his party listened that evening to a German orchestra playing Beethoven's Fifth—he reflected that if the musicians' playing sounded unenthusiastic, it was probably because their audience consisted entirely of the very enemy who had laid waste to their beautiful and ancient city.[21]

THE NEGOTIATIONS in London had become bogged down even more inextricably in small print—the actual definition of 'war crimes.' Perhaps it was hardly surprising, given that all the negotiating parties were judges or advocates.

Jackson was losing his patience with the lot of them. 'The discussions have been sterile,' he wrote, leaving for a trip to Berlin. 'One day I suggested that we were making no progress and that each ought to go ahead and try his own criminals. On another day, I suggested that I would recommend to my Government that it step out of the case, turn the prisoners over to the European Allies and let them go ahead with the trials, and on[ly] yesterday I suggested that another course was to refer the matter to [the Control Council in] Berlin for political decision'— by which phrase he meant, of course, the often touted summary liquidation of their prisoners. So little progress was being made that he sent his son and Francis Shea back to Washington, and Alderman and Bernays off to look for documents in Paris.[22]

The three power summit conference formally terminating World War

Two had just begun at Potsdam, outside Berlin.[23] On July 26 Jackson's advance party landed in Berlin after a four-hour flight from England. 'We drove through an odor of death to Potsdam,' the judge wrote. That scent seemed all pervasive in Germany, even now. Russian women acting as traffic control officers flagged them snappily through, as Jackson's convoy found its way out to the 'White House' in the Potsdam suburb of Babelsberg where Harry Truman and his new secretary of state Jimmy Byrnes, a former judge, were holding court. A small and execrable band was playing in the garden. The news from Britain was that Winston Churchill's party had lost the general election, and that Labour had swept into power in a landslide victory.

As for their Russian allies, things were getting sticky. Byrnes told Judge Jackson of the problems that the Allies were already facing. The Soviet behaviour in eastern Europe was such, he said, that they could no longer sit next to the Russians and hold court over the Germans for offences like looting a conquered country's wealth. Nor did Byrnes think much of Jackson's pious legal endeavours to get to the root of how the war began.[24]

On the following day, Jackson tried to penetrate to the heart of the matter, driving with his party twenty miles into the centre of Berlin. The capital city had crumpled into shapeless heaps of rubble, the stinking remains of former palaces, museums, churches, and apartment buildings under which thousands of bodies still lay buried. Like Murphy, he noticed that there seemed to be no young men; everywhere were lines of women toiling through the ruins like ants in an anthill, clearing away the rubble, hammering and cleaning bricks and masonry, and passing pails of bricks in endless human bucket-chains. 'The streets were lined with dumb-looking people,' described the judge, 'most of them moving their possessions, some going in one direction, some in another.' There were horse-drawn vehicles too—but a colonel called his attention to the fact that nearly every cart had a Russian at the reins. The systematic plundering and stripping of the country was continuing apace.

Hitler's Reich Chancellery, built by Albert Speer in 1939, was still a magnificent building, and although the long hall seemed neither very high nor wide to Jackson, it had a strange capacity even in its current down-at-heel condition to make him feel very insignificant inside: such was the architectural ability of Speer, now being questioned by the leisurely Allied experts in Versailles. Much of the chancellery building was still in the disordered state that Hitler's staff had left it. 'The Russians apparently had not examined with much care the papers,' observed Jackson, who wished that he could read German or indeed any language other than American. 'Hitler's overturned desk was in his room. Miss [Caroline] Fite [of the state department] picked up a number of original letters addressed to Göring, and I gathered up some typewritten documents which may or may not be important. The floor was strewn with wreckage and much motion picture film.'

He reflected that if the Russians had done no better job than this in collecting evidence here, at the very fountainhead of Hitler's evil, the trial would not be getting much from them.[25]

❖ ❖ ❖ ❖ ❖

Down the road at Potsdam, the Big Three—Stalin, Truman, and now the mousy and unprepossessing Prime Minister Clement Attlee on behalf of the British—made no proper attempt to ventilate the topic of the enemy war criminals until the last day of July 1945. Again we have a precise transcript of what was said.

'The next item,' announced President Truman, first raising the matter, 'relates to the war criminals.'

Molotov said, 'The Soviet delegation agrees to accept the British draft with one amendment. The amendment is in the last sentence after the words, "War Criminals." We wish to add specific names, such as Göring, Hess, Rosenberg, Ribbentrop, etc.'

'It is not wise,' Attlee suggested, 'to put in names.'

Stalin explained, 'We merely suggest that such people as Göring and Ribbentrop be tried. If we remain silent it will cast a shadow on our prestige. If we name persons as an example we don't leave out the others. It is no offense to the prosecution. It will be helpful politically.'

Byrnes also felt that it was unwise to name names. 'Every country has its favorite criminal. It will be difficult to explain to each country why its pet criminal was not named.'

British foreign secretary Ernest Bevin then pointed out, 'There is some doubt whether Hitler is alive. He is not on the list.'

'But he is not in our hands,' Stalin said—knowing it was a lie. 'I quite agree that Hitler should be hanged.'

Byrnes told them he had spoken that very afternoon to Justice Jackson in London. 'He expressed the hope that this afternoon or tomorrow morning his committee might reach an agreement.'[26]

BACK IN London, Jackson discussed with treasury solicitor Sir Thomas Barnes what changes might become likely in the British prosecution line-up now that Labour had won the election. The new lord chancellor was Sir William Jowitt, a man of considerably greater legal acumen than Viscount Simon. Jackson found the British to be process-oriented, still haggling over definitions. More goal-oriented, the Americans had prepared a film to educate the American public on the background to the trials; Jackson thought it terrible—it showed a particularly gruesome hanging, which he felt should be excised right away. Everybody suspected that hanging was an uncomfortable end, but there was no need to say so out loud.

❖ ❖ ❖ ❖ ❖

On the last day of July 1945 the widely respected Zionist leader Dr Chaim Weizmann lunched with Robert Jackson at the Dorchester, to plead once more for the special right of the Jews to make a presentation of their case at the trial, given that they were the only people against whom, in their view, a systematic policy of extermination had been followed. Jackson advised 'rather strongly' against any idea of having Weizmann himself appear as an advocate.[27]

His attitude to the Jews was ambivalent. Although his private papers displayed none of the antisemitism that was widely prevalent in New England and fashionable among people of his class at the time, neither did he want them muscling in on 'his' trial. He felt that his prosecuting staff was already overloaded with Jews. In fact he had set himself one perhaps surprising guideline in selecting staff, deliberately deciding to employ no Jews. Coming from a country where a substantial proportion of the legal profession was already Jewish, a percentage which would multiply over the next decades, he recognised the risk he ran, but as he explained in his most intimate post-war reminiscences: 'I had a great deal of argument and difficulty about the staff, particularly with the Jewish people and politicians.' Whenever they came individually or in committees to clamour for prominent roles in the prosecution he had to educated them about the damage this would do. 'We are prosecuting these Nazis not because they killed Jews, but because they killed men and women'—that is, for Innocenticide.[28] He was most anxious that this should not be interpreted as a vengeance trial.

ULTIMATELY AND in order not to be accused of shunning them entirely or worse, he did relent and employ one Jew, Dr Robert Kempner, in the courtroom presentation of the prosecution case.

Kempner was a lawyer of the former German ministry of the interior who had been obliged to emigrate from Nazi Germany. He had been lucky, wrote another member of the American prosecution team, to get out of Germany. 'Kempner is the only prosecutor who was born a German,' wrote this man. 'Many of the staff, of course, are ex-Germans; some even have relatives in Nuremberg and vicinity.'[29] Kempner's work, in the rebuttal division, was inconsequential. But the American-uniformed presence of this ex-German caused some friction among the justice's staff. Jackson's son privately advised his father that they regarded Kempner more as 'something of a joke'; Jackson loyally retained Kempner to the end, and he came to regret it.[30]

Robert Max Wasili Kempner, born in Freiburg on October 17, 1899, was a thoroughly embittered and rather nasty piece of work. Although a Jew, he had worked from 1928 to 1933 for the Prussian police force, so there was no doubting his intellectual qualifications.[31] Soured by his experiences at the hands of the Nazis, he had fled Germany in 1935 and become a professor at the University of Pennsylvania. He never lost his personal hatred of Hermann Göring, whom Hitler had appointed prime minister of Prussia, and whom Kempner blamed for his expulsion. On May 10, 1945 he had written to the Pentagon suggesting ways of getting at Göring, in particular the many cases 'brought to his personal attention' in which the Prussian police had 'killed and tortured' people. Kempner had suggested they bring Göring to the United States for interrogation on his morphine addiction, on Emmy's 'former intimate relationship with a Jewish theatrical man,' and on Hermann's 'relationship to the late Austrian Jewish landowner Baron Hermann von Epenstein.'[32]

Returning now to Nuremberg in 1945, Kempner swore revenge—revenge at any price. In doing so he put behind him the strict ethics by which he had been brought up in the law in Weimar, Germany. Preparing the prosecution case, he frequently resorted to threats and coercion to get witnesses to change or withdraw inconvenient evidence: Dr Friedrich Gaus, Ribbentrop's legal adviser, was one witness thus intimidated: he would be suddenly stricken with 'amnesia' about the Ribbentrop–Molotov Pact, the signing of which he had actually witnessed in Moscow.[33] Gaus later testified that Kempner had threatened to turn him over to the Russians. In the files there is also a memorandum from Colonel Telford Taylor warning Kempner that he was not to promise inmates early release as an inducement during interrogation.[34]

Kempner's behaviour with evidence was also highly questionable. He would later turn up in German foreign ministry files the original Copy No. 16 of the Wannsee Protocol, and bestow upon it a wholly undeserved reputation as a key document in the Final Solution of the Jewish problem—despite the aura which now surrounds it, the document contains no explicit reference to the killing of Jews. It is complete with GEHEIME KOMMANDOSACHE rubber stamps.[35] Not only did the R.H.S.A., the agency supposedly originating the document, use the civilian classification GEHEIME REICHSSACHE on its documents, but the statistics contained in the document bore little relation either to each other or to reality.[36]

There is further evidence of skulduggery in the documents collected by Kempner's office on the Final Solution. The Nuremberg document experts routinely produced 'staff evidence analysis sheets' on the documents that came into their hands, indicating where they were found, and which individuals were mentioned or incriminated by them. The sheet on document 4055–PS, a photostat of parts of the German ministry of the interior file on the Final Solution, shows that when first analysed by the experts it contained four important items relating to discussions on definitions of Jews; one of these four documents, originating in the spring of 1942, showed Staatssekretär Franz Schlegelberger informing his staff at the justice ministry that Dr Hans

Lammers, chief of the Reich chancellery, had phoned to inform him that the Führer, Adolf Hitler, had 'repeatedly' ordered the solution of the Jewish problem 'postponed until after the war was over.' This did not suit Kempner at all, and when the file was returned to the document centre this particular photostat was missing.[37]

For years the only evidence that it had ever existed was the brief summary in the 'staff evidence analysis sheet.'[38] Dr Kempner, challenged by this author to explain the gap, did not; at this author's prompting, the German historian Professor Eberhard Jäckel located the missing original page, still in its Reich ministry of the interior file, buried deep in the German federal archives to which it had eventually been restituted. Jäckel thereby rendered a service to the revisionist cause for which he has never been appropriately rewarded.[39]

Another high-ranking Nazi, Dr Wilhelm Stuckart, would later succeed in turning the tables on Kempner: hinting in 1947 that he had incriminating evidence against him, a pre-war document stored safely away, he would bring Kempner, who was by then prosecuting in his own right at the subsequent war crimes proceedings, to his knees. Stuckart, it must be stated, had attended the Wannsee Conference in his capacity as Staatssekretär in the ministry of the interior. Nonetheless, when he was indicted in the 'Wilhelmstrasse trial,' Stuckart boasted to his fellow inmates at Nuremberg that he was going to walk—and walk he did, sentenced to the time already served 'in view of his failing health.'[40] Two years after the trial, Allen Dulles would reveal to the Jacksons that Kempner, by now working for some far-left group in Germany, was trying to extort information from various Germans in an attempt to blackmail both him and his brother John Foster Dulles, the secretary of state; in exchange for such 'testimony' Kempner had released a certain war criminal suspect, said Dulles. Allen Dulles was by then chief of the new C.I.A.[41]

8: The London Agreement

THE ALLIES had undertaken in Point VII of the Potsdam Agreement to bring the German war criminals to a swift and sure justice. The document had expressed the hope that the London negotiations would rapidly lead to a consensus and emphasised the view that the trial of the principal war criminals should begin at the earliest possible opportunity.

Under Jowitt's chairmanship, the London conference proceeded during July and August 1945 more briskly than under the Conservatives. The Russians swallowed the Anglo-American programme 'hook, line, and sinker,' as Barnes put it privately to Jackson afterwards. Sir David Maxwell Fyfe invited Jackson over to the House of Commons for a sherry to celebrate.[1] There were several such convivial celebrations. At a dinner hosted by Jowitt on August 7, the eve of the signature of the London Agreement, Ernest Bevin, Britain's new working-class foreign secretary, a true Cockney, remarked that somebody had asked him the other day about Rudolf Hess, who had remained in Britain since May 1941 as Churchill's personal prisoner. 'You know,' Bevin replied, 'we'd forgotten all abaht 'ess.' He turned to General Nikitchenko and said with a chuckle, 'You Russians have been so successful collecting reparations, that I think I will send you a bill for taking care of 'ess.'[2]

Jowitt told Jackson a few days later that he was appointing the new attorney-general Sir Hartley Shawcross, a socialist, as Britain's official representative at the trials, but that it was inevitable that somebody else—in the event, it would fall to his predecessor Maxwell Fyfe—would have to do most of the work; Sir Hartley would visit the Nuremberg courthouse only to deliver the opening and closing speeches for the British prosecution[3]

The four powers signed the London Agreement with much fanfare at Church House, Westminster, at eleven A.M. on Wednesday, August 8, 1945. Later that day the chief prosecutors held their first joint meeting to discuss once more which names should finally go onto the list of defendants. The British representative, G. D. Roberts, wanted a 'small list,' and added dismissively: 'Everybody knows that these ten or twelve leaders of the Nazi Government are guilty.' 'In my view,' the English barrister continued, 'we ought to have a very prompt trial. The public demands it.'

The Russian, Nikitchenko, agreed: 'We should hasten the first trial. Just pick out a few names which are household words and try them.'

'We would expect the first trial,' chimed in Sir Thomas Barnes, 'to kill as many of the big birds as possible.' (They were meeting in secret, so there was no need to mince their words.)

'We should not leave out the industrialists,' argued Nikitchenko. At this point Roberts warned against allowing the trial to become unwieldy; in his experience having more than twelve defendants would result in just that.[4]

LATER THAT day the Russian prosecutor Nikitchenko stunned them all by baldly announcing that Stalin had now appointed him as the Soviet judge for the trial, and that he would be flying to Moscow immediately to organise his staff. Lieutenant-General Roman A. Rudenko would take his place as prosecutor at these consultations. Even Jackson raised his eyebrows at this. 'The Russians did a strange stunt,' he observed in a letter to his wife. 'Replaced Nikitchenko as prosecutor with one Rudenko, and made Nikitchenko a judge.' In case Mrs Jackson did not get the point he explained: 'He picked out the men to be prosecuted, so it is hard to see how he can be an impartial judge.'[5]

What right for that matter had the Americans now to sit in impartial judgement on their enemies? Two days before the London Agreement was signed, they had detonated their first atomic bomb over Hiroshima. Releasing this revolutionary new killing-weapon with the foreknowledge and agreement of their British allies, they had vaporised in a nanosecond one hundred thousand human beings, nearly all of them non-combatants protected by the international laws of warfare. In an even more questionable act, on the day after signing the agreement, the Americans repeated this feat, dropping a plutonium bomb on Nagasaki.

In his contemporary diary, Jackson made no reference to the atomic bombs. Truman had not told him about them. From his private writings, it is obvious that America's chief prosecution counsel was beginning to feel he had been trapped, but he resolutely addressed his mind to the narrow target he had set himself—the definition of a law to end wars, and its sanctification in blood when the time came.

JACKSON FOUND that the armed forces were particularly hostile to what he was up to. When he visited an American air force headquarters at High Wycombe later on the day of the agreement and tried to explain it to the officers, he found that many of the questions they put to him were sceptical.[6]

The Times now announced that the first trial of major war criminals would take place at Nuremberg, with Göring heading the list of defendants. (Although the list was far from final even now, there was no questioning Göring's entitlement to pride of place.) Two or three evenings after that, Jackson hosted yet another celebration junket, this time for the British lawyers at Claridge's. Bill Jackson, his son, surveyed the pin-striped British legal eagles, and was impressed: he too preferred the new lord chancellor, while the new attorney-general Sir Hartley Shawcross seemed to cut a more alert figure than his much older Conservative predecessor Sir David Maxwell Fyfe.[7]

On August 13, a Monday, the chief prosecutors began formal meetings to consider how to share the burden of work on the various counts between them. Shawcross, who presided, differed from Jackson, suggesting that the British and Americans conduct the case on aggressive war and war in violation of treaties, while the French and Russians should tackle war crimes and crimes against humanity. Jackson had intended there to be five committees, one for each of the four counts, and a fifth to investigate the organisations. The Russians sided with Jackson except that they would have lumped the conspiracy among the leaders together with the organisations. The French Professor Gros had yet another slant, suggesting five different topics for the committees: aggression, economic spoliation, and atrocities as against civilians, atrocities against military personnel, and medical atrocities.[8]

The final structure, which was agreed on the fourteenth, favoured Jackson's plan, with four four-power committees: one on aggressive war and the violation of treaties, chaired by the British; two committees to prosecute war crimes and crimes against humanity on the eastern and western front, under Russian and French chairmanship respectively; with the Americans chairing the planning committees on organisations and on the conspiracy to wage aggressive war.[9]

These prosecution planning conferences in London would continue, on and off, throughout August. Jackson's secretary took detailed verbatim notes on them, and these revealed many of the twists and turns that the prosecution introduced to try to protect their case, and to shield their governments too from embarrassment. The German naval judge advocate Captain Otto Kranzbühler, who would defend Grand Admiral Dönitz, would later point out that it was only after the publication of these transcripts, long after the death sentences had been handed down, that the world had learned of the very real concerns expressed by the British representatives lest the British plans against Norway in 1940 be publicly ventilated in the course of the trial.[10]

AGAIN USING his private plane, on August 17 Jackson took another party across to Nuremberg, including Sir Hartley Shawcross and Colonel Harry J. Phillimore, secretary of the British delegation, with General Nikitchenko and his interpreter Mr Troyanovsky as the Russian guests, and a number of French lawyers whose names he did not catch. Displaying the kind of xenophobia that gets nations into trouble with their neighbours, his son Bill cheerfully described his father's other guests as 'a toad-faced slimy designee of the French' and other members.[11]

❖ ❖ ❖ ❖ ❖

Little had been done even now to alleviate the lot of this city of Richard Wagner's *Mastersingers.* Nuremberg was still a cheerless place to live in, let alone to die.

One American lawyer arriving at this time described in a letter home how he had to clamber across the ruins of the old walled city, as there were still few streets that had been cleared. Smoke from cooking fires came out of the most unbelievable places, showing that buildings that looked completely blitzed were still inhabited. Holes in the walls had been plugged with loose brick or boards; there were tin stovepipes jutting out at crazy angles. The lawyer glimpsed the tangled remains of what had once been the dreaded eighty-eight millimetre high-velocity flak-gun, emplaced in the ground floor of a wrecked building.[12]

Beneath a veneer of subservience and submission the people were still insolent to the victors when they could get away with it. Americans asking the way to an address were liable to be told, 'Over there—across the rubble.'[13]

The Palace of Justice was a large, rambling building with endless cold stone corridors and innumerable offices. Reconstruction and remodelling for the coming trial were proceeding at speed. 'The army,' reported Bill Jackson, 'has sent a whole regiment in there to take care of us—drivers, telephone operators, mimeograph operators, guards, post office, post exchange, tailor shop, barber shop, etc.—everything you could possibly think of, including night club!'[14] They had torn out one wall of the courtroom, and erected public galleries in the next room. They were building a bench for the four judges and their four 'alternates' (non-voting deputy judges) along the west wall, and a thirty-six-foot-long wooden dock along the wall facing them; there was an elevator in the wall right behind the dock, through which the prisoners could be brought in from the adjacent jailhouse.

The main defendants were housed in low-ceilinged cells barely seven feet wide by thirteen; they slept on metal cots bolted to the floor along the left-hand wall. To one side of each cell's narrow steel door was a porcelain toilet bowl, set back slightly in an alcove. It was the one place which the sentinels, permanently watching their prisoner through the door's peephole, could not see. As at Mondorf, every glass window had been ripped out and replaced with Perspex. All electric wiring had also gone. Security and anti-suicide measures were paramount. While meetings with the prosecution officers were conducted across open tables, those with defence lawyers were confined to rooms where lawyer and client were separated by thick glass partitions, and a sentinel had to sniff all documents passed through the slide to make sure they had not been steeped in poison.

At seven A.M. each day a prison trusty handed each prisoner breakfast and a spoon through the Judas hole in the steel door. Water was poured through the peephole from a watering-can into a tin mug off which the handle had been ripped—another security precaution. The barber then came and shaved him. A truncheon-toting sentinel stood by to ensure that nobody spoke. 'Sentinels moving back and forth on the catwalks view the prisoners every half-minute,' reported Andrus to Jackson. At six P.M. each evening the prisoner's eye-glasses, pen, and wristwatch were removed, and the dim cell light was switched off at nine-thirty P.M.; a spotlight glared through the Judas hole all night long onto the prisoner's face, the only concession being that the current flowing through the lamps was reduced at night time from 220 to 110 volts.

Colonel Andrus had the visiting lawyers conducted through the adjoining jailhouse and they were allowed a peep at the Nazi bigwigs who had just arrived from Mondorf—Jackson, who had his son with him, recognised Hitler's haughty foreign minister among them.

'The real thrill of the trip,' wrote Bill, 'was going through the jail, where I gazed into the cell of von Ribbentrop, seated not six feet from me.' Ribbentrop was annoyed to be interrupted, as he was writing furiously, covering scores of pages in his large, jagged handwriting like Captain Nemo in the closing scenes of *Twenty Thousand Leagues Under the Sea*. 'Probably,' surmised the younger Jackson, 'he was preparing his defense. It was a strange sensation to see him caged there, and he was obviously very unhappy.' Further down the corridor, they found 'Field-Marshal Jodl' just staring glassily into nowhere; the next day Bill Jackson sat in on an interrogation of Wilhelm Keitel. Keitel seemed anxious to talk: 'Give those boys another month of solitary confinement,' opined the young American lawyer, 'and they will all be telling on each other or, as the District Attorneys say, "singing."'[15] Before leaving Nuremberg, the visiting lawyers were royally wined and dined by the U.S. Army, consoling themselves that it was all at German expense (Jackson intended to present the entire bill for these proceedings as an occupation cost.)

ON THE flimsy table in Hermann Göring's cell stood precious photos of his first wife Carin, of Emmy, and of his parents—his father in full plumed finery as governor of German South-West Africa. There was a snapshot of Edda too; she had just turned seven. 'Dear Daddy,' she had carefully written on the back , 'come back to me again soon. I have such longing for you. Many thousand kisses from your Edda!!!!' 'His health is probably not very good,' an American officer warned higher authorities on August 15, 'and on two recent occasions he was to be found in his dressing gown and pajamas in bed, as a result first of a slight heart attack … and bronchitis.'[16]

The prisoners were allowed pencils and paper to write private letters; but these, Andrus admitted, were 'promptly sent to the chief of interrogation,' Colonel Amen, leaving the prisoners puzzled and disconsolate when they got no replies. 'We've been permitted to write letters and postcards for two months,' Keitel would note in October, 'but no replies have been received.'[17] This, along with the meagre rations and lack of exercise, was part of the prosecution's programme of psychological warfare, designed to wear the prisoners down.

By the end of August, the general health and morale of all the prisoners were declining. Concerned, Andrus asked the German prison doctor Ludwig Pflücker for an explanation; Pflücker blamed the poor food and lack of human contact. Andrus allowed an improvement in the food, and relaxed the ban on Pflücker speaking to the prisoners. Pflücker would later testify that Göring was suffering repeated heart attacks at this time; but he was a urologist, not a heart specialist, and he had no heart instruments to make a proper examination.[18] On August 21 American officers marched Göring up three flights of stairs to an interrogation and to perform the meaningless ritual of 'discharging' him from the German armed forces. Short of breath and suffering stabbing heart pains when he returned to his cell, he suffered a severe heart attack that night. An American doctor ordered him to bed for two days, and confidentially warned Colonel Andrus that unless the man was permitted thirty minutes of outside exercise each day, the next heart attack might be his last.

❖ ❖ ❖ ❖ ❖

Housing the growing army of lawyers in Nuremberg still posed a difficult problem, thanks to the achievements of the bomber squadrons. While still at the Grand Hotel, Jackson's team had cast about for suitable future billets. The British thought they would need about twenty-five people, the Russians and the French about twenty each. Jackson's party would be rather larger—closer to six hundred. He found the billets assigned to the Americans would be rather cramped, and there appeared to be only one bathroom in each house. There was another very good apartment house available and they went over to inspect it, but Judge Jackson did not have the stomach to go inside, as GIs were just in the process of evicting the 'poor devils' living there.[19]

As in the eastern provinces, eviction meant an army order to leave within a specified number of hours, leaving behind all furniture and fixtures, and the keys on the outside of the door. Regardless of what the Hague Rules on Land Warfare might say, private property did not exist in a country that had just lost a war. Before they left Nuremberg the younger Jackson obtained a cache of 'liberated' German weapons, and arranged to have them shipped back to the family home at McLean outside Washington—a veritable arsenal of S.S. daggers, stilettos, swords, sabres, Mausers, and the like.[20] Even lawyers feel entitled to the plunder of war, and items like these would in years to come prove very merchantable indeed.

Returning to London through Paris, Jackson learned from the

minister of justice that France was offering the post of her chief prosecutor to François de Menthon, a resistance figure who had been minister of justice in the exiled government in Algiers and had once been professor of international law at the University of Lyons.[21]

His own staff had meanwhile shed several members through petty jealousies: Francis Shea had returned to Washington for an operation, and Colonel Murray Bernays, one of the founding fathers of the trials, had left on August 21 as already noted, ostensibly on account of health reasons—in reality sick in other ways. 'He was "sick" when we left Washington,' wrote Bill Jackson caustically, 'and the real cause, I think, is that he wasn't given [the] jobs of the importance he thought he deserved.' Jackson junior thought it was damn good riddance too, 'for he used to badger and pester Father constantly with every kind of little piddling thing.' Before leaving Europe, Bernays sent what Bill called a 'megalomaniac' cable to the Pentagon, reporting that he was being released by the justice, and that 'the mission will not suffer.'[22]

TIME WAS already pressing. Under Soviet pressure at Potsdam, the victors had undertaken to publish the actual list of defendants by the first day of September.

The final cast of the victors was taking shape, but still there was no agreement on precisely whom to prosecute and hang among the vanquished. Back in London on August 23, Jackson found that the British idea of committee meetings seemed to consist of debating individual items of evidence—on this particular day they were reading through an entire speech by Hitler. 'We did, however, get down to selecting the defendants whose names are to be published by September 1st,' noted Jackson. The press would be given advance notification of the names three days before.[23]

As for the documentary exhibits, it seemed likely that Eisenhower's armies had seized the pick of the bunch. In Paris, Colonel Storey had begun exploring these mountains of documents—quarrying from them the collection of trial exhibits that generations of historians have come to recognise by the initials PS, or Paris–Storey.[24] The case was already assuming staggering proportions: 'We have just uncovered 250 tons of documents in Germany,' wrote Bill Jackson. 'In addition, we have also come across 3,000 frames of German microfilm, each frame consisting of a whole document.' He now doubted very much that they would be ready to go to trial before the end of October.[25]

The records had indeed survived in abundance, although since they were collected only for the purposes of prosecuting war criminals it would be foolish to attempt to write a history from these alone.[26] There is anecdotal evidence that in the forests outside Nuremberg the prosecutors made a bonfire one day of all the mitigating documents which would have aided the defence case. Volumes of private papers—among them Hitler's private correspondence with Eva Braun, her private diaries, and the diaries of Hans Lammers, Heinrich Himmler, and Hermann Göring—had however vanished into the hands of American and French looters and plunderers who had descended on the valleys around Berchtesgaden.[27] The British had seized General Alfred Jodl's diaries at Flensburg, but many of these too had vanished into unknown hands. Robert Kempner illicitly came into possession of the entire diaries of Alfred Rosenberg; these Kempner would retain hidden until his death, making them unavailable to Rosenberg for his defence; even now only the iceberg's tip of them has ever been published.[28]

Among the documents retrieved by the Americans were the entire war diaries kept for the governor-general of occupied Poland, Dr Hans Frank—who had earlier been Hitler's lawyer. Lieutenant Walter F. Stein, an Intelligence officer attached to the U.S. Seventh Army, found these forty typescript volumes at the Pension Berghof at Neuhaus, near Schliersee in Bavaria; Frank had used the hostelry as an office, and he himself voluntarily handed over the diaries, believing, like Speer, that such forthrightness would curry much needed favours from the prosecutors.[29] The Hans Frank diaries were taken to the Document Center which the Seventh Army had established in the library of Heidelberg University; here Lieutenant Gerhard Schaefer, an Intelligence officer attached to Jackson's office, would find them and order them removed to the courthouse at Nuremberg on September 20.[30]

To each of these Nuremberg documents was affixed a document number, from which cognoscenti can deduce its provenance. Those prefixed with a 'C' (for Crimes), namely C–1 to C–460, came from the British admiralty; those with a 'D' from the British prosecution team at Nuremberg; the 'EC' prefix went onto economic documents used by the Americans ('ECH' coming from the Heidelberg Document Center, and 'ECR' from that at Rosenheim.) 'L' signified a document from London, like the now notorious forgery 003–L, the report on Hitler's speech to his generals on August 22, 1939 which the anti-Nazi opposition had fed to Associated Press journalist Louis Lochner in Berlin. 'M', rarely used, were further documents from the British prosecution, while the 'PS' collection, from the Paris office of Colonel Storey, was the largest (4,021 items, occupying thirty feet of shelf-space) and most authoritative. A small collection of 'R' documents consisted of 589 items screened by Lieutenant Walter Rothschild of the London Branch of the O.S.S., and finally 'TC' was a series of documents from the British foreign office's Treaty Committee dealing with international treaties like Versailles, the Hague Convention on Land Warfare, and the Kellogg–Briand Pact that had purported to outlaw wars.[31]

To match these resources, the defence lawyers would have nothing but their wits and whatever papers they could dig up by their laborious researches.

❖ ❖ ❖ ❖ ❖

Until the very eve of the trial's opening, the squabbling about whom to indict continued. The names were selected with an appalling nonchalance, and Jackson's papers reveal the crass ignorance of the Allied prosecutors about the enemies they were setting out to convict.

He had set his heart on prosecuting organisations as well as individuals—the S.S., S.D., S.A., Gestapo, and Reich cabinet, as well as what he called the leadership corps of the Nazi party and the General Staff; but his staff were still wallowing in doubt about actual details and technicalities. Terms like the 'German High Command' and 'General Staff' had been bandied about for years without any real idea of what they were. 'You will remember,' Murray Bernays had noted to the younger Donovan, 'when we conferred with Lt. Rothschild about proposed groupings of defendants, we were very vague indeed about what the German General Staff really is and consists of.'[32] In fact in Hitler's time there was no General Staff for all the armed forces as there had been in the Great War—it was a figment of the Allied propagandists' imagination. The outcome would be that rather over a hundred senior German officers were indicted in later proceedings, linked only by their possession of high rank.

THE LAST few days before the date appointed for publication of the final list of named defendants, September 1, saw hectic telephoning between Washington, London, and Nuremberg. In a memorandum entitled 'Keitel, Dönitz, Schacht, and Krupp as War Criminals,' a British Foreign Office official warned that only Keitel was fit to be included on the list, as on the available evidence the three others 'should be acquitted.' In particular, 'The case against Dönitz is very much weaker.'[33]

The case against Grand Admiral Karl Dönitz was not without piquancy. Dönitz was the former commander-in-chief of submarines who had succeeded Erich Raeder as commander-in-chief of the German Navy in 1943, and had then been appointed by Hitler to succeed him as head of state in April 1945. On August 28 Jackson was handed a sober staff analysis on this personality, which concluded with the statement that the British admiralty had determined that 'there is insufficient evidence to sustain a charge against Dönitz,' and had abandoned its efforts in this direction. The author of this analysis, a naval officer, added with a trace of sarcasm: 'Unless additional information implicating Dönitz in political, as distinguished from military acts of criminality has been uncovered in the Foreign Office or elsewhere, it is believed that there is insufficient evidence to convict him or warrant his being tried. If, as it has been somewhat facetiously said, we should have some defendants whom we can acquit, then we should be wary lest we afford other defendants the opportunity to profit by such defense evidence as Dönitz undoubtedly can introduce on his own behalf.' Thus this officer, writing on behalf of the U.S. navy department, clearly endorsed the British admiralty's view.[34] We shall see later with what methods the prosecution sought to build up a false case against the admiral.

As for Dr Hjalmar Schacht, another of the proposed defendants, right at the outset of their investigations General Donovan had confidentially proposed to Jackson that they allow the Nazi banker to give evidence from the witness box against Göring, and to 'work his passage' out of the dock that way if he could. Jackson had angrily rejected this tactic—this was one of the reasons why Donovan would storm back to Washington in a sulk.[35] He regarded the former president of the Reichsbank as the most contemptible of all the defendants. He had provided the finance for the spectacular rise and rearmament of Hitler's Germany. More than any other, this man's financial genius had paved the way for the violation of the Versailles Treaty.[36] There was evidence that even after Hitler had dismissed him before the war Schacht had continued to revere him.

The defendant Krupp was the sorest point however. Justice Jackson had always believed that the intention was to represent the major German industrial trusts by including the younger Krupp, Alfried Krupp von Bohlen und Halbach, rather than his aged and ailing father Gustav, but when the first list of names was drafted for release to the press his staff complained to Sir Hartley Shawcross that Gustav's name had crept back on to the list instead. The list read out over the transatlantic telephone on the night of August 25 certainly spoke of the younger Krupp.

LONDON: '—and Alfried Krupp von Bohlen und Halbach.'
WASHINGTON: 'I don't get that last.'
LONDON: 'That is Krupp, the metals fellow.'
WASHINGTON: '—The munitions man?'
LONDON: '... Fritz Sauckel, Albert Speer, Martin Bormann—'
WASHINGTON: 'After Speer, who comes?'
LONDON: 'Martin Bormann!'
WASHINGTON: 'Is he still alive?'
LONDON: 'We don't know!'

The British had warned against putting more than ten names on the list. By August 29, with two days to go, the list already contained twenty-two; at the last moment, two more were suddenly added—Grand Admiral Erich Raeder and Hans Fritzsche, Goebbels' principal radio commentator, both of whom the Russians now disclosed were in their hands. Jackson could see little merit in putting Fritzsche on trial; but the Russians insisted, apparently because he was one of the few high-ranking Nazi prisoners in their hands.[37]

When the list was released that day to the press—embargoed until September 1—it was inexplicably still Gustav's and not Alfried Krupp's name that it contained. Jackson urged that it was not too late to find another suitable industrialist. The French proposed Mrs Bertha Krupp. It was after all Krupp's 'Big Bertha,' named after her, which had shelled Paris in the Great War.

Jackson sensed that American public opinion would not warm to putting a woman in this trial, given that death sentences were to be expected all round; he was still thinking of Alfried, but now there was a three-to-one vote against 'substituting' this man, because of the delay this would cause as much as the unpleasant publicity that would attach to such 'tinkering' with the list of defendants.

He resigned himself to prosecuting Gustav Krupp, and sent an assistant, Jim Rowe, down to serve the indictment on him at his hunting lodge high above Salzburg.

Rowe found that the aged industrialist was a barely living 'vegetable;' he was seventy-six, had suffered two strokes in 1942 and 1943, could neither speak nor understand, and was nursed by an equally aged wife. The O.S.S. biography of the man had mentioned everything else but this. 'The army insisted on having a GI [sentinel] with him night and day,' noted Francis Biddle with a chuckle, when he arrived in Nuremberg to act as the American judge. 'The American doctor who made a report on his condition thinks probably it would kill him if he were brought here, but I think the Russians will insist on that course.' If it came to a showdown, noted Biddle, 'we shall outvote them.'[38]

Small wonder that Jackson, writing to his fellow chief prosecutors two months later, would object that 'Gustav Krupp's physical condition seems to be so bad that it would be most unwise to produce him at the trial.' The new Soviet prosecutor General Rudenko, who turned out to be a large and jovial Ukrainian, agreed but asked for expert medical evidence to explain to the public why Gustav Krupp was being dropped from the trial. The industrialist was examined by one British, one Armenian, one French, and three Russian doctors: their report left no doubt that he was senile and could not be tried.[39]

Since Martin Bormann was still absent the final line-up would thus probably be twenty-two:

Reichsmarschall Hermann Göring, commander-in-chief of the Luftwaffe and chief of the four-year plan;

Grand-Admiral Karl Dönitz, commander-in-chief of the German Navy from January 1943, and designated by Hitler in his political testament as his successor as Reich president (not 'Führer');

Grand-Admiral Erich Raeder, his predecessor;

Dr Hans Frank (governor-general of occupied Poland);

Dr Wilhelm Frick, Reich minister of the interior;

Hans Fritzsche (chief radio commentator);

Dr Walter Funk (Reich minister of economics and Reichsbank president);

Rudolf Hess (until May 1941 the Führer's deputy as chairman of the Nazi party);

S.S. Obergruppenführer Dr Ernst Kaltenbrunner (from June 1942 chief of the Reich Main Security Office, R.S.H.A.);

Field-Marshal Wilhelm Keitel (chief of staff, High Command of the Armed Forces, O.K.W.);

General Alfred Jodl (chief of the O.K.W. operations staff);

Dr Robert Ley, leader of the German labour front, D.A.F.;

Constantin von Neurath (Reich foreign minister until February 1938, later Reich protector of Bohemia and Moravia);

Franz von Papen (until July 1934 vice-chancellor; thereafter Hitler's Special plenipotentiary in Austria and ambassador in Turkey);

Joachim von Ribbentrop (Reich foreign minister from February 1938);

Reichsleiter Alfred Rosenberg (Reich minister for the occupied eastern territories from July 1941);

Gauleiter Fritz Sauckel (the Führer's general plenipotentiary for manpower);

Dr Hjalmar Schacht (Reich minister of economics until 1937, Reichsbank president until 1939);

Baldur von Schirach, Hitler Youth leader and gauleiter of Vienna;

Dr Arthur Seyss-Inquart (Reich commissar of the Netherlands);

Albert Speer (Reich minister of munitions from February 1942);

Gauleiter Julius Streicher (gauleiter of Franconia; publisher of the *Stürmer*.)

Of these thirteen were lutheran—Göring, Ribbentrop, Keitel, Frick, Funk, Schacht, Dönitz, Raeder, Schirach, Sauckel, Speer, Neurath, and Fritzsche; five were catholic, namely Ley, Kaltenbrunner, Frank (a recent convert while in custody), Papen, and Seyss-Inquart; the rest, Hess, Rosenberg, Streicher, and Jodl, listed themselves as non-sectarian.[40]

❖ ❖ ❖ ❖ ❖

At the time the list was finalised, Jackson was out of the country. He spent the end of August 1945 touring southern Europe with his pretty secretary and son. True, he might have used some of the time more usefully to sit in on interrogations and soak up some of the history of the case which he was about to prosecute. Ostensibly the purpose of his travels was to investigate the simultaneous translation equipment used by the old League of Nations at Geneva, to ask the pope whether the

Vatican had any war crimes evidence, and to have a look into the Italian war criminal situation; his ulterior purpose, however, and who can blame him, was to soak up some sun at the U.S. Army's lavish rest hotel on Capri.

He learned of the fate of the Italian fascist leaders from General Richmond, the U.S. Army's judge advocate for the Mediterranean theatre. Richmond told him informally that they had been 'thinned out pretty thoroughly,' and that in the north 'they have been pretty ruthlessly treated.' It is curious that Jackson did not inquire more closely into this encroachment on the preserves of his international Tribunal.[41] In Rome the U.S. Army's Colonel Charles Poletti, whose military government territory included northern Italy, confirmed that the 'fascist criminals' had been pretty much eliminated 'or are in the process of elimination,' and he assured Jackson that the Italians were showing pretty good judgement in the process. 'He did not,' recorded Justice Jackson, 'think there was much material for the International Tribunal in Italy.'[42] In short, most of the available necks had already been wrung.

While in Rome, Jackson, a protestant and freemason, had an audience of the Pope, who had been the papal nuncio in Berlin at the time of Hitler's accession to power. He had always been against the Nazis, His Holiness now professed, and while he had admittedly concluded the Concordat with Hitler in 1933—becoming the first great power to recognise the new Führer state—this had been done only in order to make things as endurable for his flock as possible. The Nazis, he added sadly, had not honoured the agreement. 'But,' noted Jackson, 'he was especially concerned that the whole German people should not be charged with criminality. He thought that was unwise and unfair, for he knew that many people had incurred considerable risk in opposing the Nazi regime.'

Jackson assured him that he had never considered all of the German people to be criminals. 'If the Germans had all been with him,' he argued, 'Hitler would not have needed concentration camps, the Gestapo and the S.S.'

His Holiness agreed to provide evidence to the prosecution at Nuremberg, if it were desired.[43]

The American ambassador in Rome, Alan G. Kirk, had also served previously in Berlin as chargé d'affaires. He impressed Jackson however only as something of a dilettante, a 'professional bachelor.' Over a flamboyant luncheon he told Jackson of his great liking for Hermann Göring, who was surely an aristocrat with little real liking for the Nazis and their ways; Jackson kept his own counsel on these remarks, and returned to London.[44]

Jackson's main concern was that the doctors might be whittling down Göring's drug dosage too fast, and that they might lose their biggest prey to a simple heart attack. Göring must not escape the noose. Flying home for a few days to Washington, the judge complained about the doctors to the Pentagon. 'I was concerned lest he die,' he wrote heartlessly in his diary, 'and was not in the least concerned that he be reformed.'[45]

He intended Göring to perish, but not one minute before his judges decided.

9: Those Boys Are Out for Blood

AFTER THE four powers signed the London Agreement on August 8, 1945, with its Statute setting up the first 'International Military Tribunal' at Nuremberg, diplomatic pressure was brought to bear on other countries to associate themselves with it. Altogether nineteen of Germany's enemies, representing nine hundred million people, would join their signatures to the London Agreement. Two did not—Canada and South Africa; whatever their reason, these two British dominions stayed out.

The fact that four-power agreement was secured at all was due primarily to the diplomacy and bargaining tactics of Justice Jackson. He would write privately a year later,

> Our Agreement of London of August 8, 1945 went beyond anything in history in its explicitness in outlawing aggressive war. But conditions which made for the success of those negotiations do not exist today. All governments had recently pledged to their own peoples that they would punish the Nazi war criminals. The only thing unsettled was the procedure and charges. On these matters the United States held all the aces, and we played them for all they were worth. The Americans had most of the high-ranking prisoners and we had captured the important evidence. Nobody else could conduct a really impressive trial without us.
>
> On the other hand we were in a position to conduct such a trial without the help of any other nation. Repeatedly during the negotiations I took the position that the United States would proceed alone to deal with its own prisoners if we could not come to an agreement. This was very persuasive in obtaining agreement on principles and methods. But even with these aces in my hand I was unable to get a definition of 'aggressive warfare' written into the Agreement, although I proposed the one which, in substance, had previously been agreed to by Soviet Russia in treaties with the Baltic States.[1]

Explaining later why the court was called a military tribunal, Jackson wrote that the most compelling reason was to distinguish it from civil courts everywhere—so that it would not be subject to any precedents, and so that its proceedings could not in turn create a precedent for civil courts elsewhere; moreover, the court was sitting in a country under military occupation, with no civil government.[2] It was unfortunate, as he himself admitted, that the Tribunal itself was purely a four-power court, and that the victors must thus seem to be sitting in judgement on the vanquished; but he argued, 'The scale of their attack leaves no neutrals in the world'—a view with which many countries other than the Big Four would emphatically have disagreed.

IN THE United States, as details of the Statute were announced during that second week of August 1945, strong legal doubts were voiced.

Jackson's mail began to contain letters of condemnation from colleagues of the American Bar, who felt that he had degraded the Supreme Court by accepting the role of chief prosecutor in a political show-trial; but Jackson was convinced he could both uphold the integrity of his judicial status and push out the frontiers of international law.

The chief justice of the United States disagreed, becoming quite outspoken in his criticism: Harlan F. Stone wrote that while he personally would not be disturbed if the victors put the vanquished to the sword as was customary in days of old, he was disturbed to have this action 'dressed up in the habiliments of common law.'

The plan to indict entire organisations found little favour either. In August 1945 the popular American magazine *Saturday Evening Post* published a finger-wagging article entitled, 'We Try Criminals—Not Classes.' In September the *New Yorker* added its weight with a call for frankness: 'It would be a tremendous help if the lawyers and judges entrusted with the trials would state the matter candidly and tack a big *ex post facto* sign over the courtroom door. It would be a help for instance if people were to grasp that the trial of a [Vidkun] Quisling or a Pétain differs essentially from the trial of a Göring or a Keitel. Quisling stood trial in Norway, on Norwegian law, charged with betraying his country. This was a matter of law and order. Göring will stand trial in no man's land, on no man's law, charged with befouling the earth....'[3]

In November the *New York Times* took up the assault on Jackson, quoting some of the U.S. Army's more outstanding combat generals as being wholly opposed to the prosecution of soldiers for obeying orders issued by politicians; in Germany, the newspaper pointed out, in a reference to the hated Morgenthau directive 1067 issued by the joint chiefs of staff, American officers were being ordered to accept responsibility for political measures they privately condemned as un-American, of which the worst were the 'so-called Gestapo methods used in handling Germans' employed by refugees hurriedly drafted into the U.S. Army during the war.

The cataract of criticism showed no signs of abating. In December

1945, the *Army and Navy Journal* would bluntly describe the Nuremberg indictment of the German High Command as Jackson's attempt to discredit the military profession as such. Jackson hoped that when they saw the evidence unfold these writers would change their tune.

❖ ❖ ❖ ❖ ❖

Not only were the Allies seeking to convict their enemies under laws which had not existed at the time of the alleged offences, but under the London Statute they were specifically ruling out a number of obvious defences which would have immediately been raised: the German defendants might not plead that as soldiers in a Führer state they were bound to obey the orders that were issued to them; nor could they point out that on more than one occasion each of the prosecuting powers had committed precisely the same crimes as they were alleging against the Germans (the defence of *tu quoque*.)

The Tribunal would hold that the London Statute was a valid exercise of the legislative power of the only sovereign authority for Germany, and Lord Justice Lawrence, the British president of the Tribunal, would recall that it had been laid down long before by Lord Mansfield in a famous case, *Campbell* v. *Hall*, that 'conquest' invested the conquering power with the prerogative right to 'make what law he pleases.' It was a case which Adolf Hitler might equally have invoked in his defence, had he shown much inclination to be guided by case law.

In vain would the defence lawyers argue that this was *ex post facto*, or retroactive, justice. 'As far as crimes against the peace are concerned,' they declared, 'the current proceedings have no lawful basis in international law, but are a trial based on new criminal law, a law drawn up only after the actions complained of.'[4]

They argued further that the cast-iron principle of *nullum crimen sine lege, nulla pœne sine lege* (in the absence of a law there can be neither crime nor punishment) was a general rule, which in normal circumstances would militate against the punishment of people for acts which were not against the law at the time committed. Nuremberg, said the Tribunal simply, was an exception. 'In so far as this is an appeal against the jurisdiction of the Tribunal,' ruled Lord Justice Lawrence, rejecting the defence application, 'it conflicts with Article 3 of the Statute and it can not be entertained.'[5] Besides, it might be argued, in view of the Kellogg–Briand Pact of 1928 to which Germany was a party (in terms, a renunciation of war between nations) aggressive war was already a crime by 1939.

The retroactive nature of the Nuremberg legislation nonetheless troubled many legal minds, and few greater than that of the Justice of the U.S. Supreme Court William O. Douglas. 'In our view of the law,' he would write,

> nobody can be convicted on the basis of having broken an *ex post facto* law.... In my view the Nuremberg trials applied this kind of law against the defendants. Hitler and his ilk were guilty of multiple murders and under common law deserved the death penalty. But they were not indicted under the relevant national laws. Before the Nuremberg trials the crime of which the Nazis were convicted was never considered to have been such an act under our criminal laws, nor was it held by the international community to be under threat of the death penalty. [6]

AS ALREADY mentioned the lawyers who had drafted the London Statute had taken good care to exclude in advance the defence of 'higher orders.' Article 7 of the Statute had laid down that the official position of a defendant whether as a head of state or as a responsible official of a government department would not be accepted either in exculpation or in mitigation of punishment. Under Article 8 moreover it was allowed that where a defendant could prove he had acted on the orders of his government or a superior officer this would not be accepted as exculpation, but could be used in mitigation of sentence if this appeared proper in the opinion of the Tribunal.

This rule conflicted with the manuals of military law existing at the outbreak of World War Two on both the German and the Anglo-American side. Article 47 of the German *Militärstrafgesetzbuch* provided: 'If a criminal law is violated in the execution of an order the superior issuing that order is alone responsible. But the subordinate obeying that order is liable to punishment as an accomplice, firstly if he exceeds the terms of the order issued to him, or secondly if it was known to him that his superior's order meant committing an act which would be a crime or misdemeanour under civil or military law.'

The Allied governments had however taken account of this problem already, in a curious act of foresight, during 1944. It had been pointed out to the British authorities that Article 443 of their *Manual of Military Law*—under which, according to the Geneva Convention, all British trials of enemy prisoners-of-war must take place—had specifically stated since 1914: 'It is important to note that members of the armed forces who commit violations of the recognised rules of warfare such as are ordered by their Government, or by their commanders, are not war criminals and cannot therefore be punished by the enemy.'

Article 347 of the American *Rules of Land Warfare* was similarly couched: 'Members of the armed forces are not punished for these crimes, provided they were committed on the orders or with the permission of their government or commanders.'

After the Moscow Declaration of October 1943 the Allied legal authorities had their attention drawn to the fact that if there were plans to put as many Axis war criminals on trial as possible, the principle of 'superior orders' could prove 'very troublesome.'[7] The clause was therefore surreptitiously changed in the British manual in April 1944 and in the American manual seven months later to strike this potential weapon out of any enemy defence counsel's hands after an Allied victory.

AT NUREMBERG, the defence attorneys would also be prohibited from referring in mitigation to illegal acts committed during the war by the victors. Lord Justice Lawrence would interrupt the lawyer defending the High Command to say, 'We are not trying whether any other powers have committed breaches of international law, or crimes against humanity, or war crimes, but whether these defendants have.'

Thus lawyers were refused permission to introduce a captured British official *Handbook of Instruction on How to Conduct Irregular Warfare*, instructing commandos on how to treat German prisoners: 'Adopt some of the methods of gangsters.' 'Remember, you are not a wrestler trying to render your enemy helpless, you have to kill.' 'Kick him or knee him as hard as you can in the groin. While he is doubled up in pain get him on the ground and stamp his head in.' Following diagrams in this booklet, German prisoners taken during the Dieppe raid of August 1942 were trussed in such a way that every movement would result in slow strangulation, the so-called 'death slings.'

As for Allied saboteurs, the German High Command knew that these men parachuted into occupied Europe with revolvers strapped under their armpits designed to fire forwards when the arms were raised in apparent surrender; German records contained at least one such proof, where the saboteur's parachute had failed to open and circumstances allowed the internal device to be inspected at close quarters.

Any properly constituted British or American court would have considered this to be information of material value in assessing the background of Hitler's orders for the ruthless execution of commandos and saboteurs falling into German hands.

❖ ❖ ❖ ❖ ❖

Robert Jackson returned to Washington to report to President Truman.

In his absence, his son held the fort at Nuremberg and looked around for a suitable house for them to live in. Once, on Sunday September 9, 1945, getting involved in what he unfeelingly called 'the widows-and-orphans department,' he drove out to Neuhaus, near Veldenstein in the forests outside Nuremberg, to visit Göring's wife 'at one of their ninety-nine castles,' as he wrote to his parents, adding: 'She was obviously a very fine woman, and of great character.' Bill was willing to believe that she had had no idea of the criminal acts which the Reichsmarschall had been perpetrating. As for Edda, she was as cunning as any little girl he had seen—blonde hair done in pigtails, blue eyes, infectious smile. She curtsied to the officer and offered her hand, and he was struck by the tragedy of the whole situation.[8] 'It made me feel a bit cruel,' wrote Bill, 'to be trying to hang little Edda's daddy as a war criminal, but then he never hesitated to have thousands of other people's little girls killed, because they were Jewish.' He and his fellow officers ransacked the now humble Göring household for things worth 'liberating' before leaving; they found no documents but several suitcases packed with his effects including monogrammed pyjamas and 'one suitcase packed full of dope.'[9]

Two weeks later Anneliese von Ribbentrop arrived in Nuremberg from Munich bringing her daughter, and pleaded for permission to visit her husband, the imprisoned former foreign minister, as they wanted him to change his last will and testament. They were realistic enough to realise that he would be executed. Justice Jackson refused to see them. His son explained to the two females that what he called 'this macabre bit of foresightedness' could not be accomplished as the prisoners were allowed to see no one. Again, he could not help feeling sorry for Mrs von Ribbentrop, as she too seemed 'a rather good person.' The daughter however he dismissed as a hulking, arrogant German blonde with the curling sneer so typical of the Hitler youth—'hardly a good suppliant for mercy.'[10]

The Germans already accommodated in the jailhouse seemed a very mixed bunch. Lieutenant-General Walter Warlimont, deputy chief of the O.K.W. operations staff, exemplified the German national ability to work for the enemy side by making extensive suggestions to the Americans; he even drew up in his own handwriting for Jackson a secret short-list of about twenty former colleagues and ministers he believed should be prosecuted as war criminals—including his two immediate superiors in the O.K.W., Field-Marshal Keitel and General Jodl. 'Warlimont,' summarised Keitel's attorney, '[was] very tricky, and definitely an acquired taste. Wanted just to get off the hook himself without under any circumstances exonerating [Keitel]. All the positive things had been done by him, all the negative—that was the Chief.'[11]

As his defence lawyer Keitel had chosen the elderly, highly educated Professor Otto Nelte. Nelte was concerned only to establish absolute historical truths. Keitel's son found the attorney a cultured, good-looking man with clever hands; but the field-marshal's wife Lisa found the lawyer too gentle and too intellectual and without much fight in him. After it was too late the field-marshal himself expressed doubts about whether the court had given due credit to his lawyer for his ruthless search for objectivity and the truth. Nelte, who was well informed about the goings-on outside the prison walls, described on visits to Keitel's son, who was imprisoned like his father, the situation in enemy-occupied Germany as being disastrous, with 'revolting characters' now in control. Experience showed, commented the lawyer, that those with the foulest past were the ones who hollered the loudest.[12]

❖ ❖ ❖ ❖ ❖

A paralysing regime of psycho-terror had been enforced on the defendants even before the indictment was served on them. They were held in solitary confinement in the Nuremberg jailhouse. Like the millions of ordinary German prisoners in American hands, they were kept on a near-starvation diet. Field-Marshal Keitel, sixty-three years old, lost thirty-three pounds between May and October, eighteen of them during the eight weeks after his arrival at Nuremberg. Hess was an empty husk of his former robust self. Ribbentrop was gaunt, hollow-cheeked and frail. It was self-evident that all of these factors were not without effect on the prisoners' health, morale, nerves, and powers of resistance. 'The conditions we are living under here,' wrote Keitel in his private papers, 'are not enviable given the last five months of uncertainty about the fate of our people, our family, and our own person. Apart from the interrogations we hear nothing whatever about what is going on in the world outside the prison and even then only by chance. We have been allowed to write letters and postcards for two months now; no replies have been received.'

From five-thirty P.M., as dusk fell, the older inmates could only sit and brood in the dark in their cells, because after their eye-glasses were taken away it was impossible to read in the light coming in from outside. Every evening on Andrus' orders the tables and chairs were removed from the cells. As there was nothing to hang clothing and underwear on, the prisoners were forced to lay the clothes on the dirty stone floors. 'The needs of personal hygiene which are provided for with soap, toothpaste, and a once-weekly shower are incapable of keeping pace with the unhygienic side of life in a prison cell—the filthy mattress, blankets, towels etcetera.' Exercise in the open air or outside in the gangway was limited to ten minutes a day.[13]

TRUMAN HAD nominated the former attorney-general Francis Biddle to act as the United States judge at the Tribunal. Biddle was no friend of Jackson's. Talking things over with the president on September 5 in Washington, Jackson agreed, though without enthusiasm, to the appointment; he himself proposed Judge John J. Parker, a burly, four-square American, as Biddle's alternate judge, and this was accepted. 'I discussed with him the question of whether the appointees should have military rank,' wrote Jackson, 'and he thought that was camouflaging the matter'—as it was—'and that military rank was unnecessary. He would let them sit as civilians.'[14] Thus the International Military Tribunal which had never been international in character, but four power, or even more narrowly, a victors' tribunal, was no longer military either.

Biddle's appointment was not universally welcomed. He was not popular in the war department, and Herbert Wechsler, whom Jackson had invited to assist at Nuremberg, privately suggested that it would in fact be improper for either him or Biddle to accept office on the Tribunal, since both of them had been close to the U.S. government at the time that the plan for the prosecution of the war criminals originated.[15] A properly constituted court might have accepted this as a strong ground for recusing the judge; but Nuremberg was clearly going to be no ordinary tribunal, and Biddle did not regard himself as disqualified, although he was hurt when Jackson asked him not to bring along his wife, stating that this would arouse feelings against him among the other lawyers who were not so privileged.[16]

While in Washington Jackson also warned John J. McCloy, under-secretary of war, that General Betts, the judge advocate-general in Europe, had shown him the latest instructions issued under the joint chiefs of staff directive 1067, whereby as many as two million Germans were to be rounded up as criminals. Jackson had urged that the instructions be regarded as authority rather than an obligation. The Pentagon confirmed his suspicions, that the treasury officials of Henry Morgenthau had pressed the 'severe and sweeping' terms of the directive on them.[17]

❖ ❖ ❖ ❖ ❖

Together with Elsie Douglas, Robert H. Jackson flew back to Europe from Washington, finally landing on the Orly airfield outside Paris at 1:15 A.M. on Wednesday September 12, 1945. They had the big C–54 transport plane all to themselves. The flight took much the same tortuous course as the trial looming ahead. A few hours out over the Atlantic, the pilot turned back toward Washington with a faulty fuel line, but after several more hours the line cleared and the pilot had turned back east and refuelled at Bermuda. The judge's son Bill was waiting at Orly to meet them. They spent the morning in Paris, followed by a busy day in London, during which the attorney-general Sir Hartley Shawcross informed him that the Poles were insisting on the right to appear in the case and prosecute Hans Frank—yet another complication—then flew to the city which was to be their destiny, or nemesis: Nuremberg.[18]

Bill had found him a large, roomy house to live in at No. 33 Linden Strasse, in tree-lined grounds that boasted a tennis court. The judge found it ironic that he was having to live like a prisoner. 'Our house,' he wrote to Irene, 'is surrounded with a high concrete wall and barbed wire fence. It is patrolled at all times of day & night by several guards. At the great iron gate are guards and no one can enter unless we answer the phone to admit them.'[19] Inside this house the lawyers found a music room furnished in the style of what Bill called 'a tired Louis XIV'; but there was a magnificent Steinway grand, liberated from some unfortunate German household, and a lesser piano in the drawing room, and the Americans pounded away on both instruments every night.

The table in the dining room was big enough for a bowling alley; Jackson noted he could seat twenty-five guests easily. The house was embraced by several open sun porches, and furnished in what Bill called that curious combination of calculated ugliness and utility that marks German houses, including 'all the gadgets that so delight the German heart.'

Jackson's bodyguard, Private Moritz Fuchs of Fulton, N.Y., slept next to the front door, armed to the teeth. 'Fuchs stays up as long as I do ... follows me to lunch & eats with or next to me.... They call him my shadow.'[20] Bill Jackson facetiously wrote to his mother that he thought they would be safe from everything except 'atom bombs.'[21] Hitler's armour-plated limousine had been driven up from France for Jackson's use, but he probably never used it, preferring a snappy Mercedes-Benz instead.[22] This limousine had belonged, he was told, to Ribbentrop: each new chauffeur had the same trouble mastering the six forward gears and countless gadgets installed for the luckless foreign minister whom it was now Jackson's duty to prosecute.[23]

A German housekeeper, Mrs Hassell, who had spent five years in the United States, ran the household with a maidservant, but the food was cooked and served by GIs. The food was plentiful—'I'd hate to be paying for all this fluff,' wrote Jackson junior to his mother.[24]

The first days were as disorganised as the furniture of that house. A woman wrote that the Führer was hiding at a cave near Julius Streicher's farm, the Pleikershof; Bill Jackson went off to fetch him, and returned, as his father wrote, 'Without Hitler but with some loot from the Streicher place'—Herr Streicher, languishing behind bars in the jailhouse with Ribbentrop, being in no position to prevent it.[25] Jackson and his staff finally moved to Nuremberg on September 16.[26] 'Sitting in the warm sunshine under a beautiful Bavarian autumn sky,' he dictated the next day, as he waited for the trial to get off the ground, 'the war seems remote and our mission a little weird.'[27]

UNDER ARTICLE 2 of the London Statute there were to be four judges, one for each of the four powers, each provided with an alternate without voting rights. There was still some feeling that the judges on the Tribunal should have military rank. In fact three of them were civilians. Only the Soviet judge was a soldier—the same General I. T. Nikitchenko who had left London as the chief prosecutor early in August.

The French and British prosecuting teams arrived at Nuremberg on the morning of September 21. Jackson detailed his son to show them over the jailhouse. 'Those boys are out for blood,' wrote Bill privately later that day. 'They've even suggested we use a guillotine!!'[28]*

* This proposal was not as off-base as it sounds. The Nazis had routinely used the guillotine during the Third Reich—e.g. to execute Reichstag incendiary Marinus Van der Lubbe and would-be Hitler assassin Maurice Bavard, a cousin of Hjalmar Schacht. The Germans continued to guillotine condemned criminals in the British Zone in the first post-war years.

The British had appointed Sir Geoffrey Lawrence, a lord justice of appeal, as their judge for the Tribunal; he was a popular, if elderly gentleman–judge who had won the Distinguished Service Order for heroism as a gunner in World War One. The British alternate would be Sir Norman Birkett, a witty and popular fellow, who had taken Silk twenty years before, and who got on well with both the Russians and Americans. At a meeting of the American Bar Association in Indianapolis a drunken American lawyer had once flung a confidential arm around his neck and blurted out, 'What I like about you, Birkett, is that you are not one of those condescending sons-of-bitches that they so often send over.'[29]

As for the French judge, Professor Henri Donnedieu de Vabres, an imposing figure with a Georges Clemenceau moustache, there were some unexplained question-marks in his immediate past, as with so many leading figures of the French establishment. There were indications that he had gained this prestigious posting to Nuremberg through the influence of his son, a political aide to General de Gaulle. The left wing regarded him as a reactionary, even German-minded, theorist—a sort of intellectual sympathiser with the Nazis. Dr Raphael Lemkin, one of the Jewish experts on the fringe of the American prosecution team, called de Vabres a 'narrow-gauge professor' and noted that before the war he had visited Germany at the official invitation of the chief Nazi lawyer Hans Frank—now one of the Nuremberg defendants—and that he had remained in Paris during the German occupation of France; de Vabres had even managed to publish a seven-hundred-page book in 1943 at a time when paper was scarce and its rationing closely controlled by the Germans.[30]

❖ ❖ ❖ ❖ ❖

As the expert on international law Dr Alfred-Maurice de Zayas has pointed out, although the tribunal regarded itself as a court of international law, in reality it was an inter-Allied occupation court as Germany had not agreed to the establishment of such an extra-national authority.[31] The make-up of the Tribunal flew in the face of the separation of powers which democracies had preached ever since the French revolution as the sole guarantee for the individual against the excesses of the state. 'If legislator, judge, and prosecutor are one and the same person,' naval judge advocate Otto Kranzbühler, Dönitz's attorney, later argued, 'this fact alone will be enough to entertain powerful misgivings as to the outcome of their activity.'[32]

Jackson, Maxwell Fyfe, Falco, and Nikitchenko had all participated in the negotiations on the London Statute: together these jurists had drafted the retroactive laws to be applied and had even compiled the list of defendants. Jackson and Fyfe would now surface in Nuremberg as chief prosecutors; Nikitchenko first as chief prosecutor and then as the

Soviet judge, and Falco as the French alternate judge. On top of this was the fact that Francis Biddle, who would appear here as judge, had drafted a memorandum in his capacity as U.S. attorney-general at the time of the Yalta conference in which he had set out basic propositions for the Statute and added the declaration that in his view certain Nazi organisations were criminal. 'It would be turning a blind eye on harsh reality,' said Kranzbühler, 'if one were to argue that under these circumstances the judges were independent and unprejudiced.' In any other legal system it would have been possible to reject such judges because of their evident bias. At Nuremberg however this relief was, said Kranzbühler, denied to the defence attorneys by the Statute itself.[33]

While Jackson was warmly surprised by the high calibre of the Soviet jurists he was to meet here at Nuremberg, as a team they remained an enigma to him—they were from a different world. The Americans had equipped the Russians, like the other prosecutors, with Hitler's automobiles to drive around in. With their secret-police commissar, Rasunova, they were however a law unto themselves. Counter-Intelligence Corps officers reported to Jackson that they had traced the source of a flood of counterfeit Deutschmarks in Nuremberg back to members of the Soviet prosecution team. These Russians feigned complete ignorance of the English language until untoward incidents occurred, and of these there were several.

In Nuremberg the driver of the Russian chief prosecutor, General Roman Rudenko, would be shot and fatally injured while sitting in his car outside the Grand Hotel late on December 8; he said an American soldier had opened the door and shot him. There were immediate rumours of an attempt on Rudenko's life; but more likely the intended victim was Likhatchev, a chief examining magistrate attached to the Soviet prosecution team. Likhatchev, a former interrogator at Moscow's notorious Lubyanka jailhouse, had conducted Russian pre-trial interrogations of Hans Frank among others.

His interpreter O. G. Svidovskaya recalled later,

> We spent many of our evenings in the restaurant of the Grand Hotel … where half-starved Germans entertained the Allies to the best of their abilities. One day we—that is Likhatchev, Grishayev, Boris Solovov and I—wanted to drive over to the Grand Hotel as usual. But something came up and I stayed home. Likhatchev's party drove into Nuremberg in a very conspicuous limousine; it was a black and white Horch, said to be from Hitler's own car pool, upholstered in red leather inside. Likhatchev used regularly to sit on the driver's right. This time Grishayev and Solovov alighted and walked into the Hotel. A minute later somebody pulled open the car's right hand front door and shot the driver Buben at point blank range. I myself think they were gunning for Likhatchev and assumed he'd be sitting in his usual seat. All Buben could say was: 'An American shot me.'[34]

The Soviet communist party organ *Pravda* published an angry article, and Jackson wrote to Rudenko apologising and promising an investigation.[35] Nothing came of it. In 1953 Likhatchev's career came to an untimely end when he and three others were shot by firing squad for falsifying evidence.

A FEW MONTHS after his driver's death Rudenko requested Jackson's permission to remove a body from the American Zone—the body of his assistant prosecutor Major-General Nikolai Dmitriyevich Zorya, one of the Soviet team's leading and most personable lawyers. Jackson was told the Russian had 'perished owing to the incautious usage of a firearm.'[36] Inquiring further he was informed that Zorya had been cleaning his gun when it accidentally went off: Jackson noted privately that it was unlikely that as a lawyer the man would have had a gun, or that as a major-general he would have cleaned it. 'In the third place,' added Jackson, 'it was peculiar that he should clean it with the muzzle against his forehead.' His experts reported that Zorya had been shot by somebody at close range. After mature reflection, Jackson washed his hands of the affair. If the Russians wanted to settle their disputes this way, they could: we shall return to the Zorya affair, in context, later.*

❖ ❖ ❖ ❖ ❖

For three weeks Jackson wrote no daily diary, frustrated by the cumulative delays inflicted on the opening of the trial. At the Palace of Justice the cafeteria had not been built, there were not enough translators, the prosecutors had still failed to establish their staffs at Nuremberg. Sir David Maxwell Fyfe made a flying visit from London, but only to introduce Colonel Harry J. Phillimore who would be representing him in his absence.

Before arriving, the English airily asked Jackson to get out all the documents for them to run their eye over; Jackson informed them that there was already an entire room full of exhibits, some seven thousand of them already. 'But the work is the most fascinating I ever got into and no doubt will be the outstanding work of my life,' he wrote, consoling his wife on his protracted absence from the family nest. '[My] opening speech … must be my best ever.'[37] The British pressed Jackson to go to London to work there on the indictment with them. He wanted them to centralise the work in Nuremberg. The British accepted his draft on conspiracy; he agreed to their drafts on war crimes and crimes against humanity.

There were three broad areas of disagreement. Jackson wanted to include Hitler's General Staff as a group; when the British opposed, it was put to the vote and carried by three to one. Jackson's proposal that

* Page 228.

they add certain defendants to be representative of each organisation was however defeated with three to one against. Finally, the Russians stirred up a hornet's nest by presenting a draft which speciously included Latvia, Estonia, and Lithuania as Soviet territories, and when the American negotiators demurred General Rudenko announced that he would have to return to Moscow for a couple of weeks for instructions. The state department advised Jackson to accept the Russian terms, but to hand over a letter stating that this did not amount to formal recognition of Soviet sovereignty. This was how things stood as Jackson left for Berlin on October 6 for his first meeting there of the chief prosecutors.[38]

The meeting at the Control Council offices was already in session, except that the French had already left. The prosecutors now agreed between themselves the sequence of trial events—who should speak first and who last, and in what order the evidence should be presented. The British wanted each defendant handed a proper list of documents; the Americans resisted.[39]

Jackson had bagged for himself the actual opening address, the keynote speech of the whole trial, and he invited Jowitt, the British lord chancellor, to attend when the time came. He asked Jowitt to wear all his finery, to add pomp and circumstance.[40]

10: **I'm Running the Show**

THE TWO American judges appointed for the Nuremberg Tribunal, Francis Biddle and John J. Parker, were sworn in on the last day of September 1945 in Washington.[1] Biddle was a Democrat, Parker a Republican. They took an oath which bound them among other things not to query the legal instrument under which they were to act, namely the London Statute. They left in the *Queen Mary* for Southampton—sailing rather than flying, so as to have time to discuss their whole approach to the trial.

Francis Biddle had been born in Paris, and had arrived in the United States as a child. He had taken his law degree at Harvard, served as private secretary to the legendary Supreme Court judge Oliver Wendell Holmes, and risen to the rank of Roosevelt's attorney-general in September 1941, winning for the government nineteen out of the twenty cases he had argued before the Supreme Court.[2] He had a record of concern for human rights; unlike the British he had refused to allow the handing over of Russian prisoners to the Soviets.[3] One of Roosevelt's more exuberant New Dealers, he had been dismissed as attorney-general by Truman in June 1945; unwilling to tell him to his face, Truman had simply directed his aide Steve Earley to telephone Biddle, saying he wanted his resignation by the next afternoon. Truman offered Biddle any place in the government except the next Supreme Court vacancy, which he had earmarked for somebody else. Until he was appointed to the historic Nuremberg assignment, Biddle had resigned himself to returning to his law practice.[4]

The *Queen Mary* of 1945 was a dirty but proud ship, her rails carved with the initials of the troops she had conveyed across the Atlantic to Europe's battlefields. The Canadian prime minister William Mackenzie King was making this crossing with them, as were the journalists Ed Murrow and William Shirer, who were to cover the trial for the radio and the *Herald Tribune* respectively, and—in one of those ironies unnoticed by history—the former British chief of air staff Sir Charles Portal, whose bombers had killed more than a million Germans during the war.[5] 'Parker,' noted the domineering Biddle on October 3, after two hot days cruising across the warm and fuzzy ocean, 'is ready to do anything I suggest.' A couple of days later he persuaded Parker, a reclusive man who reminded him of a lonely schoolboy in need of mothering, to call him by his first name.[6] Notwithstanding all this, Parker still found the courage to enter opinions at the coming trial which differed strongly from those of Biddle.

The American lawyers travelling with them included Quincy Wright and Herbert Wechsler, the assistant attorney-general. Both of these foresaw the obvious problems in international law posed by the trial, namely that both the procedure and any sentences were *ex post facto*, but they agreed with the notion that the protocol signed two months before in London could be viewed as merely expressing a body of law which already existed, rather than as creating new law.[7] They were disturbed however by Jackson's ambition to have the Gestapo and S.S. condemned as criminal organisations. 'If we hold these organizations to be criminal,' observed Biddle, 'it opens the door to the Russians—to everyone in fact—to shoot on proof of membership, referring to our judicial approval. Not a very desirable result.'[8]

As they were crossing the ocean, Biddle had a disturbing conversation with Mackenzie King, a simple but much trusted statesman, from which it emerged that he had had a long, intimate meeting with Hitler in 1937, during which the Führer had impressed him that he had no quarrel whatever with Britain. The British, felt Hitler, should be free to control their empire; the Führer had expressed a desire for further heart-to-heart discussions with the Canadian prime minister, and in the summer of 1939 he had sent word over to Mackenzie King in Ottawa that he would be glad to cover the cost of inviting a large deputation to Germany, as many as twenty if the Canadian so desired, provided that they were unprejudiced. The prime minister told Judge Biddle that he had gained the impression that Hitler wanted only peace with Britain.[9] The prospect of that lost alliance still clearly exercised the Canadian now, after six years of holocaust and devastation.

THE BRITISH, French, and Russian judges were planning to convene in Berlin on October 8, and they invited Biddle and Parker to fly there direct from Southampton. Jackson had arranged a special plane for them, and after a stop-over in Paris they arrived in the ruined German capital at four P.M. on October 8, where they were housed in the luxurious mansion of the former Reichsminister Bernhard Rust. They had tea with Sir Geoffrey Lawrence and Sir Norman Birkett. The French also arrived, the 'funny little' Donnedieu, and his alternate, Robert Falco. The Russian judges were late as usual, not arriving until three P.M. on the ninth, having been delayed by fog.[10]

Sir Geoffrey Lawrence took charge of these judges' meetings right from the start, 'shoving' under their startled noses a brief agenda which did not even include the appointment of a temporary chairman. The Russians were piqued, and Lawrence subsequently explained apologetically to Biddle that he was 'nothing but a simple barrister and judge.'[11]

The Charter provided for rotation of the Tribunal presidency, but the Americans preferred one presiding judge. They persuaded the French, who had been wobbling, to follow their lead.[12] Jackson had gained the unwelcome feeling during the chief prosecutors' negotiations that the British intended to offer the presidency of the Tribunal to the American judge, Biddle, who he feared would be keen to accept. This would tilt the colour of the whole proceedings so much toward the Americans, who were hosting the trial at Nuremberg and who had provided most of the impetus for the prosecution, that Jackson expressed alarm. When General Donovan had arrived from the United States on October 8, he promised to put pressure on the British and French behind the scenes to share the burden of responsibility more widely; Jackson agreed to warn off Biddle in person.[13] He had never liked the man, and was not going to let him have this feather in his cap if he could help it.

Biddle in fact willingly agreed not to preside.[14] If we follow his account, he was the one pulling all the strings: following his suggestion they chose the Russian, General Nikitchenko, to preside temporarily over the sessions here in Berlin. A different president would run the trials in Nuremberg—the Russians nominated the American, but Biddle withdrew, as agreed with his own prosecutors, and nominated the Briton, Lawrence. As junior partners the French were hardly in the running, and there could be no question of a Russian presiding for the rest of the trial.[15]

Having thus won the presidency of the historic Tribunal, the Englishman Lawrence delivered himself of a brief but modest speech of acceptance. 'Of course,' bragged Biddle privately later that day, 'it would have been fun to preside, but I have no regret as this is the wiser choice. Lawrence depends on me for everything and I'll run the show.'

He expected the trial to open in about a month. The opening would be 'the great show,' with the closing and final judgement far less interesting.[16]

DISCUSSIONS ON how to frame the indictment had continued all summer.

In its final form it ran to 25,000 words, composed in a language that was often lurid and emotional. It contained allegations which no serious historian would now unblushingly venture to sustain, but which were designed to feed the appetite of the mass media. *Life* magazine summarised some of the main points. For instance, Hitler had forged a Hindenburg last testament in his own favour. Keitel had conspired to assassinate Germany's own envoy to Czechoslovakia to create an 'incident.'[17] Göring, it continued, had suggested that Nazi hoodlums kill more Jews instead of wrecking property.[18] He had dictated over the telephone a fake telegram of Austrian capitulation.[19] Hitler had threatened to kick Chamberlain in the belly before the eyes of all the photographers. Keitel had ordered in 1941 that Japan be drawn into the war.

Most outrageously, on General Rudenko's insistence at the very last meeting of the prosecuting staffs the indictment was amended to include the murder in the Katyn forest of 11,000 Polish officers. Point 3, paragraph C of the indictment would read: 'In September 1941 eleven thousand Polish prisoners-of-war were killed in the Katyn forest, near Smolensk.'[20] The Russians were fully aware at that time—as Mikhail Gorbachev would formally confirm on April 12, 1990—that Stalin had personally ordered his secret service, the N.K.V.D., to massacre altogether fifteen thousand Polish officers and intellectuals in April 1940.[21] The former N.K.V.D. officer Pyotr Soprunenko, who signed the death warrant, still lives (1996) in Moscow as an old-age pensioner.

Jackson was aghast at this Russian effrontery. The exiled Polish leaders strongly advised the prosecution against any mention of Katyn. For several days Jackson argued with the Russian prosecution team; but the omission of Katyn would, conversely, have pointed an accusing finger at Stalin, and adamant as Rudenko was that the British should not refer to the Stalin–Hitler pact, he was equally insistent that Katyn must be charged to the Nazi account. In the event, the other three prosecutors left it entirely to the Russians to state the Katyn charge in the trial, and the Tribunal was notably silent about the murders in its judgement.

On the count accusing the Germans of deporting populations, the indictment also displayed a troubling double-standard, branding this without hesitation as a 'crime against humanity'—when committed by the Germans. When the trial began, the French and Russian prosecutors would not mince their language as they described the deportations of one hundred thousand French Alsatians to Vichy France, and of a million Poles from Hitler 'Warthegau' into the Generalgouvernement of Poland. Thus the French chief prosecutor François de Menthon would charge in January 1946: 'Within a few hours the Alsatians were hounded out of their homes with scarcely any baggage and robbed of their possessions.' 'This inhuman transportation of entire populations,' he continued, 'will remain one of the horrors of our century.'[22] And referring to the deportation of Poles the Soviet deputy prosecutor L. N. Smirnov would allege, a few weeks further into the trial, 'In the occupied Polish territories village after village, town after town, city after city was evacuated of its Polish inhabitants. This process began in October 1939 as the village of Orlowo was purged of all the Poles who lived and worked there. Next came the turn of the Polish port of Gdingen. In February 1940 the forty thousand inhabitants of the city of Poznan were driven out. Thirty-six thousand Baltic Germans took their place.'[23]

At the same time as these thunderous words were echoing in the courtroom at Nuremberg about the deportation crimes of the Nazis, the Poles were doing precisely the same in their newly acquired territories, driving the native Germans out of East Prussia, Pomerania, and Silesia, relying on the Allied decision announced in Article XII of the Potsdam agreement of August 2, 1945. The German government now accepts that in the course of this chaotic, brutal, mindless 'population transfer' of fourteen million civilians more than two million lost their lives.

THE ALLIED indictment of the Nazis for the use of slave labour was even more cynical. Roosevelt himself had indeed approved at Yalta the deportation to the Soviet Union of hundreds of thousands of able-bodied Germans as slave labourers. With an eye to the coming trial, Jackson had been able to hinder the worst excesses, but pursuant to the Allied Control Council Proclamation No. 2 of September 1945, two hundred thousand German prisoners had been shipped to the Soviet Union. In April 1947 it was estimated that the Russians still held two-and-a-half million prisoners-of-war, while no estimate was possible of the number of civilians who had been deported for forced labour from the Russian Zone of Germany. The Americans were not entirely innocent of this charge either; they were not only supplying Italian prisoners to Belgian coal mines but demanding three marks per man, five marks per N.C.O., and nine marks for each officer; a few weeks later the Americans had to halt the similar 'slave trade' in German prisoners-of war with France until they were better fed.[24]

These looked like flagrant infractions of international conventions willingly entered into, and solemnly signed and ratified. The Geneva Convention on the treatment of prisoners-of-war prohibited any country from transferring its captives to the custody of any other country. Yet when the British war minister warned the cabinet that there were 'obvious political reasons' why Britain could not give any of her 160,000 German prisoners to the Soviet Union, Lord Cherwell—famous for his role in advocating the unrestricted bombing of civilians in 1942—discounted this and wrote to Churchill a week after the war ended recommending that 'the Germans can be used in gangs and the ardent Nazis transferred to the Russians, who, I am sure, will be able to alter their views.'[25]

Monetary considerations—the adjustment of the reparations balance-sheet to Britain's advantage—underlay this proposal too. In official British files is a cabinet-level memorandum on reparations, in which the transfer of two million German prisoners 'as slaves' to Russia was to be reckoned in the final settlement at £200 per head.[26] The cabinet's basic agreement to such deportations was communicated to Washington a week later, on May 27, 1945. A copy of the TOP SECRET memorandum is in Jackson's private files: the British cabinet would raise no objection to 'the use of German labour as reparation,' and recommended that fresh 'impressment of German labour' should continue for six months. As a sop to the moralists, the cabinet expressed the pious hope that countries using this labour would sign a declaration laying down 'certain minimum standards as to food, lodging, medical treatment, work, pay and period of service.' Under this agreement, the British and American administrations transferred to France hundreds of thousands of German prisoners. As stated, the French treated them so abominably that the other Allies finally had to protest.*

With the Nuremberg trial only half over, the Allied Control Council would promulgate a new law in the western zones in February 1946, under which all German males aged fourteen to sixty-five and all women aged fifteen to fifty were subject to forced labour. Refusal to work would lead to the confiscation of ration cards—a penalty declared to be 'inhuman' by the Tribunal when applied by the Germans.

❖ ❖ ❖ ❖ ❖

The American, British, and French chief prosecutors were ready on October 10, 1945 to file the indictment with the Tribunal; once again it was the Russians who objected, stating that their prosecutor General Rudenko was not present. Jackson sent his son off to Washington to report. 'Bill can tell you about the meetings,' he wrote to his wife that day. 'Pretty much a farce. Very sad in some ways—not that it is fatal, but it could have been so much better.'[27]

Rudenko did not arrive until Friday the twelfth. It was agreed that they would file the indictment in a public session on Monday and release it simultaneously world-wide at eight P.M. that night. On the Sunday before that however Rudenko found fault with the wording, and insisted on pettifogging changes which would delay its filing until Thursday the eighteenth. Jackson was furious, writing that Sunday night: 'Rudenko raised objections to the indictment: Firstly, it was inaccurate—the inaccuracies specified being trivial and wholly in the figures he had furnished. Second, his Russian translation was not accurate and must be done over.' 'What the real reason was,' observed Jackson darkly to his wife, 'we do not know.'[28]

IN FACT we now know that the Russians were growing uneasy with the whole prospect of the trial. It threatened to open the proverbial can of worms. On September 20 Stalin's chief prosecutor Andrei Vyshinsky had flown Soviet army lawyer N. D. Zorya from Moscow to London, to discuss with the foreign minister Molotov, who was conferring there, the thorny problem of 'undesirable questions' which the defence might raise at Nuremberg; and of such questions there were legion.[29]

The Tribunal duly learned of this fresh delay and to Jackson's unconcealed pleasure publicly blamed the Russians.[30] Privately he welcomed the postponement, writing: 'It gives us a few days more on the defendants and on our case.... Am putting time in doing & redoing

* See page 147.

the opening speech. It is an opportunity of a lifetime to say something worth while on international law.'[31] Judge Biddle gathered that Rudenko had asked for the postponement on the grounds that the indictment contained inaccuracies on the figures of Nazi victims in Russia and Poland. It was obvious from his inflexibility that he was taking orders from Moscow.[32]

Thus it was on October 18, at ten-thirty A.M., that the International Military Tribunal held its first—and last—public session in Berlin, in the large assembly room of the building of the Allied Control Council in Potsdamer Strasse. From here it would move to Nuremberg, where it would commence its proceedings in proper one month later.

WHILE THE lawyers thus bargained and haggled, the prisoners languished in Nuremberg jailhouse under conditions of considerable discomfort. Neither age nor rank nor former eminence sufficed to excuse a prisoner from harassment by Andrus' bored sentinels and NCOs, most of whom nourished grievances that because of these prisoners they were being retained in Europe long after their comrades had been returned home and demobilised.

The prisoners were at first not permitted to approach within ten yards of each other. For a time it was mooted that the prisoners be handcuffed even in the dock. Andrus refused to permit the International Red Cross access to the prisoners; the Red Cross Christmas packets were confiscated when they arrived.

The elderly Hjalmar Schacht was forbidden to sleep on his side; Field-Marshal Keitel, aged sixty-three years, of which he had been a soldier for forty-three, was plagued by boils on his neck, which went untreated for there were no medicines. 'In the absence of a chair with a back-rest,' wrote Keitel, 'the permanent back pains are a physical torment for a man of sixty years and more.'[33] Most of the prisoners suffered agonies of hunger and cold, for the cell windows were unglazed and the Perspex sheeting ill-fitting and draughty.

Field-Marshal Werner von Blomberg was dying a slow and agonising death from an untreated cancer. On February 13, the first anniversary of the devastating Allied air raids on Dresden, Field-Marshal Milch learned that Blomberg had not eaten anything for days, and that he was growing weak and apathetic; Milch told the German doctor that the field-marshal must be taken out to a hospital. 'The American doctor says the same thing,' Milch wrote that evening in his diary, 'but he's frightened that "out of general hatred" Andrus won't allow it.' 'It's terrible,' Milch continued, 'to see these people suffering so badly and not be able to help them!' That afternoon Blomberg was evacuated from the prison, and he died of cancer on March 13—on the Ides of March, the very day that Reichsmarschall Göring opened his last major counter-offensive for his country in this trial.

Only Speer found his conditions suddenly alleviated. After the first week or two of solitary confinement in a filthy cell with a straw palliasse and stinking, ragged blankets, directly across the gangway from Göring's cell, he was transferred to the sunny side of the prison and given a room with a proper bed. Here he was visited for the first time by Colonel Andrus. Each man had thought he had finally bidden farewell to the other at Mondorf. The prison commandant greeted the One Who Nearly Got Away with half-concealed sarcasm. 'Very nice to see you!' he said.[34]

In part the uncomfortable conditions were a result of the necessarily stringent anti-suicide precautions enforced by Colonel Andrus. A chair was permitted in the cells only during the day time and the table was of flimsy cardboard; neither was allowed within four feet of the windows.[35] When the Tribunal later ordered that prisoners were to be allowed the use of eye-glasses, pens, and pencils in their cells to work on their cases, a sentinel was posted over each prisoner throughout the time he possessed these instruments.[36] They were allowed to use the eye-glasses in court in case they had to read any documents. Knives were forbidden. All meals were chopped up fine to enable them to be eaten with a spoon. A prison barber shaved each prisoner with a safety razor in the presence of a GI.[37]

Despite all their security measures, there were occurrences that gave Andrus nightmares. A five-inch blade from a butcher's knife was found in the lining of witness Walter Buch's suitcase. The sharp, wafer-thin metal diaphragm from one of Göring's earphone headsets in the courtroom was found to have been removed. Each episode resulted in fresh strain on the prison guards, a strain which they then took out on their prisoners. Andrus later recorded that he had particularly felt the stress after the first of his prisoners committed suicide; two of his chief prison officers suffered breakdowns and had to be hospitalised.[38]

The prisoners inevitably protested at this treatment, and more than one wrote letters addressed to the protecting power (they were not forwarded); Andrus nipped further protests in the bud by stoutly and unilaterally declaring the Geneva Convention suspended—an impropriety which only the prevailing conditions and atmosphere of mutual hatred can explain.

> 1. You are hereby informed [so Andrus warned 'all personnel concerned'] that your protest against the treatment given you at this place is not only wholly unwarranted but is improper. It is based upon entirely false premises; as you are not a CAPTURED OFFICER nor a PRISONER-OF-WAR. The ARMY, the NAVY, and the STATE of Germany have ceased to exist. You are entitled to nothing under the Geneva Convention which your nation repudiated in it's [*sic*] entirety and also repeatedly violated.
>
> 2. You represent a group of people who for more than thirty (30) years have regarded treaties as 'scraps of paper' to be used only for

their own advantage and to be violated and destroyed when they applied to peoples other than the Germans....

His pronouncement continued with a not entirely unwarranted reference to Germany's treatment of her prisoners, particularly those in the concentration camps.[39]

Higher authority had evidently enforced new regulations during the intervening weeks since they had left the ASHCAN camp at Mondorf. In rules and regulations issued there in May 1945, Andrus had stated: 'All persons incarcerated within CCPWE#32 [ASHCAN] are considered to be PWs.' After warning that any prisoner-of-war attempting to escape would be shot, Andrus concluded: 'Violations will be punished in accordance with the Geneva Convention and Rules and Articles of War.'[40] Here at Nuremberg there was no more talk of Geneva or prisoner-of-war status.[41] The number of showers per week had however been raised from one to two; and Andrus ruled that, though saluting between prisoners and Allied personnel had been forbidden, bowing was still appropriate.[42]

SINCE THIS Tribunal had been set up to conserve and further the rule of international law, it deserves more than a passing comment that the Geneva Convention to which the Allied nations and Nazi Germany were parties provided expressly that no signatory could suspend its provisions for one full year after the cessation of hostilities, precisely in order to prevent such excesses. Moreover, far from repudiating the Geneva Convention, as Hitler had been invited to do by his minister Dr Goebbels after the fire-bombing of Dresden, he had refused (after representations made by, among others, Dönitz and Ribbentrop, two of the defendants at Nuremberg); he had also refrained from making use of his huge stocks of nerve-gases because of the conventions forbidding their use.

In short, the status of prisoner-of-war, with all the rights accruing to it, was protected by the Convention, and in law it was not within the gift of either Eisenhower or his superiors or his junior officers like Colonel Andrus to abrogate it.

❖ ❖ ❖ ❖ ❖

Unpleasant though the general prison conditions were, there were compensations. Andrus was determined not to lose any prisoners this side of the noose, and the health care laid on for them was better than for the German population outside: Albert Göring, Hermann's brother, would formally apply in December to return to Nuremberg jailhouse, where he had been held as a witness, for this reason (Andrus recommended that the request be turned down.)[43]

In addition to American army surgeons, doctors, nurses, and a dentist, there were four German medical staff: The German prison doctor was Ludwig Pflücker, an army physician with the rank of major who hailed from Bad Wildungen and was by profession a urologist. Assisting him were the senior dentist Heinz Hoch, a therapist Corporal Phillip Hambach, and a physiotherapist Private First Class Walter Haar who went the rounds with Pflücker.[44]

The Americans had taken Pflücker prisoner, stripped him of all his belongings, and imported him into the prison to look after the prisoners—accused and witnesses alike; for various reasons, Pflücker is worthy of special attention. He was very popular with the jailhouse inmates. 'He is every inch a doctor,' noted Streicher.

> With his northern build, blond hair and blue-eyes, he is always bursting with good humour. It would be impossible to think of the torments, large and small, of prison life without him. If the day that's dawning through the little iron-barred window seems grim, then it's his cheerful 'Good morning, how are things today?' that picks up the gloomiest prisoner out of his brooding and puts a grin on his lips. The American prison administration trusts him implicitly, and this has made it possible for him to do the prisoners many a little favour, like getting them a cigarette or a piece of chocolate or a few broken biscuits.[45]

This growing sense of cameraderie among the prisoners is important. The Americans had under-estimated the German mentality. Field-Marshal Milch, who arrived on October 12, brought back from England in the hope that he would be a witness for the prosecution, found himself subjected to such indignities in the prison that he resolved to work only for the defence, cost him what it might.

Prisoners in the witness wing heard through the prison grapevine of the astonishing physical transformation that Göring had undergone; Milch, the ailing von Blomberg—so long as he lived—and General Heinz Guderian formed one of the factions in this wing. A less appetising faction formed around the General Staff officers like Franz Halder, Nikolas von Falkenhorst, and Walter Warlimont. These generals established their own strolling patch in a hedged-in section of the prison garden where they let it be known that they desired to be left alone—a wish that the ministers and gauleiters were happy to accede to.

❖ ❖ ❖ ❖ ❖

During October and November 1945 the O.S.S. had laboured alongside the army lawyers to perfect the case against the accused. Their methods were often more foul than fair.

The private files of Justice Jackson provide disturbing evidence of tampering with and distortion of evidence. After the main film, *The*

Nazi Plan, prepared by the O.S.S. to illustrate the conspiracy charge in count I of the indictment, was shown secretly to Jackson's staff on November 14 they warned him that there was probably little the defendants would seriously wish to deny, and there was much that would benefit the defence which should be cut. 'I would,' wrote one expert to Jackson, 'in the cutting process eliminate the scenes which follow the [German] movement across the border in Austria, Sudetenland, and the Rhine, in all of which flag-waving, smiling faces and the presentation of flowers help to nullify our notion that by these acts the people were planning or waging a war against their neighbors.'[46]

A German film on the Warsaw Ghetto was also going to be shown. A major on Jackson's staff viewed it and was taken aback by the shots of mental defectives and of the ghetto police collaborating with the Nazis. He recommended that the film be totally suppressed for that reason. This was certainly the fate of another film, specially made to illustrate 'Reichsbank loot' at Frankfurt, since at the last moment it was found that there was no proof that the loot really had come, as claimed, from concentration camp victims.[47]

Naturally there were many among the prosecution team who continued, or wanted, to believe the more far-fetched atrocity legends. One American lawyer on Kempner's team wrote home at this time from Nuremberg: 'Imagine making dentists pull out all the gold dental work from the teeth of victims before they were killed and while still conscious! We have pictures of a soap factory where they hit the victims, mostly Poles, with a blunt instrument, and the heads are cut off and boiled in one vat and the bodies in other vats. Three hundred heads were found in one vat at the time of discovery.'[48] All of this was fiction.

So was much else that was sworn at Nuremberg. The Polish member of the United Nations War Crimes Commission had sworn an affidavit that human beings had been killed by steam in the Treblinka and Belzec extermination camps.[49] Three members of Jackson's own staff had provided a sworn affidavit testifying to the existence of lethal gas chambers at Dachau concentration camp—James B. Donovan, Lieutenant-Colonel Calvin A. Behle, of the judge-advocate general's department, and Lieutenant Hugh Daly, of the 32nd U.S. Rainbow Division.[50] The Czech prisoner Dr Franz Blaha had sworn to the same chamber's existence.[51] (The German government has long since certified that no lethal gas chamber was ever operated at Dachau.)

Similarly the Tribunal readily accepted the propaganda legend first inspired by the brilliant Soviet propagandist Ilya Ehrenburg to the effect that the Nazis had fabricated soap from the remains of their victims, and even stamped the soap with the initials RJF, 'pure Jewish fat.'[52] The Russians submitted to the Tribunal exhibits USSR–196 ('recipe for making soap from human bodies'), 197 ('statement of Zyg and Mazur'), and 393 ('samples of soap made from human bodies') to support this contention. For years since, such bars of soap have been part of an unwholesome trade among curiosity-collectors in Israel, and occasionally some are even ceremonially buried to the chants of the kaddish. Why the Nazis should have wanted to rub their faces in the boiled-down detritus of their sworn enemies remains an imponderable mystery. Although it is fixed in the final judgement of Nuremberg—and hence a criminal offence in modern France to contest the historical existence of such soap—Israeli archival experts publicly announced once more in 1990 that this 'soap story' too was and always had been a propaganda lie.[53]

As the German saying has it, 'Lies have long legs,' however. As late as May 1995 the soap legend was once more being obediently touted around by authoritative newspapers in Germany.[54]

11: Hess Can't Quite Remember the Reichsmarschall

BY NOW Rudolf Hess had been brought to Nuremberg too, flown over from Wales in a special plane on October 8, 1945. The same plane brought all the medical papers and diaries recording Hess' imprisonment in Britain.[1] In his own luggage he carried with him the paraphernalia that he had collected as a prisoner in Scotland, England, and Wales since the failure of his dramatic peace mission to Britain in May 1941—manuscripts on socialism, his health, the atom bomb, economics, and reconstruction, the texts of his interviews with Lords Simon and Beaverbrook, and a number of mysterious sealed packages. The latter, which contained the evidence he needed to prove that the British had drugged and poisoned him, were taken away from him despite his protests.

Hess was now fifty-two years old, and he was maintaining that he could remember little except his own name. He found it painted on the door of the upper-floor cell into which Andrus' sentinels now ushered him.

The new Nuremberg inmate played his amnesia for all it was worth, but he still had the presence of mind to put on his famous Luftwaffe uniform for his first interrogation the next day, October 9, by Colonel Amen. The official photographer captured the improbable scene—Hitler's deputy comfortably lolling back in a hard-backed chair, wearing fur-lined flying boots with knee-length zippers. Electing to answer the questions in German, Hess gained precious seconds to work out the right answers for a Man Who Knew Too Little. The verbatim transcripts contain some of the most powerful humour and poignant exchanges that the trial was ever to produce.

He admitted to his name, but when Amen asked, 'What was your last position?' he replied: 'Unfortunately, this already comes into a period which I cannot remember any more.... There are many cases where I cannot even remember what happened ten or fourteen days ago.'

The colonel gruffly asked him what period he could not remember. Hess obliged by saying: 'Anything longer than, say, fourteen days. It has frequently happened that I met gentlemen and I could not even remember their faces when I saw them again. It is terrible! Yesterday I was told by a doctor—or maybe it was a clerk—over there, that it sometimes happened that people don't even know their own names any more, and he said that perhaps a shock would suddenly bring it all back to me.' Adopting a pathetic air he added, 'This is terrible—everything depends on it for me, because I shall have to defend myself in the coming trial.'

'You mean that you cannot even remember what your last official position was in Germany!'

'No, I have no idea. It is just like a fog.'

'Do you remember that you used to be in Germany?'

'Well,' conceded Hess, 'I think that is self-evident: because I have been told so repeatedly. But I don't remember just where I was—or even what house I was in. It has all disappeared. Gone!'

A thought occurred to Amen. 'How do you know that any kind of proceeding is coming up, as you say?'

The deputy Führer played that one with a straight bat. 'This trial has been talked about all the time. I have seen it in the newspapers ... and only yesterday I was told about it. And then when I was brought over here I was told that it was for the trial in Nuremberg. Such a big event has naturally made an impression on me, and I can remember it; I am thinking of it all the time at night.'

'But you don't know what the proceeding is for?'

'I have no idea,' said Hess; but he could not resist poking this straight-faced remark at the American colonel: 'I know that it is a *political* trial.... Perhaps I have even been told what I am accused of. But I don't remember.'

'Do you remember how long you have been in England?'

'No ... when we left there, I was told that I had been at that place for a long time.'

Pushing across his desk a book of Nazi laws and ordinances which Hess had issued as Deputy Führer in 1937, Amen asked him if he had ever seen it before. Hess pointed to his signature: 'That there is me,' he said, and after reading the first few pages at Amen's request he continued: 'This is good, and there's no question about it.' But, as for having written it, his mind was a blank, he said.

'Don't you remember having anything to do with the enactment of various laws in Germany,' asked Amen. Hess expressed astonishment: 'You mean I myself ... enacted laws?... Not a trace of it. According to this,' he continued, fingering the book's pages, 'I must have—uh, how shall I put it—I must have had a very prominent position!'

Colonel Amen changed his tack. 'Do you know who Jews are?' he asked.

'Yes. They are a people—a race.'

'You didn't like them very well, did you?'

'The Jews? No.'

'So you had some laws passed about the Jews, didn't you!'

'If you say so,' said Hess.

AND SO this extraordinary dead-pan interview, bordering often on black farce, continued. 'Do you remember the Führer?' inquired Colonel Amen.

'Yes. During all that time,' said Hess, reminiscing on his imprisonment in Britain, 'I had a picture of him hanging in my room in front of me.' 'The Führer was the leader,' he explained, and risked adding: 'He was a personality who outshone everybody in every German's mind.' He conceded that he knew that the man was dead, but he could not explain how he knew.

'Do you think you have ever talked to him?'

'According to this,' said Hess, brandishing the book at Amen, 'I must have. If somebody constantly issues laws as deputy to the Führer, then he must have talked to him.'

Amen pounced. 'You *remember* that you were deputy Führer!'

'No, I see it from this book.'

After a while the colonel asked, 'Why don't you like the Jews?'

'If I had to explain that to you in detail, I am again facing nothing; I only know that this is deeply within me.'

Getting nowhere with that bait, Amen tried names: Ribbentrop's meant nothing to Hess. Göring's? 'Göring, yes … He means something to me.'

Amen leaned forward triumphantly.

'I read his name on a door,' said Hess, his face straighter than ever. 'I merely know the fact that he is here, and that he is some personality.' 'If somebody were to come into this room right now,' he volunteered, 'and you told me, "Here is Göring," I'd just say "Good day, Göring."'

And so it went on. Goebbels, Lammers, Brauchitsch, Keitel, Jodl, the High Command—all these names seemed meaningless to the prisoner. He knew that the war was over, but from having read yesterday's newspapers.

'Do the newspapers make sense to you when you read them?' fished Amen; it seemed a tricky question, and Hess hedged. 'Partly yes,' he said, 'and partly no.'

'Did you have a family?' asked the colonel, in a manner approaching a taunt.

Perhaps a silent twinge of agony went through the prisoner. For four long years Churchill had refused to him the right to return to his own lines that is allowed to any normal military emissary crossing the lines on a mission of peace, as Hess had come in May 1941. Twenty-five more years would pass before this proud man would set eyes on his son again. 'I have had the photos of my wife and my little boy hanging in front of my eyes,' he finally answered, 'alongside that of the Führer, all the time.'

For two hours this battle of wits went on, while hidden microphones recorded every word. He spotted one signature as a forgery, because it was written *Hess* and not *Heß*. He knew what an aeroplane was, as they constantly flew over his house in Wales. The word putsch meant, to his mind, a sound like a hand slapping water.

'How do you know the difference between an original and a copy?' Amen challenged, after the prisoner described one exhibit as an obvious original.

'This,' explained Hess helpfully to the American officer, gesturing towards a photocopy with his manacled hands, 'is a copy. And this is an original. It's obvious from looking at the document.' Asked whether he was a war criminal, Hess smiled: 'Evidently—otherwise I should have to be a murderer to have these manacles on.'

'What is a war criminal?' asked the colonel.

'I would prefer,' said Rudolf Hess, winning the final point, 'to ask you this question.'[2]

Brought back after lunch for a further session, Hess noticed Göring standing to his right, clad in his familiar, though now somewhat baggy, pearl-grey uniform. The Reichsmarschall beamed brightly at him.

'Will you look over here to the right,' said Amen. 'To this gentleman here.'

'At him?' said Hess tonelessly. His face was a blank.

'Don't you know me,' Göring coached him, his vanity punctured.

'Who are you?'

'We have been together for years!'

'That must have been at the same time as that book they were showing me this morning,' suggested Hess, and, dropping a broad hint to Göring, he added: 'I have *lost my memory* for some time—now of all times, before the trial.'

'You don't recognise me?' gasped the Reichsmarschall.

'Not personally, but I remember your name.'

For an instant time stood still, but nobody spotted Hess' slip: nobody had mentioned Göring's name, they were all revelling in Göring's deflated ego. 'Listen, Hess,' he said. 'I was the supreme commander of the Luftwaffe: you flew to Britain in one of *my* planes.... Don't you remember that I was made a Reichsmarschall at a meeting of the Reichstag at which you were present!'

'This is terrible,' said Hess with a sigh, while setting the scene for a Lourdes-like miracle: 'If the doctors hadn't assured me time after time that my memory will return some time, I should be driven to desperation.'

'Hess!' roared Göring. 'Think back to 1923.... Don't you remember how we both attempted a putsch in Munich?'

'The putsch was already referred to this morning.'

'Don't you remember how you arrested the Minister?'

'I arrested the minister?' gasped Hess. 'I seem to have had a pretty complicated past.'

Göring was instructed to stand aside, and Amen ordered Professor Karl Haushofer, the famous geopolitician who had been Hess' mentor during the long years when his father was a businessman in Egypt, to be brought in.

'MEIN GOTT!' gasped Haushofer, setting eyes on the emaciated and unshaven Hess, still handcuffed to a sentinel. Hess stared at him blankly. With tears in his eyes the professor besought him: 'We have called each other by our first names for twenty years.' He added, painfully for Hess, 'I saw your wife and your child, and they are well.' He took Hess' free left hand in his. 'May I shake your hand? Your boy is wonderful. He is seven years old now. I have seen him.'

Painful though this whole scene was for Hess—the confrontation with his old friend, and the news of his wife and child—he acted out his role with grim precision to the end. 'In order to calm down an old friend,' he said, his eyes expressionless, 'I can only assure you that the doctors tell me that my memory will all come back to me … and then I shall recognise an old friend again. I am terribly sorry.'

'You will see,' said Haushofer, 'it will all come back. Just imagine, your little boy—he has grown so high,' and he indicated the height with his other hand. 'He looks half like you and half like your mother.' He talked of Hess' mother and of his own imprisonment by the Gestapo after Hess' flight. 'I should like to look into your eyes,' said the professor, 'Because for twenty-two years I have read in your eyes. And I am glad to see that a little bit of recognition is coming back into the …. Don't you remember Albrecht,' he added sorrowfully, 'who served you very faithfully? That was my eldest son. He is dead now.' (The Gestapo had murdered him in Berlin on April 23.)

'It doesn't mean anything to me,' said Hess, although the death of Albrecht must equally have been a shock to him.

SO THE confrontation with Franz von Papen went too.[3] As Gauleiter Ernest Bohle was brought in next, Hess said simply, 'There's another gentleman I don't know.'

'That is *flabbergasting*,' said Bohle in English, in his native Bradford accent.

They had failed to crack Hess. He was frog-marched back to his cell, where he took a sheet of paper and began to keep a diary (aware naturally that it was going to be read by his jailers):

> Göring and an old gentleman who is supposed to have been acquainted with me for a long time were brought face to face with me, apparently in order to ascertain whether I would recognise them. I did not recognise them.

❖ ❖ ❖ ❖ ❖

The next day, October 10, Amen asked Hess pleasantly enough:

'How is your memory today?'

'It hasn't altered at all.' After a few minutes of idle chat, Amen's patience snapped: 'When did you get this idea of losing your memory?'

Hess mildly asked him how such an idea could have helped him.

'For instance, when you directed the murder of various people—which you did!'

'I did that?'

'Yes,' bluffed Amen. 'So the witnesses say.'

'You mean,' suggested Hess, 'that, because I can't remember it, *your* witnesses are less credible?'

'Uh, somewhat,' said the colonel helplessly, losing himself in Hess' logic.

Hess pointed out that he was about to go on trial for his life. 'There is only one thing that I can do at the coming trial and that is to fight for my own skin with everything I have: and the only instrument I have to fight with is my brain and my memory.'

JACKSON WAS disturbed by this fresh problem, coming on top of what the doctors now told him about the declining mental health of the former labour front leader Robert Ley. On October 12 he wrote in confidence to Dr John Millet, the leading New York psychiatrist who had approached him in June, asking him to recommend a list of reputable specialists, since he might now have to commission examinations of 'some of the high Nazi officials' in advance of the trial.[4]

He handed this letter to his son Bill to carry on a No. 1 priority flight to the United States, together with a sealed letter to hand to President Truman; he told Bill to discuss with McCloy's office at the Pentagon the difficult problem posed by the 'mental condition of Hess and Ley,' and to represent it as Jackson's view that these two prisoners must be examined by outside psychiatrists of outstanding qualifications, not just some second-rate specialists from within the armed services. In this connection the judge mentioned the names of Edward A. Strecker, a professor of psychiatry at the University of Pennsylvania whom he knew to possess a collection of 170 human brains, and Oscar Diethelm of the Payne Whitney Clinic in New York.[5]

He and his staff kept Hess under careful scrutiny. Jackson's assistant Thomas J. Dodd asked Franz von Papen during an interrogation on October 13, 'What do you think? Do you think his mind is really gone?'

'It seems to be. I found him very changed, and his face too.... That he didn't recognise any of those people, and the way he spoke. It must be insanity.'[6]

They forced Göring onto Hess again. For an hour or more the Reichsmarschall coaxed and wheedled, but Hess still refused to recognise him. Losing patience, he bellowed: 'Now look here, Hess, it wasn't simple for me to come here and talk to you, because I too have to concentrate.' He tried again. 'Do you remember the Führer?'

'Well, I know what he looked like—I had a picture in my room.'

'Do you remember the way he spoke?'

'His picture didn't speak.'

'You refuse to remember,' Göring finally shouted. 'You refuse to *want* to remember!'

Colonel Amen, who had been listening on earphones outside the room, burst in and roared: 'Do you still think that you will be better off at the trial if you refuse to remember anything?'

Hess suggested that it would be all the same whether he remembered anything or not. He returned to his cell and entered in his diary:

> Göring tried for an hour to refresh my memory—in vain. He told me that when I fled to England I was said to have left a letter behind for the Führer.

His diary filled with bizarre notes. Were they real, or for the benefit of prying eyes? 'Great excitement,' he wrote on October 17, 'because I made a fuss over not getting the things I had asked for from my baggage. Afterwards I was told that I could make a complaint to the Commandant, but that I must not shout at people.... Have hung up small notices in the cell saying: QUIET PLEASE. DO NOT SHOUT AT PEOPLE. One of the officers who came in said this was a good idea.'

Several specialists interviewed him during the coming weeks. Captain Richard V. Worthington reported that Hess' family background had seemed stable and comfortable—he had been born in Egypt into a wealthy German business family. His earliest memory was at age three, the birth of a younger brother, and the family giving him a toy horse-drawn gun on that occasion.[7] The British doctor who had accompanied him over from Wales warned that Hess had in fact manifested symptoms of total amnesia from October 4, 1943 until February 4, 1945; and again since July 12, an amnesia from which he had not so far recovered. 'Also,' reported the army psychiatrist Major Douglas McG. Kelley, 'while in England Hess claimed he was being poisoned and sealed up numerous samples of food, chocolate, medicine etc., as "evidence" to be analysed prior to his trials.' Whatever the truth of the allegation, Kelley pointed out, either this behaviour was also simulated or it was a true paranoid reaction.

Using Rorschach cards (the ink-blot patterns) Kelley found pointers in them to a highly schizoid personality with hysterical and obsessive components. Hess complained bitterly of 'stomach cramps' which seemed to be neurotic manifestations. His amnesia was currently limited to everything that had happened after he joined the Nazi party. Kelley suggested what he called 'chemical hypnosis,' a technique requiring the injection of sodium amytol or sodium pentothal—in other words the use of intravenous truth drugs. He admitted that there had in the past been fatalities using such techniques. In conclusion, Kelley found 'internee Hess is sane and responsible, and he attributed Hess' amnesia to conscious malingering.[8] 'The American doctor,' Hess recorded blandly in his diary, 'was quite definite in his assurance that my memory would be brought back by one single injection.'[9]

Colonel Andrus was against any experimentation with drugs, given Hess' suspicions of the English. He warned Jackson: 'Treatment with drugs might call forth the same suspicion or allegations against us by him.' Moreover, in his mental condition undue alarm might well cause further injury.[10] The O.S.S. general Donovan was keen to use truth drugs on all the prisoners. Jackson instructed on October 20 that there was to be no treatment whatever involving the use of drugs which might cause injury to Hess.[11] They could not afford to lose any prisoners before the trial.

❖ ❖ ❖ ❖ ❖

After that first and last Tribunal session in Berlin, the American judges had moved down to Nuremberg. The French had gone home to vote, the British were fogbound in London, the Russians were sulking in Berlin. The American senior judge Francis Biddle liked the Soviet general Nikitchenko more the more he saw of him; the French were nice enough, but no good at getting anything started. 'The British,' he observed sarcastically, 'are all right if they get their tea every day, but if not, then not!'[12]

To Judge Biddle it seemed that Nuremberg had suffered far worse as a city than Berlin. The people looked broken in spirit and half alive, although there seemed to be more movement here than in the capital.[13] He was billeted in a large badly furnished house about twenty minutes' drive from the Palace of Justice.

In the courthouse he had been assigned a big office with two large windows: one window overlooked the prison and exercise yard, but everybody was forbidden to look out of it.[14] When they inspected the courtroom, Parker and the other alternate judges found to their annoyance that their chairs were to have shorter backs than those of the full judges. Insulted, they insisted on getting chairs of equal stature. That was just the first problem. There were no fresh eggs or milk in the city, even for the Americans, but Biddle found there were plentiful supplies of scotch, brandy, and white wine and these commodities would enable him to pass the months here virtually without pain.

Chief U.S. prosecutor Robert H. Jackson meanwhile was under a guard scarcely less close than the prisoners. Day and night, everywhere he went, he took Moritz Fuchs, his personal bodyguard, and a jeep-load of soldiers followed his heavy Mercedes-Benz around. Most mornings there was still no electricity in Nuremberg, and he had to shave by candle light. The water had to be chlorinated with tablets before they could drink it, because of the air-raid corpses still lying buried under the rubble; like Biddle, Jackson sought both solace and safety in liquor.[15]

Not speaking any German, the American lawyers had difficulty sizing up their opposing lawyers; they regarded most of them as Nazis, even when they were very definitely the opposite. The German lawyers had almost unanimous contempt for the Americans, more respect for the British, and an unspoken fear of the Russians. Jackson, said Keitel's attorney Dr Nelte, was not objective, but was vain and pig-headed, and impelled by a visceral hatred of everything German.[16]

More seriously, the American judges also began disliking Jackson. Without him and his idealism, none of them would be in this hell-hole. The U.S. Army had long made known its distaste for the whole procedure. As Judge Biddle sarcastically noted on October 21, 'The Army of course is not interested in, as a GI put it, bringing out six hundred men'—a sly reference to Jackson's growing prosecution staff—'who overrun the whole city, and sit around drinking and crapping at the Grand Hotel ... to kill twenty-four.'[17]

The prosecution staff in Nuremberg rapidly mushroomed to the scale of an industrial-sized law office. There would soon be 120 lawyers from the various armed forces and civilian agencies; there were forty interpreters in addition to the 180 translators employed by the translation divisions. The duplicating machines churned and clanked for twenty-four hours day. Together with the infantry soldiers protecting the entire operation, there were about five thousand men to be fed by the army mess each day; to these would soon be added the four hundred newspaper and radio journalists housed in the press centre, for which, since the lawyers had reejected it, the Americans had turned over the Eberhard Faber castle at Stein outside Nuremberg—a tasteless extravaganza of sunken baths and murals of youth, marriage, middle- and old-age, but also illuminated by a beautiful and much admired chandelier. Shuttle buses would convey the war- and world-weary pressmen each day to the Palace of Justice once the trial began.[18]

PRE-TRIAL interrogations of the Nazi generals were in full spate. It never occurred to these men who regarded themselves as upright Prussian soldiers to demand to have a lawyer of their own present. The prisoners were prize booty just like the Nazi medals and Mausers, and nobody read any Miranda formula to them: they were never cautioned as to their rights, because they had none. Bill Jackson sat in on some of the sessions, watching Colonel Amen's technique of extracting information from the more prominent witnesses. 'I spent two days with Göring,' he wrote, 'who has quit his dope and lost weight; he squirms and sweats when caught in a lie, but occasionally tries to crack a feeble joke.' Göring, in short, would present little problem, from his account.[19]

In fact Göring was one of their shrewder customers.

'Considering that it is eight years ago,' he said, when Amen pressed him about the danger-fraught Hossbach Protocol, 'it is almost impossible for me to pin down what the Führer said in 1937.'

He also refused to countersign the transcripts of these interrogations.[20]

When Robert Kempner, taking over the interrogations, bluffed that he had evidence incriminating Göring in the Reichstag fire from both Rudolf Diels, his first Gestapo chief, and from Erich Gritzbach, his chief aide, Göring laughed out loud and affably demanded to be confronted with the two gentlemen. That was the last he heard of them.[21]

All of the accused tended to place the blame on Hitler, whom they believed to be dead, or on Bormann, who was missing.

'Von Papen, whom I sat in on yesterday, is a slick article,' recorded Bill Jackson. 'The professional diplomat and practised liar. Johanna Wolff, Hitler's secretary, is a garrulous old bitch.'[22]

'It is amazing,' wrote one of the American attorneys after observing the interrogations of Dönitz, Göring, and Hans Frank ('a real smoothie if there ever was one'), 'how much evidence the witnesses have furnished against themselves.' Frank had kept a voluminous diary which convicted him without any other evidence; this American attorney was struck by the Nazi lawyer's fair skin and his bright, piercing eyes: 'The veins come out on his face and you can see them throb when he is questioned [and] when he is under great internal tension; I noticed that the pupils of his eyes contract and expand alternately every few seconds when he is questioned, without regard to the amount of light on them.' Hans Frank's wife, interrogated by the Americans, claimed that he was really quite harmless and that S.S. Obergruppenführer Friedrich-Wilhelm Krüger was the evil genius who had brought him to this pass.[23]

Dönitz, as a naval officer, cut a fine figure, and gave what even this prosecution lawyer called 'a very plausible and convincing story' under interrogation. Göring was their natural leader—he had a swagger and a bluster which his captors found not unbecoming, 'sort of hail-fellow-well-met type; not such as we have always pictured him. But he is a son of a bitch just the same, and so are all of them.'[24]

THE PRISONERS had their own views of the interrogators. 'There wasn't one single Jew among the British,' the obsessive Julius Streicher was pleased to note. 'Nothing but Jews among the Americans ... and only one of the Russians.' To the former gauleiter, a veritable plague of them seemed to be infesting the jail building. 'Twice a day a uniformed female lieutenant (a Jewess) walks past and smirks into my cell as though to say, "There he is. He's not getting away from us this time!"' 'The interpreter with the pince-nez is a J., a professor at Columbia University. He often comes into my cell. He thinks I haven't spotted he's a J.'[25] Streicher was impressed by the Russians, however: They radiated an enormous energy. It was just a question of time before all of Europe belonged to them.[26]

A Soviet commission came to interrogate him; they asked if he had been sacked as a teacher for sexual misdemeanours.

Streicher retorted: 'Who told you that one?'

'It's in the newspapers.'

'Uh,' said Streicher, 'if you believe everything you see in the Jewish gutter press.' He advised them to read up the judgement of the Supreme Disciplinary Court in Munich, and they would find out that he had received an honourable discharge for his participation in the Hitler putsch in 1923. After a moment's silence the Russians exchanged taciturn nods and then said: 'That's all for today.' In his private diary Streicher noted: 'They'd have liked to chalk me up as a sex criminal. In the eyes of the public that would then have been game, set, and match against this Principal War Criminal.'

It had not escaped him that the 'Russian' interrogator this time looked '*verdammt* Jewish.'[27]

It was true that Julius Streicher was commonly seen by the Allies as a professional purveyor of antisemitism and pornography—'a dirty old man,' British novelist Rebecca West wrote of him, 'of the sort that gives trouble in parks.' The dog had long been given a bad name, and it should not have proven difficult to hang him; but of what should he be found guilty to that end? The precise terms of the indictment against him presented some problems. In September two officers of the U.S. judge advocate-general's office had visited the former German chancellor Dr Heinrich Brüning, who had got out of Germany while the going was good, in the spring of 1934—after receiving a secret tip-off from Rudolf Hess—and was now teaching at Harvard. The Americans had asked him whether people like Streicher should be let off. Brüning had answered that in his view the proper course would be for Streicher to be stood before a regular German court. 'Robert Ley would definitely be sentenced to death by a German court,' commented Brüning, 'and in all likelihood Ribbentrop too.'[28]

❖ ❖ ❖ ❖ ❖

On October 19, while psychiatrists closely studied their reactions, Colonel Amen visited each internee and formally served the 25,000-word printed indictment on him, together with a list of attorneys from which he might like to choose one. Copies were also handed to lawyers appointed to represent the indicted organisations like the S.S. and the High Command. From that moment the internees became 'defendants.'

This was perhaps the first turning point of the trial. As Keitel's lawyer, Dr Otto Nelte, later explained to the field-marshal's son, the defendants now had two possible courses of action: either unanimously to refuse to be interrogated and to testify in this trial, or to tell the unvarnished truth for history. Thanks to defendants like Schacht and Papen there had been no chance of establishing a unified front; this may well, he thought, have been the reason why they had been included in the indictment.[29]

Served with the indictment, Reichsmarschall Göring asked for an interpreter whom he could trust, and for an interview with his old lawyer, Hans Frank—also awaiting trial in the same jailhouse—about the selection of defence counsel. He would eventually pick Dr Otto Stahmer of Kiel. Stahmer was sixty-six—a clear fourteen years older than the Reichsmarschall; he had never been a Nazi, but had handled patent actions, naval labour disputes and other civil cases in Hamburg. As his assistant he took on Dr Werner Bross, thirty-one, who had been born in Kiel and had studied law at Heidelberg and Berlin.[30]

Hess, handed the document at 4:46 P.M., carefully recorded in his diary: 'Indictment handed to me. One hundred pages. I thumbed through it in five or ten minutes and read the headings.' Colonel Amen had asked him whether he was willing to be interrogated. Hess said he saw no point. Amen irritably asked if he was refusing further interrogation. 'In my opinion,' replied the prisoner, 'there is no difference either way: because nothing will ever come of it. I have read the indictment and it is completely devoid of meaning for me.… However, if the gentlemen desire to put questions to me, I shall be glad to *listen* to them.' Charged on all four counts, Hitler's deputy was turning into a very awkward defendant indeed.

THE SCOPE of the Allied indictment document deeply shocked some of the defendants. Albert Speer now believed he had lost his gamble. He would write to his wife a few days later: 'I have to regard my life as at its end. Only by doing so can I shape its closing acts in the manner that I deem to be necessary.… I have to stand here as a Reich minister, and not as a private person. I cannot have any regard for you or for myself. My only desire is to find the strength to see this through along that line. I'm in fine fettle, though that may sound odd; even though I have abandoned all hope I get uneasy and restless whenever I catch myself thinking that there might be some chance after all.… Perhaps I can still do something for the German people by setting an example.'[31]

After studying the indictment Keitel's attorney advised his client to answer with the truth, pure and simple. Keitel agreed with him one hundred per cent—you could not lie away documentary evidence, he said ruefully. That was how he intended to act on the witness stand. There was no point in trying to deny, he told his attorney, as the documents were all there—they had all survived the war with typical German efficiency. Many of them bore his marginal comments, and these were often characteristic of his temperamental nature. As Keitel said to his son months later, the Führer had been well aware of the illegality of the orders he had issued during the Russian campaign, but he had expressed the view: 'If we win, then might is right anyway. You can only win this mortal struggle with exceptional methods and the

Russians themselves will quite simply force us to adopt such measures by their own methods.'[32]

The deepest insight was shown in the private reaction of General Alfred Jodl, former chief of the operations staff. He wrote: 'I am seething with rage now that I have read the indictment. It's 1918 all over again. If this war is to have any meaning for the advance of mankind, then it has got to be that it leads eventually to a lasting peace for Europe, if not the whole world. But in that case, instead of the brute force that led to the war and brought final victory, there has to be an international system of justice that is recognised by all sides. Otherwise the nations of this world will not have advanced one step. —Well,' he added, betraying the still flickering flame of hope within him, 'the prosecution is not the same thing as the Tribunal.' And: 'What has particularly infuriated me is the summary allegation that all the defendants enriched themselves from the occupied territories.'[33]

Handed the indictment, Dr Robert Ley's first reaction was to ask for defence counsel, preferably 'a respectable Jewish attorney.' He and several of the defendants suffered nervous breakdowns. One or two contemplated suicide. 'Suicide,' Keitel wrote to his defence counsel on October 24. 'How often I have found myself seriously confronted with this as a possible way out, only to reject it because—as suicides have always demonstrated—nothing is changed and nothing bettered by such action.' The armed forces would have labelled him a deserter and coward. Hitler's suicide had been his 'final disillusion.'[34]

Major Kelley warned Colonel Andrus on the twenty-fifth nonetheless that the prisoners needed to 'work off' their great psychological tension, for which he recommended more outdoor exercise: 'Such tension causes an endocrine inballance [*sic*] which produces definite physiological changes.' Kelley named Hess, Keitel, Ley, Ribbentrop, and Sauckel as particular risks.[35] On the same day General Donovan recommended that the Tribunal be invited to appoint a commission to investigate Hess' state of mental health, as well as his ability to confer with defence counsel.[36]

Only a few hours later Robert Ley cracked under the strain. He scattered suicide notes around his cell, tore rags from his clothing and stuffed them into his mouth, then twisted a sodden army towel round his neck and waited until it strangled him. It cannot have been a pleasant death. The Americans buried him like a dog in an unmarked grave. They found in his cell a bulky folder containing hundreds of pages of partly demented writings—it included letters penned by him to his beautiful wife, who had killed herself during the war. Jackson locked it away and it was never forwarded to the next-of-kin; it is still among his private files.[37] Embarrassed by this further proof that his defendants were going out of their mind, he instructed his staff: 'I do not think we should release [the Ley file] because of the effect on the case.'

The simple fact of Ley's suicide was announced to the twenty-one surviving defendants and each was ordered to sign the announcement as having been read to them.[38]

HJALMAR SCHACHT scrutinised the column of signatures. He added his own, then laconically offered to the American sergeant: 'If you wanted me to, I'd make an "X" after each one you ought to shoot.'[39]

Streicher too seems to have toyed with the idea of hanging himself, but then he decided it was worth seeing this fight through. 'I think L. hanged himself,' he mused in his diary, 'because we aren't getting anything whatever from outside, not even shirts. I'm writing on a table which consists of a cardboard on a few strips of wood.'[40]

Göring was pleased at the suicide. 'Dr Ley was unstable,' he commented. 'He would probably have broken at the trial.' He was worried that Ribbentrop was showing signs of cracking too. 'I'm not afraid of the soldiers,' he told a psychiatrist, referring to Keitel and Jodl. 'They'll behave themselves.'

12: **An Honourable Criminal**

ON THE DAY of Ley's suicide Judge Biddle went down to Rome, following in Jackson's footsteps, for a vacation. Stringy as a dried-up fruit, the pope gave him a fifteen-minute audience, for which the judge dressed in striped trousers and a black jacket. His Holiness mentioned that Mrs von Papen had been in touch with him, and he asked the American judge to do what he could to see that the former vice-chancellor of Germany was given a fair trial. He mentioned too his distress that Robert Ley, another of his flock, had been driven to suicide.[1]

General Eisenhower had turned down the requests of the British judges, Lawrence and Birkett, to bring their wives over from England into his theatre. Both were gloomy about it, and threatened repercussions through the Foreign Office; but the supreme commander probably feared even worse repercussions if Mamie were allowed to come over, and stood firm against creating any precedent.[2]

Biddle lunched with Eisenhower at his villa at Bad Homburg—sipping the first fresh milk since arriving in Germany. 'He told us many interesting things,' noted Biddle, adding without further comment: 'He had to take back from the French prison camps 100,000 prisoners-of-war because the French had stolen their coats, clothes, and food. Many were litter [stretcher] cases.'[3] The French were not however alone in such excesses. Wilfully misinterpreting the terms of joint chiefs of staff directive 1067, many of Eisenhower's officers had begun the systematic starvation of prisoners who had entered American captivity at the end of the war.[4] Up to one million of them died of malnutrition, hypothermia, and disease.[5] In the eastern territories too, something like the Morgenthau Plan was being implemented with mindless savagery: seeking revenge, the officers of some camps in what had now become Poland had begun the systematic murder of their German prisoner-of-war internees.[6]

❖ ❖ ❖ ❖ ❖

Headed by Sir David Maxwell Fyfe, the British prosecuting team arrived in Nuremberg on October 24, 1945, little suspecting that they were to become bogged down in legal battles here for nearly a year.

They were housed at the village of Zirndorf, five miles to the south-west. The British chief prosecutor was given the mayor's former villa at No. 7 Goethe Strasse.

'Phillimore talked to me for two hours after dinner,' grumbled Maxwell Fyfe in a letter the next day. 'Counting the judges' staff there are now 168 British personnel. Even cutting out the judges' people and guard, I am responsible for over 100, and have to approve billeting, transport, messing and the like.'[7] 'Everyone has something wrong,' he added a few days later. 'Lord Justice Lawrence has no top sheet and one straw pillow. Mr Justice Birkett has no separate house; if the military counsel of the delegation are billeted separately from civilian counsel, the delegation will fall into two camps. If they remain mixed, Colonel Turrill will get on Mr Elwyn Jones' sensitive socialist nerves. Miss Kentish's billet's bathroom has no curtains and none of the female staff can have a bath for fear of being overlooked.' And, as if this were not enough, 'Jackson thinks there will be trouble about Katyn.'[8]

Robert Jackson meanwhile was having a bad time building up a case against Rudolf Hess. He had sent Erich M. Lipman, of Third U.S. Army headquarters, to ransack Ilse Hess' household for documents on October 29. Lipman reported that after trawling through sixty box-folders of Hess' private and official correspondence he had to conclude that most of it would only advance Hess' case, and not that of the prosecution. 'Frankly,' declared Lipman to Lieutenant Blumenstein at Nuremberg, 'I am rather impressed with the type of friends he [Hess] had and the manner in which he frowned upon favoritism, even in the cases of his own family.'[9]

The defence counsel were not told this of course. Hess had refused to appoint a lawyer anyway, and he told the Tribunal that he couldn't care less whether they did so for him.[10] On Andrus' orders, he was not allowed to shave for four days at a time, in an attempt to break his self-esteem and morale. His response was to refuse to read the indictment. 'I may take a look at it shortly before the trial,' he said dismissively to Major Kelley. Kelley asked him if he was willing to be given an insulin injection to get his weight up before having the other 'injection to restore his memory.' Hess refused. 'I'm sure I'll get my old weight back once I am set free,' he said.

One day, on October 30, they took him out of his cell and showed him the heap of packages he had brought with him from Wales. He displayed puzzlement. 'When you came here,' said Colonel Amen, 'you brought with you various papers and documents.'

'I don't know that.'

'You told me the other day that you had,' persisted Amen.

As this was translated for him Hess turned to the interpreter. '—Told this gentleman here?' he said, indicating the colonel. 'I don't know that I ever saw the gentleman before.'

Colonel Amen's patience again snapped. 'Don't you remember that I have questioned you many times?' he challenged.

Hess shook his head.

'Your memory is getting worse instead of better. Is that right?'

Hitler's deputy pointed out that he could hardly say. He shifted to a more comfortable position in his manacles. His logic was impeccable.

THE TRIBUNAL appointed Dr Günther von Rohrscheidt to represent Hess. 'I told him,' noted Hess after the lawyer visited him on November 2, 'that I regard the entire trial as a farce; that the judgement will be a foregone conclusion; and that I do not recognise the Tribunal's authority.' Rohrscheidt asked him if he was aware that he was the only prisoner they were manacling at present. Hess told him it was a matter of indifference to him. 'He talked about my flight to England,' he wrote in his diary. 'Of which I had, however, no recollection.'

So far, Amen's staff had let Hess down lightly.

Field-Marshal Milch was given more robust treatment. He had disappointed his interrogators. He had been flown back here from England in the confident expectation that he would testify against both Göring and Speer. In the privacy of an interrogation room on November 5 he was warned by Major Ernst Engländer that he was not being frank in his testimony—he was holding back what he knew on Göring and Speer. Milch knew Engländer as 'Emery.' 'He says,' Milch wrote afterwards, 'I'm not being open with him, the question of my parentage! I told him I can't invent things about myself and I had already told him I could only clear up this matter by asking my mother! He says he's spoken with Göring about this, who told him The Letter wasn't necessary!' Engländer/Evans/Emery then warned Milch that if he continued to stick up for Göring and Speer the victors would put him on trial for war crimes too. Milch protested that he was innocent. Engländer rejoined: 'That's peanuts. We can cook up a war crimes case against any German if we want to.'[11]

On November 9 Milch added to his diary: '[Staatssekretär Wilhelm] Stuckart of the ministry of the interior has turned up here today, they were holding him in solitary over there until now. He's got very thin and ill. He's been interrogated about my parentage, evidently by Major Engländer'—he had now learned the officer's real name. Not surprisingly, the Jewish members of Jackson's staff appeared to be obsessed with this Nazi field-marshal whom they regarded as a turncoat member of their faith.

THE INTIMIDATORY American tactics appear to have been routine. Years later the former S.S. judge-advocate Konrad Morgen, whose fearless investigations had led to the wartime arrest and execution of the commandant of Buchenwald camp, rendered to the American Pulitzer prize-winning author John Toland a similar account of his experiences at the hands of the interrogators at Nuremberg. 'The officers in the [Auschwitz] camp made it easy for themselves,' reported Morgen, referring to his own wartime investigation of S.S. wrongdoing under Rudolf Höss, the commandant at Auschwitz. 'When new inmates arrived and he had no room, they took out the last batch, put them up against the wall and shot them, and made room for the new batch.' Asked however about the Six Million figure, Morgen told Toland: 'It is hard to believe such a figure.'[12] He recalled that the Jews had 'helped to kill their own people.' But he refused to give perjured testimony at Nuremberg to the effect that Ilse Koch, widow of the commandant hanged by the S.S., had made lampshades out of human skin. That was a legend, he said: totally untrue. 'The Americans almost killed me,' recalled Morgen. 'They threatened three times to turn me over to the Russians or French or Poles.'[13]

❖ ❖ ❖ ❖ ❖

Garnering usable documentary evidence became a mounting nightmare for Jackson. He had become disenchanted with the productivity and intelligence of General Donovan's O.S.S. They had promised much but had delivered little. What Donovan regarded as evidence, he certainly would not: 'I never had any feeling that anybody had trapped me into the thing,' Jackson commented later. 'But I was in the trap!'[14]

It soon became clear that the O.S.S. had intended all along to stage-manage the whole trial along the lines of an N.K.V.D. show-trial, with Jackson little more than a professional actor. As part of the stage-management they proposed to run a pre-trial propaganda campaign in the United States, with 'increasing emphasis on the publication of atrocity stories to keep the public in the proper frame of mind.' To this end the O.S.S. devised and scripted for the education of the American public a two-reel film on war crimes, called *Crime and Punishment*; it was designed to put the case against the leading Nazis. Jackson declined to participate. He refused even to read the speech that the O.S.S. had scripted for him to read into the cameras. 'As you know,' he wrote to the O.S.S. officer concerned, 'the British are particularly sensitive about lawyers trying their cases in the newspapers and other vehicles of communication.'[15]

The film proposal was followed by an explicit O.S.S. suggestion for launching a 'black propaganda' campaign during the course of the trial, with agents in selected foreign countries starting rumours designed to influence public opinion in favour of the trial and against the defendants. This would be far more effective, they pointed out, than mounting a straightforward public relations campaign which would obviously be seen as emanating from the powers conducting the trials. One of Jackson's staff secretly notified him that the suggestion was 'fantastic, if not extremely dangerous,' and the justice himself pencilled a pithy comment on the letter: 'The scheme is cock-eyed. Give them no encouragement.'[16]

Vestiges of the unsavoury methods of the O.S.S. can still be seen among the earlier Nuremberg records—for instance, at the pre-trial interrogations the defendants were not accompanied by lawyers, and were frequently persuaded by trickery or intimidation to subscribe to testimonies incriminating others which we now know to have been false. The files are full of curiosities—for instance anonymous typed extracts of documents instead of the originals, and sworn statements by witnesses like Höss, commandant of Auschwitz, in which all the 'witnesses to his signature' have signed, but not Höss himself.[17] The Americans also submitted as exhibit 1553–PS a file of invoices for substantial monthly consignments of Zyklon (hydrogen cyanide pellets) supplied to the pest-control office at Auschwitz; they concealed the fact that the same file contained invoices for identical quantities of Zyklon delivered to the camp at Oranienburg, outside Berlin, where it was never alleged there had been any gas chambers.

The defendants were sometimes first interrogated under circumstances designed to make them believe the trial had already begun. Thus Keitel referred in one private note at this time to 'interrogations by the officers (judges) of the Allied military tribunal.'[18] The transcript shows that in one August interrogation Göring challenged the interrogator: 'I would like to know if this is only a questioning, or if this is already a regular trial.'[19] The interrogator, Colonel Amen, evaded direct reply.

JUDGE JACKSON'S squabble with Donovan came to a head in the autumn of 1945 after the general returned from a long absence in China on O.S.S. business. By this time Jackson's team was well on the way to establishing on the basis of documents alone a cast-iron case against the Nazis. But Donovan was a showman and he wanted the case to rest principally on the public testimony of witnesses like Schacht and Gisevius—a documentary trial was less likely to sustain the public imagination. He had even established with Göring relations that seemed to Jackson altogether too chummy. Interrogated on the day following the service of the indictments about the truth of the sordid affair resulting in the dismissals of Field-Marshal Werner von Blomberg and General Werner von Fritsch in 1938, Göring had said he would discuss it only in privacy.[20] This intimate special interrogation duly took place on November 6 with General Donovan but no reporter present; Göring gave testimony broadly in accordance with the now well-known facts, but 'requested that [it] be kept a secret.'[21]

Relations between Jackson and Donovan now touched bottom. On November 7 the Russians staged a raucous party to celebrate the October Revolution. Since the United States was to be represented by General Donovan, Jackson refused to go, even when the Russian General Aleksandrov came to fetch him.[22] That same day in an abrupt letter to Jackson Donovan had set out his contrary ideas on stage-managing the trial. The justice replied the next day, no less abruptly. The general then tried to push through his own concept by issuing orders to the predominantly military personnel on Jackson's staff. He also ordered the prison commandant Colonel Andrus not to permit any further interrogations of Göring, causing great difficulties for Jackson since the French and Russian prosecutors were naturally clamouring for the same interrogation rights as the Americans were enjoying. 'From the beginning,' Jackson huffed in a letter to Donovan, informing him he had overruled the general's instructions, 'control of these prisoners has been in the hands of Colonel Amen who has controlled the time, place of interrogation, who could be present, etc.'[23]

As the trial opening approached, General Donovan became increasingly disaffected, because he was not in the centre of things. Inviting Donovan to dinner with Florida senator Claude Pepper and Judge Biddle on the eleventh, Jackson privately told the judge that Donovan was restless because he had nothing to do and, he said, 'is doing nothing.'[24]

Three days later the prisoner Schacht wrote an oily letter to Donovan offering assistance. Receiving a copy of this from the general's secretary, Jackson was furious. This was not what he was planning for the banker at all. On the same date Jackson received a letter from Donovan renewing his suggestion that they give Schacht 'the opportunity to fight his way out' by testifying as prosecution witness against Göring.[25]

Jackson had already once turned this idea down: to him, Schacht was one of the worst criminals, and he did not propose to let him save his own skin. He now learned that Donovan had entertained one of the senior prisoners-of-war, Lieutenant-General Erwin Lahousen, one of his opposite numbers in Nazi Intelligence, as a guest at his Nuremberg mansion; Colonel Amen had questioned Lahousen there with the German lawyer Leverkühn of Hamburg as intermediary.[26]

For Jackson this was the last straw. The integrity of the trial in the eyes of history was at stake. He issued an order putting a stop to the entertainment of and negotiations with the Nazi prisoners. When the general wrote him formally requesting permission to confer with Göring, Jackson sent a blunt refusal, and informed him: 'I won't be able to use you in any position of prominence when the trial begins. We just don't see eye to eye.'

Donovan had all the fury of the woman scorned; he had hoped to be in charge of the fiery and spectacular trial examination of witnesses. For a few days he intrigued with Jackson's enemies, and tried to win them round to his point of view. Over dinner with Colonel Andrus and Judge Biddle on November 27—in itself an impropriety on a scale worth noting here—Donovan stated that Jackson's case was 'confused and flat' from relying on so much paper evidence (the trial had by then begun, but no witnesses had been called.) '[He] is eager,' noted Biddle, 'to get Jackson to put on Göring, who he thinks would come through.'[27]

Jackson would have none of it, and the O.S.S. general stormed out of Germany. He took vital documents with him, threatening to discredit Jackson in Washington if he could. His departure forced the justice to rush a long letter to explain to President Truman on December 1, 1945 his position. 'When I asked him to work with me,' wrote Jackson, explaining Donovan's motivations, 'I was repeatedly told that he would not work in second place with anybody.... But he was the head of O.S.S. and I needed what help that organization could give.' During his absence in China, Donovan had grown out of touch, and his ideas were now so far apart from Jackson's that he had had to tell the general that he would not 'put him on the floor' to conduct any part of the case. He claimed that the morale of the prosecution staff had been much improved by Donovan's departure, 'except a few of his organization members whom I can do without if necessary.' He admitted to Truman that he had probably made mistakes but 'this is not one of them.' His only fear, he concluded, was that this trial was going to 'drag and drag.'[28]

'The affair Donovan,' Jackson confided to his wife, 'is too long to write. But if he or his friends want to ruin him, let them keep on talking. I have enough in writing to take care of him. Have sent it all to the President. But it will probably all die out in a few days—I stay, and he moves on; so why worry.'[29] 'He was a skunk,' he added three weeks later. 'Too long to particularize, but I simply could not let him take part in a case he was sabotaging. If he ever starts anything, God help him.'[30] Even then the bickering was not over. A letter came from the United States at the end of March 1946 warning Justice Jackson that Donovan was now searching New York for a suitable public relations expert whom he could hire to sabotage the Nuremberg trial.[31]

❖ ❖ ❖ ❖ ❖

Hovering over all the chief prosecutors' secret meetings was the damage that the defence lawyers could do if they managed to raise points of history which were an embarrassment to the British or Russians. The French and the Americans had less to fear in this respect.

When the prosecutors met on November 9, 1945 they discussed in some depth the problem that would arise if the defence counsel tried to turn the tables on the prosecutors on the count of aggressive war. They agreed to adopt a united front: they would protest to the Tribunal that such attacks had nothing to do with the case in hand; they also agreed that since the United States, having entered the war relatively late, would be less vulnerable to such allegations the American prosecutor Robert Jackson would be better placed tactically to ask the court to forbid such arguments. To enable them to concert their counter-attack, the prosecutors also agreed that each delegation should draw up a memorandum on the position it proposed to adopt if and when such attacks by the defence attorneys developed.[32] Maxwell Fyfe produced the British memorandum early in December. The French and Russians produced nothing.

The Russians were particularly conscious of the risk to their persons if at any time the Ribbentrop–Molotov Pact became the subject of open debate during the trial. After this meeting the Soviet deputy prosecutor Colonel Yuri V. Pokrovsky assured Vyshinsky, his Soviet controller, formally by telephone, 'The chief prosecutors are determined to avoid awkward questions and to give the defendants no opportunity of starting debates or dragging the tribunal into discussions. In this connection it has been mentioned as desirable to exchange a list, before the trial begins, of all topics which are not to be mentioned before this tribunal, so that we have the opportunity to slap these questions down immediately during the proceedings.'[33]

The local Soviet prosecutors, Rudenko and Pokrovsky, were not their own masters. Behind closed doors there was a Soviet body remote-controlling all their decisions, identified as the 'Supervisory Commission for the Nuremberg Trial.' Among its less appetising members were the chief prosecutor of the Soviet Union K. P. Gorschenin, the minister of justice I. T. Golyakov, and the president of the Soviet Supreme Court Rytschkov, who had signed many a death sentence in his time; as well as even uglier creatures like Kobulov, Merkulov, and Abakumov (who would go before a firing squad at the same time as Likhatchev in 1953.)

❖ ❖ ❖ ❖ ❖

All this time the Americans maintained the attack on Rudolf Hess and his 'amnesia' alibi.

He was losing weight fast. His cheeks were sunken, his eyes were gaunt, his chest was hollow. In an attempt to revive his memory and turn him into proper defendant material, Jackson ordered that he be given a private showing of Leni Riefenstahl's spine-chilling documentary of the 1934 Nazi party rally, *Triumph of the Will*. Jackson reminisced angrily afterwards that Hess was evidently willing to be entertained, and the fifty or so American and Russian officers watched him intently as the two-hour film unrolled. They never took their eyes off his face, illuminated by a soft lamp from below, as the screen flickered with images of a young and virile Hess marching solemnly at Hitler's side down the huge arena at Nuremberg to the strains of the Slaves' Chorus from *Aïda*, and the Reichsleiter and Reich ministers orating from the podium.

His face, after a few instants of seeming recognition, reverted to a mask. 'I should not have recognised myself,' he wrote in his diary afterwards, 'if my name had not been mentioned.' He was not going to be caught out as easily as that.

His lawyer, Rohrscheidt, asked the Tribunal to appoint a neutral medical expert, designated by the universities of Zürich or Lausanne in Switzerland, to examine his client's fitness to stand trial; the Tribunal did not want to lose Hess, and ruled that an *ad hoc* medical commission should be set up by the four powers, the victors, instead. The result was a spectacular disarray: they examined Hess on November 14, and produced four separate and differing reports on the sixteenth, seventeenth, nineteenth, and twentieth. Lord Moran, Churchill's physician, felt that Hess was completely unfit to stand trial.

The Americans still preferred shock tactics. On November 16 their psychiatrists rigged a sudden meeting between Hess and the two female secretaries who had worked for him for eight years before his flight to Scotland in 1941.

'I'll show you something that will help you to remember,' began Hildegard Fath, now thirty-six, and she began to pull out a snapshot of his little son, Wolf Rüdiger. Hess looked away and murmured urgently in German, 'No, no, no.'

After listening with difficulty to ten minutes' whispered conversation, the Americans brought in the second girl, Ingeborg Sperr.

'I just cannot remember who this Hess was,' the microphones heard the prisoner saying. 'I have the impression ...'

'I was a prisoner,' she told him, 'and have already been interrogated several times.' The 'Amis' had questioned her, she said, explaining that an Ami was an American: 'It has nothing to do with *ami*, the French for friend.'

'I've always said,' concurred Hess, happy to work in his little taunts at his tormentors, 'the Americans are riff-raff.' She told him she had been held by the Gestapo in Dachau for six weeks after his flight. 'I suffered a great deal.'

'Were you happy working for me?' he asked.

'Yes,' she said quietly. 'I have been with you since 1934.'

'A mad chapter,' he said, and expressed the hope that they would let him see her again.

Colonel Amen now intervened, snarling: 'You remember these young ladies, don't you?'

'No,' he said. 'No, I do not remember them.'

'You never saw either of them before?'

'It has just been stated in the conversation with these young ladies that I have not seen them before.'

'Are you glad to see them?' asked Amen.

'I am always glad to see Germans. Germans who tell me about my family.'

There was a nasty overtone in the reply, and Amen asked: 'What makes you think those are pictures of your family?'

'The ladies told me that. And besides, I have a picture of my son in my cell.'

'You believe what the young ladies say, do you?'

'I have not the least cause to think that Germans do not tell me the truth.'

'Do you think all Germans will tell the truth?'

'Yes,' said Hess. 'All Germans with whom I am closely acquainted.'

He had to admit however that there were a few bad characters in every country.

'How do you know they are *German* young ladies?' asked Amen.

'By their language,' explained the prisoner, turning expressionless eyes on him. 'I got the impression that they are not Americans.'

Amen picked up one point—that Hess had told one of the girls she would work for him again later. Hess nodded: 'Yes, yes. I told her she could depend on being able to work for me again one day.'

Amen asked what he meant by that.

'I have been informed,' replied Hess, 'that I formerly held a high position in the National Socialist state, and I consider that one day this will again be the case.'

The room swam past the interrogator's eyes.

'Uh, you mean you're going to have a high position in the Nazi state again? The same position? You have those plans for after the trial—is that it?'

In a matter-of-fact voice, Hess patiently repeated that he expected a 'high position in the German Nationalist state.' 'I do not know how often I should repeat,' he continued shortly, 'that I have the conviction that Germans tell the truth.'

'I could bring a lot of Germans in here that won't tell you the truth!' raged Colonel Amen.

'Yes, especially out of a prison where criminals are usually kept.'

'Such as Göring for example?' inquired Amen.

'Obviously I did not mean that.'

'Well, is Göring a criminal?'

'Yes,' added Hess, 'but an honourable criminal—a "war criminal."'

Now Amen thought he had him. 'How do you know what kind of criminal he is?'

'Because he is the same type of "criminal" as I am,' retorted Hess.

IT WAS game, set, and match to the amnesiac. 'Take him out,' shouted the colonel. 'And leave the girls.' Marched out of the room, still handcuffed to the U.S. Army sentinel, Hess whispered to his two young secretaries in German, 'You can be proud of the fact that you are prisoners.' He advised them not to expect him to write, and he never saw them again.[34]

Rohrscheidt had meanwhile formally applied to the Tribunal for the production of all the British medical files on Hess as well as those of the foreign office, and the production as witnesses of the Duke of Hamilton, Sir Ivone Kirkpatrick, Dr Henry Dicks, and others who had interrogated the prisoner. 'The above mentioned records,' stated the lawyer, 'contain, according to information received by the defence, very important conclusions as to the motive of Hess' flight and his state of health, especially about the mental disturbance and mental disorder when he arrived.' The British government eventually released only the earliest documents, the reports filed by the duke and Sir Ivone Kirkpatrick; none of the later files, revealing Hess' serious medical problems, was released to the defence.

❖ ❖ ❖ ❖ ❖

For three days the rain poured down, and by November 12 the climate in Nuremberg was bitterly raw and damp. The French and British judges were grounded by fog and the opening of the trial was delayed day after day. The comfort-loving lawyers were getting tetchy. Judge Biddle was missing the little things, like reading the *New Yorker* and *New York Times.* Sir Hartley Shawcross was getting terribly on Herbert Wechsler's nerves. Behind closed doors, the Tribunal was hearing applications. 'The boys really don't have much to do,' Biddle explained in a letter, 'except Fisher, who is arguing the mass of applications from the defendants for documents and witnesses.'[35]

Sometimes the Americans would relax by hearing Nuremberg's symphony orchestra. Once the judges had a private showing of the Soviet movie of their show trials in Kharkov, where the three German officers been tried for atrocities. 'They are horrible,' wrote Biddle after watching the newsreels, '—tortured, naked skeletons, the Kharkov defendants being hung in front of the crowds.'[36]

The Russians also publicly hanged in Leningrad several German officers whom their judges found guilty of the murders in the Katyn forest.

EVEN AT this late stage, with the curtain about to go up, the Americans were continuing to tinker with the cast. They never were satisfied with the list of defendants. Sidney Alderman, Jackson's leading counsel, urged that Hess' friend Professor Karl Haushofer, the geopolitician, should be added to the dock, as 'Hitler's intellectual godfather,' since the principal author of the conspiracy, Hitler himself, was absent. Jackson suggested that the world would look with disfavour on the Americans if they started hanging academics for their views.[37] At another stage, early in October, it was Jackson himself who tried to add names to the list, to expand the representation of the 'General Staff' and 'Police' categories; he named Field-Marshals Walther von Brauchitsch and Erhard Milch and General Franz Halder to fill the former, and General der Polizei Kurt Daluege, S.S. Obergruppenführer Karl Wolff, and two others to fill the latter. The British representatives properly pointed out that adding seven names at this late date would be 'taken as an indication that the Prosecution cannot make up its mind. This would make the case ridiculous in the eyes of many.' On October 26, Maxwell Fyfe wrote privately: 'At 11 I saw Jackson, Rudenko, and Dubost, and we decided not to join further defendants.'[38]

On Gustav Krupp, Jackson was in agonies: he had personally promised President Truman that he would prosecute the industrialists, influenced, as he secretly admitted to his fellow chief prosecutors, by the campaign at home against U.S. munitions manufacturers like DuPont, who were rumoured to have sent a certain Mr Scherrer to Europe pre-war to break up the disarmament conferences. Industrialists everywhere had to get a warning. 'There is more dynamite in this question than Krupp ever produced out of his plant!' he said on November 12, 1945, a few days before the trial began.

Therefore a Krupp, any Krupp, had to go on trial—he would have preferred Alfried, but Gustav was good enough in default.

At the Tribunal's first session, behind closed doors in Nuremberg on November 14, Gustav Krupp's lawyers moved to dismiss him from the case on the ground that he was too ill to understand what was going on. Jackson rather weakly contended that absent-mindedness was no defence—that the London Charter would allow even this Krupp to be tried *in absentia*, or that in the alternative they should replace him with his son Alfried. Sir Hartley Shawcross objected that this was a court of justice, not a game where they could substitute one man for another.[39]

Lord Justice Lawrence reserved a decision, but clearly disagreed with Jackson. One member of the American prosecution team wrote privately: 'My guess is that the elder Krupp will be dismissed, and the younger Krupp substituted, as he was head of the firm since 1943. The Krupps were unscrupulous in their dealings with forced labor, and such men and women were inhumanly treated, worse than any Georgia chain gang one used to read about.'[40] That the British and Americans had gone to very great lengths with their air forces to burn and blast to death those selfsame workers was the irony of such 'war crimes' trials as this.

Ultimately the British united front—Shawcross and Lawrence—refused to have Alfried stand in for his father, earning a grudging tribute from an unexpected quarter, Julius Streicher, who wrote in his diary: 'The British carried the day with their opinion that although one might be able to replace one NCO with another, it was just not done to have one defendant who was unfit to plead or dead replaced in the dock by his son as successor. This episode shows that the British judges at least have the good intention not to put their morals entirely on one side in the events now beginning to unroll.'[41]

There were other signs of problems to come. When defence counsel applied for one particular witness to prove that the Russians had deported slave labour from Latvia, just as the Nazis were now accused of having done, the Russian alternate judge Lieutenant-Colonel

Volchkov flew into a temper and called it libellous. 'We postpone a decision,' noted Biddle, 'till a full meeting.'[42]

❖ ❖ ❖ ❖ ❖

The world's press was informed that the show would begin on the morning of November 20, 1945. Jackson's opening speech was already a masterpiece. He had reviewed it a dozen times, Elsie had worked on it every night for weeks, and Bill had been up until five A.M. seeing it through the duplicating machine.

On the nineteenth however news arrived from Moscow which threatened the entire opening performance. The Russian chief prosecutor, General Rudenko, had been stricken by malaria, so Moscow now claimed; the Russians were demanding at least ten days' postponement, failing which they would pull out of the trial completely. Justice Jackson, who had now experienced Russian methods for five months, suddenly sensed that the Russians had got cold feet—for some reason they were trying to stop the trial.

The French deputy chief prosecutor, Monsieur Dubost—piqued by the Tribunal's refusal to allow old Alfried Krupp to be included among the defendants—supported the Russian demand for a postponement, adding that if the Soviets pulled out so would the French. 'He has orders,' Biddle recorded, 'to absent himself if the Russians are not present. The French and Russians have particularly suffered.'[43]

'It was generally believed,' Jackson privately recorded, 'that he [Dubost] was a Communist and it looked as though their position had been settled in advance.'[44]

There followed what he later described as 'the bitterest chief prosecutors' meeting of the entire trial'. Sir Hartley Shawcross warned his colleagues that including Alfried Krupp was out of the question, since there was virtually no evidence against him (this had not prevented them from including Dönitz, Papen, Hess, Jodl, and a number of others during August.) He urged that there was surely nothing to prevent Russia appointing a stand-in for Rudenko. 'Postponement,' said the Englishman, 'would arouse the derision, suspicion, and contempt of the world.'

To Jackson, the issues at stake were equally large if not larger. 'It would be an ominous thing,' he reminded his colleagues, 'if this effort of the four great Powers to co-operate should fail.'

He was as annoyed as the Russians and French that there was to be no flesh-and-blood industrialist in the dock, he said; but there were embarrassing political reasons why he, as the American representative, must insist on the Soviet prosecutor's presence. 'There are certain features in this trial, wherein Russian and American interests are not identical. There are certain matters in which the United States can neither protect nor champion the Russian viewpoint—the Polish and Finnish wars and the incorporation of the Baltic States.'

What if the defendants should raise these ticklish questions, and the Russians were not there in person? Monsieur Dubost angrily repeated that France would withdraw if the trial opened in Rudenko's absence next day. Shawcross rallied to Jackson: if Rudenko were ill, it was up to the Russians to announce publicly that they were solely to blame for any further postponement.

This was still too tame for Jackson. He solemnly announced that the United States would open the trial next day, and alone if need be, whatever happened. 'We must not start this trial,' he appealed, 'with the four Allies, who stood together in war, falling apart in peace.'

The prosecutors' meeting broke up in disorder. Late that afternoon, the Tribunal's judges themselves ordered the prosecutors in to a conference.

Jackson, expecting the worst, asked several members of his staff including his stenographer Elsie Douglas to accompany him, but Lord Justice Lawrence announced that their meeting was to be in secret—only the prosecutors might remain. Jackson was furious and asked leave to withdraw: this, he said, was the second time that he had protested against the holding of secret meetings (the first having been at Berlin.) He was not representing a private client but the United States of America; he would have to report to his own government and if necessary submit a stenographic report. If they now had two nations threatening to withdraw from the trial, he argued, it was vital for an accurate record to be made.

Lawrence remained adamant, and at a sign from him Brigadier-General William L. Mitchell, the court marshal, escorted Jackson's companions from the room. With the room cleared, Lawrence asked Jackson for his views on the Russians' request for a delay. Jackson invited Dubost to put the French view first, which the Frenchman did, displaying the same truculence he had shown as at the prosecutors' meeting, and again threatening to withdraw if the trial opened in Rudenko's absence. Shawcross repeated that any postponement must be publicly blamed on the Russians. Sir Norman Birkett pointed out to the other members of the Tribunal that they were dealing with a dangerous matter of principle: If they had to postpone hearings because of a sick prosecutor, they would be bound to do so for any illness among defence counsel too.[45] It seemed like deadlock.

Suddenly and unexpectedly Rudenko's deputy Colonel Yuri V. Pokrovsky arrived and announced with a completely deadpan face that he had just telephoned Moscow, and that 'due to a marvellous new medical discovery' Rudenko's malaria had been cured and he was on his way to Nuremberg where he would arrive five days from now. (Moscow called all the shots: In an eloquent little scene, Pokrovsky, an elegant hand-kissing former officer of the Imperial Russian Army, once wrapped his wrists in the latest ticker-tape instructions from Moscow, like a pair of manacles, and apologised to Maxwell Fyfe, 'That's how I am.') 'The trial will open,' Biddle recorded the Russian as saying, 'in a high solemn moment, of extreme importance.' Pokrovsky insisted that Rudenko must be present personally, and was refusing to delegate that function.[46]

The trial could begin next day.

❖ ❖ ❖ ❖ ❖

From the records of the Soviet government's Supervisory Commission for the Nuremberg Trial it is possible to speculate on the reasons for the Soviet agonising over the opening of the trial.[47] Once again they were terrified of an undisciplined defence lawyer lifting the lid off politically delicate matters. Three days earlier, on November 16, there had been this exchange:

> VYSHINSKY: Comrade Rudenko has no plan yet for the conduct of the trial. Rudenko is not ready to proceed with the trial. I have sent the opening speech that we have drafted to the Central Committee.
>
> KOBULOV: Our people in Nuremberg at the moment are reporting to us on the attitude of the defendants under interrogation. [He reads out a memorandum.] Göring, Jodl, Keitel, and the other persons indicted are putting on a big show in the interrogations. Their replies often contain anti-Soviet diatribes and our investigating magistrate Comrade Aleksandrov is only making very mild responses to them. The defendants are managing to portray themselves as simple officials and functionaries merely carrying out the will of the High Command. When Raeder was interrogated by the British he said that the Russians tried to convince him that he had made his statements under pressure. His testimony was recorded on film.
>
> VYSHINSKY: The chief prosecutor must interrupt the defendant where necessary and deny him any opportunity of making anti-Soviet attacks.

The possibility of effective counter-attacks by the defence lawyers against the Soviet Union continued to worry Vyshinsky, who was ultimately answerable to Stalin himself. Ten days later, on November 26, he would preside over another such secret meeting. This time the minutes read:

> Subject: List of questions to be avoided during the trial examinations (Comrade Vyshinsky):
>
> 1. Confirmation of the list of questions provided by Comrade Vyshinsky which are to be regarded as not permissible for discussion before the Tribunal.

> 2. Demand to Comrade Rudenko that he reaches agreement with the other chief prosecutors that a series of topics should not be addressed, to avoid the USSR, the United States, Britain, France and other Allied nations becoming the butt of defence criticisms.

Those present additionally insisted that for each document introduced by the other prosecution teams Comrades Rudenko and Nikitchenko—the Soviet prosecutor and judge respectively—should be required to render opinions on their admissibility with regard to the protection of Soviet interests and if necessary prevent the defence from submitting or even reading out in open court those documents ruled as 'undesirable.' [48]

JUDGE BIDDLE claimed the credit for having broken this log-jam. 'All my boys are again congratulating me tonight,' he wrote to his wife, preening himself, at nine P.M. on November 19, 1945,

> Rudenko, the Russian prosecutor, was sick with malaria and said he could not appear for the opening tomorrow. The French said they would have to walk out also. Lawrence and I were vigorously opposed to any postponement. I finally suggested as a compromise that the indictment be read in full, which would take two days; then hear the plea and adjourn about Thursday until the following Monday [November 26]. We sent for the prosecutors and told them our plans, and Gen. Rudenko's assistant, Colonel Pokrovsky , said he would telephone Moscow. Meanwhile, Birkett got the British [foreign office] to put some pressure on [Moscow], and finally the Russians came back and agreed we could go ahead. The French are behaving abominably, attacking Jackson in public. The Russians were very difficult. But tonight everyone is happy for the trial actually opens tomorrow as scheduled, and this is against all bets.[49]

13: Showtime

UNDER THE gaze of Moses holding the Ten Commandments, the International Military Tribunal at long last held its first session in the Palace of Justice at Nuremberg at ten A.M. on Tuesday, November 20, 1945. Into the renovated third-floor courtroom with its sage-green curtains, red plush chairs, and carpets imported from France trooped the twenty surviving defendants, who had been brought along a two-hundred-yard undercover passage from their cells in the nineteenth-century jailhouse block. Kaltenbrunner stayed in his cell, too ill to attend. Outside, American medium tanks squatted across the streets in a rather unnecessary demonstration of Allied might, and traffic was diverted away from the courthouse area.

The twenty defendants sat in two rows in the dock, with their backs to the wall. Göring took the most prominent place, at the right-hand end of the front row. Next to him sat Hess, who with great deliberation soon immersed himself in a rustic novel by Hans Fitz and ignored the proceedings. The British artist Dame Laura Knight, who received an official commission to fix the trial on paper for posterity, wrote in her diary of how Göring's pink and white skin contrasted with Hess's green pallor. 'Today,' she would write, 'Göring's *soignée coiffure* is slightly displaced and shows an ominous bald patch.... His fingers are short and stubby, unlike Hess's long slender fingers, as I notice when Göring helps him with his papers. It would seem Göring has considerable affection and sympathy for Hess.'

Julius Streicher inevitably saw everything on this first day differently from his fellow prisoners. For him this was the last passage of arms between himself and the Jews. He studied the Tribunal intently. 'Of the two Frenchmen, one is one hundred percent a Jew,' observed Streicher obsessively and wholly mistakenly. 'Whenever I look across at him he gets uncomfortable and turns his yellow-skinned, black-haired head to one side or the other.'[1] Like Göring, the gauleiter entertained no doubts about the outcome for himself. 'For those who can see,' he wrote of this opening day, 'there could not be the slightest doubt: there are more Jews and half-Jews in the courtroom than non-Jews. Three-quarters of the journalists and nearly all the translators [interpreters], steno typists—male and female—and other assorted helpers are members of the Jewish race. How they smirk and sneer at us defendants in the dock. You can read it in their faces: now we've got the whole gang of them, and that Streicher is there too. Almighty God! Praise be to Jehovah and praised be our ancestral father Abraham!'[2]

Three defendants, in addition to Kaltenbrunner, were missing. The seventy-five-year old Gustav Krupp von Bohlen und Halbach had been formally found unfit to plead; Robert Ley was dead; Martin Bormann could not be found. The Nuremberg lawyer Dr Friedrich Bergold had been appointed at the dictate of British deputy prosecutor Airey Neave* to represent the absent (and in fact dead) Reichsleiter.[3]

A question-mark hung over the fitness of several other defendants. Streicher's lawyer Dr Hans Marx appealed to the Tribunal to examine his client's sanity, but three of the prosecuting powers' medical experts pronounced him fit to stand trial. Kaltenbrunner had been rushed to hospital two days before with a subarachanoid hæmorrhage; during the next few months the former S.S. Obergruppenführer attended court only a few hours at a time. Göring remarked, 'If he's fit, then I'm an Atlas.' Hess' fitness to plead was no less open to question.[4] He wrote in his diary however this day: 'Start of the trial, very fatiguing. I spent most of the time reading the Bavarian peasant novel *Der Loisl*, or relaxing with my eyes closed. None of the proceedings at the hearing,' he was careful to add, 'remains in my memory.'

Three hundred press and radio correspondents crowded the courtroom for this first day. A newsreel camera whirred, recording every minute, and powerful floodlights bathed the tables crowded with prosecutors, interpreters, and German defence counsel in their traditional gowns and caps. On the bench sat the judges of the four powers together with their alternates, in chairs now of equal height, in front of their national flags—the British in wing collars, the Americans like rather anxious New York businessmen, Professor Henri Donnedieu sporting his magnificent moustache, and the two Russians in full uniform, as befitted a military tribunal.[5] Julius Streicher was impressed by these Russians—they had a soldierly bearing which was quite in keeping with their uniforms, which were designed on the old Tsarist model. As the days passed he found himself increasingly impressed by the two English judges too—both were large men, of Nordic look and aristocratic bearing. One, believed Streicher, was a lord; the other, the British alternate Sir Norman Birkett, had a large cranium and a gaze that seemed to come from deep with him; he would not have looked out of place in a cathedral pulpit, or so Streicher fantasised.[6]

The chief Russian prosecutor General Rudenko was absent in Moscow, his malaria having ostensibly returned despite the earlier miracle cure; he had authorised the trial to open this day on the understanding that the Tribunal would not tolerate the German

* In 1979 Neave, who became a Conservative member of Parliament, was killed by Irish terrorists who exploded a bomb in his car as he left the House of Commons.

defendants making any statement in his absence. Jackson studied the prisoners' faces intently. He wondered if Göring would try to challenge the court's jurisdiction. If he did not, the others would follow his lead. Judge Lawrence asked him how he pleaded to the charges. Göring took the microphone and began, 'Before I answer—'

Lawrence interrupted him. Jackson was in suspense. Göring repeated his opening words, and was again stopped by the judge.

Göring then muttered, 'Not Guilty,' adding: 'In the sense of the indictment.'

Clutched in Göring's hand, unread, was a one-page declaration. In it, he refused to recognise the jurisdiction of the Tribunal. There is no reason not to record for posterity what he had wanted to say:

> As Reichsmarschall of the Greater German Reich, I assume political responsibility for my own acts. Although answerable for these acts only to the German people and to the German courts, I am nevertheless willing, without recognising the jurisdiction of this Tribunal, to provide it with any explanations that are desired and to speak the whole truth. I do however refuse to accept responsibility for acts committed by others—acts of which I was unaware and of which I would not have approved or been able to prevent if I had known of them. Hermann Göring.

The Tribunal passed on to Rudolf Hess. To the excruciating irritation of the solemn-faced prosecution lawyers, Hess, called upon to plead, merely sprang to his feet (in a temper, as he admitted in his diary) and shouted '*Nein!*' The hundreds of spectators packing the galleries roared with laughter. Jackson was furious, feeling that Hess had 'stolen the show'—and a show it indeed was. The Tribunal president Lord Justice Lawrence, with his half-moon reading glasses every inch the Hollywood fuddy-duddy of an English judge, articulated: 'That will be entered as a plea of Not Guilty.'

Field-Marshal Keitel had also prepared a declaration, beginning with the words 'Before I reply to the question asked of me, whether I plead Guilty or Not Guilty....' Seeing Göring stopped however he did not venture to read it out.

WITH HIS son Bill at his side at the table still checking the pages, Robert H. Jackson began his opening speech. He had devoted more effort to this text than to any other in his life; and before reading it he had obtained from the Library of Congress—a human touch—a guide on *The Art of Effective Public Speaking.* His speech was later praised as one of the world's great pieces of legal literature; in Washington it was admired as no state paper had been 'since the loss of F.D.R.'s touch.' One newspaper hinted that Jackson 'might be a good bet for the Democratic Presidential nomination sometime in the future.'

Speaking in an inexorable, even, unhurried voice that did not vary for hours on end he opened this, the last battle of the European war. Occasionally Elsie would hand up to him the actual exhibit he was talking about, to bring his case to life—a bound volume of photographs of the liquidation of the Warsaw Ghetto, military orders signed or initialed by the defendants, or the registers of deaths maintained by the Mauthausen concentration camp commandant. Behind him sat the British attorney-general Sir Hartley Shawcross with, across the table from him, his predecessor Sir David Maxwell Fyfe, who would be carrying forward most of the British prosecution here.

The speech was a brave attempt at laying the foundations for the indictment on the conspiracy to wage aggressive war; it was well received, and Jackson was greatly relieved.[7] He said that the Nazis had killed an estimated 5·7 million Jews (that sounded more precise than the popular figure of Six Million.) Asked during the adjournment who had ordered this, Göring was overhead saying, 'Himmler, I suppose.' He had not confronted this issue at all in his own mind until now.

JACKSON INTENDED to make little use of live witnesses, preferring to have the documentary evidence speak for itself. At a private meeting after the trial began, Jackson offered this additional interesting explanation to the other chief prosecutors: 'Though the United States has the largest collection of potential witnesses—a whole jail full, in fact—most of them would do us more harm than good. We shall perhaps use four more witnesses in addition to [Lieutenant-General Erwin] Lahousen [chief of the Abwehr's sabotage and counter-espionage Section II], particularly on concentration-camp matters, but we shall make the bulk of our case on documents.'[8]

At one such closed session on the twenty-fourth Lawrence asked Jackson to state the political purpose of the trial. Jackson replied to the question in this sense: 'We want to prove to Germany and to the world that the Nazi regime was as wicked and as criminal as we have always maintained.' Moreover, 'We want to make clear to the Germans why our policies toward them will have to be very harsh indeed for many years to come.'[9]

This motivation for the trial must never be forgotten in contemplating the printed record. The Nuremberg archives are a historical source to be used only with caution: the published volumes contain only the prosecution's documents, and none of the defence. In the course of the trial Dr Hans Laternser, defence counsel for the General Staff and the O.K.W., would submit to the Tribunal no fewer than 3,186 affidavits sworn by field-marshals, generals and other key witnesses. Not one would be published in the blue IMT volumes.[10]

In one respect the court overruled Jackson. He had hoped to rest his case primarily on the documents, but the sheer physical burden of providing translations of twenty sets of each left the judges no option but to rule that only those portions of documents read into the record, and hence translated by the court's excellent simultaneous interpreting system, should form part of the court record.[11]

The reading of the documents into the record began. On November 29 the court was in fits of laughter over Göring's cheeky telephone conversations with Ribbentrop (in London) and Prince Philipp of Hesse during the Austria crisis of March 1938; he had ordered his Forschungsamt to monitor and transcribe these telephone conversations.[12] This put the Reichsmarschall in a boisterous mood, but it was dashed when Jackson called that afternoon for the showing of the first film exhibits prepared by the O.S.S. and by his own staff. The most effective was the film on Nazi concentration camps, a grim record made by military photographers who had accompanied the Allied armies advancing through Germany.[13] Now the defendants knew there was little hope for any of them—the last vestige of public sympathy was dispelled by the horrors that the films portrayed.

As the film compilation on the Nazi concentration camps filled the screen erected at one end of the courtroom one of the American lawyers closely watched the expressions on the defendants' faces:

> Schacht and Fritzsche refused to look at the screen at all [he wrote], and turned their heads away. All the rest seemed to have their eyes riveted to it. I wish every school child and adult could be made once a year on V.E.-day to see this film and a few others at all the theatres in the U.S. to remind them that the Germans are dangerous; and [that] the U.S. should remain well armed and well manned. Also will be shown some captured German films of the Warsaw Ghetto which the Germans obviously 'staged' to use as propaganda purposes among the German people to show what degraded and ugly subhumans the Jews were—which of course makes the film even more diabolical than if it were not so staged.[14]

Hess looked bewildered as the film was shown, and when the lights came on he said loudly to Göring on his right, 'I don't believe it.'

A suddenly thoughtful Göring urged him to be quiet.

After this film, General Jodl bitterly wrote: 'These facts are the most frightful legacy left behind by the National Socialist regime. They are far worse than the destruction of Germany's cities. The ruins can be regarded as the honourable scars of a nation struggling for its existence. This however disgraces both the Wehrmacht and its commanders alike. I have already set out how methodically we have all been duped in this regard. The allegation that we all knew these things were going on is wrong. I would not have tolerated knowing of such things for one single day.'[15]

As Kranzbühler stated a few years later, the worst thing to come out of the Nuremberg trial was the liquidation of political enemies—not the brutal but militarily necessary operations against partisans and resistance fighters but the methodical massacre of entire ethnic groups and particularly what he called 'the gigantic campaign of destruction against the Jews.' 'Anybody who was forced during the evidence stages of the trial to study the horrific pictures showing how women and their children were shot in the back of the head standing on the rim of long mass graves, or driven into gas chambers, will never get over the sense of shame that Germans—even if it was only a very few Germans—could have done such things.' But even then Kranzbühler had to add as a rider the question, Were such mass exterminations common knowledge in Germany?

Whether or not the victorious powers can grasp this fact, this question is as valid now as it was half a century ago. Nowhere in the Allied archives, which contain mountains of intercepted cipher messages and the reports on bags of mail captured from enemy ships or from overrun enemy positions, is there the slightest evidence that such atrocities were commonly known to the German public at large.[16]

ON THE last day of November the Tribunal went into closed session to hear the arguments on whether Hess was fit to plead. Rudolf Hess had however now reached a very private decision that it would be wrong to abandon his former colleagues in the dock. The general belief was that the Tribunal would find him incompetent to stand trial. As the dock cleared around Hess and the other prisoners were returned to their cells, U.S. Army psychiatrist Dr Gustave M Gilbert said to him, 'You may not be coming into this court any more. But I'll come down and see you in your cell—once in a while.'

'I am perfectly competent to defend myself,' said Hess, with a worried frown. Just as his lawyer Dr Rohrscheidt was about to begin his argument, he leaned forward and murmured to him, 'I have decided to say that my memory has returned.'

'Do as you wish,' said the lawyer irritably, and launched into his long, rambling speech as though he had not heard. For two hours the Tribunal and lawyers became mired in the hopelessly conflicting reports of the various psychiatric commissions. As Rohrscheidt on the one hand, and the prosecutors on the other, quoted the medical evidence and spouted psycho-babble at each other and to the Tribunal, Hess became more restless, in the realisation that he may well have been the sanest person present.

He slipped a note to Rohrscheidt, saying he could shorten the whole debate if he might himself speak. Rohrscheidt ignored him.

Now for the first time Hess heard it set out that under Article 12 of the Tribunal's Charter he might be tried *in absentia*, even if found unfit to plead. 'Such terrible crimes are laid at the door of the defendant that even the death penalty is to be expected,' he heard his lawyer intone.

Maxwell Fyfe responded that amnesia had never, in English law, been held to be a bar to either trial or punishment. Lord Justice Lawrence seemed to be inclining toward Rohrscheidt's view. Hess, he said, would surely be able to argue, 'I should have been able to make a better defence if I had been able to remember what took place at the time.' Jackson stooped to sarcasm in his response, referring to Hess as being 'in the *volunteer* class with his amnesia.'

The Tribunal then, at last, allowed Hess to speak. Standing up in the dock, he made a little curtsey toward the judges and read out these words:

> Mr President, I should like to say this. In order that I may be allowed to continue to attend the trial and receive judgement alongside my colleagues as is my wish, and in order not to be declared unfit to plead, I submit the following declaration to the court—a declaration which I had not intended to make until a later point in the proceedings.
>
> From this time on my memory is again at the disposal of the outside world.
>
> The reasons why I simulated amnesia are of a tactical nature.
>
> In fact only my ability to concentrate is slightly impaired. On the other hand my ability to follow the trial, to defend myself, to question witnesses, and to answer questions myself—these are not impaired.
>
> I emphasise that I assume full responsibility for everything that I have done, everything I have signed, and everything that I have co-signed.
>
> My deep-seated conviction that the Tribunal has no competency is not affected by the above statement.
>
> I have successfully maintained the illusion of amnesia with my official defence counsel; he has acted accordingly in good faith.

The Tribunal adjourned in uproar. There were peals of laughter from the public benches. Hess was marched back to his cell in handcuffs. He had made them all look very silly indeed—the judges, the lawyers, the prosecutors, and above all the teams of expert psychiatrists of the four victorious powers.

Returned to his draughty and sparsely furnished cell, Hess was shortly notified that the Tribunal wanted a copy of the text that he had just read out. He found it very satisfying that they were now having to come to him. 'I took my time,' he pencilled awkwardly into his cell diary, writing on his bed, 'and first had a meal—in peace.'[17]

❖ ❖ ❖ ❖ ❖

'We just had a dramatic day,' wrote Jackson in private that same Friday night, November 30, 1945. 'General Lahousen testified all day and certainly hung the Nazi crowd—he being an anti-Nazi German general. To cap the climax Hess repudiated his own counsel and admitted he has been faking about insanity and amnesia. It was all pretty tense. Then tonight I had dinner with the Russians—told them I would attend if I could leave at nine, which I did. Vodka, etc., dead fish—whew!'[18]

With the benefit of hindsight, we can see that there was much that should never have been introduced in evidence. On November 25 Judge Biddle wrote this private account of one of the trial's most notorious forgeries, which was in the document book introduced by Sidney Alderman. 'It is packed with interesting material from captured secret documents and accounts of meetings between the leaders and Hitler, made by his secretary, showing Germany's "aggressive war,"' remarked Biddle, writing home to his wife in the United States. 'For instance, Hitler says: "And besides, gentlemen, in Russia will happen next what I have practised in Poland. After Stalin's death we shall crush the Soviet Union." This was in August 1939. He had given orders "to kill without pity or mercy all men, women and children of Polish race or language." The secretary commented: "The speech was listened to enthusiastically, Göring jumped on the table. Bloodthirsty thanks and bloody promises. He danced around like a savage." But,' concluded Biddle, 'you'll probably have seen all this in the press by the time it gets to you.'[19]

The sheer improbability of the 264-pound Göring 'jumping on a table' was overlooked in the prosecutors' glee, as was the fact that Hitler had *not* liquidated every member of the Polish race. The document was a forgery, made available to the court by Associated Press journalist Louis Lochner, whose private papers provide adequate explanation of how he came into possession of it.[20]

The documentary finds were constantly throwing new light on the defendants. It strengthened Göring's case that he had fallen out with Hitler right at the end, and that Hitler had even sentenced him to death in April 1945. In November Hitler's political testament was finally found. This confirmed that in the last hours of his life he had formally appointed Dönitz his successor, while dismissing Göring and Himmler as traitors. Quite apart from their disloyalty toward his own person, wrote Hitler, Göring and Himmler had inflicted immense damage on the country and the entire people by conducting their secret negotiations with the enemy, without his permission and against his will, as well as by their illegal attempts to seize power.[21]

❖ ❖ ❖ ❖ ❖

As the days passed, Streicher amused himself trying to pick out more Jews from the sea of faces in the courtroom—'or which one is the bastard with Jewish blood or has married into the Jewish race?'[22] From where he sat he was by struck how hideous all the American females were—the shorthand writers and stenotypists sitting in front of the judges' bench chewing gum while their pencils flew across their pads or their fingers stroked the keyboards of the tiny stenotype machines. 'Do efficiency and ugliness go hand in hand in females of the American species?' Streicher wondered.[23]

'The defendants looked tired and nervous,' he mimicked, quoting one newspaper report. Hardly surprising, he reflected: 'Let one of these gentlemen of the press sit for three months in a prison cell with hardly any daylight and under a dim electric bulb for two hours each evening with his pen or pencil with only fifteen or at most twenty minutes a day outside in the prison yard and being wakened all night long by sentinels who are always looking in, then he too might look a bit tired and nervous when this show-trial began.'[24]

It was in netting defendants like Streicher, who under existing common law would have attracted at most a minor prison sentence, that the new London Statute showed its sinews. Jackson himself was confident that none would escape conviction. Even if any defendant was acquitted by this Tribunal, as he stated in his opening address, that man would be turned over to 'our Continental allies' for further trial—a prospect with which the British prosecutors Sir Hartley Shawcross and Sir David Maxwell Fyfe warmly concurred. 'We thoroughly agree,' they had privately written to Jackson a few days before the trial itself began, 'with the idea of conveying to the defendants that if they get "out of our frying pan" they might "jump into a Polish or Yugoslav fire."'[25]

FROM HIS private writings it is clear that Jackson by now regarded the participation of the Russian judges in the trial which he had staged as a mixed blessing at best, and as a mockery of international justice at worst. The shorthand notes of his last secret conferences with the Russians before the trial began revealed him bluntly reminding them of their own sins and warning that the United States would not identify itself with Soviet misdeeds: if the defence counsel succeeded in making capital from the secret Ribbentrop–Molotov Pact of August 1939, the Russians had only themselves to blame. He himself proposed to make no reference to it in his opening speech. As a lawyer, he was uneasy about this suppression of the truth, but he saw no alternative.

To his surprise and relief, when the British draft opening speech was circulated among the prosecution teams, Jackson found that Shawcross was proposing not only to grasp this nettle firmly, but to turn it about and brandish it defiantly in the faces of the defendants in the finest tradition of the English Bar: Whitehall's diplomats had concocted for him an arguable case suggesting that during that fateful visit to Moscow on August 22–23, 1939 the artful Ribbentrop had tricked the innocent Russians into signing the wicked pact—that Ribbentrop had thus pulled the wool over Soviet eyes while actually concealing from them Germany's predatory intent to launch an attack on Poland. Implausible though the argument was, it was at least something; it would make it impossible for the defence lawyers to allege that the prosecuting powers had concealed the existence of the document.

The Russians were not amused by this sleight-of-hand. General Roman Rudenko, their chief prosecutor, stormed without appointment into Jackson's office, waving a copy of Shawcross's proposed speech. 'I refuse to allow this calumny to be stated!' he shouted.

Jackson was astonished. He had believed the Russians would welcome Shawcross's clever jiggery-pokery. But the Russians were furious at the suggestion that a Ribbentrop could have outwitted a Molotov and a Stalin. For the British there was no alternative but to cut out the offending passage altogether. The Russians denied there had ever been such a secret pact. It had never existed, because they said so. It was *nulle et non avenue*. The skeleton was bundled back into the closet: not that it would remain there for long.

THE NIGHTMARE of awkward documents lurking in the captured German records continued to beset the Allied prosecutors throughout the trial. Fortunately the British had captured the most incriminating files, those of the German admiralty and foreign ministry, and had whisked them out of the country; they had released portions of these only with the utmost reluctance to Nuremberg. At one secret meeting of the chief prosecutors at Nuremberg we find the British representatives insisting, on instructions from London, that the archives of the German admiralty and foreign ministry be returned as soon as possible to their safes in London, because of the 'embarrassment' that their publication would cause to the British government if they should fall into the wrong hands.

❖ ❖ ❖ ❖ ❖

The dice were heavily loaded against the defendants in other ways, too. A basic difficulty for the defence lawyers was their unfamiliarity with the Anglo-American trial procedure adopted at Nuremberg: German lawyers were wholly inexperienced in the techniques of examination and cross-examination, and they were profoundly surprised by the latitude to object and interrupt shown to counsel under the Anglo-American system.

A more fundamental distinction was that even during the Third Reich the German trial procedures had been conducted with the primary objective of ascertaining truth, and all parties had united with that aim—the judges conducting the principal examination of witnesses, the opposing counsel being there to underline aspects that favoured the defence or prosecution. As Otto Kranzbühler, Dönitz's young attorney, would later comment. it was an essential feature of the Anglo-American criminal trial that it was confrontational, with each side introducing only the evidence which benefited its own case. Unlike the German custom, there was practically no obligation on the court to investigate the truth for itself. When the defence made their desiderata known to Jackson, he robustly turned them down, stating that he had no intention of 'serving two masters.'[26]

Were the scales not loaded in advance against one side or the other, this would not normally cause an injustice. In Nuremberg, it was as though the scales had only one scale-pan, on the side of the victorious powers. 'When the German defence attorneys arrived in Nuremberg in September 1945,' observed Kranzbühler, 'they had literally nothing. The prosecution on the other hand had already seized all available archives and documents and they were screening them with a huge army of experts for incriminating evidence.' Only this incriminating material was then made available to the defence attorneys; they were allowed no opportunity to look in the captured archives for defence documents in mitigation or exoneration. The foreign archives were also inaccessible to them.[27]

In a German court it would be unthinkable—and illegal—for one party to withhold part of a document which might tend to aid the other party's case.[28] But here at Nuremberg documents which might aid the defence were routinely concealed from them, or even destroyed. (It is quite wrong for Sir David Maxwell Fyfe to claim in his memoirs that 'all the documents were available to the Defence.')[29] Dr Alfred-Maurice de Zayas has expressed the view that the verdict on many of the points charged against the High Command (O.K.W.) would probably have been very different if the German defence lawyers had been allowed access to the captured records of the O.K.W.'s Office of Special Investigations into Violations of International Law (Wehrmachts-Untersuchungsstelle für Verletzungen des Völkerrechts) and permitted to select documents from those files in mitigation of the High Command's actions: 'But these files were "classified" and they were not finally released to the public domain until the seventies.'[30]

Thus at Nuremberg an extract could be quoted from a document against the defendant Alfred Rosenberg, reporting in detail clearly atrocious acts in the occupied eastern territories; the defence was able to establish—though not without difficulty—that the prosecution had omitted the beginning of the document, which showed the Rosenberg official to be protesting against the atrocities described.

Again, the Russians had submitted as an exhibit a shorthand transcript of an August 1942 conference on foodstuffs, in which a crucial page had been deleted where Göring evidently inquired about the situation in the Baltic states and in particular about the food the Jews in Riga were being given, because on the next page we find Gauleiter Hinrich Lohse replying to him: 'I can answer that point too. Only a small part of the Jews are still alive there; tens of thousands have gone. Let me however say what the native population is getting: on your instructions they're getting fifty percent less than the German population.'[31] Logically, had the missing page shown evidence that Göring was *aware* of the liquidation of the Jews in Riga, it would not have been excised. (This is not to say that Göring showed the Jews much pity. Speer—who was no angel in this respect either—would recall one remark by Göring in the prison yard, when somebody told the Reichsmarschall about Jews still living in Hungary: 'Oh, there are some left then? I thought we'd bumped them all off. Looks like somebody slipped up again.')[32]

If the robust, devious, and confrontational atmosphere of British and American courtrooms was unfamiliar to the German lawyers, they had one great advantage: they spoke the language of the documents, and they were familiar through their clients with the real facts of the case, while the Allies were forced to learn the facts for themselves and to grope their way through often highly inadequate translations and interpreters.

Against that, the Allies monopolised the captured documents and libraries, and the Germans could get no access to books and documents from abroad except through the offices of the prosecution. A vital book by Romania's former foreign minister Gafencu was on sale throughout Switzerland, but was denied to the defence lawyers in Nuremberg, as was the published war dispatch of the U.S. Army chief of staff, in which General George C. Marshall confirmed that no concerted plan had existed between Germany and Italy prior to Pearl Harbor—refuting one important point of the indictment.

When Göring's lawyer invited the Polish exile general Wladyslaw Anders to supply his evidence that the Russians themselves were the murderers of thousands of Poles at Katyn, Anders' Allied superiors forbade him to comply. Documents which Sir David Maxwell Fyfe had printed in three hundred copies for the press were virtually unavailable to the German lawyers. On January 11, 1946, Hans Frank's lawyer Alfred Seidl would apply to the court for the former governor-general of Poland to be allowed to use his own diaries, of which he had voluntarily turned over forty volumes to the Seventh Army. Those volumes were now in the courthouse document room, but he too was allowed to use only those extracts that had been picked by the prosecution.[33] Permission was refused.

While the prosecution disposed of innumerable telephone lines and comprehensive transport facilities, the defence counsel had to share two telephones between them. A document mentioned one day by the prosecution in the courtroom was rushed to the prosecutors from Vienna to Nuremberg by aeroplane on the next; defence counsel enjoyed no such streamlined facilities.

In contrast, they suffered repeated harassment. One of Neurath's lawyers was arrested and imprisoned for six weeks without being charged.[34] Dr Marx, assigned against his will to act as Streicher's attorney, was subjected to vicious press attacks, his office was ransacked, and he constantly feared arrest and imprisonment. For reasons of self-preservation he tried to dissociate himself from his client as much as decently possible.[35] As the trial drew to its close in the summer of 1946 Jodl's lawyer Professor Hermann Jahrreiss would find it necessary to make a formal appeal to the Tribunal for protection.[36] The judges did then order a degree of protection for the defence lawyers from the persecution and threats of the newspapers that the Allies had allowed to open under licence in Germany.[37]

THERE WAS too a marked difference in the treatment of defence and prosecution witnesses. Hostile witnesses found they were housed in the main jailhouse under conditions no better than the defendants'—unless they had to be kept out of sight of the more inquisitive, in which case they were moved into a 'detention home' nearby under somewhat better conditions.[38] If they were friendly witnesses, they were treated to luxury accommodation and special rations. The latter practice stopped only after this first trial, when U.S. prosecutor Walter Rapp circulated a notice warning that they were not to be coddled even if they chose to 'sing.'[39]

Key witnesses applied for by the defence were routinely declared to be untraceable. The Americans accused Keitel of involvement in the murder of a French general—S.S. Gruppenführer Hans Jüttner was said to have acted on Keitel's orders. His lawyer Dr Nelte demanded that Jüttner be called as a witness; the Americans claimed they did not know where he was. 'Nelte announced he would drive up to see Jüttner immediately,' Keitel told his son months later, 'and only then did the Americans admit that Jüttner had been interrogated months earlier.' Jüttner confirmed that he had never received any order whatever from Keitel in this connection.[40]

The same thing happened to one of General Jodl's key witnesses. Needing expert evidence of British plans to invade neutral Norway in 1940, they contacted Colonel Soltmann of the O.K.W.'s intelligence branch Fremde Heere West. The German naval High Command had deciphered Britain's naval signals; and Britain's own operational plans had been captured during WESERÜBUNG, Hitler's invasion of Norway. Subsequently Britain's aggressive intentions had been laid bare by the records of the 1940 Supreme War Council meetings, captured by the Germans in a boxcar in railroad sidings at Le Charité outside Paris.[41] Soltmann cabled his willingness to testify—and was immediately arrested by the Americans.[42] In February 1946 Göring's lawyers asked for General Karl Koller, the last chief of air staff, as a witness; the Americans made out that the general could not be traced, although their interrogator Ernst Engländer had himself questioned him at a C.S.D.I.C. (Combined Services Detailed Interrogation Centre) in England.[43]

Those defence witnesses that did arrive at Nuremberg were softened up by the prosecution interrogators before being turned over to the defence. Some ended up in solitary confinement in the prison wing. S.S. Obergruppenführer Karl Wolff, who volunteered to defend Kaltenbrunner and the S.S., was whisked away by the Americans to a lunatic asylum until, summoned to give evidence at a subsequent trial (the Milch Case) a year later, he was able to establish his sanity and released on the trial judge's orders to a normal prison. A further embarrassment was that Wolff alleged that Allen Dulles had promised him immunity in return for negotiating the surrender of the Axis forces in Italy in April 1945.[44] Field-Marshal Milch, who ignored the blackmail attempts of the American interrogator Engländer and gave evidence in defence of Speer and Göring, would be immediately removed to the notorious punishment bunker at Dachau concentration camp.[45]

True, the defence lawyers were usually well treated by their colleagues of the prosecution: they were provided with accommodation, American rations, and transportation. But they were outnumbered and outgunned. The American prosecution team now employed hundreds of men and women. Dr Nelte wrote sorrowfully to the wife of his client Field-Marshal Keitel: 'The trial effort being mounted by the victors is colossal. The evidence that has been amassed by the prosecution is a crippling burden for us, because we have no documents of comparable quality on the German side to put in against them. All we can do is to try to piece together opposing evidence by an intricate process of mosaic work.'[46]

What loaded the scales of justice most heavily against the defence however was the London Statute itself, which had established the trial procedure. Most of the usual devices open to a capable defence counsel had been smitten from his hands in advance by the skilful advance planning of their opponents the prosecutors, meeting in London to draw up the Statute. The writ of habeas corpus was not available. The Statute ruled inadmissible in advance many defences which would have been open to the Germans. The lawyers were not allowed to challenge the jurisdiction of the Tribunal or the judges' impartiality. Streicher commented in his diary: 'The usual court practice is that a defendant can challenge a judge for lack of impartiality. That would be the case if for instance the judge was related to a trial adversary. In this show trial the victors are the prosecutors and the judges of the vanquished and inevitably prejudiced. Because they are fully aware of this, they have laid down an appropriate rule denying to the defendants in advance the opportunity of challenging them.' 'And that is the purpose of the whole farce,' continued this unusually articulate gauleiter. 'In this trial there is no question of according to the defendant a blind and impartial justice; the trial has been set the task of giving to an injustice a veneer of legality by cloaking it in the language of the law.'[47]

The Tribunal also squelched every attempt by the prisoners to raise the question of their conditions of imprisonment. When Streicher tried to protest from the witness box about the beatings he had received, Jackson had the allegation struck from the record.

The mood was one of revenge: an eye for an eye. A letter reached the justice from a rich New York merchant, Ernest Schoenfeld, begging him: 'If it would be permissable [*sic*], if and when Julius Streicher is doomed to die, my most ardent wish would be to not only witness his execution, but participate in it.'[48]

The writer undertook to pay his own round-trip expenses, and offered Jackson a large sum of money as an inducement; Jackson did not reply.

14: **Much Vodka and Fun**

THE BIGGEST surprise for the defence came after the trial began. In a section titled 'A Fair Trial' the London Statute provided for the prosecution to make an 'opening statement'; in the event, this lasted for many weeks, while day after day press and radio accorded to the statement the widest publicity. When defence counsel then also asked to deliver an opening statement they were told there was no such provision in the Statute. At the end of the trial the process would be repeated: the defence lawyers were each allowed to make only a brief speech, followed by a lengthy closing argument by the prosecution to which the defence could make no reply.

The defendants were allowed to make a brief speech, a 'final statement' before judgement was passed, but Justice Jackson bitterly begrudged them even this; surprisingly, the Russians insisted on allowing it, since the last word was a fundamental right of the defendant in Russian procedure. (In a private letter to President Truman, Jackson predicted: 'I anticipate that this privilege will be used for propaganda purposes'—as though this were not the Allied purpose in staging the whole trial.)

In the course of the trial, as they were entitled to under their Statute, the judges rejected every attempt by the defendants and their counsel to challenge the jurisdiction of the Tribunal. Professor Hermann Jahrreiss, the eminent Cologne expert on international law, did however devote his closing speech—the first defence speech and as such bound to attract some publicity—to a comprehensive attack on the new laws that underlay this trial. The British prosecution were more apprehensive about Jahrreiss' speech than the American, who knew that at home the trial had long vanished from newspapers' front pages. They proposed simply to ignore the Jahrreiss argument. Sir Hartley Shawcross, the British attorney-general, was however sufficiently perturbed to fly to Nuremberg for a day himself, to urge Jackson to take Jahrreiss seriously: 'I understand Jahrreiss will say that there is no such thing in international law as a criminal war of aggression; that the Charter is the retroactive law of the victors and that in any event what these men did was legal under German law.' Shawcross for one was not satisfied with Jackson's proposal that, since the Tribunal was empowered to ignore any attack on the Charter, they too need not heed it.[1]

❖ ❖ ❖ ❖ ❖

After voting itself into a Christmas recess on December 20, 1945, against the prosecutors' protests, it was the New Year before the Tribunal reassembled.

Jackson was angry at this delay. 'We wanted to work right through except Christmas Day,' explained Jackson to his wife. 'But nothing doing with the French & British so near home.' He set off on a two-week excursion trip, beginning with a pilgrimage to the ruins of Adolf Hitler's mountainside home above Berchtesgaden.

General Joseph McNarney, the American military governor, loaned them his private train—it had until May belonged to Hermann Göring, so it was well appointed.[2] Justice Jackson's trip would take him through Rome, Athens, and the Middle East; he saw sights he had never seen before or desired to see again, including labourers working with ancient gear to build a mosque in Egypt under a slavemaster who drove them on with a whip just as their ancestors had when building the pyramids.[3]

The Tribunal took life more easily. Judge Biddle, a hard drinker, made his annual resolution to forgo alcohol for a month.[4] He was impatient to see his wife: the British and French judges had eventually been allowed to bring their wives over, but not the Americans. Travelling through Paris, he took tea at the British embassy and found on his left a very pretty secretary, as he wrote teasingly to his wife on the last day of 1945, identifying her as 'Miss Lloyd Thomas, who wants to come to Nuremberg and has my address and promised to help; lovely skin and breasts, so if you care come soon!'[5]

The faces gaunt and eyes hollow as once those of their own prisoners had been, the Nuremberg defendants languished in solitary confinement in their cells awaiting the resumption of the trial. The Red Cross packages mailed to them had been seized by the Americans. There were still no letters from their families. On what was to prove his final birthday, January 12, Göring wrote to the president of the Tribunal to complain that he had received only three letters from his wife and daughter, Emmy and Edda, since his capture. He asked the international Tribunal to order the U.S. Army to allow the letters through. 'Before my voluntary surrender to American custody,' he protested, 'I wrote asking General Eisenhower to take care of my family. Upon arrival at Seventh Army headquarters (General Patch) I was expressly promised that my request would be honoured. My wife, daughter, relatives, and next of kin were taken to Veldenstein Castle, my family property north of Nuremberg, and interned there. They were able to move around the castle freely, though isolated from the outside world, which was very satisfactory to me.'[6]

There was a reason why Emmy's letters were not reaching Göring and the others. In mid-October Counter-Intelligence Corps agent Paul H. Goldenberg had arbitrarily arrested her and her little daughter; the mother had been thrown into Straubing prison (now designated a 'civilian internment camp') and Edda had been snatched away from her and put in an orphanage. On November 24 Edda had been locked up in Straubing with her mother. The C.I.C. had also arrested Emmy's niece, sister, and nurse. The other Nuremberg prisoners' children had also been taken away and put in foster homes, while their womenfolk were sent to prison.

Hans Frank was subjected to the same kind of psychological blackmail. He learned that his sister Elisabeth had held in Straubing since September. 'My sister is completely innocent of any involvement in the accusations levelled against me,' he protested in a letter to Biddle—it never reached the judge. 'She has never been politically active and was not even a member of the Nazi Party.' Their seventy-year-old mother was now quite defenceless. 'Please be so good as to attend to this case,' Frank pleaded. 'God will reward you!'[7] These cases were not exceptions. Dr Schacht heard that his two children had been taken away from his wife. Baldur von Schirach, who had been ready to denounce Hitler and the whole Nazi ideology before the trial started, learned that his wife Henriette had been arrested on December 22 and taken to prison at Bad Tölz; under Göring's influence Schirach now wavered, and began to harden against the Americans (even though his mother was an American.)

IT HAS to be said on Andrus' behalf that when he learned that the Counter-Intelligence Corps had begun this vindictive round-up of the prisoners' wives and families his blood boiled and he wrote a furious official letter to higher headquarters to protest. The colonel demanded to know the reasons for these arrests, failing which he asked for the release of the womenfolk and children. 'Otherwise,' he predicted, 'during progress of the defense, testimony would be offered in the trial which would place the Americans on the defensive.'[8]

'You see,' Dr Gustave M. Gilbert, Jackson's resident army psychiatrist, a Jew who had fled Germany before the war, overheard Göring telling the others, 'they are just as bad as the Gestapo themselves. Don't let them pretend that they are democratic. The Americans are still our enemies. What have women and children got to do with this?'

A few days later the U.S. Army ordered Henry F. Gerecke, the fifty-four-year-old Lutheran pastor, to visit Emmy at Straubing prison, and he returned with greetings for her embattled husband.

'Now I am feeling calmer,' Göring wrote in reply. 'It's obvious why you're all in custody—just because you are mine. As the Führer is dead, I am the No. 1 principal war criminal, and you are my relatives. The hatred and the thirst for revenge—you can imagine whose—are boundless.... But I am not going to let them bend or break me.... How often I go to you in my thoughts and try to imagine the life you are leading! Have you enough books? My treasure, I cannot express how much I love you. You and Edda have always been my pride and joy. I am filled with gratitude to you both.' Why on earth, he added, had they arrested his nurse Christa?

Prison officials found that in her reply Emmy had sent him a four-leaf clover; they removed it, but he thanked her for the thought, commenting: 'Luck—ours has run out now.' 'Day and night,' he wrote her in another letter, 'two eyes stare at me through the porthole in the cell door. A spotlight shines on me all night.... Your letters are the only sunshine in my life.'[9]

THE TRIAL reopened on January 2, 1946. There was immediate unpleasantness for the defence on the third, as S.S. Obergruppenführer Otto Ohlendorf, an officer with a clever but criminal brain, testified about the mass shootings of Jews which he had himself directed on the eastern front.

Worse followed that afternoon. Albert Speer's defence lawyer rose to his feet and asked Ohlendorf whether he was aware that his client had plotted in 1945 to assassinate the Führer. Speer and Ohlendorf had been close friends. Göring spluttered with rage when he realised what Speer was up to. He stormed over to Speer as soon as the court adjourned, but the former minister turned away from him.

In direct testimony later, Speer would boast of how he had sabotaged Hitler's instruction for the scorched-earth defence of the Reich, vetoed Hitler's instructions to destroy strategic bridges, and plotted with General Gotthard Heinrici to countermand Hitler's orders for the relief of Berlin. When the trial ended Speer would admit in a wry letter to his wife: 'Most of the other defendants made things as tough as they could for me after they had heard details of my activities in the final phase of the war. It wasn't hard to imagine what they would have done if they had found out about them before the war was over. There wouldn't have been much left of my family.'[10]

Questioned in open court about his plan to assassinate Hitler and his staff, Speer feigned shyness. 'I'd prefer not to go into further details on this,' he replied, which obliged the Tribunal, after consultation, to insist: 'The Tribunal would very much like to hear the details.' After the recess which then followed Speer said alluringly: 'I am divulging these details only with the utmost reluctance, because there is a lot that is unattractive about such things. I am going to do so only because the Tribunal insists.... It is not my intention that my own case should profit from this episode.'

'*Gott im Himmel!*' roared Göring to Dr Gilbert afterward. 'I nearly died of shame. To think that a German could be so rotten, just to prolong his wretched life—to put it crudely, to piss in front and crap behind a little longer. *Herrgott! Donnerwetter!* For myself,' he added, 'I don't care if I get executed.... But there is still such a thing as honour.'[11]

NUREMBERG 1945 A cheerless place to live in, let alone to die.

RADIO TIMES HULTON PICTURE LIBRARY

FRANKLIN D ROOSEVELT LIBRARY, HYDE PARK, NEW YORK

telegram to be sent by
e Minister to Marshal Stalin.

Conference of foreign Ministers
Minister of Great Britain
g the local punishment of war
and, if possible, at the scenes
been committed. With some

small amendments this document was approved and has been published to the world with general acceptance and approval. This document however did not attempt to deal with the cases of the major war criminals "whose offences have no particular geographical localization". This matter was touched on in conversation at Teheran without any definite conclusion being reached. It has now become important for us to reach agreement about the treatment of these major criminals. Would you consider whether a list could not be prepared of say 50 to 100 persons whose responsibilities for directing or impelling the whole process of crime and atrocity is

LYNCH LAW **At Dachau regular German soldiers relieve the fleeing S.S. unit doing guard duty on the notorious camp a few days before its liberation. On April 29, 1945, 560 of the soldiers surrender to the Americans. The Americans put all but forty of them to death, includin a doctor carrying a Red Cross flag. A G.I. takes this photo as a machine-gunner (kneeling, *centre of photo*) of the 15th Regiment, 45th Infantry Division, executes 358 of the soldiers lined up against a wall.**

ALL PHOTOS UNLESS OTHERWISE STATED: U.S. ARMY SIGNALS CORPS, NATIONAL ARCHIVES, WASHINGTON DC

WORLD OUTLAWS On September 17, 1944 Churchill obtains President Roosevelt's approval for his plan to shoot the enemy leaders out of hand upon capture.

He drafts a message (*left*) to Stalin suggesting they agree on a list of 50 to 100 people whose guilt will be established merely by 'the fact of their holding certain high offices.'

The United Nations shall declare people on this list to be world outlaws. Upon their falling into Allied hands 'the nearest General officer will convene a court for the sole purpose of establishing their identity, and when this has been done will have them shot within six hours without reference to higher authority.'

Churchill himself puts this plan to Stalin in Moscow in October 1944.

But the Soviet leader takes an unexpectedly respectable line, saying: 'There must be no executions without trial otherwise the world would say we were afraid to try them.'

Having stuck his neck out, Churchill immediately draws it in. 'Of course, of course,' he lisps to Stalin. 'We should give them a trial first.'

RIBBENTROP COLLECTION, NATIONAL ARCHIVES, WASHINGTON DC

NOW YOU SEE HIM... At the summer 1945 conferences in London General **Iona Nikitchenko** (*far left*) helps fellow chief prosecutors **Robert H Jackson** (USA), Sir **David Maxwell Fyfe** (UK), and **Robert Falco** (France) decide which Germans shall go on the list to be put on trial as war criminals (IMPERIAL WAR MUSEUM)

SIR NORMAN BIRKETT British 'alternate'. He sends witty poems about champagne salesman Ribbentrop to the prosecution bench. A drunk American lawyer flings a confidential arm around his neck. 'What I like about you, Birkett, is that you are not one of those condescending sons-of-bitches that they so often send over.'

SIR GEOFFREY LAWRENCE British judge, and president of the Tribunal. 'The old goat is so dumb,' notes Biddle in his diary, 'so inept that it becomes a long series of petty annoyances at the end of a long, dull day.' Biddle thinks him spineless, but he won the Distinguished Service Order for heroism as a gunner in World War One.

... AND NOW YOU SEE HIM AGAIN At Nuremberg, Nikitchenko (*far right*), turns up as the Soviet judge, claiming the same impartiality as his colleagues **Donnedieu de Vabres** (France), **Francis Biddle** (USA) and Sir **Geoffrey Lawrence** (UK) in deciding those same Germans' criminality. Falco, not shown, is now Vabres' alternate.

FRANCIS BIDDLE American judge. Humiliated by Göring, Robert Jackson calls Biddle a first-class sonofabitch, and insanely jealous because he has the bigger car and better house. Biddle is smug: 'I do really run this show,' he records, 'and have won every point, single-handed, except for Parker, who is often a nuisance.'

JOHN J PARKER American 'alternate'. Parker, notes Biddle before the trial begins, 'is ready to do anything I suggest.' The reclusive Parker reminds Biddle of a lonely schoolboy. Biddle persuades him to call him by his first name. But Parker still finds the courage to enter opinions at Nuremberg which differ strongly from those of Biddle.

ROBERT H JACKSON OPENS FOR THE PROSECUTION AT NUREMBERG

If we want to shoot Germans as a matter of policy,' he says in April 1945, as the fighting in Europe sputters to an end, 'let it be done as such, but don't hide the deed behind a court. If you are determined to execute a man in any case, there is no occasion for a trial; the world yields no respect to courts that are merely organised to convict.'

Punished ...

SNAPSHOTS FROM A GERMAN SOLDIER'S PHOTO ALBUM

The daily routine of a cruel warfare in the Balkans. A German soldier is found mutilated. The German troops take reprisals, stringing up the menfolk in the village, like washing on a line—one by one, a chair kicked away beneath each victim and then painful death by strangulation. For crimes like these, German generals are executed at Nuremberg.

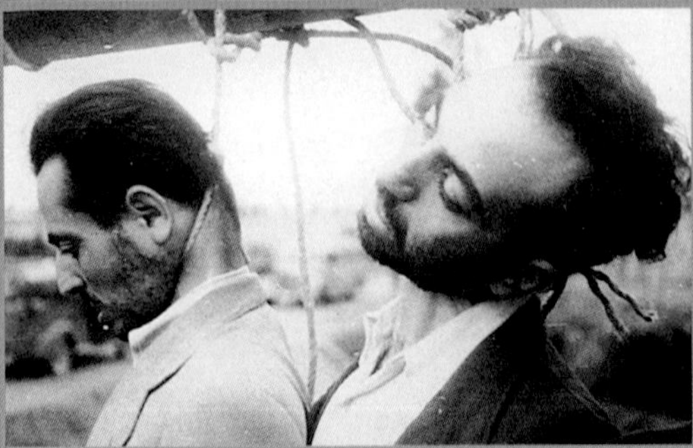

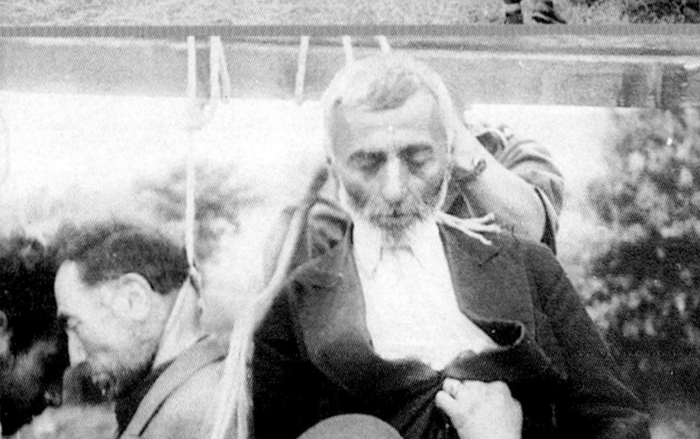

ROBERT JOHNSTON

... and Unpunished

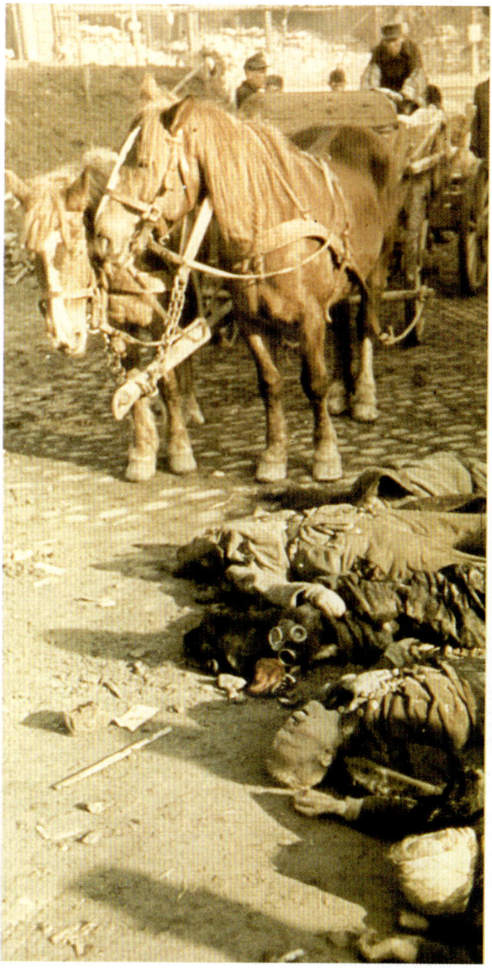

NO ALLIED GENERAL is ever called to account for the appalling fire-raids on Japan (*above*) or Dresden (*left* and *below*, scenes at the Altmarkt). In each of these 1945 raids about a hundred thousand innocent civilians are burned alive in what is only now universally recognized as a crime against international law (ORION, TOKYO; AUTHOR'S COLLECTION).

SUPERIOR ORDERS The army's new chief, Field-Marshal **Walther von Brauchitsch**, listens (*above left*) as Hitler dictates orders on July 13, 1940 to Rear-Admiral **Friedrich Wilhelm Fleischer**, Naval Commander, Channel Coast (AUTHOR'S COLLECTION).

IN THE REAR the brilliant strategist Colonel-General **Alfred Jodl** (*left*), Hitler's chief of operations, and Field-Marshal **Wilhelm Keitel** (*right*), chief of the High Command of the Armed Forces, look on. Both will be hanged at Nuremberg (WALTER FRENTZ).

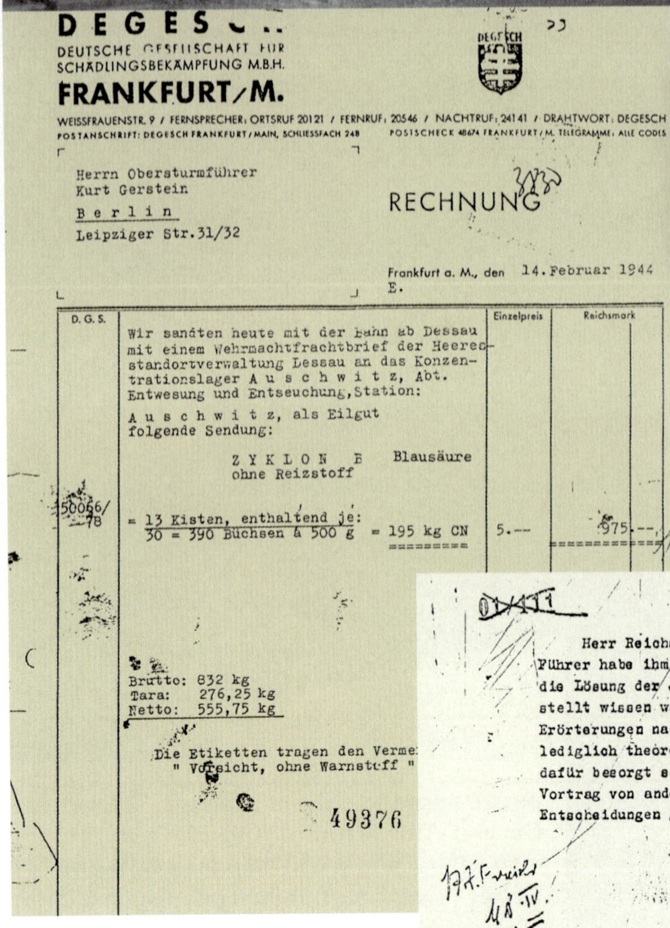

D E G E S C H
DEUTSCHE GESELLSCHAFT FÜR
SCHÄDLINGSBEKÄMPFUNG M.B.H.
FRANKFURT/M.

WEISSFRAUENSTR. 9 / FERNSPRECHER: ORTSRUF 20121 / FERNRUF: 20546 / NACHTRUF: 24141 / DRAHTWORT: DEGESCH
POSTANSCHRIFT: DEGESCH FRANKFURT/MAIN, SCHLIESSFACH 248 POSTSCHECK 48674 FRANKFURT/M. TELEGRAMME: ALLE CODES

Herrn Obersturmführer
Kurt Gerstein
B e r l i n
Leipziger Str.31/32

RECHNUNG

Frankfurt a. M., den 14. Februar 1944
E.

D. G. S.		Einzelpreis	Reichsmark
	Wir sandten heute mit der Bahn ab Dessau mit einem Wehrmachtfrachtbrief der Heeresstandortverwaltung Dessau an das Konzentrationslager A u s c h w i t z, Abt. Entwesung und Entseuchung, Station: A u s c h w i t z, als Eilgut folgende Sendung:		
	Z Y K L O N B Blausäure ohne Reizstoff		
50066/78	= 13 Kisten, enthaltend je: 30 = 390 Büchsen à 500 g = 195 kg CN	5.--	975.--
	Brutto: 832 kg Tara: 276,25 kg Netto: 555,75 kg		
	Die Etiketten tragen den Verme[rk] " Vorsicht, ohne Warnstoff "		
	49376		

Franz Schlegelberger (*above*), of the ministry of the interior, notes in 1942 (*below*) that Hitler has repeatedly ordered the solution of the Jewish problem postponed until after the war.

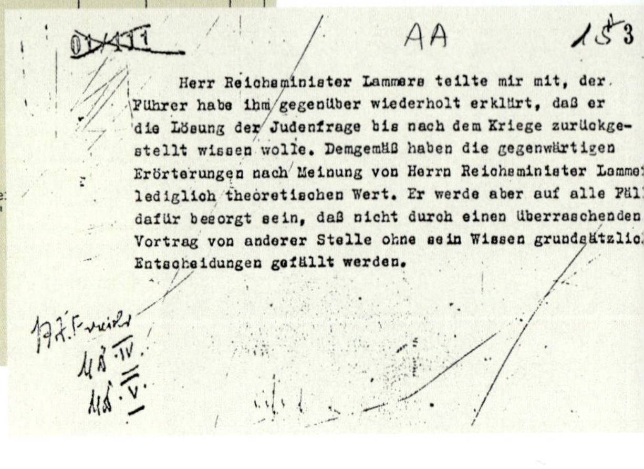

AA 153

Herr Reichsminister Lammers teilte mir mit, der Führer habe ihm gegenüber wiederholt erklärt, daß er die Lösung der Judenfrage bis nach dem Kriege zurückgestellt wissen wolle. Demgemäß haben die gegenwärtigen Erörterungen nach Meinung von Herrn Reichsminister Lamme[rs] lediglich theoretischen Wert. Er werde aber auf alle Fäl[le] dafür besorgt sein, daß nicht durch einen überraschenden Vortrag von anderer Stelle ohne sein Wissen grundsätzlic[he] Entscheidungen gefällt werden.

PEST CONTROL IN THE AUSCHWITZ SLAVE LABOUR CAMP

Tons of Zyklon B pellets, containing poisonous hydrogen cyanide, are shipped by the Degesch factory to the Pest Control division of Auschwitz and other camps including Oranienburg in 1944.

right By the end of that year British Intelligence has photos of the deadly canisters (PUBLIC RECORDS OFFICE, LONDON; AUTHOR'S COLLECTION).

After passing through the hands of Dr Robert Kempner, of Jackson's prosecution team (*extreme right*), this and other key documents vanish from sight for forty years.

PRISON COMMANDANT It is the grim duty of U.S. army Colonel Burton C Andrus (*at left*) to see that his prisoners survive long enough to mount the gallows.

SUBMARINE WARFARE In ordering unrestricted submarine warfare against Anglo-American shipping, the Tribunal rules, the German admiralty has followed the same rules as have been adopted by the British and American navies (AUTHOR'S COLLECTION).

WALTER FRENTZ

Grand-Admiral **Erich Raeder** is commander-in-chief of the German navy when Hitler seizes power in 1933. His lawyers argue that the British planned to invade Norway in April 1940, and that Hitler got there first.

Karl Dönitz succeeds him in 1943. The American Judge Biddle feels that he should be acquitted, saying: 'Germany waged a much cleaner war than we did.' Jackson admits privately the case against the admirals is the weakest they have.

TURNCOAT Lieutenant-General **Walter Warlimont**, deputy chief of the operations division of the High Command, proves helpful, drawing up in his own handwriting a list of those he thinks deserve to hang, including his own superiors Keitel and Jodl.

AUTHOR'S COLLECTION

WALTER FRENTZ

HOW THEY DO IT The Americans use dubious methods to procure evidence, even when not necessary. Major **Ernst Engländer** (*left*) ingratiates himself with freshly surrendered Reichsmarschall **Göring**, but threatens his Field-Marshal **Erhard Milch** (*above*) with war crimes indictment if he doesn't testify as required.

IN BLACK AND WHITE Colonel-General **Alfred Jodl** finds himself confronted with documents he now wishes he had never signed, like an order by Hitler for the liquidation of the Soviet commissars in May 1941 as soon as they are captured.

THE PROSECUTORS A ruthless cross-examiner, Sir **David Maxwell Fyfe** (*right*) directs the British prosecution at Nuremberg even after the Labour Government is elected. He outshines **Robert H Jackson**, the United States chief of counsel (*above*), whose courtroom skills have grown rusty from disuse.

RADIO TIMES HULTON PICTURE LIBRARY

DEAR EMMY,
DEAR EDDA
In his jailhouse cell **Hermann Göring**, stripped of all his medals, writes a postcard to his wife and child. A postman delivers it in the forests outside Nuremberg.

AUTHOR'S COLLECTION

Göring's Last Letters

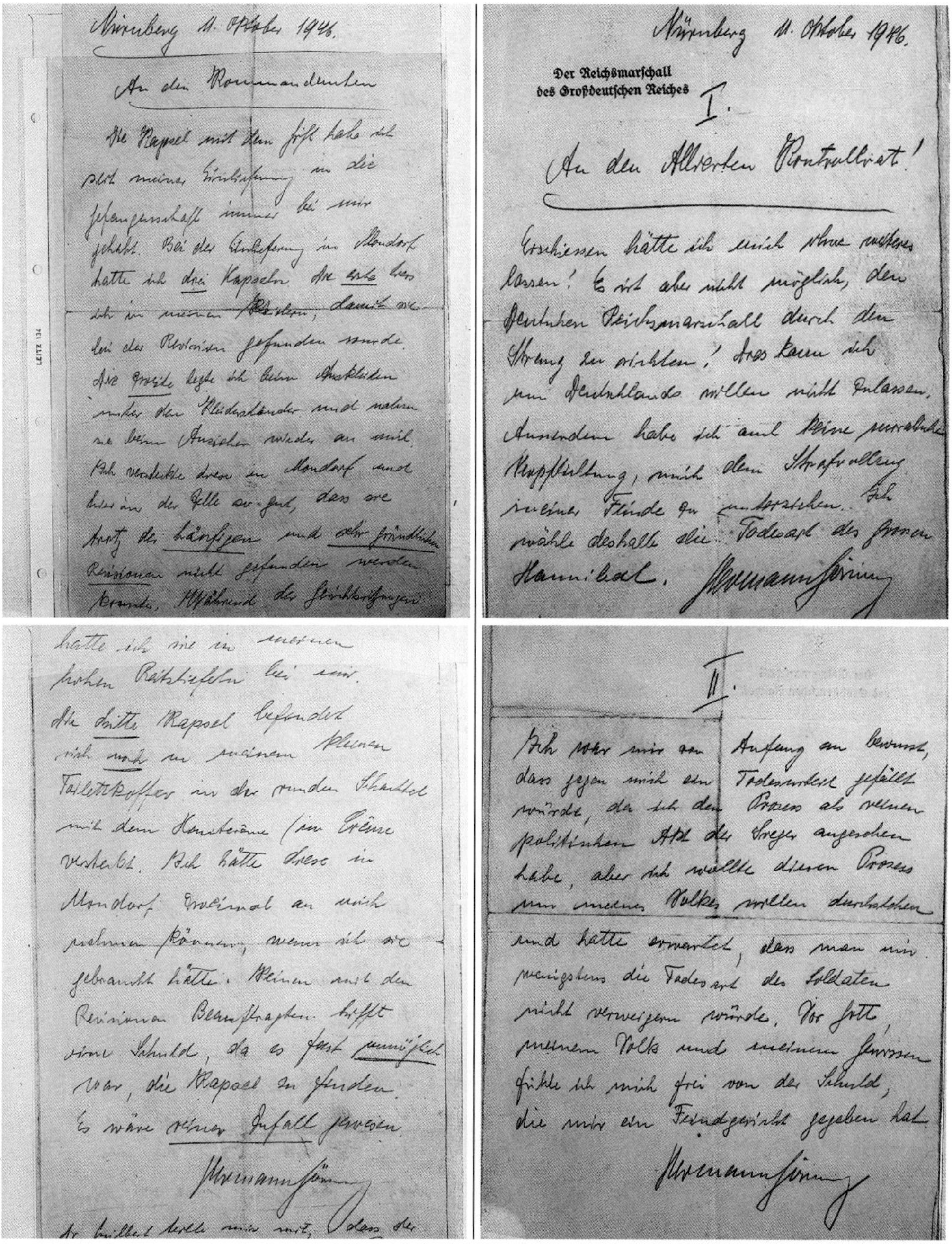

Nürnberg 11. Oktober 1946.

An den Kommandanten

Die Kapsel mit dem Gift habe ich seit meiner Einlieferung in die Gefangenschaft immer bei mir gehabt. Bei der Einlieferung in Mondorf hatte ich drei Kapseln. Die erste liess ich in meinen Kleidern, damit sie bei der Revision gefunden würde. Die zweite legte ich beim Auskleiden unter den Kleiderständer und nahm sie beim Anziehen wieder an mich. Ich versteckte diese in Mondorf und hier in der Zelle so gut, dass sie trotz der häufigen und sehr gründlichen Revisionen nicht gefunden werden konnte. Während der Gerichtsitzungen

hatte ich sie in meinen hohen Reitstiefeln bei mir. Die dritte Kapsel befindet sich noch in meinem kleinen Toilettekoffer in der runden Schachtel mit der Hautcreme (im Creme versteckt). Ich hätte diese in Mondorf zweimal an mich nehmen können, wenn ich sie gebraucht hätte. Keinen von den Revisionen Beauftragten trifft eine Schuld, da es fast unmöglich war, die Kapsel zu finden. Es wäre reiner Zufall gewesen.

Hermann Göring

Dr. Gilbert teilte mir mit, dass der

Nürnberg 11. Oktober 1946.

Der Reichsmarschall
des Großdeutschen Reiches

I.

An den Alliierten Kontrollrat!

Erschiessen hätte ich mich ohne weiteres lassen! Es ist aber nicht möglich, den Deutschen Reichsmarschall durch den Strang zu richten! Dies kann ich um Deutschlands willen nicht zulassen. Ausserdem habe ich auch keine moralische Verpflichtung, mich der Strafvollziehung meiner Feinde zu unterziehen. Ich wähle deshalb die Todesart des grossen Hannibal.

Hermann Göring

II.

Ich war mir von Anfang an bewusst, dass gegen mich ein Todesurteil gefällt würde, da ich den Prozess als reinen politischen Akt der Sieger angesehen habe, aber ich wollte diesen Prozess um meines Volkes willen durchstehen und hatte erwartet, dass man mir wenigstens die Todesart des Soldaten nicht verweigern würde. Vor Gott, meinem Volk und meinem Gewissen fühle ich mich frei von der Schuld, die mir ein Feindgericht gegeben hat.

Hermann Göring

U.S. MISSION, BERLIN DOCUMENT CENTER

left TO COLONEL ANDRUS I have always had the poison capsule with me.... I concealed it so well at Mondorf and here in the cell that despite *frequent* and *very thorough inspections* it could not be found. During the court hearings I kept it with me in my high riding boots.

right TO THE ALLIED CONTROL COUNCIL I would have let you shoot me without further ado! But it is not possible to hang the German Reichsmarschall! ... I have therefore chosen the manner of death of the great Hannibal. Hermann Göring.

JAILHOUSE NUREMBERG American soldiers keep a round-the-clock watch on the condemned men. Sentinels posted outside every cell watch their charges constantly. Göring's Cell No. 5 is furthest from the camera. A light-bulb fixed to every door grill (*right*) illuminates the interior all night long.

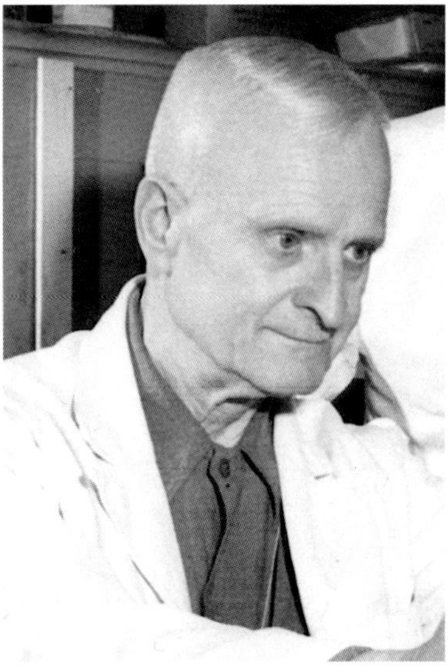

Escape!

Yet somehow Göring manages to retrieve from his impounded luggage the brass cartridge case with its lethal glass ampoule of hydrogen-cyanide.

MOST LIKELY SCENARIO
While General Jodl (*left*) and other defendants are earnestly conferring with their lawyers, Göring is shrewdly fraternising with Texan and fellow-huntsman Jack G. Wheelis, persuading him to get the ampoule out of the luggage so that Dr Ludwig Pflücker (*top right*) can smuggle it into Göring's hands.

AUTHOR'S COLLECTION

IN THE DOCK
Jodl, **Hans Frank** (dark glasses), **Papen**, **Frick** (slumped), **Seyss-Inquart** (blurred), **Speer**, **Funk** (reading newspaper) and **Neurath**.

During the trial the Allied licensed German newspapers behave despicably. Keitel's attorney finds that they are even thirstier for blood than their Allied counterparts. They leave unreported anything in the proceedings that speaks for the German people, or favours the German point of view.

below right American occupation newspaper *Die Neue Zeitung* announces Nuremberg verdicts (AUTHOR'S COLLECTION).

ON THE WITNESS STAND
About to hang, General **Alfred Jodl** writes to his young wife: 'When our friends come round to see you on the evening after my death that shall be my funeral parade. On a gun-carriage rests my coffin and all the German soldiers are marching with me—with those have died in battle out in front and the still living bringing up the rear.'

DIE NEUE ZEITUNG

EINE AMERIKANISCHE ZEITUNG FÜR DIE DEUTSCHE BEVÖLKERUNG

SONDERAUSGABE | 2. OKTOBER 1946 | PREIS 20 PFENNIG

Zwölf Todesurteile im Nürnberger Prozeß

Schacht, v. Papen und Fritzsche freigesprochen – Gefängnisstrafen für Heß, Funk, Raeder, Speer, v. Schirach, v. Neurath und Dönitz

NÜRNBERG, 1. Oktober (DANA, AP, NZ)

Am Montag, dem 30. September, und am Dienstag, dem 1. Oktober 1946, hat das Internationale Militärtribunal nach achtmonatiger Verhandlungsdauer das Urteil über die 21 anwesenden Angeklagten sowie über den nicht anwesenden Martin Bormann gesprochen. In der Montagsitzung gab der Gerichtshof unter dem Vorsitz des englischen Lordrichters Lawrence einen Rückblick über die Geschichte des Prozesses sowie über das vorgebrachte Beweismaterial und fällte dann das Urteil über die angeklagten Organisationen. In der Dienstagvormittagsitzung wurden die Schuldsprüche gegen die einzelnen Angeklagten und die Begründung dieser Schuldsprüche verlesen. Um 14.50 Uhr mitteleuropäischer Sommerzeit trat der Gerichtshof zum letztenmal zusammen, um das Strafmaß gegen die einzelnen Angeklagten zu verkünden. Im einzelnen verkündete der Gerichtshof die folgenden Beschlüsse:

Die Schuldsprüche:

Die Einzelangeklagten wurden von der Anklage unter vier Gesichtspunkten beschuldigt. Es waren dies: Anklagepunkt 1: Verschwörung gegen den Weltfrieden; Anklagepunkt 2: Planung, Entfesselung und Durchführung des Angriffskriegs; Anklagepunkt 3: Kriegsverbrechen; Anklagepunkt 4: Verbrechen gegen die Humanität. Nicht jeder der Angeklagten war aller vier Punkte der Anklageschrift beschuldigt worden. Hermann Göring war angeklagt in den Punkten 1, 2, 3 und 4 und wurde nach allen Punkten für schuldig befunden. Rudolf Heß war angeklagt in den Punkten 1, 2, 3 und 4 und wurde nach Punkt 1 und 2 für schuldig und nach Punkt 3 und 4 für nicht schuldig befunden. Joachim von Ribbentrop war angeklagt in den Punkten 1, 2, 3 und 4 und wurde nach allen Punkten für schuldig befunden. Wilhelm Keitel war angeklagt in den Punkten 1, 2, 3 und 4 und wurde nach allen Punkten für schuldig befunden. Ernst Kaltenbrunner war angeklagt in den Punkten 1, 3 und 4 und wurde nach Punkt 1 für nichtschuldig und nach Punkt 3 und 4 für schuldig befunden. Alfred Rosenberg war angeklagt in den Punkten 1, 2, 3 und 4 und wurde nach allen Punkten für schuldig befunden. Hans Frank war angeklagt in den Punkten 1, 3 und 4 und wurde nach Punkt 1 für nichtschuldig und nach Punkt 3 und 4 für schuldig befunden. Wilhelm Frick war angeklagt in den Punkten 1, 2, 3 und 4 und wurde nach Punkt 1 für nichtschuldig und nach Punkt 2, 3 und 4 für schuldig befunden. Julius Streicher war angeklagt in den Punkten 1 und 4 und wurde nach Punkt 1 für nichtschuldig, nach Punkt 4 für schuldig befunden. Walter Funk war angeklagt in den Punkten 1, 2, 3 und 4 und wurde nach Punkt 1 für nichtschuldig, nach Punkt 2, 3 und 4 für schuldig befunden. Karl Dönitz war angeklagt nach den Punkten 1, 2 und 3 und wurde nach Punkt 1 für nichtschuldig und nach Punkt 2 und 3 für schuldig befunden. Erich Raeder war angeklagt in den Punkten 1, 2 und 3 und wurde nach allen diesen Punkten für schuldig befunden. Baldur von Schirach war angeklagt in den Punkten 1 und 4 und wurde nach Punkt 1 für nichtschuldig und nach Punkt 4 für schuldig befunden. Fritz Sauckel war angeklagt in den Punkten 1, 2, 3 und 4 und wurde nach Punkt 1 und 2 für nichtschuldig und nach Punkt 3 und 4 für schuldig befunden. Alfred Jodl war angeklagt in den Punkten 1, 2, 3 und 4 und wurde nach allen Punkten für schuldig befunden. Arthur Seyß-Inquart war angeklagt in den Punkten 1, 2, 3 und 4 und wurde nach Punkt 1 für nichtschuldig und nach Punkt 2, 3 und 4 für schuldig befunden. Albert Speer war angeklagt in den Punkten 1, 2, 3 und 4 und wurde nach Punkt 1 und 2 für nichtschuldig und nach Punkt 3 und 4 für schuldig befunden. Konstantin Freiherr von Neurath war angeklagt in den Punkten 1, 2, 3 und 4 und wurde in allen Punkten für schuldig befunden. Martin Bormann war angeklagt in den Punkten 1, 3 und 4 und wurde nach Punkt 1 für nichtschuldig und nach Punkt 3 und 4 für schuldig befunden.

Vier der angeklagten Organisationen, die SS, der Sicherheitsdienst, die Gestapo und gewisse Gruppen des Korps der Politischen Leiter wurden von dem Gericht als verbrecherische Organisationen im Sinne des Statuts des Gerichtshofes beurteilt. Dieses Urteil steht nach den Bestimmungen des Londoner Abkommens durch den Tribunalspruch in Nürnberg unwiderruflich fest. Es hat jedoch, wie Oberrichter Robert H. Jackson in seiner grundlegenden Rede am 21. November 1945 erklärte, nur einen deklaratorischen Charakter und spricht weder gegen die Organisationen selbst noch gegen die Einzelmitglieder ein Strafmaß aus. Die Beurteilung einer Organisation als verbrecherisch gibt dagegen den zuständigen Behörden das Recht, Mitgliedern dieser Organisationen wegen ihrer Zugehörigkeit den Prozeß zu machen. In diesen Prozessen werden, wie Oberrichter Jackson dargelegt hat, die einzelnen Mitglieder der Organisationen die Möglichkeit haben, Umstände, die zu ihrer Entlastung beitragen, vorzubringen. Solche Umstände können der Nachweis des zwangsweisen Beitritts, der Zeitpunkt eines etwaigen Austritts und ähnliche Beweise sein. Auf keinen Fall kann jedoch ein Angeklagter in einem derartigen Verfahren noch einmal die Frage der Kriminalität seiner Organisation aufwerfen. Bestimmte Gruppen innerhalb von zwei der für verbrecherisch befundenen Organisationen waren von vornherein von der Strafverfolgung ausgenommen. Bei der Gestapo waren dies: Büroangestellte, Stenographen, Pförtner oder Personen, die ähnliche nichtamtliche Funktionen ausübten. Beim NS-Führerkorps waren es die Mitglieder der Stäbe von Ortsgruppenleitern, Zellenleitern und Blockleitern.

Die Freisprüche:

Bei den Einzelangeklagten beurteilte das Gericht das gegen die Angeklagten Hjalmar Schacht, Franz von Papen und Hans Fritzsche vorgebrachte Beweismaterial als nicht zu einer Verurteilung zureichend. Diese drei Angeklagten wurden nach allen gegen sie erhobenen Punkten der Anklage freigesprochen, und das Gericht ordnete ihre sofortige Entlassung nach Ende der Verhandlung an. Schacht war in den Punkten 1 und 2, von Papen ebenfalls in den Punkten 1 und 2 und Fritzsche in den Punkten 1, 3 und 4 angeklagt worden.

Vier der angeklagten Organisationen, die SA, das Reichskabinett, der Generalstab und das Oberkommando der Wehrmacht wurden von dem Gericht

Auszug aus der Urteilsbegründung

Begründung der Freisprüche

NÜRNBERG, 1. Oktober (DANA)

Schacht:

Der Angeklagte Schacht war lediglich nach den ersten zwei Anklagepunkten angeklagt und ist nach beiden freigesprochen worden. Der Gerichtshof hat angeordnet, daß er vom Gerichtsmarschall entlassen werde. Der Gerichtshof entschied, daß er in seiner Eigenschaft als Wirtschaftsminister und Bevollmächtigter für die Kriegswirtschaft zu der Finanzierung der frühesten Phasen der Aufrüstung Deutschlands beigetragen hatte, daß er jedoch dem Angriffskrieg ablehnend gegenüberstand und im Jahre 1937 von diesen beiden Posten zurücktrat, als es klar wurde, daß Hitler dem Kriege zutreibe. Der Gerichtshof hat entschieden, es sei nicht über einen vernünftigen Zweifel hinaus erwiesen worden, daß Schacht von den Angriffsplänen Hitlers wußte, als er das Aufrüstungsprogramm in seinem Anfangsstadium unterstützte.

Dazu sagte der Gerichtshof:

„Schacht war bei der Planung der nach Anklagepunkt 2 besonders aufgeführten Angriffskriege nicht beteiligt. Seine Beteiligung an der Besetzung Österreichs und des Sudetenlandes (die nicht in der Anklage als Angriffskriege aufgeführt werden) war derartig beschränkt, daß sie nicht als Teilnahme an dem unter Anklagepunkt 1 genannten gemeinsamen Plan zu bezeichnen ist. Es ist klar geworden, daß er nicht zu dem inneren Kreise um Hitler gehörte, der am engsten an diesem gemeinsamen Plan beteiligt war. Er wurde von dieser Gruppe mit unverschleierter Feindseligkeit betrachtet. Die Aussage Speers zeigt, daß Schachts Verhaftung am 23. Juli 1944 ebensosehr auf Hitlers Feindseligkeit gegenüber Schacht beruhte, die auf dessen Haltung vor dem Kriege zurückzuführen war wie auf den Verdacht seiner Teilnahme an dem Bombenattentat.

Der Tatbestand gegen Schacht hängt demnach von der Annahme ab, daß Schacht tatsächlich von den Angriffsplänen wußte. Mit Bezug auf diese außerordentlich wichtige Frage ist Beweismaterial für die Anklagevertretung vorgelegt worden sowie eine beträchtliche Menge von Beweismaterial für die Verteidigung. Der Gerichtshof hat die Gesamtheit dieses Beweismaterials aufs sorgfältigste erwogen und kommt zu dem Schluß, daß diese notwendige Annahme nicht über einen vernünftigen Zweifel hinaus bewiesen worden ist."

von Papen:

Der Gerichtshof hat entschieden, daß von Papen nach der Anklageschrift nicht schuldig sei und hat seine Entlassung durch den Ge-

führte zum Vertrage vom 11. Juli 1936, der scheinbar freundschaftliche Beziehungen zwischen Deutschland und Österreich wiederherstellte. Er bot dann seinen Rücktritt an, doch wurde sein Gesuch abgelehnt. Im Jahre 1938 wurde er von seinem Posten als Gesandter in Österreich abberufen und bereitete die Besprechungen zwischen Hitler und Schuschnigg vor, die am 12. Februar 1938 zu Berchtesgaden stattfanden.

Das Beweismaterial hat nicht erwiesen, daß er der gewaltsamen Besetzung Österreichs zustimmend gegenübergestanden hätte. Nach dem Anschluß zog er sich ins Privatleben zurück, bis er im Jahre 1939 zum Botschafter in der Türkei ernannt wurde. Der Gerichtshof hat erklärt: „Laut dem Beweismaterial unterliegt es keinem Zweifel, daß das Hauptziel von Papens als Gesandter in Österreich darin bestand, das Schuschniggsche Regime zu unterhöhlen und die österreichischen Nazis zu stärken, um den Anschluß herbeizuführen. Um diesen Plan durchzuführen, hat er sowohl Intrigen betrieben als auch Drohungen gebraucht. Das Statut hat jedoch solche Verletzungen der politischen Moral nicht als verbrecherisch bezeichnet.

Es liegen keine Beweise dafür vor, daß er an den Plänen, bei denen die Besetzung Österreichs einen Schritt in der Richtung weiterer Angriffshandlungen darstellte, teilgenommen hatte."

Fritzsche:

Der Gerichtshof hat Fritzsche für nicht schuldig im Sinne der Anklage befunden und seine Entlassung durch den Marschall des Gerichtshofes angeordnet.

„An der Spitze der Inlandspresseabteilung beaufsichtigte Fritzsche die deutsche Presse und hielt Pressebesprechungen ab. Er war Dietrich untergeordnet, und Dietrich stand seinerseits unter Befehl Goebbels'. Fritzsche leitete nur die ihm durch Dietrich übermittelten Instruktionen an die Presse weiter. Fritzsche wurde im Jahre 1942 Leiter der Rundfunkabteilung. Diese war eine der zwölf Abteilungen des Propagandaministeriums. Er nahm an Planungsbesprechungen keinen Anteil. Es liegen keine Beweise dafür vor, daß er die bei diesen Besprechungen erfolgten Entscheidungen kannte.

Die Anklage hat behauptet, daß er zum Begehen von Kriegsverbrechen aufgehetzt hat. Der Gerichtshof hat jedoch entschieden, daß seine Reden nicht zur Verfolgung oder Ausrottung der Juden aufgefordert haben, und daß keine Beweise vorhanden seien, daß er von der Vernichtung von Juden wußte. Er versuchte zweimal die Veröffentlichung des antisemi-

PHOTOGRAPHIC EVIDENCE The American forces who reach the concentration camp at Buchenwald, near Weimar, find thousands of emaciated victims of typhus and starvation; as one poses for the photographer, the faces of the others betray eagerness to be liberated. Two, on the bottom tier, are evidently too weak to move.

CREDIBILITY PROBLEMS As Madame **Marie-Claude Vaillant Couturier** (*below left*) testifies about her ordeal as a Communist interned at Auschwitz, Judge Francis Biddle notes that he does not believe her. S.S. officers **Rudolf Höss** (*centre*) and **Dieter Wisliceny** (*right*) testify to the Final Solution, and are hanged as a reward.

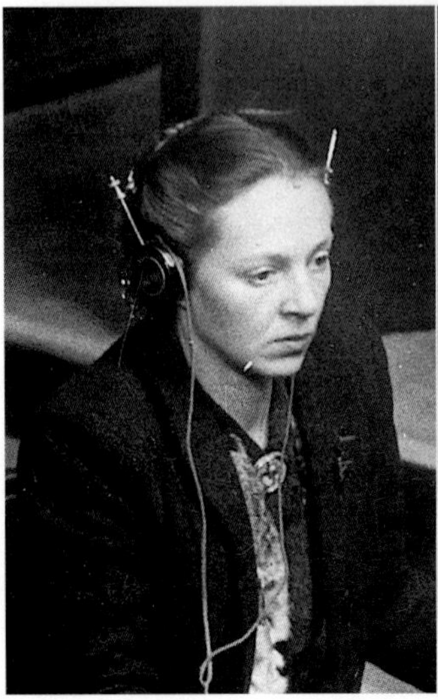

OTHERS ESCAPE THEIR JUST DESERTS **Victor Bouhler**, chief of Hitler's Private Chancellery and father of the euthanasia programme, is able to commit suicide. **Albert Speer** (with Bouhler *above left*, and being interrogated, *right*) goes through the trial without his part in the deportation of Berlin's Jews becoming known. The Americans give kid-glove treatment to former Gestapo and S.S. officials (*below left to right*) **Alfred Naujocks**, **Zeischka**, **Wilhelm Höttl**, and **Walter Schellenberg** in return for their testimony. Höttl "recalls" Adolf Eichmann telling him he killed four million Jews.

A Rake's Progress

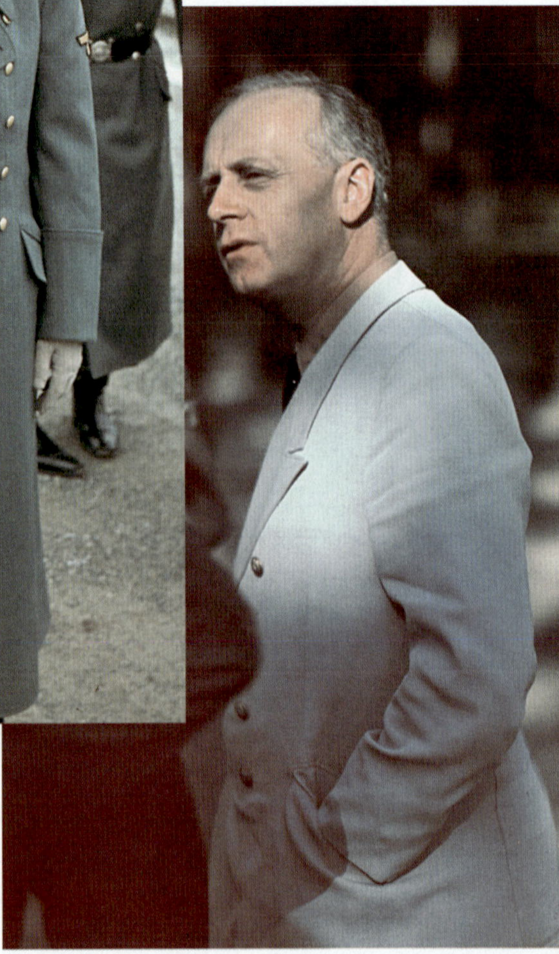

Franz von Papen (*left*) suave and worldly-wise, is mortified to find himself treated like a Nazi. After all, he escaped death by a hairsbreadth in the Röhm purge of June 1934. It was not until after Hitler violated the Munich agreement in 1939, he says, that he realised that the Führer was a 'pathological liar,' hell-bent on pursuing a reckless foreign policy with the help of his 'stupid, opportunistic, arrogant, blankety-blank foreign minister von Ribbentrop' (WALTER FRENTZ).

TURNING POINT When **Joachim von Ribbentrop** (*left*) a gifted businessman who boasts about his international society connections, replaces **Constantin von Neurath** as Hitler's foreign minister (*right*, in the witness stand at Nuremberg) in February 1938, it marks a turning point for Germany—and the start of a long and and often tortured path that ends for Ribbentrop with the hangman's noose (WALTER FRENTZ; AUTHOR'S COLLECTION).

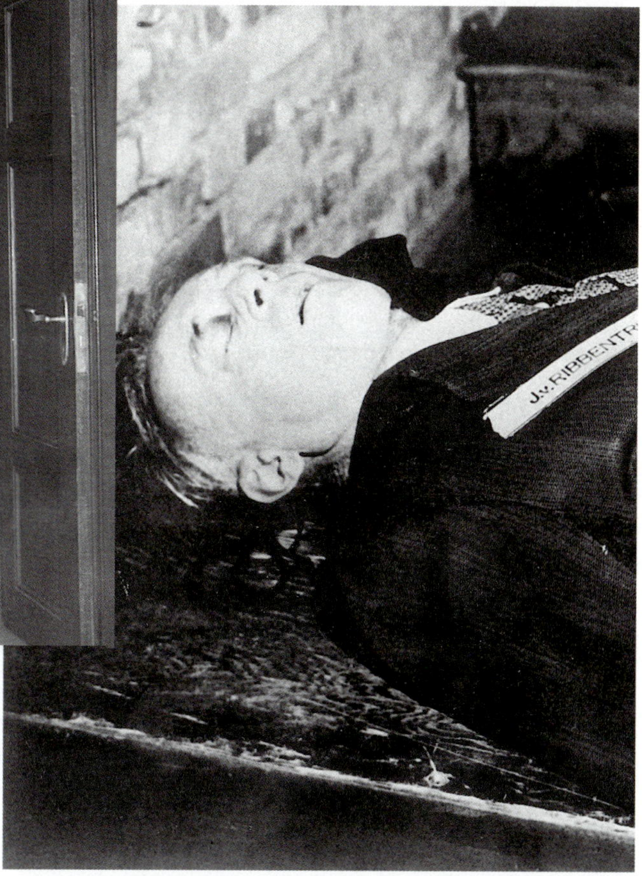

OUT OF THE FRYING PAN... A smug **Franz von Papen** hears of his acquittal. **Alfred Jodl** (*left*) and **Artur Seyss-Inquart** are more sombre.

... INTO THE FIRE Preparing to leave the Nuremberg jailhouse, **Papen** and **Schacht**, more pensive now, ask Colonel **Burton C Andrus** for U.S. Army protection. German police arrest them as soon as they leave the building.

above left British prosecutor Colonel **Harry Phillimore** secretly asks the Americans to go easy on Schacht. U.S. assistant prosecutor **Ralph Albrecht** (*right*) retorts that in Jackson's view Schacht is one of the worst Nazi criminals. Behind scenes, British judges vote for Schacht—friend of the governor of the Bank of England—to be acquitted.

ABSENT FROM THE DOCK **Ernst Kaltenbrunner** is often ill, **Martin Bormann** already dead

WALTER FRENTZ

VICE VERSA **Alfred Rosenberg** nearly gets off with jail; **Albert Speer** is nearly hanged.

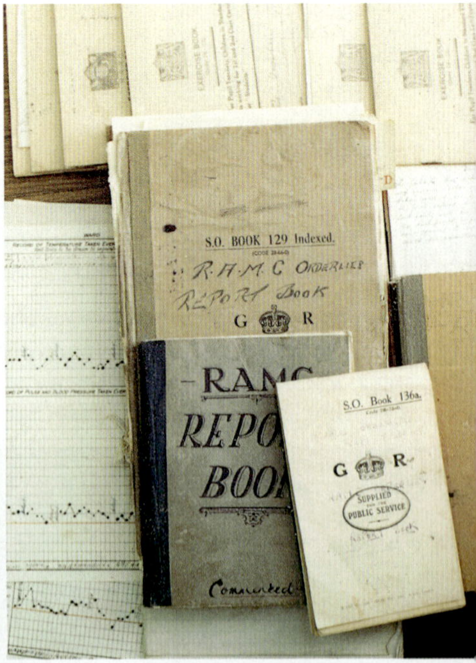

A LAST ATTEMPT AT RESTORING PEACE At midnight on May 10, 1941, Hitler's deputy **Rudolf Hess**, then aged forty-eight, makes his first ever parachute jump, landing on this Scottish moor, bringing an appeal to King George VI to end the fighting. In British custody he goes slowly mad, as the medical diaries sent with him to Nuremberg (*above*) show. But he still outsmarts U.S. Colonel **John H Amen** on October 9, 1945, *below* (RUDOLF HESS FOUNDATION; AUTHOR'S COLLECTION).

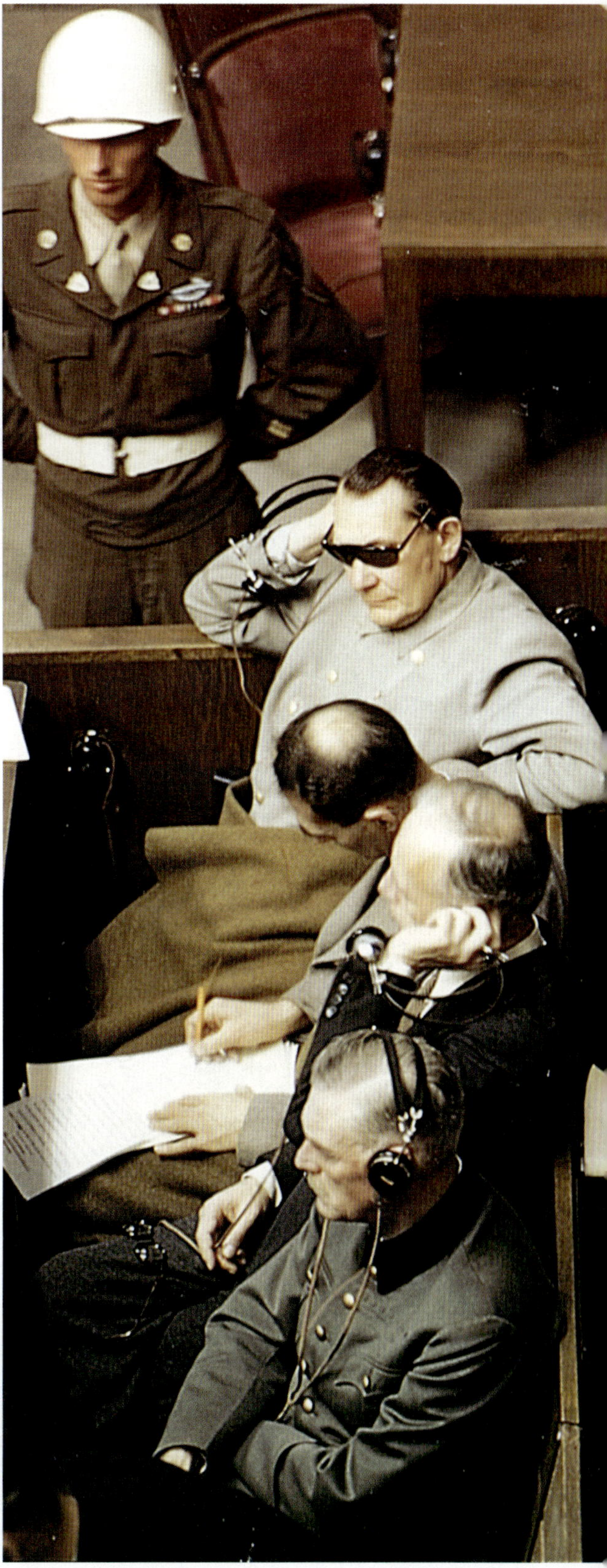

Mission with No Return

THE LONG JOURNEY By parachute into Scotland; to the war crimes dock at Nuremberg—stoutly defended by young attorney **Alfred Seidl** (*above*); and thence to Spandau jail in the British sector of Berlin (*below*) for the rest of his life (AUTHOR'S COLLECTION).

PRESS ASSOCIATION

CRIME AGAINST HUMANITY Outliving all his judges and tormentors, **Rudolf Hess** will live to the age of ninety-three. He spends forty-seven years in prison, the last twenty-one of them in solitary confinement in Spandau. He will be found mysteriously strangled to death in August 1987. Aided by Berlin police, Scotland Yard investigates until ordered by the British foreign office to stop. Hess's grave (epitaph: 'I Took the Risk') is permanently heaped with flowers from all over Germany.

JIM QUILLIN

Several of the American officers took quite a liking to him after this—particularly one six-foot-two Texan officer, Lieutenant Jack G. Wheelis, whom Göring befriended upon finding that they had much in common: a love of hunting, and of the freedom of the outdoors.

❖ ❖ ❖ ❖ ❖

The British and American prosecution teams would rest their case in mid-January 1946. Then the French would begin their case, followed by the Russians. 'The French are terrible,' groaned Jackson, 'and early in January they take over.' He was thinking of moving out to Berchtesgaden, where the air was good and the venison better, until they had finished: 'I don't want to be here [in Nuremberg] when the French mess around, so I can't be blamed.'[12] He was conscious of mounting criticism in the newspapers of the United States about his prolonged absence from the Supreme Court. Grimly aware that by succumbing to his overweening ambitions to carve out a name for himself in international law he had simultaneously vitiated his chances of advancement on the Supreme Court, he wrote to the president, expressing the desire and the intention of returning to Washington for the March and certainly for the April sitting.[13]

On January 25 the French prosecutor Dubost began a harrowing account of torturing by the Gestapo and the S.S. to force members of the French resistance—of which he had been a lowly member himself—to confess. The next evening the other judges and their wives and the prosecutors were guests at a big party thrown by Judge Biddle for seventy-five guests. Biddle remarked to Dubost's plain little wife on the contrasts between the harrowing evidence of Friday, and the delicate music from the German string quartet entertaining them to Haydn, Schubert, and Beethoven. Madame Dubost responded with a trace of irony, 'Yes, and they are said to be very good in their own families. Only it would appear they are not very good neighbours.'[14]

By early February it was plain that the trial was going to drag on well beyond the spring. Biddle wrote asking his wife in the United States to mail him two of his summer suits, as he was going to need them.

❖ ❖ ❖ ❖ ❖

The Allied military circles had been uneasy all along about putting on trial the admirals and generals who had opposed them, unless clearly specified war crimes of the old-fashioned kind could be laid against them.

Grand-Admiral Karl Dönitz, the German navy's commander-in-chief, had surrendered to them in Flensburg; but the British and American experts had then found from the captured records that he was virtually blameless of any crimes. Nevertheless Dönitz was indicted and the British lawyers—in whose hands the case against him lay—solemnly put to him the very documents which their own admiralty had secretly declared in August 1945 to be insufficient to procure a conviction.

The case boiled down to trying to implicate him in the so-called *Peleus* incident: one of his U-boats, *U–852*, had torpedoed a Greek freighter of that name, and the submarine's commander Kapitänleutnant Heinz Eck had ordered the survivors machine-gunned; he and his two senior officers were eventually court-martialled and shot by a British firing squad in Hamburg. Jackson had been shown the entry in the diary of the commander of the Submarine Force (B.d.U.) for September 17, 1942, reading: 'The attention of all commanding officers is again drawn to the fact that all efforts to rescue members of the crews of ships which have been sunk contradict the most primitive requirements for the conduct of warfare by annihilating enemy ships and their crews. Orders concerning the bringing-in of the Captains and Chief Engineers still stand.' Dönitz had signed this volume at the end in pencil, as was the custom.[15]

Against the burden of this entry however the defence could set several entries from his diary for 1945 which showed him ordering crews to adhere strictly to the Geneva Convention 'even in the present circumstances,' and to resist efforts by the S.S. to trespass on naval affairs.[16] Dönitz was one of those who had persuaded Hitler to abandon the plan to repudiate the Geneva Convention after the violation of Dresden by R.A.F. Bomber Command in February 1945.[17] The record of the British interrogations of Dönitz's chief of staff Admiral Eberhard Godt and his staff officer Fregattenkapitän Hessler states: 'Both men categorically denied that Dönitz ever countenanced the killing of survivors in cold blood.'

Since the documents on the *Peleus* incident were 'insufficient' against Dönitz the prosecution interrogators made spirited efforts to procure adequate oral evidence. Their methods were not edifying. An American army captain of Czech origin using the name 'Dr Korda' interrogated Godt at a camp code-named Fort Washington.[18] When Godt turned down the specific demand that he testify against Dönitz he was told: 'Think about it, if you would. We've got so much against you that things could get quite nasty for you too. Your situation is extremely simple. Either you testify against Dönitz—and then we'll leave you in peace. Or you don't—and then we'll string you up alongside Dönitz.' Finally the large and by now well-known War Crimes Commission bluntly confronted Godt with the question: 'Are you willing to testify against Dönitz: yes or no?' Since the admiral stood by his refusal, they left him with the parting words: 'You're going to regret this.'[19]

The British tried similar methods on the submarine crews in their captivity.[20] Only one U-boat officer (Korvettenkapitän Möhle) succumbed to these methods—agreeing with the British that Dönitz had 'orally' ordered the machine-gunning of lifeboats. Against this statement stood all the contrary evidence, often despite duress, of every other officer in the submarine arm, and in the admiralty report quoted to Jackson Möhle's statement was dismissed as highly improbable. In the trial it emerged that the British interrogators had hinted to Möhle that the evidence against Dönitz was so strong that he could not be saved, but that Möhle, the prisoner, might manage to save the lives of the three condemned U-boat men by making such a statement.[21]

In fairness to Jackson and the prosecution teams it must be said that the methods used by their interrogators were evidently unknown to them. At one stage a note was passed to Jackson in the courtroom: 'The Marshal [General Mitchell] says Streicher washes his face and brushes his teeth in the toilet bowl.'[22] It seemed rather funny, and the note did not explain that Streicher was being forced to do so, to break his resistance; besides, Streicher merited no sympathy in American eyes.

IN THE Nuremberg courtroom Dönitz's witnesses found themselves confronted by Colonel Phillimore. English trial observers disapproved of the 'cavalier fashion' in which Phillimore treated the witnesses. As an American historian would comment, Dönitz had to go before the court 'to show, if he could, that he had waged war according to rules that England herself was not always ready to follow.'[23] Had not the British themselves machine-gunned the unarmed German seamen fleeing across the ice from the freighter *Altmark* in 1940, and had they not shot at the drowning seamen from the minesweeper *Ulm* after she went down in 1942?[24] The American submarine crews, it turned out moreover, had operated under precisely the same rules and instructions as the German.

This line of defence ultimately impressed the Tribunal, as will be seen: alone of all the defendants, Dönitz was tacitly allowed the defence of *tu quoque* and he was exonerated over his conduct of submarine warfare. He was convicted on what was seemingly a technicality, of having failed to question Hitler's order for the execution of Allied saboteurs and commandos. Scores of Allied naval officers later wrote to Admiral Dönitz, disowning the Tribunal's verdict. Judge Biddle drafted a dissenting verdict with regard to Counts Two and Three against the admiral, but was dissuaded from putting it in.[25]

HITLER'S 1940 invasion of Norway, Operation WESERÜBUNG, produced a classic example of how unresponsive the victorious governments were to the needs of justice.

Field-Marshal Wilhelm Keitel's lawyers challenged the British government in March 1946 to produce certain foreign office and cabinet documents relating to Churchill's identical plans for the invasion of neutral Scandinavia. The request caused a mild panic in Whitehall. Cabinet secretary Sir Norman Brooke warned the foreign office that when he took the stand Keitel was expected to claim that Hitler's invasion of Norway had been undertaken to anticipate a Franco-British plan to go into Norway. The embarrassing thing, said Brooke, was that this defence claim was true—it would 'be supported by documents captured by the Germans in France including records of the meetings of the Supreme War Council.'[26]

Foreign secretary Ernest Bevin took the matter up with Attlee, his prime minister. 'I spoke to you the other day,' he wrote, 'about the likelihood that the Germans at the Nuremberg trial would use various documents which they captured in France to justify their invasion of Norway on the ground that they thereby forestalled an Allied invasion and I mentioned that the attorney-general wishes to have authority to put in at Nuremberg certain Foreign Office telegrams and a cabinet document to refute this defence.'

Although no partisan of Churchill, Bevin was flatly opposed to allowing such documents to be produced. Like the Russians, he feared that the Nuremberg trial might open up a can of worms. 'If we once begin,' he argued, 'it might be very difficult to know where we could call a halt as one telegram refers to another and we might bring up embarrassing references to the Finnish phase of our war plans.'[27] (In 1940 both Churchill and his predecessor Neville Chamberlain had planned to join the Finnish war against the Soviet Union.) Sir Norman Brooke advised the prime minister candidly, 'It would be very much better not to be drawn at all into the business of establishing arguments by the production of documents—especially when we do not know precisely what captured documents the other side may have.'[28]

Thus real history went by the board. Britain's name was protected, and Keitel and Jodl, denied the documents they asked for, could hang (as of course they might well have in any case.)

❖ ❖ ❖ ❖ ❖

The prosecution teams had available to them all the technical and Intelligence facilities of occupying powers. There were routine violations of lawyer–client confidentiality. Hidden microphones recorded the prisoners' conversations; psychiatrists like Gilbert and Kelley were infiltrated to question them about their innermost feelings, morale—and planned defence strategies. Their reports were made immediately available to the prosecutors. The British and American letter censorship authorities routinely forwarded to Nuremberg any items intercepted in their zones that seemed to yield similar Intelligence.[29]

Two classes of Intelligence were however not introduced in this trial—the private conversations of prisoners-of-war, monitored by ultra-sensitive hidden microphones (a violation of the Geneva Convention, these reports were kept TOP SECRET); and the ULTRA and MAGIC decrypts. On the former, the British Intelligence services had ruled that the top secret conversation-transcripts derived from the various C.S.D.I.C. interrogation camps were not under any circumstances to be openly used at the International Military Tribunal, however valuable they would have been; as a last resort the data might be used, provided that their origin remained permanently concealed.[30]

Thus General Karl Bodenschatz, Göring's chief aide at Hitler's headquarters, had been heard during May and June in England telling Field-Marshal Milch that their Reichsmarschall Göring was 'the most ungrateful man in the world.'

'Always was!' shouted Milch. 'A rotten character.'

'It wasn't paint,' said fighter-ace General Adolf Galland, when they began talking about Göring's mauve-painted fingernails. 'It was a transparent varnish.'[31]

'Bodenschatz,' challenged Milch, 'you say the Führer gave Göring a monthly allowance of thirty thousand Reichsmarks. Do you imagine he met all his expenses out of that?...The three hundred and sixty thousand marks he received each *year* wouldn't last him even a month!'

Milch noted in his diary what the others at that Camp No. 7 (at Latimer in Buckinghamshire) told him of Göring's corrupt dealings with aircraft and aluminium factories. 'Do you know,' said Milch, banging his fist on the table, 'that our commander-in-chief pocketed a fine of fourteen million Dutch guilders imposed for a rebellion somewhere in Holland and transferred them to Switzerland for his personal use? The S.S. told me all this, and backed it up with evidence. But there is such a thing as poetic justice, gentlemen!... Göring's chauffeur made off with a case containing all Mrs Göring's jewellery.'[32] (Challenged about this allegation on December 22, 1945, Göring dismissed it as nonsense and pointed out that General Christiansen, military commander of the Netherlands, came directly under the O.K.W., not the Luftwaffe.)[33]

The same restrictions were imposed on the use of the ULTRA data derived by Britain's codebreaking effort at Bletchley. For example for a year after the spring of 1942 codebreakers had read the regular reports to Berlin by the commanders of the S.S. police units engaged in partisan warfare and rounding up the Jews behind the eastern front, and they had also broken the codes used by the commandants of the seven biggest concentration camps including Dachau, Buchenwald, and Auschwitz in transmitting their daily returns in top secret code to Oswald Pohl, their ultimate chief in Berlin, about the movements and mortality rates among their slave labourers and prisoners. Although there was perhaps surprisingly no reference in any of these messages to anybody being gassed or to mass exterminations in the camps, even at Auschwitz where it was clear that tens of thousands had died in the typhus epidemics since 1942, the ULTRA data would have been useful in prosecuting individuals like Pohl or S.S. General Kurt Daluege—the latter was heard specifically ordering his police force commanders not to make detailed or statistical reports on their murderous operations in the field, since their codes were suspected not to be secure from enemy eavesdropping.[34]

The one interesting exception to this general rule was that the American government allowed the production of several MAGIC decrypts of Ambassador Hiroshi Oshima's reports to Tokyo on his conversations with Hitler and Ribbentrop prior to Pearl Harbor, as evidence of German attempts to drag Japan and the United States into the war.

The prosecutors felt they had every right to use whatever kind of secret Intelligence was at their disposal: they had to be on guard against the deceits of the Nazi witnesses and defendants. 'I just wanted to call your attention,' Colonel Amen's staff warned Robert Jackson, 'to the C.S.D.I.C. intercepts of [General Franz] Halder's conversations with other generals. He is extremely frank on what he thinks should be suppressed or distorted, and in particular is very sensitive to the suggestion that the German General Staff was involved in anything, especially planning for war.'[35]

Halder, who had been the chief of Hitler's General Staff until his dismissal in September 1942, was now acting as though he had always, but always, been an opponent of the Führer and he expressed an unseemly eagerness to testify in the witness box against his real enemy—Field-Marshal Keitel, the former chief of the O.K.W. When Keitel's lawyer Dr Otto Nelte heard of this he used two letters which he threatened to introduce in evidence, in which Halder had expressed himself in glowing language about their Führer, to dissuade the general from testifying against Keitel. (In fact it is now plain that Halder's General Staff, and not Keitel and the O.K.W., had made the running in such criminal enterprises as initiating the attack on Russia and drafting the order for the liquidation of Soviet commissars.) Nelte's warning was typical of the behind-the-scenes manœuvring that went on at Nuremberg. In another such deal Papen's lawyer Dr Egon Kubuschok was able to persuade the Americans to withdraw one threatened witness against his client, in return for withdrawing one of his own who would have damaged the American case against other defendants.[36] Such bargains were unknown under German law.

WHILE THE prosecution had hidden assets like secret sources of Intelligence, the defence was denied even the right to call every witness it wanted. Although twenty-one lives were at stake, the Tribunal's view was that the hearing of too many defence witnesses would consume too much time. The witness application lists were rigorously pruned. Jodl applied for nineteen, and was permitted four. In an international trial complicated by the involvement of a dozen European countries, only one non-German witness, the Swede Birger Dahlerus, was permitted to the defence. The Dahlerus memoirs, which had undergone the usual editorial treatment to make them suitable for publication in the climate of post-war Europe, were introduced as evidence. But for many years after the war the British government kept secret its entire contemporary file on the negotiations that Göring had conducted through Dahlerus to preserve the peace—releasing the file only years after the rest of its contemporary documents; the file revealed that in 1943 the British government had tried to blackmail Dahlerus into silence.[37]

The prosecution was strongly advantaged by the Tribunal's curious stipulation that defence counsel had to submit to them all applications for witnesses and documents in Allied hands, explaining what point each witness or document was expected to prove ('a most helpful requirement,' as Jackson called it at the time.)[38] The result is frequently a tantalising glimpse of how history might have been written differently: for example, Julius Streicher applied for his former police chief in Nuremberg, S.A. Gruppenführer von Obernitz, to be allowed to testify to the row they had had in November 1938 when Streicher had dissociated himself from the destruction of Nuremberg's synagogue as ordered by Goebbels on Kristallnacht (later he had endorsed it on architectural grounds); the witness was disallowed by the court.[39] Again, Göring's application for a witness summons against his former adjutant and physician Dr Ramon von Ondarza, of Reinbek near Hamburg, was disapproved.[40]

This does not gainsay the fact that the Tribunal did eventually offer extensive assistance and protection to the defence counsel. Some of the German lawyers who had experienced the drumhead courts (*Sondergerichte*) established during the war to try offences in the Nazi-occupied territories were overwhelmed by the courtesies extended to them by the victors.[41] A Defendants' Information Center had been opened in the courthouse in November 1945 to minister to the documentary needs of the fifty defence lawyers. This, in the eyes of one American lawyer, writing home about his experiences, made this case different from any in the United States—'the fact that we do so much for the defendants: tote their lawyers around; furnish them help and a document centre; six copies of every document forty-eight hours in advance of trial of a particular phase of the case, with German translations of every other language a document may be in, and so forth.'[42] When the Tribunal's judges toured the Center on one occasion they came across Jodl in a room next door conferring with his lawyer, and one British judge was heard to comment, 'Do you think we would have been given anything like this if Germany had won the war?'[43]

After the trial began, Jodl wrote privately, 'After these first few days I am now convinced that the Tribunal is going to be objective and conscientious. [But] the prosecutors are dangerous men, because firstly they are not experts in military affairs, and secondly because they delight in springing documents on us that we have never heard of before.'[44] A few days later however, he changed his tune: 'All that matters to me now is to prove that my own conscience is clear. That I did all I could for victory is something they can accuse me of as much as they like.'[45]

THE TRUTH was somewhere in between. Despite their overt show of impartiality, the members of the Tribunal were only human. They were the representatives of the conquering powers, come together to pass judgement on the defeated enemy; and all their black gowns, their gold braid, their impassive demeanour, and their legal prose could not alter that. They had arrived in the same planes as the prosecutors; they dined in the same hotels; they could not, as the German saying has it, jump over their own shadows. They were identified wholly with the prosecution—indeed, the president of the Tribunal, Lord Justice Lawrence, habitually and without aforethought used the letterhead of the British prosecuting team for his own correspondence.[46] As German naval judge advocate Otto Kranzbühler would later recall, 'The attitude of the judges toward their duties ranged all the way from the utmost striving for objectivity down to a barely concealed servility toward the prosecution.'[47]

It is intended as no reproach to Lord Justice Lawrence to quote one passage from a speech which he made shortly after the conclusion of the trial, and which indicates how difficult it would have been for this perhaps overly Pickwickian gentleman to understand the defendants' cause:

> Neither England nor the United States may wish in a few years' time to maintain sufficient forces to prevent another attempt by Germany to achieve the domination which she believes is her destiny. Can we afford to improvise our forces again? By the Grace of God, by the genius and nerve of our great leader Mr Churchill, and by the spirit of our people, we have for the second time in my lifetime escaped destruction. Are we going to chance it again?[48]

His sympathies for the prosecutors were balanced by no parallel feelings for the defence. When Harlan F. Stone, chief justice of the U.S. Supreme Court, now died Lawrence publicly expressed to Jackson the Tribunal's condolences. After Andrei Vyshinsky, who had prosecuted at the infamous pre-war Soviet purge trials—Jackson called him merely 'famous'—had arrived in Nuremberg, he was wined and dined at the Grand Hotel, not only by Jackson and the American prosecution team that Monday, November 26, but by the Russians on the following Friday and by the British on the Sunday after that.[49] Lord Justice Lawrence and the other judges joined the guests at the Jackson junket.

No properly constituted British (or German) court would have tolerated the display of such partiality. Perhaps Lord Justice Lawrence could hardly be held accountable for what happened at this banquet:

after a graceful speech by Vyshinsky comparing the problems of international diplomats with the easy collaboration of international lawyers, he brought everybody—Tribunal judges and prosecuting counsel alike—to their feet with glass in hand and proposed this toast in Russian: 'To the defendants. May their paths lead straight from the court house to the grave!'[50] The judges had drunk of their champagne before the translation reached them. Jackson later professed himself hideously embarrassed, but Vyshinsky's lack of diplomacy did not stop there. At Maxwell Fyfe's dinner in the Russian's honour on December 1 a Scots Guards piper marched around to the wail of his pipes; Vyshinsky now proposed a toast to the Soviet Union's most noble allies, the British and Americans. Unmentioned, the French delegation swept haughtily out of the room.[51] Sir David Maxwell Fyfe found Vyshinsky an able, cheerful, downright, and somewhat rumbustious personality—no doubt the same descriptions could have been applied to Heinrich Himmler or Roland Freisler in their heyday.

So it went on throughout the trials. The judges and prosecutors were constantly guests at each other's tables; the defence lawyers were never invited. 'We dined at [Soviet chief prosecutor] Rudenko's last night,' wrote Judge Biddle to his wife on December 1. 'Much vodka and fun and about thirty speeches!' Jackson's files are replete with the private correspondence with, and invitations from and to, the judges.[52] Once, Sir Norman Birkett, the British alternate judge, sent over to Justice Jackson a little poem about Ribbentrop as a Sekt salesman, which made quite plain what the judge's views on that defendant were.[53]

15: The Cadavers Concerned

FROM ALL over Germany, a torrent of letters had descended on Justice Robert H. Jackson, the American chief prosecutor, ever since he arrived at Nuremberg in the summer of 1945. The letters can have done little to improve his impression of the German mentality. Many were antisemitic. Scores of women wrote to him, denouncing the female next door as a war criminal too. There were letters from astrologists, graphologists, and would-be executioners offering assistance. One man had this request: 'I beg you, Your Honour, to convey to me the office of executioner in the American and British Zones and to allow me to operate with an axe. I am at your immediate disposal. The trial of Major-General Meyer—the former S.S. man who murdered Allied prisoners-of-war—is beginning here in Aurich on December 9. I would be able to use the axe to get rid of this criminal at Aurich.'[1]

A priest from Schwäbisch-Gmünd whose brother had died in a Gestapo prison after the July 20, 1944 attempt on Hitler's life stated in careful handwriting: 'I would welcome it with the greatest satisfaction if the war criminals were put to hard labour and starved and deprived of water for a while, say half a year, before being hanged. A swift execution-death by guillotine or firing squad would be too easy and merciful.'[2]

One imaginative New Jersey writer proposed that the defendants should be lined up on the bridge of a German warship off Bikini atoll when the next atomic bomb was tested, to take the salute, 'with Reporter Churchill daringly in the offing.'[3] More thought-provoking were the letters from both Germany and the United States which asked Jackson how the Americans could reconcile the proceedings at Nuremberg with their own glorification of the atomic bombing of Japan.

Perhaps not unexpectedly, the most favourable letters related to Rudolf Hess: many ordinary Germans wrote, citing instances where he had interceded on their behalf and pleading for clemency for him. By early 1946, letters were also reaching Jackson describing the conditions of German civilians deported from Poland to the Russian Zone; and there were reports of fresh inhumanities being inflicted on Germans in Poland and Czechoslovakia, including surviving German Jews. By the time the trial ended Jackson had received about five thousand letters from Germans: all of them were analysed, summarised, and filed. He rarely took action on them.

Jackson regretted that little had been done to bring home the importance of the trial to the German public. Carl Zuckmayer proposed to the Americans even before the verdict was announced a major film to report the corruption, murder, torture, and cruelties inflicted in the nation's name; but nothing came of this.[4]

The American authorities had put the radio commentary in the hands of a certain 'Dr Gaston Oulman,' who also used the name of Ullmann; he was a German émigré whose spiteful broadcasts were said to exceed the worst of Dr Goebbels in his prime. If the trial had little psychological effect on the average German, or even the opposite effect to that desired, this was thanks to Ullmann. His radio commentaries grated so harshly on German ears that they achieved the very opposite of the desired effect. Field-Marshal Milch confided to his diary that Ullmann was succeeding where even Hitler had failed, namely in turning every last living German into an antisemite. 'This was pretty plain in the big Dachau camp in 1946, at the time this swine made his broadcasts on the International Nuremberg Tribunal. If the guy had been able to see the hatred of twenty-eight thousand true Germans he would probably have reconsidered.'[5] Attorney Kranzbühler too would state that, if even those defendants who least deserved it achieved a certain popularity in the course of the trial, this was thanks to Ullmann and his propaganda.[6]

❖ ❖ ❖ ❖ ❖

Hermann Göring would pose the biggest problem, of that Jackson was sure. In November 1944 the Reichsmarschall had lectured to his generals, 'To stay alive at any price has always been the philosophy of the coward.'[7] Now, in February 1946, he told his own defence counsel, 'My philosophy is that if the time has come, the time has come. Accept responsibility and go down with guns firing and colours flying! It's the defence of Germany that is at stake in this trial—not just the handful of us defendants who are for the high jump anyway.'[8]

Dr Gilbert continued to funnel the secret Intelligence he had gleaned during his psychiatric counselling sessions to Jackson. 'Göring's defense against proposal to seize Atlantic islands for war against United States,' read one worried telegram that Jackson sent to Washington, 'apparently is that Roosevelt speeches indicated attack from us.... Also reported Göring will testify to statements by Bullitt and Davies in support of Roosevelt's threat of aggression against Germany.'[9] This was typical of the Intelligence gleaned by Gilbert in conversation with the prisoners.

That February a little feud between the psychiatrists was resolved to Dr Gilbert's satisfaction. On the sixth Colonel Andrus released Major

Douglas Kelley, who had joined his staff as consulting psychiatrist and surgeon on November 21, and sent him back to the United States. More than once Kelley had revealed details of his examinations to newspapermen despite repeated orders from Andrus to the contrary. Kelley left Nuremberg under a cloud—evidently preparing, as Andrus feared, to write memoirs and even 'misappropriating in part official files' for that purpose.[10] Some months later, as the trial neared its end, Lord Justice Lawrence would hand to Andrus an article just published by the London *Sunday Express* which showed that Kelley had not only disobeyed yet again, but was putting into the mouths of the accused words which Andrus was satisfied they had never spoken. (Thus Kelley reported how Göring had vividly described Hitler's reaction to the lynching of Mussolini—but Göring had left the Berlin bunker for the last time a week earlier.)[11]

THAT MONTH, February 1946, in the run-up to the dramatic moment when the first defendants would mount the witness stand, Jackson sent psychiatrist Dr Gilbert into the jailhouse to reconnoitre in depth the prisoners' precise intentions. Gilbert had seldom been far from the dock, his notebook in hand, writing down the prisoners' *sotto voce* comments, and observing their reactions and what would now be called their body-language. He also visited them in their cells, and conducted formal intelligence tests on them. On the October 1945 day when the indictment had first been served on them he had asked each defendant to write down his comments. Some were cynical, others evasive. Speer wrote: 'This trial is essential. There is such a thing as shared responsibility for atrocious crimes like these, even in an authoritarian state.'[12] Speer was already following his own ruthless survival-agenda: *vorwärts über Leichen*. Forward, over the fallen—even if the cadavers concerned were those of his own former ministerial colleagues.

❖ ❖ ❖ ❖ ❖

In Jackson's files are 'psychological-intelligence' reports written by Dr Gilbert on each of the main defendants.[13] These analyses are strongly subjective, revealing often as much about Gilbert as about his subject. Learning that Gilbert had attributed to him the lowest IQ (106), Julius Streicher took refuge in the comment that the analyst himself was perhaps not all that impartial. Gilbert called his 'a rigid, obsessive, insensitive, and lewd mentality.' Streicher had insisted from the start that this trial was a 'triumph of world-Jewry,' and he hinted to Gilbert that three of the judges appeared to be Jews. (None of them was Jewish.) He fully expected to die as a martyr to the cause—which in his case was the fight against the Jews. However he had had nothing to do with any mass-murder of the Jews; indeed he had been out of public office since 1939. Gilbert anticipated that Streicher's defence would be based on 'fantastic' references to circumcision and world Zionism, and to the teachings of the Talmud, and that these arguments need hardly be answered.

From what he had overheard he believed that Speer, Schacht, Fritzsche, and possibly even Frank might be ready to denounce the Reichsmarschall. 'Ribbentrop and Rosenberg [are Göring's] only real supporters; von Schirach wavering; Keitel afraid to talk up.'

For a while Schirach did join the Göring camp, then he suddenly caved in. In Keitel's view what caused Schirach to collapse was the overwhelming burden of incriminating documentary evidence of which even Schirach had previously had no inkling. 'What probably also contributed was his row [in June 1943] with Hitler, who refused to see him after that.'[14]

Ribbentrop had a fairly high IQ too (128), but his character fared badly at Gilbert's hands: he was an 'ambitious egotist and opportunist, who subordinated all moral scruples to his ruthless ambition for self-aggrandisement.' In the jailhouse he was depressed and frustrated by the defeat of his ambitions; he was alternately following Göring's lead—they had once been arch-enemies—and taking refuge in a bad memory and dishonesty. He said he had never made the antisemitic statements that had been attributed to him by General Lahousen. He denied that he had ever predicted to Hitler that Britain would not fight.*

Gilbert saw that Ribbentrop was still endlessly poring over documents and scribbling verbose defence notes in his immense pencil scrawl. Every once in a while, reported Gilbert, the prisoner threw up his hands and said: 'Why can't they let bygones be bygones? What good does it do to be so vindictive?'

In Gilbert's view the rebuttal of Ribbentrop's evasions should be easy, by pinning him down to the main facts like the Axis Pact, Munich, the Ribbentrop–Molotov Pact, and his knowledge of atrocities. 'He would like to deny the latter,' advised Gilbert, 'but it can be proven that he asked Hitler about the Lublin atrocities and was told to mind his own business, which he did.'† The army psychiatrists suspected that

* This appears to have been one of the cleverer British propaganda legends, built up to discredit Ribbentrop in the eyes of his fellow ministers. There is a memorandum signed by him in December 1937 in which he strongly warned Hitler that Britain *would* fight if it came to a war in Europe. The British foreign office 'lost' this document for forty years—to ensure that it reached posterity Ribbentrop had carried a copy into captivity in June 1945, but foolishly addressed it to Field-Marshal Sir Bernard Montgomery.

† In September 1944 a copy of the London *Daily Mail* with a Russian report on Holocaust finds at Majdanek was shown to Ribbentrop. He in turn showed it to his son Rudolf, a young Waffen S.S. officer, asking him what truth he thought was in it. Rudolf replied, 'Father, this is the same kind of atrocity story as the Belgian children with the hacked-off hands after World War One.' The foreign minister took it up with Hitler, and got the response cited above.—Author's interview of Rudolf von Ribbentrop, July 20, 1990.

Neurath, Papen, Schacht, and Speer would all be willing to sink Ribbentrop with testimony damaging to him, if the right questions were asked of them.

The other diplomat in the dock was Franz von Papen, suave and worldly-wise. He fully saw the need for such a trial as this, but was deeply wounded to find himself among those accused. He had escaped death by a hairsbreadth in the Röhm purge of June 1934, having been placed under house-arrest at the time; he had resigned as vice-chancellor immediately, he said, and he had accepted Hitler's appointment to become ambassador in Vienna, only under written conditions which he had himself drafted, for example that Hitler immediately dismiss Theo Habicht, the Austrian Nazi leader who had brought about the murder of Chancellor Engelbert Dollfuss in July 1934. It was not until after the violation of the Munich agreement, he said, that he had realised that Hitler was a 'pathological liar,' hell-bent on pursuing a reckless foreign policy with the help of his 'stupid, opportunistic, arrogant, blankety-blank foreign minister von Ribbentrop.' This was a seductive line of argument indeed. It was hard however for Papen to explain why he had later accepted Hitler's ambassadorship to Turkey. Given Papen's hostility to Göring, Ribbentrop, and Rosenberg, not to mention Hitler, Dr Gilbert suggested that they use the cross-examination of the diplomat to extract denunciations of these fellow-defendants, rather than to attack Papen's personal integrity. 'He is working on answers to such questions,' added Gilbert, 'which he is showing me, and the questions may be asked either by his attorney or the prosecution. None of the defendants will attack him.'

Rudolf Hess he found passive, apathetic, hysterical, and charged with mystic and paranoid tendencies. 'His amnesia,' he decided, 'was *not* a fake.' He was so withdrawn and secretive, sealing every document in his cell and hardly speaking, that Gilbert found it hard to predict his line of defence. 'Anything may be expected, including a relapse of the amnesia.' Being highly suggestible, Gilbert found, Hess had borrowed some of Göring's attitude toward the court and the Versailles Treaty. Apart from pointing out that he had at least tried to stop the war in 1940 and 1941, and that he had been away from Germany since May 1941, Hess had done nothing to prepare a real defence with his attorneys. He had refused the help offered by his female secretaries, who were in the witness wing. As yet, he had in fact asked for no witnesses or documents. Referring to Hitler, and possibly to himself as well, Hess had remarked that there seemed to be a streak of madness in every genius.

His fellow defendants, said Gilbert, deprecated this 'queer' Nazi's presence in their trial, and more than one feared that it would reflect poorly on their country's leadership if and when he went into the witness stand. 'It would be well to let it go at that,' suggested Gilbert, 'and not cross-examine him too much.'

He found Field-Marshal Keitel to have almost the same intelligence as Ribbentrop, and again provided to Jackson the desired stereotype, a typical Prussian bearing, concealing a basically weak character. His principal defence argument, which he told anybody who would listen, was that Hitler was his commander-in-chief, and he himself had no command functions whatever—he was just a glorified office-boy. He would like to blame everything on Hitler, but Göring was urging him not to, demanding loyalty to the Führer in return for his own support in the witness stand. It was a sad dilemma for the field-marshal, and one which he would not solve before mounting the gallows.

Strictly in private, Keitel told Gilbert that Hitler had betrayed him and the honour of the Wehrmacht. In defence matters he was collaborating with Jodl; Keitel would take the defence up to the Polish campaign. As for the murkier incidents on the fringe of the war, he was in an unhappy position: he had heard of the S.S. plans to mount a spurious 'Polish' raid on the Gleiwitz radio station; questioned at the time by Admiral Wilhelm Canaris about why the S.S. was requisitioning Polish uniforms, he had told the Abwehr chief not to stick his nose into it. He claimed not to know of how the Wehrmacht units were being dragged into atrocities. He had argued unsuccessfully with Hitler, he told Gilbert, for a reduction in the ratio of hostages to be executed in reprisals. Once again it would be Speer who would be most likely, in Gilbert's view, to provide damaging evidence against fellow-defendant Keitel.

He had kinder words for General Alfred Jodl, who had, he thought, a mind of his own in moral and military matters. He had hardly met Hitler before 1939, Jodl would argue; but he would be perfectly ready to admit to participating in the planning of an aggressive war—he was doing his duty as an officer under Hitler. He would be able moreover to prove in his own defence several ugly rows with Hitler, especially where the latter proposed to violate the rules of land warfare, with orders for the summary killing of partisans and commandos; going behind Keitel's back Jodl had issued orders effectively nullifying those decrees. 'The documents he is asking for,' warned Gilbert, 'will establish those facts.'

He would also produce documents which argued that the Nazi aggression was to some extent defensive in character: they had barely beaten Churchill to the draw in invading Norway; even before Hitler's invasion of Russia, BARBAROSSA, Stalin's massive troop concentrations had proven that he was winding up for an attack, and Field-Marshal Friedrich Paulus, now in the witness wing, was himself the General Staff officer who had worked at the time on BARBAROSSA. 'If pressed,' recommended the psychiatrist, 'he will probably not hesitate to denounce Hitler, and has no love for Göring because of the latter's pomposity and self-enrichment.' But he would not be willing to attack Keitel, as a fellow-officer.

JODL FOR his part had only contempt for these 'so-called psychologists.' 'What do these psycho-doctors and diagnosticians know about my inner being?' he wrote indignantly to his wife Luise, who worked through the trial as a secretary for the defence attorneys in Nuremberg. 'Not one jot more than the merest fly on the wall.'[15]

Summarising Alfred Rosenberg, Dr Gilbert called him 'all Weltanschauung and no moral courage,' a bigoted philosophic dilettante who indulged in false cultural anthropology and pseudo-science to rationalise an ideology. (With minor changes, Rosenberg might have used the same phraseology about American army psychiatrists.) Like Ribbentrop, he clung to Göring's apron strings in believing that the best defence would be attack. He had a quiver-full of accusations ready to fire at the four powers trying them—British concentration camps in the Boer War, Bolshevik massacres, the United States' imperialism in Latin America, the Allies' failure to honour President Wilson's fourteen points, and the raping and looting by French Moroccan troops in southern Germany in April and May 1945. All of this, Gilbert reminded Jackson, was irrelevant to the present issue, 'of Germany's guilt in this war.' He should be pinned down as having preached the ideology which made the atrocities possible. 'He has no real supporters except Streicher,' reported Gilbert gleefully, 'whose support he would rather not have.'

In Hans Frank, who had been not only a lawyer but Hitler's attorney, and governor-general of occupied Poland to boot, the psychiatrist found a most interesting subject, detecting in him signs of latent homosexuality and a split personality, with resultant sadistic and masochistic tendencies. He had converted the burden of guilt and the need for punishment to religious penitence and a mystic, transcendental philosophy. 'Frank knows he is guilty and will hang,' reported Gilbert. Posture now was everything. Motivated by the atrocity evidence, he had originally planned a passionate denunciation of Hitler as the 'devil incarnate' who had brought about the greatest orgy of destruction in the history of the world; along that road, he had also been planning to denounce Göring, Rosenberg, and the other Nazi leaders—particularly Himmler and the S.S. generals who had exterminated the Jews under his very nose (at Lublin and elsewhere) without, he insisted, his knowledge. However, Frank was moody and volatile, and time was eroding his earlier passion for penitence. His actual stance in the dock could not easily be predicted.

The defendant Wilhelm Frick, another lawyer, was dismissed by Gilbert tersely as 'unimaginative and callous, selfish and short-sighted,' with little concept of morality. His intentions too were impenetrable. While admitting that he had helped Hitler to power, he argued that he had had no powers after 1935, and that the Nuremberg Laws of 1936 were necessary in a Germany torn asunder by the Jewish problem. His general attitude—modelled on Göring's—was: 'So what?' He was the only one who would talk to Streicher, reported Gilbert. In general, Frick was concerned only with his comfort in prison, 'rather a non-entity.'

THE HIGHEST IQ (143) which Gilbert measured was that of Hjalmar Schacht: hearing of this, Speer sniffed that the results had been weighted to take Schacht's age into account; according to him, Seyss-Inquart scored most points, followed by Göring, while Speer himself wallowed in *aurea mediocritas*.[16] Ambitious and arrogant, Schacht had walled himself in behind a belief in his own righteousness. He seethed with rage at being imprisoned with Hitler's henchmen. He admitted to having violated the Versailles Treaty, but countered that since the Allies were in collusion against Germany this was no crime. He planned to introduce quotations from books like *Mission to Moscow* by Joseph Davies, the former U.S. ambassador to the Soviet capital, to prove that his own peaceful agenda was well known. He admitted rebuilding Germany's run-down economy, but not for the purpose of waging war; Hitler had dismissed him as soon as he balked at the aggressive planning that began. After that, Schacht claimed—clearly rehearsing the defence that he intended to mount—he had plotted against Hitler and was privy to several assassination plots. He had ended the war in a Nazi concentration camp.

Grand-Admiral Karl Dönitz was only a few points less intelligent than Schacht, by Gilbert's reckoning. He found him 'intelligent, fairly decent,' with his belief in his personal integrity still unshaken, although he was subdued by months in prison. He scoffed at the charge of conspiracy levelled at him, pointing out that he was only a navy commander (*Korvettenkapitän*) at the time war broke out. He felt that the rest of the indictment did not concern him either—he had not an inkling of Hitler's darker side until the trial began. He was worried about the charge that he had ordered submarines not to rescue survivors, but that was standard naval practice among the Allies too. The planning of the war, the sinking of the *Athenia* in 1939 and other episodes would be for Raeder to answer: not that he had the slightest intention of testifying against his former commander-in-chief. Albert Speer was clearly willing to speak up for him; Gilbert recommended however that they use Speer to 'wean Dönitz away' from his intention to stand up for the Führer, which was the Hermann Göring line.

Grand-Admiral Erich Raeder was almost of another generation. He had been commander-in-chief of the navy when Hitler seized power, and Hitler had kept him on until 1943. Now he was 'an irritable old man with a practical, unimaginative mentality and disagreeable disposition.' He wrote a diary in Nuremberg prison, which is now in private hands.[17] Like Hess, he spoke little and revealed nothing of his defence strategy. He had however been overheard talking with his lunch-table neighbour General Jodl, from which it appeared that both intended to produce documents to show that the British planned to invade Norway first in April 1940, and that Hitler had just beaten them to the punch by a matter of hours. It also seemed logical that Raeder would argue that the Anglo-German naval agreement of 1935, whereby Britain agreed to allow Germany to rebuild part of her naval strength up to one-third of Britain's, was in itself a breach of the Versailles Treaty. The prisoner Neurath, foreign minister at the time, would certainly verify the latter point. As for the *Athenia* incident, while it is clear that she was sunk by a German U-boat, it is also clear from German naval staff's records that this was not known to them at the time: so Raeder was not lying when he denied it. And as for Pearl Harbor, while the evidence was that Raeder had urged the Japanese to attack, it is clear that what they then did was not what he had recommended.

Gilbert disliked the former Hitler Youth leader Baldur von Schirach with visceral intensity. Their best prospect would be to get Schirach to denounce Hitler—and perhaps Streicher too—as the betrayer of German youth. 'This,' said Gilbert, 'can be handled behind the scenes.' But of late the narcissistic Schirach had become more truculent. His mother was American, and he was enraged that the American Counter-Intelligence Corps had arrested his wife Henriette and children. Göring told him this was 'persecution' and he reiterated that it made the C.I.C. no better than the Gestapo. With only limited success, Göring also pressured Schirach to act as secret 'envoy' to coax the recalcitrant Albert Speer back into a united front.

Gilbert also psycho-analysed Ernst Kaltenbrunner, the former S.S. Obergruppenführer who had succeeded the assassinated Reinhard Heydrich as chief of Himmler's R.S.H.A. Born in Austria, Kaltenbrunner's 'macrocephalic' head bore the scars of many a duel as a student in Austria. 'Stripped of his power,' wrote Gilbert, 'he reveals himself as a whining moral coward with an emotionally unstable, schizoid personality, posing as a misunderstood nationalist-idealist.' Like Adolf Eichmann when he was caught fifteen years later, Kaltenbrunner would argue legalistically that he was not responsible for concentration camps—they were Pohl's pigeon, as chief of the Economics and Administrative Main Office, or Wirtschafts- und Verwaltungshauptamt, the W.V.H.A., which was parallel to the R.S.H.A. He had taken over from Heydrich after the atrocity-system was already functioning, and the Reichsführer Himmler had by-passed Kaltenbrunner in handing down the orders to Adolf Eichmann, who was head of the Jewish desk IV-b–4 in the R.S.H.A.; Eichmann, and by implication S.S. Gruppenführer Heinrich Müller, head of Amt IV, in the R.S.H.A., had continued to oversee the Jewish deportations from Germany and other countries after Heydrich's death in 1942, without reference to Kaltenbrunner.* At the end of the war, claimed

* In Eichmann's private papers, written in 1956–7, there is hardly any reference to Kaltenbrunner, but only to Heydrich and Müller, both of whom Eichmann revered and idolised.

Kaltenbrunner, he too was in the doghouse, having obliged Himmler to cease all extermination operations in October 1944.

Gilbert pointed to the obvious logical weakness in his argument: it exploded the prisoner's contention that he knew 'practically nothing' about what was going on.

How different was Artur Seyss-Inquart, Kaltenbrunner's fellow-Austrian. Mild-mannered, bespectacled, and yet another former lawyer, Seyss-Inquart, whom Gilbert termed a brilliant and cultured intellectual with an IQ of 141, had stoically resigned himself to this fate. To his mind the Anschluss, Germany's annexation of Austria, was small beer. He was going to produce letters proving that he had warned Hitler against war if he attacked Poland. He admitted to Gilbert however that his activities as the last Nazi governor of the Netherlands were 'enough to hang him,' however hard he had tried to establish a benevolent administration. The shooting of hostages, the rounding-up of slave labour, the deportation of the Jews would be 'hard to justify now,' in Gilbert's summation.

The rest were small-fry. Conservative old-school diplomat Constantin von Neurath had stayed on as foreign minister when Hitler came to power at President von Hindenburg's request. He despised Göring and Ribbentrop, which was good; but was a member of the 'secret cabinet council' which Hitler had set up in February 1938. He pointed out correctly that it never once met. The black mark against him was his acceptance of the appointment as 'protector' of Bohemia and Moravia, after the military occupation of Czechoslovakia in 1939.

Goebbels' radio propagandist Hans Fritzsche hardly belonged in Nuremberg—his chief claim to be in the dock was that he was the only top Nazi, apart from Raeder, in Russian hands. He would be able to prove that when enemy propaganda broadcasts alerted him to the existence of atrocities, his inquiries of S.S. and Gestapo officials always met with bland assurances that these were lies. 'Now,' reported Gilbert, 'seeing the evidence in court, he has several times shown signs of emotional collapse, and recently had to be kept out of court for one day for that reason.' He would be eloquent, predicted the psychiatrist, on the way that he and the German people had been 'betrayed'; but it would take skilful cross-examination to wring out of him any admissions of personal guilt.

Economist Walter Funk felt he had done nothing irregular, and was banking on a promise from Göring to cover for him by testifying that he done nothing but carry out his orders on the four year plan. Formerly a wise-cracking, carefree type, he was now, Gilbert found, a timid, forlorn hypochondriac. The same went for Fritz Sauckel, former gauleiter of Thüringia and then Hitler's manpower commissioner. He was a man of little brain, whose argument would be that he merely recruited foreign labour and allocated it on Hitler's orders. He would even produce documents to prove that he did everything possible to ensure that the labour force was well looked after. 'He is a Göring hanger-on,' warned Gilbert, but added once again: 'Speer could probably testify against him.'

FROM ALL of this it seemed that Albert Speer held the key to the fate of many of his co-defendants, if his co-operation were sought. Here in full is what Gilbert had to say of Hitler's former munitions minister.

> (a) *Character description*: Though essentially a materialist with a lack of social sophistication and imagination, he shows a certain amount of intellectual honesty and moral courage. (IQ 127)
>
> (b) *Trial attitude and defence*: He is the only one who maintained from the very beginning that the Nazi leaders, including himself, share a common guilt for supporting a policy that resulted in destruction and murder, however innocent his own motives may have been. His own guilt lies in his blind faith in Hitler, until he realised what a destructive maniac he was—too late to do much good. He will admit his own guilt and proceed to show how guilty the administration was within his sphere of activity. He has prepared questions for his witnesses to show that war production violated 70 points of law, and will produce other incriminating evidence.
>
> He will then reveal how he plotted to assassinate Hitler, and to deliver Bormann, Himmler, Göring, and Keitel into Allied hands. His justification will be the destructive mania that Hitler exhibited after the war was obviously lost and he appealed to Hitler to quit in January 1945. At that time Hitler told him that if the German people couldn't win the war, they didn't deserve to exist. He documented this fact and his opposition to Hitler, and will produce the evidence if permitted.
>
> There will be no need to cross-examine him on his personal defense, but he can be brought to give damaging evidence against Göring, Keitel, and the Nazi leadership in general. (He will testify that Hitler considered Schacht an opponent against his aggressive plans, however.) Among other things, he has expressed his expert opinion that as a result of Hitler's prolongation of the war, Germany would be lucky to survive on a mere subsistence level for 10 years, and need not blame the occupation army for her plight. He is anxious to avoid the impression of saying these things to save his neck, and will freely admit his share of the common responsibility, because he had Hitler's confidence and did not use it to avert the catastrophe soon enough. His bitterness can be understood in terms of the destruction of his architecture and the betrayal of his blind faith by a destructive maniac.

Robert H. Jackson could hardly have wanted a better prosecution witness, and it was a misfortune that the man was now tarred with the same brush as the other defendants.

❖ ❖ ❖ ❖ ❖

Everybody had now settled into the trial's routine. The court sat five days a week and sometimes on Saturday mornings too. At mid-day the defendants took a two-hour lunch break in several upstairs rooms of the building.

Andrus had initially forbidden the defendants permission to talk with eachother at this communal lunch session. Gilbert thought this a mistake, and advised that letting them talk would give the anti-Göring and anti-Hitler factions a better chance to influence each other and not weaken. The pro-Göring forces were kept apart. 'I am always present anyway,' Gilbert advised Jackson. He also recommended that they show the O.S.S.-manufactured 'atrocity film' in the witness wing of the jailhouse to knock some of the cockiness out of the witnesses before they were dragged into the witness stand. 'I have in mind men like Gen. Milch,' wrote Gilbert, 'who would ordinarily have disparaging things to say about Göring, [and who] thinks he has a serious grievance against the Allies because of the way he has been treated as a prisoner; also Hess's secretary Fräulein Sperr, a fanatic Nazi who insists the Nazis did no wrong and everything is propaganda; [and] other militarists who think the honor of the Wehrmacht in obeying Hitler remains unsullied.'[18]

Gilbert would subsequently publish much of his jailhouse research as a book.[19] Only two items would be censored before publication on Bill Jackson's advice: a remark by Baldur von Schirach that Henry Ford's notorious tract *The Eternal Jew* was much to blame for the rise of antisemitism in Germany (Ford was alive, well, and notoriously litigious); and General Jodl's revelation that he and Eisenhower's chief of staff Walter Bedell Smith had struck a deal in May 1945 to delay by forty-eight hours the moment when the surrender instrument took effect to give time for the retreating Germans to withdraw seven hundred thousand troops as well as countless women and children from the Russian Zone. Since Bedell Smith was now U.S. ambassador in Moscow, this was an embarrassment the lawyers wished to spare him.[20] At times it seemed that the Nuremberg trials were weaving the web more tangled with each day that passed.

16: **Cooking Göring's Goose**

FEELINGS IN the United States were inflamed by the length to which the trial was running. The weeks dragged past with no end in sight. The Soviet judge General Nikitchenko sent round his colleagues on the Tribunal a letter expressing concern about the delays and the unfavourable effect on public opinion.[1]

The months of stale legal process, of abundant liquor and good food began to take their toll on judges and prosecution alike. Their keenness of intellect suffered. Each began to find the other infuriating. Their private papers tell a tale of almost non-stop tippling, and of banquets held on the slightest pretext. Sir David Maxwell Fyfe, the British prosecutor, held a dinner party on February 6, 1946 for Auguste Champetier de Ribes, the elderly French prosecutor who arrived to replace François de Menthon, and of course, most improperly, the British and American judges were invited to join the merry-making too.[2] The collaborationist French prime minister Pierre Laval had confined de Ribes to prison with the former ministers Léon Blum and Edouard Herriot for eighteen months during the war, but he admitted that his captors had made prison life relatively comfortable for him.

The carousing went on. A couple of weeks later Judge Biddle attended a dance given by the Russian prosecutors to celebrate Red Army Day, which he found 'very gay and amusing.'[3] On February 12 Robert Jackson, chief American prosecutor, held a big supper party and again invited all the Tribunal's judges. Judge Biddle, no friend by now of Jackson, thought it a very stuffy affair—too much of what he called spontaneous preparation, 'little piercing cries of delight by Mrs [Elsie] Douglas, rouged to the eyes and trying to do a little *grande dame* by gestures from the elbows.' Jackson made a speech with 'sentimental references to the "pioneer" work of the prosecution—few "veterans" are left—as if they had been taking a hill in the war … a huge build-up.'

'My dear Bob,' observed Biddle in a bitchy letter to his still-absent wife, 'is getting—maybe has got—stuffy. His mind and spirit are a little the way his face and body began to look two years ago when they were not illumined by his extraordinary lantern of intelligence. I am afraid it will continue.'[4]

Biddle was no more keenly impressed by his colleagues on the Tribunal. 'This is not an able crowd on the bench,' he wrote, as the

Russians trudged through their allegations on February 13 about tortures and the killing of prisoners. 'Lawrence never has a thought of his own, and adds nothing except that, largely guided by Birkett and me, he does make an admirable presiding officer. The French add almost nothing. Falco [the French alternate] goes along.'[5] 'I won another great victory in a three-hour debate in closed session last night,' wrote Biddle on March 13, 'over Russian obstinacy & unfairness, & *soft* British vagueness, even Birkett. I do really run this show, have won every point, single-handed, except for Parker, who is often a nuisance, & Herb [Wechsler] who is grand. But not much help on the Tribunal. They lack intelligence almost as much as they lack guts.'[6]

'The most interesting part of the trial has begun,' wrote Biddle on February 24, wishing his wife could come to enjoy the spectacle: 'Göring should be on in a week or ten days—then Hess, Keitel, Ribbentrop etc.'[7]

After that however the trial's end would seem as far away as ever. If each defendant were allowed one week, the trial would run another five months before even rebuttal began. Then there had to be evidence on the criminal organisations—Jackson's pet bugaboo—final speeches, and weeks in recess while the Tribunal wrote up its opinion. Judge Biddle's wife had now written him apologising that her bad back made it impossible for her to fly over to join him yet. On March 5 Biddle wrote again: 'I drink too much; I sleep too little; I work too hard. The obvious answer is I need you.'[8] By the middle of March Judge Biddle was downright fed up. His wife had still not come; she was playing up her back problems, forcing the judge onto the defensive in his increasingly plaintive epistles to her. All of these things posed distractions from the main event.

For whatever reason, the judges cast ever more frantic looks at the calendar. Biddle expected the case would run into July. Sir Norman Birkett was even more pessimistic, having calculated that the trial would continue right through August. Biddle reflected optimistically that the defence might at any moment collapse, if they felt that the evidence was hurting their case—'which, so far, it is.'[9] This was written one day before Hermann Göring himself mounted the stand.

SHREWDLY GAMBLING that the longer this trial lasted, the greater was the prospect of the four prosecuting powers falling out with one another, Reichsmarschall Göring was doing all he could to drag it out. Meanwhile he endeavoured to turn the trial into a major propaganda offensive against the Allies. He tried to persuade Egon Kubuschok, the lawyer defending the Reich cabinet, to apply for more and more witnesses to that end. The lawyers however no longer cared much for the reputation of the deceased Third Reich. Kubuschok, who had his own clients' interests at heart, called only one defence witness for his client organisation.[10]

As the trial now entered its critical stage the psychiatrist Dr Gilbert warned Jackson that Göring was going to be their biggest headache; the American chief prosecutor however needed no such warning. At 138, the Reichsmarschall's IQ was nominally inferior only to that of Schacht (143) and Seyss-Inquart (141.) Dr Gilbert had secretly supplied to Jackson an in-depth analysis of Göring's personality—reporting on his strengths and planned defence tactics, and on his Achilles heels as well. He called Göring an aggressive extrovert, a ruthless adventurer, and a cynical realist, a man who considered international relations to be no more than a game of opposing self-interests 'in which the clever and strong (like himself) play the hero's role.' 'The victors,' Gilbert quoted Göring as saying, 'will always be the judges and the vanquished the defendants.' He never ceased to drum into his fellow-defendants the dangerous notion that, since Germany had been a sovereign state and its Führer a sovereign ruler, the court had no jurisdiction over them.

When Gilbert had murmured to him something about aggressive wars of imperial conquest, Göring's response was: 'Don't make me laugh! America, England, and Russia have all done the same thing to promote their own national aspirations, but when Germany does it becomes a crime—because we lost.'

He intended to prove that he had been against the war with Britain, and had tried behind Hitler's back to negotiate with Lord Halifax; that he thought BARBAROSSA, the attack on Russia, was 'premature,' although inevitable sooner or later. The chinks in Göring's armour, suggested Gilbert, were two in number: the Nazi atrocities, and his greed for riches and art treasures, both of which spoiled his posture as a hero, patriot, and model officer. Hence Göring would prefer to harp on other perceived injustices, like Versailles. He would claim to have dismissed stories of the atrocities as fantastic; he had certainly never ordered any—and on the subject of atrocities, 'Were not the Russians the real experts in mass murder?' He spoke of having 'proof' that they committed many of the atrocities they were accusing the Germans of committing—probably a reference to the Katyn and Babi Yar massacres—and he hinted that there were reports and photographs proving this at Geneva. As for the art treasures, he had bought them legally, he said, and he had the receipts to prove it.

Dr Gilbert reported all this confidential data to Jackson and recommended: '[Göring] should be asked how he acquired art amounting to billions of marks from all countries; why he did not investigate atrocity reports; whether he considered the lives of millions of Germans in preparing for war.' This, suggested Gilbert, would spoil his pose.

Dr Gilbert recommended various tactics—what would today be called 'dirty tricks'—to demoralise Göring and weaken his influence, like detaching him from the other defendants at their mid-day lunch tables. Raised in a society where the business luncheon was the principal arena for wheeling and dealing, this was perhaps the most imaginative scenario that the Americans could come up with. Following Gilbert's recommendations, Jackson persuaded Sir David Maxwell Fyfe and the other chief prosecutors to agree to the prisoners being grouped differently during the lunch break, placing Göring and Streicher alone at a table where they could not influence the other prisoners. The defence counsel of course had no say in the matter.

'You are hereby notified,' the prison commandant Andrus informed his prisoners on February 16, 'that neither the Tribunal nor any other authority has required that the defendants be allowed to remain in constant communication with each other.'[11]

The new seating arrangement took effect two days later. Speer was jubilant at Göring's isolation, and Dr Gilbert found the Reichsmarschall dejected and tremulous like a rejected child. After a few days he reported to Jackson: 'Effect of separating defendants & isolating Göring marked and on the whole favorable for trial.'

Göring made a mental note of this further harassment by Colonel Andrus, the prison commandant with the lacquered red helmet, and silently vowed revenge. The jailhouse barber, a former soldier in a Luftwaffe signals unit, told the other prisoners that the Reichsmarschall was unprintable about the Americans and particularly about Andrus, whom he had dubbed 'the fireman.'[12]

THE DAY was approaching for which Göring—and the entire courtroom—had been waiting. Like an athlete coming out of training he was now nearing his peak performance. Jackson had done everything he could to demoralise, deflate, and injure Göring, already weakened by months of harsh prison conditions and a starvation diet that had cut his weight from 264 pounds to 186. He was fifty-three, but he was a man with a mission: he was convinced that he could stay the course better than this whisky-soaked American small-town lawyer. While the judges and prosecutors had been living the good life, the months of incarceration, isolation, and semi-starvation had not beaten Göring down at all; they had hardened him, and given him time to reflect, to marshal his thoughts, and to sharpen his wit. On March 6 he passed Field-Marshal Erhard Milch, his old enemy, in the jailhouse corridor. Milch, who had been brought back from England in the hope that he could be intimidated into testifying against Speer and his former commander-in-chief, was astonished to see Göring so fit and slim. Despite the manacles fastening them to their escorts, the two Luftwaffe officers exchanged forbidden salutes.[13]

The attack on Göring's witnesses began two days later, on Friday the eighth, with Göring's servile *chef de bureau* General Karl Bodenschatz on the stand. Jackson made mincemeat of him. 'Wait till he starts on *me*,' boasted Göring to Dr Gilbert afterward, accepting a cigarette with noticeably trembling fingers. Milch was brought up from the cells next.

Taking the stand he spoke up bravely in defence of the Reichsmarschall—to the rage of the Americans who had brought him over from England.

Back in his cell, Milch recorded his own impressions of the court in his diary:

> Sworn in, everybody wearing earphones; then examination by [defence] attorney Stahmer.... When I was asked about Göring's attitude to prisoners of war, Jackson interrupted, 'We've shown enough patience, but this is going too far. I object!' The Tribunal sustained his objection and poor Stahmer, somewhat confused, asked me one more short question and sat down.

The court adjourned for the weekend. 'The defendants,' observed Milch, 'were mostly very crushed. When I saw Jodl being led away his eyes were filled with tears.'[14]

On Monday the eleventh, Jackson cross-examined Milch. Nobody curtailed the U.S. chief prosecutor's questions, but that was one of the privileges of the victors. Many of the questions had little or nothing to do with the indictment; Jackson spent some time trying to nail the field-marshal on the question of his ancestry. Dr Robert Kempner, Göring's old foe, had slipped to Jackson a note reading, 'Milch was made a full Aryan on the request of Göring, in spite of his Jewish father.' There can be no doubt* that the field-marshal's late father Anton Milch was Jewish. His natural father was however another man, namely his mother's maternal uncle. Faced with the awful choice between admitting to the wrongful allegation that he was a half-Jew, and revealing that he and his siblings were all the product of his mother's incestuous relationship—she was at that time still living, and had even slipped a cyanide capsule to him during their last meeting—Milch bit his lip and said nothing.

> JACKSON: Didn't you know that the decrees which excluded Jews and half-Jews from positions were issued by Göring?
>
> MILCH: No, I did not. As far as I know the decrees were issued by the ministry of the interior, the department concerned with that.
>
> JACKSON: Uh, as a matter of fact did you not have to take certain proceedings to avoid the effects of those decrees yourself?

Pausing to consider how to frame his reply, Milch then answered:

> No. I know what you are referring to. That was a matter that was cleared up long before.

*Thanks to detailed research carried out by Professor Klaus Herrmann of the University of Montreal in family archives and Jewish records in Breslau.

JACKSON: How long before was it cleared?

MILCH: As far as I know, in '33.

JACKSON: 1933—right after the Nazis came to power!

MILCH: That's right.

JACKSON: And that time Göring had—so we'll have no misunderstanding about this—Göring had you made what's called a full Aryan? Is that right?

MILCH: I don't believe so—not that I was 'made one' by him. I *was* one already.

JACKSON: Well, he had it established, let us say.

MILCH: He was of great assistance in clarifying what was very obscure to me.

JACKSON: That your mother's husband was a Jew. Is that correct?

MILCH: That is not what I said.

JACKSON: You had to demonstrate lack of ancestry through any Jewish source. Is that correct—?

MILCH: *Jawohl*, same as anybody else.

JACKSON: —and in your case it involved the … your father, your *alleged* father. Is that correct?

MILCH: *Jawohl.*[15]

The Times reported that Milch and Jackson engaged in a battle of wits for five hours which often gave the impression that Milch, rather than Göring, was in the dock. 'I must have knocked their plans into a cocked hat!' wrote Milch, reading this newspaper report. 'Unless means is found,' warned *The Times*, 'of keeping witnesses to the point, the Nuremberg defence will become an opportunity for Nazi polemics and false trails.' Milch allowed Jackson no quarter. When Jackson asked his attitude toward air attacks on civilians, he replied, as he wrote in that evening's diary, 'I can think of nothing crueller and more objectionable than such air raids; and anybody who still has any doubts has only to take a look at Hamburg, Berlin, Leipzig, the Ruhr cities and particularly Dresden to see what I mean.'

THESE AND similar exchanges show how unreliable, if not downright deceitful, the published transcripts of the Nuremberg trials are. The only true record is the original wire recording, which was subsequently processed onto 2,011 sound discs. The 17,077-page mimeographed transcript, which was of course the only record available to the judges in reaching their conclusions, is erratic, erroneous, and incomplete; it has moreover been doctored, in some cases quite blatantly, to the disadvantage of the defence. Thus the foregoing exchange, which is now available in the National Archives on Nuremberg Trials disc 1440 B, recorded from the original wire recording, was omitted from page 5,661 of the mimeographed daily transcript. It was restored to the (blue-bound) printed volumes only after Milch, checking the transcripts, protested.

This happened more than once. When Robert Jackson asked Milch, 'Did you know that Speer turned over to the United States all his personal papers and lists including the minutes of the Central Planning Committee?', Milch replied, 'That is a matter of indifference to me.'

Jackson answered menacingly: 'That will not be indifferent to you.'

This exchange vanished from the published transcript.[16] Asked by Jackson whether he was an American prisoner, the field marshal retorted that he was a *British* prisoner, who had subsequently been declared an 'internee' by the Americans in violation of international law.[17] Challenged about the lacunæ in his memory he explained to the court that this had suffered from the severe manhandling he had received from the British commandos after his capture 'when I was beaten about the head' (by Brigadier Derek Mills-Roberts.)[18]

When the British assistant prosecutor G. D. Roberts asked him in cool and educated tones, 'You are of course aware that Norway's neutrality was violated?' Milch spat back: '*Jawohl!* To our knowledge, and in our view, it was violated twice!'—a reference to Churchill's ill-starred attempt to invade Norway before Hitler could.

This was tantamount to blasphemy, transgressing as it did against the rules on forbidden themes which the chief prosecutors had drawn up in secret between themselves. The exchange was excised from the mimeographed transcript of the trial but, on Milch's protest, subsequently restored to the printed volumes.[19]

Jackson's menaces had not been idle vapourings. As much in anger at Milch's stout defence of Göring as *pour encourager les autres*, the Americans threw him into the notorious punishment bunker at Dachau concentration camp, which was now under their management. He found his one-man cell crowded with illustrious company, including several other field-marshals. They were treated like, or worse than, cattle. 'Received from First Lieutenant H. L. Cook of HQ, 6850th Internal Security Detachment, IMT, four (4) live bodies as follows,—' certified the chit from PWE (Prisoner of War Enclosure) No. 29, as Dachau camp was now officially known; the chit listed the 'live bodies' as Dr Karl Brandt, General von Falkenhausen, General von Falkenhorst, and Field-Marshal Hugo Sperrle.[20] They would all languish here for several months, until the International Red Cross heard rumours and began investigations—or until American hangmen converted the live bodies into dead ones.

❖ ❖ ❖ ❖ ❖

'Everything had gone pretty well with the trial,' Jackson was to reflect sourly a few days later, 'until Göring took the witness stand. That, we knew, would be our hard fight. The press have been playing him up as a buffoon, but of course he really is an extremely tough and sophisticated person.'[21]

Göring was in no doubt about his own probable fate and he did not seek to ameliorate it. 'Rather die like a lion, than frisk like a rabbit!'[22] he would tell his own lawyers. Taking his seat late in the dock one morning he apologised loudly to the lawyers' tables that he had been delayed by a blood test. 'They'll be drawing enough blood from me pretty soon!' he added jocularly.[23] He expected to go before a firing squad. Viewing the courtroom from the bench, Sir Norman Birkett realised that Göring was dominating the entire proceedings. He had followed the evidence intently when required to and he had slept like a baby when not. Nobody, the Englishman added, seemed to have been quite prepared for Göring's immense ability and knowledge, or for his mastery of the captured documents.

As Göring now began to speak from the witness stand on Wednesday March 13, the whole building was packed. The lion was not only fighting back, he erupted in glistening oratory, embellishing his answers with a ready humour that evoked gales of laughter from the public galleries. He hoped that somewhere out in the forests surrounding the city his wife and little girl were proud witnesses to this, his last stand. Millions of radio listeners around the world listened to the performance. In prison camps in Britain, across liberated Europe, and in America the men poured out into the open to cluster around the loudspeakers as 'Hermann's' unmistakable voice echoed around their Quonset and Nissen huts. Former German prisoners-of-war have admitted to this author that they stood up and cheered, enthralled at the audio-spectacle of the Reichsmarschall fighting back for Germany. One Luftwaffe doctor who collected and digested the sparse news reports for fellow Luftwaffe officers interned at Latimer in Buckinghamshire observed that Göring won back much of his lost prestige at the interrogation centre on this day.[24]

The Allied and licensed German journalists crowding the press tables in the courthouse building at Nuremberg were speechless, having as Jackson wryly noted believed their own news stories that the Reichsmarschall was a dope fiend, a physical wreck, and a neurotic. His first day was a triumph; for the prosecution it produced a débâcle which threatened to dismantle the whole edifice that Jackson and his colleagues had painstakingly laboured to erect. Smoking his long meerschaum pipe afterwards, the Reichsmarschall sat on the cot in his cell and stretched out an arm for Dr Gilbert to see—it was as steady as a rock.

Still rooting around like a truffle-pig for gobbets of Intelligence, Gilbert asked him at lunch the next day what he proposed to say about the S.S. atrocities. 'That I didn't take the rumours seriously,' replied Göring, uneasily. Back on the witness stand that afternoon however he noticed the American alternate judge John Parker nodding affably to him, and he knew he was on a roll.

'Yon Göring is quite a guy,' exclaimed Speer's attorney. 'A *Mordskerl*—a real killer.'

Speer, piqued at Göring's success, said he hoped that Jackson would show him up when the cross-examination began after the weekend.

BROADCAST AGAIN live around the world, the Göring–Jackson duel began in earnest on Monday March 18. His hair slicked back, his eyes proud and defiant, Göring strode to the stand. He had the measure of this court now. He knew that Jackson, unaccustomed to the cut and thrust of courtroom advocacy for several years now, would be at a disadvantage, and particularly here—in a court where every word had first to be translated to him. Göring had a grasp of English, and that gave him a tactical edge. Alert to the crucial importance of this day, Jackson faltered. He had intended first to slap Göring into place by asking about his anti-Jewish decrees and his sumptuous art collection. In what proved a fatal change of plan, he decided at the last moment to start with weightier and more general political allegations against Göring. 'The cross-examination,' recorded Sir Norman Birkett in his own notes, 'had not proceeded more than ten minutes before it was seen that he was the complete master of Mr Justice Jackson. Suave, shrewd, adroit, capable, resourceful, he quickly saw the elements of the situation, and as his confidence grew, his mastery became more apparent.... For almost two days he held the stage without interruption of any kind.'[25]

Far from denying Jackson's sweeping charges, Göring was glad to admit them: he was *proud* of having destroyed the Weimar republic and of having suppressed the parliamentary opposition. This unexpected defence, for which Gilbert had not prepared him, wrong-footed Jackson. When Göring launched into a long discourse, Jackson peremptorily ordered him—as he would have in a New York court—to answer yes or no. He saw Biddle lean over and whisper something to the president, Lord Justice Lawrence.

'Mr Justice Jackson,' responded Lawrence. 'The Tribunal feels that the witness should be allowed to make whatever explanation he cares to make in answer to this question.'

❖ ❖ ❖ ❖ ❖

Göring glowed. Perhaps it was a fateful blunder by Lawrence. Birkett afterwards felt that if Lawrence had ruled otherwise and prevented Göring from branching off into monologues, he would have brought the Reichsmarschall more under control and helped restore Jackson's bruised confidence; but he did not, and Jackson's ordeal continued.

Fortified by his own fatalism, Göring bore up even more strongly to the American's cross-examination the next day, Tuesday March 19. Part of the case against him was founded on German documents which argued whether to allow local townspeople to lynch Allied airmen who had parachuted into their hands, insofar as these airmen had been machine-gunning civilians and passenger trains. Jackson harassed Göring at great length on these allegations, although one of his staff had warned him that the documents in evidence raised one embarrassing issue of fact: 'Did Allied planes strafe helpless civilians?'[26] (The Tribunal may have shared this embarrassment, for as on Katyn its judgement on Göring would omit all mention of this charge.)

The confrontation between Göring and Jackson which ensued was a scene that has become part of the lore of the trial, encapsulating as it did the conflict between the ordered, civilised milieu of the wing-collared country lawyer, and the swaggering, arrogant, devil-may-care world of the big-time gangster in uniform that Göring had become. Jackson was a very simple and not very educated man, a small-town advocate from upstate New York who had risen by largely political means to the highest reaches of his profession in the Supreme Court. But, perched on that lofty pinnacle, he had long lost the trial lawyer's art of cross-examination. In recent years, trials for him had devolved into a balancing of the finer points of the law, as argued by others before him.[27]

At each thrust and parry by Göring he became more incensed. Like a bull enraged by the picadors he continued to charge blindly in every direction. Here was a defendant who refused to abide by the rules of the sport, rules that seemed clearly defined by their very status—these were the victors, and those the vanquished. Göring however had determined to ridicule Jackson and destroy his authority in this court, and his silver tongue and his fearlessness about death were ready allies to that end.

When Jackson, desperately trying to salvage something from a 1935 document wrongly identified by his team as proof of Nazi planning for a remilitarisation of the Rhineland one year before that event, pointed to the TOP SECRET classification on the paper, as though this were in itself a heinous offence, Göring scoffed insolently that he could not recall having seen the secret plans of the U.S. joint chiefs of staff openly published in the pre-war years. There was raucous laughter from all over the court. Jackson ripped off his headphones and threw them down, then petulantly appealed to the judges to call the witness to order—he must answer the questions, and not attempt to deliver lengthy and irrelevant speeches.

Lawrence ruled that Göring's answer was in order.

Refusing to let the matter drop, Jackson argued heatedly and at great length that the case would get out of hand if the defendants were allowed such latitude. 'Göring's answer,' he lectured his fellow-prosecutors afterwards, 'was impudent and argumentative and the court should have used its gavel.'[28]

❖ ❖ ❖ ❖ ❖

Everybody agreed that Göring had won this round. Justice Jackson was just saved by the gong, wrote one British newspaperman afterwards.[29] There were remarkable scenes at that night's secret meeting of the chief prosecutors.

> JACKSON: The arrogance of Göring in today's session supports what opponents of this trial have always said: if you give these people a chance to speak they will propagandize and make it a farce.
>
> When I objected to Göring's attitude [and] requested the Court to instruct him to answer responsively [Judge Biddle] whispered in the ear of the presiding judge, and thereupon the Court overruled me on its own motion without even hearing an objection from Göring's counsel.
>
> If Göring is permitted to get away with this, he will encourage all the defendants to do the same thing. I have never heard of such a rule for cross-examination. The witness should be compelled to answer the question and to reserve his explanations for later (re-direct.) It is utterly impossible to cross-examine unless the Court controls the witnesses, and Göring knows he has the Court in his corner.

Furious at this débâcle, Jackson proposed to abandon the cross-examination of Göring altogether. Maxwell Fyfe was horrified. 'To cease now,' he objected, 'would be interpreted as a victory for Göring's obstructive tactics.'

'Göring is being permitted to preach,' Jackson retorted. 'He is becoming constantly more arrogant, and if this goes on it will do our countries more harm than good.'

On this, the British lawyer agreed. 'We must tell the Court that we are dealing with an experienced politician. He will make the proceedings ridiculous unless the Tribunal co-operates. The result will be that the trial is a disaster.' He recommended that they unofficially convey this warning to 'our own judges,' adding: 'The Allied Control Council, for instance, is apprehensive lest Göring's examination-in-chief do a great deal of harm in restoring Nazi prestige.' (Of course such passages from the secret stenographic record go a long way toward documenting how far the Tribunal was a political instrument, and how little store was to be set by its impartiality.) 'This,' Jackson agreed, 'is a critical point of the trial as far as achieving its objective is concerned.'

'Göring,' he stated in a further outburst to his colleagues, 'is permitted to become a hero of the Nazis because he dares to talk back to the United States. This wins him admiration from all the Nazis who remain in Germany, and he will influence the other defendants to do likewise. I almost felt this afternoon that it would have been wiser to have shot these men out of hand.'[30]

MAXWELL FYFE was made of sterner stuff than Jackson. When he took up the cross-examination he bullied beads of perspiration onto the aviator's brow by asking Göring about the execution of the fifty British airmen who had escaped from Sagan prison camp in March 1944. Even so, the British lawyer admitted later that without question the Reichsmarschall was the most formidable witness he had ever cross-examined.[31]

Maxwell Fyfe asked one particularly loaded question: was Göring still loyal to Hitler now, despite the atrocities which had come to light? After an instant's hesitation Göring answered that he believed in remaining loyal in times of hardship. He added that in all probability Hitler had known as little of the atrocities as he had himself. The Russian prosecutor then tackled the Reichsmarschall, asking why he had not refused to obey his Führer. 'If I had,' replied Göring, with his wits once more about him, 'I certainly should not have had to worry about my health.'

'We have had a most difficult time with Göring,' Jackson wrote a few days later. 'It is beyond belief that the Tribunal by this time should not have gotten his measure. For about one hour I had pretty good success getting answers and then he gave an unresponsive one and I jumped on him about it. Biddle leaned over to the Lord Justice and said, "Let him answer the way he wants to," in substance. Whereupon the Lord Justice made that ruling. Of course, with a man of Göring's driving type it was disastrous. For two days we got no answers to our questions, but lectures. It finally became so bad that the Lord Justice himself said they had been allowing him to make speeches. But it has done a great deal of harm.'[32]

Seeing Göring pinned down at last by Sir David, Jackson breathed again. 'We finally got him cornered,' he wrote to John McCloy. 'But it was a long hard battle and a great deal of irrelevant propaganda was fed out into Germany.' He added: 'We had so many documents on him, however, that we got him subdued at last and I think he is a "gone goose."'[33]

❖ ❖ ❖ ❖ ❖

After this episode, if not before, there was all-out war between Justice Jackson and the American members of the Tribunal. Each was not ashamed to spite the other. When Judge Biddle began looking for a new billet in Nuremberg, he was careful to turn one down that was too close to Jackson. The least defamatory of his feelings about Bob Jackson, his country's chief prosecutor in this, the trial of the century, was that he needed a punch on the head before he would listen to anybody else. 'He is, I think, knotted to a second-rate rotten woman,' wrote Biddle to his wife, referring to Jackson's secretary Elsie Douglas: 'She eats him, flatters him, a common possessive yes-woman, bringing out Bob's worse characteristics.'[34]

The Jacksons in turn loathed Biddle. Several times the judge had dutifully invited them round to his house, but they had always snubbed his invitation. Jackson junior blamed the unsatisfactory course the trial was taking, after the unfortunate Göring–Jackson duel, on the 'ineptitude and malice of a piss-ant like Biddle,' and the spinelessness of the British president, that 'fuddy-duddy' Lord Justice Lawrence, as a private letter written by his son at the end of March makes clear. 'The trial is not going well, thanks chiefly to Francis Biddle, who has replaced [General] Donovan as the first-class sonofabitch. He is insanely jealous of Father, and has gone out of his way to get him. It all began with his jealousy of the fact that Father had a bigger car, bigger office, bigger house etc. Also it is true that he is a bigger man, and that galled Biddle, who wanted to be Number One, and get all the publicity.'

Describing the Jackson–Göring duel, the prosecutor's son continued: 'The upshot is that he [Biddle] prevailed on the British presiding judge, who is a weak man, to let Göring say anything he wanted to, whether relevant or not. The result was that it was impossible for Father or anybody else to cross-examine Göring, and Göring proceeded to turn the things into a glorification of Hitler and the Nazi regime. It was scandalous and contemptuous, but the court, which is rather stupid, didn't know it was being insulted. But Biddle had what he wanted.' Jackson's only consolation was the belief that everybody knew what Biddle was up to, especially the press. 'He is not a popular man, any more than he was in Washington, and I think he may very well have overplayed his hand.'[35]

Judge Biddle naturally saw things in different hues. A few hours after the duel, he wrote this private account of his fellow-American's humiliation:

> Bob Jackson fell down terribly in his cross-examination of Göring today. He didn't *know* his case, didn't really study the document about which Göring was being cross-examined. Göring wise-cracked. Bob: 'And you kept those military plans secret?' Göring: 'Did the American army broadcast their military plans?' Bob: 'The witness is not responsive. He has been steadily contumacious, & is not answering the questions yes or no.' Etc. He asked us to protect him, in substance. Lawrence looked to me for help; but I thought he better do his own job, & said nothing, & we adjourned, everyone feeling that Göring was winning the bout of wits, which he was.

Jackson's trouble was, the judge wrote, that he wanted to be pope; it was not easy, philosophised Biddle, to pitch in and be tough with a clever gangster like Göring, a 'brilliant sixteenth-century extrovert.' Göring had listened to every question closely, took his time, and answered well; while Jackson did not listen to the answers. He was totally dependent on his notes, and he had failed to absorb the case in the way that a chief prosecutor should before beginning a cross-examination.[36]

Jackson's chief interrogator Colonel Amen dined with the judges that night. Biddle—like Jackson—agreed that the English judge Lawrence was weak and listless in court. 'A guide is needed,' he felt, 'and I'm boiling over: Birkett agreeing, but hesitating to say anything.' It was an awful situation. Amen, one of Jackson's best assistants, was frantic—his boss, he complained, had nothing but 'yes-men' around him, and that was the reason why he was not well prepared. The publicity had gone to Jackson's head: 'He is losing ground,' said Amen, 'and needs help.'[37]

From all of this it is evident that the Göring–Jackson duel had torn Tribunal and prosecution asunder. It laid bare very raw nerves—nerves which this long-drawn-out trial was testing to the limit. If there was one good thing about the judges' spinelessness, reflected Bill Jackson cynically, it was that in the end they would not dare do anything other than convict most of the defendants 'and so eventually the trial will have served its purpose.'[38]

FOR TWO weeks Jackson writhed under the burden of Göring's public triumph and his own humiliation. Aboard the plane that bore him out of Nuremberg to Paris on March 30 to accept an accolade from the French legal profession, he wrote an indignant letter to his wife: 'The Tribunal is permitting by its weak and indecisive rulings the trial to just droll along.' The biggest job still facing him, he realised, would be the last—the final argument. But at this rate it was impossible to guess when they would be through. 'There is a real drive on among [the] prosecutors to finish by July 1st. If only we had a presiding judge like Judge Sears, and not this diddling Biddling business. Gods!'[39]

Ernst Engländer, the American air force's star interrogator, who had by 1946 been returned to private life in Wall Street as a financier, was astonished as much by Göring's triumph as by Milch's performance on his behalf. He wrote a furious letter to Jackson to inquire whether the unchallengeable evidence which had been obtained by the hidden microphones at the C.S.D.I.C. camp in Britain had been available to the prosecution at Nuremberg. 'Göring and Milch hated each other,' he wrote, 'and we have it in their own words—there can't be any question about that.... I feel sure that with the evidence taken down in Milch's own words one could break him down in court to such an extent that he would have to reverse himself and admit perjury,' he wrote to Jackson. 'I should like to see those boys hang and sweat rather than to make themselves out as heroes and martyrs.'[40]

Hopeful even now of scoring a final victory over Göring, Jackson sent a woman to question Milch at Dachau; but the field marshal had to explain that so far as he knew there had been no shorthand record taken of his talks with Engländer, which he had always believed to be informal and off the record. He had not known about hidden microphones. Engländer's suggestions were therefore rejected as unhelpful.[41]

From all over the world fan mail poured into the prison addressed to the Reichsmarschall, with messages like 'keep your chin up Hermann,' and 'good for you Hermann.' He was not allowed to see the letters.[42]

Jackson too received letters of support, though fewer than Göring did. There was a spinster in southern England who wrote to him from Brighton on blue Basildon Bond notepaper:

> Dear Sir—In your prosecution of the unscrupulous Georing [*sic*], people seem to have forgotten that the signing of the Munich Pact was filmed, & I saw it here in Brighton, either at the 'Regent' or 'Savoy'. That would mean either 'British Gaumont' or 'Pathé' Gazette. In that particular film Georing was in the background, clad in his white uniform. He was walking to & fro, smiling smugly to himself, & rubbing his hands *together*—It was NOT the gesture of a man desiring Peace, but it *was* that of a Cur, who had succeeded in *trapping* an unsuspecting, believing man, such as the then Prime Minister, who cried to his public on arriving home,—'This means Peace in our Time.'—I am, Sir, Yours truly, & in sympathy at having to tackle such a slimy individual as Georing, A. FERIDA RASSAM (Miss.)

Jackson winced, marked it 'crank,' and filed it away.[43] Göring's victory was not final, but it would haunt him for the rest of his life.

17: Schacht Saved on the Square

ONE LETTER which Hermann Göring did receive came from his daughter, with a flower pressed from the forest. 'Mummy was sad she didn't hear you on the radio,' wrote Edda, 'I would have given up all my toys just to hear your voice. Mummy has told me she's going to be allowed to see you. I'd like to see you frightfully too. Can't I come as well? I'm *sooooo* fond of you and it's so awfully long since I saw you. Oh, Papa, if only I could come too!' 'I promise you, papa, that I always try to comfort Mummy and I'll always protect her. How much nicer it would be if you were there to protect us!!! I pray every evening to Dear God that Mummy and I can see you soon and give you a big hug.'

The stenographic record of the secret meeting of the chief prosecutors on April 5, 1946 reveals how deeply Göring's opponent, Robert Jackson, still felt the injury to his pride, and the anxiety he felt for the future of the trial.

He had now heard that Rosenberg's lawyers had put in eight hundred pages of documents for translation, of which three hundred pages were extracts from philosophical works. Dr Gilbert told him of how the prisoners were gloating.

> JACKSON: If the Court knew what the defendants say among themselves (and it will be printed some day) they will feel differently. For instance Göring told Ribbentrop that if he wanted to get away with a long spiel the way he (Göring) had, he should make his story interesting.
>
> MAXWELL FYFE: In the closed session with the Court the other day, I tried to suggest, when the Court requested a limitation of cross-examination, that Göring had been on direct [cross-examination] by his own counsel for two-and-a-half days and had caused so much trouble for the occupying Powers that the prosecution simply had to take the time to counter his testimony....[1]

Jackson searched for some proper way of tipping off the judges about what the defendants were saying about them behind their backs.[2] There is little doubt that he told the judges privately during their innumerable drinking and dining sessions together.

If all or most of the other defendants had acted as Göring had, the trial would have been reduced to a shambles; this was Sir Norman Birkett's view.[3] But not all of them viewed their prospects as bleakly as did the Reichsmarschall. Indeed some of them, being the more astute, recognised that he was now the Tribunal's *bête noire* and they were careful to make plain their disapproval of him.

Albert Speer referred in his evidence to Göring's vanity, his corruption, and his drug addiction; Schacht would report on May 3 gossip that he had heard, and this was by no means untrue, of Göring appearing in private dressed in a Roman toga like the Emperor Nero, wearing lipstick, with his sandals displaying painted toenails, and with rouge embellishing his cheeks. (Göring angrily denied the lipstick, talking with Dr Gilbert that evening.) After that, Göring passed word to Jackson that, if guaranteed a firing squad, rather than the hangman's rope, he would give the prosecution some *real* dirt on Schacht. Jackson did not heed him—the mode of execution was not within his gift.[4]

The other defendants watched Schacht's wriggling performance with contempt. 'Schacht made a poor impression,' Keitel told his son a few weeks later. 'He thinks he's the brightest defendant of the lot.... Sometimes he was completely unpolitical, and sometimes just an economist.'[5]

IN APRIL the court heard evidence from Hans Bernd Gisevius, the renegade Abwehr officer whom Jackson had first met in Wiesbaden.

His O.S.S. 'handler,' Allen Dulles, had originally expected to use Gisevius for the prosecution but Jackson, hoping to keep oral evidence to a minimum, had decided not to call him himself. Late in March 1946 however both Schacht and Frick had applied for him to be brought in from Switzerland, where he had taken refuge from his fellow-Germans, for their defence. This was an unexpected twist. 'Personally,' Dulles wrote to Jackson, 'I regret that he has been drawn into the case by Schacht but he is the type of fellow who feels it is his duty to go to Nuremberg and I assume that he will testify that from 1938 on Schacht flirted with the anti-Hitler forces.' While Gisevius might be of use to Schacht's defence, he expected that his testimony could hardly benefit Frick.

Knowing the robust treatment routinely meted out at Nuremberg by the Americans to witnesses summoned for the defence, Dulles besought for Gisevius such courtesies as could be shown to him under the circumstances.[6] As a former Abwehr officer, he might be subject to automatic arrest by the American authorities, and the O.S.S. had to ask that he be given special clearance; they also expressed their strong feelings that no attempts should be made by 'our people at Nuremberg' or by the army to discredit any testimony Gisevius might give, 'in view of his activities on our behalf.'[7]

Gisevius as a witness did substantially more harm to Göring's defence than good to those of either Frick or Schacht. Jackson, delighted, wrote a letter of appreciation to Allen Dulles on April 28: '[Gisevius] fulfilled the expectations stated in your letters,' he wrote. 'Göring is in a badly depressed state.' The German officers in the dock were outraged when Gisevius unrolled all the dirty linen about Blomberg's 'unbecoming' marriage to a young Berlin girl. Keitel told his son later that when Gisevius dragged up the Blomberg affair in court he told Nelte to object that all this had nothing whatever to do with the indictment. 'Gisevius,' said Keitel, 'was a dirty character whom Canaris, who had been playing a double-game from the very outbreak of war, sent into Switzerland with intelligence missions concerning Britain and America. When Nelte asked him how much the foreigners had paid him for his activities Gisevius had refused to answer. Almost to a man the lawyers had risen in arms against Gisevius.'[8]

❖ ❖ ❖ ❖ ❖

With tempers running more ragged with each day that passed, and still smarting from Göring's victory, on April 24 Jackson wrote a personal letter to President Truman to complain about the conduct of their judge, Biddle.[9] Biddle's wife had now joined him in Nuremberg, and despite—or because of—this he too was now regularly in a foul temper. He lost control completely on the bench on May 21, when Lord Justice Lawrence refused point-blank Biddle's request to ask his own questions of a witness. In low tones, Biddle angrily said that he had every right to ask questions as did Lawrence himself. Lawrence, wounded, asked the questions for him, and Biddle later apologised. 'I must watch this,' noted the American. 'But the old goat is so dumb, so inept that it becomes a long series of petty annoyances at the end of a long, dull day.[10]

Everybody was getting nervy. While interned in Moscow Grand-Admiral Raeder had written for his own purposes a scathing indictment of his fellow commanders-in-chief, and particularly of Field-Marshal Keitel.[11] Rather naïvely, Raeder had believed that this *aide-mémoire* would be safe from prying eyes. The Russians had seized it, and, on May 21, Colonel Pokrovsky tried to introduce the document as prosecution exhibit USSR-460. The Tribunal refused his application on a technicality. Keitel was still devastated on hearing of Raeder's comments, pointing out to his counsel Dr Nelte in a private letter that the admiral had never voiced such criticisms during the war although such would have been his duty. 'I have seen my character so grievously smeared by a very senior representative of the armed forces,' he wrote, 'that I can no longer expect to meet with any understanding from this Tribunal.' He offered to let Nelte resign the defence; the attorney of course refused.[12]

Few people grasped the point that, for all his highfaluting title as chief of the High Command, Keitel had been little more than Hitler's military office-manager. On May 25 Raeder tried to soften his criticisms of Keitel, in an affidavit taken by Pokrovsky, stating that naturally nobody had any prospect of staying long in office if he was to have a row with the Führer every other day.

General Jodl poured balsam on some of the doomed Field-Marshal Keitel's wounds by his stout testimony during the first week in June. Jodl, who had been chief of the High Command's operations staff, had set before the Tribunal clearly and frankly all the things which Keitel had been too flustered to say. 'I feel,' Keitel wrote to Jodl's young wife on June 9, 'that I must and should write to tell you how delighted I have been with the course of the defence during this last week. [Your husband's] constancy and dignity, and the way he has preserved his honour as a soldier, were as impressive as his clear and irrefutable answers were convincing. The great effort you have made with your co-operation has also repaid itself one hundredfold.'[13]

❖ ❖ ❖ ❖ ❖

Seeing no value, as they put it, in staying in the Palace of Justice and listening to the defendants ignoring the issues of the trial and lecturing the courtroom and the world on the glories of the Nazi state, the two Jacksons, father and son, left Nuremberg and went over to Prague to observe the trial of Karl-Hermann Frank, the 'Butcher of Lidice.'

The Americans took a perhaps closer than usual interest in this trial: Frank had been in their custody, and they had extradited him to Prague under Czech pressure. They also had a morbid curiosity about seeing a Soviet-style People's Court at work—these, his son noted, were notorious for being 'drumhead affairs,' which 'give the defendant a fair trial and then hang him.'[14] Judge Jackson found that the trial was 'a revelation in efficiency and fairness of trial procedure.'[15] Frank was sentenced and hanged—or rather strangled, no drop being involved—soon after.

EASTER CAME and went, and there was no sign that their ordeal in Nuremberg was approaching an end. 'There is a good deal said about how long the trial is taking,' Jackson admitted to his wife. 'But one year ago this building was in the hands of Germans.' In a throw-away remark which revealed precisely how worried he now was, he continued: 'I am not worried about the verdict of history, but of course it is damned annoying to come over here for a few months and be kept so long.'[16] Not much later, he would begin to write half-seriously about his own 'imprisonment' at Nuremberg.[17]

NEXT WEEK, wrote Jackson on April 18, 1946 he would probably take on the cross-examination of Hjalmar Schacht—'after Göring the toughest of them.'[18]

He had always regarded Schacht as one of the most despicable defendants. The banker's arrogant attitude since the trial had begun only vexed him all the more. When the gruesome concentration camp films were shown, for example, Schacht had contemptuously folded his arms and turned his back on the screen in the courtroom.[19]

Even more irritating for Jackson was that Schacht was overheard in the cells confidently predicting that he would be acquitted. Irritating rumours circulated that the prosecution of Schacht was not in earnest. Letter-writers taunted Jackson that he would never succeed in convicting a big banker—whether friend or foe, they were the new Untouchables.

He soon became aware that the Nazi banker did indeed have friends in the most unlikely places and influence everywhere. One day one of his team, the eminent New York international lawyer Ralph Albrecht, reported to him that the British assistant prosecutor Colonel Harry J. Phillimore—later a lord justice of appeal in London*—had accosted him in the hall outside the courtroom and urged the Americans to relax their remorseless pressure on the banker. When Albrecht, perplexed, asked 'Why?', Phillimore uneasily explained that certain representations had been made by Sir Montagu Norman, governor of the Bank of England from 1920 to 1944. 'It would be most unfortunate,' murmured the British colonel, 'if anything were to happen to Schacht.'[20] In fact Schacht had been an informer of Sir Montagu, secretly apprising him of the political and financial decisions taken at the highest level in Berlin for sixteen years before the war.[21]

There is in the records of His Majesty's treasury in the British archives an illuminating file on the efforts made by Sir Montagu Norman to get Schacht released.[22]

Albrecht held out little hope to the Englishman. As he had predicted, Jackson refused even to consider interceding on Schacht's behalf. He regarded the case against the banker as a test of the good faith of the entire prosecution. As he had said in a secret meeting of all the chief prosecutors in April, of which there is a shorthand record in his files, 'If the court, for instance, holds that we have no case against Schacht, then it seems clear that we can have no case against any industrialist, as the case against him is stronger than the others.' Sir Hartley Shawcross agreed with him.[23]

So Jackson rebuffed Phillimore's plea: indeed, he decided from now on to handle the case against Schacht in person. He privately recorded

* Twenty-five years later Phillimore was one of the three judges who heard this author's appeal in the landmark 'Convoy PQ.17' libel action, *Cassell & Co.* v. *Broome*. Phillimore, Schacht, Montagu Norman, and Sir Norman Birkett, one of the British judges who held out for Schacht's acquittal in 1946, were all freemasons. Jackson was also a leading mason; his diary entry for June 16, 1945 records a conversation in which Truman, Grand Master of the Masons of Missouri, showed him his gavel (Library of Congress, Manuscript Division, R H Jackson papers, box 95).

later, 'I would at least stand out forthrightly in demanding his conviction, convicting him if I could.'[24] He harried the banker mercilessly in the witness box, addressed him as 'Schacht,' *tout court*, confronting him with the evidence of his participation in Hitler's aggressive planning until eventually the defendant had to admit that he had been untruthful about his dealings with the Führer.[25]

Jackson showed the Tribunal newsreel film of Hitler's triumphant return to Berlin in July 1940 after the defeat of France—long after Schacht would have had them believe he had fallen into disfavour. There was Schacht, in Prince-Albert morning coat and top hat, the only civilian among the generals waiting on the station platform to pump the Führer's hand—indeed with two hands he caught hold of the Führer's, stepped out of line, and followed him 'in almost lickspittle fashion,' as Jackson remarked later.[26] And this was the Nazi gentleman for whom the British lawyer Phillimore and banker Sir Montagu Norman were interceding.

All the more acute was Jackson's fury when the Tribunal—with only the Russian judge publicly dissenting—acquitted Schacht.[27] Biddle, who read out this part of the judgement, claimed some months later that he had also wanted to convict, but the British had insisted on an acquittal and had left him no choice.[28] Dr Raphael Lemkin, later the U.N.'s part-time consultant on the draft convention on genocide, subsequently confirmed that Biddle had voted for conviction; he averred however that it was de Vabres who voted to acquit Schacht.[29] The actual sequence of events behind the closed doors of the judges' chambers will be revealed later in this narrative.

❖ ❖ ❖ ❖ ❖

It was now late spring, and Robert H. Jackson longed to be home in his beloved Virginia countryside. By early May he had little more cross-examination to do, and hoped there would be little if any rebuttal. He might be home as early as July. 'The case is going along alright,' he wrote to his wife on May 8. '—Slow, but really making an unanswerable record on nearly all defendants. Schacht and Funk both showed up as tricky, lieing [*sic*] bankers.' The British prosecution team were now giving the German admirals Karl Dönitz and Erich Raeder a working-over, he told her, adding a sniping side-shot at the British: 'The case against them [the admirals] is among the weakest we have.'[30]

Tiring of it all, Jackson left the British team at it, flying over to Paris for a furlough and then on to London. It would be May 18 before he returned to Nuremberg. All the time he was working on his summing-up speech, his closing arguments before the Tribunal. It would be his last personal appearance at the trial.[31]

The world now took only a desultory interest in the proceedings in the Palace of Justice at Nuremberg, but Jackson had by now grown contemptuous of public opinion. He found that one characteristic news item that had aroused interest in the United States was that Göring had thumbed his nose at Hjalmar Schacht: 'In the first place, he didn't,' huffed Jackson in a letter to his wife, 'and the report is a lie. In the second place, if he had, of what importance is it beside the historic facts that every day are being put in the record here? But, the press!'

❖ ❖ ❖ ❖ ❖

Dr Alfred Seidl, the diminutive young (thirty-five year old) Bavarian lawyer defending Rudolf Hess and Hans Frank, tossed the cat among the pigeons by applying to put before the court the text of the secret additional protocol to the pact signed between Ribbentrop and Molotov in Moscow on August 23, 1939, which had enabled Hitler to invade Poland a week later. Under the terms of this document, Hitler and Stalin had carved up eastern Europe and the Baltic states between themselves. Seidl asserted that he had received the top-secret document from an officer of the United States whom he declined to name.

The Soviet government had always denied the existence of such a secret additional protocol. They had striven since the summer of 1945 to keep it out of this trial. Early in March 1946 however Jackson had learned through his Intelligence sources what Seidl was planning and on the eighth he had written to his French and Soviet colleagues, reminding them of what he had said on this topic at the November 8 secret prosecutors' meeting, and adding that he had reason to believe that the defence was preparing a major attack on Soviet foreign policy and intended to depict the Soviet Union as having waged aggressive wars against Finland, Poland, the Balkans, and the Baltic states.[32]

General Rudenko reminded Jackson in a letter three days later of the topics which the Soviet delegation considered inappropriate for discussion in open court and which the prosecutors should therefore jointly object to. Shorter than Vyshinsky's original embargo-list by three points, it still listed six topics: references to the Soviet Union's social structure; the Ribbentrop–Molotov non-aggression pact and related matters; Ribbentrop's visit to Moscow and Molotov's to Berlin; the Balkan question; the Soviet Baltic republics; and Soviet–Polish relations.[33]

As Jackson had predicted, on March 15 Seidl now handed in written testimony about the history and origins of the pact of August 23 and a subsequent pact of September 28, 1939, in the form of an affidavit sworn by Dr Friedrich Gaus, who had been Reich Foreign Minister von Ribbentrop's senior legal adviser, to the effect that he had personally witnessed the signing of the document in Moscow.[34] Seidl read out the preamble of the secret protocol to the treaty, as described by Gaus, while Ribbentrop was being examined on April 1. Ribbentrop confirmed that from memory that was roughly what it said.

At this point Rudenko interrupted to protest that this had nothing to do with the defendant Rudolf Hess, whom Seidl was now representing; nor with Hans Frank, his other client. He claimed that this was an attempt to distract the court. The court withdrew to consider, then Lawrence allowed Seidl to ask the questions. In his response, Ribbentrop now made lengthy statements about the pact which he had signed with Molotov, and its secret additional protocol.

Seidl had real dynamite in his hands—an American officer had anonymously passed to him a photocopy of the pact's secret additional protocol. Years later Seidl concluded that the U.S. state department had itself planted the document in his hands as the opening shot in the Cold War. One legal problem at Nuremberg was that the document was only a photocopy, neither sealed nor authenticated. Such legal niceties had not, of course, prevented the prosecution from tabling dubious exhibits like the Hossbach Protocol. Seidl applied to Maxwell Fyfe; the Englishman had to confirm the authenticity of such documents (the British, like the Americans, had copies of the original German foreign ministry microfilm); the Briton advised Seidl to request Rudenko to attest to the document's authenticity. Seidl did so.

In the first week of April he went to the Soviet prosecutor's offices in the Palace of Justice and asked to see General Rudenko. The air crackled with hostile vibrations, as silent alarm bells rang. Rudenko's secretary vanished, and returned with word that Rudenko was out, very definitely out, but that Comrade General Zorya would see him.

'I have in my attaché case,' Seidl told the luckless general, 'photostat copies of the two secret "additional protocols" which were signed on August 23 and on September 28, 1939 after the conclusion of the Non-Aggression Pact and the Treaty on Friendship and Frontiers by Reich Foreign Minister von Ribbentrop and by your Soviet People's Commissar for Foreign Affairs.' He admitted that both were only uncertified photocopies of the original documents (in fact prepared from the Loesch microfilms), but he added that Sir David Maxwell Fyfe had confirmed their authenticity to him. When he invited the Soviet delegation to verify these exhibits, Zorya thought for a moment and then responded, 'I am afraid this is a totally pointless conversation.'[35]

This meeting was Zorya's undoing. Rudenko, rejecting the poisoned chalice which Seidl's compromising documents must have looked like to him, had thrown his deputy, Zorya, to the wolves instead. Unlike his colleagues, who all came from the public prosecutor's office in Moscow, Zorya was an outsider here at Nuremberg. Before being posted to Nuremberg in September 1945, he had been in the armed forces, and then legal adviser to the Lublin Committee for the National Liberation of Poland. He was expendable.

Unaware of the political abyss that was yawning open beneath the unfortunate Zorya, for having allowed this document to leak into the trial, Seidl continued hammering at the wedge. He went back to Dr

Friedrich Gaus with the photocopies, and obtained a new affidavit, certifying that they were authentic. The affidavit itself got mysteriously bogged down in the translation section, which the prosecution controlled, but Seidl was able to show the court Gaus' signature on the photocopies authenticating them

Events now took a dramatic turn. On the evening of May 21 Seidl had Ribbentrop's Staatssekretär Ernst von Weizsäcker in the witness stand, and put to him questions about the secret additional protocol. Again the Soviet prosecutor Rudenko objected. The judges conferred, then allowed Seidl to go ahead and ask the question. Seidl told the diplomat that he had in his hands a text which Gaus had declared to be, almost beyond doubt, the text of this treaty. 'I shall now show to you this text—'

Lord Justice Lawrence suddenly woke up from whatever daze he had been in and interrupted to ask what precisely was this document which Seidl was showing to the witness. Was it the same item which he had already shown to the court before and which the court had on that occasion refused to accept? 'Is it,' he pressed, 'the same document?'

Seidl confirmed: 'It is the selfsame document which I produced to the Tribunal together with other documentary exhibits and which was refused as a document, and I apprehend that it was refused by the Tribunal because I declined to disclose the provenance of this document.'

When he continued to justify producing this document, saying that he just wanted to use it to refresh the witness Weizsäcker's memory, Rudenko angrily interrupted again: 'First of all we are dealing with crimes committed by the principal German war criminals and we are not here to investigate the foreign affairs of other states.'

The court, he said, had already rejected the document as a forgery devoid of any evidentiary value. Thomas Dodd, the American assistant prosecutor, sided with Rudenko, as they had all agreed beforehand. Seidl refused to reveal how he had obtained the document, except for saying that it came from a trustworthy member of the Allies. The court withdrew, then ruled that the document was not to be shown to the witness on account of its unknown provenance. The cat was however out of the bag. On the following day, May 22, the Saint-Louis *Post-Dispatch*, one of America's great newspapers, published for the first time the authentic text of the 'secret additional protocol,' with all its cynical plotting by Stalin to join in and profit from Hitler's aggressions.

THE SOVIET generals at Nuremberg needed no clairvoyant powers to guess how pleased Stalin was going to be about their failure to prevent this. On May 23 Major-General Zorya was found dead in his office in the Palace of Justice, a bullet wound in his head. On May 24 the Soviet chief prosecutor Rudenko signed a travel warrant for his deputy Pokrovsky authorising him to 'travel to Leipzig to convey to the military authorities in the Soviet Zone the body of the assistant chief prosecutor of the U.S.S.R., N. D. Zorya, who had lost his life in an accident at Nuremberg.'[36] The Russians' internal investigation of the death ended on May 28; the file was entitled, 'Inquiry into a Case of Suicide.'[37]

When interpreter Svidovskaya asked Colonel Likhatchev, chief of the Soviet commission of investigators which kept tabs on all of them while at Nuremberg, what had caused Zorya's death, he replied cryptically: 'He got himself into a mess and took fright.' Years later Zorya's son received a letter of condolence from D. M. Reznichenko, the former Soviet military prosecutor in Leipzig. 'One evening in May 1946,' he wrote, ' I received a phone call in my Leipzig home from Stalin's anteroom in Moscow at eight P.M. We had a direct line. There was nobody but me in the prosecutor's office at the time. From Stalin's office I got the instructions to get a tin coffin ready for next morning, to carry your father's remains back to Moscow for burial.'

The plane was delayed in Leipzig for three hours by bad weather. 'Then a new directive came from Stalin's office instructing us to bury the man there and then.' Soviet state-counsellor Third Class Major-General Nikolai Dmitriyevich Zorya was buried as an anonymous ordinary Russian soldier—not as a general—somewhere on German soil. Zorya's in Moscow was told nothing; they received a suitcase some time later with his personal effects and the oral message that he had died in a shooting accident.[38]

Rudenko did what he could by way of damage-control in Nuremberg. On the last day of May he called for a special meeting of the chief prosecutors in Room 231 and protested that Seidl's application was a mischievous attempt to split the united prosecution front. Had not Jackson at their meeting on November 8 predicted precisely such attacks? There was general agreement among the prosecutors that Seidl's tactic was deplorable, and they should try every possible legal device to head him off. Maxwell Fyfe called the German lawyer's application irrelevant and harmful. Dodd promised punitive steps against any American army officer who was found to have assisted the defence by providing the photocopy.[39] On June 1 all four prosecutors signed a protest to the Tribunal for having upheld Seidl's applications. A day or two later Jackson circulated a memorandum to all the chief prosecutors endorsing General Rudenko's complaint to the Tribunal that the defendants were getting out of hand.[40]

❖ ❖ ❖ ❖ ❖

After his return to Nuremberg from Paris and London, Jackson busied himself with the cross-examination of the defendant Albert Speer.

To Jackson, the former munitions minister was one of the more problematic personalities in the dock. He seemed candid, decent, and westernised, and above all he had refused to join the Göring 'front.' Under the circumstances this could only warm Jackson to him. The British prosecutors also had a soft spot for Speer. 'My wife,' recorded Sir David Maxwell Fyfe, 'was one of many people who were profoundly impressed by Speer's evidence and manner, and remarked to Griffith-Jones that he would be the sort of man Germany would need in the future.'

There was no doubt that Speer was a clever individual indeed. His willow-like intellectual flexibility was demonstrated as much by his rapid rise within the Nazi hierarchy, as by his ability to survive in the mælstrom of Nuremberg jailhouse politics. He would nearly pull it off—were it not for the judges who rightly found otherwise.

History can now be in little doubt about the immensity of Speer's guilt, particularly for the use of slave labour in the underground missile plants which mass-produced the V–2 rocket missiles and the jet engines for the Messerschmitt 262 planes, and for the eviction of fifty thousand Jews from their apartments in Berlin in pursuit of his slum-clearance projects—which became the first stage of the expulsion of those Jews from Germany to uncertain fates in the eastern territories and at Auschwitz.

In a desperate though smoothly executed attempt to save his neck, Speer ratted on his colleagues at Nuremberg. Private letters which he addressed to Jackson, pencilled in the block letters prescribed by his jailers, had testified to his anxiety to do a deal with the Americans in preference to one of the other Allied powers.[41] Thomas Dodd, initially assigned to conduct the interrogation of Speer, reported that the former architect's guiding emotions were vanity and jealousy of Göring. Since Speer obviously felt slighted by Jackson's decision to relegate his cross-examination to a subordinate, Dodd urged Jackson to recognise this foible, and to tackle the Reich minister in person. 'It will buck up Speer's morale,' he said, 'and make him feel important and turn him into a much more candid witness.' This was a very accurate assessment of Speer's character.

Jackson yielded to Dodd's advice and sent private word to Speer to that effect. Speer, as predicted, replied through the prison 'grapevine' that he was therefore now ready to spill the beans. He would write in his memoirs, 'On the eve of the cross-examination an American officer dashed into my cell to break it to me that Jackson had decided to take over my examination in person.'

In the witness box Hitler's former friend and minister proceeded to reveal so much, and was so emphatic in his denunciation of the Führer and of his fellow defendants (quoting for example Hitler's own verdict on Göring as 'a failure and a corrupt drug addict') that the American chief prosecutor was delighted. 'He made a good witness for us,' Jackson wrote after this cross-examination.[42] Later, he would privately state: 'If I had been picking one of the defendants for acquittal, I would have acquitted Speer.'[43]

What Speer had, for all his intellect, failed to grasp was that the ultimate verdict would lie in hands other than those of the Americans.

❖ ❖ ❖ ❖ ❖

In mid-June 1946 there was a disappointment for the prosecution.

The Tribunal had allowed the prosecution three days to make their closing arguments, which they conceded was plenty. But the Tribunal then agreed to let the defendants have fourteen court days—about three weeks of real time—for their closing arguments, not that there was much that even the most dedicated defence lawyers could do to save their clients now. In Dr Otto Nelte's closing speech for Keitel on July 8, he stressed the tragic role that even a field-marshal had to play under a dictatorship. His defendant, he said, was fighting to save not his neck but his face. He asked not for Keitel's acquittal, but for the recognition of the field-marshal's dilemma, and a modicum of sympathetic understanding.[44]

The American lawyers listened to these pleadings with impatience. They had all had their say, and they wanted to get home. 'Why they should have so long,' wailed Jackson in a letter to his wife, 'I can't see.' In Britain and France, he learned, no time limits were imposed on the defence at all. Judge Biddle, who on this issue shared Jackson's sentiments, tried to have each defendant limited to a two-hour closing argument, but failed. This meant that the trial could not finish before the middle of July at the very earliest. 'The plain fact is,' Jackson surmised, in a mood of cynicism, 'these Europeans are in no hurry at all—U.S. food is good and, why hurry?' He rebelled against sitting for two to three weeks more than necessary at the prosecution table while the German lawyers conducted what he called their 'filibuster against death.' 'I do not intend,' he resolved, 'to sit and listen to them day after day.'[45]

He wished he were back in Washington, and it was high time. There was mounting criticism of his absence from the Supreme Court, and this had increased to a furore when the chief justice, Stone, died; there was a flurry of slashing and sniping and backstabbing by the absent Justice Jackson's rivals on the court to prevent him from succeeding Stone. In effect, he was sentenced *in absentia*. Judge Hugo Black, who had been a leading Ku-Klux Klan official in earlier years, wrote a letter condemning Jackson.[46] On June 11 Jackson sent off what he called a 'blunt and undiplomatic' cable to President Truman, hoping to force the whole controversy out into the open.[47] 'By God, they have nothing on me,' he lamented to his wife, 'and there is plenty more besides this.' 'I'm a long ways away but by God I am not dead! Of course,' he recognised, 'this telegram will be regarded as only a gripe—but what the hell. The important thing is whether the [Supreme] Court is in someone's pocket.'[48]

In the event, the Tribunal would take nearly three months pondering its judgement.[49] The plum position on the Supreme Court slipped out of Jackson's grasp for ever. It was extraordinary, as Göring had once remarked, how little things could have such a disproportionate effect on one's own fate (he himself had once stalked off after an unknown blonde as a youth, and thus literally missed the bus and with it his chance of becoming a freemason—which would have prevented his joining the Nazi party: which would have saved him from Cell No. 5 at Nuremberg.)

One way and another, mused Jackson, these Nazis had a lot to answer for.

18: **Final Solution**

The Jewish organisations in New York had suggested to Robert Jackson in June 1945 that he adopt the figure of six million victims of the Nazis. After months of reviewing the evidence he noted in April 1946: 'The Nürnberg trial involves the murder of between four and five million people according to some estimates, and as high as six million according to others. These are apart from any persons killed in combat and apart from the persons who died as the result of tortures in concentration camps, with the exception of the extermination camps. For example, at Dachau 268,000 were killed.'[1] These figures were however still far short of being generally proven.*

In retrospect it may seem remarkable that the Nazi 'factories of death' played a much smaller part in the Nuremberg trial than did the shooting of a number of R.A.F. officers who had escaped from the prisoner-of-war camp at Sagan, and the conditions under which Speer's slave-labourers worked in the munitions industry. Perhaps this was because the commandant of Auschwitz was still at large when the trial opened. Besides, the prosecution of such atrocities had been delegated to the Russians and French. Atrocious though they were, the conditions found within the concentration camps that had been overrun by the American and British armies did not lend themselves to the framework of the international trial.

Dachau, the camp outside Munich, was a case in point. Examined at Nuremberg, Dr Franz Blaha testified in one affidavit that he had helped with gassings there, stating at one point: 'Of the eight or nine persons in the chamber there were three still alive, and the remainder appeared to be dead.... Many prisoners were later killed in this way.'[2] But reputable historians now generally agree that there was no homicidal gas chamber at Dachau; and there never had been.[3] True, what looked like one had been found by the liberating troops. A GI had been photographed in front of a gas-tight door bearing a death's-head emblem and such

* This estimate was wrong. Around 75,000 prisoners were in the camp when liberated, including 43,401 political prisoners and 22,100 Jews. Most of these were innocent of any crime. Health and sanitation conditions in these camps were appalling. The German government now computes the overall total of deaths at Dachau 1933–45 at 31,951, two-thirds of them during the uncontrollable typhus plague of the last seven months; of this total, 2,226 died in one month after the Americans assumed control of the camp.

inscriptions as GASZEIT: ZU ... AUF... (Gassing time: closure ... opening...), and VORSICHT! GAS! LEBENSGEFAHR! NICHT ÖFFNEN! (Caution! Gas! Deadly Danger! Don't Open!)[4] In fact this chamber had been used to fumigate prisoners' clothing to kill the typhus-bearing lice, but the photograph was widely published.

The American authorities assigned a forensic pathologist, Dr Charles P. Larson, to carry out autopsies on bodies exhumed at Dachau (regrettably, no such exhumations have been conducted at Auschwitz or other sites). After a bulldozer uncovered one mass grave, Larson carried out twenty-five autopsies a day at his own estimate. He determined that in most of these cases death had been from wartime's 'natural causes,' primarily typhus, and that the grave would have been better left severely alone.[5]

The whole of the Nazi drive to liquidate their enemies had proceeded in such a ramshackle, haphazard, and disorganised manner that it is difficult even now to state with certainty precisely what happened and what did not. The historian's task is not eased by the laws imposed, fifty years after the event, by some European countries specifically stifling informed conjecture and investigation. Despite the precedent set by the Dachau gas chamber, in the Federal Republic of Germany it is a criminal offence to question anything about the gas chambers.* In France it has been a criminal offence since 1990 to *contester* (challenge) any of the crimes against humanity as defined by the Nuremberg Charter; thus it is an offence to attribute the Katyn murders to the Russians, and to question the authenticity of the 'Jewish soap' samples.†

AT NUREMBERG the S.S. officer Dr Wilhelm Höttl, who had in 1944–5 been a deputy section leader in Amt VI of Kaltenbrunner's R.S.H.A., operating in south-eastern Europe, had placed on record that at the end of August 1944 in his home in Budapest he had had a conversation with S.S. Obersturmbannführer Adolf Eichmann on the topic of Romania's recent defection from the Axis; Eichmann had expressed the conviction that Germany had finally lost the war and that he himself was doomed since he had 'millions of Jews' on his conscience. Höttl claimed to have

* The author was fined DM30,000 (around £13,500) by the Munich courts in January 1993 for stating in one lecture that the gas chamber shown to tourists at Auschwitz is a fake. He was also banned from German archives and territory in perpetuity. The Auschwitz authorities have since then conceded that this chamber was built three years after the war as a 'reconstruction' on Polish government orders; they admit that they have yet to devise a formula for explaining this to visitors. See *L'Express*, Paris, January 26, 1995.

† The Fabius-Gayssot law was introduced by communist deputies and signed by President François Mitterrand on Bastille Day, 1990. There have been several prosecutions under this French law. The author was in 1995 fined about £500 by a Paris court for an opinion expressed in an interview granted in his London home to a reputable French newspaper three years earlier; he had not visited France for years.

asked him how many Jews he was talking about. Himmler, Eichmann had replied, had also recently wanted to be given a precise figure, and he had drawn up a report for him . 'In the various extermination camps,' Eichmann had continued, according to the version written down by Höttl for the Americans, 'they had killed around four million Jews while two million more had met their deaths in other ways, most of them being shot to death by the task forces (Einsatzkommandos) of the security police during the campaign against Russia.' 'Himmler had not been satisfied with the report,' Höttl's affidavit continued, 'as in his view the number of Jews killed should have been greater than six million.' Himmler had thereupon sent a man over from his statistical office to draw up a new report on the basis of Eichmann's material.*

Höttl claimed to have reported on these matters even before the end of the war to the O.S.S., 'with whom I was in contact at this time.'[6]

IT IS necessary to see Höttl's testimony in the light of his attempt to secure an early release from American confinement. In this he was remarkably successful, despite his background in the murkier and more murderous reaches of the S.S. operations in the Balkans. He had written to Colonel Andrus on September 26, 1945, reminding him of his services for the O.S.S. in Switzerland and Italy, of the hundreds of pages of Intelligence he had turned over to General George S. Patton, commander of the U.S. Third Army in southern Germany, and of the evidence which he had already rendered against S.S. Obergruppenführer Kaltenbrunner. Höttl added plaintively that for several years he had suffered from stomach ulcers: '[I] am subject to periodical attacks in late spring and autumn.' Since the autumn was now upon them, he asked to be released from jail before the ulcers returned. He ended this remarkable letter with a plea to be allowed 'to report verbally and explicitly and at the same time to discuss details as to an eventual collaboration.'[7]

On October 18, the day before the indictments were served on the twenty-one defendants at Nuremberg, Andrus, an officer who would not normally be expected to show sympathy toward a mere ulcer-victim, signed a *laissez-passer* for the former S.S. officer. 'Dr Wilhelm Höttl,' this read, 'is a German citizen and ... has the permission of this office to go and come anywhere within the confines of Nuremberg, Germany, without police escort or security control.'[8] Ulcers or no, Höttl has survived to this day.

By early 1946 Jackson also had the oral estimate provided by another of Eichmann's wartime cronies, S.S. Sturmbannführer Dieter Wisliceny.

* The only statistical analysis of the Final Solution of the Jewish problem known to have been commissioned by Himmler was that conducted by his inspector of statistics Dr Richard Korherr in January 1943, which was required to provide Hitler with a survey of the S.S. achievements in the first ten years of the Third Reich. No such analysis made in the summer of 1944 has yet been found in the archives.

He would be one of the very few witnesses actually called by the prosecution, and he would testify 'that Eichmann, in charge of the whole program, had told him between 4 and 5 million Jews [were] killed.' In fact, Wisliceny testified, Eichmann had once said, 'I shall jump joyously into my grave in the knowledge that I have five million Jews on my conscience.'

UPON READING Wisliceny's testimony Eichmann, still hiding in Argentina, at first called it *Blödsinn*—rubbish—but then, in a later secret conversation, conceded that he probably had made some such statement.

Eichmann's initial excuse, speaking into a tape recorder in Argentina ten years after Wisliceny's testimony, was that this statement by his former intimate, superior, and subsequently subordinate was of little value as it must have been extracted under duress. With difficult-to-follow logic Eichmann questioned whether the enemy would really have strung up a few weeks later in Slovakia 'a man who had already once in a trial of such a scale as the Nuremberg Tribunal made the claim that his boss had spoken of liquidating five million people—a cardinal allegation of our adversaries … a witness as valuable as this.' 'It is equally untrue,' said Eichmann in the course of a different taped conversation , 'that I said "I shall jump joyously into my grave in the knowledge that I have killed five million Jews." My own men would have looked at me as a megalomaniac loudmouth.'[9] He noted on this occasion that there had been a similar allegation by Dr Höttl. 'That is the same madness,' Eichmann would later write. 'Perhaps Höttl heard Wisliceny's "statements" being broadcast or read them in the press or in the enemy's books, and then he chimed in with his own contribution.'[10]

After thinking things over, however, Eichmann later conceded that he had after all uttered some such incriminating sentence—although he now claimed to have spoken only of 'enemies of the Reich' and not of 'Jews'.[11]

❖ ❖ ❖ ❖ ❖

It had been left to the French and Russian prosecutors to present the case on crimes against humanity.

It was on January 3 that the court heard the testimony of Wisliceny. He related how Himmler had ordered Eichmann to assemble a task force at Mauthausen camp in Austria ready for the Nazi invasion of Hungary in March 1944.[12] Judge Biddle's notes show his impressions of this witness's revelations : 'Impossible food and shelter conditions. Eichmann then suggested to Hungarian government they be transported to Auschlitz [*sic*] which was done, Hungarian police assisting.' Altogether 450,000 Jews, Biddle jotted down, had been 'brought to final solution,' according to this witness. 'Eichmann thought about four or five millions Jews killed, and witness thinks four million were covered by the final solution. In Feb 1945 Eichmann said he would laugh at the fact that he had five million people on his conscience.'[13]

On January 28 the French introduced their first female witness. Marie-Claude Vaillant Couturier was a thirty-four-year-old former member of the French National Assembly. The Nazis had arrested her in February 1942 and sent her to Auschwitz with two hundred other prisoners on January 23, 1943. Of these, she said, forty-nine had survived the war. These prisoners had had to build roads and clear the marshes, constantly standing ankle-deep in water and quicksand. She described vividly how they had been forced to stand for a roll call throughout one freezing day in February, and then struck to make them run. 'Those who could not were taken to Block 25, the ante-room of the gas chamber, where they were killed. Corpses in courtyard,' noted Biddle, 'a hand or head would now and then stir in the corpses, seeking to free itself.' The moaning, in all languages, continued from morning to night: 'Water! Water!' They 'sang Marseillaise when the gas truck [*sic*] started to move.'

As the judges jotted all this down their minds became too numbed by the horror of it all to ask pertinent questions or to analyse: 'The sick would often die of exposure in front of the hospital.' (Why was a hospital needed at an 'extermination camp'? Neither Biddle nor his colleagues made any comment.) 'The women often preferred to die at work.' 'Straw mattresses full of vermin, lice etc.' 'During disinfection of clothes all remained naked and the sick died.' 'Was employed in infirmary and saw young Jewish women who were waiting for sterilisation. The men were castrated often—experiments—high rate of mortality.'

Some of her story was evidently based on hearsay. 'Abortions were common. Babies drowned in bucket of water. Order came from Berlin to kill mothers and babies, someone told her.' 'The women in S.S. [*sic*] were as savage as the men under its system. Atmosphere of terror and corruption. S.S. distributed punishment in the form of fifty blows of stick on back by a sort of machine.' Once, finally articulating his feelings about this woman's testimony, Biddle noted his own scepticism, and wrote: 'This I doubt,' But he continued to write down what the witness told the court:.

> Selected, out of convoys of Jewish women, the old and sick and children, who were gassed at once, not even taken to camp. Orchestra with internee personnel played cheerful tunes like the 'Merry Widow' when they arrived to be gassed, so they would not know their fate. Went to red brick building, undressed, given towel, gassed. Died in agony. Gold teeth extracted from ashes of burned bodies. One night there was not enough gas and the children were

> hurled alive into the furnaces. Workers who were too weak, and Jewish women gassed. Typhus cases gassed. In Xmas 1943 naked women were stacked on trucks, and Hessler [*sic*] beat the women who were trying to escape as they knew they were going to their deaths, and we heard the 'lugubrious clamor' from the death trucks.... Gypsies from all over Europe were all gassed.

Cross-examined, this female witness admitted 'curtly (in German!)' as Biddle noted with surprise, that she had been arrested for resistance activity, as a communist.

Streicher's defence attorney Marx asked her: 'How do you explain you came through so well?'

'Says she's been out a year,' Judge Biddle jotted down, recording her answer. 'Most of her statements based on personal experience,' noted Biddle in quotation marks—which implied that he assessed that quite a lot were not.[14]

GÖRING TOO had only mistrust for this kind of testimony and especially for the film evidence belatedly introduced by the Russians. 'Anybody can make an atrocity film,' he remarked to Dr Gilbert on February 15, ' if they take corpses out of their graves and then show a tractor shoving them back in again.' On the twentieth the court was shown a Soviet-made atrocity film, replete with torture instruments, mutilated bodies, guillotines, and baskets of decapitated heads. Göring yawned out loud, and scoffed to Kelley's successor, Major Leo N. Goldensohn, that evening: 'They could just as easily have killed a few hundred German prisoners of war and put them into Russian uniforms for the atrocity picture. You don't know the Russians the way I do!'

On February 27 Biddle paraphrased in his notebook the evidence of a Polish woman who had been at Auschwitz. 'Selection for death made by doctors and S.S.,' recorded Biddle. 'Youngest and strongest entered camp. Women with small children were sent to the crematory where the children were separated and taken separately into the gas chamber. In 1940 it was ordered that the children should be thrown living into the furnace without being first gassed.' (Neither the Auschwitz camp nor its Birkenau offshoot existed in 1940.) 'You could often hear the cries. Whether this was to save gas or because there was no space in the gas chamber is hard to say.... Often they worked in the gas chamber "from dawn to dusk."'[15]

❖ ❖ ❖ ❖ ❖

Given the central role in Himmler's criminal scheme evidently played by the slave-labour camps at Auschwitz, the Allies had made a determined search for the former S.S. Obersturmbannführer Rudolf

Höss, the first of its three commandants. By early 1946 British military police had finally located his wife and children in Schleswig-Holstein. They kept her under close surveillance and on March 11 forced her to reveal that her husband working as a farm labourer near Flensburg under the assumed name of 'Franz Lang'.[16] The posse found Höss at eleven P.M. that night, sleeping on a bunk in the farm's slaughter-house. Two days earlier he had accidentally broken the phial of cyanide which he possessed; he was unable now to escape the consequences of his ill-starred career. To make doubly sure, he was immediately handcuffed and the cuffs were not removed for the next three weeks.[17] He was dragged off his bunk, stripped naked, dumped onto one of the slaughter tables in the barn and manhandled until a medical officer accompanying the unit murmured, 'Call them off unless you want to take back a corpse.'[18]

As the car pulled into the British unit's barracks at Heide, a blizzard was blowing. Höss was marched naked across the parade ground to a cell.[19] For the next three days he was kept awake and repeatedly interrogated in German—he understood no English. Kenneth Jones, a private with the Fifth Royal Horse Artillery, and two other soldiers were detailed to take turns to sit in his cell, armed with pick-axe handles to jab him every time he fell asleep. 'After three days and nights without sleep,' said Jones, 'Höss finally broke down and made a full confession to the authorities.'[20]

Höss himself wrote later, 'At my first interrogation, evidence was obtained by beating me. I do not know what is in the record, although I signed it. Alcohol and the whip [his own] were too much for me.' The 'record' was an eight-page text typed in German, which Höss signed in the early hours of March 15, having the presence of mind even now to add the time, '2:30 A.M.' after the date.[21]

This confession, which subsequently came to be submitted to the Nuremberg tribunal as document NO–1210, had taken three days of torture, as his captor, Sergeant Bernard Clarke himself would describe, to obtain. It contained numerous perhaps deliberate errors, for instance the identification by Höss of an extermination camp at 'Wolzek near Lublin,' in addition to those at 'Belzek' and 'Tublinka,' all spelt thus. Wolzek has never existed; and the other two camps, Belzec and Treblinka, were not in existence at the time that Höss testified to.

Having signed this document, Höss was transferred to British Intelligence regional headquarters at Minden-on-the-Weser. 'There,' he would later complain, 'I received further rough treatment at the hands of the English public prosecutor, a major.' His interlocutor here was Gerald Draper, a thirty-one-year-old lawyer who was chief interrogator of the British War Crimes Group. Höss' confession would be listed as the high point of his career.[22] This encounter was probably the source of a brief statement, set down in an English (i.e. not American or German) hand, which has survived and which reads in full as follows:

Statement made Voluntarily at [sic] Gaol
by Rudolf Hoess, former Commandant of
Auschwitz Concentration Camp on 16th day of March 1946.

I personally arranged on orders received from Himmler in May 1941 the gassing of two million persons between June/July 1941 and the end of 1943 during which time I was commandant of Auschwitz.

signed.

Höss signed this statement: 'Rudolf Höss, SS-Ostubaf., fr. Kdt. v. Auschwitz–Birkenau'.[23] He was also interrogated on March 20, 1946 at Minden, but that report is lost or not yet in the public domain.[24]

Shackled to another prisoner Höss was driven eleven days later to the American Zone in southern Germany, where he was housed in the Nuremberg jailhouse as a witness. His companion on this road journey was Moritz von Schirmeister, Dr Joseph Goebbels' former press officer, for whose production Hans Fritzsche had applied as a defence witness. 'Sure,' Höss told Schirmeister before they were unshackled, 'I signed to the effect that I had bumped off two and a half million people. But I could equally well have signed that it was five million. There are methods to get anybody to confess to anything regardless of whether it is true or not.'[25] Höss would describe the regime imposed on the jailhouse inmates by the American colonel Andrus as a 'rest-cure' compared to what he had been through in the British zone.[26]

AT NUREMBERG Höss was questioned, not once but several times.[27] He was visited almost every day by interrogators from the different nations and pointed out to people as 'an especially interesting animal,' as he boasted. He found these sessions most unpleasant—not so much physically as psychologically.[28] They left him, he would write, in no doubt whatever about the fate lying in store for him. He lost interest in his fate. Dr Gilbert found Höss 'apathetic,' as he wrote on two pages of his memoirs, and manifesting a 'schizoid apathy,' as he added on a third.[29]

His memory was patchy about dates and places, and about the events of four or five years earlier. He remembered, he said on April 1, 1946, that the terrain around Auschwitz was very swampy, but claimed that he could not recall the precise sequence of the transports of Jews. In July 1941 (elsewhere however he said: 'Just before the Russian campaign') Himmler had given him the order to liquidate the Jews at Auschwitz after the holding capacity of the three camps in the Government-General of Poland had turned out to be inadequate. In this connection Höss had again bafflingly referred to the three camps as 'Belzek, Treblinka, and Wolzek.' At Auschwitz, he said, he had sometimes handled two trainloads a day. He had performed the gassings in two old farmhouses at Auschwitz. Höss then spoke of 'a little hole [through which] the gas was blown in,' only to elaborate in his next sentence that they were using Zyklon-B, which was 'a crystalline substance.' (In the proprietary Zyklon pesticide, the cyanide compound was impregnated into inert slow-release pellets the size of sugar-cubes; it was consequently incapable of being 'blown in' through 'little holes,' shower-heads or the like.) After an interval of three to fifteen minutes all the occupants were dead, Höss said; standing some distance away outside he could hear the screams dying away. Those awaiting their turn outside, he also said, could not hear a thing. After half an hour the corpses of those who had been gassed were removed and burned in open pits at the back: he was not asked, nor did he explain, how they could burn bodies in water-filled pits in marshy terrain.

It was all rather incoherent, but coherence came as the days of interrogation went on. By the second day, April 2, Höss knew that two transport trains held a total of between 1,600 and 1,700 people. But his notion of overall figures was still hazy. At Minden, he said, an Englishman had told him of one hundred thousand Russian prisoners-of-war being killed; he thought that figure impossible, 'perhaps it was ten thousand.' He was then quoted as saying that Himmler had ordered him to destroy all statistical files even as they were compiled—then why compile them?—and not to keep any records of the liquidations.[30] Subsequently Höss talked in his interrogations of three or four openings which had been cut into the roofs of the gas chambers, and through which the gas had been poured in; he also said that wire mesh shafts had extended from these openings down to the floor of the gas chambers. By means of electric ventilators the poisonous gases had been exhausted from the chamber within half an hour. Evidently the danger to the body-removal squads had by now dawned on the interrogators too.[31]

According to Höss the two big crematoria, each equipped with five double retorts, could have incinerated two thousand bodies every twelve hours. Asked how long each such cremation-cycle took Höss was unable to volunteer a precise figure. Elsewhere he testified however that each retort could hold a maximum of three corpses at any one time, and that this took up to six hours; this gave a maximum figure of 120, not two thousand, in twelve hours.

On April 3 and 4 Höss was questioned about his earlier career, about the Dachau concentration camp, about his relationship to Eichmann, and about the mass shootings of Jews at Riga. He again spoke of the extermination camps at 'Treblinka, Wolzek and Belzek' and now estimated, despite his insistence two days earlier that he could not give any overall figures, that 2·5 millions had been murdered at Auschwitz and that half a million more had died of diseases. (On April 2 he had testified that Eichmann had once told him that he was reporting to Himmler that he had sent 2·5 million people to Auschwitz; but since that figure included both the able-bodied and those unfit for work,

Höss' April 4 estimate of 2·5 million liquidated appears to have been unreliable too.)

ON APRIL 5 the Americans placed before him a three-page affidavit, which they themselves had drafted and typed, for his signature. Written in English throughout, it contained the admission by Höss that he had 'gassed' 2·5 million people at Auschwitz in addition to the half million who had died there of diseases.

'We have prepared an affidavit written in English—,' they began by informing their prisoner; whereupon, according to the verbatim transcript, the witness (Höss) 'read through' the statement that followed and replied that he had read it and understood it.

'Yes,' continues the transcript, 'I understand everything that I read.'

In reality Höss could not understand English. It merits passing comment that this English affidavit by Höss was *not* in fact signed at any point by him, although the Nuremberg interrogating officers and interpreter all pre-signed the document as witnesses to his 'signature'.

Not for three days was Höss shown a German translation of the English affidavit ('which you signed'); the transcript of this new conversation on April 8 shows Höss belatedly insisting on changes to the text. An anonymous hand interpolated entire lines, while other lines were deleted by a stroke of the pen; there are no initials in the margin to endorse such changes, but Höss signed this entire German document in its new form on each page ('after reading over the statement'.) It included the following curiously worded statement typed in English at its foot: 'I understand English as it is written above. The above statements are true; this declaration is made by me voluntarily and without compulsion.'[32]

The prosecution may well have decided that Höss would make an unconvincing, perhaps even a dangerous witness at Nuremberg, and they abandoned plans to call him. But he was called by the defence, by the lawyer acting for S.S. Obergruppenführer Ernst Kaltenbrunner, Dr Karl Kaufmann, in the surely rather lame hope that his examination of Höss might shift the blame away from the living defendants here in the dock to the late Heinrich Himmler. 'I have never been able to grasp,' Höss would later write, 'and it is still not clear to me, how I of all people could have helped to exonerate Kaltenbrunner.'

A well-groomed Rudolf Höss finally entered the witness stand on April 15, 1946, and he now repeated his testimony in public, willingly estimating that at Auschwitz three million people had been exterminated, 2·5 million of them by gas chambers.

His cross-examination by Colonel Amen was little more than a formality. Amen read into the court record, paragraph by paragraph, the document which he represented to the Tribunal as an English translation of a German affidavit by Höss, skipping two paragraphs, numbers 8 and 9, where the document had become hopelessly garbled in the translation—and merely asking Höss from time to time whether he had so stated. The prisoner replied merely '*Jawohl*,' or '*Ja, es stimmt*—yes, that's right,' apart from a brief one-sentence and a two-sentence reply.[33]

There were no further questions. Like countless prisoners in countless docks at Moscow, Prague, and Budapest in the years before and in the years after, he made no reference to what he had been through in custody; nor was he asked. The shell-shocked or battle-weary defence counsel made no attempt to challenge his shocking admissions.

❖ ❖ ❖ ❖ ❖

On the day after entering the witness box, on April 16, Höss was again secretly interrogated and on this occasion he was brought face to face with Otto Moll, the Auschwitz camp gardener, who had specialised in executing prisoners by a single shot in the back of the head; he had become the manager of one of the two farmhouses at Auschwitz—the 'bunkers' which Höss said had been converted to gas chambers (and which Höss on April 30 located as having been 'behind [the crematoria] numbers 3 and 4, some distance away from 3 and 4'.) Moll was claiming to have buried thirty to forty thousand bodies in the mass graves; Höss corrected the figure during this confrontation to 106,000–107,000 bodies. During his interrogation of April 30 Höss changed his story yet again, relating this time that the '105,000–106,000' bodies had been interred, not incinerated, in the pits; on instructions from Himmler or Eichmann in the winter of 1941–42 he had then given Moll orders to exhume the bodies and burn them. Höss claimed that these cremations personally supervised by the Reich surgeon-general of the S.S. Dr Ernst-Robert Grawitz—who had killed himself at the end of the war—because of the danger of epidemics.

In fact Eichmann had no authority to issue orders to Höss, as they were in different branches of the S.S. It has moreover to be said that the volume of a hundred thousand corpses can readily be assessed at around ten thousand cubic metres, which would have required the mass graves to occupy a surface area of about five thousand square metres. There is no trace on the Allied aerial photographs either of such burning operations or of the pits themselves. Perhaps for security reasons, the Allies made no attempt to introduce these highly detailed aerial photographs of Auschwitz in this or the later war crimes trials.[34]

On May 5 the concentration camp films were again screened, this time for the benefit of Höss, Wolff, and Jüttner.[35] Höss had come to the end of the road in Nuremberg; at the airfield a few days later, on May 25, 1946, the Americans handed him over to Polish officers who flew with him in an American plane to Warsaw.[36] He was sentenced to death at Cracow on April 2, 1947, and hanged two weeks later—at the site of his crimes, the Auschwitz concentration camp.

Höss had attempted to smuggle out of Nuremberg prison a letter to his wife in which he apologised to her and to his family for 'confessing' to the atrocities at Auschwitz; he claimed that he had been tortured into making spurious admissions. Seized by prison officers and never delivered, the letter is still in private hands in the United States; the owner offered it in 1996 to Ben Swearingen, one of the country's foremost autograph experts. He refused to touch it, fearing that it was 'political dynamite.'

19: Behind Closed Doors

THE JUDGES began deliberations on their final opinion behind closed doors on June 27, 1946. Coupled with their confidential discussions on the verdicts and appropriate penalties for each defendant, these deliberations developed into a rather longer task than they had anticipated. They were now settled in however and rather enjoyed the life here after all.

The intention was that these deliberations should remain for ever secret—that the outside world should never discover what reasons led to the acquittal of these men, and the hanging of those. Among the private papers of the American judge, Francis Biddle, are however his daily notes taken during their deliberations. It is astonishing, even rather horrifying, to see from them how far the judges were undecided; how much they disagreed on the very simplest issues; how they wavered and vacillated up to the last moment; and how, despite the weeks and months of hearings, they continued to nurse misconceptions for which there was no evidence at all. Their discussions reveal an almost unreal atmosphere, an unworldly detachment from the harsh realities of war and peace: at one stage the British judge, of all people, felt that a defendant needed punishing for having called for the bombing of a town in England. Politics often overrode the requirements of law. Sentences had to be harsh. The Tribunal was too important, said one judge, to award light sentences.

In general, the French judges were the least draconian, while the Russians at least from the outset called for the stiffest sentences—death sentences across the board and on all counts: the idea of acquittals, even on some of the counts charged, seemed foreign to them. As the months passed the Russians aligned themselves more with the American viewpoint. The Americans were unexpectedly hard, voting for the death penalty more frequently than their colleagues.

Although Judge Biddle's notes allow to us an unhoped-for glimpse behind the scenes, it is plain—particularly from the wrangling over Schacht—that there were further levels and sub-levels of plotting and intrigue, to which we are still not privy.

The British and Americans had prepared a draft opinion, but at this first session on June 27 General Nikitchenko objected to its length, believing in brevity and objectivity. They should merely list the charges, said the Russians, state how long the Tribunal had sat, describe how the evidence had been collected, and then give their findings. Lord Justice Lawrence felt that they should give the greatest prominence to the waging of aggressive war. Francis Biddle, the American judge, felt uneasy that the opinion followed too closely the prosecution's evidence, and tended to ignore the evidence assembled by the defence. The French judge Donnedieu de Vabres also felt the opinion was too long.

Several of the judges were unhappy about the charge of conspiracy to wage war, since it was not known to international law and would arguably therefore be *ex post facto*. It was also unnecessary, Donnedieu suggested, since the defendants had all, except perhaps Franz von Papen, committed other crimes; he continued to stick to this view throughout their weeks of deliberations. Had there in fact been a conspiracy? he asked; all that the prosecutors had so far proven was that there had been 'an announcement by Hitler' of his views on November 5, 1937 (the Hossbach Protocol.) 'We are free to knock out any accusations in the indictment,' he said, 'and we should find that no conspiracy exists.'

The Russian alternate Colonel Volchkov then spoke, urging rather obsessively that they work into the document suitable mentions of 'gas chambers, soap, women's hair, etc.'[1]

Since Donnedieu had moved to strike out the whole count of conspiracy, the American, Biddle, asked him for his reasons in writing. De Vabres explained that such a charge was unknown to both European and international law—that under international law there was sometimes every justification for waging an aggressive war. Quite apart from that, said de Vabres, the prosecution had not provided any proof that the 'common plan and purpose' essential in any conspiracy was present in Hitler's operations: even the Hossbach Protocol, of November 5, 1937, which came the closest to providing such proof, showed nothing more than Hitler convening his commanders-in-chief and ministers and informing them of his plans for the conquest of Europe. The rest had just clicked their heels. To talk about a conspiracy, involving many brains, on the one hand, was to negate the whole concept of the Führer Principle.

What, asked de Vabres, remorselessly pressing his point home, was the merit in proving a conspiracy anyway, if all the defendants could be shown to be guilty on the counts of waging aggressive war and war crimes?

He was troubled too by the 'psychological effect' of blaming the war on a conspiracy, something essentially 'dark, hidden, and secret,' since this would serve to let the German people themselves off the hook. This was to him as a Frenchman most undesirable.

Biddle sided with de Vabres, but fretted lest this might resulted in Papen's being acquitted, since the 1938 Anschluss with Austria, which was seen as his brainchild, was not alleged to have been 'aggressive war.'

'It would of course eliminate many difficulties,' he observed, commenting on the French viewpoint in a secret letter to Herbert Wechsler in New York asking for advice, 'and get rid of all the trash and looseness gathered in the indictment'—for which he implicitly blamed Jackson.[2]

AFTER RETIRING to rework their opinions, the judges met again on July 11. The French judge urged them to cut out the polemical tone: they should state facts and avoid opinions. But those opinions differed. Lord Justice Lawrence wanted to highlight the Nazi 'seizure of power'; Biddle thought this less important, holding that they should stress the violence. General Nikitchenko, the Soviet judge, wanted proper mention made of the party's racist theories, and he insisted that they bring in the meetings of industrialists, and the part played by German diplomats.[3]

Six days later they again went over the draft opinion. Again it was the Frenchman, de Vabres, who brought fresh thinking to the Tribunal's deliberations, asking that the document attend less to Austria and Czechoslovakia, which were not alleged as wars of aggression, and recognise that the war had in fact started with Hitler's attack on Poland. He doubted the wisdom, he said, of relying too heavily on what he characterised as 'unofficial' documents like the Hossbach Protocol, and he diplomatically invited them to refrain from any 'discussion of the aggressive intentions of England in Norway, Germany against Russia, England against Belgium, etc.' Judge Biddle however felt that they should allow more discussion of the evidence concerning Norway that spoke in favour of the defence.

TO THE outsider reading these notes made by Judge Biddle, it seems remarkable that after nine months of trial the judges should still have been floundering on even the most essential issues. General Nikitchenko wanted them to quote more from *Mein Kampf* to prove that it had always been Hitler's plan to seize Lebensraum. At present, he pointed out, their opinion was paying less attention to the Soviet Union than to Poland. 'Norway,' he allowed, 'is of course different from Russia: Germany had to get a right flank in Norway.' Disagreeing with de Vabres, he described the Hossbach Protocol as 'a most important document, made by a responsible official.' As for Hitler's attack on Greece in 1941, John Parker felt that, even though Britain had actually got her troops into Greece first, the Tribunal could still claim that Hitler's attack was a war of aggression. Biddle disagreed, arguing: 'This is dangerous and academic and bad international law.'[4]

After this conference the two American judges cornered Sir Norman Birkett and proposed that they redraft the opinion's section on aggressive war, 'to save pressure on him.' Birkett willingly agreed.

❖ ❖ ❖ ❖ ❖

In general these discussions behind the scenes about the Tribunal's final opinion were marked by a surprising willingness to compromise. Biddle deprecated the document's general hectoring tone, and constantly urged its authors to tighten it up and eschew emotional expressions like 'an event of the highest possible significance,' and 'shocked the conscience of mankind.' General Nikitchenko also brought a dispassionate mind to their debates, pointing out on July 20 that the Jews were not the only ones persecuted by the Nazi 'master race'—the Nazis had described others as *Untermenschen*, subhumans, too. He also protested at attempts to make a martyr out of the unlamented S.A. chief of staff Ernst Röhm, whom Hitler had liquidated as part of his 1934 purge. Röhm was 'a typical Nazi,' Nikitchenko said, and should be dealt with 'very briefly.'

Lawrence agreed to make these cuts, going easy on the purple prose and throwing in, as he put it, a little 'master race.'

Nikitchenko asked furthermore that the opinion state categorically that Hermann Göring had caused the Reichstag fire*—as Hans Bernd Gisevius had alleged—to incriminate the leftists. His deputy Volchkov however led the counter-argument, that they ought to leave out any specific reference to Göring, and say that the historic blaze had been followed by repressive measures.[5]

THE JUDGES were in no hurry. 'Life at the Villa Conradty is completely spoiling me,' wrote Judge Francis Biddle to Herbert Wechsler on July 10. 'For instance, last night for dinner we had a most excellent cauliflower soup, cold trout with mayonnaise, stewed veal, fresh peas, a delicious salad with just the right amount of garlic, and gooseberry tarts. On the other side, Dry Martinis Cliquot and some Martel brandy which Madame de Fels had sent over. Does it make your mouth water?' His cellar, he added, had been enriched by Sauterne, Burgundy, claret, and some delicious Rhine wine from Brussels—a city through which that river did not normally flow.[6]

The prisoners and their distant families were enjoying a less Epicurean existence. Göring was putting up with the unaccustomed straitened conditions more stoically than his wife. Emmy and her daughter had been released from prison and were living in a

cottage deep in the forest at Sackdilling, without water or electricity. She implored the Tribunal to let her visit her imprisoned husband. 'I haven't seen my husband for a year and a quarter,' she wrote, 'and I am longing so terribly for him that I don't see any way out. I need strength to carry on without my husband.... My husband is very much worried about my child and myself, as we are without protection and help.' The Tribunal authorised her to come to see her husband. The prison commandant Colonel Andrus however disallowed it.

* He had not.

Göring already viewed the coming end of the trial quite dispassionately. There was a significant little scene on July 22, after Dr Friedrich Bergold had made his final plea for his absent client Martin Bormann. Göring called him over to the dock, and quoted to him with a smirk, gleefully rubbing his hands: 'These Nurembergers hang no one before they really have them.' It was an old German saying, but something about the way he said it told Bergold that Göring for one did not intend to hang.[7]

As the judges continued their deliberations, it was obvious that there were major differences between them on matters of principle, even though they had not begun to consider any questions of individual guilt. 'I find no improvement in the vagueness of the English mind,' wrote Judge Biddle, criticising the Tribunal's president, 'nor in the tight logic of the French. I sometimes feel that the Russians understand what it is all about better than any of us.' 'Volchkov,' he added by way of apology for this heresy, 'taking me home from a very gay, wet Russian party the other night, kissed me firmly.'[8]

BY AUGUST 8 the draft final opinion was available in a form where each of the judges could make specific objections. After first excluding everybody but the two interpreters from their room, they resumed their often heated discussion.

Donnedieu still felt they should throw out the whole charge of conspiracy, and submitted a new memorandum on this. He also disliked the way that after the document had dealt with Hitler's first 'diabolical' war plans against Austria, Czechoslovakia, and Poland the rest of the wars seemed something of an anti-climax. The judges were still tying themselves up in knots dealing with 'England's plans to attack Norway,' as Biddle noted, and planning to reproduce Hitler's secret speech of August 22, 1939: but Hitler had made explicit reference in that speech to the secret Ribbentrop–Molotov Pact, and Nikitchenko and his deputy Volchkov wanted these words omitted from the text. On orders from Moscow, they had little choice if they did not want to share General Zorya's fate.

There were other tangles in the web they were weaving: Parker felt they should make some reference to Hitler's wars against England and France; but Biddle and de Vabres disagreed (no doubt because it was Britain and France who had declared war on Hitler, and not vice versa.)[9] After endless circular discussions like these it was refreshing to emerge into the warm sunshine of Nuremberg's streets and be driven back to their villas in the outlying villages.

A week later the judges met again and finally faced down Donnedieu's insistence that they throw out the conspiracy charge, Count One. Lord Justice Lawrence invited him to open this final debate, but the French judge turned to his alternate Falco and allowed him to proceed. Doing so, Falco broadly agreed with him. His argument was simply that conspiracy was hard to define, and that the count was unnecessary, since the accused could be found equally guilty as accomplices to waging an aggressive war. He doubted moreover, noted Biddle, that the prosecution had actually proved that any such conspiracy existed. They should reject therefore the conspiracy charge on the ground that it had not been proved.

Arguing on a more philosophical level Donnedieu came to the same conclusion. He pointed out that the London Charter listed only three crimes—against peace, war crimes, and against humanity; the conspiracy charge had popped up in the indictment, 'one great conspiracy,' as he described it, 'to commit at the same time three crimes that are not even defined.' The Germans had always been warned that they would eventually be punished for substantive crimes, 'but not for mere conspiracy.' French jurisprudence, he explained, expanding on his theme for a moment, reposed on two honoured principles: the precise definition of crimes, and the fact that criminal law could not be retroactive. During the Nazi occupation of France, he reminisced, the Nazis had once attempted to introduce a retroactive law against communist propaganda. He himself had protested and he had been denounced for this by the German-controlled press. 'The choice has but a slight technical interest for you others,' he argued. 'And you should make a concession to us for whom it has an enormous moral value.'

Intrigued, the American alternate John Parker inquired if Donnedieu would therefore hold all the defendants Not Guilty under the first count of conspiracy. He replied, 'Yes,' adding once again that they could find sufficient other formulæ to convict.

Lawrence summed up, finding little common ground with Donnedieu. They were, quite simply, bound by the London Charter. True, as drawn, it might be regarded as retroactive. 'If it says conspiracy is a crime, we must follow it,' he argued. 'We can't take a false view of the facts to help the situation. *Ex post facto* is a view of justice.' They were occupation powers, and they could enforce whatever Charter they wanted. Thus Judge Biddle recorded Lawrence's arguments, adding his own terse though probably unspoken comment in parenthesis: 'British at their worst.'[10]

WHEN THEY reconvened the next day Nikitchenko took the argument in favour of retaining a conspiracy charge further; he did so at great length, speaking for two hours. He illustrated it with the example of the radio journalist Hans Fritzsche, one of the defendants. 'It is no crime to speak over the radio,' argued the Russian. 'But as long as he's a member of the conspiracy he's guilty of the other crimes.' As for the objections about introducing *ex post facto* legislation, the Russian asked: 'Why do we object to this innovation? The Tribunal is not an institution to protect old law and to shield old principles from violation.' Descending from the sublime to the obscene, he reiterated the Nazis' crimes, the 'crematories and bone-crushers of the Nazi regime,' as Biddle summarised his remarks.

For fifty minutes Sir Norman Birkett very wisely lamented that this controversy on such fundamental matters should have arisen so late in the trial: they had been sitting in judgement for ten months, and there had been no public discussion of these issues. 'Count One,' he argued, 'is the basis of the indictment.' If that count were to be rejected as Donnedieu was suggesting, 'the whole value of the trial will go.' Their purpose was to show that World War Two had not come out of a clear blue sky, but as the result of careful planning by the Nazis. Certainly this common plan existed by 1937, the time of the Hossbach Protocol, said Birkett. There was, in his own pithy definition, '(a) a common plan, (b) to commit war, (c) when, (d) what defendants, and (e) degree of guilt.'

Put like that, it sounded simple. The heart of this trial would be torn out, he pleaded, if they repudiated Count One. 'You say then [that] this dreadful war isn't planned. You bring about a national disaster. You acquit [the Nazi] party.' Squaring up to the other judges, Sir Norman challenged: 'Do you want to acquit the Nazi regime?' He feared that they were about to inflict infinite harm on the Tribunal.[11]

To and fro, and round and round, the debate continued on August 19, with John Parker speaking for an hour in defence of Count One. He thought the conspiracy proven 'beyond all peradventure.' Following him, Francis Biddle tried to reconcile these extreme viewpoints. Clearly they would have difficulty in finding a defendant like Dr Schacht guilty if they had to rely on Count Two. He was thereby unwittingly establishing how very much the laws had been written *ex post facto*, with these defendants in mind. 'I suggest,' he ventured, 'we write an opinion emphasising the separate plans rather than one single great loose conspiracy.'

Biddle mused afterwards, 'How can we meet Donnedieu de Vabres' purposes and sustain Count One?'[12]

Count One, or not Count One: that was a very moot question.

❖ ❖ ❖ ❖ ❖

Robert H. Jackson had been recalled to the United States. The sensation-hungry American public felt cheated because he had proclaimed that the trial would end in 1945. Moreover he had published a disagreeable article about the new chief justice of the Supreme Court in the Nuremberg newspapers. The defence counsel believed that he felt aggrieved at not having received the nomination himself; he had been recalled in a manner properly cloaked in public expressions of regret. 'On top of this,' noted Lieutenant-Colonel Karl-Heinz Keitel after a conversation with his father's attorney, 'there is a deep-seated feeling in the American armed forces that you can't call officers to account.' Jackson's retort to that was that these weren't officers but criminals who had been put into uniform. He felt that the American generals were stabbing him in the back with such irresponsible remarks.[13]

A few days later, on September 1, Keitel began writing his memoirs. 'For myself and for my family,' he wrote at one point, 'how I wish that I had been granted an upright and honourable soldier's death; why did Fate deny me that on July 20, 1944, in the course of the attempt on the Führer's life?'[14] His pencil racing across sheet after sheet of lined paper, by September 7 he had reached the Blomberg–Fritsch crisis, of January 1938.

While the judges continued to meet and debate the finer points of the law, the prisoners waited in their cells. General Alfred Jodl wrote to his wife on August 28 that if he were to be asked what sentence he really reckoned with, he had to admit quite frankly 'with one as much as the other.' 'Perhaps it will turn out to be more favourable than we feared in our darkest hours; perhaps it will be worse than we hoped for in the brightest.' He had packed his bags, whatever the outcome, he said; one swift grab and he could be out of here. But if death came knocking at his cell door, he wrote, that would not surprise him either.' 'It will find in me not a broken and rueful prey, but a proud man looking straight into its eye-sockets.' Nothing would persuade him that he had deserved such a fate.[15]

For his closing address to the Tribunal, Alfred Jodl crafted these words: the German armed forces had found themselves confronted by an impossible task, namely 'to wage a war which they had not wanted under a supreme commander whose confidence they lacked and whom they did not unconditionally trust, who often flouted basic principles of command and tried and tested viewpoints, using troop units and police forces which were not completely under their command, and guided by an intelligence service which was working partially for the enemy.'

Speaking for himself, Jodl intended to say: 'And that is why I, Members of the Tribunal, regardless of what sentence you pronounce upon me, shall leave this courtroom with my head held as high as when I entered it so many months ago.... In a war like this, in which hundreds of thousands of women and children were killed by saturation bombing and in which the partisans used every—and I mean every—means to their desired end, tough methods, however questionable under international law, do not amount to crimes of morality or conscience.'[16]

Göring knew precisely what verdict and sentence to expect. In his own closing address, he would state: 'The German people trusted the Führer. Given his authoritarian direction of the state, they had no influence on events. Ignorant of the crimes of which we know today, the people have fought with loyalty, self-sacrifice, and courage, and they have suffered too in this life-and-death struggle into which they were arbitrarily thrust. The German people are free from blame.' By his execution he hoped to expiate their crimes.

Boldest of all in his closing speech, delivered on August 31, was Rudolf Hess, who had hardly spoken during the trial. With his script broadcast around the world, he concluded with these words:

> To me was granted to work for many years of my life under the greatest son my country has brought forth in a thousand years of history. Even if I were able, I should not want to erase this epoch from my past existence. I am happy to know that I have done my duty to my people—my duty as a German, as a National Socialist, and as a true disciple of the Führer.
>
> I regret nothing. Were I to live my life again I should act once more as I have acted now, even though I knew that at the end a funeral pyre was already flickering for my immolation: I care not what mere mortals may do. The time will come when I shall stand before the judgement seat of the Eternal. I shall answer unto Him and I know that he will judge me innocent.

On September 2 the Tribunal heard the suggestion of Colonel Andrus that the defendants should now be allowed to see their wives and lawyers and to talk together. They saw no reason to disapprove.

❖ ❖ ❖ ❖ ❖

That afternoon the judges began to debate their verdicts on the individual defendants. From now on all the interpreters and typists would be confined behind locked doors.

Most of the verdicts on guilt or innocence were arrived at with speed and unanimity. Göring, they agreed, should be found guilty on all counts; though for a while Donnedieu held out, on principle, for an acquittal on the charge of conspiracy.

The case of Rudolf Hess, who had been seated next to Göring and was therefore considered next, gave considerably more trouble. Most agreed to his guilt on Counts One and Two—the conspiracy, and crimes against peace—but there were profound disagreements on Three and Four (war crimes and crimes against humanity): General Nikitchenko wanted him found guilty on these, and when Colonel Volchkov argued that Hess' signature on the Nuremberg race laws made him 'guilty of the killing of millions of Jews' Biddle entered in his notes, probably with a sigh, the realisation: 'Russians are going to be very extreme.'

Ribbentrop was agreed to be guilty on all four counts. Donnedieu now made plain that he was reserving his opinion on Count One, the main conspiracy charge, on all of the defendants. Keitel, likewise, was found guilty on every count. Opinion on Alfred Rosenberg was divided: Falco, Lawrence (who suggested life imprisonment), Nikitchenko, and

Volchkov argued for finding him guilty all four counts; Donnedieu suggested that Count Two was doubtful. The Americans both passed.

On Hans Frank, Volchkov, Birkett, and the Americans voted for guilty on Counts One, Three, and Four; Donnedieu again refused to include Count One, and Nikitchenko wanted him declared guilty on all four.

Frick was generally felt to be guilty on Counts One and Three by Falco and Parker, and on all four counts by the Russians and English. The former S.S. Obergruppenführer Ernst Kaltenbrunner presented a problem. Biddle, Falco, and Donnedieu held him to be guilty on war crimes and crimes against humanity but innocent on Counts One and Two. Birkett felt they could add Count One, as did Parker and Volchkov and, to a lesser degree, Lord Justice Lawrence. Nikitchenko predictably found Kaltenbrunner guilty on all four Counts.

There was a surprising unanimity between the Americans, the Russians, Birkett, and Falco for finding General Jodl guilty on all four counts; Donnedieu would have acquitted him on One and Four, and Lawrence on Four.

Reaching the case of the absent Reichsleiter Martin Bormann, Parker and Biddle wanted the Tribunal to satisfy itself with a declaration that he was dead, but Donnedieu, and Birkett too, wanted him declared guilty on all counts. The Russians stated there was not enough evidence that he was dead, and he should therefore be convicted.

Artur Seyss-Inquart, considered next, was rapidly found guilty on all four counts, though Biddle expressed reservations on Counts One and Two.

The judges all wanted to hang Julius Streicher for something, but disagreed strongly about what. Falco, Donnedieu, Parker, Biddle, Birkett, Lawrence, and the Russians scattered their choice between Counts One, Three, and Four seemingly at random. In a diary note which reveals both the mood at these sentencing sessions and the superficial reasoning which decided between life and death, Biddle recorded,

> The Russians, Falco, and even the British, are talking of holding defendants guilty on account of the positions they held. 'Streicher,' Volchkov says, 'for instance, was personally connected with Hitler.' I blurt out that I think it's preposterous to hold a little Jew-baiter as a conspirator because he was a friend of Hitler, or a Gauleiter, or a Nazi. Lawrence bridles and says I have bad manners. Parker pours oil on the water, and says we must limit the theory of conspiracy, and that Streicher had nothing to do with planning or conspiring.

Resuming their deliberations, Falco, Parker, Lawrence, Birkett, and the Russians considered Walter Funk guilty on all four counts; de Vabres once again excepted Count One, as did Birkett. Fritz Sauckel was regarded by nearly all of them as guilty only on Counts Three and Four;

the Russians threw in One and Two. Speer too attracted guilty votes only under Counts Three and Four. Parker and Birkett were inclined to add One and Two, but they reserved their decision on this. Neurath, Hitler's first foreign minister, was held by Falco and the Russians and British to be guilty on all four counts; the Americans would have been more lenient.[17]

ON THE following day, September 3, they considered their interim verdict on the indicted organisations. The Americans argued that the Charter gave the Tribunal wide powers of discretion; the Russians disagreed, stating that the Tribunal was bound to make a finding on each organisation. 'We can only say whether an organisation is criminal or not.' Lawrence was worried that any finding by the Tribunal would be used to pass summary judgements on possibly totally innocent members of the organisations it found to be criminal. Judge Biddle thought the whole thing stank, and noted: 'I suggest to throw them all out. A shocking thing, this group crime.'[18]

They met again on September 4 to try once more to overcome Donnedieu's fundamental objections to Count One. Later that day, they tried to agree the wording of the section on war crimes, and crimes against humanity. Again the French and Americans pleaded for a toning down of the emotional language, while Birkett and the Russians wanted to adhere to its more lurid hues. Donnedieu perhaps tactlessly suggested that the judgement ought to describe what partisan warfare was like, 'so as to give a true picture'; the Russian General Nikitchenko objected to that, and his deputy Volchkov again obsessively demanded that they include a detailed account of the gas chambers, as well as mentions of how the Nazis' had used the corpses to make soap.[19]*

On September 6 the Tribunal resumed discussion on the individual defendants whom they had sat facing for ten months across the courtroom.

Lord Justice Lawrence admitted straight away that he wanted to see Dr Hjalmar Schacht—the freemason, former Nazi banking chief, and pal of the governor of the Bank of England—acquitted. Hearing this Donnedieu objected to the very notion of acquitting any of the defendants; he would however go along with light sentences on 'several defendants' including Schacht and Papen. The French judge revealed that he had been particularly angered by that newsreel scene of Schacht shaking hands with Hitler after the conquest of France. On moral values, he continued, he would be shocked to see a Keitel condemned to death and a Schacht acquitted.

Judge Biddle inclined to the same view, but asked for more time to consider the evidence on Schacht; his colleague Parker remarked that Schacht did appear to have opposed the war. 'If he was guilty,' he

*They did not. See page 131.

continued, 'he should get the works. If he were not guilty, he should be acquitted. Conviction might greatly discredit the Tribunal.' Schacht, he pointed out, had denied financing Hitler's rearmament specifically to wage an aggressive war. 'He was a banker, therefore a man of character.' Robert Falco, the French alternate, said he did not attach much importance to Schacht's alleged anti-Hitler plotting. Sir Norman Birkett appeared at first to be sitting impartially on the fence: '[Schacht] must be acquitted, or severely punished.' Having said that, he listed all the reasons why he thought Schacht should be allowed to go free. 'Thinks a reasonable doubt is raised,' noted Biddle, 'and believes we should acquit.' The Russians were horrified by this, and wanted Schacht convicted at least on Counts One and Two.

The verdict on Franz von Papen also raised delicate issues. Falco felt that while he should be convicted on Count Two, for having actively prepared the Anschluss with Austria in 1938, and for having helped propel Hitler into power, a moderate sentence seemed called for. Donnedieu broadly agreed, calling Papen 'a corrupting creature,' and suggesting that the Tribunal had an overriding duty to lay down moral standards. The Americans however held out for an acquittal, since there was no evidence that he had actually done anything wrong in any of his offices. Lord Justice Lawrence pointed out that at the time of the Anschluss Papen had been effectively dismissed from office. 'Had nothing to do with it,' noted Biddle. 'To take over embassy at Ankara was hardly a criminal act. No evidence that he tried to bring Turkey into war. *Acquit.*'[20]

On the following day Nikitchenko, supported by his deputy Volchkov, made a half-hearted attempt to hang Papen, asking whether they could not agree that the Nazi regime, after the seizure of power, had violated the Versailles Treaty and rearmed Germany with a view to aggressive war; because in that event—so the Russians argued—each and every official of the party was culpable in some degree. The Russians felt that they should find Papen guilty on all four counts.

WITHOUT REACHING a decision on this, they moved on to Sir Norman Birkett's draft of the opinion on aggressive war. Once again General Nikitchenko tried valiantly to keep out of the text the part of Hitler's speech of August 22, 1939, where he crowed over the isolation of Poland that was a consequence of the Ribbentrop–Molotov Pact ('Now I have Poland where I want her ...').[21] On the following day it was Biddle's turn to object, when Birkett proposed that they eliminate from the draft the finding that in declaring war on the United States Germany was guilty of an act of aggressive war. Nikitchenko then tried to gerrymander the voting procedures, claiming that there had to be a vote of at least three to one in favour of any acquittal: two to two was not sufficient. (The next day, Biddle pushed through a vote whereby the judges agreed that there must, on the contrary, be a vote of three to one to convict. Nikitchenko dissented.)[22]

❖ ❖ ❖ ❖ ❖

The guilt or innocence of Grand-Admiral Dönitz split the Tribunal wide open. Robert Falco considered the admiral's guilt self-evident, at least on Count Two, because of the invasion of Norway in April 1940. He considered too that Dönitz's order of September 1942 implicated him in not saving survivors of torpedoed ships: at the very least, Falco felt, the order was ambiguous, and Lieutenant-Commander Eck had certainly construed it as an order to liquidate all survivors. Dönitz had also transmitted Hitler's Commando Order of October 1942, and he had drafted minutes of a conference with the Führer on measures to adopt against Danish saboteurs. As to the employment of concentration camp labour, Dönitz, asking for twelve thousand workers to be made available, had said he personally would not worry about their 'origin.'

Falco's colleague Donnedieu de Vabres was less severe, though still holding Dönitz guilty on Count Three. Dönitz had had nothing to do with the wars of aggression, being only a subordinate officer when Norway was invaded in 1940. As for committing war crimes against neutral ships in reserved zones, Donnedieu confessed himself somewhat at a loss: Was not the British blockade itself a breach of the Hague Rules, he asked, and of the agreements which Britain had signed at the pre-war Washington and London conferences? Were not reprisals justified? He felt that Dönitz's orders, though equivocal, could not be construed as orders to kill survivors. There was a doubt, he pointed out, and it was their duty to resolve it in favour of the defendant. Despite what Falco had said, Lieutenant-Commander Eck had denied that his conduct was the result of an order from Dönitz. Donnedieu argued therefore for 'a very mild sentence' on Dönitz.

Francis Biddle went even further, arguing vigorously for acquittal. 'The essence of the charge is Dönitz's conduct of the submarine warfare,' he summarised. 'The other charges are trifling. Eck's testimony proves that he did not have any orders from Dönitz. How silly for us to say he was guilty for not giving warning and saving survivors, when doing so would have made use of submarines impossible, when Britain ordered all merchantmen to be armed and to fight back, and [U.S. Admiral Chester W.] Nimitz was giving orders to sink without warnings and not to save survivors. Germany,' concluded Biddle, 'waged a much cleaner war than we did.' It is fair to say that his alternate, Parker, took a much sterner view of Dönitz, and wanted him found guilty on Count Two. The Russians took what Biddle termed wearily 'the usual line,' arguing that to acquit Dönitz would be to say that his submarine warfare was legal and proper.

Lord Justice Lawrence showed that he too favoured finding the admiral guilty, arguing that for submarines to give warning was obligatory, and talking of the announcement that submarines would sink anything as 'a murderous declaration.' As for the killing of survivors, Dönitz was, agreed Lawrence, entitled to the benefit of the doubt. But everything he did was typically National Socialist, harsh and inhumane. Dönitz's order to kill a communist spy, said the lord justice, 'only illustrated the harshness of the man.' His deliberations might seem to have lacked the forensic touch one might expect in a judge of his eminence; but his own opinion was clear: 'Guilty therefore on Counts Two and Three.'

Biddle felt that the old Englishman had totally lost touch with reality. The American admiral Nimitz had sunk opposing vessels without warning. The Germans had to adopt the same methods as their enemy. They were sitting in judgement on the Germans in a city in which tens of thousands of civilians still lay buried in the ruins as a result of Britain's bombing campaign, and were talking of the enemy as though such standards did not apply to the victors. He felt strongly that Dönitz was innocent, and should be acquitted.

❖ ❖ ❖ ❖ ❖

Grand Admiral Raeder was given only the shortest shrift. All the judges found him guilty on the Second and Third Counts; Falco, Lawrence, the Russians, and the Americans on Count One as well. (Francis Biddle felt that Raeder should be shot; his alternate, Parker, however opposed the death penalty in this case.)

Turning finally to Baldur von Schirach, they all except Lawrence agreed he was guilty under Count Four; the Russians added Count One, Nikitchenko arguing that Schirach had once conferred with Hitler on deporting four hundred thousand people.[23]

THUS BY September 10 when they convened to take a final vote on the defendants and the proposed penalties, many of the verdicts were broadly agreed.

This left a few stubborn decisions, like that on Hans Fritzsche. He was just a propagandist, suggested Falco, but an accomplice all the same in war crimes and crimes against humanity. Donnedieu murmured that this man was the least guilty of all. John Parker pointed out that the year he had spent in jail was already a severe punishment, given the mildness of the crimes. 'Hitler wouldn't have wasted five minutes with him,' he said. '[He was] only indicted because Goebbels is dead.' Like the case of the two Krupps, they were being asked to make a vicarious sacrifice. 'Freedom of speech and the press is of the greatest importance to liberty. A man shouldn't be convicted for what he says or writes unless it is an incitement to crime.' Biddle was proud of his fellow-American, and agreed vigorously.

General Nikitchenko took the opposing view, asking that they find Fritzsche guilty on Counts One, Two, and Three, and saying: 'His propaganda led to atrocities.' Volchkov tried a more silky line, saying:

'We of course must not try journalists for what they write, but Fritzsche is being tried as a leader of the Press for his false ideas of racial superiority, etc., which led to the extermination of so many victims.' He had moreover, said Volchkov, conducted a 'libellous, slanderous campaign against the Russians, accusing them of atrocities.'

Lord Justice Lawrence revealed himself moved by the American arguments: he felt Fritzsche was guilty on Three and Four, and originally on Count One too, but now he wanted time to reconsider in the light of what Parker and Biddle had said.

With relief they turned to Hermann Göring's case: here there could be no mitigating factor. All agreed he was guilty on all counts, all agreed on the death penalty. 'A high-class brigand,' summarised Donnedieu, while confessing: 'He has a certain nobility.' He proposed the firing squad—in fact he felt that all the executions should be by firing squad. Biddle intervened that in general he preferred hanging, though he too felt that the firing squad should be allowed in some cases as mitigation. Donnedieu displayed a tendency to inflict some 'honourable' and some 'dishonourable' penalties; when he even tediously suggested they distinguish between different types of imprisonment, imposing on occasion what the French called *reclusion* (dishonourable detention), Nikitchenko wearily interrupted: 'Don't let us get into such ridiculous trifles.' He too preferred hanging as the 'main form,' and certainly not the guillotine.

As for other punishments, although Article 28 of the Charter allowed them to confiscate the defendants' property, they all agreed to disregard this provision and leave it up to the Control Council in Berlin; when the Russians pressed that the judgement should at least say that all stolen property was to be confiscated, Biddle irritably retorted: 'How silly, stolen property should always be returned. Why express a platitude?' Besides, they had been offered no evidence to identify any stolen property. Voted down three to one on Biddle's motion, Nikitchenko sulked and objected: 'It will be understood that this stolen property will remain in the hands of the brigands.'

At last their discussion reverted to Göring. All agreed that he was guilty on all four counts and should hang (except Donnedieu, who asked that he be shot.) 'These are final votes,' noted Biddle at this point, 'unless reservation.'[24]

20: **Deadly Alliances**

THE VOTING—it was still September 10, 1946—then proceeded apace. Turning next to the case of Rudolf Hess, the Russians asked for the death penalty on all four counts; Lawrence favoured life imprisonment. The Americans and Donnedieu acquitted him on Three and Four, the former asking for life, the latter 'perhaps twenty years.' A vote proved inconclusive. 'Then Lawrence proposes life, and Nikitchenko again sticks to death,' wrote Biddle. 'We finally—except French—agree on life sentence.' Probably none of them realised that this simple sentence, so easily agreed on, would mean Rudolf Hess languishing in a prison cell for the next forty-one years, as he did, and outliving every one of those judges present, spending over twenty of those years in solitary confinement.

Ribbentrop was disposed of as rapidly as Göring: guilty on all four counts, to be hanged. The debate on Keitel went the same way, except that the French preferred shooting. All the judges found Kaltenbrunner guilty on Three and Four; Lawrence would have added One, and the Russians wanted all four. They settled for hanging the S.S. Obergruppenführer on Counts Three and Four. In the case of Alfred Rosenberg, surprisingly the French showed a degree of leniency, finding him guilty on all four counts but asking for a life sentence; Parker agreed, 'as he displayed humanitarianism.' Francis Biddle thought he should be hanged on Three and Four, and probably on One and Two as well, though he reserved his final opinion on the punishment. The Russian judges and Lawrence went to the other extreme, finding that the Nazi philosopher should be hanged on all four counts. On Hans Frank too, Biddle found Donnedieu 'curiously tender,' suggesting 'perhaps' a life sentence more appropriate than hanging, while all found him guilty on Counts Three and Four, and the Russians threw in Count One for good measure as well. The majority decision prevailed, and Hans Frank was marked down for hanging on Counts Three and Four.

Arriving at the case of Wilhelm Frick, opinions varied: Falco wanted the former lawyer and Reich minister hanged on all four counts. Parker agreed on the guilt, but felt a life sentence more appropriate 'as he was really but a bureaucrat.' Donnedieu reserved his opinion; Biddle acquitted him on Count One, but hanged him on the other three; the Russians and Lawrence again joined forces in finding the defendant guilty on all four counts. Lord Justice Lawrence noted with evident disapproval that Frick had not gone into the witness stand. 'We conclude to convict him on Two, Three and Four and to hang him,' Biddle jotted in his notes.

Streicher's case merited only two and a half lines in those notes. The judges agreed his guilt under Count Four; the Russians added Count One too. There was enough to hang him. Walter Funk also attracted the death sentence at first on all four counts, although Professor Donnedieu, pointing out that Funk 'didn't participate in aggressive war,' hesitated on the sentence and then John Parker spoke out for life imprisonment instead. Nikitchenko objected gravely, 'The role of Funk seems to have been underestimated,' and he, Volchkov and Lawrence all voted for the death penalty. Given Donnedieu's reservations however, the decision on sentence was held over.

There was virtually no discussion on Fritz Sauckel, the colourless manpower commissioner: all agreed on Counts Three and Four, all wanted him hanged, the Russians throwing in Counts One and Two as well. Although only Lawrence found him guilty under Count Two, the final verdict mysteriously omitted Three and hanged Sauckel under Counts Two and Four.

Of greatest historical interest was the case against General Alfred Jodl, the upright 'soldier's soldier.' Even the bloodthirsty Robert Falco found him less guilty than Keitel, and held that Jodl 'deserves life, or [a] term of years' on all four counts. Donnedieu agreed that the general should be given what he called an 'honourable sentence,' a term of years. The Americans, Russians, and British however found Jodl guilty on the first three counts (Biddle, Lawrence, and the Russians on all four) and asked for hanging (Biddle wrote a question mark after the word.) They still felt uneasy perhaps, because they postponed a final decision on Jodl by several days.

The line-up against the former lawyer Arthur Seyss-Inquart was unanimous for the death penalty on Counts Three and Four, while Parker added Count One, and Lord Justice Lawrence and the Russians, forming their usual alliance, added in all the other counts as well.[1]

ON ALBERT Speer opinion was hopelessly divided, an indication of how far he had won over some of the judges with his methods, but failed to deceive others. There evolved a general agreement that he was guilty on Counts Three and Four, particularly for the use of slave labour. The French wanted to imprison him. While John Parker found himself impressed by Speer's personality and the extent to which prosecutor Robert Jackson had respected him, his senior colleague Francis Biddle felt that Speer deserved to hang on those two counts; unusually, he found the Russian general and his deputy strongly supporting him while expanding the guilt 'as usual' to all four counts. Lord Justice Lawrence, finding perhaps some affinity with Speer's suave persona, agreed with

Professor Donnedieu, suggesting that the slave-labour system which Speer took over was already in existence. He proposed fifteen years; de Vabres seconded him. Forming an unholy alliance, Biddle and Nikitchenko held out for the death penalty. The debate swayed to and fro. 'We can't agree,' recorded Biddle finally. Norman Birkett, who had been absent working on drafts, came in and voted for ten years. Unable to resolve their differences, they adjourned until the morrow.[2]

Biddle began the next day's conference, on September 11, with his conclusion, having reviewed the evidence again, that Rosenberg was guilty on all four counts and should therefore be hanged; Donnedieu still held out for a life sentence on the philosopher.

They moved back to Speer, and agreed on a penalty of fifteen years' imprisonment, on Counts Three and Four (that was not however the final sentence.) Proceeding to Neurath, the former foreign minister, Biddle, Parker, and Falco found against him only on Counts Three and Four, and suggested respectively fifteen years, five years, and a 'rather heavy' penalty; Donnedieu agreed on ten or fifteen years, but on Counts One to Three. Sir Norman Birkett felt that all four counts applied, earning fifteen years; his colleague Lawrence felt that those four counts earned Neurath life imprisonment, the Russians wanted, characteristically, the rope. The final vote was a compromise, guilty on all four counts and fifteen years in jail.

Their deliberations on Bormann were largely academic, since the Americans felt sure he was dead and they should simply say so. The British disagreed; the Russians were unconvinced by the evidence that he was dead, and wanted to hang him on all three counts with which he was charged (One, Three, and Four.) The outcome was that Bormann was found guilty on Counts Three and Four, and sentenced to hang. The evidence that he was already dead would not be announced in the opinion.

Robert Falco felt that Baldur von Schirach had earned life imprisonment on Counts One and Four, perhaps even death. This defendant had published a letter approving of Streicher's programme in the *Stürmer*; he had agreed with Hans Frank on the deportation of fifty thousand Jews, saying that it was better for the Jews to be sent to concentration camps. Since he regularly received the reports of the *Einsatzgruppen* (task forces), Schirach 'must have known' what was going on. Professor Donnedieu however urged caution, expressing the fear that they might be making an error of perspective. 'Put ourselves in Schirach's position at that time,' he said, and suggested that a sentence of twenty years to life was more appropriate than hanging. Biddle showed himself negatively impressed by Schirach's role as gauleiter of Vienna. Sir Norman Birkett, reading from the evidence, reminded them that this defendant had even boasted that the deportation of the Jews from Vienna was a step forward in European culture. 'Twenty years,' he suggested. 'Russians: the works, as usual,' noted Biddle, and with the same hint of sarcasm he quoted Lord Justice Lawrence as urging the death penalty on Counts One and Four, since Schirach had '*actually* urged [the] bombing of [an] English town when Heydrich was killed.' It was indeed a rare perspective from a judge whose country's air force had burned alive and blasted to death around a million civilians in air raids over the past five years. When the debate subsided, they agreed on twenty years for the youth leader.

All of the judges found Raeder guilty on Counts One to Three. The French spoke of twenty years, Lawrence and the Americans of life imprisonment, and the Russians of hanging. The final compromise was life imprisonment.

WHEN THE discussion turned to Dönitz, Sir Norman Birkett joined them. Falco pointed out that his guilt was much less than Raeder's; he and Donnedieu suggested five to ten years at most. Parker agreed. Sir Norman Birkett thought ten inadequate, and proposed twenty. For once the Russians agreed, feeling that Dönitz deserved less than Raeder's life sentence. Lawrence also supported ten years, while still describing Dönitz as a 'Nazi of a ruthless order.' Biddle bravely argued against even this sentence, urging that it would be an injustice to convict Dönitz on submarine warfare, but he lacked Parker's support, who talked vaguely about a 'damnable warfare,' and showed frankly that, whatever Nimitz had testified to the contrary, he did not believe it possible that 'our country,' meaning the United States of America, could have done anything as heinous as Dönitz. Biddle warned that he would draft a dissenting opinion. The other judges held to a ten-year prison term, subject to hearing from him.

ALTHOUGH IN the interests of Tribunal unanimity Biddle's dissenting opinion was never filed it is nonetheless a document worthy of examination.

This, wrote Biddle, was intended to be an impartial trial, and yet clearly it was not. Until Dönitz succeeded Raeder in January 1943, he had taken no part in preparing any wars of aggression; from 1943 onward Germany was however 'fighting a purely defensive war,' Biddle pointed out. Therefore it was impossible, argued Biddle, to find Dönitz guilty under Counts One and Two of the indictment. (The Tribunal reached the opposite conclusion, stating in its verdict that Hitler 'almost always' consulted with Dönitz in the earlier years;[3] a claim for which even now, half a century later, there has not been found a tithe of supporting evidence.)

As for Count Three, the charge of war crimes, Biddle pointed out tersely that the Germans had done no more, and often considerably less, than their enemies: 'It is clear to me, as it seems to be to my colleagues, that the British Admiralty had prepared before the outbreak of war to arm its merchant ships, that it had integrated them into its naval and aircraft intelligence system by directing them through wireless to make position reports on all sighting of submarines. These actions as well as the use of the convoy system, merchant ships escorted by naval escorts, would seem to remove the immunity from attack without warning granted "merchant vessels" by the London Agreement.' Churchill himself had admitted having ordered to be sunk all German ships by day, and all ships by night 'as opportunity served.'

Turning to the killing of survivors, Biddle's dissenting opinion continued that there was no question in his mind that Dönitz himself had never ordered this.

The United States Navy had carried on unrestricted submarine warfare in the Pacific from the first day that nation entered the war. 'All ships in the zone were torpedoed without warning,' Biddle had found, 'and the entire Pacific Ocean was declared a zone of operations.' While implying no criticism of Winston Churchill, Admiral Ernest King, or Admiral Chester Nimitz, the respective naval leaders, Biddle felt entitled to cite their actions to show that the Allies did precisely what they accused the Germans of having done. 'It is, in my opinion,' he wrote, 'offensive to our concept of justice to punish a man for doing exactly what one has done himself.'

To convict Grand Admiral Dönitz, in short, argued Judge Biddle in his dissenting judgement, would be to convict him not for starting a war, but for losing one.[4] Having written these brave words Biddle, displaying rather less valour, decided not to file the document; it would have been a pointless exercise, one against three, and Article 4, para. 4 of the London Statute had defined that three votes were enough to convict. Judge Biddle later made no secret of his opinion, being quoted as having said: 'The Germans fought a much cleaner war at sea than we did.'[5]

In the event, this was the only case in which the defence succeeded in invoking the principle of *tu quoque*. The Tribunal found itself faced with troubling evidence, as its verdict against Dönitz concluded, in particular with an order issued by the British admiralty on May 8, 1940—in other words by its then first lord Churchill—to the effect that any ship found in the Skagerrak was to be sunk on sight, and with the answers given by Nimitz to a defence questionnaire in which he confirmed that in the Pacific Ocean the United States Navy had from day one of entering the war waged unrestricted submarine warfare. Therefore the Tribunal specifically did not levy any punishment on Dönitz on account of his violations of international laws for submarine warfare.[6] It was a small consolation, but a consolation all the same.

❖ ❖ ❖ ❖ ❖

Hans Fritzsche was at first accorded a modest prison sentence by the Tribunal. That interesting concept, the freedom of the press, told strongly in his favour. At most the judges felt inclined to let him off with a sentence of two to five years, including time already served.

Then even more interesting concepts supervened: Donnedieu warned that it would be a pity to inflict a very light sentence—it would be preferable to acquit him cleanly. Parker agreed: 'Why use a cannon to shoot a sparrow?' he asked. Biddle nodded, and said simply, 'Acquit.' The Russians argued heatedly against acquittal, Volchkov stating that it would hold Fritzsche up to the German people as a defender of freedom of speech. Lord Justice Lawrence argued vaguely, 'It is an important case.' But to acquit a propagandist working for the war was no less dangerous. 'Did he not know the wars were illegal?' he asked rhetorically, as they adjourned for the night.[7]

Outside the courtroom the next day, September 12, Donnedieu stopped Biddle to say that he was now inclining against acquitting Fritzsche. Lawrence resumed where he had left off, arguing that Fritzsche had lied on the stand. Biddle stoutly defending his arguments for acquittal: they were not trying Fritzsche for false propaganda, he said. Parker chimed in, saying that the world would not understand a conviction. When he said that the journalist was like a private in the army, this provoked a long speech from Nikitchenko. Professor Donnedieu 'wobbled round a good deal,' according to Biddle, saying he would never convict Fritzsche if they decided to acquit Papen—as seemed increasingly likely.

With the decision on Fritzsche therefore left in suspense, they moved on to the appropriate verdict and penalty for Hitler's banker, Dr Hjalmar Schacht. Falco, speaking first, found him guilty on Counts One and Two, arguing on the latter point that the banker had known where the war was leading. (Biddle disagreed.) However, given the mitigating circumstances, he felt five years would be appropriate. Donnedieu agreed in general, pointing out that if Hitler had been successful Schacht would have had none of the misgivings about Nazism that he was so voluble about in court. Parker was still in favour of acquittal, finding nothing wrong in the Mefo-bills (*Mefo-Wechsel*), the financial wizardry with which Schacht had engineered the Nazi economic miracle after 1933. Francis Biddle, the other American, disagreed, stating that Schacht had earned a life sentence on Count One.

Up then piped the voice of Sir Norman Birkett, who declared, rather lamely, that the 'only way' was to *acquit* Schacht; the choice, he argued, was between acquittal and a very severe sentence indeed, on the basis that he was the 'chief architect' of aggressive war. It seemed a curious argument, if a clever one, for it left reasonable men among them with no choice but to acquit.

Schacht was of course the *bête noire* of the Americans, and for once the Russians came out of their shell. During the lunch recess General Nikitchenko approached Biddle and asked him how much they ought to go down in their demands. 'Suggest a stiff [prison] term,' responded

Biddle, 'as a compromise, and see what happens!'

Donnedieu now hinted that he would be prepared to go up to as much as a ten-year sentence.

When they resumed Nikitchenko put up a valiant fight, rehearsing in great detail the evidence against Schacht on Counts One and Two. As there were mitigating circumstances, he volunteered, he would propose life imprisonment instead of his normal recommendation, hanging. Volchkov agreed, even referring to Schacht's advanced age.

The British judge Lawrence, like Sir Norman Birkett, still held out for acquittal however. The primary question, he asked, was what were Schacht's intentions in assisting Germany's rearmament? Had it been shown that he intended that armament to be used for aggression? He may have intended merely to strength Germany's hand at the international negotiating table. 'It is power that counts at international negotiations,' said Lawrence. 'It is not Utopian, but it is the truth.' Germany, he recorded, was suffering in 1933 under a feeling of injustice—probably mistaken—but one which had found much sympathy in the United States and elsewhere. Indeed, if Germany had gone about things in the right way, these other countries might even have agreed to waive the onerous treaties. 'We are not trying Schacht for negligence,' intoned the lord justice, in his clipped English accent. 'Intent is necessary.'

After a few more words from Donnedieu, the judges solemnly agreed on their verdict on Schacht: eight years from the day he was arrested, or about six years more in jail. Reviewing his notes years later, Biddle drew four thick lines next to this passage: because, behind the scenes, something happened between that decision recorded on September 12, 1946 and the moment eighteen days later when Schacht would be let off scot-free.

THE RENEWED discussion on Franz von Papen caused equal heartburn to the judges. Falco suggested that as the wily old diplomat had not gone along altogether with Hitler, he should be jailed for five years. Donnedieu felt that Papen's guilt was graver than that of Schacht. In mitigation, it might be said that Papen could have had no way of knowing that the war would result in inhuman and criminal acts—or was Donnedieu now confusing him with Schacht, since he then said that he had already spent several years in a concentration camp and took no part in the war after it began? Bringing the talk firmly back to Papen, Parker said bluntly that the prosecution had failed to make its case against him. Biddle agreed: 'Papen never advocated *aggression* in Austria.' Apart from Austria in 1938, there was nothing.

Sir Norman Birkett, musing out loud, said, 'He was, of course, an intriguer.' Hitler himself had acknowledged that Papen had helped him to power. Having said that, he agreed that that wasn't enough for a conviction; since the prosecution itself had expressly stated that they attached no significance to anything that happened while Papen was Nazi ambassador at Ankara, it all boiled down to 'dislike of the kind of man Papen is.' They had no alternative, Birkett argued, but to acquit. Seeing their prey escaping, General Nikitchenko tamely suggested a modest penalty, perhaps ten years, but already Lord Justice Lawrence was pronouncing that they had no choice but to acquit—to which he added the ominous words, 'I dislike von Papen more than I dislike Schacht.' He was still manœuvring to secure Schacht's acquittal.

An acquittal of Papen raised collateral difficulties in British eyes. In that case, they ought to acquit Fritzsche too, said the lord justice, since the radio journalist's guilt was certainly no greater than that of the Nazi ambassador von Papen. 'It would be unfortunate to acquit only Papen,' suggested Lawrence—again revealing on what improbable and silken threads these life-and-death decisions were being reached.

A vote was taken: three of the judges were in favour of acquitting Fritzsche, which was more than enough under the rules. Seeing another victim escape, General Nikitchenko loudly objected to Lawrence's facile argument. 'I can see no reason to acquit Fritzsche simply because we acquit Papen,' he protested.

Sir Norman Birkett gently prised Lord Justice Lawrence out of what Biddle called 'his hole.' 'Papen isn't a reason for acquitting Fritzsche,' he pronounced, 'but the conclusion is wise from a political point of view.'

Nikitchenko indicated that he would want to file a dissenting opinion on Fritzsche, which should not however be made public, as part of the judgement; he explained that this was usual in Soviet law—a dissent could be kept secret, but be considered on appeal. 'I don't care how it is done,' he said, 'but I would like it to go to the Control Council as part of the judgement.' He even had some hopes that the Control Council might recommend the committee of chief prosecutors to consider a retrial of Fritzsche. If the Americans recalled the Anglo-Saxon prejudice against 'double jeopardy,' nobody mentioned it at this point. Donnedieu objected to the very idea of anybody filing a dissenting opinion, saying that the whole Tribunal had to reach each decision. A dissenting opinion would deprive the Tribunal of its authority.

They swiftly moved on to less contentious matters, the sentence on the guilty 'generals,' Keitel and Jodl. The French chivalrously thought they should be shot, as befitted soldiers; the other judges voted for the gallows, except for Biddle who would have hanged Keitel and allowed Jodl the firing squad. In this however Biddle however conceded defeat. The two men would hang. On Funk, all but the Russians now voted for life imprisonment on Counts Two to Four.[8]

❖ ❖ ❖ ❖ ❖

On September 7, 1946 Colonel Andrus departed for a week's

vacation, taking his family to Switzerland. In his absence, for the first time in over a year, the prisoners were allowed the chance to see and speak to their families. Of course no kind of intimacies were allowed. There were half a dozen open cells erected in the meeting room; the prisoners could speak with their next-of-kin through a window measuring perhaps sixteen by twenty-four inches. The rest of the partition consisted of wire-mesh. Each prisoner was manacled to a white-helmeted sentinel sitting next to him with a Tommy gun.[9]

Looking much thinner, on September 12 Emmy Göring was shown in for half an hour to see the Reichsmarschall. On the seventeenth Edda, now eight years old, was allowed to come into Room 57 with her, to see her father for the first and last time. 'Stand on a chair,' commanded her father, 'so I can see how you've grown.' She recited to him the poems she had learned, out in the forest, and then their brief visit was over. 'Papa,' she said, before being led away, 'when you come home, will you please put on your rubber medals in the bath like people say you do?'

❖ ❖ ❖ ❖ ❖

That night something happened to upset the decision to jail Schacht.

As the judges went in to resume their deliberations on September 13, Lord Justice Lawrence took his senior American colleague aside and revealed that Professor Donnedieu had 'changed his mind' on Schacht. He now felt that the banker—the man who had shaken Hitler's hand after the defeat of France—should be acquitted. Biddle was astonished, and recorded his suspicions in the following telling words: 'I wonder what the English have done to him.'

The French judge's reasons, said Lawrence, were that originally he felt that all the defendants were guilty in some degree and all should have been convicted; but now that they had decided to acquit Papen and Fritzsche, Schacht had to go free too, as he was less culpable than Papen. Acquittal was the only option since, in Donnedieu's view, 'the Tribunal is not created to pronounce light sentences.' He, Lawrence, had allowed himself to be persuaded by his colleagues' opinion. Schacht was guilty of 'serious imprudence,' no more; and he, Donnedieu, would not bear the responsibility for imposing any sentence on such an old man.

In this conversation with Francis Biddle, Lawrence swore that he had not spoken 'at all' to Professor Donnedieu—the very fact that Biddle noted those words suggests that he had his own opinion on the matter. He was furious, calling the Frenchman a sentimental old fool who was using his heart, not his mind. 'It is shocking to say that the fate of other defendants should affect Schacht's fate.'

General Nikitchenko, informed of this unusual turn of events, described it as unjust, and unsupported on the evidence before them.

He threatened to put in another dissenting opinion, basing it on his fellow judges' 'methods of arriving at such a conclusion.' Judge Biddle however urged him not to. 'Let us not air publicly our frank private discussions,' he said. He could see his American colleague Parker grinning; Parker said he was proud to be associated with a man like Donnedieu who had the courage to change his mind. Lord Justice Lawrence was also smiling broadly; he patted the French professor on the back, and said that he was now expressing a correct legal result.

'I thought it was my duty,' said Donnedieu, 'to say only what I thought—frankly, without hypocrisy—and considerations of policy do come in. We talk here privately, not for publication.'

Biddle stated that they should *never* refer to anything except what is found in the record of judgement, and they should never reveal what occurred at these secret sessions. Fortunately he wrote those words down too, and all is now revealed.

LIKE GÖRING, Field-Marshal Wilhelm Keitel now spoke of himself as a candidate for the firing squad. The death sentence would not surprise him in the way it would General Jodl.[10]

Keitel's defence attorney had noticed in the final weeks of the trial how upset his client had become as each day brought fresh documents to light, both positive and negative, genuine and forged, and documents deliberately held back until the last moment to trap the field-marshal in denials and contradictions. 'I am fighting not to save my neck,' he told his son, 'but my face.' The banker Schacht had lost his face, he felt for example. He spoke mockingly of the despicable way that both Albert Speer and Hans Frank had wriggled, saying 'Frank is beyond hope, he revoked his own testimony at the end in his closing statement.' Speer had evidently hoped to buy his way out to freedom. The field-marshal recalled with wan contentment how Speer had gaily waved farewell to the rest of them when he was driven away alone from Mondorf, as though that was the end of the affair as far as he was concerned; he had then turned up in Nuremberg after all. He had straightened up a little toward the end, once he saw that his earlier posturing had got him nowhere.[11]

Keitel's eldest son Karl-Heinz wrote daily notes on these last conversations with his father. Worn down by the mental torment of the trial and lif in the prison cell, the field-marshal was twice close to tears. Father and son spoke quietly about the future of Germany and about the inevitable conflict between east and west that seemed to be approaching.[12] Privately Keitel once added in a resigned sort of way that the Führer had seen much of this coming quite realistically and very accurately too. Given that every other country had begun to rearm, Hitler had in his opinion no choice but to launch a preventive war, since Germany could never win in an all-out arms race. The Führer had roundly dismissed all the misgivings that his advisers had incessantly put before him. 'One man must have the will and must then allow nothing to distract him. One must have faith, otherwise one might as well give up there and then. Hitler had considered himself the only man capable of generating the faith that was an essential requisite for victory.'[13]

His face pale and gaunt, the field-marshal warned his son that Germany must on no account opt for east or west as yet: she must bide her time.[14] Over in the United States many of Germany's finest experts were already working under pressure for future wars, for example the best technicians from Speer's ministry. General Jodl was even firmly convinced, said Keitel, that the Russians were keeping in being the German army which they had encircled in the Courland in April 1945 and that it was still in existence as such. 'It may come to pass,' believed Keitel, 'that Germans will be forced to fight against Germans if it should come to a military conflict, which God forbid.' He pleaded with his son to keep a weather eye on the situation.[15]

Keitel was in no doubt whatever what lay in store for him: he had countersigned or p.p.'d too many orders issued by Hitler and by Göring too, and the allegations against him about slave labour and the notorious order for the liquidation of Soviet commissars were accordingly far graver than those against Göring or Fritz Sauckel.[16] He still maintained that Hitler had ordered some things of which virtually all the defendants were unaware. 'Life at the Führer's Headquarters,' said Keitel, 'was literally like living behind barbed wire, just like at Nuremberg—only as the chief of the High Command.'[17] Three days later Keitel added: 'In World War One, as chief operations officer I shared with my commanding officer tactical responsibility for an entire division. In World War Two as a field-marshal and chief of the O.K.W. I was permitted to issue orders only to my driver and my valet.'[18]

Father and son also talked about the true stories behind many a historic episode—about the background to the Blomberg–Fritsch affair, about the execution of General Friedrich Fromm, about Keitel's letter to Rommel ordering him to commit suicide, and about the putsch planned in June 1934 by S.A. Chief of Staff Ernst Röhm against Hitler and the Reichswehr, as the armed forces were then known. 'Himmler can't have had a finger in the Röhm putsch,' Keitel's son recorded after their talk on September 19, 1946. 'Daddy was at the time commander of an infantry division in Potsdam, and he and his operations officer Major von Rintelen got wind of the putsch in good time and reported it to Blomberg [the Reich defence minister] who at first refused to believe it. It was a putsch by Röhm against the regular army. He wanted to turn his S.A. into a militia, a people's army, get rid of the professional army and become war minister himself. His S.A. officers were to become the officer corps of the future.'[19]

From 1933 on Germany had pursued the right foreign policies, summarised the field-marshal, according to his son Karl-Heinz Keitel after their last conversation on September 28, 1946. If only they had not had to resort to these terrible methods: the methods only made sense when viewed in the context of the constantly deteriorating situation and, said the field-marshal, the Führer had seen everything he had warned of confirmed by the decisions announced at the Yalta conference in February 1945. Once the ferocity of his methods had dimmed with the passage of time, Adolf Hitler would be viewed by history as a genius. Every great revolution in history had gone agley, said Keitel; but Hitler had simply not had the time to do things in an evolutionary way.[20]

❖ ❖ ❖ ❖ ❖

Having decided the fates of the twenty-one defendants, the judges had now turned to the fate of millions—the members of the indicted organisations. The French alternate judge Robert Falco set the ball rolling by finding only three such organisations to be criminal, the Gestapo, the S.S., and the political leaders. John Parker agreed that they should leave out the Reich cabinet, the S.A., and the General Staff, while the High Command as such was not 'an organisation.' Francis Biddle went much further, urging that they leave the organisations out of the judgement entirely. 'It is a shocking view,' he said once again, 'to convict men without trial, which is what we are doing.'

Sir Norman Birkett however felt that since the organisations had been indicted, to avoid making any declaration about their criminality now would be 'a political mistake.' They should however specifically exclude the small-fry people like Nazi block-leaders (*Blockleiter*) and cell-leaders (*Zellenleiter*), the lowest rungs on the street- and factory floor-level of the Party organisation. There was no case against the S.A., certainly not after the Röhm purge of 1934. The Gestapo should be declared criminal, and the S.D. He felt that to declare the entire S.S. to have been a criminal organisation was 'very troublesome,' and they should be more specific where they could. The S.S. had committed crimes at Oradour-sur-Glane, and in the Warsaw Ghetto. It had provided, he said, about thirty thousand guards—principally Waffen S.S. men—at the concentration camps; and in November 1938 the S.S. and Gestapo were chiefly responsible for the outrages against the Jews. (Despite having listened to all the evidence, Birkett was wrong on both counts: the concentration camp guards were never provided by the Waffen S.S., and Himmler was perhaps surprisingly one of the loudest to protest at Dr Goebbels' excesses during the 1938 Kristallnacht pogrom.)

The Russians showed themselves surprisingly moderate on this issue. Lord Justice Lawrence spoke on behalf of the British, agreeing that they were being asked to lay down a 'novel form of jurisdiction,' but the situation itself was novel. That should not make them hesitate to exercise discretion. 'It is only a matter of procedure,' his Lordship argued (at which point Biddle entered the silent comment: 'Gawd!') 'So we shouldn't shrink from it. We shouldn't distrust other courts. We shouldn't,' he continued, with a self-deprecating smile at this moralising lecture, 'allow ourselves that attitude of mind.'

After a lengthy exposition on the political consequences of making the wrong decisions, Biddle suggested they put it to a vote. He, Lawrence, and Professor Donnedieu voted for declaring the Gestapo, S.S., S.D., and the political leadership criminal organisations, and for declaring all the others not criminal. Nikitchenko voted to include them all.[21]

FROM WASHINGTON Justice Jackson cabled to Nuremberg the recommendation that the prison psychologist Dr Gilbert be allowed to remain on duty until the day of sentencing, 'and perhaps afterwards until the executions,' to which he dutifully added the rather hollow qualification, 'if any.' Jackson thought some of Gilbert's most important observations might be made during that period.[22]

But Judgement Day was repeatedly postponed. Drawing up the final opinion and judgement was taking longer than the judges had expected. Biddle went to Paris on unspecified duties for a few days. He didn't return until mid-day on September 16, when he found his colleagues again bogged down in a discussion on war crimes and crimes against humanity. He remarked that they would have to postpone the Judgement Day again; on the following day Lawrence and Birkett agreed, and they settled on a week's postponement.[23]

As the day approached Colonel Andrus, back in Nuremberg, called secret conferences of his security officers to go over all their plans. He wanted nothing to go wrong—no dramatic assassinations of the defendants, no suicides, no disturbances to detract from the solemnity of the occasion. Nobody was to be allowed to bring handbags or cases or any kind into the courtroom. No visitors or unauthorised people were to be allowed onto the floor of the Tribunal.[24] For the two critical days he ordered the numbers of German civilians in the building reduced, an army cordon thrown round the whole area, a show of force starting at the Grand Hotel, road blocks established on all roads into the Nuremberg–Fürth enclave, and additional searches of all defence counsel when they arrived.[25]

Since pressure for seating would be intense on the final morning and afternoon Andrus ordered all unnecessary tables taken out and extra chairs brought in, with extra seats added to the prosecution and defence tables, and seating for up to six defence lawyers, the rest having to sit on the floor. The army would issue tickets of different colours to admit to the two sessions. On the final day, when the Tribunal would pronounce the sentences on each defendant, tickets to the visitors' gallery could admit one person in the morning and a different person in the afternoon. No Germans would be admitted at all except for newspapermen, who would be packed into the press gallery. '[The] defendants will all be downstairs,' ordered Andrus, 'and each in their turn will come up to be sentenced. Two sentinels with a club for each man.'[26]

On September 29 the prisoners' wives were ordered to leave Nuremberg. Emmy Göring came to see her husband before leaving.

'Don't you believe,' she pleaded, 'that we three shall one day be together—in freedom?'

'I beg of you,' he adjured. 'Give up hope.'

21: **Prize Day**

TEUTONIC SAGAS relate that after the great battle with the Mongols on the Lechfeld plain, where the armies of two different worlds had clashed in violent and bloody massacre, the spirits of the fallen warriors had continued the struggle for three more days above the clouds. So it had been in Nuremberg too: where the city's face bore the terrible scars of the mortal struggle between Germany and her enemies which had ended in May 1945, the ghosts had continued the struggle for sixteen more months. But there the parallel ended: the armies were unequal now; one side was unarmed and had few friends.

As the members of the Tribunal, decked out in all their finery, filed onto their rostrum on the last day of September 1946 to begin pronouncing judgement, many if not most of the twenty-one prisoners in the dock at Nuremberg had long known in their hearts just what their fate would be; the prosecutors knew it, the judges knew it, and the German people knew it too.

An ugly little row had already soured the atmosphere. Under the provisions of Article 25 of the London Charter, the Control Council had appointed a Quadripartite Commission of four generals—the American General Roy V. Rickard, the British General E. J. Paton-Walsh, the French General L. Morel, and the Russian General P. Malokov—to administer the executions. This commission had demanded the right to sit prominently on the courtroom floor with the prosecution staff while sentence was pronounced. As chief U.S. prosecutor Robert Jackson had refused this demand point-blank: 'The impropriety of playing up the executioners before the judgement of guilt had been rendered or sentence imposed does not seem to have occurred to such mentalities, if that is what they can be called by courtesy,' he acidly recorded.[1]

On this last day of September 1946, as the Tribunal began to read out its judgement, the courtroom was packed to capacity with ambassadors, generals, newspapermen, lawyers, and—to Jackson's vexation—the executioners. Under pressure from above he had finally allowed them to occupy inconspicuous seats in the gallery, where they now gloated and glowered like the *tricoteuses* of the French Revolution.[2]

Five separate passes were required to enter the courtroom that day. Every ticket had been snapped up. The competition for seats had been tougher than for Max Schmeling's championship fight with Joe Louis in 1938. The world's photographers wanted to take telephoto pictures of each defendant as he learned his fate, but the Tribunal had refused to allow them in. For the first time cameras and arc-lights had also been excluded. The courtroom was shrouded in unnaturally sombre hues. An air of expectancy hung over the whole building.

Taking it in turns, the judges read out the lengthy document. As Lord Justice Lawrence began reading the judgement in his dispassionate voice, Jackson recognised with relief that despite the frontal assault by Professor Donnedieu the Tribunal had both allowed and sustained the main conspiracy charge—in fact to Jackson it seemed that they had relied in large part on Göring's own admissions under cross-examination.[3]

After a lengthy introduction, the judges turned to the culpability of the individual defendants. Göring's was addressed first. He was found guilty on all four counts of the indictment, and in particular of the charge of conspiracy to wage aggressive war. As Jackson later claimed, still mentally fighting that duel with the Reichsmarschall, this charge would have been difficult to prove had it not been for the admissions boastfully made by Göring during those difficult days when he had been given the run of the witness stand.

'His guilt is unique in its enormity,' pronounced Lawrence. 'The record discloses no excuses for this man.'

The other verdicts followed. Altogether nineteen of the twenty-two defendants were found guilty, and four of the indicted organisations were declared to have been criminal in character—the leadership corps of the Nazi party, the S.S., the S.D., and the Gestapo. To Jackson's dismay, however, the Tribunal acquitted the S.A., the Reich cabinet, the General Staff, and the High Command (the O.K.W.), arguing that their structure was too loose to be considered a 'group' or 'organisation.' While Jackson welcomed the Tribunal's condemnation of the officers of the General Staff and the O.K.W. as 'a ruthless military caste' who had been 'responsible in large measure for the miseries and suffering that have fallen on millions of men, women, and children—they have been a disgrace to the honorable profession of arms,' he reported to President Truman that he found the acquittal 'otherwise regrettable.'[4]

There were three acquittals of individuals. Schacht, Fritzsche, and Papen were acquitted on all counts. As he had threatened to do, the Soviet judge Nikitchenko put in a strong dissenting opinion against their acquittal (and calling for the conviction of the Reich cabinet, the General Staff, and the O.K.W. as criminal organisations too.)[5] As Schacht's acquittal was announced, Göring was seen to tug off his earphones in annoyance and slam them down.

ACQUITTED DID not mean free; these three men were not eager to venture forth into an inhospitable new Germany, and they pleasded with Colonel Andrus to extend the hospitality of Nuremberg jail until such time as they could be escorted away under American protection to freedom. They wrote:

> To Colonel Andrus:
> We herewith request accommodation at the Nuremberg jailhouse until such time as transportation under American protection can be laid on.
> FRANZ VON PAPEN, HJALMAR SCHACHT, HANS FRITZSCHE

The Americans offered to transport them to any place in the American Zone and told them they would be turned loose at 9:15 P.M. on October 4.[6] For some reason Schacht turned down the American offer. Perhaps he had already learned that the disgruntled victors were putting pressure on the German authorities to resume the prosecution where they had failed. As he was released from his cell, German police stepped forward and arrested him. A German court sentenced him to eight years' imprisonment as a major offender under the denazification laws enacted by the Control Council in Berlin. He served two years in solitary confinement, and was eventually released in 1948. The world of banking absorbed him again as though there had never been a blemish on his character.[7]

❖ ❖ ❖ ❖ ❖

In their judgement, the Tribunal had been less severe on Speer than on any of the other defendants. Speer believed his tactics had worked. His jubilant lawyer Dr Hans Flächsner told him, 'After listening to that I think you'll get perhaps four to five years!'

On October 1 the Tribunal reassembled to pass sentence.

One by one the prisoners were brought up by sentinels into the dock to hear their fate.

Göring was first, stepping through the lift doors at three P.M.

Lawrence read out the sentence: 'Defendant Hermann Wilhelm Göring, the International Military Court sentences you to death by hanging.'

Hanging—not a firing squad. His face betrayed no emotion. He was followed by Ribbentrop, who attracted the same sentence—to Jackson's surprise—without flinching, Keitel and Kaltenbrunner, the Gestapo chief, heard the same words; the latter bowed barely perceptibly before he turned on his heel and returned to the elevator. Altogether twelve of the defendants—Göring, Ribbentrop, Keitel, Kaltenbrunner, Bormann, Rosenberg, Jodl, Frank, Frick, Streicher, Sauckel, and Seyss-Inquart—were sentenced to the gallows. Martin Bormann, trapped by Russian tanks in a Berlin street one day after Hitler's suicide, had in fact swallowed cyanide before the war was over.

General Jodl stood to attention in the dock, and as he too was sentenced to death by hanging his bald, kindly features relaxed briefly into an expression of disbelief, to be replaced as swiftly by an expressionless mask.[8] Justice Jackson had privately felt the greatest respect for General Jodl, who was obviously not a political soldier like Keitel.[9]

Schirach and Speer were sentenced to twenty years in prison, Neurath to fifteen, and Dönitz to ten. Hess, Funk, Raeder were given life sentences.

Jackson gathered his papers, said farewell to his colleagues, and flew back to Washington. The executions were no concern of his—they were for Colonel Andrus and the army, whom he despised, to administer.

THE SENTENCES confounded Jackson's expectations. Schacht, whom Jackson had found the 'most contemptible,' had been let off scot-free. Dönitz, who the British and American naval experts had warned could not be branded a war criminal on the available evidence, had been sentenced to ten years in jail; Jodl, in Jackson's eyes a respectable 'soldier's soldier,' would be delivered to the rope; and Speer, whom he would have acquitted, would be consigned to Spandau prison for twenty years.

Was Jackson dismayed? Are lawyers ever disagreeably surprised by their handiwork? Probably not. He had fought these men to establish a legal principle, and he had seen that principle upheld.

That the trial had been fair, Jackson was convinced. Looking at the similar trials in France, and the exclusively U.S. Army trials conducted at Dachau, he was proud of his own record in comparison: In France the courts condemned 2,853 people to death and executed 767; but the French resistance summarily executed 8,348 people without trial.[10] The U.S. Army war crimes trials at Dachau were a mockery of the law: defendants and witnesses there were savagely beaten or intimidated to make them sign false confessions; hooded prisoners were subjected to mock trials, 'condemned to death,' and offered a 'reprieve' if they would sign statements incriminating other prisoners.[11] Jackson recognised that U.S. Army officers in Nuremberg had brutalised aspects of his own trial, but on balance he was satisfied with the objectivity of the result. All the defendants agreed they would have suffered far greater indignities at the hands of their fellow-countrymen, had they been put before German courts.

In most cases, the basic justice of the sentence passed at Nuremberg was undeniable: German courts, constituted under German laws existing in the war, could have disposed of many of the defendants for their actual responsibility for known murders—the killings after the Röhm putsch, the widespread liquidation of political enemies or racial groups, the murder of enemy prisoners-of-war.[12] Even so, Jackson was grateful that the prosecution had not been required by the Charter to recommend a penalty for each defendant. In the first place, he did not believe in the death penalty as such, but as long as it existed in the world he would have had little alternative but to demand it for all these defendants without distinction. In a secret meeting of the chief prosecutors he had once pointed out: 'We should take the position that we have indicted nobody who is not guilty.' And he shrewdly jested 'We ought to let the dock decide this question on a majority vote. They are so bitter against each other that in this way a majority could easily be found to hang each man in the dock.'[13]

Over the years that followed, there were curious inequities which are apparent only in retrospect: For health reasons Grand-Admiral Raeder was allowed home from Spandau jail as early as 1955 and Funk in 1957; but the half-blind and half-deaf deputy Führer Rudolf Hess, who was the only man to have undertaken, at risk to his own life, a step to end the madness of war in 1941, would be held as a prisoner at Spandau, crippled with arthritis, until his still unexplained death there by strangulation in August 1987.

❖ ❖ ❖ ❖ ❖

The silence that encased each of the condemned men now seemed even more impenetrable as they returned to their cells. Göring found Gilbert hovering around the door, satisfied his curiosity with one brief word, 'Death,' and asked to be left alone.

Keitel had ceased writing his memoirs on September 29, as he learned that sentence was to be pronounced. Learning now that he had only a few more days to live he would spend the next ten days feverishly writing down his memories of the last days in Hitler's headquarters. 'The death sentence,' he wrote to his counsel on the day it was pronounced, 'has come as no surprise to me, but I am very deeply upset about the way it is to be executed. I beg of you under these circumstances to avail me of your selfless assistance once more, to help me make a plea for my execution to be changed to a soldier's death by firing squad. I consider it pointless to ask more than that.'[14] His wife joined in his plea, adding her request to his that there should be no demeaning plea for clemency.[15] Ending his hand-written memoirs with the Latin word *Finis,* Keitel put down his pencil on October 10, then lifted it for one last time to add these doleful words: 'I began my term as a prisoner of war on May 13, 1945 at Mondorf; I was transferred to a prison cell at Nuremberg on August 13, and am awaiting my execution on October 13, 1946.'

After hearing the death sentence pronounced, General Jodl had returned to his cell in a daze; he did not want to fill his numb heart with hopes, he wrote, but would just allow its beat to fade away. It is obvious that he had not really expected this sentence. 'It's my fault that you didn't yet receive my wristwatch and lighter,' he wrote to his young wife

Luise, 'because I didn't want to lose sight of them as I was expecting the sentence to go differently.'[16] He threw himself onto his straw palliasse and resumed his reading of the *Book of the Orient* by Base; he planned to write to Luise again the next day and he could not rid himself of a desire to take her up in his arms and comfort her. 'Let's not talk about me,' he wrote her now. He had written much the same once during the trial: 'I am not what is at stake here; my own person is of no consequence whatever in this trial.'

He had lost his appetite. Dr Pflücker came bustling round to offer help, but Jodl told him he wanted only to be alone.

'You're a true Roman,' the German doctor told him.

'I'm not as good as they were at controlling my emotions,' the general found himself replying. 'I've got too bold a spirit and too big a heart.'

How much misery it would have spared his young bride, he reflected (as indeed did Keitel), if Count von Stauffenberg's bomb had killed him on July 20, 1944 as it had Lieutenant-General Rudolf Schmundt, Luftwaffe General Günther Korten, and the stenographer Heinrich Berger. He involuntarily remembered the last letter he had received from Irma, his first wife, as she lay dying. 'I'll keep on writing,' her letter had ended, 'so long as anything occurs to me to write, and thus this letter will never end, just as our love will never end.' 'I too would like to keep on writing,' the condemned general wrote to Irma's young successor. 'But I am running out of paper.'[17]

The next evening, writing to her again, he sensed something like a clamp tightening on his heart 'just as it always does when I am suffering bitterly.' He had felt like this as Irma died, and he had felt it again as he had had to sign the death sentence on Germany, the surrender document, at Rheims on May 7, 1945.

Indignation about the injustice of it all seethed within him. What then was he supposed to have done differently? When his defence attorney had asked this question, it had been greeted with a blank and unhelpful silence by the entire courtroom. Whether one assassinated the legal head of state or obeyed his orders it seemed to make no difference: in both cases one was headed for the gallows.[18] 'Perhaps,' he mused, 'a just man has to die in order that his tomb can become the cradle of a new international law.' Perhaps with his own sacrifice he was saving the lives of countless others. Perhaps there would now follow a long interval of peace.[19]

THEIR DUTY done, on October 2 Lord Justice Lawrence, Sir Norman Birkett, and the other judges left Nuremberg by air, as did their wives and staffs.[20] Sir David Maxwell Fyfe and his prosecution team also left Nuremberg that day.

The executions were to take place fifteen days, excluding Sundays, from the day of sentencing. Undisputed king of his own castle now that the lawyers had gone, Colonel Burton C. Andrus stepped up security precautions in the jailhouse still further, to ensure that nothing went wrong before then. He refused Göring all further outside exercise, and did not allow him the regular showers due to him on the fourth and eleventh. Prisoner-health was now a matter of indifference. Sudden searches were the order of the day. On the fifth Andrus ordered the straw palliasse on Göring's cot changed without warning. During each of the remaining seven interviews outside his cell, Göring was securely handcuffed to a sentinel.

Under Article 29 of the London Charter of August 8, 1945, the four-man Allied Control Council in Berlin had been vested with the powers to 'reduce or otherwise alter the sentences.' Many of the condemned men proudly asked their lawyers not to submit pleas for clemency. Often the lawyers overrode their wishes. Between October 2 and 5 seventeen appeals were submitted; most of them were two or three pages long, but Ribbentrop's ran to fifteen pages and Hess' to forty-seven.[21]

Among those of the condemned men who forbade their lawyers to enter appeals was Jodl but he changed his mind. 'I wasn't at first too happy about the appeal,' he wrote to his Luise on October 3,

> but when [Professor] Exner read out to me today once again the grounds for the sentence it was clear to me that I owe it to you and to my own name to set out in a document what is false and what is unjust about the verdict. Because, let them do what they want to me, it is my ambition that one day you will see my name cited in Germany with awe; it is for that alone that I shall have died, not for fame or fortune, for Party or for Power. Since I have learned that not even those who were acquitted have dared venture forth into the new German 'freedom' without being hounded with hatred everywhere they go I have begun to cherish death.[22]

His former chief Field-Marshal Keitel had calculated on October 3 that the hangings would take place in fourteen days' time, once the sentences had been confirmed. 'It has been a great help in squaring up to the Tribunal as I did,' Keitel wrote to his son on October 3, 'that I have for a long time been aware of what my fate would be.' If he was still proud of one thing, it was to have spoken nothing but the truth throughout the ordeal.[23] To the Control Council, and especially to those members who had been soldiers themselves, he addressed this request: 'I will willingly give up my life in the expiation demanded by my sentence, if my sacrifice will speed the prosperity of the German people and serve to exonerate the German armed forces from blame. I have only one plea: to be granted a death by firing squad.'[24]

Grand Admiral Raeder actually appealed to the Control Commission for the death penalty, as he could not face a life sentence. Göring's attorney applied on October 4 for the Council to commute the sentence or alter it to a firing squad; writing on his behalf, defence attorney Dr Otto Stahmer protested to the Council that Göring had been a brave officer in World War One, and one universally respected for his chivalry; he referred once more to his very real efforts to restore peace to Europe, and argued that there was not the slightest evidence that Göring had ever known of 'the extermination of the Jews carried out by Himmler.'[25] Jodl too asked for the firing squad.[26]

All of the appeals were rejected by the Allied Control Council in Berlin. In effect, there was no appeal. The Russian and British governments had ordered their representatives, the military governors, not to reduce the sentences. The British military governor, Air Chief-Marshal Sir Sholto Douglas, later revealed that after the sentences were announced Ernest Bevin, the British foreign secretary, had sent him a top-secret cable instructing him to confirm the sentences and to ignore any appeals. The archives broadly confirm this: Fearing that the Control Council might actually reduce the sentences, the Labour cabinet, meeting in London on October 7, decided to send a telegram instructing Douglas that 'from a political point of view it would be an advantage if there were no alterations of the sentence.'[27] This was the ultimate injustice of Nuremberg, the final interference of the legislature with the judiciary.

The Control Council's records show that the appeals came before it on October 9 and 10: after a short discussion the four wise men decided not to hear any of the German defence counsel, and to confirm the execution date for the sixteenth. All the petitions, whether for clemency or the firing squad, were denied, though not before there had been some discussion on the petition of General Jodl in particular, since there was a degree of consensus that he had been a brave and upright soldier and as such was entitled to stand before a firing squad. With his instructions from London firmly in mind, Sir Sholto Douglas argued that since the general had neither protested against Hitler's criminal orders nor resigned, the gallows was more appropriate. 'In my examination of the evidence,' he claimed in an early version of his memoirs, 'I had discovered that Jodl had been instructed by Hitler to sign the order for the execution of the 50 RAF prisoners after the mass escape from Stalag Luft III. He had protested to Hitler that this was illegal, but he had then done as he was told and signed the order. In doing that, so far as I was concerned, he had signed his own death warrant.'[28] He later denied that he was motivated by a sense of personal revenge. There is in fact no evidence to substantiate Douglas' claim that it was Jodl who had signed the warrant, nor was any introduced before the Tribunal.

The American member, General Joseph McNarney, spoke in favour of Jodl's request; the Soviet general Sokolovsky demanded hanging, because of the German general's role in the planning of BARBAROSSA. The French general Pierre Joseph Koenig was inclined to allow Jodl the firing squad, but the chairman gave his casting vote in favour of the rope. So hanging it would be. The Russian tried even at this late stage to reverse the acquittals of Schacht, Papen, and Fritzsche, and to obtain a death sentence on Hess instead of life imprisonment, arguing that Hess, Hitler's deputy in the party and the third most important man in Hitlerite Germany, was 'responsible for all the crimes committed by the Nazi regime.'[29]

JODL'S OWN attitude towards the Tribunal had been conditioned by the urge to establish the historical truth of the war as he knew it. As early as March 1946 he had written to his wife:

> My thoughts are still in a whirl about past events. I keep finding myself wondering whether it wouldn't have been my mission to have acted without any regard for my own personal defence but in such a manner as to establish the real historical truth. I would have done so, if two powerful forces had not acted in the opposite direction. Firstly this was not the principal task of the Tribunal, and it could have blocked any such attempt with the legal objection of 'irrelevant.' And it would inevitably have failed, because the archives of the other side are closed.
>
> Secondly I ask myself, did you ever really know this man [Hitler] at whose side you led such a thorny and ascetic existence? Did he perhaps just trifle with your idealism too, abusing it for dark purposes which he kept hidden deep within himself? Dare you claim to know a man, if he has not opened up the deepest recesses of his heart to you—in sorrow as well as in ecstasy? To this very day I do not know what he thought or knew or really wanted. I only knew my own thoughts and suspicions. And if the shrouds now fall away from a sculpture we fondly hoped would be a work of art, only to reveal nothing but a degenerate gargoyle—then let future historians argue among themselves whether it was like that from the start, or changed with circumstances.
>
> I keep making the same mistake: I blame his humble origins. But then I remember how many peasants' sons have been blessed by History with the name, The Great.[30]

Jodl's long path to the gallows had begun as soon as he reached Nuremberg prison. The truth about him was that before the Nazis came to power in 1933 he had actually been an opponent of Hitler and his movement, and at first after formally swearing the oath of allegiance to him on August 3, 1934 he had regarded him only like any other head of state. Before October 1938 he had never attended any military conference with him. 'On September 3, 1939,' he would recall, 'Keitel introduced me to the Führer in his train on the way to the Polish front line.' From that day on until April 23, 1945 General Jodl had remained in close official contact with Hitler as chief of the Wehrmacht operations staff. Most of his service diaries had fallen into Allied hands in 1945.[31]

At denazification proceedings in Munich in 1953 a German court effectively cleared the late General Jodl of the Nuremberg charges and rehabilitated him posthumously, basing its decision in part on the fact that four years earlier the eminent and universally respected French member of the Nuremberg Tribunal, Professor Donnedieu de Vabres, had stated that in his view the conviction of Jodl had been without merit and a miscarriage of justice.[32]

❖ ❖ ❖ ❖ ❖

During the entire Nuremberg proceedings the licensed German press had behaved in a despicable manner, which was however intelligible given that they and their publishers were dependent on the favours of the victorious powers, and have remained residually so until far into the Nineties. Dr Nelte depicted the German journalists to Keitel's son in the following terms— they were thirstier for blood even than their Allied counterparts, and left unreported anything in the proceedings that spoke for the German people, or from the German point of view.

Berlin workers had gone on strike in protest at the three acquittals. Hearing this, Jodl commented bitterly that these same men had barely two years earlier voluntarily worked fourteen or sixteen hours a day in the arms factories; this just showed once more how politics and propaganda could be made the whores of any government in power. 'What a majestic character any beast of prey is compared with homo sapiens,' he mused.[33] Judging by this episode, said Dr Nelte, a German trial would have led to an even bigger bloodbath—a pure show-trial. With the exception of the Russians, all the judges had taken fright at their own bravery. But much had been shown to be different from the way that Jackson and the prosecutors had naïvely portrayed. There were many misconceptions that had been set right. Yet there was now a palpable sense of fear that they might have inadvertently set a precedent by pronouncing the death sentences. 'The prosecution failed to achieve their ambition of setting the defendants at each other's throats,' said Nelte, and perhaps this was the very reason why they had indicted such defendants as Schacht and Papen in the first place. Despite everything the defendants had been perceived to display a dignified and proper attitude and a real comradeship toward each other.[34]

GENERAL JODL lay on his bed, cleaned his cell for the umpteenth time, and dozed in and out of sleep while he pondered whether he still had enough time to write to Luise an account of his mountain-climbing exploits; instead he listened to the organ in the church next to the prison 'as it wafts its pure and gentle notes through the walls to me.'[35] He slept like a babe without any kind of sedative because he was worn out, because he had strong nerves, and because he had come to terms with a fate whose closing act had never caused him a moment's fear in life.[36]

The little cardboard table began to fill with greetings cards from all over Germany. It was like a birthday. He admitted to a sense of complete apathy toward death, perhaps even an eagerness to be with his little Irma once again: he was leaving his living wife, to rejoin his departed one.[37]

He wrote to Luise again on October 8:

> Back on April 21 [1945] in Berlin I thought I'd be able to take you with me. It was obvious to me that it was going to be a fight to the bitter end, and that was why I had got hold of the Tommy gun. But I was thinking that it would be a battle for the Berghof [on the Obersalzberg] and after that for the Kehlstein eyrie, which François-Poncet [a Richard Wagner devotee] so aptly dubbed the Gralsberg. So I was thinking that you'd be with me in the tunnels of the Obersalzberg and that I would be fighting this last fight in my own beloved countryside surrounded by my mountains, perhaps even with my head buried in your lap. As simple and as beautiful as that. That was how I had pictured it.[38] Those were the days! But then Hitler had announced on April 22 his fateful decision to stay on in Berlin, and fight the last battle there.

THE ALLIED Control Council ruled that the convicted men would be allowed to see their lawyers until the afternoon of Saturday October 5, to set their affairs in order. They would be allowed to see their families only once more, for an hour-long farewell visit on any day of their choice between Sunday the sixth and the twelfth.[39]

Streicher, who had consistently refused to lodge an appeal, was treated less leniently; his oldest son, a Luftwaffe officer, was allowed to see him for only three-quarters of an hour before the execution.[40] In one of these last conversations, Streicher referred to his sworn enemy Benno Martin, the police chief (*Höherer S.S.- und Polizeiführer*) in Nuremberg, who had tried to 'work his passage' by making out that he was a resistance hero. 'If I were to open my mouth,' hinted Streicher, 'Martin would be for the high jump.' He took the precise meaning of these words to the grave.[41] Streicher said he had originally contemplated suicide, but never attempted it, deciding it was more important to testify once more about why he had combated the Jews.[42] He never changed his mind about the Jews: least of all here at Nuremberg, which he regarded from start to finish as the final proof of all that he had ever taught about them.[43]

He told his son as they parted that at the foot of the gallows he would swear fealty to Adolf Hitler once more. 'Göring, Keitel, and Jodl will also die like men,' Streicher believed.[44]

❖ ❖ ❖ ❖ ❖

Altogether Dr Otto Stahmer had seen his client Göring 145 times, including twice each on October 4 and 5; on the last occasion, Göring handed to him through the sliding panel his wedding ring and his blue-leather attaché-case to take out of the prison to Emmy. Nervously clutching that wedding ring she came on the seventh, spent a while with Father Sixtus O'Connor, the prison padre, then was allowed in to Room 57 at 2:45 P.M. to say good-bye to her doomed husband. On his way over from the jailhouse, the Reichsmarschall strutted ahead of the sentinel chained to him, Private Russell A. Keller, pulling the little soldier along and roaring: 'You see, I am still a leader.'[45]

General Jodl had precisely the same feeling, as he was taken in handcuffs to see the two professors Exner and Jahrreiss. 'I was a bit sad,' he wrote his wife, 'that they told you about the manacles. But believe me these things don't hurt me, and I don't regard myself at all as the one who is in handcuffs; I regard myself as the one leading my escort, both intellectually and physically.'[46] He took leave of his two loyal law professors and asked his wife afterwards in a letter to tell the two men that he hoped they would forgive him for having deprived them of a year of their lives.[47]

As Göring said farewell to his wife, three men stood in a semi-circle behind him holding Tommy guns. He said that he hoped life would not be too hard on little Edda. 'You may die with your conscience pure,' Emmy assured him. 'You have done here in Nuremberg all that you could for your comrades and for Germany.' She felt that in a way he too would be dying in action.

'I had no idea that you were so brave,' he said, lifting his voice so she could hear him through the glass.

'Listen closely,' she then said, putting her mouth close to the glass. 'Do you still have your comb?' 'Yes.' 'And brush?' 'Yes.'—It was a curious little exchange, but Russell Keller probably understood no German. Without altering the cadences in her voice Emmy asked, 'Do you still have what Ango gave you?' 'Ango' was Reichsleiter Victor Bouhler, who had swallowed cyanide to kill himself in June 1945.

'No,' he said. 'I would have liked to say yes, because that would make it easier for you.' (He was not lying at this moment: he did not have a cyanide pill. He would still have to get that brass cartridge, somehow, out of the store-room.)

'Do you have yours?' he asked; and as she shook her head, he stated confidently: 'They won't hang me. Not that. It's the *Bullet* for me. They won't hang a Hermann Göring.' Did she understand what he meant by The Bullet? He had chosen his words most carefully. Emmy seemed relieved. 'Shouldn't I go now?' she asked. 'I'm quite calm, Emmy,' he said as he stood up to go.[48]

Back in his cell, Dr Pflücker brought him a sedative. 'I've just seen my wife for the last time, my dear doctor. Now I am dead. It was a difficult hour, but she wanted it. She bore up magnificently. She only faltered toward the end.'

On October 11 at mid-day the American psychiatrist Dr Gilbert had already notified the condemned men that the Control Council had denied their appeals. 'Perhaps he thought he was doing me a favour,' wrote Jodl. 'Perhaps he was looking for a particular psychological bon-bouche. Whatever.'[49]

JODL HAD saved up the final visit from his wife to the next day, the very last permitted day, Saturday October 12. He was glad now, as he looked into her eyes for the last time, that they were both innocent of even the slightest ray of a craven hope. It was time to write *finis* properly.

On the evening before her visit he wrote her a letter, beginning with the words: 'When you receive this letter we shall have said farewell to each other for ever and we shall know that nothing can ever change that fact.' The general was now almost looking forward to death. 'The thought that I am now free will console you, as free as any man can be. No cell and no sentinel, and always I can be with you and protect you. Every evening when the bells peal you will sense that I am there.' He had a bath, and he bathed almost as fastidiously as though it was his wedding on the morrow. He caught himself actually being careful not to waste the soap, although there was no longer any need for economy. He told her he was going to leave in his cell all his linen and anything else that he did not require for dying in, so that Luise could use them to help others who were in need.[50]

All of the condemned men parcelled up their remaining possessions, and wrote final letters. Not everything reached the next of kin. When Colonel Andrus left the prison in November to return to the United States he would take with him folders of original letters pencilled in the obligatory block letters by the more prominent prisoners—letters from Richard Walther Darré to his brothers and sisters, from the Hungarian Regent Nicholas von Horthy to 'Field-Marshal Stalin,' a note from Walter Buch giving his wife power-of-attorney, an emotional letter from Franz von Papen to his wife, and similar letters addressed by the other prisoners to their wives, children, and sweethearts, as well as historical statements by Kurt Daluege and Rudolf Höss (the former commandant of Auschwitz.)[51] Many other such documents are now in private hands, indicating that the American officers who received them did not forward them but retained them for their souvenir and autograph value. Among these is a one-page sheet written by Ribbentrop:

> To the Prison Administration.
>
> Please hand all my personal effects as listed below to my attorney Dr Georg Fröschmann, of No. 36 Weilandstrasse, Nuremberg, to hand to my wife Anneliese von Ribbentrop:
>
> 36,000 marks in cash less the amount handed to my wife Anneliese von Ribbentrop by Colonel Andrus. I believe the latter amount was 3,600 marks.[52]

One gold wristwatch by Longines. Dr Fröschmann or Mr Kuntze has the prison's receipt for this gold watch;

Various pictures and letters, which are in the linen bag in my prison cell;

Two defence documents (blue) also in the linen bag;

One suit, one pair of grey trousers;

Diverse linen;

My memoirs, pages 108 – 126;

One note on policies on the Jews;

Two gold dental bridges. J. VON RIBBENTROP[53]

To the same prison office, Seyss-Inquart addressed the following pencilled instructions:

My personal effects here are to be handed over to Frau Gertrud Seyss-Inquart, Austria. Frau Gertrud Seyss-Inquart is my wife and has the free right to dispose of all these effects among my next of kin as she alone decides.

The following valuables are on hand according to the Statement of Inventory dated May 31, 1945

1 wristwatch (Zentra);

1 wristwatch (Lusina–Geneva);

1 table clock (Jungklaas);

1 table clock (Haller);

1 medal (Cross);

500 plus 710 equals 1,210 Reichsmarks as per receipts on hand. One leather coat, one raincoat, one leather vest, one black attaché case, one brown attaché case, one black dispatch case, one boot bag with lock, one pair of boots, one black document pouch, Goethe's *Faust*, poets' anthology, etc.

Nuremberg, October 13, 1946 DR ARTHUR SEYSS-INQUART[54]

ON OCTOBER 13 Keitel sent one last letter to his son. Perhaps sad not to have received word from Karl-Heinz—the Americans were being selective about whose mail they forwarded—the field-marshal commented only that the women of the family had written to him, and added: 'Enough said. What cowards we men are.'[55]

Unaware that Gilbert had beaten him to it, at mid-day that day Colonel Andrus visited each of the condemned men and informed him that the Control Council had rejected all appeals for clemency. Jodl portrayed the grim little scene for his wife. 'At twelve-thirty this afternoon the colonel and his retinue came into my cell. I buttoned up my collar, and stood at ease by the wall under the window with my hands behind my back. He briefly informed me that the Control Council had rejected the appeals lodged with it. I nodded, he nodded back, and I then said: "This decision too is an honour for me."' After that the general returned to his reading of Knut Hamsun's *The Wanderer.*[56]

That night the prisoners could hear heavy trucks shunting to and fro in the prison yard a hundred feet away. The gallows equipment was being unloaded. Kept awake by the hammering, as three sets of gallows were erected in the gymnasium, Fritz Sauckel began screaming. Göring heard the screams, and wished there was something he could do to help the former gauleiter.[57] His erstwhile Staatssekretär Erhard Milch heard the hammering coming from the gymnasium that night—he had been returned here from Dachau to face a trial of his own—and wrote in his diary: 'Is that the gallows? I wonder what mood the poor condemned men are in when they hear it too!'[58]

The next day First Lieutenant John W. West unlocked Göring's cell and conducted a snap search of all the Reichsmarschall's belongings; he shook out the bed to search for contraband or suicide instruments. T he condemned Reichsmarschall talked volubly throughout, West later testified, and seemed unduly happy.[59]

From this night on Jodl found that he could not sleep without sedatives after all. Unlike Streicher, he was now receiving a deluge of mail; some evenings he was already getting replies to letters that he had sent out only that morning. The American army censorship authorities were being curiously helpful in his case. 'It was hatred that cut me down,' he wrote, wonderingly, to Luise, 'but it will be love that bears me up to the stars.' There was such an abundance of affection in the countless letters that now reached him that his cell seemed to him like a garden, blossoming and fragrant with spring greenery and shoots. 'And it is all for me, the man who was supposed to be despised and deserted by everybody out there.'[60]

Did Jodl know how many days he still had? Almost certainly.[61] He had also made a mental picture of the execution itself—'the final hour, which is to be leered at by the camera lenses and taken down by the pencils of the newspaper reporters.' He intended that they should take due note of his pride and his contempt for his executioners.[62]

On the fourteenth, Göring casually asked Pastor Gerecke if he knew the execution hour. The American pastor replied that he did not, and to Göring's dismay also refused him Holy Communion. 'I refused him the Lord's Supper,' the pastor testified afterwards, 'because he denied the divinity of Christ who instituted this sacrament.... he became more discouraged because I insisted he couldn't meet Edda, his daughter, in heaven if he refused the Lord's way of salvation.'

It was now October 15, the last day alive on earth for the condemned men. Suddenly uncertain, Jodl wrote: 'I still don't know whether the moment of departure comes in tomorrow's morning hours or not. Father Sixtus, who was here this afternoon, said nothing. I have received all the farewell letters, including yours—but I'm saving reading that up for the end until I know when for certain.' Father Sixtus said he would come round once more, 'so that might mean this evening.' A few hours later, at seven P.M. the general added: 'Father Sixtus just saw me and now I know for sure.' The padre handed to him the very last letters from his wife and many, many more. After he had gone, Jodl nervously wrote a few more lines to the letter: 'That I have made mistakes I know, but if there is a God in Heaven, as I think He is, and as only He can be, then he will forgive me my sins.'[63]

Göring also realised that tonight was the final night. He sat down in his cell No. 5 and began writing one last document. It was found later in the cell:

> I find it tasteless in the extreme to stage our deaths as a show for sensation-seeking reporters, photographers, and the curious. This grand finale is typical of the abysmal depths plumbed by court and prosecution. Pure theatre, from start to finish! All rotten comedy!
>
> I understand perfectly well that our enemies want to get rid of us—whether out of fear or hatred. But it would serve their reputation better to do the deed in a soldierly manner.
>
> I myself shall be dying without all this sensation and publicity.
>
> Let me stress once more that I feel not the slightest moral or other obligation to submit to a death sentence or execution by my enemies and those of Germany.
>
> I proceed to the hereafter with joy, and regard death as a release.
>
> I shall hope for my God's mercy! I deeply regret that I cannot help my comrades (particularly Field-Marshal Keitel and General Jodl) to escape this public death spectacle as well.
>
> The entire effort to stop us from doing harm to ourselves was never motivated by concern for our welfare, but purely to make sure that all would be ready for the big sensation.
>
> But *ohne mich* [count me out]! HERMANN GÖRING.

Further down the gangway, Jodl watched the last hours of his life ebbing away, reading the last letters and the final lines from his wife until his eyes were filled with tears. 'In my head I can already hear the funeral march of the infantry and then more faintly the familiar melody—I wonder if you can hear it too: *Ich hatt' einen Kameraden*, Once I Had a Comrade.' He laid down his pen for ever with the words which he would shortly proclaim from the steps of the gallows: 'I offer greetings to my loved ones. I salute my comrades. I send greetings to my eternal Germany.'[64]

The Americans instructed the German doctor, Pflücker, that the condemned men were to be awakened at 11:45 P.M. and notified that their execution was imminent.

THE AUTHORITIES (the 'Quadripartite Commission for the Detention of Major War Criminals') had nominated forty Allied officers to attend that night's executions—including a Soviet, British, American, and French general; two newspapermen of each nationality; twenty-four assorted American officers; and two Germans, Dr Wilhelm Högner and Dr Jakob Meister, respectively the prime minister and chief prosecutor of Bavaria's puppet government.[65]

Since Jackson had refused the demand of the four generals of the Quadripartite Commission to be allotted prominent seats on the floor of the courtroom on the day when sentence was passed, they took their revenge now and denied to both the Tribunal and the prosecution staffs access to the execution chamber erected in the prison gymnasium (not that Jackson had wished to be present.) Jackson's own representative, Whitney R. Harris, had flown specially to Nuremberg to be present, but the door was closed in his face.[66]

The Americans had advised all newspapers that no information would be given out before a certain 'M' time—five A.M. Nuremberg time. Andrus had ordered the eight hand-picked journalists to be locked up until the cadavers of the hanged men were safely spirited out of the building. At 5:50 P.M. Selkirk Panton of the London *Daily Express* had sent a final dispatch to his editor using the curious telegraphese developed by journalists: 'OFFICIALLY ANNOUNCED TONIGHT UNDER SECRECY BAN ADEIGHT [to eight] REPORTERS TO WITNESS HANGINGS,' to which he added, 'AM NOW BEING TAKEN INTO PRISON WHENCE EYE UNPERMITTED FILE ANYTHING UNTIL HANGINGS OVER.'[67]

The journalists were taken into the jailhouse at eight P.M. for a final peep at the condemned men. Kingsbury Smith, reporting to International News in New York, was so anxious to scoop his colleagues that before being escorted inside he sent off a fictitious account. He had 'seen,' so he cabled to New York, Göring slumped on his small iron cot, his heavy shoulders sagging against the bare whitewashed wall, reading a well-thumbed book about the birds of Africa. '[I] stood looking at Göring over [the] shoulder of [a] prison sentinel whose duty it was to observe Göring constantly.... With the eyes of an American security guard watching him like a cat watches a rat, Göring had little hope of emulating Ley's act [that is, suicide] even if he had entertained such an idea.' The journalist was struck, he continued, by the prisoner's 'criminal features, the mean and mad face, the lips with a rat-trap tightness about them.' He informed New York that the Reichsmarschall would have the longest walk to the gallows, as Cell No. 5 was at the far end of death row.[68] Having sent off the cable in advance, he joined his seven colleagues for the actual visit to the cells, after which they would all be locked in for some hours. It was a cable he must have regretted for the rest of his life.

❖ ❖ ❖ ❖ ❖

The prisoners were in no doubt that they were about to star in their final roles. General Jodl took extra care to shave; he wanted to be spick and span to the very last minute of his life. 'They shall not see some run-down and pitiful sinner,' he had written privately a few days earlier, 'but a proud soldier who is calmer and more composed than his tormentors.'[69]

In Cell No. 5 Göring too knew that these were the final hours. Private First Class Gordon Bingham had seen Dr Pflücker hand him a white envelope late that afternoon; Göring poked into the envelope, then poured a white powder out of it, probably sugar, into his tea.[70] When Private Edie went off duty at four-thirty P.M. he had seen Göring asleep with his arms across his chest.[71] About three hours later the pastor Gerecke visited the cell. 'He seemed lower than other days,' he testified but that was not surprising in view of things to come. They spoke quietly about the other condemned men, and Göring asked particularly about poor Fritz Sauckel. Once again the Reichsmarschall criticised the method of execution, saying: 'It is most dishonourable for me, because of my former position with the German people.' Gerecke broke the silence that followed those words, to ask once more if he had completely surrendered his heart and soul to his Saviour. Göring replied that he was a Christian, and felt at ease.[72]

When the guard changed again at eight-thirty P.M. Private Gordon Bingham looked through the peephole and saw Göring lying on his bed, wearing his boots, pants, and coat and now holding a book in both hands. After twenty minutes, recalled Bingham, the prisoner sat up and laid the book at the head of the bed; then stood up, urinated—which took him out of sight for a few seconds—sat on the bed and took off the boots and pulled on his slippers. Picking up the book, he walked to the table and picked up his eye-glass case two or three times, looked at the glasses in it, and put it down again; perhaps it was just absent-mindedness, agreed Bingham. Then he began tidying his cell, moving the writing materials from the table to the chair, and standing his boots in one corner of the cell. Then he prepared for the night: sitting on the bed he took off his slippers and socks, removed his coat and laid it at the foot of the bed, then pulled off his trousers and put them with other clothes into the box on the floor by the table.

For a few minutes he pottered around like this, then climbed heavily up into the bed, pulling the blanket up beneath his arms. Private Bingham could see the prisoner shifting restlessly for fifteen minutes, stroking the blanket between himself and the wall with his left hand, while occasionally massaging his forehead with the other.

Escorted by Lieutenant James H. Dowd, at 9:05 P.M. Dr Pflücker came round for one last time, delivering pheno-barbital tablets to the prisoners who could not sleep. Pflücker gave Göring's cell a miss. 'I'll see him later,' he said as they passed Cell No. 5: Göring usually took his red and blue pills at eleven P.M. Dowd glanced through the peephole; he was struck by the composure of the Reichsmarschall, lying flat on his back seemingly asleep.[73]

At nine-thirty Pflücker was already back with the pills for Göring and Sauckel. Escorted this time by Prison Officer First Lieutenant Arthur J. McLinden, the German doctor murmured to the prisoner for about three minutes. Göring had guessed that the execution night had arrived. 'I know it,' he told Pflücker, and asked if he ought to undress or not. Pflücker, forbidden to reveal yet that this was the night, answered evasively—so he testified. 'But there is certainly something up,' Göring persisted. 'One sees all sorts of strange people in the passage, and there are more lights burning than usual.'[74]

The sentinel saw the doctor hand over a pill or capsule which Göring put into his mouth there and then. (Pflücker later admitted in testimony that he had filled Göring's pill with baking soda, not sedative, as he did not want to risk his really falling asleep this night: a significant admission.) After speaking a few more words, Pflücker took his pulse on the left wrist, then left the cell followed by McLinden. The Reichsmarschall wished both men 'Gute Nacht' as they left.[75] Before leaving Cell No. 5 Pflücker and Göring shook hands, which must have confirmed to Göring that his death was nigh. Shaking hands was of course absolutely forbidden, but what punishment could they inflict on either man now? 'The last time, it was difficult for a doctor not to shake hands,' he would explain simply to the board of investigation. That the prisoner could still speak indicated of course that he did not yet have anything bulky concealed in his mouth.

The investigation shows that Göring's left hand now stayed out of sight at his side. Perhaps Pflücker had slipped the brass cartridge containing the ampoule to him as he took his pulse. The condemned man lay for fifteen minutes, his head turned slightly to the left, facing the wall, perhaps to keep the light off his eyes. Once he pointed the fingers of his right hand at the sentry when the inspection light clattered accidentally aside. Once he laced his hands together and held them over his eyes for a few minutes.

Twice more the other sentinel, Lieutenant Dowd, passed by, at 9:35 and at 9:40 P.M., glancing in each time. Göring had not moved. He just lay there, thinking, listening to the prison sounds. It seems logical that Pflücker's visit was the historical turning point in his suicide endeavour: had Göring obtained the cyanide ampoule many hours before, he would surely have used it earlier, rather than risk leaving it too late—the door bursting open, men pinioning his arms behind his back, the handcuffs clamping his wrists together.

At ten-thirty P.M. he decided the time was coming. Would it be eleven, or midnight? Brave though he was, he still lingered on. Cyanide makes for an unpleasant death. The Tribunal had made this plain enough in its every reference to the Holocaust. The prisoner heard the guard being changed. Glancing up once, he saw Bingham looking through the porthole. Private First Class Harold F. Johnson came on duty: he saw Göring still lying on his back in the prescribed position. Once, five minutes later, Göring casually lifted his left hand, clenched, as though to shield his eyes from the light beam. 'He lay perfectly motionless till about 10:40,' testified Johnson, 'when he brought his hands across his chest with fingers laced and turned his head to the wall.' The ampoule, unbroken, must by now have been transferred to his mouth. 'He lay that way for about two or three minutes,' said Johnson, 'and then placed his hands back along his sides. That was at 10:44 exactly, as I looked at my watch to check the time.'[76]

A FEW minutes earlier, at about ten-thirty P.M., Captain Robert B. Starnes, the chief prison officer under Andrus, had walked to the covered catwalk that led from the jailhouse to the rear entrance of the Palace of Justice. A 'trapdoor' had been built into this catwalk, and here he met the six members of the hanging crew, the Third Army Execution Team, and let them in. He walked them over to the gymnasium, and pointed out some objects that were to be placed inside—no doubt the eleven coffin-crates and stretchers. Göring, their prize prisoner, was due to go to the gallows first. Inside the gymnasium, the newsreel cameramen were loading their cameras and testing the arc-lights. The ten lamps bathed the scene in an unnaturally bright white light. Everything was running like clockwork. It was about ten-fifty P.M. when Starnes set off for the jailhouse where the eleven condemned men were in their cells. A rope round his neck, Göring was slated to drop through the trapdoor to his death at midnight.

❖ ❖ ❖ ❖ ❖

In the criminal wing of the jailhouse, Starnes found pandemonium. The lights were blazing at full voltage, telephones were ringing unanswered, army boots were clattering on metal catwalks. As the captain broke into a run toward Cell No. 5, he picked up the pungent odour of bitter almonds. He could smell it from half the cell-block away. It was the unmistakable calling-card of hydrogen cyanide.

First Sergeant Daniel E. Hauberger met him.

Göring, he screamed, was dead.[77]

22: The Lion Escapes

THERE IS no doubt that Hermann Göring's 'escape'—for that is how he at least had regarded it—sent a thrill through Germany at a time when starvation stalked the ruined streets and prison camps, and the humiliation of defeat and the rigours of the Allied occupation were barely being endured. Even in the United States, wrote Dr Gilbert, the ordinary people were impressed by the bravado with which Göring had pulled off this coup.[1]

As Douglas Kelley too would write, Göring had stoically endured his long imprisonment in order that he might face down the Allied tribunal and browbeat the prosecuting lawyers on their own terms. This he had done, and by doing so he had re-established himself with the German people. 'In his last moments of life,' wrote Kelley in his memoirs of the trial, 'he took matters into his own hands and, once again the dominant figure, cheated the hangman of the Allied nations. His suicide, shrouded in mystery and emphasizing the impotency of the American guards, was a skillful, even brilliant, finishing touch, completing the edifice for Germans to admire in time to come.'[2]

GÖRING HAD once confessed to a certain curiosity about what it was like on the Far Side.[3]

At 10:47 P.M. on the night of October 15, 1946 he found out. Private First Class Harold F. Johnson, watching steadily through the peephole, saw Göring, lying with his back turned toward him, seem almost imperceptibly to stiffen. Then he heard a hideous blowing, choking sound escape the prisoner's lips. Johnson ran to the phone and called for the corporal of the relief. Sergeant Gregory Tymchyshyn came clattering down from the second tier, taking the iron steps two at a time.[4] They could see Göring writhing in agony, already dying.

The sergeant ran off to the Prison Office and came back with Lieutenant Norwood G. Croner, the prison officer, and the American chaplain Gerecke. Croner looked through the peephole; his first thought was that Göring was having a fit. He sent word to First Lieutenant Arthur J. McLinden. As Croner went off to fetch the German doctor from the Prison Office, McLinden unlocked the cell door and went in with the chaplain.[5] Private Johnson followed them in, holding the inspection lamp.

Göring's right arm was hanging limply out of the bed. Gerecke took the pulse and announced, 'Good Lord, this man is dead.'[6]

Pflücker arrived. 'I went to Cell No. 5,' he testified a few days later. 'The Chaplain [Gerecke] was standing on the right side of Göring. Göring lay back and made one short expiration. I took his pulse. It was fading away; his face was getting blue-green and looked like artificial light.'

'Göring is dying,' the doctor announced. 'There is nothing we can do.' He turned to the officer standing in the doorway: 'Get Roska!'[7] First Lieutenant Charles J. Roska was the American prison surgeon, who was standing by in the gymnasium to perform his other duties of the night.

While examining the dead or dying Reichsmarschall, Pflücker would later maintain, he heard a 'rustling noise under the blanket' and on pulling it aside he found two envelopes immediately under Göring's hand, clutched to his abdomen. So he told Captain Robert B. Starnes, the chief prison officer.[8] Pflücker's own testimony continued: 'I removed the blanket because I had to examine his heart and then I saw the envelope [*sic*] in one hand. I told the Chaplain to look at the envelope that I found. He took the envelope and felt it and saw that there was a cartridge case in it and two or three sheets of paper. I did not take the paper out. I tried to open the cartridge shell. There was nothing in it. I saw there was no powder or anything in it. I put it back in the envelope and gave it to the Chaplain and asked him to please remember that I had found it in Göring's hand.'

Perhaps this was an odd insistence on his part. He evidently expected to be blamed and even arrested for what had happened. Remembering how Himmler had committed suicide, he asked Dr Roska, who arrived at five to eleven, to check Göring's mouth for glass splinters.[9]

Roska determined that Göring had no pulse and no audible heartbeat. He could see splinters of glass in his mouth.

He would testify, 'I had just taken an envelope from Göring's hands containing a brass cartridge,' but there was nothing else in his hands.[10]

Gerecke's testimony confirmed this.[11] By now Chief Prison Officer Starnes had arrived, having left the six-man hanging crew, as it were, hanging around. As he plunged into Cell No. 5 the cyanide fumes were so strong that they stung his left cheek. He found Gerecke and the German doctor fumbling around Göring's heart and checking his pulse. 'He's dead,' said the chaplain; and Dr Pflücker echoed him, 'He really is dead.'[12]

AS THE clock struck midnight—according to Selkirk Panton's dispatch finally sent off at 3:15 A.M. to the *Daily Express* in London—a white-faced and breathless Colonel Andrus, speaking without notes, admitted to the eight newspapermen: 'Göring is dead by suicide.'[13] He said that Göring was due to have been hanged first.

Andrus told the pressmen that they had found 'one' envelope in the cell, torn open at the top, marked in pencil 'H. Göring,' containing three pencilled notes 'and a small brass container.'

Suddenly the newspapermen were on top of the biggest story of the whole trial. Basil Gingell cabled this to Reuters early on October 16: 'HOW HE OBTAINED POISON ET [and] HOW HE MANAGED ADKEEP IT ADESCAPE DETECTION IS NOW BEING INVESTIGATED.' He was among the eight newspapermen who had been conducted around the condemned men's cells at nine-thirty P.M. and they had seen Göring sleeping peacefully in his two-tone blue silk pyjamas. 'EYE HAD MYSELF PEERED THROUGH LITTLE GRILL ... HIS PODGY HANDS RESTING ON COUNTERPANE, HIS RIGHT HAND WAS CLENCHED. EYE NOTICED IT [and] IT MUST HAVE BEEN IN GRIP OF HIS CLENCHED FIST.'[14]

Anxious to divert the blame from his army officers, Andrus identified unnamed German prison workers as the chief suspects.[15]

❖ ❖ ❖ ❖ ❖

Göring's suicide threw the whole timetable out of kilter. The generals ordered the executions delayed. At 11:45 P.M., a hastily convened Board of Investigation consisting of Colonel B. F. Hurless, Lieutenant-Colonel W. Tweedy, and Major Stanley T. Rosenthal unlocked and entered Göring's cell. They found Göring's lifeless form lying on the cot, his skin already taking on the bluish-grey hue of cyanosis, and with one eye broadly winking in lifeless humour at them. In a two-hour search they turned over every inch of the cell: they checked every box and carton, the empty toilet-roll core, the pack of playing cards, but found no clue to how he had pulled off this stunning conjuring trick.

Intending to treat the condemned men with the same dignity as hitherto, Colonel Andrus had planned to permit each man to walk freely from his cell to the execution chamber in the gymnasium. After Göring's suicide however the four generals of the Quadripartite Commission instructed him to shackle the remaining condemned men. Their handcuffs were to be unlocked and removed only once they were inside the execution chamber, and exchanged for the 'silken cords' with which their hands were to be bound for the actual drop.

This inevitably led to an unbecoming delay while each man faced the gallows, and after the first two the Commission would tell their representative to hasten over to the jailhouse and bind each condemned man in his cell.[16]

Each condemned man was now frog-marched to the execution chamber separately. The Americans were in a worse state of jitters than the men they were about to kill. 'Every man-jack of them died very bravely,' recorded Field-Marshal Milch proudly a few hours later. 'One Ami said: "They had ice in their veins."'

FIRST TO be brought in and offered to the rope, at 1:29 A.M., was Hitler's foreign minister Joachim von Ribbentrop, his hands bound tightly behind him with a leather strap.

He and most of those who followed through one or other of the three trapdoors died with their Fatherland on their lips. Ribbentrop's last words were written down: 'God save Germany and be merciful on my soul. My last wish is for a united Germany, understanding between east and west, and peace on earth.' Then he was led up the thirteen steps to the trapdoor; it opened the moment the black hood had been thrown over his head, and he dropped out of sight beneath the black drapes.

The second execution team was already waiting with Field-Marshal Keitel at the next gallows. His hands were strapped behind him. A few halting words came out, ending with: 'More than two million German soldiers died for their Fatherland. I now follow them and my sons who gave their all for Germany!' In soldierly fashion he marched up the steps. As he dropped, the heavy trapdoor swung back, smashing every bone in his face. The same thing happened to the next condemned men: the gallows had been wrongly designed.

The colonel conducting the executions swayed on his feet, and asked General Rickard if it was permitted to smoke. By way of answer first Rickard, then several other observers, pulled out packs of Lucky Strike and lit up. The doctors went behind the drapes to check for signs of life.

Rosenberg went to the rope without a murmur.

Hans Frank had a smile on his face and it seemed he was genuinely penitent; he paused at the door of the chamber only to thank Colonel Andrus for the kindness with which the jail staff had treated him.[17]

Frick called out in a loud and clear voice, 'Long live the eternal Germany!'

Streicher, who had an injured knee, worried that he might not go upright to his execution as he had assured his wife and son at their last farewell; he had told them he had been specially practising walking without his cane.[18] He put a spin on the day's grim end which had probably not occurred to the rest: today was Purim, one of the high holy days of the Jewish calendar commemorating the deliverance of the Jews in Persia from destruction by Haman. 'Heil Hitler!' he called out. 'This is a joyous Jewish festival, but it is my Purim festival! The day will come when the Bolsheviks will hang the lot of you!' As the black bag went over his head, he began, half choked, to shout, 'Adele, my beloved wife—!' then he too had dropped.

Fritz Sauckel, about whom Göring had expressed the most concern, followed his fellow gauleiter, stammering only: 'I die an innocent man. God save Germany and make her great again!'

Then came Jodl, upright as Keitel before him, proclaiming at the foot of the steps, 'I send you greetings, my Germany!'

Seyss-Inquart was the last to be despatched. A soldier took off his eye-glasses, and the former lawyer said: 'I hope that this execution is the final act in the tragedy of World War Two and that people will learn from this example, so that truth and understanding can be restored among the nations. I believe in Germany.' He was hanged at 2:57 A.M.

AT 2:54 A.M., meanwhile, as Colonel Andrus meticulously recorded in a memorandum on 'Deliverance Times of Convicts,' Göring's carcass was 'delivered to the execution team.' It was dragged into the execution chamber twelve minutes after Seyss-Inquart's hanging, so that it might be viewed by the committee of four Allied generals and the two eager representatives of the new Germany, the Social Democrat Dr Wilhelm Högner, prime minister of Bavaria, and Dr Jakob Meister, his chief public prosecutor.[19]

Hermann Göring's lifeless remains were set down between the first and second of the three gallows that had been built.[20] His bare feet protruded stiffly from beneath the khaki blanket. One arm clad in blue silk hung over the side of the stretcher. The pyjama jacket was soaking wet, apparently from the army doctors' frantic attempts to revive him so that he could be hanged.[21]

The other coffin-crates were lined up next to Göring's and the bodies were put on top. Onto each cadaver was put a label with the man's name. Official photographs were taken of each. Streicher, Sauckel, Frick, Jodl, and Seyss-Inquart still had the ropes knotted round their necks. The faces of Keitel, Jodl, and Frick had been battered in.[22] The pillow beneath Frick's head was soaked with blood. Later the bodies were stripped naked and photographed again. On orders from higher authority, Andrus kept word of the executions secret until the bodies could be 'spirited away.'[23] The closed coffins would be removed to the American-controlled Dachau concentration camp and incinerated in the crematorium; the ashes were strewn into Munich's river where it ran past the foot of a garden in Solln.

JACKSON TOOK grim satisfaction from the criticism that was heaped upon the army for the botched hangings. In Britain and Germany the publication of the photographs was wisely forbidden, but in America many newspapers carried them, much to his annoyance; he had no sympathy with the condemned men, of course, but as a shrewd man he knew that the photographs would stir sympathies. 'People saw the dead Nazis and didn't see the six million dead victims,' he privately pointed out. 'I had a very low opinion of the Army's handling of the executions and of the publicity.'[24] He even drafted an angry letter to a national newspaper protesting about the 'ghoulish' treatment of Göring's remains—as befitting neither Göring's life nor whatever authority ordered it—but as a Supreme Court judge he had to avoid controversy and the letter was never sent.[25]

The now anti-Nazi German press representatives, what Dr Goebbels used to call the Journaille, abandoned what professional ethics they had ever had, particularly the journalist from the press agency DANA. Desperate for a scoop, he put out a lurid and totally fictitious account of the executions; unaware that the gallows had been erected indoors, he claimed to have witnessed the executions from a rooftop vantage-point. The next day he took refuge in claiming to have spoken of seeing not the actual executions, but the men being led into the execution chamber. This too was impossible, as Colonel Andrus established by checking all the rooftop views in question.[26]

The grisly deeds performed, one of Andrus' officers issued what is known to philatelists as a 'first-day cover,' a specially printed envelope bearing the Tribunal's emblem, a Nuremberg postmark, and the names of the hanged men; fortunately for his profits, he had waited first, and was thus able to include Göring's suicide as well.[27]

❖ ❖ ❖ ❖ ❖

Rumours abounded about the letters alleged to have been found in Göring's cell. People said there had been a witty, sarcastic, triumphalist letter to Churchill (there was such a letter circulated later—a forgery).[28]

What were the three notes that Göring had left behind? At the time nobody was told. The Control Council in Berlin, locking the letters in its safe, ordered that they be kept secret in perpetuity. Colonel Andrus was given the contents of only one letter, the letter addressed to him, dated October 11, 1946.[29]

Written, or at least dated, on the same day was a letter to his wife enclosed in an envelope with a letter to the chaplain:

> Nuremberg, October 11, 1946
>
> Dear Pastor Gerecke!
>
> Forgive me, but I had to do it like this for political reasons. I have prayed long to my God and feel that I am doing the right thing. (I would have let them shoot me.) Please comfort my wife and tell her that this was *no ordinary suicide*, and that she can rest assured that God will still gather me up in His great mercy.
>
> God protect my dearest ones!
>
> God bless you, dear pastor, evermore. Your HERMANN GÖRING.
>
> ---
>
> My only sweetheart!
>
> Upon mature consideration and after profound prayers to my God, I have decided to take my own life and thus not allow my enemies to execute me. I would always have accepted death by firing squad. But the Reichsmarschall of Greater Germany cannot allow himself to be hanged. Moreover, the killings were to be carried out like a spectacle with the press and film cameras there (I assume for the newsreel pictures.) Sensation is all that matters.
>
> I however want to die quietly and out of the public eye. My life

came to an end the moment I said my last farewell to you. Since then I am filled with a wondrous peace and I regard death as the final release.

I take it as a sign from God that throughout the months of my imprisonment He allowed me the means to free myself from this mortal coil, and that this means was never discovered. In His charity, God thus spared me the bitter end.

All my thoughts are with you, with Edda, and all my beloved friends! The last beats of my heart will mark our great and eternal love. YOUR HERMANN.

The letter to Colonel Andrus was one sheet of paper, which had been folded once vertically and once horizontally to fit into an upper pocket or a very small envelope. It read:

Nuremberg, October 11, 1946

To the Commandant

I have always had the poison capsule with me, ever since my delivery into imprisonment. On delivery into Mondorf I had *three* capsules. I left the first in my clothing so it would be found upon inspection. I put the *second* under the clothes rack when undressing and retrieved it when dressing. I concealed it so well at Mondorf and here in the cell that despite *frequent* and *very thorough inspections* it could not be found. During the court hearings I kept it with me in my high riding boots.

The *third* capsule is *still* in my little toilet case, in the round pot with the skin cream (hidden in the cream.) I could have taken this twice at Mondorf if I had needed it.

None of those entrusted with the inspections is to blame, as it would have been almost *impossible* to find the capsule. It would have been pure chance.[30]

To which Göring added this postscript:

Dr Gilbert told me the Control Council has refused to convert the manner of death to firing squad!

That settled old scores with Gilbert too. The letter was obviously designed to make Andrus look a complete fool, and at the same time to shift attention away from whoever had smuggled the lethal capsule out of the store-room to Göring between October 11 and 15.

Then, taking one of the last sheets of his headed notepaper (DER REICHSMARSCHALL DES GROSSDEUTSCHEN REICHES) and writing on both sides he had composed this defiant letter:

Nuremberg, October 11, 1946

I.

To the Allied Control Council.

I would have let you shoot me without further ado! But it is not possible to hang the German Reichsmarschall! I cannot permit this, for Germany's sake. Besides, I have no moral obligation to submit to the justice of my enemies. I have therefore chosen the manner of death of the great Hannibal. Hermann Göring.

It was clear from the outset that a death sentence would be pronounced against me, as I have always regarded the trial as a purely political act by the victors, but I wanted to see this trial through for my people's sake and I did at least expect that I should not be denied a soldier's death. Before God, my country, and my conscience I feel myself free of the blame that an enemy tribunal has attached to me.

The letter had also been folded once vertically and once horizontally, to fit into a regular-sized envelope. The other two letters were given the same date, October 11. There is of course the possibility that Göring wrote them at the end, and antedated them as a prank, to poke his finger in his captors' eye. Given his sense of history however, it is more likely that he did indeed write them on October 11, four days before the end. Where had they been since then? Surely not in his cell: their discovery would have led to the most urgent search for a means of suicide. The most likely hypothesis is that developed, without knowing of the dates on these letters, by American researcher Ben Swearingen: that Göring struck a bargain with an American officer, either directly or through Dr Pflücker, to get his hands on one of the cartridges he knew he still had in the baggage-room.

From this it follows that the American officer needed an alibi-letter or letters to protect him from inevitable investigation; that Göring then smuggled the letters out to him, several days ahead, in which he would 'confirm' to Andrus that he had had the poison ampoule with him 'all the time.' Late on October 15 Dr Pflücker then smuggled the envelopes back into the cell—first the one addressed to 'H. Göring' with the cartridge and then, after the suicide, the one containing the letters, which he thrust beneath the dying Reichsmarschall's hand, turning to the Chaplain Gerecke even as he did so and asking him 'to please remember that I had found it in Göring's hand.'

THERE REMAINED certain housekeeping functions for the generals of the Quadripartite Commission. On October 18 they met in Nuremberg, inspected the photographs, presumably those of the poison capsule and Göring's other effects, ordered the lesser ones and their negatives destroyed, and forwarded the rest to the Control Council in Berlin; they swore a suitable interpreter, a Mr N. Jacobs, to secrecy and appointed him to translate the first sheet of the letter which Göring had addressed to Colonel Andrus, and the originals of all the other Göring letters were sent off to Berlin, with no copies being made.[31]

In Hess' cell was found the speech he had intended to make at the end of the trial—describing his 'torture' at the hands of his British captors, and analysing what he saw as the causes of the war. These were an amalgam of Versailles, Soviet expansionism, Britain's chronic jealousy of Germany, and Germany's lack of Lebensraum. Rather startlingly he claimed that neither Hitler nor anyone in Germany had intended to hurt the Jews or anybody else, but that by means of mysterious 'hypnotic influences' the Jews had caused basically decent Germans to do these terrible things in order to discredit National Socialism. The same hypnotic influences had caused Hitler's military blunders, and the criminal behaviour of the otherwise honourable Englishmen.[32]

As for the captured regalia of the late prisoners, they made a sad little list: all of Keitel's medals won in two wars were ordered to be destroyed as well as his two Iron Crosses, his four wound-medals, his Luftwaffe dagger, and his field-marshal's baton; to the finance director of the U.S. zone, to help defray the costs of the trial, would go his two gold party badges. Jodl's three Iron Crosses, wound-medal, and 'various campaign ribbons' were ordered destroyed, as were Göring's famous Blue Max—the Pour le Mérite awarded him as commander of the Richthofen Squadron in World War One—and his two Iron Crosses; forwarded to the finance directorate 'after destruction of Nazi insignia' were his two spread-eagle Nazi party badges, made of platinum and studded with diamonds, and other gewgaws.[33] At a subsequent meeting the Commission ordered that since Mrs Alfred Rosenberg had written that she did not desire any of the personal possessions of her late husband these, 'being of insignificant value,' were to be destroyed, as well as the diamond-encrusted U-boat medal belonging to Admiral Dönitz, which was to be forwarded to the finance director 'after the swastika had been obliterated.'[34]

As for the papers left by the other men, which included their trial working notes, private letters to their next of kin, letters to the American military government, and autobiographical papers, the generals agreed that a working party should sort these into categories.[35] Among these papers forwarded to the Control Council were a diary kept by Keitel from August 12, 1945 to the date of his sentencing, October 1, 1946; a note to the German people by Sauckel, dated October 14, 1946; a sixty-two-page essay by Hans Frank on 'Material Leading up to the Outbreak of War'; all that was found in the cell of economist Walter Funk was a seven-page essay on 'The Birth of the Banknote'; in the cell of Speer, fifteen sheets of production figures 1940–45.

❖ ❖ ❖ ❖ ❖

Since the suicide of Göring, his cell had been kept locked and a guard posted to prevent unauthorised entry. On the morning of October 18, two days after the suicide, Brigadier Paton-Walsh, the British general, told his fellow generals on the Quadripartite Commission of his own deductions after viewing Göring's body, stating that the mortician had 'confirmed many of his deductions.' 'These,' he stated, 'inclined him to consider the enquiries in regard to the umbilical as of special importance.' He expected the laboratory tests would confirm or refute this 'solution.'[36] The laboratory tests however did not support his theory.

What had happened to the two envelopes, particularly the second envelope, the one with the hand-written address 'H. Göring'? To this latter envelope might cling the implication that an outsider had passed the cartridge to its addressee.

They searched Göring's personal effects in the Prison Office baggage-room, and found concealed in his toilet case, just as he had bragged, yet another identical brass cartridge, still charged with a glass cyanide ampoule. It was taken to the 385th Station Hospital for analysis.[37] Evidently the cartridge he had used had found its way from that store-room to his cell, a discovery which carried with it the ugly inference that an American officer was involved.

All of those who had held the store-room key were questioned under oath, and all testified in a stereotype answer 'that Göring received nothing from, nor had access to, the baggage-room during this period.'[38] The affidavits were all identical, except one: under re-examination, Captain Starnes, who had held the key to the room from October 1 to 15, testified: 'I ... can state positively that I did not personally give Göring anything from the luggage room, nor did he have access to that room during this period.'[39] Why the word 'personally'? Why did Starnes not use the standard denial that the others had?

Andrus was quick to point out that the psychiatrist Dr Gilbert had notified the condemned men as early as October 11 that their petition for clemency had been disapproved as soon as he learned of it through the newspapers, which was several days before the official notice arrived for Andrus to publish to the prisoners. 'This, of course,' he wrote to an American army doctor, 'gave Goering a good deal longer to make his plans and screw up his courage.'[40]

How Göring had managed to pull it off was a mystery, which was solved only years later by Ben Swearingen, who tracked down the fountain pens and watches which Göring had brought into captivity and had used to bribe that six-foot-two Texan officer, Lieutenant Jack Wheelis, to procure the vital cyanide capsule from the jailhouse baggage-room in the nick of time.[41] Charles Bewlay, a former Irish ambassador to Berlin and friend of the Görings, knew more than he ever admitted, but revealed in his biography of the Reichsmarschall that 'a non-German in the prison' had helped him get the capsule 'in the night before his execution.'[42] Göring's wife knew the officer's identity, but never revealed it. Their daughter Edda has stated that a letter revealing the name is in the hands of their family lawyer, with instructions not to open it before the man's death. In 1948 Werner Bross, the young north German lawyer who had been associate counsel of Göring in the trial, talked about the suicide with the American desk officer in the client–lawyer consultation room during the subsequent proceedings; Bross recalled, years later, that this officer tapped his large, expensive wristwatch and said, 'A present from Göring. Understand?'[43]

Wheelis is now dead, but it was probably no coincidence that his widow later put up for sale a very large, expensive wristwatch that Hermann Göring had given to him.[44]

GÖRING'S SUICIDE ruined Colonel Andrus' week, month, year—and indeed the rest of his life. Months earlier, the Templars had invited him to attend their dinner at the Criterion Restaurant in Piccadilly, London on October 19, in honour of Lord Justice Lawrence, Sir David Maxwell Fyfe, Sir Norman Birkett, and the Tribunal's other members of the Inner Temple's masonic Lodge.[45] 'Even with the Quadripartite Commission busy here,' he now wrote, apologising, 'and making great demands upon my time, I still would have arranged to come, but the suicide of that horrible criminal created so many complications that it was absolutely impossible for me to be away.'[46] In an act of petty revenge, he ordered the surviving prisoners' rations cut, and all bread and sugar allowances cancelled.[47]

Letters rained in on Andrus from far and wide with theories about how the wily Reichsmarschall had obtained the cyanide—hidden in the rim of his spectacles, passed mouth-to-mouth in a farewell kiss by Emmy; he patiently thanked their senders.

For days the wildest theories ran round the prison. People said that Göring had kept swallowing the cartridge whole: but it was about one and a half inches long, and how could he guarantee to recover it in time when needed? Moreover the brass threads showed no trace of fæcal matter nor was any found under his fingernails. This also scotched the second theory, casually (but perhaps significantly) ventilated by Dr Pflücker to the Board, that Göring might have kept the brass, screw-capped cartridge hidden under the rim of the toilet bowl; but the risk of flushing it away was great. On October 24 the Board re-entered the locked Cell No. 5 and solemnly examined Göring's toilet bowl and satisfied themselves that he could have placed the cartridge case in one of the two recesses at the rear of the integral porcelain seat. But this did not answer two questions: the cartridge had been in one of the envelopes; and how could he be sure that he would not suddenly be frog-marched into a different cell? The toilet-bowl theory was a red-herring planted by Pflücker. Besides, at no time during the hours before his suicide was Göring observed to have sat on it, only to have urinated into it.

Dr Pflücker testified that he had handed to the prison officer what he had found in Göring's hands. Starnes testified that these were 'two' white envelopes, letter size. 'I reached into one of the envelopes and withdrew a brass cartridge case with a cap on it.' (Had Göring really bothered to screw the cap back on?) 'I noticed also that both envelopes had folded paper inside with the writing on them that I recognized as Göring's own handwriting.' The envelope which had contained the poison ampoule was slightly torn at the end, where the cartridge case, had been extracted, and it was marked on the outside, 'H. Göring' or 'H. Goering'—a significant difference, indicating perhaps whether a German or American had written the name; regrettably, that envelope, which was later turned over to the British general E. J. Paton-Walsh, was not photographed along with the letters and other evidence. Starnes and Andrus had enlarged the tear slightly to see if anything else was inside; but it was otherwise empty.[48]

Starnes testified that he had handed the 'two' envelopes to Andrus with the cartridge case and cap.[49] By the time he wrote his memoirs, Andrus would recall only having been given 'a single folded sheet of paper,' found in Göring's bed. 'I took the paper along, unread, to the [Quadripartite] Commission Office, where the suicide investigation would almost immediately begin. I did not even try to read the note because if I did, it could have led to "prejudice."'[50]

There seems to be an important contradiction here, which might even indicate a wilful cover-up: although several witnesses testified without question that the cartridge had been inside the envelope with a torn corner, through which it had been extracted, the investigations began to centre on whether Göring had concealed it in his digestive system or in his navel all along; were they not aware of the envelope? If they were, did they discount it as a red herring? If they were not, why not? Had the army officers, beginning a cover-up, now concealed or even destroyed it? (The torn envelope has not been seen since; it is not in the safe with the three original letters, in the Berlin Document Center.) Even the Nuremberg jailhouse staff were instructed that the Reichsmarschall had hidden the capsule in his anus and then in the toilet bowl of his cell. After his suicide, all incoming prisoners were subjected to an anal examination.

The initial findings were that Göring had had the poison 'in his possession all along,' that he might have concealed it at one time in the 'cavity of his umbilical,' that at another time it was 'in his alimentary tract' (despite the absence of fæcal matter), and that he could have concealed it in the obscure recess of the toilet under the overhanging rim (which did not necessarily mean that he did). The document absolved the American sentinels, the other prison guards, and the German workers of any blame. The Board of Inquiry recommended Xraying prisoners in future.

'There was no abdominal wound,' wrote Andrus on October 24 in a confidential briefing of Brigadier-General Rickard, the American member of the Quadripartite Commission, 'much less any blood or bleeding wound, on the body of the suicide.' He did not believe that a messenger or the German cook could have smuggled the phial to him. He admitted that in theory it could have been passed to him by one of the lawyers in court, but it was rather thick to be concealed in a document, and it would have required sleight of hand as the lawyers were not permitted to shake hands or to reach across the barrier at the dock at any time. Clearly Colonel Andrus was at a loss to explain how Göring had pulled it off.[51]

He wrote to Dr Robert Kempner, once Göring's deadliest foe, a bitter, vindictive letter containing statements that stood in gross contradiction of the evidence. 'Your suppositions are all sustained. That man had the poison on him all the time. His navel had been subjected to an operation of some kind and readily provided a repository big enough for the cartridge case, and it is certain that he carried it at least part of the time there; also a considerable time in his rectum, as it was proven by laboratory tests. So, in his horrible self destruction, he was mouthing own dung.'[52]

Again in violation of the scientific evidence, the agreed findings of the special working party of the Quadripartite Commission on October 26 were:

> (a) The container holding the poison was in the possession of Göring from the time of his apprehension.
> (b) The container could have been inserted in the umbilical cavity and at some time was certainly contained in his alimentary tract.
> (c) There was no blameworthy action or negligence on the part of the U.S. guards and in particular of the guard on duty at the time of Göring's death.[53]

RELATIONS BETWEEN Andrus and his army superiors had always been strained, particularly since the beginning of the year. The Göring suicide spelt the end for him. *Time* magazine ran a blistering and in parts downright unfair attack on his professional capabilities. The Pentagon recalled him. At the end of November he quietly left Nuremberg and returned to the United States, his services as governor of the jailhouse prematurely terminated 'owing to the grave illness of his wife.'[54]

Andrus never forgave Hermann Göring for putting one across him. He blamed General Eisenhower, for having insisted on executions by hanging. Had a firing squad been permitted, he was sure that the Reichsmarschall would have gone along with that. Göring's successful suicide—if *in extremis* a suicide can be considered as a success—would prey on the colonel's mind until the end of his life. Moments before he died of leukæmia twenty-one years later Burton C. Andrus blurted out to his son, in the final delirium of death, 'I have just been told that Göring has committed suicide—I must go and see to this matter,' and he looked around for his uniform to get dressed.[55]

❖ ❖ ❖ ❖ ❖

At its meeting on October 25, 1946 the Quadripartite Commission instructed Andrus how to dispose of the hanged men's personal effects: all their medals and insignia 'bearing Nazi emblems' were to be destroyed; their clothing and personal possessions 'less precious jewels' were to be turned over to the next-of-kin along with any cash up to one thousand Reichsmarks. The rest of the precious stones and cash were to be turned over to the finance directorate. The money and valuables of those sentenced to prison terms were to be frozen and forwarded to the Reichsbank.[56]

Andrus afterwards turned over to Emmy Göring the late Reichsmarschall's personal effects—minus those things that the Reichsmarschall had given away to the American officers and those that others had purloined. She signed for them—the list read in full: '750 Reichsmarks, 1 traveling clock, 1 toilet case, 1 gold cigar case, 1 gold cigarette case, 1 pill box, 1 wrist watch, 1 square watch with chain, 1 cigar cutter and pencil holder, 4 semi-precious buttons, 2 cuff links, 1 gold pin ("evergreen twig"), 1 pearl stick pin, 1 silver cigar cutter, 1 antique pin, 1 watch in an antique case, 1 heart-shaped silver pin, 1 small watch set with diamonds, 1 cigarette lighter, 1 pocket divider and compass combination, 2 horse buckles,' together with two large suitcases, one hat box, and one fitted bag.[57]

It seemed appropriate that the convicted men's wealth should be confiscated to pay for the trial. According to a memorandum in Jackson's files, it had cost $4,435,719.[58] But the personal cost to Jackson, as to Colonel Andrus, had been incalculable. Through his absence at Nuremberg, he had lost his chance of becoming chief justice of the United States, perhaps even president, and through his sponsoring of the trial he had become a figure of controversy. His motives were misunderstood; he was linked in many eyes with the scandalous series of war crimes trials held concurrently with his own, by the military authorities. Worst of all, his dream of establishing a precedent for the prosecution of aggressive warmongering went unfulfilled; the International Military Tribunal remained the first and last court of its kind until the closing stages of the war in the former Yugoslavia.

Further international trials had been envisaged at the time of the London talks, but as the primary trial dragged on first the American public—who in real terms had to bear the cost—and then the British lost their enthusiasm for a second trial, which would have figured the principal German industrialists and financiers. The Americans began looking round for other groups of criminals to put on trial, as representatives of German industrial, economic, and diplomatic professions. The British declined to join in. Asked about putting on trial a number of German industrialists before a second International Military Tribunal, the British government were reluctant to get involved, proffering the rather vague argument that it would be an anticlimax and detract from the first IMT. The entire British prosecuting team refused to remain at Nuremberg, no doubt because of the loss of fees involved.[59]

Under considerable American pressure, the British agreed to put one field-marshal on trial, the redoubtable Erich von Manstein; there were some unquestionable ugly patches in Manstein's career, notably some executions of Jews in the rear army areas of which he had known and approved. But his was the first and last such trial in the British Zone, apart from a number of swift hearings—the estimate is 541 British trials, 275 Australian, five Canadian[60]—against concentration camp officials and other lesser criminals, around three hundred of whom were hanged by Albert Pierrepoint, Britain's official hangman, at the Hamelin jailhouse. The French, it is pertinent to observe, did not put one German general on trial.[61]

The Americans conducted at Nuremberg a number of 'subsequent proceedings' against one hundred and ninety-nine further defendants—generals, diplomats, civil servants, and industrialists.[62] Although they were formally dressed up as 'The People of the United States v. Erhard Milch,' and so on, it suited the Americans in later months to purport that these too had been international proceedings. The Americans hanged several hundred Germans at Landsberg fortress prison over the next two years. Pictures of these hangings in U.S. government archives display one haunting feature. In each case the man to be hanged—who often richly deserved his fate—was formally photographed, full-length, facing the camera at the foot of the gallows steps; the two sentinels gripping his handcuffed arms however stood with their backs turned to the camera, as did all the hangmen and their assistants on the scaffold.

The British government very deliberately and publicly washed their hands of the subsequent American trials. Replying to a Question in the House of Lords by Bishop Bell of Chichester, a spokesman said that His Majesty's government bore no responsibility for the proceedings conducted at Nuremberg since the end of the International Tribunal.[63] Asked his opinion on the Far Eastern International Military Tribunal which the Americans had concluded against twenty-eight Japanese generals, admirals, ministers, and diplomats in Tokyo, Justice William O. Douglas, chief justice of the Supreme Court, uttered the scathing condemnation: 'It did not sit as a judicial tribunal. It was an instrument of power.'[64] The eleven judges sentenced seven of the Japanese defendants to death, and acquitted none; the Tribunal was however notable for the dissenting opinions filed by the Indian and Dutch judges.

WHAT WAS the balance-sheet of Nuremberg? It was established there that the German attack on Poland was an aggression pure and simple. The defence thesis that the war against Russia was essentially a preventive war—which has now been conceded by Russian historians after fifty years' delay—was rejected by the Tribunal. Rather less convincingly the Tribunal also rejected the defence arguments that the German invasion of Norway in April 1940 was also essentially preventive in character—the British having refused to open their own secret files on this affair. Less well known is the important fact that the Tribunal was unable to describe the German wars against either Britain or France as wars of aggression.[65] Every allegation levelled against Germany's conduct of submarine warfare was also dismissed as unfounded during the trial. 'For obvious reasons no serious allegations were raised against Germany's aerial warfare,' said defence lawyer Otto Kranzbühler delicately, while reluctant to break the taboo imposed by the Allies on Germany's historians on this awkward topic.[66] Thus there was no mention in either the indictment or the judgement of the German V-weapons or the Luftwaffe's aerial attacks on Rotterdam, Coventry, Warsaw, and London. Scarcely less momentous for the German people was the judges' confirmation that the liquidation operations in Germany were generally unknown to the public, which meant that there could be no talk of a collective guilt for those crimes.[67]

The world saw Nuremberg as the old-fashioned practice of the victors putting the vanquished to the sword, behind a façade of retroactive law and elegant speeches. As the years passed this view was entrenched by the absence of similar trials where aggressive war was clearly established. The Soviet Union planned an aggressive campaign against South Korea, but as the *New York Times* was to comment in 1951: 'A powerful aggressor, if undefeated in war, cannot and will not be punished.'[68]

When the armed forces of Britain, France, and Israel conspired together and launched their attack on Egypt in 1956, Rudolf Hess' lawyer Alfred Seidl inquired of the British Foreign Office whether the British prime minister Eden was to be brought before any tribunal to account for himself.[69] The tragic truth was that Nuremberg had set no real precedent in international law. A resolution presented in 1946 to the United Nations Organisation relating to the codification of the principles established at Nuremberg was referred to the organisation's International Law Committee, and buried without ceremony.[70]

THE LAST word rests with the defendants and the writings they left behind them—some better left unpublished, like Robert Ley's demented outpourings, others improbably written for better times, like Rudolf Hess' various proclamations to the German people from his Nuremberg cell, written for the eventuality that he be 'appointed to take over the reins of government in the western zones.'[71]

The parade moved on. Two days before his execution, Jodl had written these moving words to his wife: 'It is already late and the lights are soon going out. When our friends come round to see you on the evening after my death that shall be my funeral parade. On a gun-carriage rests my coffin and all the German soldiers are marching with me—with those have died in battle out in front and the still living bringing up the rear.'[72]

Notes to Sources

Notes to Chapter 1

1 On R H Jackson, see: Felix Belair, 'Jackson Sets Forth His Political Philosophy,' in *New York Times*, Magazine Section, Feb 13, 1938; *Fortune*, Mar 1938; *Look*, Mar 12, 1940; Marquis Childs, in *Forum*, Mar 1940; 'Robert H Jackson,' in *Pathfinder*, No. 2422, Jun 1, 1940, page 8; *Brotherhood of Locomotive Firemen and Engineers' Magazine*, vol. 108, May 1940, page 313; the profile by Richard Lee Strout, in *Christian Science Monitor*, Jul 13, 1940; Karl Schriftgiesser, 'Robert H Jackson,' in *North American Review*, winter 1939–40; the Hon William L Ransom, 'Associate Justice Robert H Jackson,' in *American Bar Association*, Aug 1941; 'Robert H Jackson, US Prosecutor of Major War Criminals,' in *Judge Advocate Journal*, vol. ii, No. 2, summer 1945; Jackson's own article, 'Nuremberg in Retrospect: Legal Answer to International Lawlessness,' in *American Bar Association*, vol. 35 (Oct 1949); and Telford Taylor, 'Robert H Jackson and the Nuremberg Trials,' in *Columbia Law Review*, vol. 55 (Apr 1955). After Jackson's unfortunate death in 1954, Sir David Maxwell Fyfe wrote a fine tribute to him in the *Stanford Law Review*, Dec 1955.

2 R H Jackson passport application, May 1945 (Library of Congress, Manuscript Division, R H Jackson papers, box 103, 'Misc. papers').

3 R H Jackson speaking on Apr 13, 1945 before the American Society of International Law.

4 R H Jackson diary, Apr 27, 1945 (Library of Congress, Manuscript Division, R H Jackson papers, box 95).

5 R H Jackson, Oral History project, 1952 (University of Chicago Law School, R H Jackson collection). This is microfilmed on the author's film DI–87.

6 Stimson diary, Jun 7, 1944 (Yale University Library, Henry L Stimson papers, microfilm reel 9); Memorandum of Conversation Between the President and the Secretary of War on the Occupation of Germany, Jun 8, 1944 (National Archives, Washington [hereafter NA], RG.59, Records of the State Dept., Office of European Affairs, file 17).

7 Stimson diary, Jun 9, 1944.

8 Halifax diary, Mar 16, 1943 (Univ. of York, Borthwick Institute, Hickleton papers, Lord Halifax, file A7.8.12). Cordell Hull's remark calls to mind Heinrich Himmler's rationale for killing Jewish women and children as well as their menfolk, as stated in his infamous Posen speech in October 1943.

9 Sir David Maxwell Fyfe is wrong therefore in writing in *The Memoirs of the Earl of Kilmuir. Political Adventure* (London, 1964) [hereafter Maxwell Fyfe], page 79, that Cordell Hull counselled Roosevelt strongly against the summary execution of the enemy leaders.

10 Butcher diary, Jul 10, sealed pages released for the author in 1977 (Dwight D Eisenhower Library, Harry C Butcher papers); cf Halifax diary, Jul 10, 1944.

11 H R Morgenthau, *Germany Is Our Problem* (New York, 1947); indignant at being branded the originator of the Morgenthau Plan, Eisenhower had his staff search his files for all pertinent records: see Dwight D Eisenhower Library, Pre-Presidential papers, file 152, 'Morgenthau Plan.' And see War Dept. to Eisenhower, Jul 30, 1944 (NA, RG.331, SHAEF/SGS, file 353.02/5, 'Morgenthau Visit, Jul–Sep 1944').

12 Morgenthau diary, Aug 12, 1944 (Roosevelt Library, Henry R Morgenthau papers, vol. 763).

13 Fred Smith, 'The Rise and Fall of the Morgenthau Plan,' in *United Nations World,* Mar 1947, pages 32ff. Smith, present as an assistant of Morgenthau, took notes.

14 Eisenhower to War Dept, ca. Aug 1947 (Dwight D Eisenhower Library, Pre-Presidential Papers, file 152, 'Morgenthau Plan'). There is a version of this conversation in Kay Summersby's diary, Aug 7, 1944 (ibid., Personal Files, box 146: 'Kay Summersby diary, Jun 1944–Apr 1945').

15 PM's appointment card, Aug 10 (copy in the author's possession); Morgenthau diary, Aug 19, 1944.

16 Harry Dexter White, Memorandum for the Secretary's files, Aug 13, 1944 (Princeton University, Seeley Mudd Library, Harry Dexter White papers; see too John Foster Dulles papers, ibid., 1953, box 77).

17 Morgenthau diary, Aug 19, 1944.

18 Stimson diary, Aug 23, 1944.

19 'Brief for Conference with the President on Aug 25,' Aug 23, 1944 (Yale University Library, Henry L Stimson papers).

20 Stimson diary, Aug 25, 1944. Cf James Forrestal diary, Aug 25 (Princeton University, Seeley Mudd Library, James V Forrestal collection, box 19); and Wickard diary, manuscript, Aug 25, 1944 (Roosevelt Library, Claude R Wickard papers).

21 H L Stimson, 'Memorandum of Conversation with the President,' Aug 25, 1944 (Yale University Library, Henry L Stimson papers).

22 Stimson diary, Aug 31, 1944.

23 Lord Halifax to FO, Sep 1, 1944 (Public Record Office, London [hereafter PRO], file FO.371/39080).

24 Stimson diary, Sep 4, 1944.

25 Ibid., Sep 5, 1944.

26 Cordell Hull, 'Suggested Recommendations on Treatment of Germany from the Cabinet Committee for the President,' Sep 4, 1944 (Library of Congress, Cordell Hull papers); comments by Stimson thereon, Sep 5, 1944 (Yale University Library, Henry L Stimson papers). For early drafts of the Morgenthau Plan, entitled 'Suggested Post-Surrender Program for Germany' (5 pages), and 'Punishment of Certain War Crimes and Treatment of Special Groups' (appendix B, 3 pages), signed by Morgenthau in the original and dated Sep 11, 1944, see Roosevelt Library, President's Safe File, box 44, 'Germany 1944–45.'

27 Lord Halifax to FO, Sep 1, 1944 (PRO file FO.371/39080).

28 Stimson diary, Sep 7, 1944.

29 Ibid., Sep 9. For Stimson's subsequent memoranda to Roosevelt dated Sep 9 and 15, 1944 on the Morgenthau Plan see Roosevelt Library, President's

Safe File, box 44, 'Germany 1944–45'; they are also printed in Senate Internal Security Sub-Committee print, 90th Congress, 1st Session, *Morgenthau Diary (Germany)*, vol. i, pages 612–15, and 621–3.

30 Morgenthau diary, Sep 9, 1944.

31 On Sep 29, 1944 Hull expressed his anger at how Roosevelt had adopted Morgenthau's 'mad German plan' while at Quebec: note by Arthur Krock of the *New York Times* (Princeton University, Seeley Mudd Manuscript Library, Arthur Krock papers).

32 For the developing British policy on the treatment of German prisoners-of-war, Jul 1943–Sep 1945, see PRO file WO.106/4037; for policy on the arrest of the German leaders, May–Jun 1945, see WO.106/4463.

33 PRO file WO.32/14552 is closed for seventy-five years.

34 Sir Archibald Clark Kerr to FO, Nov 5 (PRO file FO.371/33036; and see PREM.3/219/6); David Irving, *Hess. The Missing Years* (London, 1987), pages 230f. Eden submitted paper CWC(42)12, summarising Clark Kerr's discussion with Stalin, to the War Cabinet Committee on Treatment of War Criminals on Nov 24, 1942 (PRO file CAB.98/23).

35 Anthony Eden, War Cabinet Paper WP(43)286, Jun 29, 1943 (PRO file CAB.66/38); summarised in note for Lord Cherwell, Jul 5, 1943 (Nuffield College, Oxford, Cherwell papers, files 63, 65, 'Germany, post-war treatment and reparations policy'). For British FO discussions on the treatment of war criminals see PRO files FO.371/34363–80.

36 Duff Cooper (Chancellor of the Duchy of Lancaster), War Cabinet Paper WP(43)293, 'Warning to Neutrals Not to Grant Asylum to Enemy Leaders and War Criminals,' Jul 5, 1943 (PRO file CAB.66/38).

37 Churchill to Roosevelt, Jul 26, 1943, No. 383, filed Jul 26, 6:25 P.M., GMT (NA, RG.218, Joints Chiefs of Staff, 'CCS 389 Italy, Jun 10, 43 (Sec.1).'

38 Roosevelt to Churchill, Jul 30, 1943 in *Foreign Relations of the United States, Conferences at Washington and Quebec, 1943* (US Government Printing Office, Washington, DC, 1970).

39 Halifax diary, Sep 10, 1943 (Univ. of York, Borthwick Institute, Hickleton papers, Lord Halifax, file A7.8.13).

40 War Cabinet, Oct 8, 1943.

41 Minute by Eden, Oct 9, 1943 (PRO file PREM.4/100/9).

42 Churchill to Roosevelt and Stalin, Oct 12, 1943; printed in Winston S Churchill, *The Second World War*, vol. v: *Closing the Ring* (London, 1952), pages 263ff.

43 Churchill, 'The Punishment of War Criminals,' War Cabinet Paper WP(43)496, Nov 9, 1943 (PRO file CAB.66/39).

44 Ibid. 'By this means,' argued Churchill, 'we should avoid all the tangles of legal procedure, and the responsibility for the execution of the outlaws would rest upon the decree of the 32 United Nations, which constitutes a solid and unchallengeable foundation for an Act of State.'

Notes to Chapter 2

1 Churchill's parliamentary private secretary Colonel George Harvie Watt related this to Hugh Dalton: Dalton diary, Nov 11, 1943 (London School of Economics, Political Science Library, Hugh Dalton papers).

2 Sir Edward Bridges, secretary of the War Cabinet, minute, Feb 15, 1944

(PRO file CAB.66/47).

3 Annex to Bridges' minute, WP(44)105, 'War Criminals,' Feb 15, 1944 (ibid.).

4 Eden, War Cabinet Paper, WP(44)555, 'Draft of a Suggested Telegram to Be Sent by the President and the Prime Minister to Marshal Stalin,' Oct 3, 1944 (PRO file CAB.66/56).—For American transcripts of the CCS and Plenary (Big Three) sessions at Teheran see NA, RG.218, Joints Chiefs of Staff, Official Papers of Admiral W D Leahy, file 89.

5 As told by Roosevelt later. Henry Wallace diary, Dec 18, 1943. John Morton Blum (ed.), *The Price of Vision. The Diary of Henry A Wallace, 1942–1946*(Boston, 1973).

6 Cf Winston S Churchill, *The Second World War,* vol. v: *Closing the Ring* (London, 1952), page 330.

7 Charles Bohlen, Minutes of Tripartite Dinner meeting, Nov 29, 1943, in *Foreign Relations of the United States. The Conferences at Cairo and Teheran, 1943* (Washington, 1961), pages 552ff. Those present included Roosevelt, Churchill, Stalin, Hopkins, Eden, Averell Harriman, Bohlen.

8 Wallace diary, Dec 18, 1943. Herbert Bayard Swope also had the story: quoted in R H Jackson diary, Jun 10, 1945 (Library of Congress, Manuscript Division, R H Jackson papers, box 95).

9 Churchill to Cadogan, Apr 19, 1944, in David Dilks, *The Diaries of Sir Alexander Cadogan, 1938–1945* (London, 1971), page 620.

10 Alfred-Maurice de Zayas, 'Der Nürnberger Kriegsverbrecherprozeß,' in *Macht und Recht. Große Prozesse in der Geschichte* (Munich, 1991) [hereafter Zayas], page 252. For material on the Soviet 'Kharkov' trials and the problems which these caused for Allied propaganda, see NA, RG.84, US embassy in London, secret files, box 21, file '820.02 A–Z.'

11 Jackson diary, May 17, 1945.

12 Maxwell Fyfe, op. cit., page 79.

13 Hans Fritzsche testimony on Jun 26–28, 1946, *The Trial of Major War Criminals before the International Military Tribunal at Nuremberg*, 42 vols (Nuremberg, 1946–49) [hereafter, *IMT*], vol. xvii, pages 200f.

14 Frank K Roberts (FO) to PWE, Mar 18, 1944 (PRO file FO.898/422).

15 Lord Simon, 'The Punishment of Hitler and His Chief Associates,' Sep 4, 1944 (PRO file LCO.2/2981, 'War Crimes: Trial of Major War Criminals, Hitler & Others').

16 Morgenthau diary, Sep 12, 1944 (Roosevelt Library, Henry R Morgenthau papers).

17 Mackenzie King diary, Sep 11, 1944 (Public Archives of Canada, Ottawa, William Lyon Mackenzie King papers, MG.26, J1).

18 Morgenthau diary, Sep 13, 1944.

19 H D White, 'Conference in Secretary Morgenthau's suite, Quebec, Sep 14, 1944,' in Morgenthau diary, Sep 14, 1944, pages 1514–15.

20 Ibid.

21 Eden diary, Sep 15, 1944 (Birmingham university, Avon papers, files 20/1/22). Like many politicians, Eden privately harboured antisemitic feelings. On Mar 8, 1942, after visiting Eton College, he wrote: 'Watched the boys troop in. We were not impressed. Dirty and sloppy, with an ever increasing percentage of Jews, was our conclusion!' (Ibid., 20/3/8.)

22 Memorandum, initialed 'OK., F.D.R.' and 'W.C., 15.9.' (copies will be found in Dwight D Eisenhower Library, Eisenhower files, Box 152,

'Morgenthau Plan'; ibid., Box 76, 'Morgenthau'; Henry Morgenthau's book, *Germany Is Our Problem* (New York, 1945); Nuffield College, Oxford, Cherwell papers, files 63, 65: 'Germany, post-war treatment and reparations policy,' 'Morgenthau Plan'; Forrestal diary, October 20: 'Morgenthau ... handed me a copy' (Princeton University, Seeley Mudd Library, James V Forrestal collection); Morgenthau diary, Sep 15, pages 1454-5; and Lord Halifax's papers (Univ. of York, Borthwick Institute, Hickleton papers, Lord Halifax, file A4.410.4.6).—For Churchill's telegrams to Eden about the talks with Morgenthau at Quebec, Sep 1944, see Eden's papers (PRO files FO.800/412, 413).

23 Eden, hand-written minute, Nov 19, 1944 (PRO file FO.371/391228).

24 H R Morgenthau, Treasury Plan, sent to Lord Cherwell with covering letter dated Sep 26, 1944 (Nuffield College, Oxford, Cherwell papers).

25 JCS Interim Directive to SCAEF [Eisenhower] regarding the Military Government of Germany in the Period Immediately Following the Cessation of Organised Resistance (Post-Defeat), Sep 17, 1944 (Dwight D Eisenhower Library).

26 Major A K S Morrice, Asst Sec. General Staff, SHAEF, for Chief of Staff, Oct 14, 1944, enclosing JCS directive 1067/2 (Dwight D Eisenhower Library).

27 Churchill, 'Draft of a Suggested Telegram to Be Sent by the President and the Prime Minister to Marshal Stalin,' [Hyde Park, NY], Sep 17, 1944. The original is in Roosevelt Library, President's Safe File, file A/16, 'Germany.'

28 Stimson diary, Sep 20, 1944 (Yale University Library, Henry L Stimson papers, microfilm reel 9).

29 Morgenthau to Lord Cherwell, Sep 26, 1944 (Nuffield College, Oxford, Cherwell papers, 'Morgenthau Plan'). The Plan's name was 'Treasury Plan for the Treatment of Germany' (original carbon copy in Nuffield College, Oxford, Cherwell papers; copy in author's possession). Cf. David Irving (ed)., *Der Morgenthauplan* (Bremen, 1986).

30 Hansard, *House of Commons Debates*, Sep 28, 1944, cols 414–15.

31 Eden, War Cabinet Paper, WP(44)555, re: 'Draft of a Suggested Telegram to Be Sent by the President and the Prime Minister to Marshal Stalin,' Oct 3, 1944 (PRO file CAB.66/56).

32 Meeting between Churchill, Stalin, Molotov *et al.*, Oct 9, 1944, 10 P.M. (PRO file PREM.3/434/2, 'TOLSTOY Records of Meetings at the Kremlin, Moscow, Oct 9–17, 1944').

33 Meeting between Churchill, Stalin, Eden, Molotov *et al.*, Oct 17, 1944, 10 P.M. (ibid.).

34 Library of Congress, H H Arnold papers, box 225.

35 Churchill to Roosevelt, Oct 21, 1944 (Roosevelt Library, microfilm, and PRO file CAB.120/170).

36 Simon, memorandum, Sep 4, 1944 (PRO file LCO.2/2981).

37 Herbert Wechsler, secret memorandum, Dec 29, 1944 (University of Syracuse, New York, George Arents Research Library, Francis Biddle Collection, box 14, 'Trial Documents').

38 Forrestal diary; and Henry L Stimson diary, Jan 16, 1945 (Yale University Library, Henry L Stimson papers, microfilm reel 10).

39 Meeting in Secretary Stettinius' Office, State Dept, Jan 17, 1945, 3:30 P.M. (Princeton University, Seeley Mudd Library, Harry Dexter White papers).

40 H L Stimson, E Stettinius, F Biddle, Memorandum for the President on War Crimes, Jan 22; and S Rosenman, quoted in Jackson diary, Apr 27, 1945.

41 Roosevelt–Stalin discussion, Feb 4, 1945 (NA, RG.59, Charles Bohlen papers; see too Roosevelt Library, Harry L Hopkins papers, box 337).

42 Adm. Leahy diary, Feb 9, 1945 (Library of Congress, Manuscript Division, William Daniel Leahy papers).

43 ARGONAUT conference, 'Minutes of 2nd Plenary Session between the United States and Great Britain,' 12 noon, Feb 9, 1945 (PRO file CAB.120/170).

44 From James F Byrnes' shorthand record of the Yalta conference. Feb 9, 1945 (Harry S Truman Library, Naval Aide files, box 9).

45 ARGONAUT conference, 'Minutes of 2nd Plenary Session between the United States and Great Britain,' 12 noon, Feb 9, 1945 (PRO file CAB.120/170).

46 Transcripts of the conversations of Hess with Simon, on Jun 9, 1941 (PRO file PREM.3/219/5; and Oxford University, Bodleian Library, Simon papers, box 88); and with Lord Beaverbrook, Sep 9, 1941 (House of Lords Records Office, Beaverbrook papers, file D.443).

47 This author located the diaries of the doctors treating Hess and the medical attendants guarding him throughout this period, 1941–44, in the Federal Records Center, at Suitland, Maryland, in the files of OMGUS: Office of the Chief of Counsel for War Crime, Secretariat of the IMT, General Records, box 113, pieces 5021 and 5022. See David Irving, *Hess. The Missing Years* (London, 1987).

48 The truth-drugs experiment was conducted on May 7, 1944. Lieut. Col. Henry V Dicks, report, May 10, 1944; J R Rees, *The Case of Rudolf Hess* (London, 1948), pages 87ff.

49 Irving, *Hess*, page 230.

50 FO (Frank Roberts) to Clark Kerr, No. 331, Nov 4, 1942 (PRO file FO.371/30920).

51 FO Research Dept, 'Hess, Rudolf,' Jul 7, 1945 (Library of Congress, Manuscript Division, R H Jackson papers, box 100).

52 Rudolf Hess, circular 174/38 to all Gauleiters, Nov 10, 1938 (Berlin Document Center [hereafter BDC] file 240/I).

53 Eden, War Cabinet Paper, WP(44)330, Jun 16, 1944 (PRO file LCO.2/2981).

54 Memorandum on a meeting on Apr 5, 1945 (PRO file LCO.2/2980, 'Attorney General's Committee and British War Crimes Executive').

55 Simon to Rosenman, Apr 6, 1945 (PRO file LCO.2/2981).

56 Memorandum on a meeting on Apr 5, 1945 (PRO file LCO.2/2980).

57 John Colville, 'diary,' Apr 8, 1945. *The Fringes of Power. 10 Downing Street Diaries 1939–1955* (London, 1985).

58 Winston to Clementine Churchill, Apr 9, 1945; cited in Martin Gilbert, *Winston S Churchill* (London, 1986), 7 vols, vol. vii: *Road to Victory*, page 1286.

59 Rosenman, quoted in Jackson diary, Apr 27, 1945.

60 Morgenthau diary, Apr 11, 1945, pages 1499–1503.

61 See too Rosenman to Herbert Wechsler, Apr 23, 1945, with attached report (NA, RG.238, US Chief of Counsel at Nuremberg, Main Office Files, box 202).

62 Rosenman, quoted in Jackson diary, Apr 27, 1945.

63 Stimson diary, Apr 25, 1945.

64 Ibid., Apr 22–9, 1945.

Notes to Chapter 3

1 R H Jackson diary, Apr 27, 1945 (Library of Congress, Manuscript Division, R H Jackson papers, box 95).

2 Ibid.

3 Ibid.; and letter of acceptance, Jackson to Harry S. Truman, Apr 29, 1945 (ibid.; and NA, RG.238, US Chief of Counsel at Nuremberg, Main Office Files, box 201).

4 Jackson to Truman, Apr 29, 1945.

5 Jackson diary, Apr 30, 1945.

6 It is in NA, RG.238, US Chief of Counsel at Nuremberg, Main Office Files, box 201.

7 R H Jackson, Memorandum, May 1, 1945, re Document entitled, 'Punishment of War Criminals,' dated Apr 28, 1945 (ibid.).; and diary, May 1, 1945.

8 Jackson diary, May 4, 1945.

9 Ibid., May 7, 1945.

10 David Irving, *The War Between the Generals* (New York, 1981), page 11. 'If it is found that United States personnel were guilty of negligence,' the US Legation in Berne informed the Wehrmacht High Command, 'appropriate action will be taken with respect to them. The Supreme Commander [Eisenhower] profoundly regrets this incident and has taken steps to prevent its recurrence' (NA, RG.218, Joints Chiefs of Staff, file 383.6, Mar 21, 1945). This incident became known to the prisoners in Nuremberg; Milch noted in his diary on Dec 9, 1945, 'A reliable gentleman reports that in March 108 German prisoners-of-war of the Americans arrived suffocated to death in a rail transport!' (author's microfilm DI–59).

11 Howard A Buechner, *Dachau. The Hour of the Avenger* (Metairie, La., 1986), a vengeful but well-researched account written from an unsympathetic viewpoint; see too the eye-witness evidence collected by Milch in his Dachau diary, 1946–47. The most graphic photograph of the mass-shooting is Signals Corps negative number SC.208765, in NA, Still Pictures Branch. The Seventh Army's archives at Suitland, Maryland, reveal that the U.S. Army ordered a full inquiry after a report on the massacre appeared in the forces' newspaper *Stars & Stripes*; the men who did the shooting were exonerated, as having been following superior orders. Their superiors were never charged. I am indebted to Charles Provan for this information.

12 On Katyn, see the extensive Congressional Hearings of the Eighty-Second Congress, Washington, DC, held from Oct 11, 1951 to Nov 14, 1952 (copies in the University of Syracuse, George Arents Research Library, Francis Biddle Collection, box 15; the interim and final reports are in Box 16). In Jackson's papers are applications by Göring for the witnesses Böhmert and Stockert, May 13, 14, 1946, to testify on Katyn (NA, RG.238, US Chief of Counsel at Nuremberg, Main Office Files, box 180).

13 Cadogan diary, Jun 18, 1943 (Churchill College, Cambridge, Sir Alexander Cadogan papers, ACAD.1/10).

14 Beside Churchill the later prime minister Harold Macmillan bore a measure of the moral blame for this episode, as Britain's minister-resident in the region; Nikolai Tolstoy, *The Minister and the Massacres* (London, 1986).

15 In Hamburg 48,000 civilians died in the British fire raids of July 1943; in Dresden, up to 100,000 in one night, Feb 13, 1945; in Pforzheim, ten days later, 20,000 of the city's 65,000 inhabitants.

16 Information from the mass grave's memorial, and from N H V Shapton to the author, Dec 7, 1989. Out of a misplaced sense of grievance the British commander Brigadier Derek Mills-Roberts beat the Luftwaffe field-marshal Erhard Milch, crippled by a car accident, unconscious with his own field-marshal's baton after seeing the bodies washed ashore. Roberts denied this to this author, but his next of kin sold the stolen baton (which had snapped in two during the assault and been repaired) at Phillips' auction house in London in the 1970s.—And see Rudi Goguel, *Cap Arcona* (Frankfurt am Main, 1972).

17 British Chiefs of Staff report on Chemical Warfare to the Cabinet, Jul 27, 1944 (PRO file PREM.3/89).

18 Cherwell to Churchill, Aug 4, 1944 (Nuffield College, Oxford, Cherwell papers). Eisenhower flatly opposed the use of such a weapon. See Barton Bernstein, 'Churchill's Secret Weapon,' in *Bulletin of the Atomic Scientist*, Jan/Feb 1987.

19 Churchill to Chiefs of Staff Committee, Minute D.217/4, Jul 6, 1944 (PRO file PREM.3/89). The First Sea Lord noted afterwards, 'There is no doubt [that the] PM is in no state to discuss anything—too tired and too much alcohol.' Diary of Admiral A B Cunningham, Jul 6, 10 (British Library, Dept of Manuscripts, Additional MS 52575, vol. xix). Eden's diary, Jul 6, 1944, describes Churchill on this 'ghastly' occasion as being 'tight.'

20 See the JIC report, 'Use of Chemical Warfare by the Germans,' Jan 29, 1945, in Anderson Diary, Jan 29, 1945 (Hoover Library, Frederick Anderson papers).

21 So the Combined Chiefs of Staff were informed in 1943 in a report by Colonel L Mitkiewicz, Polish liaison officer to the Joint Chiefs of Staff (NA, RG.218, Joints Chiefs of Staff, file CCS/381 'Poland—6.30.1943—Sec.1').

22 Harry S Truman to War Dept, Jul 31, 1945, IN–178 (Harry S Truman Library, Map Room Files).

23 Jackson diary, May 4, 1945.

24 Morgenthau diary, May 9, 1945, page 1580 (Roosevelt Library, Henry R Morgenthau papers).

25 Jackson diary, May 7, 11, 1945.

26 Ibid., May 10, 1945.

27 Ibid.

28 Ibid., May 12, 1945.

29 R H Jackson, Memorandum for Edwin W Pauley, United States Representative on the Reparations Commission, re: 'Draft of Instructions,' May [12] (Library of Congress, Manuscript Division, R H Jackson papers, box 95); and Oral History project (University of Chicago Law School, R H Jackson collection); and diary, May 12. The leaked memorandum was quoted verbatim by Drew Pearson in his column in the *Washington Post*, May 23, 1945.

Notes to Chapter 4

1 R H Jackson diary, May 3, 7, 1945 (Library of Congress, Manuscript Division, R H Jackson papers, box 95).

2 Author's interview of Ralph G Albrecht, New York, May 22, 1971.

3 Jackson diary, May 7, 1945. On May 11, however Jackson noted: 'Donovan's studies from O.S.S. are very complete and encouraging.'

4 Ibid., May 11, 1945.

5 Ibid., May 14, 1945.

6 Ibid., May 15, 1945.

7 Ibid.

8 Marshall to Eisenhower, May 12, 1945 (NA, RG.153, Judge-Advocate General, Internal Affairs Division, box 1476); this file contains several telegrams laying the foundations of the war crimes trials.

9 Jackson diary, May 14, 1945.

10 Hitler's Commando Order, Oct 18, 1942.(Nuremberg Document [hereafter ND]: 503–PS.)

11 Ibid., May 21, 1945.

12 Jackson diary, May 17, 1945. In NA, RG.238 however is a binder of documents and proposed charges against many leading Nazis compiled by the War Crimes section of the Judge Advocate-General's Office, submitted in 1945 to Jackson.

13 Jackson diary, May 18, 1945.

14 Ibid., May 17, 1945.

15 Ibid., May 16, 1945.

16 Ibid., May 15, 1945.

17 Ibid.

18 Ibid., May 18, 1945; and Jackson, Oral History project (University of Chicago Law School, R H Jackson collection).

19 Oral History project.

20 Fabio Andriola, *Appuntamento sul Lago. L'Ultimo piano di Benito Mussolini* (Milan, 1990); and *Carteggio Segreto* (Casale Monferrato, 1996). Max Salvadore, the SOE's representative in northern Italy, when asked by the CLN, the Partisan committee in Milan, gave clearance for the murders. See the series of disclosures by 'Mandrake' (Nicholas Farrell) in the *Sunday Telegraph* in the autumn of 1995, and Prof. Renzo de Felice, *Il Rosso e Il Nero* (Milan, 1995.)

21 Karl-Heinz Keitel, 'Conversation with My Father,' Sep 23, 1946, 1 P.M. (Institut für Zeitgeschichte, Munich [hereafter IfZ], Irving Collection).

22 It will be found in the files of the Attorney General's Committee and British War Crimes Executive (PRO file LCO.2/2980).

23 Dönitz to Eisenhower, May 15, 1945 (BA file R.62/11a); M Steinert, *Die 23 Tage der Regierung Dönitz*, page 289; and Zayas, op. cit., page 267.

24 Several were lost; the surviving Jodl diaries and papers, 1937–45, are ND: 1781–PS to 1811–PS, filmed on two reels of microfilm in NA, RG.238, A–235.

25 Robert Murphy, *Diplomat among the Warriors* (London, 1964) [hereafter Murphy], page 300.

26 Rupert Butler, *Legions of Death* (London, 1983) [hereafter Butler], pages 238f.

27 Word of the treatment of Streicher got around. Field-Marshal Erhard Milch, imprisoned as a witness at Nuremberg, wrote in his diary in Oct 1945, 'The Party Treasurer Schwarz admires Streicher for having held himself erect despite five days in handcuffs, only rotten potato peelings, whippings, and having Negroes spitting into his mouth' (author's microfilm DI–59).

28 Julius Streicher, manuscript, Jun 16, 1945 (in author's collection).

29 Jackson diary, hand-written, May 22, 1945.

30 See Oral History of Bernard Bernstein (Harry S Truman Library, Oral Interviews, No. 188).

31 Jackson diary, hand-written, May 24, 1945.

32 Ibid., May 25, 1945.

33 On Feb 5, 1948.

34 Jackson diary, hand-written, May 25, 1945.

35 Jackson diary, Jun 14, 1945.

36 Jackson diary, hand-written, May 26, 1945.

37 Ibid.

38 See the extensive 1944 files on Wilhelm Canaris, Edda Ciano and the Ciano diaries, Hans Bernd Gisevius, and Dulles' other skulduggery, in Princeton University, Seeley Mudd Manuscript Library, Allen W Dulles papers, boxes 20–1, 23.

39 Jackson diary, hand-written, May 27, 1945.

40 Ibid., May 28, 1945.

41 Ibid., May 29, 1945; and see Maxwell Fyfe, op. cit., page 80.

42 Jackson diary, hand-written, May 28, 1945. The wartime Churchill national government had dissolved and Churchill had appointed the former solicitor-general Barnes as acting attorney-general in the 'caretaker' government pending a general election. Two-page note, 'War Crimes,' on a meeting with Jackson *et al.*, May 28, 1945 (PRO file LCO.2/2980).

43 Jackson diary, hand-written, May 29, 1945.

44 Minutes of meeting on May 29, 1945, in House of Lords (PRO file LCO.2/2980).

45 R H Jackson, memo, 'Meeting at House of Lords,' May 29, 1945, 2:30 P.M. (Library of Congress, Manuscript Division, R H Jackson papers, box 95). In keeping with the O.S.S. nature of these early American war crimes trial operations, the document's top-secret classification is authorised by 'CO, OSS, ETOUSA.'

46 Ibid.

47 Ibid.

Notes to Chapter 5

1 JCS.1067 stipulated that except for the purpose of facilitating the occupation, 'you [Eisenhower] will take no steps looking toward the economic rehabilitation of Germany nor designed to maintain or strengthen the German economy.'

2 Stimson diary, May 9, 1945 (Yale University Library, Henry L Stimson papers, microfilm reel 10).

3 Henry Stimson to Harry S Truman, May 16, 1945 (ibid.).

4 R H Jackson diary, May 16, 1945 (Library of Congress, Manuscript Division, R H Jackson papers, box 95); and Oral History project (University of Chicago Law School, R H Jackson collection).

5 Surles to Eisenhower, SHAEF, Jun 1, 1945 (Dwight D Eisenhower Library, file 125, 'Daily APD').

6 Jackson to Truman, Jun 6, 1945 (Library of Congress, Manuscript Division, R H Jackson papers, box 95); and dated Jun 7, 1945 in NA, RG.238, US Chief of Counsel at Nuremberg, Main Office Files, box 201.

7 Jackson diary, Jun 6, 1945.

8 Ibid.

9 'The Crucifixion of the Jews Must Stop,' in *American Hebrew*, Oct 31, 1919. We are indebted to the Polish Historical Society of Stamford, Connecticut, for this information and a facsimile of the journal concerned.

10 Ibid.

11 Ibid.

12 Ibid. Swope's point was not short of the mark. Göring had levied a 'one billion Reichsmark' fine on the Jews for the murder of Ernst vom Rath in 1938. The Jews who were expelled from Germany were expropriated, and millions of marks of assets were formally confiscated by the Revenue Office of their home city. (For the revenue files relating to the assets of the 50,535 Jews expelled from Berlin alone, see the deportees' card-index in the Landesarchiv Berlin, previously held in the property administration department of the Senator für Finanzen in Fasanenstrasse.)

13 Dr John A P Millet to R H Jackson, Jun 11, 1945 (Library of Congress, Manuscript Division, R H Jackson papers, box 107: 'Psychiatric and Personality Studies of Nazi Leaders').

14 Jackson diary, Jun 14, 1945.

15 Jackson to Millet, Jun 23, 1945.

16 D M Kelley to B C Andrus, Oct 25, 1945, 'Secretarial Aid for Medical Section' (Burton C Andrus Collection, Colorado Springs).

17 W E Jackson to Colonel Paul Schroeder, 'Psychiatric Examination of Defendants,' Dec 17, 1945 (Library of Congress, Manuscript Division, R H Jackson papers, box 107: 'Psychiatric and Personality Studies of Nazi Leaders').

18 DAG(A), unsigned memo on meeting with General Donovan, Jun 9, 1945 (PRO file LCO.2/2980, 'Attorney General's Committee and British War Crimes Executive,' pages 453ff).

19 P Dean to Sir D M Fyfe, Jun 19, 1945 (ibid.).

20 Jackson diary, Jun 11, 1945.

21 Jackson diary, Jun 16, 1945. Dr Ečer interrogated Keitel, Lammers, and others in Aug 1945 (NA, RG.319, XE.009308).

Notes to Chapter 6

1 R H Jackson diary, Jun 24–7, 1945 (Library of Congress, Manuscript Division, R H Jackson papers, box 95).

2 Maxwell Fyfe, op. cit., pages 83ff; and see Sidney Alderman, *Negotiating with the Russians* (New York, 1951), chapter iii.

3 R H Jackson to Irene, his wife, Jul 4, 1945 (Library of Congress, Manuscript Division, R H Jackson papers, box 2).

4 [Record of meeting of] Jun 21, 1945 (PRO file LCO.2/2980, 'Attorney General's Committee and British War Crimes Executive').

5 Jackson diary, Jun 21, 1945.

6 Ibid., Jun 26, 1945.

7 Jackson to Irene, Jul 4, 1945.

8 Maxwell Fyfe, op. cit., pages 86ff.

9 Jackson diary, Jun 28, 1945.

10 Ibid., Jul 6, 1945.

11 Its numerical designation was CCPWE#32. For the weekly roster of prisoners arriving at and leaving this camp see PRO file WO.208/4153 and NA, RG.332, ETO G–2 section, box 97. Walter Lüdde-Neurath loaned the author a manuscript he wrote in 1947 on this camp. For the full series of Detailed Interrogation (DI–) reports at ASHCAN see NA, RG.332, ETO G–2 section, box 96. For a witty account of a visit to ASHCAN, dated Oct 23, 1945, evidently by

Leonard Ingrams of the Foreign Office Political Intelligence Dept., see PRO file FO.898/425; the file also contains many otherwise unknown interrogation reports on the inmates.

12 B C Andrus, private letter, Nov 1, 1946 (Burton C Andrus Collection, Colorado Springs). The *Time* article by John Staunton appeared on Oct 28, 1946.

13 Andrus, 'SOP [standard operating procedure] for the reception of prisoners,' ASHCAN, Jun 5, 1945 (Burton C Andrus Collection, Colorado Springs).—See too Burton C Andrus, *The Infamous of Nuremberg* (New York, 1969), pages 32f (also published as *I Was the Nuremberg Jailer*).

14 Karl-Heinz Keitel, 'Conversation with My Father,' Sep 15, 1946, 9:30 A.M. (IfZ, Irving Collection).

15 Ibid., Apr 21, 1945.

16 Cf Milch diary, Apr 3, 1945: 'Reich Air Ministry. Transportation staff. Speer tells of his duel with F[ührer] on account of demolitions' (author's microfilm DI–59).

17 Ibid., Apr 8, 1945: 'Speer here [hunting lodge Bärenwiese outside Berlin], dictates broadcast.'

18 Ibid., May 22, 1948. This conversation must have been on about Apr 22, 1945.

19 For Ohlendorf, see his PW Paper 133 (PRO file WO.208/4176).

20 For Speer's visits to Dora, see Chronik der Dienststelle des Reichsminister Speer, 1943.

21 (Genuine) Speer Chronicle, 1941; Matthias Schmidt, *Das Ende eines Mythos* (Bern & Munich, 1982), pages 186, 188. Speer to Otto Wetzel, Reichstag deputy, Apr 21, 1942 (Bundesarchiv [hereafter BA] file R.3/1605).

22 (Genuine) Speer Chronicle, Nov 27, 1941; it boasts that JG was 'extremely surprised' at the scale of the effort.

23 Conversation of Lieut.-Gen. Werner Bruns overheard on Apr 25, 1945, CSDIC (UK) report SRGG.1158 (PRO file WO.208/4169). See too his interrogation on Feb 13, 1948 (NA film M.1019, roll 20), and the interrogations of Rocques and Elke Sirewitz. The transportation lists confirm that 3,715 Berlin Jews left for Minsk (Nov 14), Kaunas (Nov 17), and Riga (Nov 27, 1941). For Hitler's order, see Himmler's note on his telephone call from Hitler's 'bunker' to Heydrich at 1:30 P.M., Nov 30, 1941: 'Judentransport aus Berlin. Keine Liquidierung' —Transport of Jews from Berlin. No liquidation (NA film T84, roll 25).

24 Correct. Professor Karl Brandt, Hitler's personal surgeon since 1936; bosom friend of Speer, sentenced to death by a drumhead court martial on Hitler's orders in March 1945 for having sent his family to a location behind American lines. Sentenced to death again by the Americans in 1947 for his leading role in the euthanasia operations (last words on the gallows: 'I — am — ready').

25 O Hoeffding to W T Stone, 'Interrogation of Speer,' Jun 1, 1945. CIOS report (NA, RG.84, US embassy in London, secret files, box 324, file '800 Treasury'); further SHAEF interrogations of Speer are in ibid., box 30, file 800, 'Policy on Germany').

26 Hoeffding.

27 Karl-Heinz Keitel, 'Conversation with My Father,' Sep 23, 1946 at 1 P.M. (IfZ, Irving Collection).

28 ETHINT interrogation report on Alfred Jodl (NA; microfilmed on author's film DI–8). Keitel told his son on Sep 28, 1946 that the Americans had asked

him to write a strategic assessment of Germany's current position; he had declined and turned the task over to Jodl, who as chief of the operations staff was more suitable. 'Jodl has already received confirmation that his study has been received in Washington.' Karl-Heinz Keitel, 'Conversation with My Father,' Sep 28, 1946, 1 P.M. (IfZ, Irving Collection).

29 Julius Streicher diary, Nov 30, 1945 (Höffkes Collection).

30 Interrogation of Göring, SAIC/X/5 (NA, RG.332, ETO G–2 section, box 73).

31 Inventory of Göring's personal effects on capture (Burton C Andrus Collection, Colorado Springs).

32 Testimony of Col. Burton C Andrus, annex to 'Report of Board of Proceedings of Hermann Göring (Suicide),' Oct 1946. Copies are in BDC Director's Safe, Berlin; NA, RG.260, Records of OMGUS Allied Control Council, file 2/92–1(2); and in the Wheeler Bennett papers at St Anthony's College, Oxford.

33 David Irving, *Göring* (London, 1989), page 476.

34 CCPWE#32 report DI–36 (NA, RG.332, ETO G–2 section, box 96).

35 Lieut.-Col. Ernst Engländer to R H Jackson, May 18, 1946 (NA, RG.238, US Chief of Counsel at Nuremberg, Main Office Files, box 179).

36 Ernst Engländer, 'Göring, Almost Führer,' in *Interavia*, Jul 1946.

37 Seventh Army interrogation of Robert Ley, SAIC/30, May 29, 1945.

38 Streicher diary, Nov 30, 1945.

39 Ibid.; and Adele Streicher, comments on Arnim von Manikowski, *Das Gericht der Sieger*, page 82.

40 Andrus, Progress Report, Jul 26, 1945 (ibid.).

41 Andrus to Col. Fritzsche, Aug 4, 1945 (ibid.).

42 Ribbentrop manuscripts and a political interrogation dated Aug 11, 1945 are in Jackson's papers (NA, RG.238, US Chief of Counsel at Nuremberg, Main Office Files, box 182).

43 USFET–MISC/X–P 25, Conversation between British Army officer and Ribbentrop, Top Secret, Aug 4, 1945 (NA, RG.238, OSS, XE–file: 'Ribbentrop'). More such X–P transcripts are in NA, RG.332, ETO G–2 section, box 97.

44 The reasons for the ban on his teaching were solely Streicher's politics and his part in the Hitler putsch. The files on Streicher as a senior teacher are in family possession.

45 Adele Streicher, comments on Manikowski, page 131.

46 Adele Streicher, comments on G M Gilbert, *Nürnberger Tagebuch* (Stuttgart, 1948), page 127 (Höffkes Collection).

47 Adele Streicher, comments on Whitney R Harris, *Tyranny on Trial* (Dallas, 1954), page 233.

48 Adele Streicher, comments on Gilbert, op. cit., pages 300, 407, 437.

49 Ibid., on page 12 (Höffkes Collection).

50 Adele Streicher, comments on Karl Anders, *Im Nürnberger Irrgarten* (Höffkes Collection).

51 Streicher was probably largely innocent, framed by the manager of his publishing firm, Fink. Streicher's son writes, 'At the trial of his case that Streicher demanded it turned out that Fink was one hundred per cent aligned with Streicher's worst enemy [Benno] Martin, the senior S.S. and police chief [of Nuremberg]. Streicher was firmly convinced that Fink had been blackmailed by Martin.'

52 *Vierteljahrshefte für Zeitgeschichte*, Munich, 26th year, No. 4, Oct 1978.

53 Streicher diary, Nov 30, 1945; and Adele Streicher, comments on Manikowski, page 82.

54 Walter Lüdde-Neurath MS (in the author's possession).

Notes to Chapter 7

1 For the file on Keitel see NA, RG.319, XE.009308.

2 R H Jackson to Irene, 'Friday Eve' [Jul 6], 1945 (Library of Congress, Manuscript Division, R H Jackson papers, box 2).

3 R H Jackson diary, Jul 7, 1945 (Library of Congress, Manuscript Division, R H Jackson papers, box 95); and Oral History project (University of Chicago Law School, R H Jackson collection).

4 ND: 386–PS. The memorandum was written up afterwards by Colonel Friedrich Hossbach, Hitler's Wehrmacht adjutant. *IMT*, vol. xxv, pages 402–13. See Walter Bussmann's analysis of this document in *Vierteljahrshefte für Zeitgeschichte* (1968), pages 373ff. For the arms-production background of the conference see Milch to Göring, Oct 30, 1937 (Bundesarchiv-Militärarchiv, Milch Documents, vol. 53, page 0849), and the paper by Dr Treue in ibid., file WiIF.5/1196.

5 BDC, file 240/II.

6 Jackson diary, Jul 7, 1945. The diary does not name any of the four. There is a 1945 file on Schlabrendorff in Princeton University, Seeley Mudd Manuscript Library, Allen W Dulles papers, box 22.

7 Allen W Dulles to R H Jackson, Mar 27, 1946 (Library of Congress, Manuscript Division, R H Jackson papers, box 102, 'Gisevius, Hans Bernd').

8 For Gisevius' dispatches on and after the Jul 20, 1944 bomb plot, see Donovan to Roosevelt, Jul 22, 1944 et seq. (Roosevelt Library, PSF box 168); for OSS telegrams from Berne, May–Jul 1944, on Beck, Olbricht, Fromm, Goerdeler, etc., and the OSS summary on the 'Wotan Group,' Jul 23, 1944, copies of which were supplied via Ambassador John G Winant to the British Intelligence service, see NA, RG.84, US embassy in London, secret files, box 8, file '800 Germany.'

9 'These services were rendered solely on account of his anti-Nazi sentiments and no question or financial compensation of future protection entered into our discussions.' Allen W Dulles, To Whom it May Concern [memo on Gisevius], Feb 27, 1946 (ibid.).—There is a file on the Peenemünde raid in Princeton University, Seeley Mudd Manuscript Library, Allen W Dulles papers, box 19. On the Nazi decoding of US diplomatic telegrams see the interrogation of Laun, who worked under Geheimrat Selchow in the Pers–Z section (cryptanalysis) of the Auswärtiges Amt, the German Foreign Ministry (NA, RG.84, US embassy in London, secret files, box 22).

10 'We interviewed some strange witnesses ...' R H Jackson to Irene, Jul 12, 1945.

11 Ibid.

12 W J Donovan to Truman, Jun 22, 1945 (OSS director's files, quoted by Anthony Cave Brown, *Wild Bill Donovan. The Last Hero* (New York, 1982), page 285.

13 Jackson diary, Jul 7, 1945; and letter to Irene, Jul 12, 1945.

14 For the Russian and German texts of the Ribbentrop–Molotov Pact of

Aug 23, 1939, see Loesch film F11, equivalent to NA film T120/616, pages 0048–52; for its secret additional protocol, see Loesch film F19 (or NA film T120/624), pages 0182–8; documents pertaining to the secrecy of the latter, T120/616, pages 0037–46. For the texts of the German–Soviet boundary and friendship treaty of Sep 28, 1939, see Loesch film F2 (or NA film T20/607), pages 0315–16, 0331–2, 0327–8; for the additional protocol concerning Lithuania and Poland, see ibid., pages 0310 and 0329.

15 All that survives is Schmidt's listing of these transcripts: BA file Kl. Erw. 501. See too NA, RG.84, US embassy in London, secret files, box 30, file '800, German Documents.' Among other sensitive files was one on the shooting of Stalin's son Lieutenant Jakob Djugashvili in a German prison camp—he tried to escape after being taunted by British prisoners about his primitive personal habits.

16 Jackson diary, Jul 8, 1945.

17 Ibid.; and Oral History project.

18 Jackson to Irene, Jul 20, 1945.

19 Maxwell Fyfe, op. cit., page 90.

20 Jackson diary, Jul 21, 1945.

21 Ibid., Jul 22, 1945.

22 Jackson to Irene, 'Thursday Eve' [Aug 9?], 1945.

23 *Foreign Relations of the United States*, 1945, vol. ii: *Potsdam.*

24 Jackson diary, Jul 26, 1945.

25 Ibid., Jul 27, 1945.

26 Eleventh Meeting of the Big Three, [Potsdam], Jul 31, 1945 (Harry S Truman Library, Independence, Missouri, Naval Aide Files, box 3).

27 Jackson diary, Jul 31, 1945.

28 Jackson, Oral History project.

29 F L Felton, private letter [Jan 1946] entitled 'Third Report on the Battle of Nuremberg' (Hoover Library, Frederick L Felton Collection, Ts Germany F 326).

30 Kempner wrote frequently on the trials afterwards. See e.g. his review, 'The Nuremberg Trials as Sources of Recent German Political and Historical Material,' in *American Political Science Review*, vol. xliv, No. 2 (Jun 1950).

31 Obituary on Kempner, *Daily Telegraph*, Aug 19, 1993. Throughout the 1970s he fought to prove that the Nazis, and not the Dutchman Marinus van der Lubbe, burned the Reichstag in Feb 1933; the Joseph Goebbels diaries, first researched by this author in Moscow in 1992, finally proved Kempner wrong.

32 Kempner to Col. Melvin Purvis, May 10, 1945 (NA, RG.153, Judge-Advocate General, Internal Affairs Division, box 1390); there is a similar note about Göring dated May 3, 1945 from Kempner to Thomas Dodd (NA, RG.238, US Chief of Counsel at Nuremberg, Main Office Files, box 183). Epenstein was involved in a triangular liaison with Göring's mother, and became something of a (Jewish) godfather and benefactor to him.

33 See Friedrich Gaus, affidavit, Mar 15, and declaration in lieu of oath, May 17, 1946 (NA, RG.238, US Chief of Counsel at Nuremberg, Main Office Files, box 180); and his testimony for Ribbentrop, Mar 15, 1946 (box 182). For an early interrogation of Gaus at CSDIC(WEA) see NA, RG.332, ETO G–2 section, box 15.

34 In NA, RG.238, entry 199, Records of HQ, 6850th Internal Security Detachment, IMT, box 3.

35 The original memorandum on the [Wannsee] conference of Jan 20, 1942

is in the files of Abt. Inland II, geh. (Auswärtiges Amt, Pol. Archiv AA, 'Final Solution of the Jewish Problem,' Serial 1513; NA film T120, roll 780, 372024ff). Those present included Gauleiter Meyer, Stuckart, Freisler, Bühler, Klopfer, Kritzinger, 'Gestapo' Müller, and Eichmann.

36 In this connection Eichmann, still hiding in Argentina, exclaimed: 'Eastern territories, 420,000… What d'they mean, eastern territories? Bialystok 400,000—[…] I'm supposed to have mentioned Bialystok additionally?' asked Eichmann. 'Impossible, I can't name cities.' As further figures from the alleged Wannsee protocol are read out to Eichmann, he interrupts and says, 'No, no, no. This table of figures has been wangled into it.' 'Hungary, 742,800!!' 'Well, the intent seems quite clear: If there were that many Jews there originally, and now there are only this many, then the others must have been killed. That's been wangled in. As true as I am standing here.' Eichmann transcripts (1956), in the author's possession, pages 275–6.

37 ND: 4055–PS; USA Exhibit 923.

38 Staff Evidence Analysis Sheet on ND: 4055–PS (IfZ).

39 [Franz] Schlegelberger Manuscript, undated (Spring 1942) (BA file R.22/52). For Kempner's views on the Nuremberg documents, see his 'The Nuremberg Trials as Sources of Recent German Political and Historical Material.'

40 Milch diary, Apr 14, 1949: 'Stuckart gets three years, eight months because of bad health.'

41 W E Jackson memo on talk with A W and J F Dulles, Nov 1, 1948 (Library of Congress, Manuscript Division, R H Jackson papers, box 2).

Notes to Chapter 8

1 R H Jackson diary, Aug 2, 1945 (Library of Congress, Manuscript Division, R H Jackson papers, box 95).

2 Ibid., Aug 7, 1945.

3 Ibid., Aug 7, 1945; Maxwell Fyfe, op. cit., page 92.

4 Minutes of Chief Prosecutors' Meeting held on Aug 8, 1945 (Library of Congress, Manuscript Division, R H Jackson papers, box 98; these are microfilmed on the author's films DI–70 and 71).

5 R H Jackson to Irene, 'Thursday Eve' [Aug 9?], 1945 (Library of Congress, Manuscript Division, R H Jackson papers, box 2).

6 Jackson diary, Aug 8, 1945. His visit was to HQ, US Eighth Fighter Command.

7 W E Jackson to mother, Aug 21, 1945 (Library of Congress, Manuscript Division, R H Jackson papers, box 2).

8 Jackson diary, Aug 13; and Minutes of Chief Prosecutors' Meeting held on Aug 13, 1945.

9 Minutes of Chief Prosecutors' Meeting held on Aug 14; and memo from R H Jackson to all members of the staff, Aug 14, 1945 (University of Chicago Law School, R H Jackson collection).

10 German naval judge advocate [Flottenrichter] Otto Kranzbühler, lecture at Göttingen University, printed as *Rückblick auf Nürnberg*, Nuremberg, Sep 1949, page 8 [hereafter Kranzbühler].

11 W E Jackson to mother, Aug 21, 1945.

12 F L Felton, private letter [Jan 1946] entitled 'Third Report on the Battle

of Nuremberg' (Hoover Library, Frederick L Felton Collection, Ts Germany F 326).

13 F L Felton, private letter dated Jan 21, 1946 (ibid.).

14 W E Jackson to mother, Aug 21, 1945.

15 Ibid.

16 Report on Hermann Göring, Aug 15, 1945 (US State Dept., author's microfilm DI–34).

17 Keitel letter, Oct 10, 1945 (Karl-Heinz Keitel papers; in author's possession).

18 Testimony of Ludwig Pflücker, Exhibits AC to 'Report of Board of Proceedings of Hermann Göring (Suicide),' Oct 1946 (NA, RG.260, Records of OMGUS Allied Control Council, file 2/92–1[2]).

19 Jackson diary, Aug 18, 1945.

20 W E Jackson to mother, Aug 21, 1945.

21 R H Jackson diary, Aug 20, 1945.

22 W E Jackson to mother, Aug 21, 1945.

23 R H Jackson diary, Aug 23, 1945.

24 W E Jackson to mother, Jul 12, 1945.

25 Ibid., Aug 21, 1945.

26 Jackson's records of US Chief of Counsel, the court archives of the Tribunal (IMT) and of the subsequent American proceedings, as well as the bulk of the OCCWC (Office of Chief of Counsel for War Crimes, which replaced the Office of Chief of Counsel in January 1946) are in the National Archives as RG.238, World War II War Crimes Records. There is held as RG.260 at the Federal Records Center, Suitland, Maryland, a residue of records of OMGUS, the Office of Military Government for Germany United States, including the papers of the IMT secretariat, as well as the Evidence and Language Divisions, and the records of the Defense Center.

27 This author has spent thirty years locating, retrieving, and copying these looted items which are in American private hands, and making them available to historians.

28 Kempner brazenly included in his works quotations from the Rosenberg diary which are not included in the only published version, as edited by Professor Hans-Günther Seraphim: *Das politische Tagebuch Alfred Rosenbergs* (Göttingen, 1956).

29 Alfred Seidl to IMT President (Lawrence), Jan 11, 1946 (Federal Records Center, Suitland: RG.260, OMGUS files [OCCWC], shipping list 74–3/7, box 117).

30 Lieut. Gerhard Schaefer, memos, 'Authentication of the Frank Diaries,' Dec 19, 1945; and 'Acquisition of the Frank Diaries,' May 22, 1946 (ibid.). Frank himself had not written or even countersigned the diaries—they were kept by the Reichstag (parliamentary) clerk Gnauck. There were forty volumes, including 1939, 1940 (5), 1941 (5), 1942 (3), 1943 (7), 1944 (4), and 1945 (1), as well as the minutes of his *Regierungssitzungen und Ansprachen*. They are on twelve reels of 16-millimetre microfilm in NA, RG.238.

31 Memo by Fred Niebergall, Chief of the Document Control Branch of R H Jackson's Evidence Division, Apr 22, 1948 (Federal Records Center, Suitland: RG.260, OMGUS files [OCCWC], shipping list 74–3/7, box 117).

32 M C B[ernays] to W B Donovan, Jul 2, 1945 (University of Chicago Law School, R H Jackson collection).

33 Memo, 'Keitel, Dönitz, Schacht, and Krupp as War Criminals,' with a

covering slip dated Aug 23, 1945 (PRO file LCO.2/2980, 'Attorney General's Committee and British War Crimes Executive,' pages 337ff).

34 Lieut.-Commander John P Bracken, USNR, to R H Jackson, Aug 24, 1945 (NA, RG.238, US Chief of Counsel at Nuremberg, Main Office Files, box 179).

35 R H Jackson, Oral History project, page 279; and Jackson to Truman, Nov 1945 (University of Chicago Law School, R H Jackson collection). In the R H Jackson files is a list of papers, including: 'The Donovan File: statements signed by Göring, by the various German generals; the letter from Schacht; his letter to you and your reply' (Library of Congress, Manuscript Division, R H Jackson papers, box 2).

36 Jackson, Oral History project, page 345.

37 Ibid. In Jackson's files is a 'Moscow confession' made by Fritzsche.

38 Francis Biddle diary, Oct 21, 1945 (University of Syracuse, New York, George Arents Research Library, Francis Biddle Collection, 'Personal Notes of Conferences').

39 Francis Biddle, letter, Nov 8, 1945 (University of Syracuse, New York, George Arents Research Library, Francis Biddle Collection, 'Personal').

40 HQ, 6850th Internal Security Detachment, IMT, 'Roster of Accused Showing Religious Preference,' Nov 27, 1945 (Burton C Andrus Collection, Colorado Springs).

41 Jackson diary, Aug 27, 1945.

42 Ibid., Aug 29, 1945.

43 Ibid., Aug 28. The Pope forwarded a packet of documents through Harold Tittman, the US chargé at the Vatican (ibid., Aug 29, 1945).

44 Ibid., Aug 29, 1945.

45 Ibid., Sep 5, 1945.

Notes to Chapter 9

1 R H Jackson writing in Nov 1946.

2 Unsigned memo, Apr 20, 1946, on International Military Tribunal, Nurnberg, Germany (Library of Congress, Manuscript Division, R H Jackson papers, box 103, 'misc.').

3 *New Yorker,* Sep 15, 1945 (NA, RG.238, US Chief of Counsel at Nuremberg, Main Office Files, box 213).

4 *New York Times*, Nov 22, 1945; cited Zayas, op. cit., page 255.

5 *IMT*, vol. ii, page 111.

6 William O Douglas, *An Almanac of Liberty* (New York, 1954), page 96, cited Zayas, op. cit., page 255.

7 S Glueck, *War Crimes. Their Prosecution and Their Punishment* (London, 1944), page 157.

8 W E Jackson to mother, Nuremberg, Sep 21, 1945 (Library of Congress, Manuscript Division, R H Jackson papers, box 2).

9 Ibid.

10 Ibid.

11 Karl-Heinz Keitel, 'Conversations with Dr Dr Nelte at Nuremberg,' Sep 19–27, 1946 (IfZ, Irving Collection).

12 Ibid., and Karl-Heinz Keitel, 'Conversation with My Father,' Sep 14, 1946, 1:30 P.M. (ibid.).

13 Keitel manuscript, undated (ibid.); and see Walter Görlitz (ed.), *The*

Memoirs of Field-Marshal Keitel, transl. David Irving (London, 1965) [hereafter Görlitz]; original, *Generalfeldmarschall Keitel. Verbrecher oder Offizier* (Göttingen, 1961).

14 R H Jackson diary, Aug 7 (Library of Congress, Manuscript Division, R H Jackson papers, box 95). McCloy and Donovan both expressed displeasure about the appointment of Biddle (ibid., Sep 5) as did Sam Rosenman (Sep 9, 1945).

15 Jackson diary, Sep 5, 1945.

16 Ibid., Sep 6, 8, 1945.

17 Ibid., Sep 5, 1945.

18 W E Jackson to mother, Sep 21, 1945; R H Jackson diary, Sep 11–12, 1945. Jackson refused to consider allowing the Poles in, which would have added another language and other difficulties.

19 R H Jackson to Irene, Oct 12, 1945 (Library of Congress, Manuscript Division, R H Jackson papers, box 2).

20 W E Jackson to mother, Sep 21, 1945 (ibid.).

21 Ibid., Aug 21, 1945.

22 Ibid., Sep 21, 1945.

23 R H Jackson to Irene, Oct 12, 1945.

24 W E Jackson to mother, Sep 21, 1945; and R H Jackson diary, Sep 13–15, 1945.

25 Jackson diary, Sep 16, 1945.

26 Francis M Shea to Coleman, Sep 15, 'Personnel Movement of Sunday, Sep 16, 1945' (NA, RG.238, US Chief of Counsel at Nuremberg, Main Office Files, box 201).

27 Jackson diary, Sep 5, 1945.

28 W E Jackson to mother, Nuremberg, Sep 21, 1945.

29 Francis Biddle, letter, Dec 28, 1945 (University of Syracuse, New York, George Arents Research Library, Francis Biddle Collection, 'Personal').

30 W E Jackson to R H Jackson, Aug 11, 1947 (Library of Congress, Manuscript Division, R H Jackson papers, box 2).

31 Zayas, op. cit., page 253.

32 Kranzbühler, op. cit., S12.

33 Ibid., page 12.

34 O. G. Svidovskaya, MS, quoted in Vladimir Abarinov, 'In the Corridors of the Palace of Justice,' in *Raduga* (Horizon), No. 9, Moscow 1989, pages 12ff [hereafter Abarinov]. Interpreter Yelizaveta Yefimovna Stenina-Shchemeleva said Buben crawled to the hotel's revolving door groaning, 'But they're our allies!'

35 *Pravda*, Moscow, Dec 12, 1945. R H Jackson to R Rudenko, Dec 10, 1945, quoted by Abarinov.

36 R H Jackson, Oral History project (University of Chicago Law School, R H Jackson collection).

37 Jackson to Irene, Oct 12, 1945.

38 Jackson diary, Sep 18–Oct 5, 1945.

39 Ibid., Oct 6, 1945.

40 Ibid., Oct 8, 1945.

Notes to Chapter 10

1 Biddle was born on May 9, 1886, Parker on Nov 20, 1885.

2 See the Francis Biddle Collection in the George Arents Research Library

at the University of Syracuse, New York. Among the items used for this work are Biddle's journal, 'Notes on Conferences,' in which the judge depicted the trial preparations; photographs, private letters from Nuremberg to his wife Katherine and son Randy; and trial documents. Of great importance are his 'Notes on Evidence,' ten bound volumes of typescript summaries of the evidence he had heard each day, organised in respect of each defendant, with often scathing personal comments. There are virtually complete sets of verbatim and summary minutes of the organisational proceedings from Oct 9, 1945 to Aug 30, 1946. See Biddle's articles, 'The Nurnberg Trials,' in *Virginia Law Review*, vol. 33, No. 6 (Nov 1947), and 'The Nurnberg Trial,' in *American Philosophical Society*, vol. 91, No. 3 (1947). Biddle died on Oct 4, 1968.

3 Francis Biddle diary, Oct 6, 1945 (University of Syracuse, New York, George Arents Research Library, Francis Biddle Collection, 'Personal Notes of Conferences').

4 R H Jackson diary, Jun 4, 1945 (Library of Congress, Manuscript Division, R H Jackson papers, box 95).

5 Biddle diary, Oct 2, 1945.

6 Ibid., Oct 3, 1945.

7 Ibid. See Quincy Wright, 'Legal Positivism and the Nuremberg Judgment,' in *American Journal of International Law* (undated); and 'Some Important Events in 1946; the Nuremberg Trial,' in *Journal of Criminal Law and Criminology of Northwestern University*, vol. 37, No. 6 (Mar–Apr 1947) (ibid., box 17).

8 Biddle diary, Oct 4, 1945.

9 Ibid. For the Canadian Prime Minister's diary record of his meetings with Hitler, Göring, and other top Nazis see Mackenzie King diary, Jun 1937 (Public Archives of Canada, Ottawa, William Lyon Mackenzie King papers, MG.26, J1), as well as Sir Nevile Henderson to Eden, Jun 27, 1937 (PRO file FO.954/10), and Sir Francis Floud (Ottawa) to FO, Aug 8, 1937 (PRO file FO.371/20750).

10 Biddle diary, Oct 7–9, 1945.

11 Ibid., Oct 9, 1945.

12 Ibid., Oct 10, 1945.

13 Jackson diary, Oct 8, 1945.

14 Biddle diary, Oct 10, 1945.

15 In a telegram dated Sep 9, 1946 Jackson proposed to Biddle that they write this in a preface to a documentation on the IMT: 'Upon assembling it was generally known that representatives of all nations were ready to agree upon the American member Francis Biddle as Presiding Officer. However the United States was to be host to all the nations at Nuremberg, had as its prisoners most of the defendants, had captured the bulk of the evidence, and had been delegated a leading part in the prosecution. Under these conditions, for the United States also to take the presidency of this Tribunal would tend to make the trial too predominantly an American enterprise in the eyes of Europe' (University of Syracuse, New York, George Arents Research Library, Francis Biddle Collection, 'Personal').

16 Biddle diary, Oct 13, 1945.

17 Cf ND: L–79; author's microfilm DI–78.

18 Cf ND: 1816–PS.

19 Cf ND: 2949–PS.

20 *IMT*, vol. i, page 58.

21 On Katyn, see Alfred-Maurice de Zayas, *Die Wehrmacht-Untersuchungsstelle. Unveröffentlichte Akten über alliierte Völkerrechtsverletzungen im Zweiten Weltkrieg* (Munich, 1979), chapter 23.
22 *IMT*, vol. v, pages 461f, Jan 17, 1946.
23 Ibid., vol. viii, page 286, Feb 26, 1946.
24 Milch diary, Oct 10, Nov 19, 1945 (author's microfilm DI–59).
25 Cherwell to Churchill, May 17, 1945 (Nuffield College, Oxford, Cherwell papers).
26 Memorandum, ibid.
27 R H Jackson to Irene, Oct 12, 1945 (Library of Congress, Manuscript Division, R H Jackson papers, box 2).
28 Jackson to Irene, Oct 15, 1945.
29 Abarinov, op. cit., pages 12ff, quoting Zorya's diary, Sep 14–20, 1945.
30 Jackson diary, Oct 14, 1945.
31 Jackson to Irene, Oct 15, 1945.
32 Biddle diary, Oct 15, 1945.
33 Wilhelm Keitel, Manuscript, Oct 10, 1945 (Karl-Heinz Keitel papers, in IfZ, Irving Collection).
34 Albert Speer, *Erinnerungen* (West Berlin, 1969) [hereafter Speer], page 509.
35 B C Andrus, 'Rules for Prisoners,' Sep 11, 1945 (NA, RG.238, entry 199, Records of HQ, 6850th Internal Security Detachment, IMT, box 7).
36 B C Andrus to Commanding General, HQ Command, IMT, Jan 31, 1946 (ibid.).
37 B C Andrus, 'Prisoner Routine, Nurnberg Jail,' Nov 10, 1945 (Burton C Andrus Collection, Colorado Springs).
38 B C Andrus, 'Proposed Broadcast, BBC' (ibid.). The passage is deleted.
39 B C Andrus to Peter-Josef Heisig (and all other Personnel Concerned), Dec 3, 1945 (ibid.).
40 B C Andrus, Headquarters Continental Central PWE#32, 'Rules and Regulations Governing PWE#32,' May 30, 1945 (Burton C Andrus Collection, Colorado Springs).
41 B C Andrus, 'Rules for Prisoners,' Sep 11, 1945 (ibid.). Only those Germans operating the prison were now still 'prisoners of war,' the rest were simply 'prisoners' and 'internees.'
42 Ibid.
43 Andrus to Commanding General, US Third Army, Dec 26, 1945 (ibid.); and Albert Göring to R H Jackson, Sep 6, and to IMT, Sep 19, 1945 (NA, RG.238, US Chief of Counsel at Nuremberg, Main Office Files, box 207).
44 Lieut.-Col. Rene H Juchli, 'Medical Service for the Palace of Justice and Court Jail,' Nov 24, 1945 (Burton C Andrus Collection, Colorado Springs).
45 Streicher diary, Nov 24, 1945 (Höffkes Collection).
46 Gordon Dean to Jackson, Donovan, Amen, *et al.*, 'Photographic Evidence,' Nov 18, 1945 (NA, RG.238, US Chief of Counsel at Nuremberg, Main Office Files, box 213). *The Nazi Plan, 1919–45* was a twenty-two-reel 35-millimetre film compiled from Germans newsreels and other German films with English subtitles.
47 Commander James B Donovan, USNR, to Colonel Storey, Dec 12, 1945 (NA, RG.238, US Chief of Counsel at Nuremberg, Main Office Files, box 213). 'Needless to say,' commented Donovan, 'after having the movies made in Frankfurt at their direction, cutting the film, preparing a script on it, etc., I was

rather shocked to learn of the absence of supporting evidence.'

48 F L Felton, undated private letter (Hoover Library, Frederick L Felton Collection, Ts Germany F 326).

49 Dr Tadeusz Cyprian, affidavit (ND: 3311–PS).

50 J B Donovan, Lieut.-Col. Calvin A. Behle, and Lieut. Hugh Daly, affidavit (ND: 2430–PS).

51 Dr Franz Blaha, affidavit (ND: 3249–PS).

52 The initials RIF on industrial-grade artificial soap stood for *Reinste Industrie Fett*.

53 Statement by Shmuel Krakoski, archives director at Yad Vashem Museum, Jerusalem; published in newspapers around the world, e.g. *Chicago Tribune*, Apr 25, 1990. Krakoski claimed it was sadistic Nazi propaganda, though it is hard to see how it would have benefited the Nazis. Justifying the forty-five-year delay, Krakoski said: 'When so many people deny the Holocaust ever happened, why give them something to use against the truth?'

54 Artur ('Atze') Brauner, in a statement published in German newspapers, e.g. *Frankfurter Allgemeine Zeitung*, May 6, 1995.

Notes to Chapter 11

1 These are now in the files of OMGUS at the Federal Records Center, Suitland, Maryland: Office of the Chief of Counsel for War Crime, Secretariat of the IMT, General Records, box 113, pieces 5021 and 5022.

2 Interrogation of Rudolf Hess, Oct 9, 1945 (NA film M.1270, roll 6); see David Irving, *Hess. The Missing Years, 1941–5* (London, 1987). For Jackson's recollections of the episode, see his Oral History project, chapter xxxix, 'Rudolf Hess: Balmy Exhibitionist' (University of Chicago Law School, R H Jackson collection), and box 100 of Library of Congress, Manuscript Division, R H Jackson papers.

3 Pre-trial interrogation of Franz von Papen, Oct 12, 1945 (NA film M.1270, roll 14).

4 R H Jackson to Dr John A P Millet, Oct 12, 1945 (Library of Congress, Manuscript Division, R H Jackson papers, box 107: 'Psychiatric and Personality Studies of Nazi Leaders').

5 R H Jackson to W E Jackson, Oct 12, 1945 (Library of Congress, Manuscript Division, R H Jackson papers, box 103: 'Office files, Jackson, William E'). In a hand-written working note in Jun 1945 Jackson observed that Strecker considered that 'a mass disorder plays a part' (ibid., box 107: 'Psychiatric and Personality Studies of Nazi Leaders').

6 Pre-trial interrogation of Papen, Oct 13, 1945.

7 Captain Richard V. Worthington, History, Rudolf Hess, Dec 31, 1945 (Library of Congress, Manuscript Division, R H Jackson papers, box 107: 'Psychiatric and Personality Studies of Nazi Leaders').

8 Major Douglas McG. Kelley, 'Psychiatric Status of Internee,' Oct 16, 1945 (ibid.).

9 Rudolf Hess prison diary, Oct 18, 1945 (copy in author's possession).

10 B C Andrus to R H Jackson, Oct 17, 1945 (Library of Congress, Manuscript Division, R H Jackson papers, box 107: 'Psychiatric and Personality Studies of Nazi Leaders').

11 Colonel Robert J Gill [to B C Andrus], Oct 20, 1945 (ibid.).

12 Francis Biddle, letter to Randy, 'Sunday Oct 2,' 1945; the date must be an error (University of Syracuse, New York, George Arents Research Library, Francis Biddle Collection, 'Personal Notes of Conferences').

13 Biddle diary, Oct 21, 1945 (ibid.).—See also his paper, 'The Nuremberg Trial,' in *Virginia Law Review*, vol. 3, 1947, pages 679–96.

14 Biddle, letter, Nov 2, 1945 (University of Syracuse, New York, George Arents Research Library, Francis Biddle Collection, 'Personal').

15 R J Jackson, undated letter, 'Thursday eve' [Nov 22, 1945] (Library of Congress, Manuscript Division, R H Jackson papers, box 2).

16 Karl-Heinz Keitel, 'Conversations with Dr Dr Nelte at Nuremberg,' Sep 19–27, 1946 (IfZ, Irving Collection).

17 Biddle diary, Oct 21, 1945. A year later, on Oct 7, 1946, Jackson would report to Truman that at its peak the US staff directly engaged on the case at Nuremberg numbered 365 civilians and 289 military personnel, a total of 654.

18 Biddle, letter, Nov 12, 1945.

19 W E Jackson to mother, Nuremberg, Sep 21, 1945 (Library of Congress, Manuscript Division, R H Jackson papers, box 2).

20 Pre-trial interrogation of Göring, Aug 28, 1945; these verbatim interrogations will be found on NA microfilm M.1270, roll 6. For all such *British* pre-trial interrogations by Mervyn Griffith-Jones and others see collection FO645 at the Imperial War Museum, London.

21 Interrogation of Göring, Oct 8, 1945.

22 W E Jackson to mother, Nuremberg, Sep 21, 1945.

23 Interrogation of the wife of Dr Hans Frank (NA, RG.153, Judge-Advocate General, Internal Affairs Division, box 1345, file 100–66).

24 F L Felton, undated private letter (Hoover Library, Frederick L Felton Collection, Ts Germany F 326).

25 Streicher diary, Nov 30, 1945 (Höffkes Collection).

26 Ibid.; for a two-page interrogation log on Streicher, Dec 13, 1945–Oct 5, 1946, see NA, RG.238, entry 199, Records of HQ, 6850th Internal Security Detachment, IMT, box 7.

27 Streicher diary, Nov 11, 1945. G[ustave] M[ahler] Gilbert, *Nuremberg Diary* (New York, 1947); German: *Nürnberger Tagebuch* [hereafter Gilbert], page 15, was one who referred to Streicher's alleged sexual perversions. Streicher's widow comments, 'In actual fact there is not the slightest basis for such allegations. By modern standards Streicher was normal to the point of ennui. There is probably nobody who ever heard a dirty joke from his lips.'

28 Heinrich Brüning, *Briefe und Gespräche, 1934–1945* (Munich, 1974), pages 542–3.

29 Karl-Heinz Keitel, 'Conversations with Dr Dr Nelte at Nuremberg,' Sep 19–27, 1946 (IfZ, Irving Collection).

30 Werner Bross, *Gespräche mit Göring während des Nürnberger Prozesses* (Flensburg, Hamburg, 1950) [hereafter Bross].

31 Speer to his wife, Oct 27, 1945; Speer, op. cit., page 512.

32 Karl-Heinz Keitel, 'Conversations with My Father,' Sep 21, 1946, 1:30 P.M. (IfZ, Irving Collection).—Hitler offered similar excuses to Ribbentrop's liaison officer Walther Hewel, see his 1941 diary (Irving Collection); and see Keitel's remarks on Sep 25, 1946, 1 P.M., who quotes Hitler as saying: '*Jawohl*, I know it's illegal, but either we win or it's all over for the German people anyway!'

33 Manuscript by Jodl (Luise Jodl papers; copy in IfZ, Irving Collection).

34 Keitel to Nelte, Oct 24, 1945; in Görlitz, op. cit., page 235.

35 D M Kelley to B C Andrus, Oct 25, 1945, 'Exercise of Internees' (Burton C Andrus Collection, Colorado Springs).

36 W J Donovan to Colonel R G Storey, Oct 25, 1945 (Library of Congress, Manuscript Division, R H Jackson papers, box 107: 'Psychiatric and Personality Studies of Nazi Leaders').

37 Much of it was nonetheless of historical value (NA, RG.238, US Chief of Counsel at Nuremberg, Main Office Files, box 181). The author has made the complete Ley file available on his microfilm DI–79. The file includes papers on the suicide, as well as a curriculum vitæ (16 pages); letter Ley to his wife, Aug 14; 'Inga, a Dialogue' (25 pages), Aug 14–16; Ley to Henry Ford, Aug 17; 'My Children! My Testament,' (17 pages), Aug 22; 'To My People! My Political Testament' (21 pages), Aug 25; a typescript, 'Thoughts on the Führer' (18 pages); 'Life or Fame—a Political Inquest' (18 pages); 'A Farmer's Fate' (73 pages); various letters to his children; Ley to Dr Flicke on Principles of the Law, Oct 24; statement by Ley, Oct 24; 'Abschied (Farewell),' (7 pages); and 'Farewell' (6 pages).

38 See the formal log of these notifications in Burton C Andrus Collection, Colorado Springs (folder iii).

39 For Schacht's own memoirs on the trial, see his memoirs, *Abrechnung mit Hitler* (Hamburg, 1948), or *Account Settled* (London, 1948).

40 Streicher diary, Nov 30, 1945.

Notes to Chapter 12

1 Francis Biddle, letter, Oct 25, 1945 (University of Syracuse, New York, George Arents Research Library, Francis Biddle Collection, 'Personal'). See too the message of Nov 27, 1945 from R H Jackson to Harold H Tittmann, the US chargé d'affaires at the Vatican, replying to a note from His Holiness about Papen (NA, RG.238, US Chief of Counsel at Nuremberg, Main Office Files, box 182).

2 Biddle, letter, Nov 1, 1945.

3 Biddle, letter, Nov 6–7, 1945.

4 Eisenhower's political adviser Robert Murphy, reported, op. cit., pages 360–1, visiting one such camp. 'I was startled to see that our prisoners were almost as weak and emaciated as those I had observed in Nazi prison camps. The youthful commandant calmly told us that he had deliberately kept the inmates on starvation diet.... After we left, the medical director asked me, "Does that camp represent American policy in Germany?"'

5 James Bacque, *Other Losses* (Toronto, 1989).

6 On which see *New York Times*, Nov 1, 1994; and the revelations by the Jewish author John Sack in *Eye for an Eye* (New York, 1994). He indicts Solomon Morel, commandant of the camp at Swietochlowice. Eighty thousand German men, women, and children, states Sacks, were tortured and put to death in internment camps run by vengeance-seeking officers like Morel, who now lives in Tel Aviv and is under investigation by Dr Stanislaw Kaniewski, the Polish government's senior prosecutor at Katowice.

7 Maxwell Fyfe to Sylvia (his wife), Oct 25, 1945; Maxwell Fyfe, op. cit., page 103.

8 Maxwell Fyfe to Sylvia, Nov 1, 1945;.

9 Erich M. Lipman to Lieut. Blumenstein, Oct 29, 1945 (NA film M.1270, roll 6).

10 Rudolf Hess diary, Oct 21, 1945 (copy in the author's possession).

11 Milch diary, Nov 5, 1945 (author's microfilm DI–59); and affidavit, Mar 1947. Taxed by the author with this episode during an interview in New York, Engländer threatened proceedings for defamation but did not enforce his threat.

12 Despite the most strenuous efforts, the Yad Vashem Museum, Jerusalem has compiled a list of no more than three million possible Holocaust victims. The same names appear in this list many times over.

13 Transcript of John Toland's interview with Konrad Morgen, attorney, Frankfurt, Oct 25, 1971 (Roosevelt Library, John Toland papers, box 53). For Morgen's Nuremberg testimony see *IMT*, Aug 7–8, 1946, pages 488–515.

14 R H Jackson, Oral History project (University of Chicago Law School, R H Jackson collection).

15 Memo for Jackson, Jul 12, 1945, 'OSS Proposals for Propaganda,' and Jackson to Donovan (NA, RG.238, US Chief of Counsel at Nuremberg, Main Office Files, box 213).

16 Ibid.

17 Affidavit by Rudolf Höss, Apr 5, 1946 (ND: 3868–PS); for the original interrogations of Höss see NA film M.1270, reel 7.

18 Wilhelm Keitel, Manuscript, Oct 10, 1945 (Karl-Heinz Keitel papers, in IfZ, Irving Collection).

19 Pre-trial interrogation of Göring, Aug 27, 1945 (NA film M.1270, roll 6).

20 Ibid., Oct 20, 1945.

21 Ibid., Nov 6, 1945; a Private Sonnenfeldt was also present as interpreter (ibid.).

22 Maxwell Fyfe, op. cit., page 107.

23 Jackson to General W J Donovan, 'Interrogation of Witnesses,' Nov 14, 1945 (Burton C Andrus Collection, Colorado Springs).

24 Biddle, letter, Nov 12, 1945.

25 Donovan to Jackson, Nov 14, 1945.

26 'Amen's interrogation of Lahousen *re* Thanksgiving dinner at Donovan's house,' is listed in note, 'papers desired from R H Jackson Files,' in Library of Congress, Manuscript Division, R H Jackson papers, box 2.

27 Biddle, letter, Nov 28, 1945.

28 Jackson to Truman, Dec 1, 1945 (Library of Congress, Manuscript Division, R H Jackson papers, box 101).

29 R H Jackson to Irene, Dec 20, 1945 (Library of Congress, Manuscript Division, R H Jackson papers, box 2).

30 Ibid., Jan 10, 1946.

31 The letter was from Horsky, and is listed in note, 'papers desired from RHJ Files,' in Library of Congress, Manuscript Division, R H Jackson papers, box 2.

32 Minutes of Chief Prosecutors' Meeting on Nov 9, 1945 (Library of Congress, Manuscript Division, R H Jackson papers, box 98); and see Jackson to Rudenko and Champetier de Ribes, Mar 8, 1946; the Russian translation is in CGAOR [Central State Archives of the October Revolution], f. 7445, op. 2, d. 8, l.47.

33 Abarinov, op. cit., quoting: 'Information from Pokrovsky, CGAOR, f. 7445, op. 2, d. 391, l.57'.

34 Pre-trial interrogations of Hildegard Fath and Ingeborg Sperr, Nov 16, 1945; and Hess diary, Nov 16, 1945.

35 Biddle, letter, Nov 18, 1945.

36 Ibid., letter, Nov 12, 1945.

37 Alderman to Shea and Telford Taylor, Sep 7, on Dr Lemkin's study of Karl Haushofer; and to R H Jackson, Sep 13, 1945, 'Karl Haushofer as a Major War Criminal' (NA, RG.238, US Chief of Counsel at Nuremberg, Main Office Files, box 190).

38 Maxwell Fyfe to Sylvia, Oct 26, 1945.

39 Biddle diary, Nov 14, 1945 (University of Syracuse, New York, George Arents Research Library, Francis Biddle Collection, 'Personal Notes of Conferences').

40 F L Felton, private letter, Nov 14, 1945 (Hoover Library, Frederick L Felton Collection, Ts Germany F 326).

41 Streicher diary, Nov 19, 1945 (Höffkes Collection).

42 Biddle, letter, Nov 18, 1945.

43 Biddle diary, Nov 19, 1945.

44 Jackson diary, Nov 19, 1945.

45 Biddle diary, Nov 19, 1945.

46 Ibid.; Maxwell Fyfe, op. cit., page 102.

47 The commission's records are in the former Central State Archives of the October Revolution in Moscow; reproduced in Abarinov, op. cit.

48 Soviet Supervisory Commission for the Nuremberg Trials, Protocol No. 1, Session of Nov 26, 1945 in Nuremberg; Annex 1 to Abarinov, op. cit. The subject continued to cause heartburn after the trial began. On Dec 3 the Soviet delegation would demand the deletion of passages 'that are unacceptable to the USSR' from the speech of the British chief prosecutor Sir Hartley Shawcross, and on Dec 7 similar passages from the speech by Alderman.

49 Biddle, letter, Nov 19, 1945. Name spellings have been corrected.

Notes to Chapter 13

1 Streicher diary, Nov 27, 1945 (Höffkes Collection).

2 Ibid., Nov 21, 1945.

3 Francis Biddle diary, Nov 17, 1945 (University of Syracuse, New York, George Arents Research Library, Francis Biddle Collection, 'Personal Notes of Conferences').

4 Birkett raised this point. Ibid.

5 See H Donnedieu de Vabres, 'Le procès de Nuremberg devant les principes modernes du droit pénal international,' in *Recueil de Cours*, vol. 70 (Paris, 1947), pages 447–582; copy in University of Syracuse, George Arents Research Library, Francis Biddle Collection, box 16.

6 Streicher diary, Nov 27, 1945.

7 R H Jackson, undated letter, 'Thursday eve' [Nov 22, 1945] (Library of Congress, Manuscript Division, R H Jackson papers). His opening speech is recorded on twenty-four discs in NA, RG.238.

8 Minutes of Chief Prosecutors' Meeting, Dec 5, 1945 (Library of Congress, Manuscript Division, R H Jackson papers, box 98; these are microfilmed on the author's films DI–70 and 71).

9 Kranzbühler, op. cit., page 24.

10 Zayas, op cit., page 264.

11 Francis Biddle, letter, Nov 25, 1945 (University of Syracuse, New York, George Arents Research Library, Francis Biddle Collection, 'Personal').

12 ND: 2949–PS.

13 The 35-millimetre film runs to seven reels.

14 F L Felton, undated private letter (Hoover Library, Frederick L Felton Collection, Ts Germany F 326). For an official summary of the reaction of each of the accused when shown the concentration camp film, see the Burton C Andrus Collection, Colorado Springs (file iii). The Warsaw Ghetto film was not staged in the sense that Hollywood staged SA brutalities and Japanese atrocities with hired screen-actors for their documentary series *The March of Time*; Dr Goebbels had sent his cameramen into the ghetto to obtain raw film footage for use in the Deutsche Film-Gesellschaft production *Der ewige Jude*. Elke Fröhlich (ed.), *Die Tagebücher von Joseph Goebbels. Sämtliche Fragmente*, 4 vols (Munich 1987), vol.3: *1.1.1937–31.12.1939*; entries for Oct 17, 24, Nov 2, 3, 9, 11, 12, 18, 19, 28, Dec 18, 1939.

15 Luise Jodl papers; copy in IfZ, Irving Collection.

16 One can screen the entire series of SD-*Meldungen aus dem Reich* for example and find no reference by the public to the Final Solution.

17 Hess diary, Nov 30; for his statement of Nov 30, and Lord Justice Lawrence's ruling on Hess of Dec 1, 1945 see NA, RG.238, US Chief of Counsel at Nuremberg, Main Office Files, box 180.

18 R H Jackson to Irene, 'Friday night,' [Nov 30], 1945 (Library of Congress, Manuscript Division, R H Jackson papers, box 2).

19 Biddle, letter, Nov 25, 1945.

20 ND: 003–L.

21 Adolf Hitler's Political Testament, Apr 30, 1945, as cited by R H Jackson in *IMT*, vol. ix, pages 480f.

22 Streicher diary, Nov 27, 1945.

23 Ibid., Nov 29, 1945.

24 Ibid., Nov 30, 1945.

25 H Shawcross and D Maxwell Fyfe to R H Jackson, Nov 1945 (IfZ, Irving collection, Jackson papers, vol. iii).

26 Kranzbühler, op. cit., page 6.

27 Ibid., page 7.

28 'He says the trial was conducted fairly,' noted Keitel's son after one conversation, 'so long as the defendants weren't physical wrecks from the conditions at Nuremberg.' He commented however, 'Particularly important in this respect the withholding of defence documents of the last twelve years.' Karl-Heinz Keitel, 'Conversation with My Father,' Sep 16, 1946, 1:30 P.M. (IfZ, Irving Collection).

29 Maxwell Fyfe, op. cit., page 106.

30 Zayas, op. cit., page 261.

31 'Die Juden leben nur noch zum kleinen Teil; zigtausend sind weg. Ich darf aber sagen, was die einheimische Bevölkerung bekommt; sie bekommt auf Ihre Anweisung 50% weniger als die deutsche.' Stenographic record of Reichsmarschall Göring's Conference on the Food Situation with the Reich Commissars for the Occupied Territories and the Military Governors, on the afternoon of Thursday Aug 6, 1942 in the Hermann-Göring Room of the Reich Air Ministry (ND: Exhibit USSR 170). Note that although the crucial page 144 is missing, the Russian pencil pagination continues without a break.

32 Speer, op. cit., page 514.

33 Alfred Seidl to IMT president (Lawrence), Jan 11, 1946 (Federal Records Center, Suitland: RG.260, OMGUS files [OCCWC], shipping list 74–3/7, box 117).

34 Von der Lippe, diary, page 193; copy in IfZ, Irving Collection.

35 Adele Streicher, comments on Hans Fritzsche, *Das Schwert auf der Waage* (Heidelberg, 1953), page 165.

36 Biddle to Jahrreiss, Aug 2, 1946, with a memorandum on the protection of defence counsel against press attacks (University of Syracuse, New York, George Arents Research Library, Francis Biddle Collection, 'Trial Documents,' box 15).

37 Report by Officer-in-Charge, Defendants' Information Center, to R H Jackson, Jul 24, 1946 (University of Chicago Law School, R H Jackson collection).

38 Felton, undated private letter, op. cit.

39 Walter Rapp memo on housing witnesses, Nov 22, 1946 (NA, RG.238, entry 199, Records of HQ, 6850th Internal Security Detachment, IMT, box 7).

40 Karl-Heinz Keitel, 'Conversation with My Father,' Sep 14, 1946, 1:30 P.M. (IfZ, Irving Collection).

41 For the original records of the Supreme Council meetings, see the papers of French Prime Minister and War Minister Edouard Daladier at the Fondation Nationale des Sciences Politiques, Archive d'Histoire Contemporaine. Boxes 2–DA–5–Dr 3, 4, 5, and 7 contain the minutes of the Conseil Supreme meetings of Feb 5, Mar 27, 28, Apr 5, 9, 22, 23, 27, and May 6, 1940; these were in German hands from Jun 1940 onward, as were the copies in Prime Minister Paul Reynaud's files, now in the Archives Nationales in Paris, Paul Reynaud papers, box 74 AP 22. Copies taken by the Germans of the records of the French General Staff, 1939–40, and of the French Foreign Ministry, 1939–40, are on NA microfilm T120, rolls 115 and 127 respectively. The German Foreign Ministry published them in a series of White Books: No. 4, *Dokumente zur englisch-französischen Politik der Kriegsausweitung*; No. 5, *Weitere Dokumente zur Kriegsausweiterungspolitik der Westmächte: Die Generalstabsbesprechungen Englands und Frankreichs mit Belgien und den Niederländen*; and No. 6, *Die Geheimakten des französischen Generalstabes* (all Berlin, 1940).

42 Luise Jodl, unpublished biography of her husband Alfred Jodl (Luise Jodl papers; copy in IfZ, Irving Collection). For the international-law aspects of the invasion of Norway, see Hermann Mossler's unpublished paper, 'Comments on Document Entitled, "International Legal Evaluation of the Norway Action",' Apr 6, 1946 (University of Syracuse, George Arents Research Library, Francis Biddle Collection, box 16).

43 Statement by Dr Kurt Kaufmann, Kaltenbrunner's lawyer (standing in for Dr Stahmer), Jan 19, 1947 (Erhard Milch papers; copy in author's possession).

44 Dulles' letters about this allegation are listed in note, 'papers desired from R H Jackson Files,' in Library of Congress, Manuscript Division, R H Jackson papers, box 2. There are 1943–45 files on 'Unconditional Surrender,' 'Sunrise,' and Karl Wolff in Princeton University, Seeley Mudd Manuscript Library, Allen W Dulles papers, boxes 19–21.

45 Milch diaries, Nov 5, 1945; Mar–Apr 1947 (author's microfilm DI–59).

46 Nelte to Frau Lisa Keitel née Fontaine, cited in Görlitz, op. cit.

47 Streicher diary, Nov 22, 1945.

48 Ernest Schoenfeld to R H Jackson, Dec 1, 1945 (NA, RG.238, US Chief of Counsel at Nuremberg, Main Office Files, box 184).

Notes to Chapter 14

1 For two memoranda by Donnedieu de Vabres dated Jul 8, 1946 on Jahrreiss' arguments, see University of Syracuse, New York, George Arents Research Library, Francis Biddle Collection, 'Trial Documents,' box 14; therein is also a memorandum by Nikitchenko on 'the Conception of Conspiracy', Jul 17, 1946.

2 R H Jackson to Irene, Mary, and Nancy, Dec 20, 1945 (Library of Congress, Manuscript Division, R H Jackson papers, box 2).

3 Ibid., Jan 10, 1946.

4 Francis Biddle, letter, Jan 1, 1946 (University of Syracuse, New York, George Arents Research Library, Francis Biddle Collection, 'Personal').

5 Ibid., letter, Dec 31, 1945.

6 Göring to President of Tribunal, Jan 12, 1946, hand-written (BDC, Director's Safe).

7 Hans Frank to Biddle, undated, hand-written (ibid.).

8 Andrus memo, 'Arrest of Families of Prisoners,' Jan 12, 1946 (Burton C Andrus Collection, Colorado Springs).

9 These letters are all now in private collectors' hands.

10 Speer to his wife, Aug 1946; Speer, op. cit., page 595.

11 Milch initially believed in Speer's story of his assassination plot (Milch diary, Mar 6, 1946, May 9 and 14, 1947: '[The] assassination helped him a lot' in the trial; but by May 22, 1948 his diary showed that the field-marshal was deeply disillusioned by his former friend and now regarded the story as a fiction (author's microfilm DJ–59).

12 Jackson to Irene, Mary, and Nancy, Dec 20, 1945.

13 Jackson to Irene, Jan 12, 1946.

14 Biddle, letter, Jan 27, 1946.—Memo for R H Jackson, Aug 24, 1945: 'Grand Admiral Dönitz as a war criminal' (NA, RG.238, US Chief of Counsel at Nuremberg, Main Office Files, box 179).

15 War Diary of C-in-C, U-Boats (Dönitz), Sep 17, 1942; quoted in above-cited memo for Jackson. Interrogated at Mürwik on Aug 3, 1945, Eberhard Godt explained that the order resulted from the RAF's bombing the U-boat commanded by Hartenstein when he was rescuing the survivors of the torpedoed liner *Laconia*; the orders, he said, merely reflected that the safety of the U-boat had to come first. As British naval Intelligence officer Lieut.-Commander Patrick Beesly pointed out, 'It is improbable that [Masters and Chief Engineers] were to have been rescued if the remainder of the survivors were to have been machine-gunned' (ibid.).

16 War Diary of C-in-C, German Navy, May 4, 10, 1945; cited ibid.

17 Interrogation of Kapitän zur See Alleweldt, Aug 16, 1945; cited ibid.

18 Interrogations of Konteradmiral Godt and Fregattenkapitän Kessler, Aug 10, 1945; cited ibid.

19 Information from Admiral Godt to the author, May 4, 1969; he also described this incident late in 1945 to Field-Marshal Milch, who noted it in his diary (author's microfilm DI–59).

20 For the CSDIC (UK) transcripts of these interrogations, taken by hidden

microphones, see PRO file WO.208/4198; more documents on the Eck case are in NA, RG.84, US embassy in London, secret files, box 30, file '711.6 United Nations Commission.'

21 *IMT*, vol. xiii, page 460. Möhle evidently bore Dönitz a grudge. Milch recorded in his diary on Feb 9, 1946: 'Captain Möhle, commander of a submarine flotilla, also thinks that Dönitz made a bad C-in -C, but that all his submariners think the world of him.'

22 Amen to W E Jackson, Apr 30, 1946 (NA, RG.238, US Chief of Counsel at Nuremberg, Main Office Files, box 184).

23 Eugene Davidson, *The Trial of the Germans* (New York) [hereafter Davidson], page 422.

24 German Naval Staff (Seekriegsleitung) War Diary, Sep 1942, passim.

25 The undated six-page typescript dissent is among Biddle's papers with a note in his hand reading, 'This was not filed. Probably suggested by [Judge] Parker' (University of Syracuse, George Arents Research Library, Francis Biddle Collection, box 19).

26 Sir Norman Brooke to Sir Orme Sargent, Mar 16, 1946 (PRO file PREM.8/393).

27 Ernest Bevin to Clement Attlee, Mar 27, 1946 (ibid.).

28 Brooke to Sir Leslie Rowan, Attlee's private secretary, Mar 29, 1946 (ibid.).

29 E.g. a letter from Dr Werner Knieper's office in Dortmund to Dr Hans Laternser at Nuremberg, Jul 15, 1947, intercepted by US Civil Censorship Division of USFET; Knieper suggested that they discourage defence counsel Dr Rauschenbach from calling Warlimont as a defence witness in the South-Eastern Generals' Case. It was passed to the Office of the Chief of Counsel for War Crimes (Trevor Roper papers, IfZ, Irving collection).

30 Patrick Dean, top-secret minute, Jun 18, 1945 (PRO file LCO.2/2980, 'Attorney General's Committee and British War Crimes Executive').

31 CSDIC (UK) report SRGG.1238 (PRO file WO.208/4170).

32 CSDIC (UK) reports SRGG.1234c, 1279, 1311 (ibid.); Milch diary, Jun 5, Jul 29, 1945. There is an interrogation of the chauffeur Joseph Skock in NA, RG.153, Judge-Advocate General, Internal Affairs Division, box 1534.

33 Interrogation of Göring, Dec 22, 1945, ibid., box 1534; and CSDIC/CMF/X reports 166–172, Jun–Jul 1945 with letters W J Donovan to J B Donovan, warning him to limit access to the prisoners severely (ibid., box 1495).

34 Sir Frank H Hinsley *et al.*, *British Intelligence in the Second World War. Its Influence on Strategy and Operations* (Cambridge, 1979–84), vol. ii, appendix on SS and police codes.

35 Unsigned note to Col. J H Amen, in NA, of pre-trial interrogations of Halder (IfZ, Irving Collection, R H Jackson papers, vol. ii, page 709). The report in which Generals Burckhard Müller-Hillebrand and Franz Halder cynically discuss how to twist the facts to exonerate the General Staff from any charge of war-mongering is CSDIC (UK) report SRGG.1350, of Sep 9, 1945 (PRO file WO.208/4170).

36 Author's interview of Dr Egon Kubuschok, Mar 31, 1971.

37 See the FO dossier, 'Translation of Report of Negotiations between Great Britain and Germany,' Nov 16, 1942–Apr 16, 1943 (PRO file FO.371/34482).

38 Minutes of Chief Prosecutors' Meeting, Oct 26, 1945 (University of Chicago Law School, R H Jackson collection; now Library of Congress, Manuscript Division, R H Jackson papers, box 98).

39 Witness-application for Fritz Herrwarth, Streicher defence, Jan 24, 1946 (NA, RG.260, OMGUS files, box 117). For Jackson's files of IMT rulings on Defence Applications, see Library of Congress, Manuscript Division, R H Jackson papers, box 100.

40 On Mar 7, 1946 (Library of Congress, Manuscript Division, R H Jackson papers, box 100).

41 Author's interview of Dr Kubuschok, Mar 31, 1971.

42 F L Felton, private letter [Jan 1946] entitled 'Third Report on the Battle of Nuremberg' (Hoover Library, Frederick L Felton Collection, Ts Germany F 326).

43 W E Jackson to Gordon Dean, Nov 2, 1945 (NA, RG.238, US Chief of Counsel at Nuremberg, Main Office Files, box 213).

44 Jodl to his wife, 1945 (Luise Jodl papers; copy in IfZ, Irving Collection).

45 Ibid.

46 E.g. on the letter which Lord Justice Lawrence wrote to R H Jackson, Jul 26, 1946: the printed heading was 'British War Crimes Executive (ES)', which was also used by Sir David Maxwell Fyfe and Sir Hartley Shawcross (University of Chicago Law School, R H Jackson collection).

47 Kranzbühler, op. cit., page 11.

48 Lord Oaksey (as he had become), speaking at Birmingham, Jun 21, 1947.

49 The Americans held a dinner for Vyshinsky at the Grand Hotel that Monday, the Russians on the following Friday, Nov 30, and the British on Saturday after that, Dec 1, 1945; undated letter of R H Jackson, 'Thursday' [Nov 22, 1945] (Library of Congress, Manuscript Division, R H Jackson papers).

50 R H Jackson, Oral History project, page 480 (University of Chicago Law School, R H Jackson collection).

51 bid.

52 See the documentation in the University of Chicago Law School, R H Jackson collection, especially the files 'British Delegation 1945–1946,' 'French delegation 1945–1946,' 'Misc. Correspondence 1945–1946,' and 'USSR Delegation 1945–1946.'

53 Norman Birkett to R H Jackson, Jul 26, 1946.

Notes to Chapter 15

1 Kurt Erdt to R H Jackson, Borkum, Dec 7, 1945 (Library of Congress, Manuscript Division, R H Jackson papers).

2 Pastor Dr Berthold Müller to R H Jackson, Schwäbisch-Gmünd, Dec 29, 1945 (ibid.).

3 J P Hubbel to R H Jackson, New Jersey, Jan 30, 1946 (ibid.).

4 Carl Zuckmayer to R H Jackson, Sep 1946 (IfZ, Irving Collection, R H Jackson papers, vol. iii).

5 Milch diary, Apr 5, 1947. Gaston M Ullmann (born Behrmann, 'the bosom-buddy of Mr Kempner') was later unmasked as an international swindler and jailed (ibid., Apr 20, 1948); on May 19, 1948 the newspapers reported his arrest for fraud, his flight, and subsequent suicide attempt. Milch commented: 'It's all catching up on these crooks and traitors.'

6 Kranzbühler, op. cit., page 24.

7 Reichsmarschall's speech to the Air Staff officers, Nov 25, 1944 (General Karl Koller papers, author's microfilm DI–17).

8 Bross, op. cit., pages 85ff (Feb 20, 1946).

9 R H Jackson to US State Dept., Feb 13, 1946 (NA, RG.238, US Chief of Counsel at Nuremberg, Main Office Files).

10 B C Andrus to Lord Justice Lawrence, Aug 29; and to Public Relations Officer, War Dept., Sep 6, 1946: 'Misconduct of Dr Douglas M Kelley' (Burton C Andrus Collection, Colorado Springs).

11 Howard Whitman and Dr Douglas M Kelley, 'What Goering & Co. Talk about in their Cells,' *Sunday Express*, Aug 25, 1946.

12 Speer, op. cit., page 512.

13 G M Gilbert, 'psychological-intelligence' reports (Library of Congress, Manuscript Division, R H Jackson papers; copy in IfZ, Irving collection, Jackson papers, vol. iii). They are undated but from internal evidence were written in Feb 1946.

14 Karl-Heinz Keitel, 'Conversation with My Father,' Sep 16, 1946, 1:30 P.M. (IfZ, Irving Collection).

15 General Alfred Jodl to his wife Luise, Oct 8, 1946; published in *Der Turmwart*, No. 4/5, Zürich, April/May 1949.

16 Speer, op. cit., page 512.

17 In the possession of Berlin journalist Henrik Pastor, who in 1987 showed it to this author along with seven audiotapes of Rudolf Hess talking with Spandau commandant Eugene Bird.

18 Gilbert confidential memorandum to Jackson, undated [Feb 1946] (Library of Congress, Manuscript Division, R H Jackson papers; copy in IfZ, Irving Collection, Jackson papers, vol. iii).

19 Gilbert, op. cit.

20 W E Jackson to R H Jackson Jan 16, 1947 (Library of Congress, Manuscript Division, R H Jackson papers, box 2).

Notes to Chapter 16

1 General Nikitchenko to fellow judges, May 27, 1946 (University of Syracuse, New York, George Arents Research Library, Francis Biddle Collection, box 14, 'Trial Documents').

2 Francis Biddle, letter, Feb 7, 1946 (ibid., 'Personal').

3 Ibid., Feb 24, 1946.

4 Ibid., Feb 13, 1946.

5 Ibid.

6 Ibid., Mar 13, 1946.

7 Ibid., Mar 5, 1946.

8 Ibid., Feb 24, 1946. His wife finally came out to join him, returning to the States in mid-May.

9 Ibid., Mar 17, 1946.

10 Author's interview of Dr Egon Kubuschok, Mar 31, 1971.

11 Andrus to prisoners, Feb 16, 1946 (NA, RG.238, entry 199, Records of HQ, 6850th Internal Security Detachment, IMT, box 7).

12 Milch diary, Aug 23, 1946 (author's microfilm DI–59).

13 Ibid., Mar 6, 1946.

14 Ibid., Mar 8, 1945.

15 *IMT*, vol. ix, page 63, German text, checked against sound recordings in NA.

16 Ibid., pages 54–5; Milch diary, Jul 11, 1948.

17 *IMT*, vol. ix, page 125 (NA disc 1430B).

18 Ibid., page 88 (NA disc 1437B).

19 Ibid., page 137. The entire exchange can be heard on NA disc 1440B. It is missing from the mimeographed transcript, page 5660, line 20.

20 The Lists of Transferred Internees are in NA, RG.238, entry 199, Records of HQ, 6850th Internal Security Detachment, IMT, box 8.

21 R H Jackson to John J McCloy, Mar 27, 1946 (University of Chicago Law School, R H Jackson collection).

22 Bross, op. cit., May 14, 1946, page 196.

23 Author's interview of Dr Kubuschok.

24 Information from Professor Dr med. Gerhard Rose to the author.

25 H Montgomery Hyde, *The Life of Lord Birkett* (London, 1964).

26 Seymour Krieger, comments on documents ND: 057–PS, 1676–PS, and L–154 (IfZ, Irving Collection, R H Jackson papers, vol. ii).

27 Author's interview of Ralph Albrecht, New York, May 22, 1971.

28 Minutes of Chief Prosecutors' Meeting held on Mar 19, 1946 (Library of Congress, Manuscript Division, R H Jackson papers, box 98).

29 In a letter to this author, Jun 23, 1983.

30 Ibid.

31 Maxwell Fyfe, op. cit., page 114.

32 R H Jackson to Gordon Dean, Mar 25, 1946 (University of Chicago Law School, R H Jackson collection).

33 Jackson to John J McCloy, Mar 27, 1946 (ibid.).

34 Biddle letter, Mar 19, 1946.

35 W E Jackson to mother, Mar 29, 1946 (Library of Congress, Manuscript Division, R H Jackson papers, box 2).

36 Biddle letter, Mar 19, 1946.

37 Ibid.

38 W E Jackson to mother, Mar 29, 1946. 'But most of us are hardly on speaking terms with Biddle these days.'

39 R H Jackson to Irene, 'aboard the plane bound for Paris' [Mar 30, 1946] (Library of Congress, Manuscript Division, R H Jackson papers, box 2). 'In Paris I was guest of the French Bar … and collected more medals than Goering.' Ibid., Apr 18, 1946.

40 Lieut.-Col. Ernst Engländer to Justice R H Jackson, May 18, 1946 (NA, RG.238, US Chief of Counsel at Nuremberg, Main Office Files, box 179).

41 Milch diary, Jun 4; Lieut.-Col. J Amen to Thomas J Dodd, Jun 7; Dodd to R H Jackson, Jun 10, 1946 (ibid.).

42 *Daily Express*, Mar 25, 1946. A dispatch by Selkirk Panton (National Library of Australia, Canberra, Collection 5808, Selkirk Panton papers, folder 3).

43 A. Ferida Rassam to R H Jackson, Mar 30, 1946 (Library of Congress, Manuscript Division, R H Jackson papers, box 99: 'Public Reaction to Trial, Mar 1946').

Notes to Chapter 17

1 Minutes of Chief Prosecutors' Meeting, Apr 5, 1946, 5:15 P.M.; both the stenographic text and a duplicated summary are in this file (University of Chicago Law School, R H Jackson Collection).

2 Ibid., summary.

3 Norman Birkett MS.

4 R H Jackson, Oral History project (University of Chicago Law School, R H Jackson collection).

5 Karl-Heinz Keitel, 'Conversation with My Father,' Sep 21, 1946, 1:30 P.M. (IfZ, Irving Collection).

6 Allen W Dulles to R H Jackson, Mar 27, 1946 (Library of Congress, Manuscript Division, R H Jackson papers, box 102, 'Gisevius, Hans Bernd').

7 Strategic Services Unit, War Dept., USFET, to Capt. Sam Harris, Office of Chief of Counsel, Mar 28, 1946 (ibid.). Gisevius had a difficult time after the war. Lunching with W E Jackson on Jan 18, 1949 he revealed that he had withdrawn his own book *Bis zum Bitteren Ende* in Germany because Field-Marshal von Blomberg's widow had gained an injunction as the book called her an ex-prostitute (she was not); he was surprised to find himself being constantly slandered by 'the neo-Nazis.' W E Jackson to parents, Jan 18, 1949 (Library of Congress, Manuscript Division, R H Jackson papers, box 2).

8 Karl-Heinz Keitel, 'Conversation with My Father,' Sep 15, 1946, 9:30 P.M. (IfZ, Irving Collection).

9 This is listed in a note, 'papers desired from RHJ Files,' in Library of Congress, Manuscript Division, R H Jackson papers, box 2.

10 Francis Biddle, letter, May 22, 1946 (University of Syracuse, New York, George Arents Research Library, Francis Biddle Collection, 'Personal').

11 ND: USSR–460; see *IMT*, vol. xiv, page 243.

12 Keitel to Nelte, May 21, 1946; Görlitz, op. cit., page 236.

13 Keitel to Luise Jodl, Jun 9, 1946; ibid.

14 W E Jackson to his mother, Mar 30, 1946 (Library of Congress, Manuscript Division, R H Jackson papers, box 2).

15 R H Jackson to Irene, Apr 18, 1946 (ibid.).

16 Ibid.

17 Ibid., May 8, 1946.

18 Ibid., Apr 18, 1946.

19 Jackson, Oral History project, page 304

20 Author's interview of Ralph Albrecht, New York, May 22, 1971. Albrecht's papers are now in the Hoover Library. He volunteered the information on this episode without being prompted (prefacing it with the words, 'You British are odd folks—'). It is fair to note that when the author asked him for corroboration Lord Justice Phillimore threatened action for defamation (a course his solicitors did not however pursue), and that Albrecht wrote asking to withdraw what he had related.

21 So Norman told the U.S. ambassador in London. Telegram, Joseph P Kennedy to US State dept., Feb 27, 1939.

22 See especially the memorandum by J. R. Leith Ross, Dec 3, 1945, interceding on Dr Schacht's behalf as war criminal; and Sir Montagu Norman's attempts to get the case against him dropped. There is a reassuring note that there was 'no risk of his being hanged' (PRO, Treasury papers, papers of Leith Ross, file T188/288).

23 Shorthand record of Chief Prosecutors' Meeting, Apr 5, 1946, 5:15 P.M. (University of Chicago Law School, R H Jackson Collection).

24 Jackson, Oral History project, page 347.

25 Professor Andrew Gibb, op. cit. (1954).

26 Jackson, Oral History project. On this newsreel see R H Jackson to W E

Jackson, Apr 30, 1946 (NA, RG.238, US Chief of Counsel at Nuremberg, Main Office Files, box 183).

27 Jackson, Oral History project, page 350. Birkett's typescript drafts of the judgement are in Biddle's papers along with his own drafts (University of Syracuse, George Arents Research Library, Francis Biddle Collection, box 19).

28 Biddle, the American judge, had stood for UNESCO. The Poles opposed his candidacy on the grounds that it was he who had read out the judgement acquitting Schacht. It was then that he made his disclosure, in a statement to the *New York Herald Tribune*.

29 W E Jackson to R H Jackson, Aug 11, 1947 (Library of Congress, Manuscript Division, R H Jackson papers, box 2). Of Lemkin, he notes: 'I never could quite figure the bugger out when he was in London and then Nuremberg.'

30 R H Jackson to Irene, May 8, 1946.

31 Ibid., May 17, 1946.

32 Jackson to Champetier de Ribes and Rudenko, Mar 8, 1946. Russian text in CGAOR, f. 7445, op. 2, d. 8, l. 47.

33 Lieut.-Gen. R Rudenko to R H Jackson, Mar 11, 1946. Russian text in CGAOR, f. 7445, op. 2, d. 8, l. 36.

34 Alfred Seidl (ed.), *Die Beziehungen zwischen Deutschland und der Sowjetunion, 1939–1941. Aus den Archiven des Auswärtigen Amtes und der Deutschen Botschaft in Moskau* (Tübingen, 1949), pages iv–v.

35 Alfred Seidl, *Der Fall Rudolf Hess*; he confirmed details to Abarinov, op. cit., saying that Zorya answered without a moment's hesitation. 'I am quite sure that he had already discussed this response with General Rudenko in advance.'

36 Quoted by Abarinov, op. cit.

37 Now in files of the former Soviet Public Prosecutor's Office, says Abarinov.

38 Abarinov, op. cit., pages 12ff; Mark Raginskii, *The Nuremberg Trial* (Moscow, 1987), page 53, states only that Zorya died while cleaning his gun. Abarinov, born 1955, a trained Soviet journalist and special correspondent of the Moscow *Literaturnaya Gazeta*, based his account on investigations by the general's son Yuri Nikolayevich Zorya.

39 Minutes of Chief Prosecutors' Meeting held in Room 231 at 1630 hours on 31.5.46 (Library of Congress, Manuscript Division, R H Jackson papers, box 98); the Russian translation in CGAOR, f. 7445, op. 2, d. 8, l. 18–19, is wrongly dated May 30, 1946.

40 Listed in note, 'papers desired from RHJ Files,' in Library of Congress, Manuscript Division, R H Jackson papers, box 2.

41 Copies of Speer's two letters to R H Jackson are in IfZ, Irving Collection, R H Jackson papers, vol. i. Col. Amen sent them to Jackson on Nov 17, 1945 (NA, RG.238, US Chief of Counsel at Nuremberg, Main Office Files, box 184).

42 R H Jackson to Irene, Jun 22, 1946.

43 Jackson, Oral History project, page 362.

44 *IMT,* vol. xvii, pages 654ff.; xvii, pages 7 et seq. See also Nelte, *Die Generale. Das Nürnberger Urteil und die Schuld der Generale* (Hanover, 1947).

45 R H Jackson to Irene, Jul 12, 1945.

46 Jackson referred to it in his letter to Irene, Jun 22, 1946.

47 R H Jackson to President Harry S Truman, Jun 15, 1946 (Library of Congress, Manuscript Division, R H Jackson papers, box 26).

48 R H Jackson to Irene, Jun 11, 1946.

49 Francis Biddle, 'Notes on Judgment,' a 67-page typescript on the meetings of the Tribunal to discuss the judgment, Jun 27–Sep 26, 1946 (University of Syracuse, New York, George Arents Research Library, Francis Biddle Collection, 'Trial Documents,' box 14).

Notes to Chapter 18

1 Unsigned memo, Apr 20, 1946 (Library of Congress, Manuscript Division, R H Jackson papers, box 103, 'misc.').

2 *IMT*, vol. v, pages 172f.

3 As the semi-official West German historian Professor Dr Martin Broszat, director of the IfZ, Munich, stated in *Die Zeit* (Hamburg), Aug 19, 1960.

4 Signals Corps negative number SC.206194, by T/4 Sidney Blau (NA, Audio-Visual Branch); see *After the Battle* magazine (London, 1980), No. 27.

5 John D McCallum, *Crime Doctor* (Mercer Island, Washington, 1978), pages 46ff. Upon being honoured in 1980 for his work as a pathologist by the University of Kansas, Larson remarked that while hundreds of thousands, even millions, of Jews had died at the hands of the Nazis, 'most died of the results of the conditions to which they were subjected rather than mass exterminations.' 'In one camp,' he said, '90 percent died of tuberculosis. It went from shack to shack.' *Wichita Eagle*, Apr 1, 1980.

6 Affidavit by Dr Wilhelm Höttl, Nov 26, 1945. Höttl: 'I had already, prior to the German collapse, given detailed data about it [his conversation with Eichmann] to American Quarters in a neutral foreign country with which I was in touch at that time' (ND: 2738–PS).—There are two files on Höttl in Princeton University, Seeley Mudd Manuscript Library, Allen W Dulles papers, box 21 (1945); and box 57 (1953), a manuscript of Höttl's memoirs, 'I Was Hitler's Master Spy.'

7 Höttl to Andrus, Sep 26, 1945 (NA, RG.238, US Chief of Counsel at Nuremberg, Main Office Files; quoted by Anthony Cave Brown, *Wild Bill Donovan. The Last Hero* (New York, 1982), page 754).

8 Pass issued by Jackson's office, OUSCC, Oct 18, 1945 (ibid.).

9 Eichmann papers, in possession of the author, pages 317, 325, 340,

10 Ibid., page 311.

11 Ibid., page 365.

12 The Mauthausen death books, 1939–45, giving the names, birthdate, and date of death 'of each individual who died at Mauthausen,' were introduced as evidence at Nuremberg. Two reels of microfilm, NA, RG.238.

13 Judge Francis Biddle, 'Notes of Evidence, vol.1,' Jan 3, 1946 (University of Syracuse, New York, George Arents Research Library, Francis Biddle Collection, box 3). The Auschwitz death books were captured by the Russians in Jan 1945, and returned by Moscow to the German government in 1989: they list the names, dates of birth, dates of death, and alleged causes of death of some forty-siz thousand people in the camp, dying mainly from epidemics and similar causes.

14 Ibid., vol. 2, Jan 28, 1946.

15 Ibid., Feb 27, 1946.

16 Butler, op. cit., page 235; based on information from Clarke.

17 Rudolf Höss, *Commandant in Auschwitz*, with introduction by Lord

Russell of Liverpool (London, 1959), pages 713–15; German edition, Prof. Martin Broszat (ed)., *Kommandant in Auschwitz* (Stuttgart, 1958) [hereafter Höss, *Commandant*]. This pencilled manuscript was written in captivity in Crakow, in 1947; the original has remained in Polish hands since then.

18 Butler, op. cit., page 235; based on information from Clarke.

19 Ibid., page 237.

20 Interview of Kenneth Jones published in *Wrexham Leader*, Oct 17, 1986. Mrs Vera Atkins, of Winchelsea, Sussex, was present at the interrogations but declines to provide information.

21 Rudolf Höss deposition, Mar 14 (or 15?), 1946 (ND: NO–1210).

22 Draper, born May 30, 1914, died in 1989; the obituaries all referred to Draper's achievement in getting Höss to confess under his 'stern questioning' (*Daily Telegraph*).

23 Facsimile in Lord Russell, *Geisel der Menschlichkeit* (Berlin, 1960), page 161; English edition: *The Scourge of the Swastika*.

24 The Nuremberg files state that Höss was interrogated on Mar 20, 1946 in British hands at Minden, Germany; this transcript No. D.479B appears not to have been released yet by the British authorities.

25 Moritz von Schirmeister, letter in author's possession.

26 Höss, *Commandant*, pages 713–15.

27 Interrogations of Rudolf Franz Ferdinand Höß (NA microfilm M.1270, reel 7).

28 'I cannot really blame the interrogators,' he would write. 'They were all Jews.' Höss, *Commandant*.

29 Gilbert, op. cit., pages 229–30, 239.

30 This too was improbable, because who else compiled the daily statistical summaries which were radioed in cipher from Auschwitz to Berlin and duly deciphered by the British in the winter of 1942–43? Sir Frank H Hinsley *et al.*, *British Intelligence in the Second World War. Its Influence on Strategy and Operations* (Cambridge, 1979–84), 3 vols, vol. ii, appendix., especially page 673: 'The returns from Auschwitz, the largest of the camps with 20,000 prisoners, mentioned illness as the main cause of death, but included references to shootings and hangings. There were no references in the decrypts to gassing.'

31 *L'Express*, Paris, Jan 26, 1995. There is no visible trace of roof-openings on the aerial photographs made by Allied planes of the buildings in question, nor in their ruins today; and neither in these ruins nor on the blueprints of the original buildings, are there any traces of such ventilating equipment.

32 Affidavit by Rudolf Höss, Apr 5, 1946, 'subscribed and sworn before me this 5th day of April, 1946, at Nürnberg Germany,' Lieut.-Col. Smith W Brookhart (ND: 3868–PS; NA microfilm M.1270, reel 7). As introduced to the court 3868–PS was a forgery inasmuch as it was represented as a 'translation' into the English (although it does not exist in German), and the hand-written interpolations had been wrongly incorporated, rendering para. 9 incomprehensible. The version of the document printed by Henry Monneray in *La Persécution des Juifs dans les pays d l'Est présentée à Nuremberg* (Paris, Centre for Contemporary Jewish Documentation, 1949), pages 159–62, gets round this by omitting the end of para. 9 and all of para. 10.

33 *IMT*, vol. xi, pages 457–61.

34 Nor did they introduce other compelling evidence about Auschwitz, for example, the testimony of S.S. Sturmbannführer Kurt Aumeier, who had for several weeks acted as deputy commandant of Auschwitz. Aumeier was initially

as incoherent as Höss under interrogation by the British in Norway and England. The memoirs and manuscripts which he pencilled in the Kensington interrogation centre commanded by Lieut.-Col. Scotland also displayed an increasing precision with each week that passed. The final manuscript (or fair copy) signed by Aumeier was pencilled in British Army style with all proper names in block letters (PRO file WO.208/4661.) Aumeier was extradited by the British to Poland and hanged.

35 Robert B Starnes, list of the internees who viewed the film that day (NA, RG.238, entry 199, Records of HQ, 6850th Internal Security Detachment, IMT, box 7).

36 List of Transferred Internees, May 1946 (ibid., box 8). In Polish captivity, Höss penned—or rather pencilled—his memoirs, a document from which substantially evolved much of the present knowledge of the Holocaust. No doubt he agreed to write the manuscript as a means of postponing his fate. Modern German historians like the late Professor Martin Broszat, who edited it in 1958, would however skirt around and even omit without comment the manuscript's egregious anachronisms, inconsistencies, and other generally implausible passages. Even so Adolf Eichmann, hiding in Argentina, would write scathing comments about the inaccuracies and downright untruths that he claimed to have found in his copy of the Höss memoirs. A photocopy of Eichmann's handwritten marginalia is in the author's possession; the original, authenticated by the Bundesarchiv, Koblenz, is owned by Günter Pleyer, of Hennef, Germany.

Notes to Chapter 19

1 [Francis Biddle:] First Meeting to Discuss the Opinion, Jun 27, 1946 (University of Syracuse, New York, George Arents Research Library, Francis Biddle Collection, box 14, 'Notes on Judgement—Meetings of Tribunal').

2 Francis Biddle to Herbert Wechsler, Nuremberg, Jul 10, 1946 (ibid.).

3 [Biddle:] Second Meeting re Draft of Opinion, Jul 11, 1946 (ibid.).

4 [Biddle:] Third Conference on Opinion, Jul 17, 1946 (ibid.).

5 [Biddle:] Second Section—Preliminary View, Before Aggressive War, Jul 20, 1946 (Ibid.).

6 Biddle to Wechsler, Jul 10, 1946.

7 An unidentified press clipping of Oct 16, 1946, in NA, RG.153, Judge-Advocate General, Internal Affairs Division, box 1561.

8 Biddle to Wechsler, Jul 10, 1946.

9 [Biddle:] Conference—Aug 8, 1946 (University of Syracuse, New York, George Arents Research Library, Francis Biddle Collection, box 14, 'Notes on Judgement—Meetings of Tribunal').

10 [Biddle:] Session on Opinion—Conspiracy, Aug 14, 1946 (ibid.).

11 Ibid., Aug 15, 1946.

12 [Biddle:] Meeting on Opinion, Aug 19, 1946 (ibid.).

13 Karl-Heinz Keitel, 'Conversations with Dr Dr Nelte at Nuremberg,' Sep 19–27, 1946 (IfZ, Irving Collection).

14 Görlitz, op. cit., page 53.

15 General Alfred Jodl to his wife Luise, Aug 28, 1946; published in *Der Turmwart*, No. 4/5, Zürich, April/May 1949.

16 Alfred Jodl, 'Closing Statements,' Nuremberg, undated (Luise Jodl papers; copy in IfZ, Irving Collection).

17 [Biddle:] Meeting on Defendants, Sep 2, 1946 (University of Syracuse, New York, George Arents Research Library, Francis Biddle Collection, box 14, 'Notes on Judgement—Meetings of Tribunal').

18 [Biddle:] Meeting on Organisations, Sep 3, 1946 (ibid.).

19 [Biddle:] Meetings on Sep 4, 1946 (ibid.).

20 [Biddle:] Sep 6, 1946, Meeting (ibid.).

21 [Biddle:] Sep 7, 1946, Conference on Judgement (ibid.).

22 [Biddle:] Meeting of the Tribunal, Sep 9, 1946 (ibid.).

23 [Biddle:] Meeting, Sep 9, 1946 (ibid.).—This was a reference to a letter from Dr Hans Lammers to Schirach, Dec 3, 1940 (ND: USA–681).

24 [Biddle:] Final Vote on Individuals, Sep 10, 1946 (ibid.).

Notes to Chapter 20

1 [F Biddle:] Final Vote on Individuals, Sep 10, 1946 (University of Syracuse, New York, George Arents Research Library, Francis Biddle Collection, box 14, 'Notes on Judgement—Meetings of Tribunal').

2 Ibid.

3 *IMT*, vol. i, page 351.

4 Biddle, typescript, 'Dönitz—Dissent by Judge Biddle,' marked in handwriting: 'This was not filed. Probably suggested by [judge] Parker' (University of Syracuse, New York, George Arents Research Library, Francis Biddle Collection, box 19).

5 Bradley Smith, *Reaching Judgment at Nuremberg* (New York, 1977), page 261.

6 *IMT*, vol. xxii, pages 636f.

7 [Biddle: Final Vote on Individuals], Sep 11, 1946 (University of Syracuse, New York, George Arents Research Library, Francis Biddle Collection, box 14, 'Notes on Judgement—Meetings of Tribunal').

8 Ibid., Sep 12, 1946.

9 Karl-Heinz Keitel, 'Conversation with My Father,' Sep 14, 1946, 1:30 P.M. (IfZ, Irving Collection).

10 Ibid.

11 Ibid., Sep 23, 1946, 1 P.M.

12 Ibid., Sep 14, 1946, 1:30 P.M.

13 Ibid., Sep 25, 1946, 1 P.M.

14 Ibid., Sep 27, 1946, 1 P.M.

15 Ibid., Sep 28, 1946, 1 P.M.

16 Ibid., Sep 14, 1946, 1:30 P.M.

17 Ibid., Sep 16, 1946, 1:30 P.M.

18 Ibid., Sep 19, 1946, 1 P.M.

19 Ibid. On Sep 23, 1946 he added, 'His [Himmler's] connection with the Röhm Affair was this: he made sure he was on the right side, against Röhm.... Schleicher and Bredow were on Röhm's side.'

20 Ibid., Sep 28, 1946, 1 P.M.

21 [Biddle: Final Vote on Individuals and Organisations] Sep 13, 1946.

22 R H Jackson, cable to Office of US Chief of Counsel, Nuremberg, for Thomas Dodd, Washington, Sep 3, 1946 (IfZ, Irving Collection, R H Jackson papers, vol. iii).

23 [Biddle:] Sep 16–17, 1946.

24 'Conference held in Colonel Andrus's Office,' Aug 23; and F Jay Nimitz to Andrus, Sep 17, 1946 (Burton C Andrus Collection, Colorado Springs).

25 B C Andrus, Results of a meeting on Sep 26, 1946 (NA, RG.238, entry 199, Records of HQ, 6850th Internal Security Detachment, IMT, box 7).

26 'Conference held in Colonel Andrus's Office,' Aug 23; and F Jay Nimitz to Andrus, Sep 17, 1946.

Notes to Chapter 21

1 R H Jackson to Whitney R Harris, Nov 18, 1946 (IfZ, Irving Collection, R H Jackson papers, vol. iii).

2 R H Jackson, Oral History project (University of Chicago Law School, R H Jackson Collection).

3 In general on the judgement at Nuremberg see Harold Leventhal, 'The Nürnberg Verdict,' in *Harvard Law Review*, vol. lx, No. 6 (1947).

4 R H Jackson final report to Truman, Oct 7, 1946.

5 A mimeographed copy of Nikitchenko's dissenting opinion is in NA, RG.238; it is published in *Nazi Conspiracy and Aggression. Opinion and Judgment* (US Government Printing Office, Washington DC).

6 Papen to Andrus, Oct 1; Fritzsche to Andrus, Oct 1; Schacht to Andrus, Oct 4; joint letter to Andrus signed by all three, Oct 3, 1946 (Burton C Andrus Collection, Colorado Springs).

7 See Davidson, op. cit., page 240.

8 Author's interview of Dr Rudolf Merkel, Nuremberg, Mar 14, 1971.

9 R H Jackson, Oral History project, page 366.

10 Ibid.

11 See the article 'America Dishonored' in *Chicago Tribune*, Oct 13, 1948. The complete records of the Judge van Rohden Commission of Inquiry into the American excesses at Dachau are in the National Archives, Washington. See too Reginald T Paget, QC, *Manstein—His Campaigns and Trial* (London, 1951), a fine volume which first brought this author's attention to the egregious injustices of some of the post-war trials.

12 Cf Carl Haensel, 'Das Gericht vertagt sich,' a mimeographed typescript of lawyer Haensel's Nuremberg diary.

13 Minutes of Chief Prosecutors' Meeting, Jul 1, 1946 (IfZ, Irving Collection, R H Jackson papers, vol. iii).

14 Keitel to Nelte, Oct 1, 1946; Görlitz, op. cit., page 237.

15 Lisa Keitel to Nelte, Oct 1, 1946; ibid.

16 General Alfred Jodl to his wife Luise, Oct 9, 1946, published in *Der Turmwart*, No. 4/5, Zürich, April/May 1949.

17 Ibid., Oct 1, 1946.

18 Ibid., Oct 5, 1946, evening.

19 Ibid., Oct 2, 1946.

20 Andrus diary, Sep 7, 14, Oct 2, 1946 (Burton C Andrus Collection, Colorado Springs).

21 Copies are in Judge Biddle's papers (University of Syracuse, New York, George Arents Research Library, Francis Biddle Collection, 'Trial Documents,' boxes 14–15) and in NA, RG.260, OMGUS, box 15.

22 Jodl to his wife, Oct 3, 1946, evening.

23 Field-Marshal Keitel to Karl-Heinz Keitel, Oct 3, 1946; Görlitz, op. cit., page 237.

24 Keitel to Control Council, Oct 5, 1946; ibid., page 238.

25 Dr Stahmer petition to Allied Control Council, Oct 4, 1946 (NA, RG.260, OMGUS, box 15).

26 Wilhelm Keitel to Allied Control Council for Germany, Oct 8, 1946 (ibid.).

27 British Cabinet to Sir Sholto Douglas, Oct 7, 1946 (PRO file PREM.8/392).

28 Sholto Douglas, memoirs as serialised in *Sunday Express*, Sep 19, 1965. This author challenged him in *The Times* to produce the 'evidence' of which he had written. He did not reply, but his subsequently published volume of memoirs omitted the whole passage.

29 Minutes of the Allied Control Council in Berlin, 42nd (Extraordinary) Meeting, Oct 9–10, 1946 (NA, RG.153, Judge-Advocate General, Internal Affairs Division, box 1561, file 119–1a).

30 Jodl to his wife, Mar 10, 1946.

31 For example ND: 1809–PS, Jodl's 1940 diary. President Harry S Truman later signed a rare executive order expropriating the copyright in the Jodl diaries for the US government.

32 Prof. Dr Erich Schwinger, 'Declaration,' Marburg, Jun 15, 1951, reporting what Donnedieu had told him (Luise Jodl papers; copy in IfZ, Irving Collection).

33 Jodl to his wife, Oct 7. On Oct 11, 1946 Jodl added: 'From what you have written me about those who were acquitted, I would not want to change places with them. There probably isn't any place for people like me in Germany any longer, at least not until one day my ghost begins to go around and knock on the doors of all these opportunists.'

34 Karl-Heinz Keitel, 'Conversations with Dr Dr Nelte at Nuremberg,' Sep 19–27, 1946 (IfZ, Irving Collection).

35 Jodl to his wife, Oct 5–6, 1946, evening.

36 Ibid., Oct 8, 1946, evening.

37 Ibid., Oct 7, 1946, evening.

38 Ibid., Oct 8, 1946, evening.

39 Order read by Andrus to Little, Tweedy, Teich, and Chaplain Gerricke [*sic*] Oct 3, 1946 (Burton C Andrus Collection, Colorado Springs).

40 Adele Streicher, comments on Arnim von Manikowski, *Das Gericht der Sieger*, page 200 (Höffkes Collection).

41 Adele Streicher, comments on G M Gilbert, *Nürnberger Tagebuch* (Stuttgart, 1948), page 125 (Höffkes Collection).

42 Adele Streicher, comments on Douglas M Kelley, *Twenty-two Cells in Nuremberg* (New York, 1947), page 164 (Höffkes Collection); and on Hans Fritzsche, *Das Schwert auf der Waage* (Heidelberg, 1953), page 25.

43 Adele Streicher, comments on Eugene Davidson, op. cit., page 57.

44 Adele Streicher, comments on Joe Heidecker and Johannes Leeb, op. cit., page 487 (Höffkes Collection).

45 Dispatch by Selkirk Panton to *Daily Express*, Oct 7, 1945 (National Library of Australia, Canberra, Collection 5808, Selkirk Panton papers, folder 3).

46 Jodl to his wife, Oct 4, 1946, evening.

47 Ibid., Oct 4–5, 1946.

48 Emmy Göring's memoirs; David Irving, *Göring* (London, 1989), page 501.

49 Jodl to his wife, Oct 11, 1946.

50 Ibid.

51 Burton C Andrus Collection, Colorado Springs.

52 The records of the Quadripartite Commission show that of Ribbentrop's valuables only 22,000 marks were turned over to the Finance Directorate, and 810 marks handed to the family with the Longines wrist watch. There is no explanation for the discrepancy of some ten thousand marks (or the gold teeth). Andrus, memo, 'Disposal of Valuables left by Condemned Men,' appendix 'B' (NA, RG.238, Col. Teich files: 'Ribbentrop').

53 Original in the possession of R C 'Duke' Schneider, Florida (copy in the author's possession).

54 Ibid. Only 500 marks (and all the timepieces) were turned over to the widow, the rest was missing.

55 Field-Marshal Keitel to Karl-Heinz Keitel Oct 13, 1946; Görlitz, op. cit., page 237n.

56 Jodl to his wife, Oct 13, 1946 evening.

57 Milch diary, Oct 13–14, 1946 (author's microfilm DI–59).

58 Ibid., Oct 14, 1946.

59 Testimony of First Lieutenant John W West; all these testimonies are annexed to 'Report of Board of Proceedings of Hermann Göring (Suicide),' Oct 1946. Copies are in BDC Director's Safe, Berlin; NA, RG.260, Records of OMGUS Allied Control Council, file 2/92–1(2); and in the Wheeler Bennett papers at St Anthony's College, Oxford.

60 Jodl to his wife, Oct 14, 1946, evening.

61 For example he wrote on October 13, 'It just occurs to me that you won't get this letter until Tuesday [Oct 15] and that there will then be further letters for you when I am no longer on this earth'.

62 Ibid., Oct 14, 1946, evening.

63 Ibid., Oct 15, 1946, evening.

64 Ibid., Oct 15, 1946, evening.

65 The TOP SECRET list of all the names is in the Burton C Andrus Collection, Colorado Springs. The Russians were Major-General P Malokov, Dr Vorbtzov the medical officer, Captain Afanasier, for TASS, and Major Temin for *Pravda*. The British were Brigadier E J Paton-Walsh, with the newspapermen Selkirk Panton and Basil Gingell; the American newspapermen were Arthur Gaeth and Kingsbury Smith. The French member was Général de Brigade L Morel, the American was Brigadier-General R V Rickard.

66 Whitney R Harris to R H Jackson, Oct 1946 (IfZ, Irving Collection, R H Jackson papers, vol. iii); see too W R Harris, *Tyranny on Trial* (Dallas, 1954).

67 Selkirk Panton to *Daily Express*, 5:50 P.M., Oct 15, 1946 (Selkirk Panton papers, folder 3).

68 Dispatch by Kingsbury Smith, Oct 16, 1945 (NA, RG.153, Judge-Advocate General, Internal Affairs Division, box 1561); the file contains many clippings on the IMT's documents and on the executions.

69 Jodl to his wife, Oct 4, 1946.

70 Testimony of Private First Class Gordon Bingham, Exhibit V.

71 Testimony of Edie, Exhibit T.

72 Testimony of Gerecke, Exhibit K; cf Gilbert, op. cit., page 435.

73 Testimonies of Pflücker and Dowd.

74 Ibid.; and Pflücker, in *Waldeckische Landeszeitung*, Oct 1952, No. 16.

75 Testimony of First Lieutenant Arthur J McLinden, Exhibit P; supported by that of Bingham, Exhibit V.

76 Testimony of Private First Class Harold F Johnson, Exhibit U.

77 Testimony of Captain Robert B Starnes, Exhibit AD.

Notes to Chapter 22

1 G M Gilbert, *The Psychology of Dictatorship* (New York, 1950), page 107.

2 Douglas M Kelley, op. cit., pages 76f.

3 Reichsmarschall Göring's speech to the Air Staff officers, Nov 25, 1944 (General Karl Koller papers, author's microfilm DI–17).

4 Testimony of Private First Class Harold F. Johnson, Exhibit U, and Sergeant Gregory Tymchyshyn, Exhibit S. Whitney Harris, writing to Jackson at second hand on Oct 19, 1946 after questioning the witnesses himself, confirms the time, 10:45. 'When the doctor arrived the death rattle was in his throat. Göring had cheated the hangman. They found in the cell a small envelope marked "H. Göring" on the outside, inside of which three notes, one addressed to Colonel Andrus from Göring, and the cartridge case in which the vial of potassium cyanide had been preserved' (University of Chicago Law School, R H Jackson collection).

5 Testimony of First Lieutenant Arthur J McLinden, Exhibit P.

6 Testimony of Private First Class Harold F Johnson, Exhibit U.

7 Testimony of Pflücker, Exhibit AC.

8 Testimony of Captain Robert B Starnes, Exhibit AD.

9 Testimony of Pflücker, Exhibit AC.

10 Testimony of First Lieutenant Charles J Roska, Exhibit AB.

11 Testimony of Gerecke, Exhibit K. 'When Dr Pflücker arrived,' he recalled, 'he found an envelope and some letters under the blanket.'

12 Testimony of Captain Robert B Starnes, Exhibit AD.

13 Selkirk Panton to *Daily Express*, 3:15 A.M., Oct 16, 1946 (National Library of Australia, Canberra, Collection 5808, Selkirk Panton papers, folder 3).

14 [Basil] Gingell to Reuters *et al.*, Oct 16 (ibid.). Whitney Harris confirmed this in his letter to Jackson, Oct 19, 1946: 'At nine-thirty the correspondents were permitted to inspect the cell-block and observe the condemned.... Göring simulated sleep, his hands outside of the blanket.' (University of Chicago Law School, R H Jackson collection).

15 Statement reported in *New York Times*, Oct 17, 1946.

16 Andrus to Keathley, Oct 29, 1946 (Burton C Andrus Collection, Colorado Springs).

17 Ibid.

18 Adele Streicher, comments on Joe Heidecker and Johannes Leeb, op. cit., page 494 (Höffkes Collection).

19 Hanging times from Whitney Harris to R H Jackson, Oct 19, 1946; time of delivery to execution team from Andrus memo, 'Deliverance Time of Convicts,' Oct 17, 1946 (Library of Congress, Manuscript Division, R H Jackson papers; and Burton C Andrus Collection, Colorado Springs).

20 Draft telegram by Selkirk Panton [Oct 16, 1946] (Selkirk Panton papers).

21 Dispatch by Kingsmith [Kingsbury Smith] to International News, New

York (ibid.). The Board stated (Exhibit H) that the remains were taken to the gymnasium for preparation for disposal.

22 The photographs were published in a brochure in Germany. K H Gentz, *Endstation Nürnberg* (Detmold, 1951).

23 Andrus to Keathley, Oct 29, 1946.

24 R H Jackson, Oral History project, page 548 (University of Chicago Law School, R H Jackson collection).

25 In reply to a review of the book *The Rise and Fall of Hermann Goering*, published by the *New York Times* on Sep 14 (1948?).

26 Andrus to Keathley, Oct 29, 1946.

27 One such cover is in the Göring collection of Keith Wilson, Kansas City.

28 Alleged letter from Hermann Göring to 'the former prime minister of Great Britain' Winston Churchill, dated 'Nürnberg Oct 10, 1946.' The author first saw a copy of this in the Karl-Heinz Keitel papers, vol. iii; there is also a copy in the papers of Julius Schaub (IfZ, Irving Collection), and over the years other copies have surfaced, with minor textual variations. It is almost certainly a forgery, generated by right-wing circles in South Africa at the time.

29 H Göring to Andrus, Oct 11, 1946; original in BDC Director's Safe, Berlin; copy in Burton C Andrus Collection, Colorado Springs.

30 Ibid. Andrus wrote in his memoirs that Goring admitted in this note that he had concealed the brass capsule 'in his anus and in his flabby navel.'

31 Quadripartite Commission, Minutes of Seventh Meeting, Oct 18, 1946 (NA, RG.238, Col. Teich files: 'Ribbentrop').

32 These manuscripts have, after a long odyssey through secret archives, landed in the National Archives, in Washington DC. See the summary of them dated Sep 9, 1966 (NA, RG.238, Col. Teich files).

33 Quadripartite Commission, Minutes of Seventh Meeting, Oct 18, 1946 (NA, RG.238, Col. Teich files: 'Ribbentrop').

34 Quadripartite Commission, Minutes of Eighth Meeting, at Nuremberg, Dec 4–5, 1946 (ibid.).

35 Quadripartite Commission, Minutes of Seventh Meeting, Oct 18, 1946 (ibid.).

36 Ibid.

37 Testimony of First Lieutenant Charles J Roska, Exhibit AB.

38 Sworn affidavits by John West, Exhibit Z3; Lieut. Jack G Wheelis (Z3); Charles W Pace, Arthur J McLinden, John S Carver, Charles H Backstrom, Dale W Shore, Norwood G Croner, and Daniel E Hauberger.

39 Testimony of Captain Robert B Starnes, Exhibit Z1.

40 Andrus to Dr W H Dunn, Oct 24, 1946 (Burton C Andrus Collection, Colorado Springs).

41 Lieutenant Jack G Wheelis, Service No. O–1330498, was a huntsman like Göring. He had been assigned to HQ, 6850th Internal Security Detachment, IMT, on Nov 26, 1945 (Roster of Officers, Jan 17, 1946: in Burton C Andrus Collection, Colorado Springs); on Jul 4, 1946 Wheelis, now a first lieutenant, was detailed Asst Operations Officer for the Detachment (Special Orders, Jul 4, 1946, ibid.). On Feb 8, 1946, Wheelis signed a note certifiying that he 'to the best of my knowledge did not enter into a conversation with George Tucker, correspondent,' four nights earlier (ibid.). A letter from Andrus to Major Charles L Hammes, of the war crimes team at the Luxembourg ministry of justice, Nov 5, 1946, shows that Wheelis presented a continuing disciplinary problem in other respects too (accidentally unpaid bills) (ibid.). He died in 1954.

42 Charles Bewlay, *Hermann Göring* (Göttingen, 1956; London, 1962), page 502.

43 Werner Bross to Ben Swearingen, Dec 3, 1979.

44 Ben Swearingen, *The Mystery of Hermann Göring's Suicide* (New York, 1986). Swearingen states that Göring gave Wheelis a photograph showing them perusing a sheaf of papers together, signing it as 'Reichsjägermeister' Göring, and dedicating it to 'The Great Huntsman from Texas.'

45 H A Twelftree, Master of the Templars Lodge, invitation (typed on British War Crimes Executive notepaper) to Andrus, Aug 31, 1946 (Burton C Andrus Collection, Colorado Springs).

46 Andrus to Twelftree, Oct 22, 1946 (ibid.).

47 Milch diary, Oct 18, 1946; he deduced, 'Presumably a punishment for Göring's suicide.'

48 Testimony of Captain Robert B Starnes, Exhibit AD. The question of one or two envelopes occupied the Board of Inquiry only briefly. Starnes admitted that one of the two could have been just a folded piece of paper, but he stated: 'It looked like an envelope to me. Many prisoners however fold paper for envelopes.' This author has seen all three original letters: they were *not* folded 'like envelopes.'

49 Testimony of Captain Robert B Starnes, Exhibit AD.

50 Burton C Andrus, *I Was the Nuremberg Jailer* (New York, 1979), page 250.

51 B C Andrus to Brig.-Gen. Roy V Rickard, Oct 24, 1946 (Burton C Andrus Collection, Colorado Springs).

52 Andrus to Kempner, Oct 28, 1946 (ibid.). He used the next day almost identical terms to Lieut.-Col. James J Pintel, writing of 'the revolting condition that this suicide concealed the container for his poison in his rectum, as proven by laboratory tests of matter still clinging to the container when it was found in his possession after death. So, we have the horrible condition of a human being mouthing his own dung' (ibid.). As late as Feb 1, 1968 he was quoted (in the Canberra *Daily Mirror*) as saying: 'At other [times] he [Göring] was to admit to me later in a suicide note he secreted the brass-and-glass phial in his navel.'

53 Quadripartite Commission, Minutes of Fourth Meeting of the Special Working Party held at Nuremberg on Saturday Oct 26, 1946 (NA, RG.238, Col. Teich files: 'Ribbentrop').

54 Quadripartite Commission, Minutes of Eighth Meeting, at Nuremberg, Dec 4–5, 1946 (ibid.).

55 Interview of Burton C Andrus Jr., Nov 18, 1986.

56 Quadripartite Commission to B C Andrus, Oct 25, 1946 (NA, RG.238, Col. Teich files: 'Ribbentrop').

57 Receipt for valuables: Hermann Goering, signed Emmy Göring [Oct 1946] (Burton C Andrus Collection, Colorado Springs).

58 Lieut. Colonel Hilton, memorandum dated Aug 31, 1946 in University of Chicago Law School, R H Jackson collection, file, 'HQ Command IMT'. The figure included court costs, personnel, hotel accommodation, heating, etc.

59 The PRO file on this is PREM.8/391.

60 Zayas, op. cit., page 263; added to which figures were 271 French, 35 Dutch, 25 Polish, 11 Norwegian, 2 Chinese, and one Greek trial.

61 See Reginald T Paget, QC, *Manstein—His Campaigns and Trial* (London, 1951). The British records of the Manstein Trial are now housed in the Liddell Hart Centre for Military Archives, at King's College London.—See too Kranzbühler, op. cit., page 23.

62 The Americans also conducted trials, e.g. the notorious Malmedy Trial, at Dachau.

63 Kranzbühler, op. cit., page 25.

64 Ibid.

65 Ibid., page 8.

66 Ibid.

67 Ibid., page 9.

68 *New York Times*, Jul 7, 1951.

69 Davidson, op. cit., page 125.

70 Letter from R H Jackson's secretary to Miss H Amelia Durbin, Pennsylvania, Feb 5, 1952 (University of Chicago Law School, R H Jackson collection).

71 For many years the only evidence of the existence of this Hess typescript was in the BDC catalogues. The document then turned up in the National Archives, and is now in RG.238, Colonel Teich papers.

72 General Alfred Jodl to his wife Luise, Oct 14, 1946 (Luise Jodl papers; copy from Karl-Heinz Keitel papers in IfZ, Irving Collection).

Index

C

H

I

J

T

Conflicting Views on **Goebbels: Mastermind of the Third Reich**, by David Irving

"THIS IS A REPELLENT BOOK, AND NOT ONLY BECAUSE OF ITS SUBJECT. Irving (*Göring*) has been increasingly under fire for exploiting seemingly indefatigable research to distort history. In the book in hand, he uses enough pejoratives to sustain the illusion of objectivity regarding Hitler's propaganda chief, yet suggests that the admittedly bad man had a cause not entirely bad in itself. Nazi brutality is almost always retaliation for the plots of international Jewry and the criminality of domestic Jews. Even the books notoriously burned are "decadent and anti-German.' The term *Redakteur* (editor) 'to Goebbels' sensitive ear had a Jewish ring.' Protesters in Saarbrücken are 'a clamoring ragbag of communists, Jews, freemasons, and disgruntled émigrés.' There is always, in Irving's own words, a 'Jewish problem' that Goebbels struggles to solve. Much of the book, heavily indebted to the self-serving Goebbels diaries, is in such a vein….

"The real insidiousness of the biography is that its formidable documentation will gain it acceptance as history."

— Anonymous, *The Publishers Weekly*, New York

"SILENCING MR IRVING WOULD BE A HIGH PRICE TO PAY FOR FREEDOM from the annoyance that he causes us. The fact is that he knows more about National Socialism than most professional scholars in his field, and students of the years 1933–1945 owe more than they are always willing to admit to his energy as a researcher and to the scope and vigor of his publications.... There is nothing absolute about historical truth. What we consider as such is only an estimation, based upon what the best available evidence tells us. It must constantly be tested against new information and new interpretations that appear, however implausible they may be, or it will lose its vitality and degenerate into dogma or shibboleth. Such people as David Irving, then, have an indispensable part in the historical enterprise, and we dare not disregard their views."

— Professor Gordon C Craig, *The New York Review of Books*

"IRVING ATTRACTS CREDIBILITY AND ATTENTION BY HIS indefatigable energy, intelligence and resourcefulness. Compared with most British historians, often a dull, lazy breed, Irving has spent a lifetime ceaselessly criss-crossing the globe to gather eyewitness evidence about World War II."

— Tom Bower, *The Daily Mail*, London

"HE IS THE FIRST TO USE GOEBBELS' FULL DIARY, 75,000 PAGES, RECENTLY found in Moscow.... Irving's trademark research into original manuscripts is uniquely impressive."

— George Stern, *The Literary Review*, London